The Ultimate Guide

OREGON ROCK CLIMBS

FIRST EDITION

Oregon Rock Climbs™
© 2021 East Wind Design

All rights reserved. No part of this book may be reproduced or transmitted in any form by any means, electronic or mechanical, including photocopying and recording, or by any information storage system, except as may be expressly permitted by the Copyright Act. Requests for permission must be made in writing to the author and publisher.

Book Design: East Wind Design
Technical Maps and Illustrations: EWD

Cover Photograph: *Chad climbing at Rock Creek Crag*
Frontispiece images:
Bob M. at *MCS*, Nick B. at *Ozone*,
Hugh B. at *Beacon Rock*,
Ian G. at *Carver*.

ISBN-13: 978-0-9997233-6-4
ORC v1.2

Manufactured in the USA

OREGON ROCK CLIMBS

Table of Contents

- Disclaimer ix
- Acknowledgments ix
- Info About The Local Crags 4
- Regional History 6
- NW Oregon Climate 14
- Geology — NW Oregon 16
- Climbing Route Ratings 23
- Equipment & Specialized Gear 27
- Climbing Style And Ethics 28

Portland's Urban Crags 31

Broughton Bluff 33
- North Face 36
- Hanging Gardens Wall 39
- Red Wall 50
- Bridge Cliff 55
- Spring Rock 57
- Bat Wall 59
- Broken Rock 68
- Trinity Wall 69
- Berlin Wall 69
- Jungle Cliff 71
- New Frontier Cliff 77

Rocky Butte Quarry 79
- Silver Bullet Wall 83
- Video Bluff 87
- Dream Weaver Wall 89
- Wizard Wall 92
- Far East Wall 92
- Warrior Wall 96
- Freeway Wall 97
- Mean Street 97
- Easy Street 102
- Toothpick Wall 102
- Breakfast Cracks 105

Carver Bridge Cliff 109
- Rockgarden Wall 112
- Yellow Wall 117

Madrone Wall 125
- Left Corner Wall 126
- Orange Wall 130
- Fourth Class Wall 133
- Main Wall - Scott Free Area 134
- Shining Wall Section 141
- Hardscrabble Wall 148
- Hardscrabble - South End 154

Columbia Gorge Crags 157

Ozone Wall	159
Shire Wall	163
Middle Earth	164
Snake Wall	165
Masterpiece	166
Old Tree Area	171
The Shield	172
Heaven's Ledge	175
Old School Wall	178
Mordor Wall	181
Sport School Wall	184

Far Side Crag	187
East End Formation	187
Indian Head	188
Giant Fir Tree	189
The Landing	192
Central Buttress	194
Maple Tree Zone	196

Beacon Rock	201
SE Face Area	216
First Tunnel	222
Second Tunnel	225
Third Tunnel	229
Northwest Face	235
West Face	242
ALL OTHER GORGE CRAGS	245
Rooster Rock	245
Crown Point	247
Pillars of Hercules	249
The Rat Cave	250
Little Cougar Rock	255
St. Peters Dome	257
Little St. Pete's	259
Katanai Rock	259
Apocalypse Needles	261
Cape Horn	262
Rabbit Ears	263
Jimmy Cliff (Twilight Zone)	264
Rock Creek Crag	266
No Star Slab	271
Skookum Pinnacle	272
Wind Mountain	273
Windy Slab	275
Dog Spine	276
The Bypass	279
Wankers Columns	281
OH8	285
Lyle West Crag	292
Lyle Tunnel Crag	294

Horsethief Butte 295
Monte Cristo Slab 311

SW WASHINGTON CRAGS 339
Chimney Rocks 341
LaCamas Plug 349
Tower Rock 350
Sunset Bluffs 353

MT HOOD REGIONAL CLIMBS 359
French's Dome 361
Salmon River Slab 371
Illumination Rock 373
Razorblade Pinnacle 379
Hunchback Wall 383
Enola (The Swinery) 393
Kiwanis Crag 403
Castle Canyon 405
Kinzel Tower 406
Mosquito Butte 408
Coethedral 412
Collawash Cliff 418

EAST SIDE ROCK CLIMBS 419
Newton Pinnacle 425
Lamberson Butte 425
Pete's Pile 430
Klinger Springs 445
Bulo Point 455
Heliotrope 463
Area 51 463

SANTIAM ROCK CLIMBS & SUMMITS 477
North Santiam Region 479
Needle Rock 479
Little Needle Rock 481
Elephant Rock 482
Dog Tooth Rock 484
Spire Rock 486
X-Spire 489
Breitenbush Ears 489
Thor's Hammer 490
Stack Rock 492

South Santiam Region 495
The Menagerie 495
Santiam Pinnacle 512
Iron Mountain Spire 514
Smokestack 515
Twin Sisters Pinnacle 515
Two Girls Mtn 516
Pirates Pinnacle 518

Horse Rock Pillar 519
SOUTHERN WILLAMETTE CRAGS 521
Skinner Butte Columns 523
Wolf Rock 529
Moolack.. 541

Disclaimer

Rock climbing is an inherently dangerous activity. The publisher and author of this guidebook assume no responsibility for injury or death resulting from the use of this book. This book is not intended to serve as an instructional manual and should not take the place of proper training. If you are unsure of your ability to handle any circumstances that may arise, seek professional instruction or attain the services of a professional guide.

Errors may exist in this book and we cannot be held responsible for injury or death while using this guidebook. You and you alone assume complete responsibility for your safety.

The author and publisher makes no representations or warranties, expressed or implied, of any kind regarding the contents of this guide. They make no representations or warranties, expressed or otherwise implied regarding the accuracy or reliability of this guide. The user assumes all risk associated with the use of this book and all activities contained within.

Acknowledgments

The culmination of beta in this book exists primarily because of the shared knowledge and assistance of many friends and individuals. Thank you all for sharing your expertise about the exhilarating edge of this sport.

This guidebook is the end formulation of insight from all those rock climber's and boulderers who relish this sport and choose to maintain valued historical notes on the sport. Numerous tidbits of data exist in various small articles, but a major portion of the information is through close contact with friends and acquintances who have collected a rather impressive amount of climbing information and data, each focused toward their relative prospective view of the sport.

Over many years various individuals provided expandable authoritative information, or climbing energy, or valued insight into various crags and climbs. A brief contributors list from the **PRC** book: W. Wallace, R. McGown, M. Schoen, G. Lyon, G. Rall, S. Mrazek, N. Charlton, J. Opdyke, M. Cartier, S. Tracy, P. Hranicka, C. Ellars, C. Franklin, E. Vining, C. Buzzard, S. Polizzano, E. Linthwaite, S. Ligon, J. Bell, K. Evensen, B. Smith, J. Stewart, M. Deffenbaugh, K. Rauch, T. Abbott, B. Coe, J. Rust, G. Murray, and D. Sowerby. The contributors list from the **NWOR** book: J. Neiland, D. Gonthier, D. Smoland, C. Miller, G. Fergusan, K. Benesch, K. Pogue, A. Sanderson, D. Sword, B. Englund, K. Hann, M. Noel, N. Watt, S. Peterson, K. Helser, H. Brown, C. Mallegol, J. Tripp, K. Kucera, P. Cousar, P. Waters, S. Elder, etc. And of course a number of authors who wrote various older guide books to this region: C. Neuberger, N. Dodge, J. Thomas, R. McGown, etc. Many other persons not referenced here have collectively added to the wealth of knowledge of local climbing and bouldering in this region as well. Photograph credit appreciation goes to several individuals: Mr Abbott, Mr Cousar, etc.

A number of individuals were highly instrumental in sharing various crucial aspects of knowledge, ideas and energy that have helped to strengthen the quality and vibrant nature of this book. Those individuals are a virtual walking encyclopedia of superb detailed knowledge on multiple tangents of the sport in this region. Their wealth of local history, in-depth beta, photograph collections, as well as an express determination to continously explore unknown places to find the next hotspot crag or summit were instrumental in this project. Considerable portions of this book are reflective of that energetic personality and invaluable expertise. That information knowledge base yielded data that could be compiled accurately into a quality product that would satisfy the interest of all climbers in this region.

INTRODUCTION

The Complete Master Collection

The Complete Collection of all the Climbing Crags, Elusive Summits, Alpine Pinnacles and other Adventure Climbing opportunities in NW Oregon & SW Washington

The **ORC** book combines the core aspects of rock climbing, alpine, and adventure climbing opportunities from the best of two worlds (the ever popular **Portland Rock Climbs** book and **NW Oregon Rock** book). This Complete or Premier edition can be accurately described as an extensive collection of climbing data detailing an impressive array of this regions numerous climbing options combined under one title — all the destinations pertinent to today's rock climber.

By enfolding this regions climbing options together in one book, the ORC becomes the ultimate quintessential all-encompassing all-in-one climbers and collectors guidebook to the entire facet of rock climbing, alpine climbing, and adventure thrashing sports found in this U.S. micro-region. Blending PRC and NWOR book characteristics into one ultimate premier thesis creates a complete major edition as no other book ever has.

A unique book of this kind might be thought of as a 'collector's edition', and in some way it may be well suited as a coffee-table reading book, or the centerpiece of your bookshelf's exhaustive climbing book collection. Yet the book is much more. Its design and structure combine a vast wealth of knowledge to make it the great go-to book for all of this regions climbing

Rebecca Gibson leading *Blind Ambition 5.10b*

2 INTRODUCTION

Paul Couser on *Bloodline* at Broughton Bluff

destination information.

From Portland, to The Dalles, from Longview, to Eugene, this book brings to life a plethora of opportunities well suited to all sport, trad, and adventure climbers. Even the specialized rock climber who relishes all the wild aspects of the sport will find this book highly valued.

Only rarely in a generation does a guidebook — like this one — reach a stage of par excellence to become a well appreciated high quality thesis. Some books make an immediate substantive impact, but also become an essential component of great value to the scene of rock climbing in a region and its those rare books that become legendary classics.

Though most of this regions lesser crags are not a goldmine by any standard, especially if compared to superb places like City of Rocks in Idaho, the overall extent and variety of cragging options that are packed into this region in a mere 80 mile circuit, do make this Portland -to- The Dalles -to- Eugene core region uniquely capable of entertaining even the most ardent sport focused climber.

Luckily, with the plethora of over 25 small crags scattered throughout this region, we think this hefty load of cragging options will keep you quite busy, traveling the climbing circuit tour to your string of favorite little crags, or working on a favorite project route or two, or interacting with local site stewards, while meeting new acquaintances and friends.

This book discusses climbing sites in the metro area of the city of Portland and its broader urban area, a fine string of quality crags in the entire Columbia Gorge, a series of crags to the east, south, and west side of the Mt Hood (along highways U.S. 26 and U.S. 35), and climbing options on the Clackamas, Santiam and McKenzie river basins (including Eugene). Set into core chapters, oriented by zone or section this all-in-one go-to guide compiles the beta-data into common zones or river valley corridors.

Portland urban crags, Columbia Gorge crags, SW Washington, Mt Hood - U.S. Hwy 26 corridor crags, U.S Hwy35 crags and Eastside Crags, Clackamas River crags, Santiam crags, and Southern Willamette (Eugene and McKenzie basin crags).

OLDER BOOKS ON CLIMBING

Our corner of the Pacific Northwest offers numerous tantalizing climbing destinations, and several of the finest little crags are readily accessible in or very

Nick Sommerhiser on *Orient Express*

CRAG HISTORY - PORTLAND ✦ INTRODUCTION

close to Portland. Many of the climbs available in the Portland area transcend well beyond the ordinary scope of rock climbing. I encourage you to explore these favorite crags and experience the unique treasures right here in our region. Crags like Broughton Bluff and Carver Bridge Cliff are prime reasons that the sport of rock climbing continues to be popular in the Portland area.

At the heart of this guidebook is the latest climbing information and it's presented in a new way. Previous authors have laid the groundwork for making this a successful guidebook. Carl A. Neuberger's "A Climbers Guide to the Columbia Gorge," was published in the December 1958 issue of the *Mazama Annual* Volume XL, Number 13. Neuberger's article provided the first comprehensive guide detailing the great Columbia River Gorge classics. He described key features of the gorge that were of great interest to climbers—objectives like St. Peter's Dome, Rabbit Ears below Table Mountain, Little Cougar Rock, and other famous Columbia River Gorge climbs—all within a compact, well-written guide.

The next Oregon guidebook with a compilation of climbing history and route statistics was the twice published *A Climber's Guide to Oregon* by Nicholas Dodge. Printed in 1968 and 1975, Dodge's book contains a wealth of interesting content from the earlier years of climbing and mountaineering and describes many fascinating areas in Oregon from Illumination Rock to Wolf Rock.

In 1983, after years of prolific mountaineering and rock climbing, Jeff Thomas compiled and published *Oregon Rock: A Climber's Guide*. Chock-full of excellent photos and descriptions, the broad scope of Thomas' guide allowed for its marketing success while focusing attention on two of Portland's great climbing areas: Broughton Bluff and Beacon Rock.

The *Rocky Butte Quarry: A Climber's Guide to Urban Rock*, published in 1987 by Mike Pajunas and Bob McGown, contributed equally toward filling in the gaps in crag information and made a reasonable comeback with an updated edition in 1989.

The 1993 edition of *Portland Rock Climbs* took that next step and incorporated information about all the local rock climbing areas in one publication.

These guidebook authors have helped to draw considerable climber and community attention to our favorite local crags, not only for access but also for their natural preservation.

Portland Rock Climbs encompasses a select group of our favorite crags. These are the crags that stand well above other climbing areas by providing consistent rock climbing opportunities. These are: Broughton Bluff, Rocky Butte, Carver Bridge Cliff, Madrone Wall, Ozone Wall, Far Side, Beacon Rock, and French's Dome. This extensive group of crags make up the major core of Portland area rock climbing. The Madrone Wall, though it had been closed for many years, has now reopened to public access. A quality climbing site (managed by the County) that has quickly become one of our premier climbing areas in the Portland region.

CRAG HISTORY (PORTLAND)

Every generation of rock climbers strives to reach out and discover bold new horizons

Kim Crihfield at *Horsethief Butte*

that prove both challenging and rewarding. Rock climbers today have great access to a myriad of cragging opportunities. There are over 850 rock climbs available locally to test your endurance and skill, many of which are steep, multi-pitch climbs, some of them located in the very heart of the spectacular Columbia River Gorge.

Exploring and scrambling has been a gratifying pursuit in northwest Oregon since before the turn of the twentieth century. In the Columbia River Gorge, interest for exploration expanded in part because of the building of the Columbia River Highway, which began in 1913. Recreational pursuits in northwest Oregon have continued to become focused and energized ever since.

From the early 1950s onward, rock climbers have consistently shown great interest in the local crags such as Broughton Bluff and Rocky Butte. As the resilience of rock climbing equipment improved, and as lead climbers' skills began to reach well above the 5.9 level, these crags soon became favorite focal points for practicing the sport of climbing. The old classic climbs of the gorge became less popular. For example: the number of summit ascents on St Peters Dome in 1963–64 was five groups; from 1965–68 just three groups; in 1972 one group; in 1977 one group; and in 1994 one person (Wayne Wallace's roped solo ascent)! In early 2008 Radek & Shirley Chalupa, and Jeff Thomas accomplished another rare ascent of this summit. At that rate of diminishing ascents we must wonder if anyone is interested in ever climbing to the summit of St Peters Dome again.

The trend toward climbing on solid rock is in many ways a great benefit to the sport, for over time these places have developed into excellent, high-quality cragging sites, perfect for testing rock climbing skills and endurance. Most present-day climbers visiting these favorite crags find great satisfaction when free-climbing there. The old classic gorge summits still do exist, of course. To truly experience the wild edge of raw adventure you will probably have to do as the early explorers did, and take to the hills.

Eugene Dod near *Gothic Rock*

INFO ABOUT THE LOCAL CRAGS

Broughton Bluff is the most frequented climbing crag in Portland, especially during spring, summer, and fall. It is the one place that has enjoyed continuous popularity ever since the 1960s. The area is protected by a canopy of Douglas fir trees that provide excellent shade on hot and sometimes humid summer days. Poison oak and nettles grow prolifically here, but year-round use at the popular sections of the crag has generally kept them pushed back.

Rocky Butte Quarry is a unique crag located in northeast Portland near the junction of I-205 and I-84. This easily accessible crag is a great place to top-rope or

Jim Nieland on *Lower Twin Pillar*

to learn the sport. As the name implies, it was a rock quarry site prior to 1956, but now trees envelop the crag in a canopy of cool shade, perfect for summer climbing.

Climbers visited this north-facing crag during the 1960s and '70s to practice their free- and aid climbing skills, but only a few of those early climbers' ascents are known. It was not until the mid to late 1980s that the crag was thoroughly explored for climber use. Video Bluff, Toothpick Wall, and Breakfast Cracks have become favorite areas to climb on a hot summer afternoon. If you can overlook the rough outer appearance—such as the freeway, spray paint, broken glass, and other litter—you will begin to see the inner beauty of this favorite haunt.

Carver Bridge Cliff is a small, secluded, and perpetually shaded basalt cliff of intricate beauty deep in a forest of fir and maple trees. This crag offers very steep and mostly difficult rock climbing for the skilled climber. The best season for climbing here is usually mid-April through October. It is a great place to climb on a summer morning when the temperature at the crag is cool and comfortable.

Dave Sowerby at *The Rat Cave*

The *Madrone Wall* is a superb multi-season climbing crag in Portland. Thanks to concerted efforts by citizens involved with the Madrone Wall Preservation Committee and the local chapter of the Access Fund, the Madrone Wall Park (managed by Clackamas County) has been opened in October 2017 for public access and enjoyment. This crag offers a southwest facing orientation, which is perfect for those fall and winter sunshine days. During the summer it can be quite hot and humid, especially on sunny afternoons. But, overlooking the biting red ants and the minor amount of poison oak, this place is hauntingly beautiful. The reddish-orange rock walls and the stately Pacific madrone (Arbutus menziesii) trees combine to create a wonderful forested setting.

Wayne Wallace during an October ascent of Eliott Headwall

The *Ozone Wall* is one of Portland's more recent additions and certainly one of the better sites for multi-season climbing. With great south facing exposure directly overlooking the Columbia River the steep andesitic bluff provides a great user friendly place to climb in a forest canopy that softens the notorious Gorge winds.

Beacon Rock, the great monolith of the Columbia River Gorge, is situated among some of the most vivid scenery in the Pacific Northwest. This is a favorite well-traveled climbing site during the summer months. Strong winds and cold temperatures keep Beacon Rock nearly void of rock climber presence in the winter months, except for an ardent select core of individuals who relish nailing in the late Fall and early winter season.

The best months to climb here are normally mid-April through September, but the south face of Beacon Rock is closed to climbing (except the northwest section near the main highway) from February 1st until approximately July 15th due to peregrine falcon nesting. Visit Washington's Beacon Rock State Park website for the specific seasonal closing and opening dates of this crag.

Kay Kucera on Bloodline

Beacon Rock offers steep, highly sustained, full pitch and multi-pitch, technically demanding rock climbs at varying levels of difficulty. This is bold climbing! Beacon's easiest route (SE Face route) is 5.7, but it involves nearly 600 feet of multi-pitched leads and requires considerable route-finding skill. The majority of the more frequently ascended climbing routes here range from 5.10 to 5.11+ in difficulty. To date the most difficult lead climbs established are 5.13- with virtually unlimited potential beyond that, whether free climbing or nailing.

The climbing routes are of the highest standard, easily taking first place locally in bold, technical rock climbs. Many of the dihedral systems were nailed in the 1960s and '70s. Later, many of these nailing routes were free climbed at surprisingly moderate ratings, thus establishing some of the finest stemming and jamming problems in the entire Columbia River Gorge basin.

REGIONAL HISTORY

ABOUT NW OREGON & SW WASHINGTON

Every generation of rock climbers strives to reach out and discover bold new horizons that prove both challenging and rewarding. Rock climbers today have great access to a myriad of alpine summits and backwoods cragging opportunities. But the exploring and scrambling idea has been a gratifying pursuit in northwest Oregon since before the turn of the twentieth century. In the Columbia River Gorge, interest for exploration expanded in part because of the building of the Columbia River Highway, which began in 1913. Recreational pursuits in northwest Oregon have continued to become focused and energized ever since.

In the Gorge one wave of exploration began in earnest when turn of the 20th century pioneer photographers and explorer-geologists, men like Benjamin Gifford, G. M. Weister, the Kister Brothers and Ira A. Williams reached places that are extremely difficult to access, even today.

The first recorded ascent of Beacon Rock occurred on August 24, 1901 by Frank Smith, George Purcell, and Charles Church. The route ascended steep brush slopes and exposed 4th and low 5th class corner systems on the west side of the rock formation.

Back in the 1880s high upon the slopes of Mt. Hood, the renowned O.C. Yocum began guiding his guests up to the summit of the mountain, one of them being a young man of 16 years age. This legendary young man, Elijah [Lige] Coalman, is remembered for his strength and zeal. He was instrumental while working for the Forest Service as a lineman striving to establish a lookout station on the summit of Mt. Hood, which he manned for a short time when it was completed. His abilities quickly gained a reputation among the all the great climbers and mountain guides in the Northwest.

"The great vitality of Coalman was demonstrated by one day he spent in 1910. He and a climbing client ate breakfast at the hotel in Government Camp. They then climbed to the summit of Mount Hood and down to Cloud Cap Inn, where the client wanted to go. After lunch at Cloud Cap, Lige climbed back over the summit and arrived for dinner at Government Camp at 5:00 p.m." [Quote from *Mount Hood, A Complete History*, by Jack Grauer.]

In the years from 1913 to 1930 T. Raymond Conway is said to have ascended Illumination Rock nearly a dozen times. From August 1933 to 1936, Gary Leech, another virtual climbing legend in his own right, recorded climbing numerous routes on Illumination Rock, many of these solo, including a solo traverse from the south side up and over the summit and down the East Ridge to the saddle.

In the 1930s another generation of adventures began to take on the serious rock summits of the Gorge, and also high on Mt. Hood. With tremendous vitality Don Onthank, Lee Darling, Ray Conkling, John Ohrenschall, Carl Neuberger, Joe Leuthold, Bill Cummins, Art Maki, the Darr's, Don Comer and many others were instrumental in exploring and conquering some of those great classics. The summits they ascended are unique, tantalizing, and serious in every way, and yet are still available to climb with caution.

These early era rock and mountain climbing pioneers found that by their tremendous endeavors they could go to the edge and beyond.

Beginning in December 1930 an elite mountaineering fraternity was formed known as the Wy'East Climbers. The original founding members were: Don Burkhart, Ray Atkeson, James Harlow, Ralph Calkin, Barrie James, Alfred Monner, Norman O'Connor. Other members who quickly joined the ranks were Joe Leuthold, Olie Lien, James Mount, Everett Darr, Bob Furrer, Ray Lewis, Henry Kurtz, Curtis Ijames and others. This group was known for

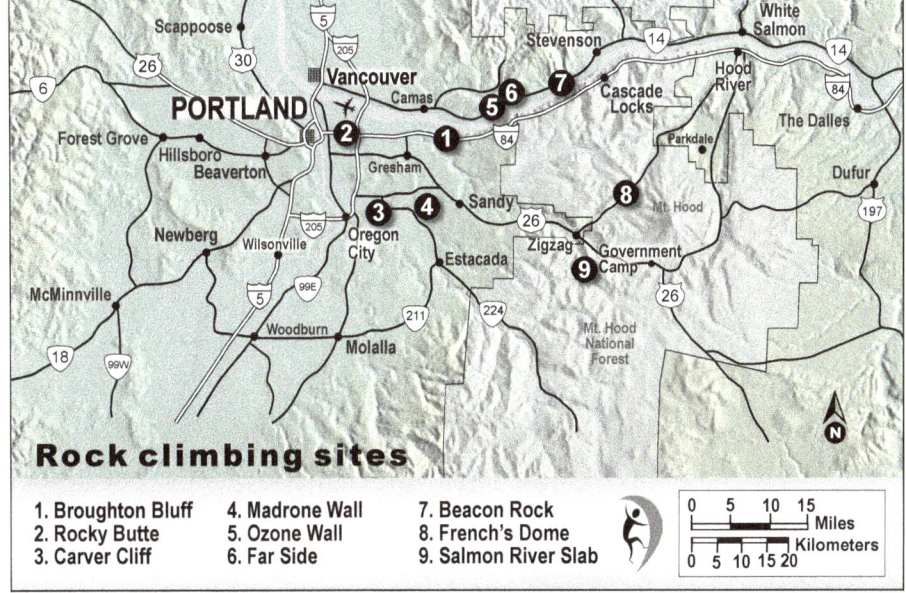

Rock climbing sites

1. Broughton Bluff
2. Rocky Butte
3. Carver Cliff
4. Madrone Wall
5. Ozone Wall
6. Far Side
7. Beacon Rock
8. French's Dome
9. Salmon River Slab

bold adventures, but also showing community founded generosity.

They were highly successful in pioneering a number of new routes on Mount Hood, including Eliot Glacier Headwall. They were instrumental in establishing a First Aid & Rescue equipment cache at a rock shelter near the base of Crater Rock.

On September 28, 1937 Timberline Lodge was formally dedicated by Franklin D. Roosevelt. In 1938 the Wy'East Climbers were instrumental in forming Ski Patrol. This organization initially focused on Search & Rescue emergencies, accident prevention, training, and public education, but has today expanded into the National Ski Patrol Association.

After the Second World War, the fraternity gained new members such as the Petrie brothers, Richard Pooley, David Nelson, James Angell, the Levin brothers, Richard Dodd, John McCormick, Ray Conkling, Al, Kirnak, Albert Weese and others.

In the early 20th century interest for a round-the-mountain trip at the 9,000' elevation level among the glaciers of Mt. Hood was suggested. It was first mentioned by Will Languille. Lige Coalman and O.C. Yocum took a personal 2-day excursion and found an adventure filled with lightning storms, rockfall, and collapsing glacial serac walls. In later years, a very select group of skiers have continued this adventure by skiing from Timberline Lodge up to Illumination Rock saddle, then across the Reid Glacier and around the mountain (Previous seven paragraphs based on brief articles in *Mount Hood: A Complete History*, by Jack Grauer, 1975).

One of the early conquests by some of these historical climbers was on St. Peters Dome in the Columbia River Gorge. On June 23, 1940 a team consisting of Eldon Metzger, Everett and Ida Darr, Glen Asher, James Mount, and Joe Leuthold made the first ascent of St. Peters Dome. Due to the extreme difficulty of succeeding on a wall of loose rubble the number of summit ascents on St Peters Dome gradually grew smaller; in 1963–64 there were five groups; from 1965–68 just three groups; in 1972 one group; in 1977 one group; in 1994 one person (Wallace's roped solo ascent). In early 2008 Radek & Shirley Chalupa, and Jeff Thomas accomplished another rare ascent of this spire, then in 2011 Scott Peterson and partner summited on it, as well.

Alpine exploring, rock climbing, and adventure driven spire climbing quickly became popular again after World War II. Don Comer and friends took to exploring the Crown Point West Chimney in 1950. Ray Conkling and Bud Frie made a second ascent (and likely the first, too) of the minor Conklings Pinnacle in 1951 near Kinzel Tower.

John Ohrenschall (a Swiss guide) and Gene Todd completed the first ascent of the south face of Beacon Rock in 1952. To this day the SE Face route (5.7) is the most frequently climbed technical route on the river face at Beacon. Ray and Leonard Conkling teamed up later to establish the ever

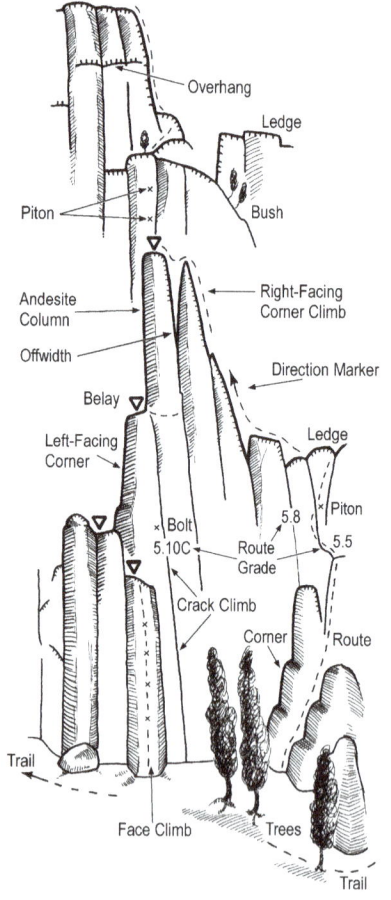

REGIONAL HISTORY ✦ INTRODUCTION

popular Giants Staircase in 1958, the first technical route at French's Dome. Dave Bohn and partners explored a new variant in 1958 on St Peters Dome.

In 1961 Eugene Dod, Bob Martin, and Earl Levin teamed up to explore a particularly steep crack system near the third tunnel at Beacon Rock leading up to Big Ledge.

The development of "Dod's Jam" route is particularly interesting in that it began as a mixed aid and free climb from the railroad tracks at the bottom of the face. On one of the early attempts (in 1961) Earl Levin recalled evaluating a 65-foot overhanging jam crack, which would probably have been aided, but for Eugene Dod, who insisted on flailing away at it, with all his might. "Starting out was most difficult, as Eugene had to stand on my shoulder to work his way into the crack. Up he went and struggling every inch of the way. At the halfway

point he was almost completely exhausted and felt that he would fall any moment. Somehow he made his way to the top where he rested before setting up a third belay position on a tiny ledge appropriately named "The Perch". At the same time I belayed Bob Martin to my position. Bob then decided to go on to Eugene and received a belay to "The Perch". He was so tired at this point that Eugene took the next lead. Through a tree growing inconveniently in our path and sixty-five feet higher up an overhanging face (A1) we found ourselves on 'Big Ledge' and peaceful serenity (Nick Dodge, *A Climbing Guide to Oregon* (1975), pg 26).

Driving From	Driving To	Total Miles	Est. Time
Seattle, WA	Portland, OR	180 miles	3.5 hours
Tacoma, WA	▲	150 miles	3 hours
Yakima, WA		185 miles	3.75 hours
Hood River, OR		56 miles	1 hour
The Dalles, OR		81 miles	1.5 hours
Pendleton, OR		210 miles	3.5 hours
Redmond, OR		130 miles	3 hours
Bend, OR		163 miles	3 hours
Salem, OR		51 miles	1 hour
Albany, OR		73 miles	1.5 hours
Eugene, OR		115 miles	2.25 hours
Roseburg, OR		185 miles	3.75 hours
Grants Pass, OR		253 miles	5 hours
Lincoln City, OR		83 miles	1.75 hours
Astoria, OR	▼	98 miles	2.25 hours
Driving time from city center Portland to the crag listed in PRC			
Broughton Bluff		approximately	30 minutes
Rocky Butte Quarry		▲	15 minutes
Carver Bridge Cliff			25 minutes
Madrone Wall			30 minutes
Ozone Wall			45 minutes
Beacon Rock		▼	60 minutes

Starting in the early 1960s Kim Schmitz, Dean Caldwell, Bob Martin, Charles Carpenter, Wayne Arrington, Alan Kearney and others forged alliances to continue exploring the bold new frontier of Beacon Rock. Schmitz and Levin extended the Dod's Jam route with a variation in 1965 that ends by rappeling onto Grassy Ledges above Flying Swallow. Wayne Arrington and Jack Barrar developed a direct finish variant in 1972 that follows close to the upper headwall and lands on the trail near an overlook.

More climbers met and forged formidable climbing teams during the 1960s-70s. Jim Nieland, Bill Cummins, and Dave Jensen formed climbing partnerships with the indefatigable Eugene Dod as they succeeded on numerous bold ascents throughout northwest Oregon and southwest Washington. Some of their contributions include the Zucchini Route (NE Face route) in 1968 on Crown Point, three routes on Twin Pillars in the Ochoco Mtns also in 1968, and Needle Rock near Detroit, Oregon also in September of 1968.

Jim Nieland traveled often, and this afforded the opportunity to explore rock pillars even in the remote hinterland of southeast Oregon. He still found untraveled rock climbs closer to Portland. He and Francisco Valenzuela completed the first ascent of the northwest face Tower Rock on June 19th & 20th, 1982. His remembrance about the ascent, "...[we] started the climb thinking it would take 5-6 hours to complete. At dark we found ourselves in the middle of the face, with no easy way to retreat down the overhangs below. We spent a cold night on a ledge. We reached the top early afternoon the next day, a little dehydrated but none the worse for wear..." Though an impressive plainly visible roadside wall, Tower Rock is a seldom repeated climb to this day.

The Columbia Gorge seems to have its own share of mysterious places, too. Jim Davis and Wayne Haack attempted the West Face of Wind Mtn during the summer of 1975. The goal was to reach the prominent upper left leaning corner system. They rapped after placing some fixed gear on the initial technical lead at the top of the main ravine after an encounter with rockfall. Davis returned a year or two later with friends Priest and

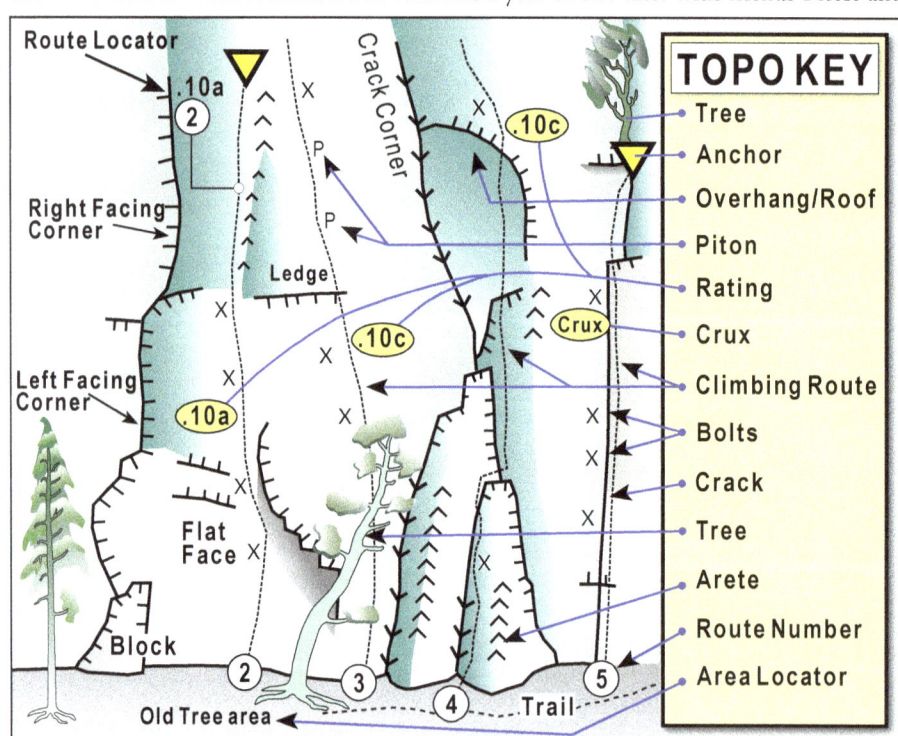

> ### Dod's Jam Route
>
> In 1961 Eugene Dod, Bob Martin, and Earl Levin teamed up to explore a particularly steep crack system near the third tunnel at Beacon Rock leading up to Big Ledge.
>
> The development of "Dod's Jam" route is particularly interesting in that it began as a mixed aid and free climb from the railroad tracks at the bottom of the face. On one of the early attempts (in 1961) Earl Levin recalled evaluating a 65-foot overhanging jam crack, which would probably have been aided, but for Eugene Dod, who insisted on flailing away at it, with all his might.
>
> "Starting out was most difficult, as Eugene had to stand on my shoulder to work his way into the crack. Up he went and struggling every inch of the way. At the halfway point he was almost completely exhausted and felt that he would fall any moment. Somehow he made his way to the top where he rested before setting up a third belay position on a tiny ledge appropriately named 'The Perch'. At the same time I belayed Bob Martin to my position. Bob then decided to go on to Eugene and received a belay to "The Perch". He was so tired at this point that Eugene took the next lead. Through a tree growing inconveniently in our path and sixty-five feet higher up an overhanging face (A1) we found ourselves on 'Big Ledge' and peaceful serenity."
> Nick Dodge, *A Climbing Guide to Oregon* (1975), pg 26.

Tyerman determined to succeed, but still could not surmount the friable R/X section above the initial ravine. Years later Jim Nieland and Francisco Valenzuela completed a 3-pitch route in 1984 immediately to the right of the West Face crack in another deep corner system. As a low elevation backup plan Wallace and Olson opted to try the West Face crack in 1994, but the adventure was cut short when Wayne took a leader fall on the X-rated pitch. Later that same season, Steve Elder completed the first ascent of the West Face crack by rope-soloing the route in September 1994 in his usual daring style.

The original half dozen routes on Illumination Rock were established prior to the second world war. In relatively recent days, and after honing ice climbing skills in the Columbia Gorge, another generation of climbers found the rime ice gullies on I-rock to be stellar when the conditions are good. Wayne Wallace teamed up with Richard Ernst, Lane brown and Leesa Azaar to punch a stout string of extreme mixed ice routes up the face left of the South Chamber. Steve Elder quietly shook the scene and made a rope-solo run on the northeast face in his typically classic style (he is also the only person known to have soloed Yocum Ridge in summer and winter). Nate Farr and Collin Bohannon found the stone cold icy northwest face of I-rock to their liking, and added to the spectrum of minimalist routes on that shaded side.

The north western portion of Oregon state has a great variety of rock bluff formations ranging from basalt to andesite, as well as a few minor andesitic bouldering opportunities which have boosted the sport of rock climbing in all aspects. A broad group of individuals from the 1960s onward took great interest in rock climbing near their home base whether that was Portland, Hood River or Government Camp. Each little core group, driven by team members in a closely knit, and sometimes exclusive enclave, set new trends by exploring and establishing a string of fine climbing areas in this region that continues even to this day. Idealistic teams such as the legacy of Paul LaBarge and Jim Tripp have brought great little climbing sites like The Swine (Enola) to the forefront of regional climbing. Even the minor Misty Slab outcrop above French's Dome was rumored by Bob McGown to offer a nice 5.9 crack climb. Enticing rumors make it all a worthy hunt.

At French's Dome, climbers like Hermann Gollner, Vance Lemley, Pat Purcell, Tom Kingsland, and other coaches from the Mt Hood Summer Ski Camps found the dome perfect for their first ascent climbing purposes beginning in the late 1990s. Tymun Abbott and Dave Sowerby added a string of powerful quality routes during that same period. The Dark Side (aka The Siege) carries a unique bit of history. The route was bolted by Hermann who shortly later departed out of state. The route was cleaned and projected by Florjan Jagodic but he could not do it. Florjan, still eager to attain the first ascent on the route asked Hermann, who is a training master, "How to attain the 5.13 mark." Hermann said, "Just loose a few pounds." So, Florjan feverishly worked the route all the while dieting, but down south Hermann also got still stronger. As he subtly put it, "He surrounded the castle and starved him out," like a Seige. The next spring Hermann came back to work at the Ski School and

sent it sometime in the late spring of 1997. But oddly enough, during the very same months a local Scotsman (Dave Sowerby) began working the project and also managed to free it. So the FFA saga, whoever might have sent it free still makes a great saga in classic European style.

Menagerie hardman Jim Anglin departed from the Sweet Home area for finer climes, and quickly took to helping with route development at Area51 in the year 2003. Paul Cousar and Kay Kucera, a team filled with virtually infinite energy, have taken giant steps from the years 2001-2005 to set Area51 and OH8 firmly on this regions climbing map. Their strong emphasis on biodiversity dynamics, user impact, and trail maintenance (as well as rock climbing) keep these sites readily accessible, while bringing various ethical awareness considerations to all visitors.

The Wolf Rock massif is an imposing feature subtly inviting to adventure climbers who like forging new routes. Wolf Rock saw a wide variety of climbers such as Gil Staender, John Barton, Nick Dodge and others forged climbs up the steep moss ravines of the north side during the '60s and early '70s. Yet it was Wayne Arrington, Mike Seeley who during a two-day effort that they established the classic Barad-Dûr route, punching a line through the improbable great roofs on the southeast face of Wolf in June 1972. The 1970s-'80s brought Dean Fry, John Barrar, Jeff Thomas, Doug Phillips and Jay Peterson to Wolf's south face scene where the rock was suitable to their taste, though still occasionally friable with runout sections. Wolf Rock continues to be popular, especially for those of us who are determined to walk in the footsteps of Mr. Arrington by repeating his great 900' long Barad-Dûr route. The monolith attained greater interest from a widely diversified generation of climbers who arrived on the scene from early 2000s onward to establish a stellar string of high quality bolt routes near the Conspicuous Arch. Some of those players were John Rich, the Fralick brothers, Jim Anglin, and Kent Benesch.

The Menagerie Wilderness climbing area offers an extensive selection of rock bluffs and spires, from an enjoyable mix of moderate climbs around Rooster Rock in the lower area, and the very bold spicy flavored climbs with plenty of serious leading endeavors in the upper Menagerie area on tuffaceous rhyolite formations. Rooster Tail was initially explored in 1949 by Bill Sloan and Byron Taylor. In the 1950s energetic climbers like Pat Callis and associates, quickly joined by the Bauman brothers starting in the early '60s the vertical edge trend of climbing at the Menagerie continued unabated well into the early 2000s. Tom and Bob Bauman are certainly the two most prolific Menagerie climbers who began exploring here, finding its steep spires and cliff formations an exhilarating worthy objective. The Bauman brothers were also highly instrumental toward encouraging the formation of this small Wilderness area. Pat Callis, Willi Unsoeld, Bob Ashworth, Eugene Dod, Jim Nieland, Dave Jensen, Wayne Arrington, and Jeff Thomas (Oregon Rock and Oregon High author) were a few of the contenders from the 1960s and onward. The Dod-Jensen-Pratt team succeeded in summiting on the infamous Turkey Monster spire in 1966. Pat Callis and Soren Norman teamed up the conquer the North Rabbit Ear in 1960, quickly followed by the Bauman brothers on the South Rabbit Ear in 1966. Jim Anglin teamed up with the Bauman brothers to establish a tremendous selection of additional climbs. Jim was certainly one of the primary players who helped place the Menagerie firmly on the modern rock climbing map. The Menagerie site is quite possibly the single most diverse (from quality to friable rock) place in the mid-western Cascades that has over 150 climbing routes on rock 40+ formations.

The central Cascade range of western Oregon have long been a suitable back door haunt for the OSU Mtn Club at the University in Corvallis. This club, initially founded by Willi Unsoeld and associates, became an energetic club where students could mix a bit of studies with the great outdoors. Members of the club explored and climbed a variety of spires in the Menagerie and Detroit areas and well beyond, often leaving a powerful climbing legacy in their own time.

Southern Willamette climbers such as Dave and Dee Tvedt, Mark Ashworth, Randy Rimby and the Fralick brothers enjoyed establishing climbs at Hills Creek Spires from 1995 onward. This odd cluster of steep tuffaceous volcanic spires lay perched on the south facing ridge crest slopes of Kitson Ridge near Oakridge, Oregon. Flagstone climbing site provides a tremendous selection of fine climbing opportunities on a steep slab of snow and ice polished densely compact fine-grained andesitic rock formation. Initially explored in the late 1970s, the site eventually experienced a surge of activity from the mid-1980s onward. Alan Amos, Walt Corvington, the Tvedt's, the Fralick brothers, and many other climbers helped establish the 70 odd fine quality slab climbs. The route Hydrotube (5.9) first climbed by Corvington and Amos in the late 1980s is certainly one of the great classic gems at Flagstone and likely to be one of your fist leads if you visit there.

Although this book details some of these fascinating old summit rock climbs, today's trend toward climbing on solid rock is beneficial to the sport, for it has opened a great new door to back forest rock climbing opportunities at excellent, high quality rock crags in a fresh air environment that benefits everyone.

Most climbers visiting these crags described in this book find great satisfaction visiting these quiet forested crags that are within a relatively easy 1-day outing from the city of Portland.

NW OREGON CLIMATE

The northwest U.S. has a temperate climate that receives an abundance of precipitation mainly because a warm subtropical air mass and a cold polar front jet stream air mass intermix producing variant seasonal changes in the climate. The Oregon climate west of the Cascade Range is predominantly wet for most of the year. Pacific marine air weather systems bring an abundance of rainfall that saturates the region, especially from late-October through May. Most rock climbers in northwest Oregon generally seek the local crags during the warm season (May through October). During this portion of the year mild marine air often mixes with inland Great Basin hot weather to bring a climber-friendly cycle that keeps the region quite comfortable.

During the summer months, temperatures will average in the seventies to mid eighties (Fahrenheit) with occasional short peaks of hot, sunny days in July and August reaching the nineties. Temperatures above 100°F are infrequent.

By late October, the Pacific marine air storm tracks become more active, usually bringing a consistent series of rain showers. The typical winter storm systems generate frequent cold, rainy days with average temperatures in the 35–50°F range. Occasional strong low weather systems sweep south from the inland polar region to produce short periods of intense cold in the twenties to mid-thirties east of the Cascade Range, but these brisk temperatures seldom penetrate into the valleys of western Oregon. Average annual precipitation in the Willamette Valley near Portland is about 40 inches; at times the winter weather is prohibitively wet. During these periods, most rock climbers seek the refuge of a local rock gym or sports gym for fitness continuity.

Although the winter may seem long in Oregon, virtual year-round rock climbing is readily available and without driving all the way to Smith Rock. Broughton Bluff and the Madrone Wall both offer a southwesterly orientation. With a little winter sunshine these crags quickly dry out and both provide a respite from the notorious howling east winds of the Columbia River Gorge.

Most of the crags around Portland may be utilized during May through October. In spite of the typical rain showers, the cliffs are generally vertical enough to quickly dry out during seasonally mild temperatures. Several popular sites at the crags are so precipitous (such as the Bat Wall) they seldom get damp from rainfall except in the depth of winter.

Lower elevation (3,000' to 4,000') rock climbing sites west or east of the Cascade mountain range such as French's Dome or Pete's Pile are usually accessible as early as mid-May through October. Expect heavy snow pack to hinder easy access to high-altitude (5,000' to 6,000') pinnacles or climbing sites such as Lamberson Butte or Needle Rock until mid-July.

Certain summits like Illumination Rock offer winter mixed alpine climbing opportunities which yields a year-round opportunity for those dedicated to the extreme sport of rime ice climbing. In spite of region-

NW OREGON CLIMATE ✧ INTRODUCTION

al rain showers, the spires and cliffs generally dry out quickly during the seasonally mild May through October temperatures.

POLAR JET STREAM

The polar jet stream gradually descends southward each month in the Fall and Winter; Ketchikan Alaska in October, near Vancouver, British Columbia in November, Astoria in December, and Eureka, California in January.

When this jet stream develops a sharp southward swing over the mid-continent some of this Arctic cold air mass will pour over the Cascades from the east (and through the Columbia Gorge). Initially is produces a mix of snow or freezing rain, but if the Arctic air mass if strong enough it can provide a term of intense cold (20° F – 30° F) but otherwise sunny weather in the Columbia Gorge and slightly warmer temperatures in the northern Willamette Valley. A Gorge wind chill factor (30+ mph) increases the sense of cold and assists in distributing water droplets on cliff scarps that freeze quickly in two to three days. Local ice climbers usually will closely watch for this weather pattern.

TRIP PLANNING

How does this data break down for quick use by a rock climber? If it is not raining, go climbing. Is the forecast on the west side of the Cascades predicting gray skies and showery conditions in May and June? Then consider driving to an east side destination where you can often find sunnier skies and certainly less rain than the west side climbing sites.

Unique places such as Pete's Pile or the remote well-concealed Bulo Point climbing crag make great drier climbing destinations because of the effect of the rain shadow created by the Cascade mountain range. In essence, your visit to east side climbing destinations for rock climbing opportunities is sure to be a success, although during summer thunderstorm activity can

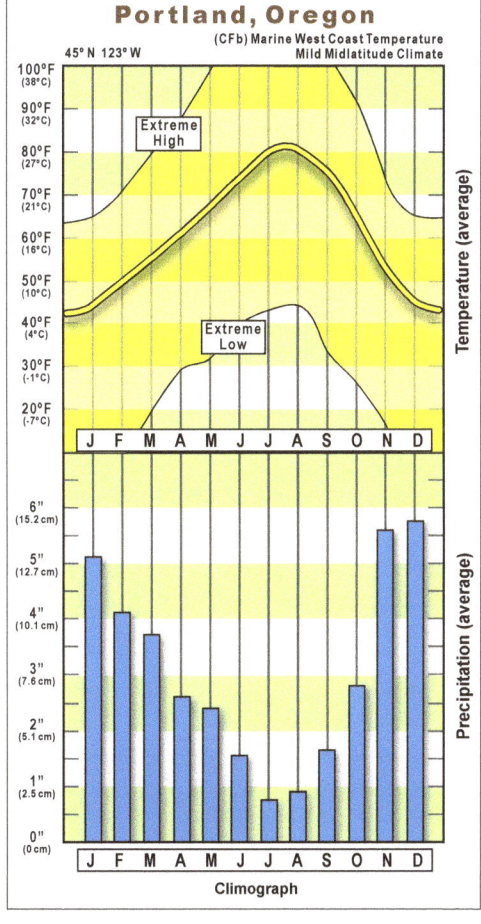

Portland, Oregon
45° N 123° W
(CFb) Marine West Coast Temperature
Mild Midlatitude Climate

Climograph

develop rapidly along the eastern slope of the High Cascades on a hot summer afternoon.

GEOLOGY — NW OREGON

A formative discussion on the physical geology and natural processes of rock structures is beneficial to all climbers by providing a better understanding of the cliffs and mountains we climb on. This analysis is a brief summary of Plate Tectonics and continental volcanism designed to enhance your understanding of localized geologic characteristics of rock stratum and lava formation.

PLATE TECTONICS

The geological landscape of Oregon, like a thin fabric has been stretched and reshaped by continental and oceanic movements described systematically as Plate Tectonics. This diverse region of volcanic activity is structurally composed of igneous, sedimentary, and met-

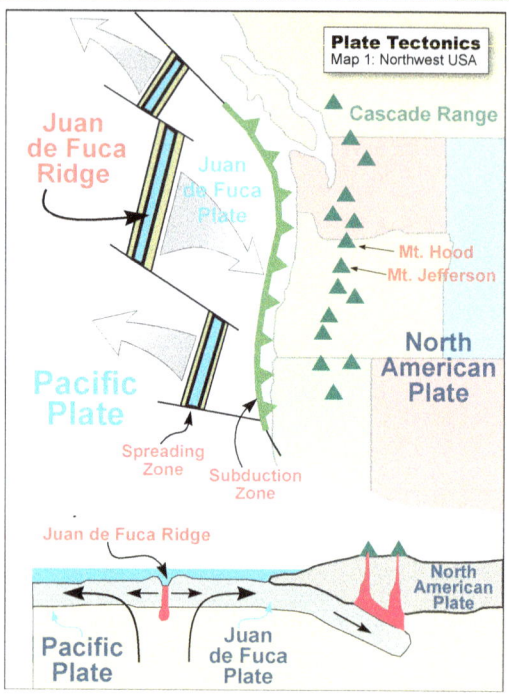

amorphic rock formations creating an interwoven and complex matrix. Though our lowlands and valleys of northwestern Oregon (including the northern Coast Range) are commonly formed of sedimentary rock, much of the Cascade Mountain Range is built on multiple layers of basalt (~50% silica), andesite (~60% silica), some dacite, and infrequent formations of welded tuff rhyolite (~70%+ silica) stratum such as Steins Pillar.

The lithosphere between the upper plates and the earth's mantle moves in relation to deep ocean volcanism, while the oceanic and continental plates ride piggyback on top. Plate tectonics gradually shift and build all rock formations into similarly understandable patterns and concepts. The thicker continental plate is composed of very old granitic stock surrounded by younger uplifted sediment, and when it collides with the offshore oceanic crustal plate the heavier (denser) plate is

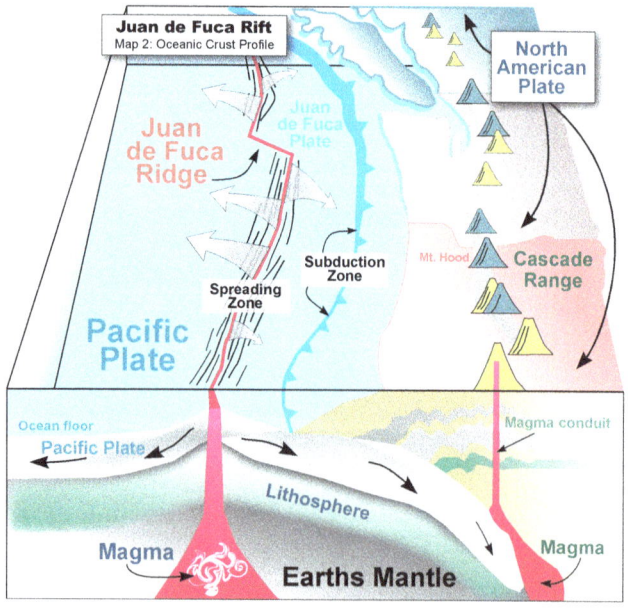

SiO₂ Content	Magma Type	Volcanic Rock
~50%	Mafic	Basalt
~60%	Intermediate	Andesite
~65%	Felsic (low Si)	Dacite
~70%	Felsic (high Si)	Rhyolite

Most magmas are composed of ten elements: Oxygen (O), silicon (Si), aluminum (Al), iron (Fe), magnesium (Mg), titanium (Ti) calcium (Ca), sodium (Na), potassium (K), and phosphorous (P). Oxygen and silicon are by far the two most abundant elements, thus for clarity the different magma types are described by their silica content (SiO_2).

Igneous Rock Classifications

	Felsic	Intermediate	Mafic	Ultramafic
Fine Grain	Rhyolite	Andesite	Basalt	
Intermediate		Dacite	Diabase	
Course Grain	Granite	Diorite	Gabbro	Peridotite
Glassy	Obsidian			
Frothy	Pumice		Scoria	

subducted beneath the former. Some of the compositionally lighter weight sedimentary rocks (oceanic & continental) that are subducted back down into the earths mantle will melt and remix with the magma pool or core, then rise as infrequent magma intrusions through fissures or fault lines in the continental crust. Most oceanic seafloor sediment accumulates from organic marine animals and plants, as well as from terrigenous (land) or submarine volcanic sources.

If the magma congeals underground it is referred to as intrusive igneous rock in the form of dikes, sills or batholiths, but when the magma erupts volcanically through breaks or fissures in the earths surface it is known as extrusive igneous volcanism.

When the magma breaks the continental crust they are observable as volcanic vent openings which can develop into mountains that expel material composed of lava flows, flood basalts, lava domes, explosive pumice, ash or tuff clouds, and debris formations. This offshore fault line subduction zone folds and warps the sedimentary perimeter continental landscape creating our coastal range. These coastal foothills of sedimentary rock are folded and uplifted by the oceanic plate to form the low profile Coast Mountain range.

Certain mountain ranges such as the Olympics in Washington state are created less by volcanism and more by the ongoing tectonic folding and faulting process. The northern Cascade Mountain range of Oregon has a series of major strato-volcanoes (i.e. Mt. Hood, Mt. Jefferson) but also shield volcanoes (Newberry Crater in central Oregon) and numerous smaller cinder cones such as Olallie Butte.

THREE TYPES OF ROCK

Igneous rock formations are classified geologically into three main groups to emphasize the mode of origin: igneous, metamorphic, and sedimentary.

Intrusive or plutonic rock forms as magma migrates upward from Earth's mantle, but cools and solidifies slowly at depth to form subsurface rock masses. Extrusive volcanic rock forms when the magma breaks out upon the Earth's surface and cools quickly. The principal forms of hardened extrusive igneous rock are basalt, andesite, dacite, and rhyolite, while intrusive igneous magma congeals below the surface slowly to form granite, diorite, and gabbro.

Metamorphic rock is formed when deeply buried, then folded and compressed by stresses, high temperatures, and chemical conditions. Sedimentary rocks are formed by processes that are active at the earth's surface. These are usually formed by erosion, decay, breakdown of other rock material, or an accumulation or buildup of rock, shells, or corals that over time are compacted and hardened to form sedimentary rocks. Examples are limestone, gypsum, flint,

18 INTRODUCTION ✦ GEOLOGY - NW OREGON

conglomerate, sandstone, and shale.

The primary factors affecting the melting ratio of rock structures are water (volatiles), changes in pressure, and heat. Partial melting occurs when the rocks melting point breaks down certain silica-rich minerals first, then stops the process by a shift or change in parameters. As magma cools and solidifies two groups of silicate mineral elements form; dark and light silicates.

Dark silicates are rich in iron and magnesium (prevalent in olivine, pyroxene, amphibole, biotite, garnet), and light silicates are rich in potassium, sodium, and calcium (prevalent in quartz, muscovite, feldspar). The formation of dark or ferromagnesian basaltic (mafic) magma is composed from dry, silica-poor ultramafic rock of the Earth's upper mantle peridotite, which contains mostly olivine and pyroxene. Ultramafic rock is uncommon at Earth's surface, but is thought to be the primary constituent of the upper mantle. Light granitic (felsic) magma is likely composed from the crystallization of silica-rich andesitic magma or continental rocks.

BORING LAVA FORMATION

The low silica basalt lava cliff formations in and around Portland were deposited from a flow called the Boring Lava Flow. Prominent hills such as Mount Scott, Mount Tabor, Rocky Butte, Chamberlain Hill, and buttes near the town of Boring are cinder cone volcanoes part of the Boring Lava Field formation which generally deposited cinder, ash and lava flows. Larch Mountain, further to the east is a shield volcano which allowed for fluid lava to travel along a gentle gradient slope to deposit alternating layers of basalt and debris.

The degree to which the Boring Lava formation congealed resulted in deep layers of compact basalt with broad smooth surfaces with widely-spaced generally vertical joint cracks. The flow was deposited upon the Troutdale Conglomerate formation, a mixture of well-rounded pebbles of water transported volcanic material. The slope below the north face of Broughton Bluff reveals some of this layer of pebbled product. Thick sheets of this low silica basaltic lava flow also exist on Mount Sylvania, as well as near Oregon City. Broughton bluff, Carver cliff, and Madrone wall are part of this extensive formation. Surface color striations, such as at the Madrone Wall show a distinctly golden-tan undertone with a smattering of artistic yellowish-brown, red, orange, and gray painted upon the surface of the rock cliff caused from iron oxidation interaction with water.

COLUMBIA GORGE BASALT GROUP

Highly fluid dense black magma erupted as flood basalts during the middle Miocene Epoch in southeast Washington and northeastern Oregon. These very active flows traveled laterally for hundreds of miles eventually covering extensive portions of southeast Washington and much of eastern Oregon. The cumulative effect of the CGBG deposited lava formation varies from 2,000' thick to a thickness in excess of 5,000' near Tri-Cities. This basalt formation, when deposited congealed quickly to form dense dark-colored 6-, 5-, 4-sided vertically oriented polygonal structured columns (6 inches to 2 feet in diameter) of dark colored basalt capped with an entablature on top of each flow. Each individual lava

Bob McGown on *Turkey Monster*

flow has congealed in distinct layers commonly 40' to 200' thick and is readily visible on numerous cliffs throughout the Columbia River Gorge and eastward to Wallula Gap, the lower Palouse River, and the channeled scablands of central Washington. The largest of these flood basalts formations is known as the Grande Ronde flow.

The cliffs in the Gorge near Yeon Mountain reveal well over 2,000 feet of horizontal layered bands of this basalt flow, bringing beauty and rugged harmony to this scenic area. The vertical beauty of the Gorge terrain was enhanced by Columbia River erosion processes, by multiple Missoula Flood inundations, and a gradual uplift of the Cascade Range. Although some rock climbing is possible on these flood basalt formations (such as Horsethief Butte) the nature of the narrow columnar rock formations, decomposition, and weathering processes tends to limit rock climber interest.

The outstanding exception in the gorge of course is Beacon Rock, an old volcanic neck core that is the second largest monolith in the world after the Rock of Gibralter. The volcano, originally erupted and built in a distant Epoch was weathered by erosional processes and flood waters of ancient Lake Missoula, leaving this prominent remnant core neck in the central Gorge. The 848-foot high monolith is composed of a medium-colored, vesicular andesite and is steeply featured on all sides. On the south face massive vertically-jointed columns make this site a perfect haven for skilled rock climbing enthusiasts. Today, the mile-long zigzag trail leading to the top of Beacon provides hikers with one of the finest panoramic views of the Columbia River Gorge.

CASCADIAN MOUNTAINS

The Cascade range is formed from these active plate tectonic movements and typically align roughly parallel to the general off-shore descending oceanic plate. Andesite and basalt formations are common in the northern part of the High Cascades while rhyolite, andesite, and basalt formations surface south of the Three Sisters peaks.

The northern Oregon coastline rock formation, though often sedimentary in nature has prominent headland basalt formations as well. The impressive mass of Onion Peak near Nehalem (including Saddle Mtn. and Humbug Mtn.) is an intrusive body of submarine pillow basalt. North of Mt Hebo old flows, tuffs, and breccia formations are common in the hills, while the central Oregon Coast Range south from Mt Hebo reveals a greater percentage of sandstone formations. The crest of certain prominent peaks west of Salem, Corvallis and Eugene have gabbro, diorite, syenite and basalt caps. These usually formed as dikes or sills and have eroded into minor rock outcrops and an occasional boulderfield some of which is viable for climbing. The southern Oregon Coast range has a large percentage of volcanic and sedimentary seafloor uplifted rock formations strongly metamorphosed into schist, sandstone, serpentine, some limestone, and in the Klamath Mountains outcrops of granite.

CASCADE MOUNTAIN RANGE

The Cascade Mountain range can be structurally divided into two north-south oriented regional masses; the older or Western range which have low hills near 1700' at the western margin and 5800' near the eastern margin, and the presently existing High Cascades with

10,000'+ tall peaks. The High Cascade formation contains the series of peaks climbers often ascend, such as Mt. Hood, Mt. Jefferson, 3-Sisters, etc.

The volcanic history of the Cascades can be subdivided further into three general building phases: a coastline Klamath-Blues-Wallowas lineament, the Western Cascade gradient, and the High Cascade fault zone lineament.

The original phase of volcanic activity began during the Eocene Epoch built a mountain chain from the Klamath's to the Wallowas, including the Ochoco Mountain remnant in central Oregon. Once completed sometime in the Pliocene Epoch most of this series of very old coastal range (prior to the existence of the Willamette Valley) produced major granitic peak formations on a scale rarely seen since in Oregon.

After considerable inactivity, the next eruptive phase in the Miocene Epoch produced the old Western Cascade mountain range, some of which fell as ash-tuff deposits in Central Oregon of which the John Day ash formation is a primary example.

This Western range of mountains gradually reduced in size through weathering and glacial processes, now look like mere foothills or ridge crests cut by deep ravines nearly lacking in visible summits showing volcanic origin. But the evidence is in the rocks.

Oregon's northwestern Cascade province are separated by three major river drainage valleys; the Clackamas River, the Santiam Rivers, and the McKenzie River. This diverse region is a heavily forested eco-system that lies entirely below timberline, but do occasionally provide sub-alpine craggy peaks and pinnacles, thin-soiled steep slopes covered with Bear-grass (Xerophyllum tenax) and beautiful scenic views. Some of the low foothills southeast of Stayton and south past Eugene are composed of tuffaceous sandstone, rhyolite and basalt formations.

Our present High Cascade skyline is the result of relatively recent Pliestocene Epoch activity in the timeline of eruptive cyclical volcanism. Initially, this final eruptive phase produced Shield or low-profile mountains. Belknap Crater and Newberry Crater are several classic examples of low-profile shield volcanoes that produced much cindery tuffaceous material, including high silica content obsidian flows.

Soon the conical stratovolcanoes built much larger (and taller) andesitic-dacitic mountains intermixed with basalt lava flows as well as considerable tuff ash fall deposits. Several late stage High Cascade volcanoes have produced some rhyolite, but this is usually found south of the 3-Sisters region, while Andesite formations are commonly found in the northern part. The southern Oregon volcanoes seem to be using a silica-rich but water-poor coastal subduction material which is remixed with magma and resurfaced as light-colored rhyolite-andesite lava.

Rhyolitic volcanism can be violently explosive though. Mt. Mazama, our present day water filled Crater Lake is an example of an old rhyolitic volcano that was comprised of sufficient quantities of water and gasses to produce a highly explosive tuff explosion.

MISSOULA FLOODS

Broughton Bluff and even Rocky Butte Quarry were partially exposed by dramatic erosional processes of the Missoula Flood (see J. Harlen Bretz papers 1923, 1925, & 1956) which scoured the Columbia River Gorge and east side regions with 400' to 1000' high inundations of flood waters emanating originally from near the northeastern Idaho-Montana border. These flood waters occurred during the last Ice Age when lobes or tongues of the Cordilleran Ice Sheet extended across the Clark Fork River drainage channel blocking and forming the infamous Lake Missoula in western Montana. The ice dam broke repeatedly sending powerful forces of water moving abruptly southwestward along the river system all the way to the Pacific Ocean.

Fine examples of the effects of this flood are Lake Pend Orielle, the channeled Scablands, Grand Coulee, and the steeply scoured walls of the Columbia River Gorge. Numerous large erratic boulders rafted on icebergs were left scattered along the entire route and in the northern Willamette Valley.

The Sandy River carved additional steepness into Broughton Bluff, while erosional processes on the Clackamas River exposed the mighty cliffs of the Madrone Wall and Carver Bridge Cliff.

GEOLOGIC NATURE OF VARIOUS CLIMBING SITES

Mt. Hood volcanism is composed of andesitic rock with medium silicon content 57-62% (SiO_2) mostly in the nature of lava flows, domes and pyroclastic deposits. The south debris slope fan from Crater Rock (a hornblende dacite dome) down past Timberline Lodge is composed mostly of dacite and andesite debris material. Illumination Rock and Steele Cliffs are andesite flows that congealed abruptly due to surrounding abstract terrain movement limitations. Mt. Hood is a composite or stratovolcano which has alternating layers of lava flows and pyroclastic deposits.

French's Dome is a fine example of a late stage 'plug' dome neck core of an old volcano that was likely a 'satellite' vent of the larger very old Sandy Glacier Volcano on the west flank of Mt. Hood. The ancient flows of this volcano exist below the Sandy River Glacier at the 1,650 meter elevation as a narrow profile dike or core composed of olivine andesite lava. Additional satellite vents are the Pinnacle and Cloud Cap.

The andesite lava of Enola (the Swinery) east of Rhododendron is a moderately porphyritic (58.7% SiO_2) formation.

The Pete's Pile bluff is a widely joint-spaced 60-meter high columnar andesite formation that is a moderately porphyritic lava flow exposed on the east canyon wall of East Fork Hood River near Polallie Creek. The bluff was exposed by the effects of avalanche flood debris and river cutting forces from Mt. Hood eruptive volcanic cycles. Compositionally the Pete's Pile bluff has an abundance of 2-3mm blocky plagioclase phenocrysts of silicate mineral (5-10%) with traces of olivine and amphibole in a dense medium-gray colored groundmass.

Porphyritic andesite with various sized phenocryst minerals in a dense mesocratic matrix of medium gray to light gray colored rock are quite common in the northern part of the state. The Cascade mountain geographic zone experiences a continuous cycle of seasonal hot and cold temperate fluctuations that strongly influence the process of mechanical and chemical weathering.

At Bulo Point chemically active water solutions increased the process of granular decomposition of the superficial structures. Rock formations in the 15-mile creek watershed are porphyritic silicic andesite (62.6% SiO_2) in a blocky plagioclase phenocryst matrix of light and dark-colored minerals. The Bulo Point formation is likely an extrusive lava flow or intrusive near-surface sill later exposed through erosional processes that removed the less resilient layers. A steady weathering process from water, heat and other factors gradually rounded the overall cliff features. Bulo Point has a course-grained surface texture akin to a particularly rough grade of sandpaper that increases friction ability so long as you are careful with how you jam your fingers or fists into rough-edged cracks.

Crown Point is a CGBG flood basalt formation with some conglomerate and Boring Lava formations at the top near Vista House.

Skinner Butte is polygonal sided steeply oriented columnar course-grained basalt that formed from a congealed near-surface intrusive flow and is likely a laccolith (the tip of a larger batholith) that is weathered erosionally along with limited quarrying activity.

Spire Rock and X-Spire, which are located near Triangulation Peak east of Detroit, Oregon are likely old basalt volcanic necks or feeder vents of resilient rock that resisted erosional effects which removed the surrounding softer landscape.

At the west end of Detroit Lake is a small granitic stock or core of an ancient volcano.  This granitic structure about one mile in diameter near the dam was formed by subsurface magma activity and crystallized by cooling slowly at great depth. The summits above Tumble Lake (Needle Rock, Elephant Rock, Split Spire, Tumble Rock) are likely fissures or vents from a deep volcanic formation. These summits are basaltic formations heavily weathered by the elements, but still offer reasonably massive outcrop structures ideal for adventure climbers. Other subsurface granitic stock formations exist near Blue River on the McKenzie and near Leaburg Dam.

Steins Pillar is an imposing 350' tall (with a 120' girth) erosional remnant composed of moderately welded tuff (ignimbrite) from hot pyroclastic flows typically vented from dacite or rhyolite volcanic ash eruptions. This natural pillar of light-colored rock and the two formations immediately to the south are silicic (65%+ SiO_2) tuff flow remnants from the John Day Formation.

There are a total of three distinct banding colorations due to three violent eruptive volcanic phases of silica-rich hot pumice fragments, ash, and glass shards built upon the other is short succession. Nearby buttes such as Forked Horn Butte are the likely former sources of these eruption cycles. Each distinct layer of the ash eruption was still hot when the next eruptive phase deposited additional frothy fragments. The pumice, readily altered by compression, heat, and chemical agglutination, flattened the fragments and gaseous pockets, thus cementing the crystaline ash elements together. Steins Pillar is capped with a weathering-resistant fourth layer of reddish hardened ash giving the spire a pronounced steeply overhung feature. The pillar walls have a notable hardened yellow-brown stain from the oxidation process of iron bearing minerals in the tuff.

If you are looking for big granite alpine spires Oregon is not the place. The sand dunes on the Oregon coast are closer to Portland than the nearest outcrop of pure granite. But, Silver Star Mtn does have some granodiorite related formations in the 3,500'-4,500' elevation, such as Chimney Rocks.

CLIMBING ROUTE RATINGS

This guide uses the well-known Yosemite Decimal System (YDS) as the standard method for rating rock climbs. This system, first developed at Tahquitz in the 1950s, is a two-system concept connecting a Difficulty Grade and a Free Climbing Class.

Difficulty Grades

A Difficulty Grade (Roman numerals I through VI) indicates how long it will take to climb a route and is determined by the difficulty, the involvement, and the length of a route. For example:

- **Grade I**   Can be climbed in a few hours.
- **Grade II**   Can be climbed in a half day or less.
- **Grade III**   Can be done in less than a day.
- **Grade IV**   One long, hard day. The hardest pitch is no less than 5.7 in free climbing difficulty.
- **Grade V**   In one long day if the climbers are experienced and fast, otherwise 1½ days plus should be expected while the hardest pitch is usually at least a 5.8 difficulty.
- **Grade VI**   Requires multiple days to ascend and often includes extreme mixed free climbing and/or difficult nailing.

The Yosemite Decimal System concept, though designed to assist, is highly subjective and will vary from area to area. Some climbers may be able to climb very efficiently on two Grade IV routes while others may barely manage a Grade II without bivouacking. Most of the climbs found in this guide are Grade III or less in difficulty.

Free Climbing Difficulty Class

The Free Climbing Difficulty Class is based on an ascending scale from 1 to 5 and is then subdivided into an open-ended scale from 5.0 to 5.15 and beyond. This scale is designed to reflect the hardest free move on a pitch or the overall sustained character of the pitch. See the graph in the Appendix for detailed comparisons with other international ratings.

This open-ended scale allows for future routes of increasing difficulty. If a particular pitch contains a series of moves of the same difficulty, a higher rating is usually assigned. Further sub-grading separates the easier 5.10s from the harder 5.10s by using the letters A, B, C and D. Occasionally a slightly broader definition is applied with a minus (-) or a plus (+) emblem after the numeral. For example: 5.10a/b (**.10-**), 5.10b/c (**.10**), 5.10c/d (**.10+**). Some free-climbing routes at the local crags are underrated due to top-roping before leading. The best solution is to rate the climb according to an on-sight lead by a climber unfamiliar with the route in question.

Aid Climbing Difficulty

The art of modern nailing, Aid Climbing Difficulty or Class 6, is quite unlike its neighbor mentioned above. Both the technical severity of the piton or pro (protection) placement and the climber's security are linked to the same rating. In the sport of nailing, the letter A indicates aid climbing, while the number, (0 through 6 and higher), indicates the degree of nailing. The letter C indicates that it can be ascended clean without the need for pitons or other gear driven with a hammer. All of Class 6 aid climbing uses equipment as the means for progressing up the rock scarp to a higher point.

- A0 Pendulum, shoulder stand, tension rest, or a quick move up by pulling on pro-

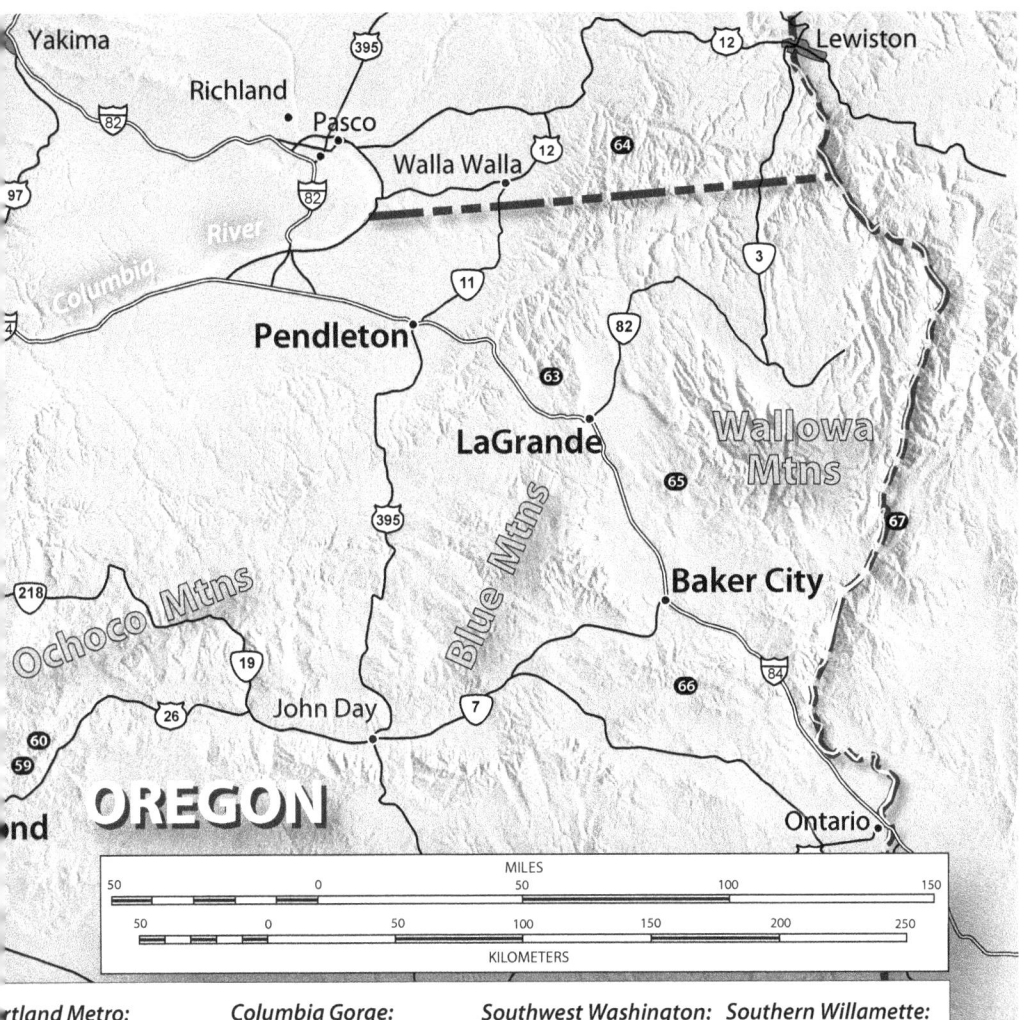

rtland Metro:
Broughton Bluff
Rocky Butte
Carver Bridge Cliff
Madrone Wall

Hood Region:
French's Dome
Salmon River Slab
Hunchback
Enola
Kiwanis Crag
. Illumination Rock
. Razorblade Pinnacle
. Mosquito Bluff
. Lamberson Butte
. Newton Pinnacle
. Pete's Pile
. Klinger Springs
. Bulo Point
. Area51
. Collawash Cliff
. Coethedral

Columbia Gorge:
21. Rooster Rock
22. Crown Point
23. Pillar of Hercules
24. St Peters Dome
25. Katanai Rock
26. Apocalypse Needles
27. Ozone Wall
28. Cigar Rock
29. Beacon Rock
30. Jimmy Cliff
31. Rock Creek Wall
32. Wind Mtn
33. Windy Slab
34. Wankers Column
35. OH8
36. Little Lyle Wall
37. Lyle Tunnel
38. Horsethief Butte
39. Monte Cristo Slab

Southwest Washington:
40. Chimney Rocks
41. Tower Rock
42. Shark Rock
43. Pinto Rock

North Santiam Region:
44. Thor's
45. Dog Tooth Rock
46. Needle Rock
47. Spire Rock
48. Breitenbush Ears

South Santiam Region:
49. Menagerie
50. Santiam Pinnacle
51. Iron Mtn Spire
52. Two Girls Mtn
53. Smokestack

Southern Willamette:
54. Wolf Rock
55. Skinner Butte
56. Moolack

Central Oregon:
57. Trout Creek
58. Smith Rock
59. Steins Pillar
60. Twin Pillar
61. Gothic Rock
62. Shepard Tower

Northeast Oregon:
63. Spring Mtn
64. The Dikes
65. High Valley
66. Burnt River
67. Hell's Canyon

tection.
- **A1** Solid equipment placements.
- **A2** Is more difficult to place but offers some good protection.
- **A3** Involves marginal placements and the potential for a short fall.
- **A4** Frequent marginal placements; will only hold body weight.
- **A5** Pro supports body weight only; risk of 50-foot-plus fall.
- **A6** Involves full pitch leads of A-4 and serious ground fall potential.

Modern nailing equipment has profoundly changed the way in which climbers approach a prospective route. Knifeblades, RURPs, Bird Beaks, and a variety of hooks and ultrathin wires offer new ways to aid climb at the extreme edge. Since free climbs are often maintained as free climbs, certainly some nailing routes should be maintained as nailing routes.

For those routes requiring a "seriousness" rating, they are as follows:
- **PG**: Protection may be adequate near the difficult sections, yet involve risky or runout sections which can increase the potential for an accident.
- **R**: A bold lead with a serious fall potential; may involve questionable or poor protection; serious injury is possible.
- **X**: Involves high risk of ground fall potential; very poor to no protection available; serious or fatal injury possible.

The climbing difficulty class rating listed in this guide is not to be considered as absolute. All climbing routes are subject to unforeseen challenges that can quickly make the climb inherently dangerous.

Confidence, ability, intuition, and good judgment are crucial for managing the degree of risk that you and your climbing partner are willing to accept. Develop those invaluable skills so that you can foresee your risks or liabilities, because careless judgment becomes a harsh learning curve. Proceed with caution; climb at your own risk!

An additional concept utilized frequently in this guide:
- **TR**: Indicates the route is generally a top-rope climb, although the climb may have been free climbed in the past.

The "Star" or Quality Rating used throughout this book is designed to help climbers selectively choose the more aesthetic climbs. This is a highly subjective system for many of the un-starred routes are worthy of attention, so be sure to check out some of the lesser-known climbs as well.

- **No Stars**: An average route.
- **One Star** (★): Good quality route, better than the usual.
- **Two Stars** (★ ★): Excellent route, good position with quality rock climbing, a highly recommended route.
- **Three Stars** (★ ★ ★): Superb position, a classic line on excellent rock, a must-do route on everyones list.

Of these starred routes, not all will be bolted face climbs. Some will be crack climbs, several will be short but worthy, and a few will be two routes connected together making an even better classic climb.

The star ratings for a climb at Broughton Bluff will vary from the quality routes at Beacon Rock or Smith Rock as they represent the favorable, interesting routes at that particular cliff.

Hard or Soft Ratings

If Portland area ratings for rock climbs seem a bit skewed you're not alone in this analysis, and perhaps they really are to some extent. As one local climber once said, "If you can climb

5.12 at Broughton you can climb 5.12 anywhere."

Each local climbing site tends to reflect a slightly different rating scale. Some sites tend to have ratings that are **HARD** for that specific grade (5.10b may seem like a 5.10c), while other crags tend to be slightly **SOFT** for that grade. The following analogy should provide a quick means to compare overall ratings at the local Portland area crags: *Broughton* routes are typically hard for the grade; *Carver* is usually hard; *Madrone* is solid; and *Beacon* is hard for the grade. Possible reasons? The slick surface texture of local basalt, inobvious moves that involve diligence to solve, crag styles (such as stemming), or climbers who tend to rate a new route hard or soft (for whatever reason).

VISUAL BIO

These quick and convenient graphical emblems provide a fast visual bio to basic site characteristics that we seldom think to ask. The emblems cover basics such as effects of localized weather on each crag or route, cliff orientation, shaded by trees or directly facing the full sunshine.

In simple terms the upper emblem string conveys a message: The site is open or climbable for 8-months (depending on weather or regulations), it is five minutes to the nearest section of cliff, the cliff orientation is west facing, receives afternoon sunshine, it is shaded by a forest of trees, and has special regulations. A cam emblem is for trad gear route, while the carabiner emblem indicates sport routes. If the site is forested (no sun) such as Carver it will be simply a 'Trees' emblem. The last emblem (umbrella) will be found next to certain actual route names. The umbrella emblem will help to point you to rock climbs that may be dry even if it has rained or is raining lightly, although extended heavy winter rains will soak most crags.

EQUIPMENT & SPECIALIZED GEAR

Both personal safety and your quality of enjoyment depend on your being adequately prepared with the appropriate gear when rock climbing at the local Portland crags. Essential equipment such as locking carabiners, belay-rappel devices, and even double ropes will help to ensure that your outing is a successful one.

In recent years, climbers have seen quality improvements in rock climbing equipment, both innovative and beneficial to the sport. Standard rock gear protection ("pro") such as spring-loaded camming devices (Camalots, Friends, TCUs, etc.), HBs, RPs, curved wired stoppers or nuts (or wires), bolts, and tailored rock shoes have contributed greatly to climbers' overall safety and climbing enjoyment. The following gear recommendations should be used as a broad list from which you can generally determine your needs for a specific climb. Gear sizes appear under each route name as a guideline, but choose your gear by analyzing your skills and needs for each rock climb *before* ascending it. Ask other climbers what they may have used for route protection, and be willing to take extra equipment and perhaps even larger-sized gear.

For traditional free climbing at Portland area crags you will likely need a variety of the following gear: A single 60-meter rope, helmet, a set of 12–15 quick draws (QDs), wired stoppers up to 1½ inches, small camming devices like TCUs up to 1½ inches, and larger spring-loaded camming devices ranging from 1–4 inches.

It is wise to bring extra slings as well as some of the big stuff like Hexcentrics or Big Bro, especially if a particularly fine offwidth crack is your challenge. Tiny specialized pro (like HBs, RPs, or Steel Nuts) may be useful on a few of the desperately thin routes. You can go with a rather lean rack of the above gear when visiting Carver Bridge Cliff, while a more comprehensive gear rack, including two ropes, would prepare you nicely for the long, steep leads at Beacon Rock.

For those interested in pursuing a career in nailing, a number of outrageous routes are available at all the local crags. Consider some of the following to assist you in your climb: Knifeblades, Hooks, RURPs, bashies, tie-off loops, etc.

For the climbing enthusiast who needs the latest new gear products (or even quality used equipment) there are many local retail outdoor stores available that offer competitive prices.

Remember, wherever you climb, always exercise good judgment before and during the climb. Practice route analysis, ask for consultation and advice from others, develop foresight, and when you begin your ascent, climb with a reasonable degree of caution, fully aware of the risks of this sport!

BOTANICAL ELEMENTS

Our northwest Oregon crags are saturated with diverse botanical flora enhanced by the north pacific weather systems that impact this region each year. Tall canopied forests of Douglas fir, Western Red Cedar, White Oak, Red Alder and Bigleaf Maple are dominate trees in our lower elevation forests. In addition, Oregon Ash, Vine Maple, Pacific Dogwood, Hazelnut, and a few Cascara Buckthorn add vibrance to the beauty and dimension of the forest structure.

Moss clings to the edge of steep cliffs, hanging from branches of trees like a thick beard. Common low growing shrubs and plants such as Saskatoon, Solomon Seal, Mahonia, Yarrow, Miner's Lettuce, and a veritable family of fern varieties create a dense layer of ground foliage. Other unique varieties are Oregon Stonecrop, Woolly Eriophyllum, Penstemon (p. ovatus) and of course the ever-present Poison Oak.

A magnificent broadleaf evergreen tree with reddish peeling bark called Pacific Madrone (arbutus menziesii) grows on the sunny slopes of the Madrone Wall county park. Various other local crags hold a unique treasure of Trillium that bloom in the Spring. Deep forest shade is also home to Three-leaved Anemone, Alumroot (micrantha), Thimbleberry, Currant, Salal and Sword Fern.

Next time you are heading to a crag bring a flora book to peruse, and take time to enhance your awareness of the local flora habitat at our crags.

CLIMBING STYLE AND ETHICS

Contemporary climbing ideology consists of two forces: style and conceptual ethics. Style is how you climb on the rock while climbing ethics are what you do to the rock. Conceptual patterns in regional rock climbing develop into presently accepted style trends such as top-roping, rappel inspection, fixed gear, free climbing, and soloing. Some of these concepts are likely to evolve in the future. Fixed gear (pitons & bolts) trends, and new product technologies will continue to reshape the sport climbing ethical patterns of the future.

In order for new climbs to attain a comparable rating there must be another point of reference nearby for comparison. For example: The Sickle at Broughton is considered to be an accepted 5.8 rating, therefore, ratings for new rock climbs nearby are usually established based on a comparison with its rating criteria.

Several basic examples of locally accepted trends are: route cleaning, bolting, fixed top belays, and pre-inspection. Climbers at crags like Beacon Rock are more inclined toward a traditional climbing method, where a number of the rock climbs were established when the first ascent party placed the fixed gear while on lead. Many crags are situated on government managed lands where long-term scenic values of a public resource are important (and some of these lands may have climbing rules that apply).

Placing more fixed gear on established routes is non-typical, although it is considered reasonable to replace old fixed gear on rock climbs (such as upgrading ¼-inch bolts to ⅜-inch bolts). Fixed anchors are usually maintained by local climbers, because this regions rainy climate eventually effects certain fixed metal products in 50–100 years. Any route, whether established via free or nailing, is usually considered as such; it was the teams choice at the time. A number of aid nailing routes over time became quality free routes, which fits well into the popular trend of free climbing. Chiseling is uncharacteristic — people will continue to climb at very high standards in the years to come.

The advent of power drills has transformed the sport by making route development more efficient. Some restraint should be exercised when bolting, because every new route does not necessarily need bolts. Vandalism of climbing routes fixed with bolts or pitons has occasionally occurred — this is neither style nor ethics. Just be aware that some climbing routes you may wish to climb may not be leadable due to missing fixed gear.

Ongoing community involvement in stewardship opportunities at the crags — which includes all of us — will help keep these places available for many generations to come. Enjoy the sport of rock climbing for its social and outdoor benefits by respecting others as well as the rock.

WILDERNESS ETHICS & RESOURCE MAPS

When traveling into the wild areas of Northwest Oregon always strive for a minimal form of impact travel, using good judgement skills, and wilderness values. Just a short distance from our homes we have a vast and diverse ecosystem in a unique temperate rain forest climate. Forest management agencies have readily available information that promote resource concepts such as backcountry preparation and safety, leave no trace (LNT) ethic, and other guidelines useful for wilderness travel. Analysis, consultation, foresight, and preparation are wise steps that should be taken before you venture into wilderness areas.

If you are planning to travel into the wilderness or other back country areas, a wide variety of invaluable maps are available concerning your area of exploration. Some of these are national forest maps, topographic maps (USGS or private source), or the highly useful digital maps now available online linkted to an App, or on a CD disk.

ABOUT THIS GUIDE BOOK

This books purpose is to provide information that will help influence rock climbing for the public good with the goal to educate users about long-term stewardship of our natural resources we enjoy climbing upon, while offering insight about the nuances of each different climbing site, route development limitations, private property or ownership issues, provide a written communication bridge to rock climbers with the hope of eliminating or reducing potential friction with area residents, and encourages users to become involved in trail maintenance and other crag stewardship opportunities. It explains regulations such as seasonal raptor/flora closures, suggests where overnight camping options may exist, and points out basic community and emergency services at nearby towns. We aim to broaden user interest throughout the entire region, seeking results that bring beneficial tourism-based stimulus to our local economies.

This book is all about creating a good public resource that will be helpful toward preserving access in both public and private venues, brings crucial reference material forward for public officials, and is highly useful with emergency response agencies for developing emergency rescue or evacuation plans. You are not merely a visitor, but a valued partaker with an interest in how public lands are being managed.

"It is a long road that leads to the peaks."
~Gaston Rebuffat

OREGON ROCK CLIMBS

1

PORTLAND'S URBAN CRAGS

This first section details all of the popular rock climbing crags within or near the urban Metro area of Portland, Oregon. These crags are Broughton Bluff, Rocky Butte Quarry, Carver Bridge Cliff, and the ever popular Madrone Wall.

Each crag is unique in its own way. The Madrone Wall is superb for winter and fall season climbing due to its southwest facing cliff orientation that is warmed by the rays of sunlight filtering through a canopy of fir and madrone trees. The Broughton Bluff site is so extensive it fits well for all skill levels of climbers from beginner to experienced (even though a fair portion of the routes cater to crack gear leading). Carver Cliff is sport climbing central by design, and well suited to summer season rock climbing. The inner city crag of RBQ — due to its north facing aspect — lends well to summer rock climbing, and due to its top-down access (easy roadside 1 minute access) the routes are often top-roped these days, which makes the crag a convenient place for after work route climbing opportunities.

BROUGHTON BLUFF

PERCHED MAJESTICALLY ALONG THE EASTERN SHORE of the Sandy River is a rock climbing paradise that has provided years of enjoyment for all who visit. This steep-walled crag, with its close proximity to the City of Portland, is one of the best local crags to offer an excellent variety of climbing opportunities for every rock climber.

Located just minutes east of Troutdale at the entrance of the majestic Columbia River Gorge, Broughton Bluff offers great rock climbs on an extensive and secluded 160-foot-high series of cliffs on Oregon State Parks land. This excellent year-round rock climbing crag provides individuals of all ages the opportunity to explore the intriguing facets of rock climbing.

In the late 1950s Broughton Bluff was approached by a few dedicated rock climbers who began to utilize this crag, often for aid climbing but also to refine essential rock skills in order to succeed on the great walls and mountains in other states. Broughton is a great place to learn new climbing skills, develop physical strength, challenge your ability to persevere, and even excel beyond your greatest climbing aspirations.

BRIEF HISTORY OF THE CRAG

The broad sweep of this heavily forested bluff, located at the Lewis and Clark State Park, was named after Lieutenant Broughton. As a member of the Captain George Vancouver expedition of 1792, he had traveled up the Columbia River to a place just east of the Sandy River. The honorary name was bestowed in 1926 by the Scouts and accepted by the U.S. Board of Geographic Names.

The crag, which is bordered on the west by the Sandy River, continues to be historically important, especially to rock climbers. Of the earliest known ascents at Broughton Bluff, most were done using a variety of mixed aid and free climbing. One of those early ascents to be-

Drew Hansen leading *Loose Block Overhang*

come established was the Hanging Gardens II 5.6 A1 (now a free climb at 5.10a) route ascended by Bob Waring, John Wells, and Bruce Holcomb in 1965. Today, it is considered a trade route classic. This climb stands as a tribute to those early days of exploratory aid climbing. Perhaps the finest achievement at Broughton took place in 1968 when Steve Strauch and Jim O'Connell ascended the North Face via the superb classic and ever-popular Gandalf's Grip (5.9+). This route is one of the best crack climbs of this rating at Broughton Bluff.

In the 1970s a small number of active climbers established many more routes. Jim Mayers, Gail Van Hoorn, Alan Campbell, Dave Jensen, Talbot Bielefeldt, Dean Fry, and others "opened the door" by aid climbing routes like Peach Cling (now a free climb at 5.11b), Mr. Potato (5.11a), and Sesame

Street (5.9+), all of which were ascended in 1972; Peer Pressure (5.10d) in 1973, Face Not Friction (5.11d) in 1975, as well as ever-popular Classic Crack.

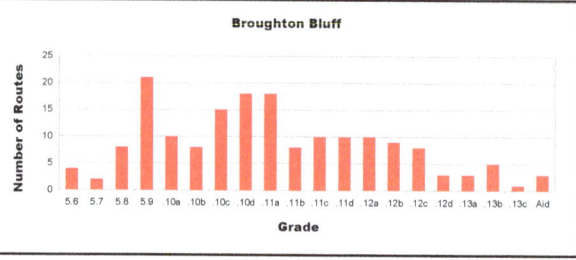

The mid-1970s brought serious free climbers who began to push beyond the known boundaries of their time, firmly establishing a whole new dimension of free climbing adventure. Many of the older routes were now being ascended free without the use of direct aid, while the latest climbs were pushed considerably beyond the 5.9 realm.

Red Eye (5.10c) and Sheer Stress (5.10a) were done in 1976; Sandy's Direct (5.10c) and Physical Graffiti (5.10d), a short, difficult roof problem, were put up in 1977. Beyond the Red Wall stands the superb cliff known as the Bat Wall, where climbers established Superstition (5.11a) and Hanging Tree (5.10d) in 1977 as well. It was this massive and secluded wall that became the key to the next generation.

Some of the climbers who were instrumental here in the 1970s are Doug Bower, Monty Mayko, Bruce Casey, Robert McGown, Mike Smelser, Jeff Thomas, Ken Currens, Mark Cartier, Jay Kerr, and Dan Foote. They and others focused their energy toward free climbing the untapped routes.

Nearly ten silent years descended upon Broughton Bluff but the summer of 1990 brought another group of climbers who noticed a realm of blank space waiting to be conquered. A few extra bolts quickly unraveled the final mysteries of Broughton, firmly bringing the 5.12 rating to the crag.

The Unnamed Aid Route on the Bat Wall quickly fell from its old aid status. After several free climbing attempts by local climbers, G. Rall succeeded first on this key rock climb. Afterward, a name with real bite stood out: Dracula (5.12a). A virtually endless series of climbs soon followed. Bela Lugosi (5.12c), Bad Omen (5.12b), and Kashmir (5.12b) were all established in 1990. In 1991, Heart of Darkness (5.12b) brought renewed interest to the Jungle Cliff, while Bloodline (5.12b) continued the legacy in 1992 at the Bat Wall.

Gary Rall, Wayne Wallace, Dave Sowerby, Jay Green, and many others have helped to push the standards of the 1990s. The mysteries of Broughton met a new destiny.

Compositionally, Broughton Bluff is a form of blocky, densely compacted volcanic basalt,

Climber leading *Edges & Ledges* 5.8

very dark in color, and occasionally stained with brilliant hues of reddish-orange sections on its surface. From a climber's perspective, the entire bluff formation is composed of thirteen aptly named walls, ten of which are detailed in this guide with climbing topographical reference maps. The sections of cliff at Broughton that offer the greatest variety of free climbing opportunities lay north from the Bat Wall. The access trail south of the Bat Wall is a bit rough and the rock climbs tend to receive less attention. Several other cliffs even farther to the south (Aerie, Perihelion, and Eclipse Wall) are located on private land and are not available for climbing purposes. Detailed route information provided on the ten cliffs are from left to right: North Face, Hanging Gardens Wall, Red Wall, Bridge Cliff, Spring Rock, Bat Wall, Trinity Wall, Berlin Wall, Jungle Cliff, and New Frontier Cliff.

VISUAL BIO

These emblems represent most of Broughton Bluff. The North Face is fully shaded, but does receive minor late afternoon sunshine in the summer. The Hanging Gardens Wall receives some mid-morning sunshine that filters through a tall canopy of fir trees. The southernmost cliffs (Berlin Wall, Jungle Wall and New Frontier) will take about 15 minutes to approach. Broughton offers considerable variety for traditional gear leads, but also a respectable amount of sport routes particularly on the Red Wall and Bat Wall. There are a few nocturnal scorpions (as the route name Scorpion Seams can atest) at Broughton, but you may not see one unless you climb there frequently.

HOW TO GET THERE

From the city center of Portland, drive east on I-84 toward the town of Troutdale. Continue on the interstate highway until you cross the Sandy River, then take exit #18 onto the Historic Columbia River Highway. (This is a popular scenic river road that curves south along the river before heading east through Corbett.) At exit #18 drive south a very short distance until you cross under a railroad trestle that spans the Sandy River. Just beyond (on the east side of the road and river) is the Lewis and Clark State Park. This wayside facility offers ample free parking and is used by boaters, hikers, and climbers. Take note of the curfew hours on the entrance sign. The park rangers will lock the gate at dusk and vehicles remaining in the parking lot after closing

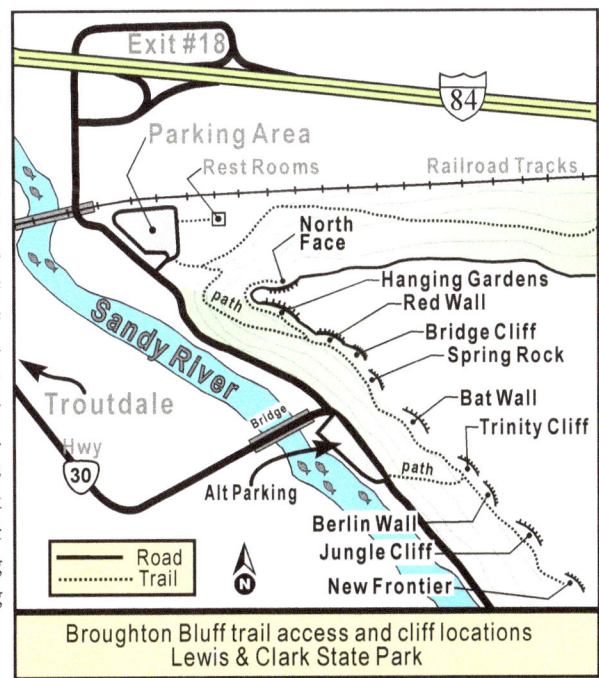

Broughton Bluff trail access and cliff locations
Lewis & Clark State Park

will be cited.

APPROACH

From the parking lot walk south along the gravel path to the base of the steep hillside, then up the climber-maintained zigzag path. This trail angles around onto the south slope then continues up to meet the cliff base near the south edge of the Hanging Gardens Wall. The trail to the right quickly leads to the Red Wall, while the left path meanders along the base of Hanging Gardens Wall then around the corner farther to the North Face.

If you plan to top out from a rock climb on either the North Face or the Hanging Gardens Wall, the best option for a scrambling descent is down a third-class ridge crest between these two cliff formations. Most of the rock climbs at Broughton have excellent established belay anchors from which you can rappel back down to the ground near your original starting point without actually topping out on the climb.

NORTH FACE

1. **Frodo's Journey 5.9 ★★**
   60' (13m) in length, QD's and Pro to 2"
   Start up left from the cave and clip the first bolt on Traffic Court. Then step left and climb directly up over a small roof and V-shaped slot to a small perch. Continue up the slab (3 bolts) to a slight overhang. Clip the 4th bolt then surmount the bulge, and continue up several face moves to a belay anchor at mid-height on the left face.

2. **Traffic Court 5.8 ★★**
   60' (18m) in length, Thin Pro to 2", TCU's suggested
   Start as for Gandalf's left variation and climb past a bolt to a stance. Ascend a vertical corner till it eases to a slab. Muscle over a final bulge directly above then step right to rejoin with Gandalf's Grip at the belay.

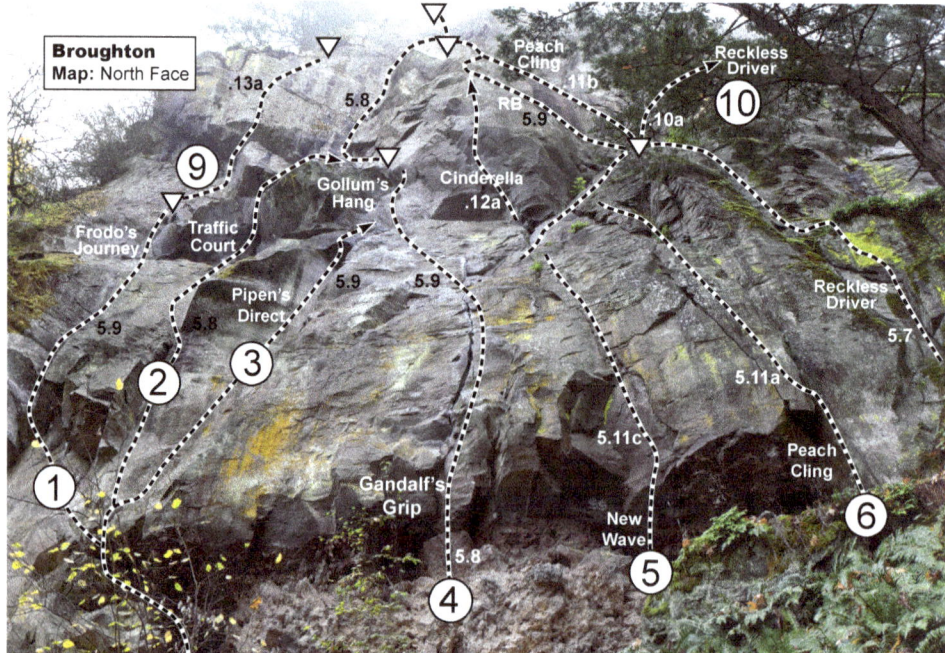

◆ **BROUGHTON BLUFF** 37

3. **Pipen's Direct 5.9** 🌂
   Pro to 1½"
   Start up left from the cave past a bolt to a small ledge. Continue up the right leaning dihedral to a overhung tricky lip crux move, then rejoin into the Gandalf's Grip route just below the Gollum's Hang crux section.

4. **Gandalf's Grip II 5.9 ★★★** 🌂
   Multi-pitch, Pro to 3½", TCU's or small wires suggested
   This route is a Broughton super classic.
   Pitch 1: Commence up steep ground to the right of the alcove using a vertical crack. At a small narrow stance move up left (bolts) via tiny edges and sloping insecure holds (5.9+) to the Gollum's Hang. Surmount the bulge (bolt) and belay on a sloping ledge.
   Pitch 2: Move left and climb a steep crack corner through two small overhangs (5.8) then

North Face

angle up right to a belay on a nice small flat ledge.

Pitch 3: Above is an obvious wide crack. Climb this to the top and walk off, or rappel from here to the previous anchors.

5. **New Wave   II 5.11c** ★★
   30' (9m) for the 1ˢᵗ Pitch, Pro to ¾"
   A thin seam to the right of Gandalf's Grip start. P2 is now called Skullduggery. The crux of this climb is a powerful hung stemming sequence to reach better holds.

6. **Peach Cling   II 5.11b PG** ★★
   Multi-pitch, Pro to 2", mostly small wires
   Excellent route. Starts 15' right of Gandalf's. Layback up a desperate thin left-leaning tips flake until it ends in a shallow corner. Continue up to a good belay on a ledge. Move up left via strenuous and off-balance moves (bolts) ending on a ledge and bolt belay (2ⁿᵈ anchor on Gandalf's). Continue up leftward (pitons) on down sloping smears (5.10) to the top. Walk off.

7. **Cinderella   5.12a** ★★
   30' (9m) in length, QD's and pro to 1½"
   Excellent quality route ascending the center bulge on the North Face between Gandalf's Grip and Peach Cling. Joins with Risky Business. Either rappel from Gandalf's second belay anchor with two ropes or climb up and walk off.

8. **Risky Business   5.9** ★★
   40' (12m) in length, QD's and pro to 1", cams recommended.
   The first pitch is a great climb! Start at the first belay on Peach Cling. Step left onto a sloping series of ledges (5.9) passing several bolts. Continue up good holds until able to join with Peach Cling then to the belay anchor on Gandalf's Grip. A surprisingly quality climb of only moderate difficulty. The 2ⁿᵈ pitch turns immediately right from the belay stance, around a corner (5.8) to a hidden jug, then ascends a mossy crack dihedral leading to the summit.

9. **Dark Tower   5.13a/b**
   102' (31m) in length when starting from the ground to the top anchor
   Sport route using 5 QD's from lower belay to upper belay
   Difficult route that ascends the slightly overhung left side of the north face wall. Start from a belay anchor (see diagram), move up a left facing corner, then surmount the first roof. Continue up the headwall on crimpers to a crux move just below the belay anchor. Located immediately left of the 2ⁿᵈ pitch of Gandalf's Grip.

10. **Reckless Driver   II 5.10c**
    Multi-Pitch, Pro to 3", cams or TCU's helpful
    No traffic jam on this route. Start 5' right of Peach Cling. Move up an easy corner to a ledge then up a right-facing corner (5.6) then leftward to the Peach Cling belay. Up to the right is a bush. Thrash over the bush past a crux (5.10a) up an easy right angling ramp system to a belay anchor. Exit off down right to a large fir tree (rappel), or from the top of the ramp step left and climb up a thin crack system (5.10c) to the summit.

11. **Skullduggery   5.12b**
    165' (50m) in length, Pro to 2" small cams and nuts
    A stout thin seam up right of P2 Peach Cling. Eases to a 5.7 dihedral near upper anchor.

12. **Sweet Emotion   II 5.10b PG**
    165' (50m) in length,   Pro to 2½", Needs bolts on 2nd pitch
13. **American Graffiti   5.8+**
    30' (9m) in length, Pro to 2"
    Climb the crack just below the large fir tree on the west edge of the North Face.

    HANGING GARDENS WALL
14. **Giant's Staircase   5.6**
    35' (8m) in length
    Numerous ledges provide basic entertainment and several variations.
15. **Edges and Ledges   5.8   ★ ★ ★**
    60' (18m) in length, 4 QD's and pro to 2"
    Start right of Giant Staircase, but on the left side of a large detached top heavy column of rock. Climb up the left corner of this detached block, and step onto a large ledge, then embark up left onto the bolted prow and face climb on interesting edges to the belay anchor above.

16. The Sickle 5.8 ★★★
60' (18m) in length, Pro to 4"
This popular climb is the obvious curving wide crack about 30' up the wall, and just above a large ledge. This area has numerous cracks and ledges that offer climbers an excellent area to top-rope with relative ease.

17. The Hammer 5.9 ★
60' (18m) in length, Pro to 3"
A rather difficult, short jam crack high step crux problem off the upper main ledge leads to easier jams and smears near the anchor.

18. Columns & Slab Area 5.7 to 5.9
60' (18m) in length, usually top-roped
A 1960s climb near the "Hammer & Sickle" routes was called **Prometheus Slab** (historical info suggests it meandered a bit). Several of the vertical columns (and upper short slab) offer minor but fun leads and/or top-rope climbs. These climbs are located between the Hammer and Spud. Use fixed belays accessible via a trail above the wall. The topo lists these merely as #18a-b-c-d (none are named).

Leading Hit The Highway 5.10a

19. Spud 5.9
60' (18m) in length, Pro to 3"
A bit tricky at the start reaching the 'spud' pocket, then land on a small ledge in a corner. Stem corner till it merges into Tip City.

20. Tip City 5.10c ★★
60' (18m) in length, Pro to 1½"
An excellent thin crack. Locate two parallel cracks that join with Chockstone Chimney at a ledge. The left crack is Tip City and the right is Lean Years. The climb is slightly easier if you utilize both cracks.

21. Lean Years 5.10c ★★
60' (18m) in length, Pro to 1½"
The right parallel crack. Both routes make excellent options to practice thin crack climbing.

22. Hangover 5.11
40' in length (TR)

23. Chockstone Chimney 5.9
80' (24m) in length, Pro to 4"
An original 1960's climb.

24. Milestone 5.7
80' (24m) in length, Pro to 3"

25. Loose Block Overhang 5.9 ★★★
120' (36m) in length, Pro to 2½"
This very popular climb offers two optional starting points. **Pitch One**: 1.) climb a flared corner to an offwidth fist crack (5.8) for 25' to the top of a large block and belay. 2.) Ascend on the left via steep steps into an odd tight corner capped by an overhang. Surmount

this hang on the right by using hand edges and fist jams till you can smear onto the top of the block to the belay.

Pitch 2: jam a slightly overhung crack (5.9 crux) until it eases onto a ledge and bolt belay. Maneuver up a very short 5.8 left-facing corner, swing right onto a slab (piton) then up an easy blocky section and walk off left. Or from the same belay exit up a left slanting crack (20') on steep rock and thin holds as an odd alternative.

26. Grace and Danger 5.11b R

25' (7m) in length, Pro to 1½" Cams recommended

Ascend the outside arête next to the 1st pitch of Loose Block.

27. Slapfest 5.12b ★★

40' (12m) in length, 6 QD's and minor pro to 1"

Climb the superb bolted face immediately right of the crux pitch of Loose Block Overhang. A rather stiff, unusual route. Joins with Least Resistance at its crux move.

28. Least Resistance 5.10a

30' (9m) in length, Pro to 1"

Climb the first 50' of Hanging Gardens route but angle up left to a left-leaning seam (bolts) that pulls around an outside corner up to a stance at the second bolt anchor on the Loose Block Overhang.

29. Dynamic Resistance 5.10d ★★

80' (24m) in length, QD's and Pro to 1½"

Climb the first 40' of Hanging Gardens route and move up left to a steep corner between Least Resistance and Sandy's Direct. Power up the strenuous tight corner (bolts), move right around an odd bulge, then exit up left over a final crux roof to a bolt anchor. Rappel. An excellent climb.

30. Sandy's Direct 5.10c PG ★

120' (36m) in length, Pro to 2" including small stoppers

A challenging lead climb. Climb the first 40' of Hanging Gardens route (stay left of the maple tree belay) and continue straight up a vertical corner system 80' to a sloped ledge with a belay anchor. Rappel.

Bryan Smith leading *Sesame Street*

Hanging Gardens Wall Left Half

CHAPTER 1 ✧ ORC

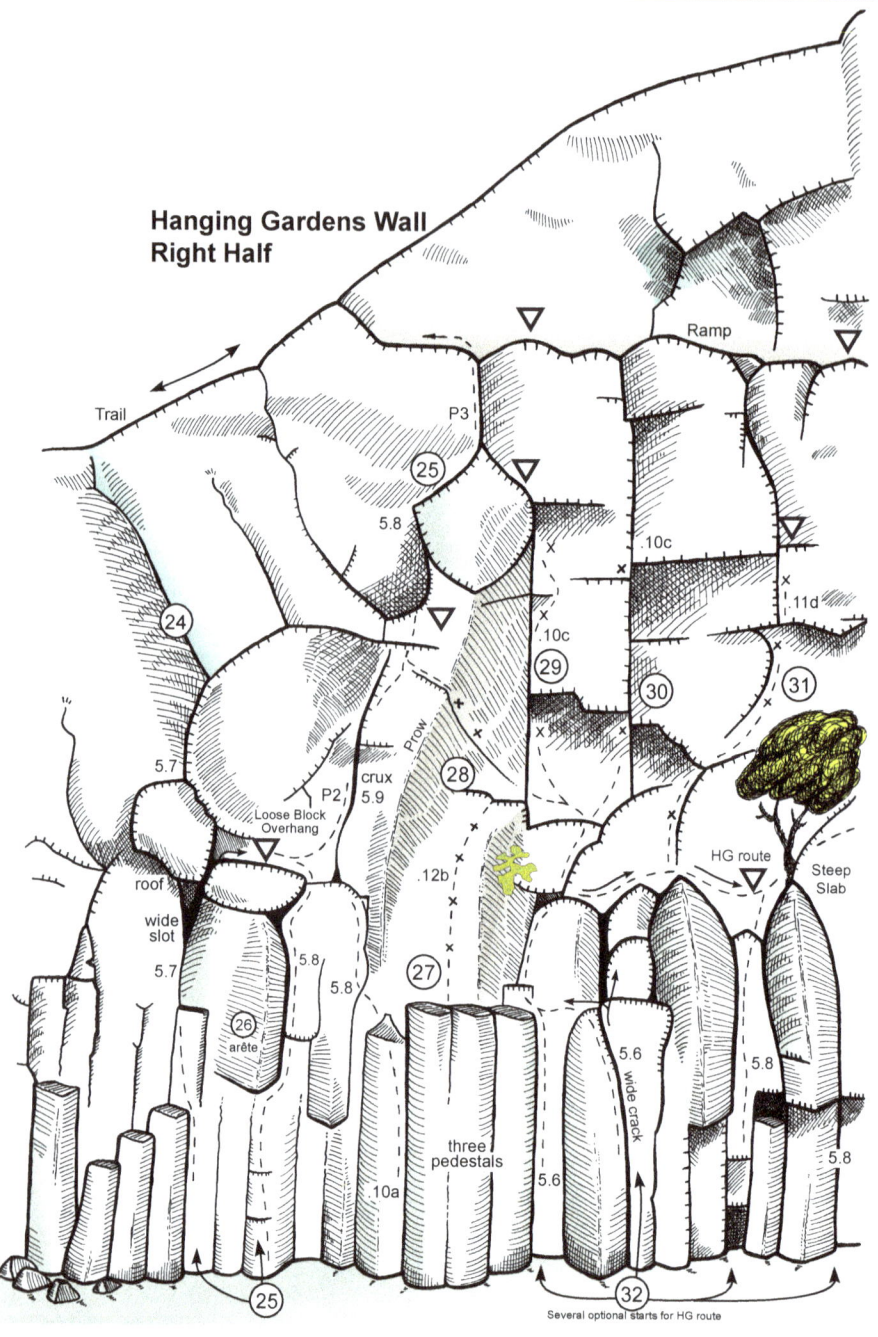

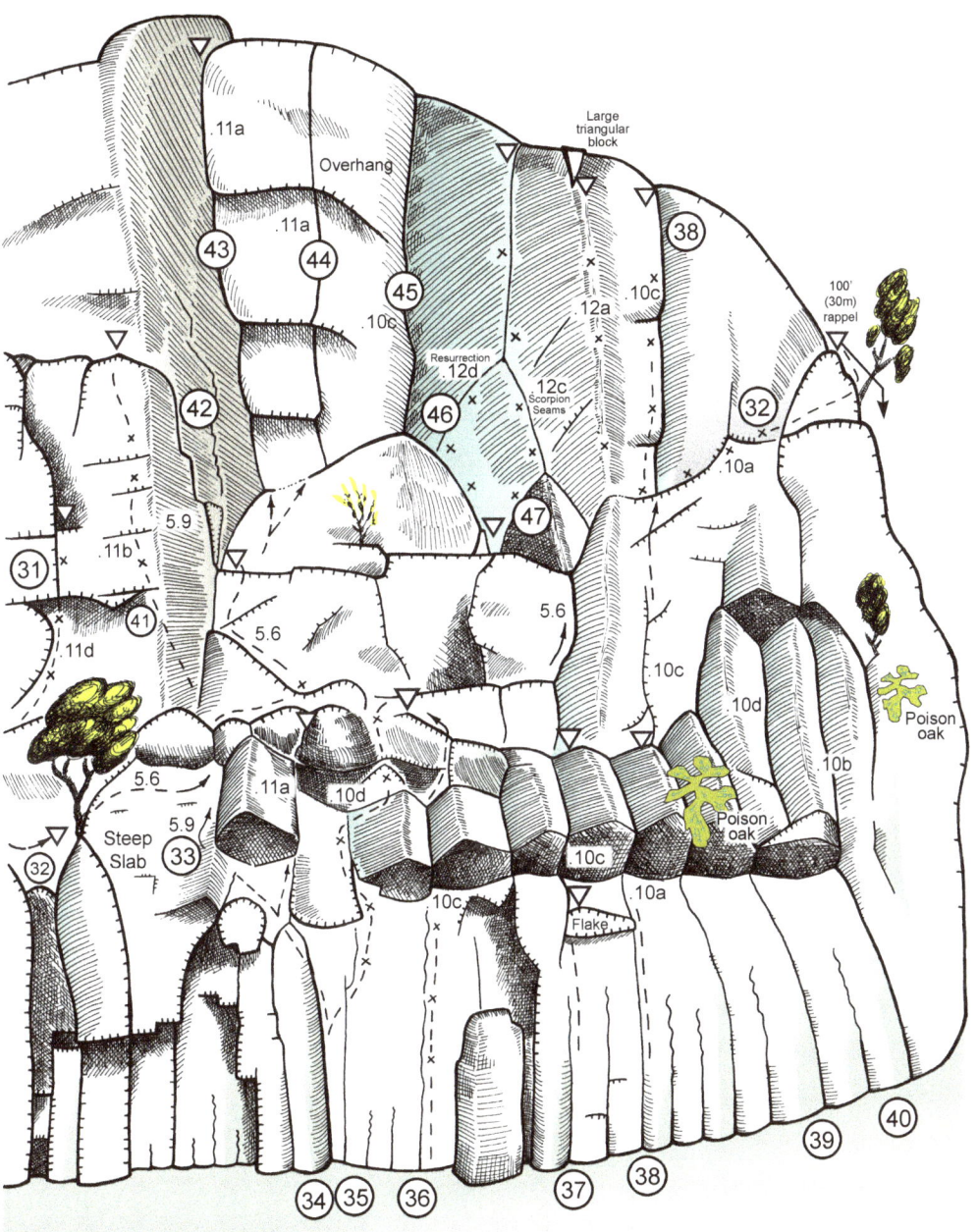

31. Face Not Friction 5.11d ★★
60' (18m) in length, QD's and minor pro to start
Quality climbing, worth the effort. Up and left of the maple tree belay is a partially fixed face-seam problem on vertical rock. Climb this to a bolt anchor at a small ledge. Rappel or continue up left on steep, bushy cracks to an upper ledge, then exit left to walk down.

32. Hanging Gardens Route II 5.10a (or 5.6 A0) ★★★
Multi-pitch, Pro to 1½"
One of the original Broughton favorites put up in 1965. This very popular climb offers multiple optional starting points (see topo).
Pitch 1: The standard route ascends a wide 3-4" crack with edges (5.8) to a stance, then [or angle up left to a corner with ledges] directly up over several balanced blocks. Move right to the bolt belay next to the small tree. Reference photo for other options that lead directly to the first belay anchor via some wide cracks (5.8).
Pitch 2: From the tree move right across a steep slab (5.6) and jam up a slightly overhung bulge (5.7) to a narrow crawl. The original route traverses right passing the Mr. Potato anchor then up a short corner and bolt belay on the left (or go up left from the pitons to the Sesame Street belay anchor on a large ledge about 20' higher up).
Pitch 3: Move right and up around a blind corner. Free climb (5.10a) or A0 (fixed bolts & pitons) diagonally right 20' along the "bicycle path" to a stance on a small ledge at a bolt anchor belay. A vertical 80' rappel takes you directly to the ground just to the right of Shining Star.

33. BFD 5.9
30' (9m) in length, Pro to 1"
A short challenging climb. Small cams can be quite helpful for the crux section.

The following 5 routes have belay anchors located on a narrow series of sloped ledges about 40' up the cliff.

34. Mr. Potato 5.11a
40' (12m) in length, Pro to ¾"
Unusual yet interesting climb. Start up the same crack as you would for BFD, but continue directly up a right facing near vertical corner. Pull over several bulges to join with Hanging Gardens route where two pitons are secured at a small stance.

35. From Something to Nothing (aka Something) 5.10d ★★
40' (12m) in length, Pro to 1" and QD's
A very popular face and corner problem immediately right of Mr. Potato. Climb up the same crack corner as Mr. Potato, but move up right (bolts) on face edges to an awkward stance at a slot with a bulge above. From the slot work left onto the steep face around the slight bulge to another tenuous stance on an arête. Surmount the next bulge on thin face edges (crux) to a bolt anchor.

36. Fun in the Mud 5.10c ★★
40' (12m) in length, Pro to 1" and QD's
This is a good route with a stiff bulge problem involving thin jams to surmount the crux. Starts up a steep bolted slab, pulls the overhang then steps right slightly and up a corner step, then move directly left to catch the "Something" bolt anchor.

37. Circus Act 5.10c ★
40' (12m) in length, Pro to 1" including cams
The first pitch thin crack on a short slab is a common lead (to a belay below the overhang).

BROUGHTON BLUFF 47

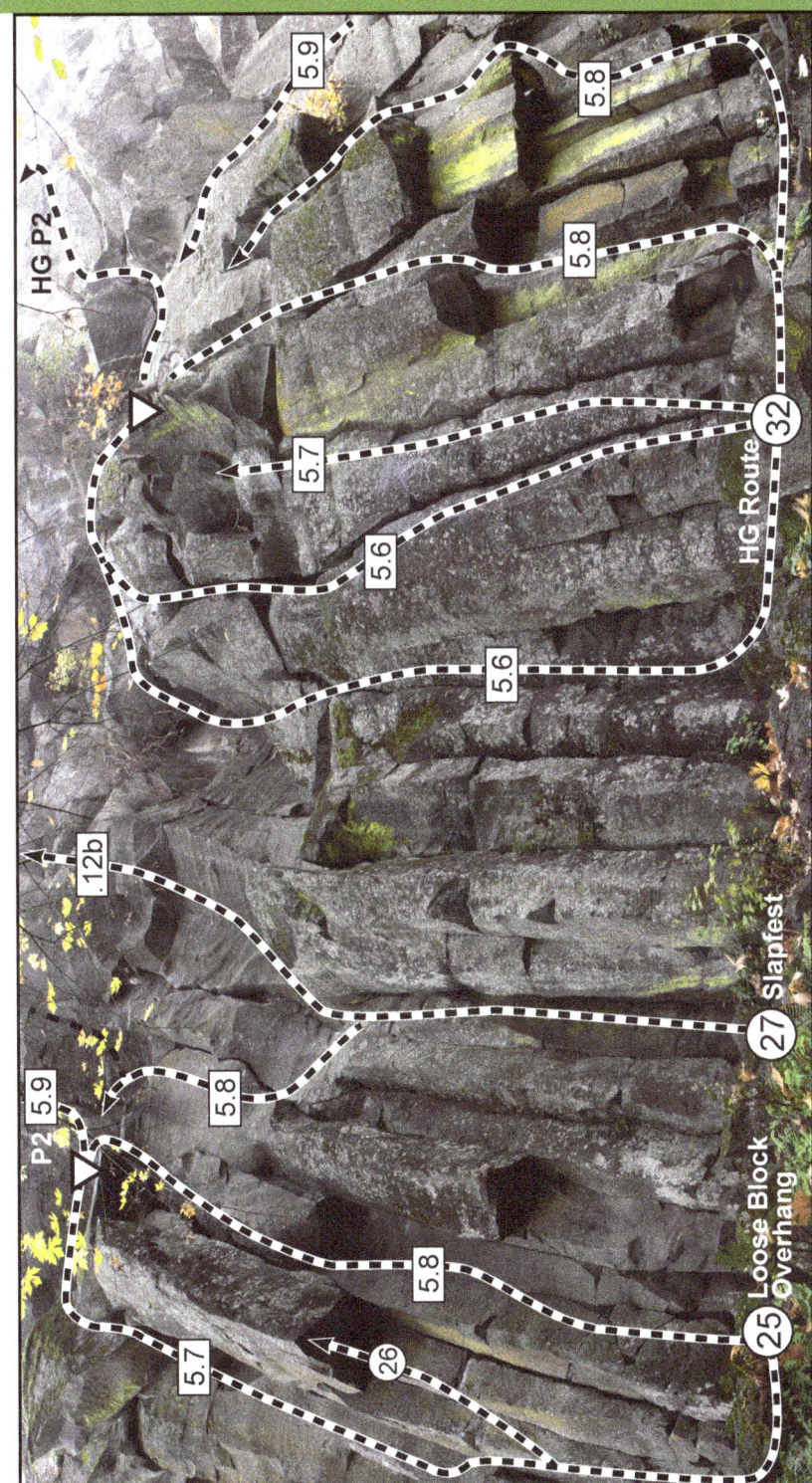

Panograph: *Loose Block Overhang to Hanging Gardens Route*

38. **Shining Star   5.10a**
140' (42m) in length, Pro to 2"
A good first pitch. Located on the right side of Hanging Gardens Wall. Climb a crack on a mossy slab immediately right of a maple tree. Pull through the bulge (5.10a) and continue up to a stance on sloping ledges. Step left to join Hanging Gardens route or step right and climb a broken crack system (5.10c) via edges and corners. Crosses over the Hanging Gardens route at the "bicycle path". Note: immediately left of the second portion of Shining Star is a minor prow with bolts called **Show Me The Money** 5.11. It can be used to access certain upper routes such as The Black Prow or upper Hanging Gardens route.

39. **Hung Jury   5.10d**
130' (39m) in length, Pro to 2½" including pitons

40. **Hang 'Em High   5.10b**
130' (39m) in length, Pro to 2"

The following seven routes are located in a overhanging amphitheater above the second pitch of the Hanging Gardens route. Refer to Map #1 for a visual tour.

Broughton
Map: HG Wall
Lower right aspect

41. Main Vein   5.11b
30' (9m) in length, Pro to 2"

This is the obvious prow right of Face Not Friction and above the maple tree belay. Follow the standard Hanging Gardens route past the tree, but at the old bees nest move up left around the corner by way of a crack. Once on the steep slab angle left then right and finish up a bolted arête until it joins with Sesame Street.

42. Sesame Street   5.9   ★★
Pro to 3"

Excellent but short. Climb the first pitch of Hanging Gardens. At the piton anchor for Mr. Potato step up left on easy ledges to a bolt belay. To your left is a slightly overhung zigzag jam crack. Climb this 15' to another belay. Rappel with two ropes or traverse left along ledges to the descent trail.

43. Demian   5.10d PG   ★★
30' (9m) in length, Pro to 3" TCU's optional

Superb, strenuous route ascending a desperate overhanging crack.

44. Endless Sleep   5.11a R
30' (9m) in length, Pro to 2"

45. Peer Pressure   5.10c R
30' (9m) in length, Pro to 2'

Poorly protected at the start but exciting stemming above. From the bolt anchor at the base of Scorpion Seams angle up let on slabs then ascend the overhung corner (pitons) to the top.

46. Scorpion Seams   5.12c   ★★
30' (9m) in length, 6 QD's

On the right face of the overhanging alcove are two bolted seams that merge halfway up the route and finish to the same belay anchor. The left start is called **Resurrection** (5.12d) while the right start is called **Scorpion Seams** (5.12c).

Broughton Bluff Map: Upper Right section of the Hanging Gardens Wall

47. Black Prow 5.12a
30' (9m) in length, Pro to 2"
A nice prow lead when it's combined with **Shining Star** and **Show Me The Money**.

RED WALL

One of the best places to experience the flavor of rock climb at Broughton Bluff.

Broughton
Map: Red Wall Left

48. Arch de Triumph 5.7
20' (6m) in length Pro to 4"
Right facing corner crack system.

49. Arcturas 5.10d
20' (6m) in length (TR)
Thin seam on a face that is better when its done as a TR (less risk).

50. Anastasia 5.9 ★
25' (7m) in length (TR)
Climb a thin crack to a flared crux problem on a steep slab. Best as a TR.

51. Dry Bones 5.10d/.11a
25' (7m) in length (TR)
Minor TR face with a brief high step smear crux.

52. On the Loose 5.11- ★★
30' (9m) in length
An excellent climb to the left of Classic Crack. Powerful climb with tricky pro; quality route though seldom done as a lead these days.

53. _____ 5.11 [TR]
Minor direct start TR to the previous climb.

54. Classic Crack 5.9+ ★★★ (Dry)
30' (9m) in length, Pro to 2"
Classic...that's exactly what it is! A beautiful jam crack that splits a smooth wall. A well-traveled slippery route. Can be top-roped by scrambling up an access trail to the left.

55. Thai Stick 5.10d ★★★ (Dry)
30' (9m) in length, QD's
A very popular lead climb. Climbers often combine this with Critical Mass for a stellar full power packed lead.

56. Mr. Bentley 5.11+ ★★ (Dry)
30' (9m) in length (TR)
Excellent top-rope route involving sequential endurance.

57. Sheer Stress II 5.10a PG ★★★ (Dry)
Multi-pitch, Pro to 2½"
Very popular route. One of the super classics. Commence up the shallow left-facing corner (crux) 15' right of Classic Crack. Climb up until it eases under a bulge, then move right to a bolt anchor. Belay. Move right to a semi-detached block, and then climb up over

Broughton Map: Red Wall

a bulge, then up a steep jam crack (5.10a) until possible to exit right on good holds to a ledge. Rappel with 2 ropes from bolt anchor.

The following routes are located generally above Classic Crack or Sheer Stress and can be accessed by most of the previous routes on the Red Wall.

58. Physical Graffiti II 5.10d ★★★
Multi-pitch, Pro to 2"
A fascinating route highlighted by a hand jam roof problem. Move up an easy corner (5.7) on the left corner of Red Wall and above Arch De Triumph. Upon reaching a roof traverse right to a ledge and bolt belay. Jam a crack busting through a big overhang. The climb eases onto a steep crack and an anchor. Rappel or finish up one of the upper variations (5.10a and dirty).

59. Habitual Ritual 5.11a
30' (9m) in length, 4 QD's and minor pro to 2"
A short bolted prow (above Anastasia) that leads directly up to merge in with Physical Graffiti at its belay anchor.

60. Physical Direct 5.9
30' (9m) in length, Pro to 2" TCU's recommended
Minor cracks and edges immediately right of Habitual Ritual.

61. Hit the Highway 5.11a ★
30' (9m) in length, Pro to 1½"
Good yet surprisingly hard lead. Begin on the intermediate ledge at the top of Classic Crack, but left of the belay anchor. Ascend directly up a steep bolted face (5.10a) then move right to the Red Eye belay. Step right and up (5.10a) a few moves until possible to move left to an ominous looking steep corner. Climb this and exit left to join with Physical Graffiti or jam

Broughton
Map: Red Wall Right

directly up a vertical crack to a ledge. Angle up left to a bolt belay. Rappel.

62. Red Eye II 5.10c ★★
Multi-Pitch, Pro to 2½" (1st pitch is 4 QD's)
A very popular route, especially the first pitch. Lead Classic Crack or start at the ledge above Classic, and climb a bolted face past a round red "eye" to a bolt anchor on a ledge to your left. Belay, then step right and up a crack system to easier ground. Belay at stance. Finish up a wide off width corner (5.10c) with numerous edges. Exit left and up to the tree at top of bluff. Rappel with two ropes or walk off.
Note: The Conspiracy (5.12b) is an alternative connector (between Red Eye and Critical Mass) to get to the stellar Kashmir route if you are climbing up via Thai Stick. The difficulty depends upon whether you reach out right to Critical Mass.

Shootin' 5.10c

63. Kashmir 5.12a ★★★
40' (12m) in length, 5 QD's and minor pro to 2½" (#5 Rock and 2½" Friend)
This superb line is located on the brilliant orange face in the upper amphitheater. Ascend Red Eye approximately 30' until possible to enter onto the steep bolted Kashmir face on the left. Rappel from bolt anchors with 2 ropes unless you rappel to the Red Eye anchor. See the note above for an alternative connector route variation to get to Kashmir.

64. Critical Mass 5.11c ★★★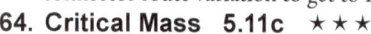
80' (24m) in length, 8 QD's and optional pro to 1½"
Impressive bolted climb on a steep orange wall. Originally this route powered out the 5.11a scoop then exited up left into a corner crack. Redirecting it focuses you on a balancy 5.11c crux at the final bulge above the initial overhung scoop.
Start by ascending Sheer Stress or Thai Stick, then power out the upside down scoop on positive holds, then dance over the thin crux bulge to a sloping stance. A few more tenuous moves end when you grasp a large block. The bolt anchor is at the top of the large block and below the prominent off width.

Classic Crack 5.9

65. Pinhead (E. Pluribus Pinhead) 5.11d ★★★

100' (30m) in length, 8 QD's and minor pro to 1½"
A fabulous route ascending the beautiful upper orange face of the Red Wall. Commence up the first pitch of Sheer Stress to the bolt anchor. From the anchor continue up left (bolts) on a steep section that eases to a minor stance. Step up right and climb a vertical bright reddish-orange colored face to a bolt anchor.

Sheer Stress 5.10a

✧ BROUGHTON BLUFF 55

66. **Trailer Park Sunset 5.13a** ★★ 🌂
    100' (30m) in length, 7 QD's
    A high quality route that parallels Pinhead. From the belay (for P1 Sheer Stress) climb up right via moderate block climbing (4 bolts) to a ledge rest and then ascend a steep burly crux (bolt) culminating with a dynamic throw to the jug rail on Pinhead. Exit right on independent climbing (2 bolts) to a belay.

The next several routes are just to the right of Sheer Stress on a darker shaded section of wall.

67. **Opus 5.11+ R** 🌂
    45' (13m) in length, 3 QD's to 1st anchor
68. **Sheer Energy 5.10a** ★★ 🌂
    45' (13m) in length, Pro to 1½"
    A great climb and surprisingly popular. Step to the top of several free-standing columns of basalt, then climb a short crack and face climb up left (bolts) to the Sheer Stress belay anchor.
69. **Hard Body 5.11b/c** ★★★ 🌂
    50' (15m) in length, 6 QD's
    Very popular route with an unusual crux. Commence up a shallow corner to a strenuous move, then pull through a bulge and up steep rock to an anchor capped by a roof. Rappel.
70. **Shootin' (aka Shoot from the Hip) 5.10c** ★★ 🌂
    45' (13m) in length, Pro to 1" and QD's
    Fun climb with big holds and a crack to start.
71. **Friction 5.9** ★
    45' (13m) in length, Pro to 1" and QD's
    A tenuous crux move but still a popular climb.
72. **That's the Way 5.8**
    45' (13m) in length, Pro to 2"

    BRIDGE CLIFF
73. **Under Your Belt 5.9+ R**
    165' (50m) in length, P1 gear to 2", P2 14 QD's
    A long climb ascending the blocky 5th class section on the lower left. Belay at 40'. P2 trends up through a blocky section, and then up a clean dihedral to the top of the cliff.
74. **Polar Vortex 5.9**
    40' (13m) in length
    Ascend a fl at crimpy face, then easy steps to belay at 40'. Minor variation that merges with the previous route. Rappel. Or continue up Under Your Belt to the top of the cliff .
75. **Edge of Eternity 5.11c** ★
    Multi-pitch, Pro to 2"
    A long climb that begins on the lower section of wall. Climb the dihedral and move right around a diffi cult corner (5.11) to ledge belay. Above an easy wide corner is a clean angular face with bolts. Climb

Ian Goss leading Dracula 5.12a

this (crux) to the next belay. Move up onto a big ledge, step right and climb (bolts) the right face of an arête (5.11a) to a tiny ledge, then a short face to the tree belay. Rappel.

76. Eagle's Wing 5.12a
40', Pro 5 QD's
Climbs the crimpy face to the right of the start of Edge of Eternity.

77. _____ 5.9
P1 35', 4 QD's, P2 35' 7-8 QD's
Climb face to a wide slot (of detached block). Belay at 35'. Step right and continue to angle up right till you merge into WOTWS route (bolts). Continue up Walk On The Wild Side.

78. _____ 5.11+
45 in length, 7 QD's
Climb Eagle's Wing (or other nearby route) to the Little Ledge belay. Climb directly above the belay up several ledges, then up a steep prow system to an upper belay. Rappel.

79. Walk on the Wild Side 5.10c/d PG ★ ★
45' (13m) in length, Pro to 2"
The standard approach to this classic route begins near the first pitch of Fruit Bat. P1: Traverse left to a right facing corner and climb the vertical corner (bolts). Belay on the big upper ledge. P2: traverse left about 15' past a central corner (Spider Monkey) to a left-leaning corner. Ascend this to the cliff top

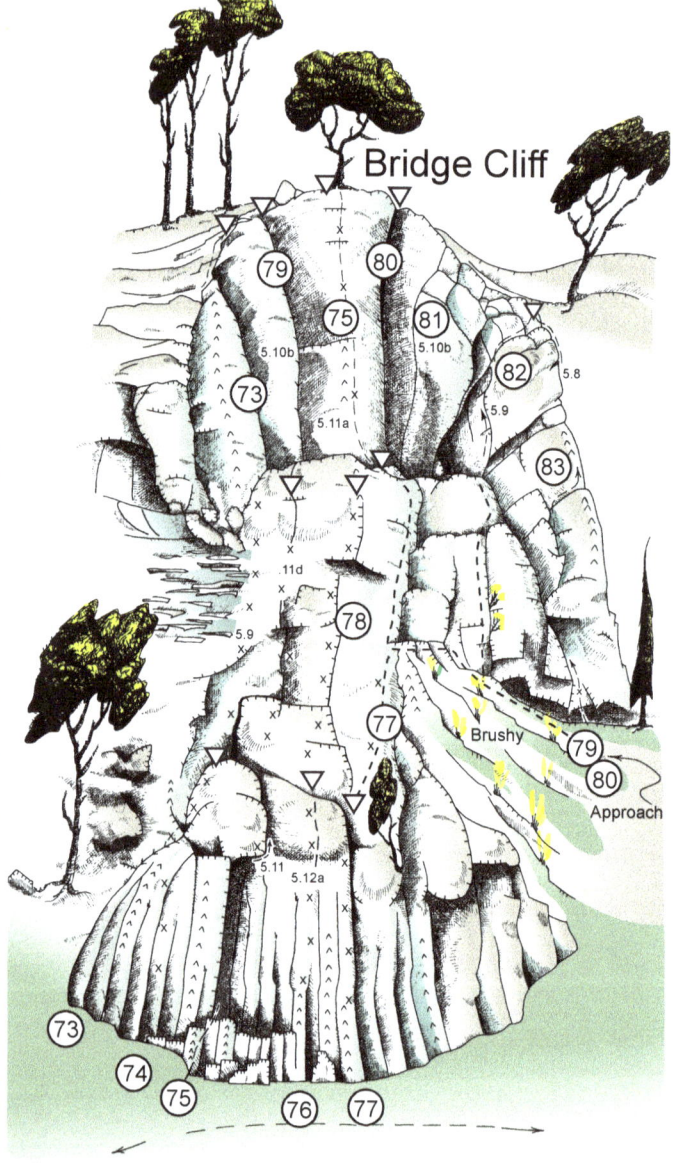

belay. Rappel.

80. **Spider Monkey 5.9** ★
    40' (12m) in length, Pro to 3"
    A large dark dihedral on the upper face above the big belay ledge. Stem this crack corner system to the top of the cliff.

81. **Fruit Bat II 5.10b** ★
    Multi-pitch, Pro to 2"
    Approach via a path from the left edge of Spring Rock that arrives at a small landing below a big overhung roof. Start past a bolt into a sloping crack corner, and continue left via grassy ledges and crack corners to a big ledge with a belay. On the right face of the deep dihedral (Spidermonkey) is a thin finger crack. Ascend this and top out.

82. **Seventh Sojourn 5.9**
    Pro unknown

83. **Shandor 5.9**
    Pro to 3"

    SPRING ROCK

84. **Toe Cleavage 5.8+**
    30' (9m) in length, Pro to 1"
    A fun minor route with a tricky crux smear move to easier climbing.

85. **Velcro Fly   5.10d PG**
    30' (9m) in length, QD's and minor pro to 1"
    The route is highlighted by a thin crux move in a shallow corner at a bulge. Wander up easier slabs to a bolt belay.

86. **Free Bird   5.11a   ★★**
    40' (12m) in length, Pro to 1"
    Excellent route. Step up to a small corner, reach left, then climb a second corner to a roof. Exit left onto slabs that lead up left to a bolt anchor.

87. **Ground Effects   5.12a/b   ★★**
    40' (12m) in length, 4 QD's
    Probably the most unusual and fascinating route on Spring Rock. The climb involves two roof moves using very unorthodox technique. Solve the puzzle.

88. **Jumping Jack Thrash   5.11d R   ★★** *Dry*
    40' (12m) in length, Pro to 1" TCU's and RP's recommended
    A great climb, but it is usually TR due to a very risky landing on large rocks. Ascend a thin crack in the center of the face to a bolt anchor under an overhang. Rappel.

89. **The Spring   5.10b/c   ★★** *Dry*
    40' (12m) in length, Pro to 3"
    This punchy little flared crack climb is great for strong climbers who like powerful moves in a moderate sense. Takes good camming unit protection.

90. **Short Fuse   5.10c   ★★** *Dry*
    35' (10m) in length, QD's and minor pro to ½"
    Yes, it is quite short, but it is still a worthy climb. Ascend the blank face and exit right to a ledge, step up left to a bolt anchor. Remember to bring a small selection of gear!

91. **Short Circuit   5.10b**
    35' (10m) in length, QD's
    A short crux face climb, then a sloped ledge, and a few corner crack moves to a belay.

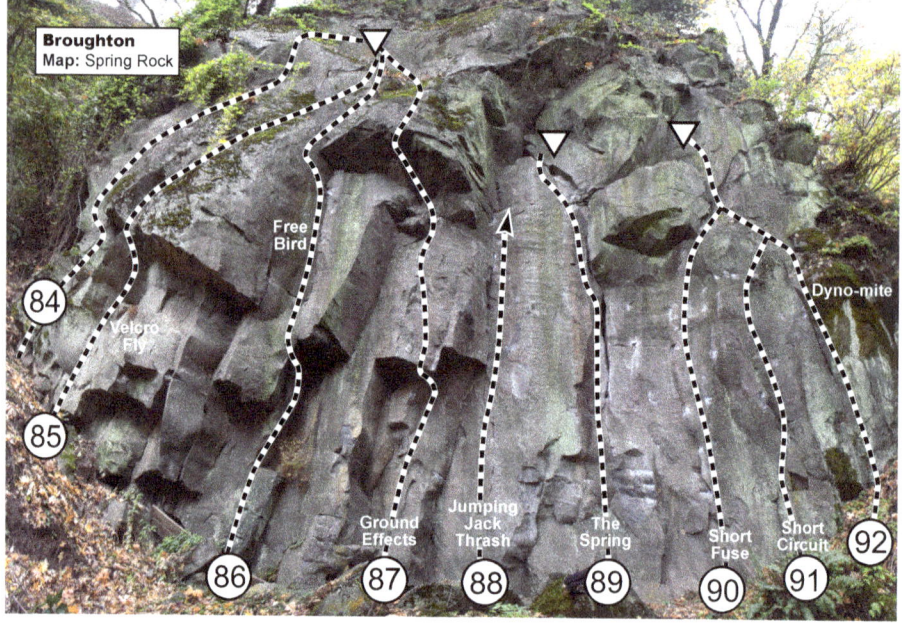

Broughton Map: Spring Rock

92. Dyno-mite 5.10b
35' (10m) in length, Pro to 1½"
Ascend a slight seam groove (crux) to a sloped stance, then easier large steps up left to belay.

BAT WALL

One of the most impressive walls at Broughton Bluff, and the ideal place to learn some of the powerful tricky nuances of the 5.12 game at this crag.

93. Hanging Tree III 5.11a ★
Multi-pitch, Pro to 3" (and/or QD's)

Stephanie D'Cruz on *Superstition*

If it stays clean it is a quality powerful route offering excellent quality stemming and face climbing. P1 (5.8): climbs over a large block and up a crack to a sloped ramp. P2 (5.10b/c): climb a right facing corner, then move right around roof then up a crack to a perch belay. P3 (5.10d): Traverse right, then climb the prominent dihedral (just left of the Dracula anchor). P4 (5.9): Starts a tough move, then eases to 5.7 climbing, then move right to a belay ledge. P5 (5.9): Climb a short corner to an exit move onto the top of cliff.

94. Scottish Variation 5.10c/d
40' (12m) in length, gear to 3"
Climb a brief slab, move up left at a fat crack, then trend right (bolts) up a seam on a flat face. Climb eases onto a sloped ledge, and merges into Hanging Tree.

95. Hanging Judge 5.11a/b ★
40' (12m) in length, 5 QD's
A fine route starting with a step, then cruise up a slightly hung crack using edges and crimps to surmount over a minor bulge. Eases onto a sloped ledge at a belay.

96. Go Back to the Gym II 5.7 A3 for 40'
40' (12m) in length, Pro to 1" includes TCU's, KB, LA, Leepers, Hangers, Bathooks, (III A4+ on the upper portion)
Great aid route. The second part (II A3), branches onto a ¼" deep tied-off pin stack seam, then up to a hanging belay. Die in the Gym (III A4+) goes over the smooth bulge on hooks (seven in a row) and bad pins to a sloping stance belay at 65'. Finish up the upper wall by criss-crossing the Hanging Tree route to the summit anchor (160').

96b. Undercount 5.13b
55' in length, 5 QD's (plus more QD's for Count Chalkula)
Begin immediately left of Dracula and climb up to the no-hand stance, then trend up slightly left-ish to a sloped slight pod, then trend up right-ish on thin crimps till it merges with the Count Chalkula route.

David working on *Lost Boys*

97. Dracula 5.12a ★★★ Dry
65' (19m) in length, 10 QD's
The premier Broughton Bluff classic rock climb! A difficult free climb of the highest standard. Originally called the Unnamed Aid Route. Commence up a small right-facing corner to the right of the dead leaning tree. From a small ledge embark up a diagonal right leaning hand ramp, then up left, then right to a seam. Balance up the seam and surmount the final obstacle, a flared pea-pod corner. Bolt belay anchor.

98. Count Chalkula 5.13b Dry
65' (19m) in length, about 10 QD's
Begin on Dracula but cut left after the long rail. Four bolts from here to belay. The crux surmounts the small roof and requires hard lie-backing off bad feet. Extension may be 5.14?

99. Bela Lugosi 5.12c ★★ Dry
65' (19m) in length, 10 QD's
Fascinating route to climb. Ascend a shallow corner gracefully to a thin stance. Pull through a desperately thin crux then up left via a zigzag seam (crux) until it joins with

Dracula to the pea-pod finish.

100. Fright Night   5.13a [right var], 5.13b [left var]

65' (19m) in length, 8 QD's

The full direct finish (5.14?) is a difficult route. Alternate #1: at the 4th bolt traverse right (5.13a) into Bad Omen. Alternative #2: climb to the 5th bolt and move left (5.13b) to Dracula. This commits you to the opportunity to send the Dracula 'pod' one more time.

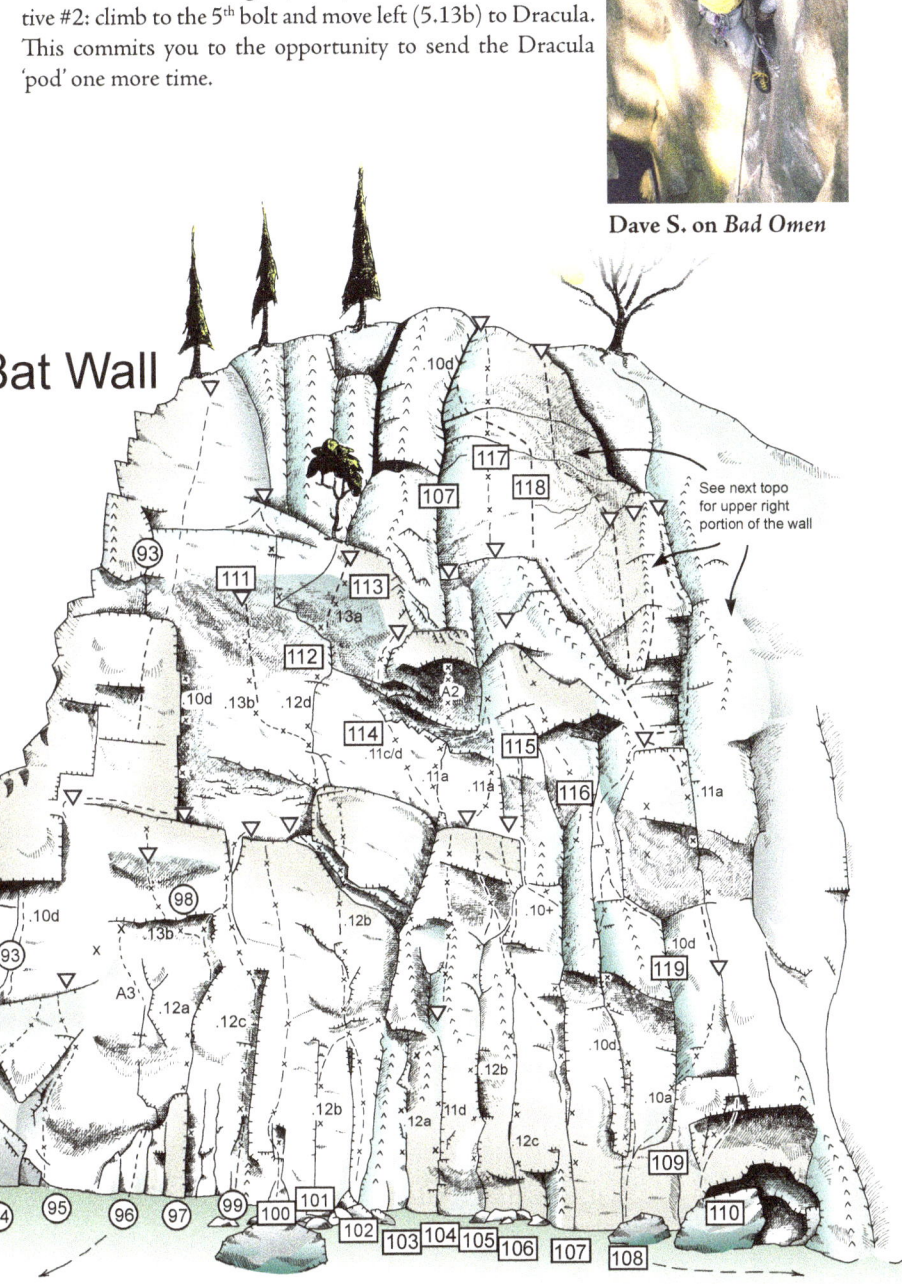

Dave S. on *Bad Omen*

Bat Wall

101. The Haunting 5.12b ★
65' (19m) in length, 5 QD's and pro to 2"
Originally called Snap, Crackle, Pop (aid climb), this fascinating vertical seam has yielded a sequential and difficult free climb of modern standards. Ascend the seam 25', then angle right across Bad Omen and enter a fist jam that eases to a hand crack (5.9) corner ending at the Superstition belay ledge.

102. Bad Omen 5.12b ★★★
65' (19m) in length, 10 QD's
Superb! Another Broughton super classic. Begin up a steep face via side pulls to a thin stance, move over the bulge (crux) and up small edges to an unorthodox high step (crux). Carefully work up a left leaning flared slot until a protruding roof forces you left and up to a sloping ledge and bolt belay.

103. Danse Macabre 5.12a
40' (12m) in length, 3 QD's (plus 3-4 QD for short P2)
Short climb with a techy crux move, then a deep corner, then past a roof to the belay. Short pitch two climbs a brief arête up over a small lip to an upper belay.

104. Bloodsucker 5.11d
40' (12m) in length, 3 QD's
Short climb with a brief trick hung crux flake that eases into a deep corner at the belay.

105. Bloodline 5.12b ★★★
65' (19m) in length, 7 QD's
Originally called Beeline, this gusto climb offers the local rock jock a bold start and a fantastic roof to exit through. One of the most exciting and interesting routes on the Bat Wall. Layback up an overhung face to several natural pockets then crack up to a stance. Balance up a smooth section then up a thin crack to a stance below a large roof. Start on the right and power up left then over the lip and finally to the ledge and bolt belay for Superstition.

106. **Predator 5.12c** *Dry*
    60' (19m) in length, QD's
    A unique powerful bulge crux sequence for the initial opening moves, then a slight stance, then some more face/crack moves till it merges into Superstition (P1) at the slot.

107. **Superstition III 5.11a ★ ★ ★** *Dry*
    Multi-pitch, P1 9-10 QD's (minor pro to 1"?), P2 5.11a (4 QD's), P3 pro to 2"
    A great route and quite popular, particularly the first pitch. Step up onto an outside corner and ascend a shallow groove corner system until possible to smear left via under clings (5.10+), then up a brief thin crack to a narrow ledge (belay). P2: power up right on a steep 4-bolt crux pitch to the next belay. P3: continue up a crack corner to a steep, and surprisingly strenuous wide crack problem (5.10d). Rappel.
    Note: a squeezejob variant [Vlad the Impaler 5.10] branches up left at mid-route [P1] onto Predator, then continues up bypassing a large roof [Bloodline's final crux roof] to end on the large ledge belay where Superstition [P1]ends.

108. **Lost Boys 5.10d ★ ★** *Dry*
    70' (21m) in length, 8 QD's
    An excellent warm-up. On the right side of the Bat Wall are several large boulders in front of a cave. Begin behind the left one, face climb up to an overhang (crux) with a slot. Move up, then right, mantle, then up until you can exit right via an under cling and reach (crux) around a corner to a bolt anchor on a ledge.

109. **Mystic Void 5.10a**
    45' (13m) in length, 4 QD's
    Ascends the face left of, and then joins with the Well Hung route above the large roof. Rap from belay anchor, or tackle one of the routes above.

110. **Well Hung 5.10b ★ ★**
    45' (13m) in length, Pro to 1"
    An original Bat Wall favorite. Step directly off the large boulders onto the face under the large roof. Traverse right then swing onto the roof via jug holds to a stance. Move up the corner to the belay anchor.

The following routes are located on the upper portion of the Bat Wall. Some are independent routes, and some branch off variations from an existing lower route. Beta is listed Left to Right for this section.

111. **Nosferatu 5.13b ★ ★**
    100' (30m) in length, 17 QD's (if using variation from Bad Omen)
    Excellent test-piece that requires power and technique. Nosferatu branches left after the first bolt on Manson. Link via the variation with Bad Omen for the full deal. Use 70-meter rope to rap to the ground (or shorter rope to get to Dracula anchor).

112. **Manson Reunion 5.12d ★ ★**
    60' (18m) in length, 7 QD's
    A high quality route that is located above Fright Night. Though seldom climbed, this route ascends a surprisingly stunning section of the Bat Wall. From the Bad Omen anchor climb up a short corner to a stance, then crimp up past a blank crux section. Embark up left on incut crack edges out a smooth round overhang to a belay at a ledge.

113. **Sutured by the Vampress 5.13a ★ ★**
    60' (18m) in length, 7 QD's (from Dracula belay)
    Cuts up right just after crux bolt on Manson, and cruises an intricate thin seam via jugs, slopers and a lunge. Much more exciting finish.

64 CHAPTER 1 ✧ ORC

114. Vampyr 5.11c/d
40' (12m) in length, Pro 4 QD's (from Superstition P1 belay)
This bolt route climbs up left into an overhung zone from the first pitch belay on Superstition. There are four bolts to the next belay anchor.

115. Missing Children 5.12b
Pro 5 QD's
Where Supersition P1 ends, this route steps out right then powers up a difficult series of moves, easing back to the P3 belay for Superstition.

116. Remain in Light 5.12 b/c
35' (10m) in length, Pro 11 QD's
Where Superstition (P1) moves abruptly left this route continues up a steep corner, then steps right, then continues up a slightly overhung section. If you climb straight up past the last bolt to the anchor it's 5.12b/c, but if you move left and climb up 5' before moving back right to the last bolt it's considered 5.11d/12a.

117. Epitaph 5.12c
35' (10m) in length, Pro 5 QD's
Begin on the Ledge of Light. Initial sloper crux, then a second crux, and a final slab with small edges.

118. Demon 5.12c
35' (10m) in length, Pro: to 2"
From same ledge as Epitaph climb a seam (bolts) till you reach a left trending crack. Traverse this crack up left till it merges into Supertition P3. An alternate ending is to continue straight up into the last section of Van Helsing.

119. Mystic Pizza 5.10d
70' (21m) in length, QD's, and pro to 1½"
An interesting variation with good pro. Start as for Mystic Void; instead of traversing to the right to join Well Hung, continue up an obvious corner system then exit up left (crux) to join Lost Boys. Minor 2-bolt variant busts up right from Mystic Pizza.

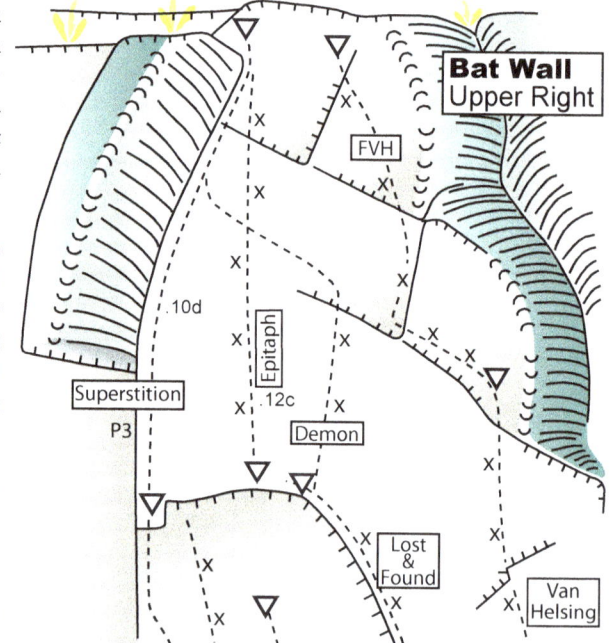

The following routes either begin at the Well Hung belay station, or are located above that belay (or can be accessed by any route from Lost Boys to Well Hung).

120. Natural Mystic 5.11a
30' (10m) in length, 4 QD's
A short hung corner lead above the P1 be-

lay on Well Hung. Route ends on Lost Ledge (a 70' rappel to ground).

121. Lost & Found 5.8
40' (12m) in length, 7 QD's
From Lost Ledge take large steps up left, up a brief arete, and into a right facing corner till you land on a big ledge and belay (at base of Demon / Epitaph).

122. Van Helsing 5.11+ ★
65' (18m) in length, 10 QD's
At the 3rd bolt on Lost & Found route, step right and continue up steep face past some tricky moves to the base of a left diagnaling crack on the upper headwall (just right of

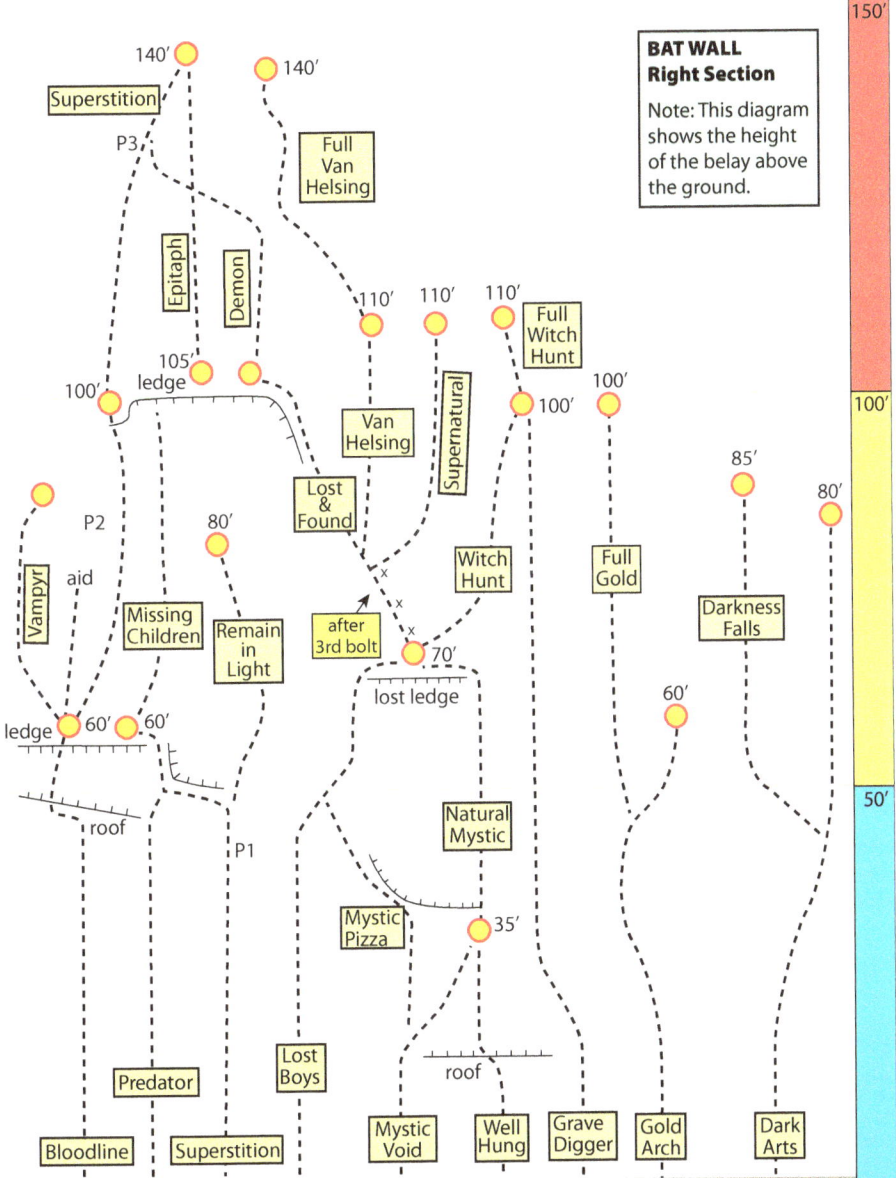

Epitaph and Demon). Follow the steep crack features past several bolts to the top of the headwall

123. Supernatural 5.12a ★★
45' (13m) in length, 8 QD's
Just after the 3rd bolt on Lost & Found route, head up to the steep hanging arête using a difficult sequence of moves to reach good jugs and a wild finish.

124. Witch Hunt 5.11a ★
30' (10m) in length, 5 QD's
From the Lost Ledge, step right and climb the corner system with tricky moves till you reach the Grave Digger belay near the lip of a roof (60m lower to the ground). A brief extension exists (see next). Or continue through the roof and up the final headwall moves past 2 more bolts for the **Full Witch Hunt** extension (8 bolts, 70m lower or rap twice).

BROUGHTON BLUFF

The following routes start on the ground immediately right of Well Hung route.

125. **Grave Digger   5.11a   ★★**
100' (30m) in length, 16 QD's
A long high quality lead. Begin immediately right of the Well Hung roof. Climb past two small overhung sections, then move up left above the Well Hung roof, and climb up a long corner system with several overhung lip sections.

126. **Gold Arch   5.12b/c   ★★**
60' (21m) in length, 10 QD's
A route established in the 80's. Begin immediately right of Grave Digger up a short steep slab, then power up a strenuous barn door lie back on a gold-streaked face, over a minor lip to a belay. The original P2 (still unclean) continues up ledges to the cliff top.

127. **Full Gold   5.10d   ★★**
100' (30m) in length, 16 QD's
The cool extension of Gold Arch. From the last bolt on Gold Arch move up left and climb a steep face, over a minor lip, then a corner with edges till you reach a belay anchor.

128. **Dark Arts   5.10d   ★★★**
80' (30m) in length, 12 QD's
A superb quality route. Climb a steep slab, then power up a vertical corner (past a gold streaked face), surmount an overhung lip, then continue up a long series of steep crimps and seams to a belay.

129. **Darkness Falls   5.11b/c   ★★**
85' (27m) in length, 12 QD's
An extension of the previous Dark Arts route. At bolt #6, move up left under a roof (chain draws) then up a series of minor lips in a right facing corner.

130. **Witching Hour 5.10c   ★**
75' (21m) in length, Pro 9 QD's
Immediately right of Dark Arts is a fine short lead that utilizes a series of blocky overhangs. Stem up till under a small roof, power up to a slab, then (crux) sustained climbing to belay.

131. **Revenant 5.10-**
65' (19m) in length, 8 QD's
Climb a corner till you reach a small roof. Use a small crack to surmount the roof, and continue up easier vertical terrain above to the belay.

The next climbs are found at the extreme southern end of the

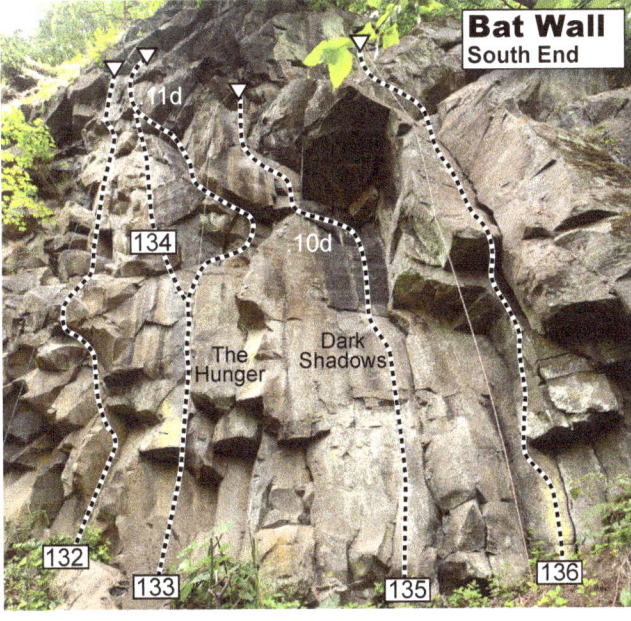

Bat Wall.

132. Tombraider 5.11b
55' (16m) in length, Pro: 9 QD's
Powers through a series over small overhangs, then a set of small stances, followed by several more small bulging overhangs.

133. The Hunger 5.11d
55' (16m) in length, Pro to 1½" and cams suggested
Begin on a small rock pedestal. Climb a short thin finger crack (gear) to a stance, step right and climb an overhung crack that veers hard left till it lands in a ramp, then cruise ramp till it surmounts a final bulge (bolts) to a belay.

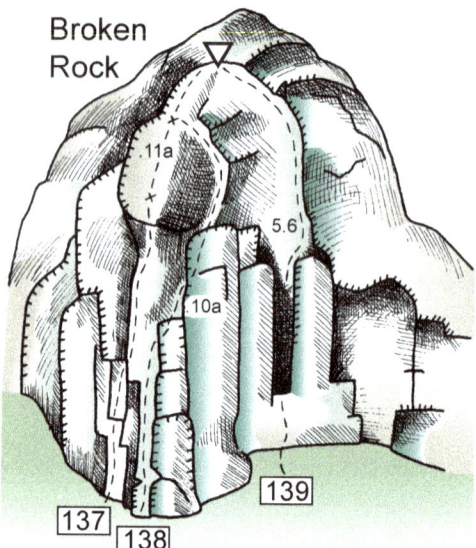

Broken Rock

134. _____ 5.11+
55' (16m) in length, 11 QD's
A bolted left trending variation of The Hunger (where that route moves right to an overhung crack) that utilizes crimps and edge face climbing till it re-merges into The Hunger at the final bulge just below the belay.

135. Dark Shadows 5.10d ★
40' (12m) in length, Pro to 1½" TCU's recommended
Originally called Shadow Dancing (5.8 A2), this climb was easily freed to produce a unique problem. Ascend a face to a left facing corner capped by a large roof. Step left, then up, then left (crux) past fixed pitons and up to a belay anchor on a small ledge. Rappel.

136. _____ 5.9
40' (12m) in length, Pro to 3"
Immediately right of Dark Shadows is a wide corner crack. Climb this to its top, then surmount a bulge (2 bolts) that lands on a sloped ledge sytem at a belay. Rappel.

Just south of Bat Wall is a series of small outcrops and one large cliff. The first small blocky short vertical chunk is Broken Rock, followed by T Wall, Berlin Wall, Jungle Cliff, and New Frontier Wall.

BROKEN ROCK

137. Static Cling 5.11a
35' (10m) in length, pro to ¾", small TCU's
Height is a factor when moving past the first bolt. A variation using part of Plan B route is 5.10d.

138. Plan B 5.10a
35' (10m) in length, Pro to 2", 1½" Friend and #0 TCU recommended
Minor fun climb.

139. Lickity Split 5.6 ★

35' (10m) in length, Pro to 2", including a 3½" Friend
An interesting route.

TRINITY WALL
140. Bust A' Move 5.11b ★

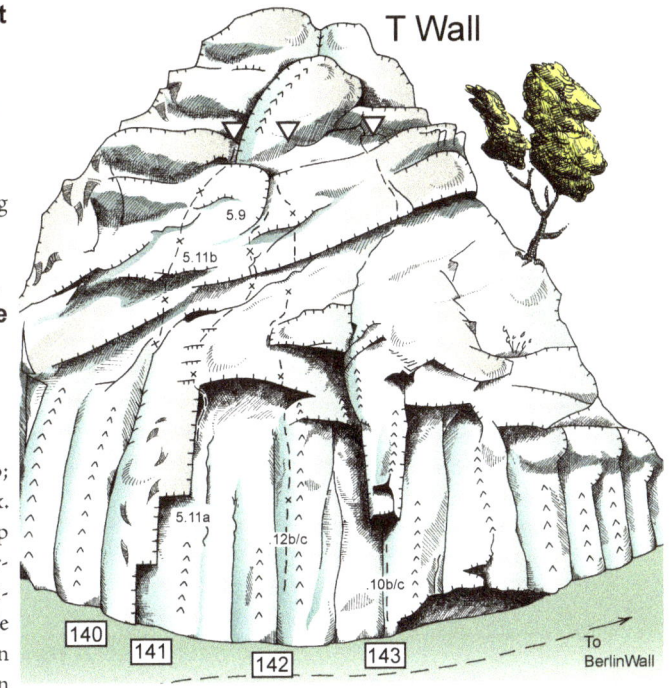

40' (12m) in length, 4 QD's and pro to 1"
Good climb; surprising crux. Commence up a shallow corner over a minor bulge. Angle rightward via thin holds (crux), then up an easy corner to a belay. Rappel.

141. Father 5.11a

40' (12m) in length, Pro to 1½"
Quality climb. Ascend the strenuous right-facing corner until possible to exit up left onto a slab. Move up right on easy ground then up left (bolt) in the center of the face, and left to the bolt anchor in a corner.

142. Livin' in Sin 5.12b/c

40' in length, 4 QD's
Powerfully difficult face climbing followed by an overhung roof, that eases onto relatively enjoyable face climbing for the upper half of the route.

143. Thoughts & Prayers 5.10 b/c PG13

40' in length, Pro: 4"
Climb the ominous hanging pillar on its left side, then through a minor roof, and jaunt up left to merge with previous route or climb to the original belay up high on the right.

BERLIN WALL
144. Closet Nazi 5.12a ★★

45' (13m) in length, 5 QD's
Remarkable and highly challenging route. Climb the bolt line on the left side of the wall up very clean, overhung rock. Can be a virtual stream of water during the winter months.

145. Recipe for Airtime II A3

30' (9m) in length, Pitons and natural pro
Minor aid line.

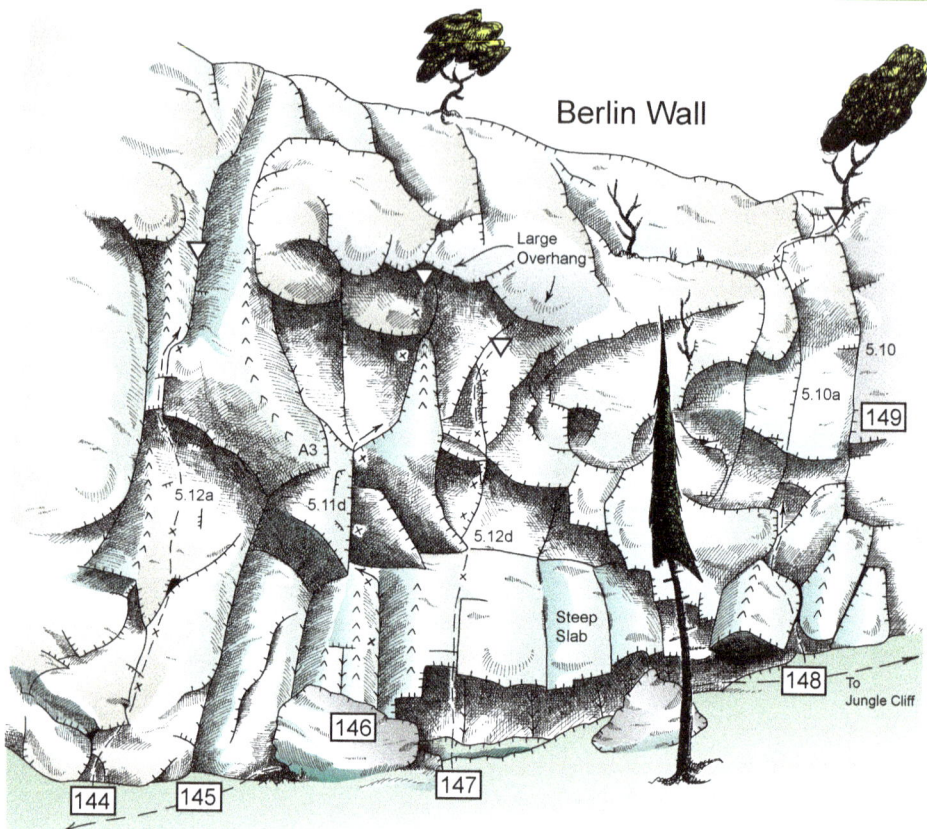

146. **Twist and Crawl   5.11d**
    40' (12m) in length, 5 QD's
    Located in the center of the wall directly under the huge roof. Unusual yet quite good. Move up a dihedral around a crux corner then up and out the overhang to the anchor.

147. **Genocide   5.12d / 5.13a**
    40' (12m) in length, 5 QD's (1" nut or cam to start)
    To the right of Twist and Crawl is another route on this virtually upsidedown wall. Start up a crack on a slab then up via physically articulate moves out the overhang to a bolt anchor.

148. **Pride and Joy   5.10a**
    40' (12m) in length, Pro to 1",   Small wires recommended
    On the far right side of Berlin Wall is a smooth vertical section of rock broken with several thin cracks. The left is a 5.10a, the right is a top-rope. Takes good pro. Rappel from the tree anchor directly above the top-rope problem.

149. **_____   5.10**
    40' (12m) in length (TR)

The next two crags are located on private land (tread wisely). The Jungle Cliff has seen a substantial increase in the number of bolted routes which make this wall enticing for the power climber seeking extreme and well hung beastly routes.

JUNGLE CLIFF

150. Zimbabwe II 5.10a
Multi-pitch, Pro to 3", Cams recommended
Ascends the steep face on the far left corner of Jungle Cliff via numerous ledges.

151. Minimancer 5.9+
55' (16m) in length, 8 QD's
Ledges and jugs, but with a hard knee bar start out of the little cave. Will eventually have a second pitch. Alternate start traverses in from left to 2nd bolt. A route extension (5-bolts more) continues above the belay station.

152. Welcome to the Jungle 5.11a/b ★
80' (24m) in length, 9 QD's
Punch out of a little cave, then up ledge & edge terrain, then punch through a steep overhung section up a long buttress system.

153. Slash and Burn 5.12a ★
80' (24m) in length, QD's and minor pro to 2"
A good route on fantastic steep rock. Begin at the cave, pull up (5.9), move up the slab to the right, then up the slab to a belay. Continue up the overhanging corner above, move left at difficult section and finish up a vertical dihedral to a final crux move. Rappel from belay.

154. _____ 5.14-
80' (24m) in length,
Open project (one of Dave's old projects). Cruise the lower part of Slash & Burn, then it launces up right to punch through a series of substantially overhung roofs.

155. _____ (aka Headhunters) 5.12d
100' (30m) in length, P1 5 QD's, P2 10 QD's
P1 punches up out of the small cave on the right side, then over a crux lip onto a slab to a belay. P2 tackles the overhung upper section, but branches left at the 5th bolt. The last few bolts is the crux section.

156. Jungle Boogie 5.13b/c ★
100' (30m) in length,
Same start as previous route (on P1). As you power up the overhung P2 branch right at the 5th bolt and continue up more overhung terrain to another belay.

157. Yum Yum 5.10b ★
50' (15m) in length, 7 QD's
A fun retro-bolted climb. Start right of the cave and ascend a slab via a thin seam and minor corner system. FA was done by Wallace ground up onsight with mostly gear.

Dave on Heart of Darkness P2

Dave on Heart of Darkness P1

Jungle Cliff

158. Tarzan 5.12d ★★
50' (15m) in length, 7 QD's
The obvious and impressive arête. Tarzan is definitely one of the most unusual routes of its kind at Broughton.

159. Crime Wave 5.10c PG
50' (15m) in length, QD's, TCU's, #2 Friend recommended
An awkward variation left of Gorilla Love Affair. Bolts don't make it any easier.

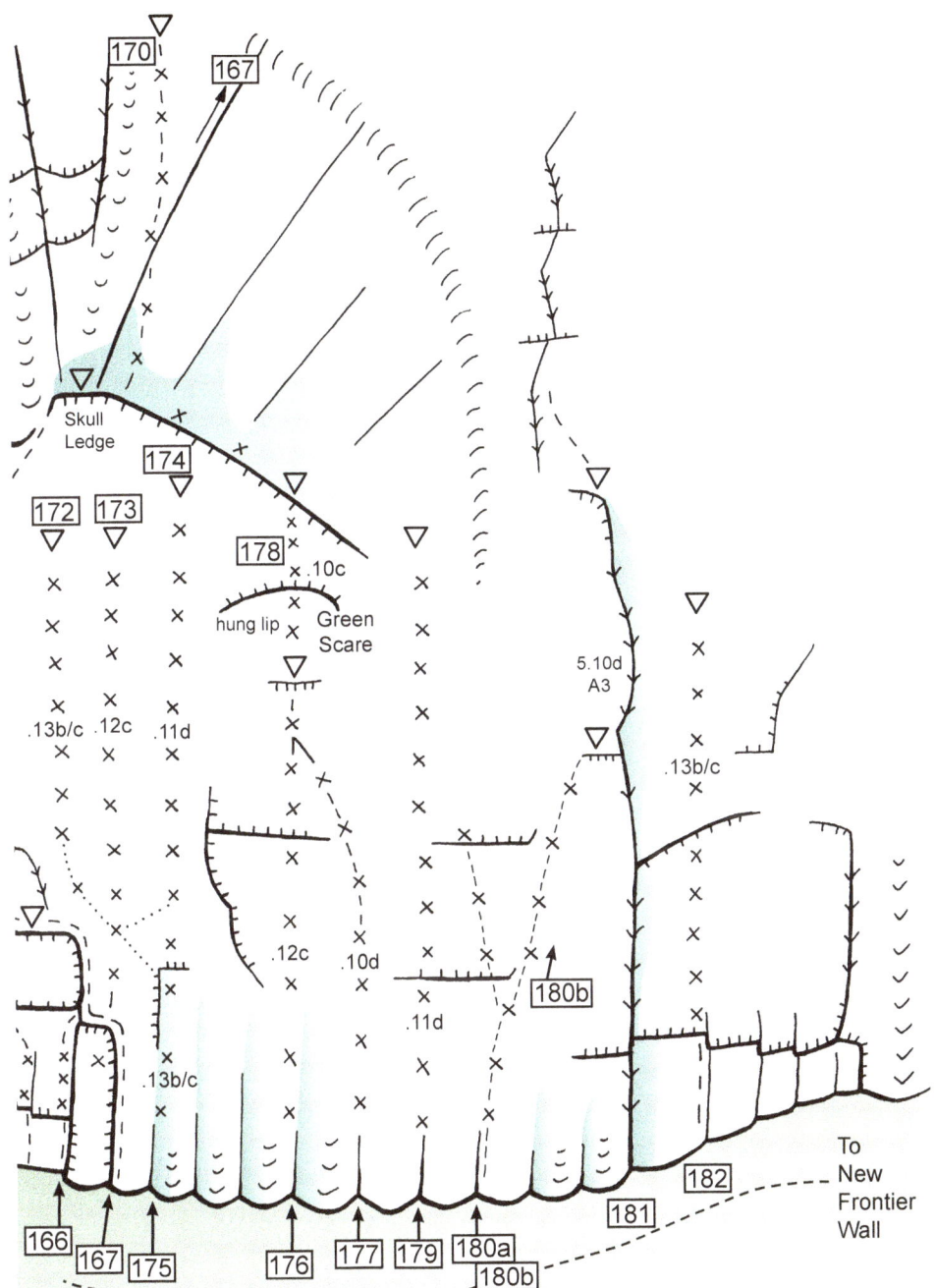

160. Gorilla Love Affair 5.10d ★★★
50' (15m) in length, 6 QD's, optional TCU's
A very exhilarating climb. Stem up to a small roof, move left, then up to another roof. Step right and up a smooth dihedral (crux) until possible to step left to finish up a crack

leading to the belay anchor for Yum Yum Tree. Rappel.

161. Wretched of the Earth 5.11d ★ (Dry)
80' (24m) in length, 8 QD's
A bizarre crux flated chimney, then easier crack/slab terrain, then a brief cruxy move just before the belay. Was the old Out of Africa aid line.

162. Heart of Darkness 5.12b ★★ (Dry)
P1 80' (24m) in length, 10 QD's
A beautiful route that leads up an overhung arête in the heart of Jungle Cliff country. Desperately struggle out the overhung start to a stance, then up and left along a hand ramp. Pull through the crux (thin) then up the right side of the arête to a stance. Make a quick move up a smooth face and up to a tiny

stance belay. Proceed up left out the fiercely overhung headwall (5 bolts and 5.11d) via face and jug holds. Rappel with 2 ropes.

163. ____ A3
An old aid line in a hung slot corner.

164. Mowgli Direct 5.12b (Dry)
40' (12m) in length, QD's
Located between Heart of Darkness and Mowgli's Revenge.

165. Mowgli's Revenge 5.11b (Dry)
40' (12m) in length, 4 QD's
Underneath a large roof to the right of Heart of Darkness, you will find two bolt routes. The left one is Mowgli's Revenge. An interesting climb that exits the roof on the left side. Rappel from bolt anchor.

166. **Amazon Woman 5.10d** ★

40' (12m) in length, 4 QD's and minor pro to 1½" Cams recommended

Commence up a vertical stem problem via small edges to a stance. Reach up right under the roof, then traverse right and exit to a good stance. Step up a wide crack to a huge ledge and bolt belay. Rappel.

167. **Amazon Man 5.11d (or III 5.11 A3)** ★ ★ ★

Multi-pitch, Pro to 3", Bring KB & LA

This formidable achievement, put up in 1979, penetrates through the heart of Jungle

Cliff. Begin up a corner (immediately right of Amazon Woman) past a fixed piton to a stance, then up a wide crack to a big ledge with a good anchor. Mowgli's Revenge joins here. Continue up by one of two cracks to a stance, then delicately traverse left via sloping ledges (bolts) to the Heart of Darkness belay. Ascend directly above you (5.10+) to another belay then move right around the sweet headwall and up a difficult section. Belay at bolts on Skull Ledge. Storm the dihedral (5.11 D) directly above that leads to the summit. Monkey Paws route (5.11b) is the face climb at right side of skull ledge. Rappel with 2 ropes. Note: a considerable portion of this route is fixed with bolts.

The next several routes are located above P2 and P3 of Amazon Man.

168. _____ **5.12 (?)**

100' (30m) in length, __ QD's
Project.

169. **Enter the Void 5.11a** ★

40' (12m) in length, about 6 QD's

Located on the right face of the huge overhanging center prow. Climb any lower route to the Amazon Man P2 belay, then climb up right around the below the huge overhang, then up a crimpy quality face to the belay.

170. **Total Liberation 5.11c** ★
    50' (15m) in length, 6 QD's
    From Skull Ledge climb the initial portion of Amazon Man (right slanting crack) then continue directly up (left-ish) to a belay anchor.

The next routes are located to the right of P1 and P2 of Amazon Man.

171. **_____ 5.13+ (?)**
    100' (30m) in length, ___ QD's
    Unfinished project. Tackles a blank-*ish* vertical face above the P1 belay for Amazon Man.

172. **The Groove 5.13b/c**
    100' (30m) in length, 11 QD's
    Climbs the initial part of Amazon Man to a stance, then up Oracle to its 2nd bolt then move over left and climb a vertical to slightly hung sequential face.

173. **Oracle 5.12c** ★★
    100' (30m) in length, 11 QD's
    A superb line with powerful bouldering moves, powerful crimpy moves on lower section, and a difficult crux section closer to the belay. Shares start with Necromancer.

174. **Necromancer 5.11d** ★★
    100' (30m) in length, 11 QD's
    Start on Amazon Man to a small stance, then climb directly up a face, but at 2nd bolt (see diagram) bust right on good edges, and climb directly up edges along a unique fin-like feature. Original aid line Killer Pygmy.

◆ **BROUGHTON BLUFF** 77

175. Warlock 5.13b/c ★★
100' (30m) in length, 11 QD's
Fierce alternate start to Oracle, Warlock tackles a slightly overhung prow, and when you get to about the 3rd bolt move left into Oracle and send it.

176. Firestorm 5.12c ★★
60' (18m) in length, 8 QD's
Sends a substantial overhung roof system on fairly good holds. Involves a tough committing crux section under the large roof.

177. Ecocide 5.10d ★★
60' (18m) in length, 8 QD's
Technical thin opening crux section in minor corner, then gradually moves up leftward under the roof on good holds to several small corners where it merges with the Firestorm route at the last bolt. (P2 is called **Green Scare** 5.10).

178. Green Scare 5.10
30' (10m) in length, 5-6 QD's
The pitch above Ecocide that lands on the ramp near Skull Ledge.

179. Forged In The Flames 5.11d ★★
90' (27m) in length, 12 QD's
Begin up a shallow corner, rest just under a major bulge, power through it onto a brief slab section, work past a few more small bulges to a corner that eventually eases to a ledge belay.

180a. _____ 5.12 [?]
Climb the same vertical corner as the next route but trend up left at the third bolt.

180b. Total Depravity 5.11c ★★
50' in length, 7 QD's
Climb a vertical stem box corner, and at the third bolt continue up right on technical climbing that bypasses a large roof on the right edge. Continue up on better holds till it lands at a belay station on a large ledge that also used by Mujahadeen route. Rappel.

181. Mujahadeen II 5.10d A3
80' (24m) in length, Pro to 4", including KB, LA, and Angles
Portions of the right side of Jungle Cliff have a thin layer of dried mud on the surface. This line tackles a series of prominent corner systems.

182. Silverback 5.13b/c ★
80' (24m) in length, 9 QD's
Climbs a water streak up the far right side of Jungle Cliff. Route has three distinct cruxes. Begin up a dirty dihedral to a steep, powerful bulge (stick clip the first bolt), then moderate climbing up an arête. Attain a rest stance below the headwall, then do a series of powerful moves up the headwall face on thin edges till you reach a jug near the belay station.

Monty Mayko climbing the popular Sheer Energy 5.10a

NEW FRONTIER CLIFF

183. Luck of the Draw 5.11a ★
80' (24m) in length, QD's and pro to 1"
Vertical face and slab (leftmost route).

184. **Touch and Go (variation)   5.10c**
80' (24m) in length, QD's and pro to 1"

185. **Alma Mater   5.10d   ★ ★ ★**
80' (24m) in length, QD's
Beautiful steep slab on the left side of New Frontier Cliff. Commence up an odd balance start (5.10d) until it eases to a continuous, fun 5.8 climb ending on a ledge. Rappel.

186. **Split Decision   5.8**
30' (9m) in length, Pro to 4"
Climb the wide crack immediately right of Alma Mater.

187. **Tin Star   5.8**
60' (18m) in length, Pro to 1½"
Climb the outside of the block to the belay ledge, then continue up left onto a face (bolts) and up to an anchor.

188. **True Grit   5.9**
80' (24m) in length, Pro to 2"
From the top of the block step up left into dihedral and up this to the top.

189. **Pony Express   5.6**
30' (9m) in length, Pro to 2"
This is the route on the right side of the block.

190. **Happy Trails II 5.10a**
Multi-pitch, Pro to 3"
Interesting climb with some grungy, loose sections. Walk to the right side of the wall (trail's end). Above is a short clean jam crack that pulls through a slot to a left-facing slab corner. Climb this up into a loose chimney; belay at the oak tree. Continue up right a few moves until you can under cling left then up a broken slab above to top out. Rappel or walk off.

191. **Wild Wild West   5.10c**
60' (18m) in length, Pro to 3", cams suggested
Climb the first pitch of Happy Trails. From the oak tree, step left to a crack then up to a large roof. Under cling out right (crux) and around corner (rope jams easily) then up easy cracks to the top.

192. **Pioneer Spirit   5.11b**
45' (13m) in length, 4 QD's and minor pro to 1"
Climb the short, clean jam crack of Happy Trails. Step right and then up this tantalizing face climb. The crux is a blind lunge. Rappel from bolt anchor.

193. **Promised Land   5.11c R**
80' (24m) in length, Pro to 3", cams and small wires, RP's recommended
Good climb on good rock, yet located "at the end of the Broughton world." Start to the right of Happy Trails and behind several trees. Pull up an easy bulge, move up left on a slab to a vertical step. From a ledge, climb the exciting and steep crack system to a huge block. Lean out right (bolt) and layback up the arête to a bolt anchor. Route is overgrown.

Rocky Butte Quarry

THIS UNIQUE INNER CITY CRAG located in northeast Portland provides enjoyable roadside rock climbing opportunities for all age groups. Whether your rock climbing skill level is beginning, intermediate, or advanced, the one-hundred-plus crack and face climbs on this steep basalt crag provide excellent scope and variety that will challenge you on to ever greater goals in the sport of rock climbing.

North facing, and overlooking a distant Columbia River, the surprisingly extensive and tall Rocky Butte Quarry is the ideal place for rappelling, top-roping, or lead climbing. With just a one-minute walk from the parking area you can access the upper edge of this crag to explore some of these favorite climbs.

Though the cliffs of the main quarry are located close to the busy I-205 freeway corridor, a canopy of trees provides ample cool and comfortable shade as well as a green barrier from the nearby freeway. Even during hot summer days this enjoyable crag continues to be a popular climbing area offering a great respite from the humid summer temperature.

The Joseph Wood Hill Park on the very top of Rocky Butte is a great place to view the city of Portland. Along the inner side of the loop road is the "castle," a majestic, circular-shaped stone walled platform that was at one time rumored to be part of the defenses for the Bonneville Dam in the late-1930s.

BRIEF HISTORY OF THE CRAG

In 1931, Rocky Butte was purchased by Joseph Wood Hill where he built and operated a military academy. Portions of land on the butte were donated to Multnomah County in 1935. With federal funding through President Roosevelt's administration, the New Deal idea promoted a Work Project Authority (WPA) to start construction of a road to the top of the butte.

Rock from the quarry on the north side of the butte was used for road abutments and retaining walls. With the guidance of an Italian stone mason the scenic road and the castle-like formation at the top of the butte proved a resounding success for the people of the area. The west side road project, started in 1938, now provides tourists a unique road with the turn enclosed entirely inside the tunnel.

The scenic views of the Columbia River Gorge and the evening lights of the City of Portland from the heights atop Rocky Butte are splendid.

Today, the Portland Bible College and City Bible Church with its large round church domes are now located at the site of the old Hill Military Academy. Other stonework facilities, such as the Rocky Butte Jail, were built from locally quarried material. The old jail site on the east side of the butte is now part of the I-205

Bri Stekly on *Orient Express* 5.8

freeway corridor.

After rock quarrying at the butte ended in 1956, the Mazamas and other groups began frequenting the north-facing bluff to practice rappelling. Numerous old bolt lines and ring pitons provided evidence of those early years of aid climbing at the quarry.

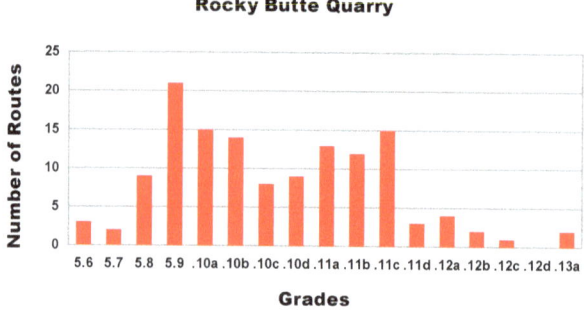

The late 1970s brought a new era to the quarry: the sport of free climbing. Some of those early free climbs quickly attained popular recognition, such as Blackberry Jam (5.10a), first ascended in 1974 by Jim Davis and T. Crossman. Other climbs such as Espresso (5.9) and White Rabbit (5.10b) in 1977; Bird of Paradise (5.10c) in 1979; and Toothpick (5.11c), Close to the Edge (5.11+), and Blueberry Jam (5.10a) were soon to follow.

Those young people who proved instrumental during the 1970s phase were key to the future of climbing here. Doug Bower, Bill Coe, Jay Kerr, Robert McGown, Mike Smelsar, John Sprecher, Scott Woolums, and others continued to expand the scope of rock climbing at Rocky Butte. Though climbing activity at the crag fell quiet from 1979 to 1984, these same people as well as Mike Pajunas, Wayne Wallace, Joe Parsley, Gary Rall, and others eventually tamed the Rocky Butte "frontier" in the late 1980s.

Scores of urban classic climbs were produced: Bite the Bullet (5.11a), Fandango (5.10c), Live Wire (5.11a), Edge of Might (5.11b), Stranger than Friction (5.10a), Zeeva's (5.10b), Phylynx (5.11b), Crack Warrior (5.11b), Emotional Rescue (5.10b), Vertical Therapy (5.9), Red Zinger (5.11c), and many more.

Rock climbers who frequent the quarry these days generally use it as a top-rope climbing area. The popular rock climbs have fixed bolt anchors or tree affixed top-rope chains near the top of the route. There are a number of routes that are still leadable climbs, such as Emotional Rescue or Flakey Old Man, if you are so inclined.

The close proximity to the city and the increased presence of human traffic unfortunately brought several environmental drawbacks. Spray-painted graffiti on the walls, garbage dumped over the cliff edge, broken glass, and traffic noise from the busy I-205 freeway are the most obvious. Most of these can be easily overlooked by using a ground tarp. The pesky plant *Rhus diversiloba* (poison oak) is prevalent throughout the area and grows along the ac-

Tyler leading *Flakey Old Man 5.7*

cess trails and on some of the climbs, but it is generally kept beaten back by regular climber presence. This crag is very accessible to the public, especially for the local rock climber seeking a quick escape from the office blues.

On a positive note, the Oregon chapter of the Access Fund promotes a Bi-Annual Rocky Butte Quarry Cleanup day. You are welcome to join the work party to help remove junk and clean up the access trails. For many years now this event has provided the positive means for us to keep this city park a climber-friendly environment.

At the top edge of the quarry cliff, numerous trees offer a convenient means for climbers to set up a strong top-rope anchor belay point. Many of the popular climbs also have excellent fixed bolt anchors near the upper edge of the climbs, but be cautious when accessing these anchors as they tend to be very near to the edge of the precipice. In certain places these anchors were established on the vertical face at the top of the climb. In all cases, use additional precautionary measures when approaching the edge of the cliff to locate and set up your top-rope anchor.

Thanks to the interest sparked by the *Rocky Butte Quarry: A Climber's Guide to Urban Rock* (1987) by Mike Pajunas and Bob McGown, climber activity at this crag has increased rapidly. The trails have improved with use, while the overall image of our Rocky Butte Quarry has changed for the better.

This chapter on the quarry describes thirteen sections of wall in detail with topographical reference maps for the areas that are most frequently visited by rock climbers. The following are described from right to left as you would encounter the bluff from above. They are: Poodle Pinnacle, Trivial Wall, Silver Bullet Bluff, Video Bluff, Dream Weaver Wall, Wizard Wall, Far East Wall, Warrior Wall, Freeway Wall, Mean Street, Easy Street, Toothpick Wall, and Breakfast Cracks. The Wall of Shadows and the Grotto area have

Overview Map of Rocky Butte

David leading *Emotional Rescue*

not been detailed because much of this far west section of cliff is located on private property.

VISUAL BIO

These emblems represent virtually all of the Rocky Butte Quarry climbing site when accessed from NE Rocky Butte road. If you plan to start your proposed climb at the bottom of the bluff (such as Emotional Rescue) it will take about five minutes to descend to the base on one of the narrow steep trails.

HOW TO GET THERE

The Rocky Butte Quarry is located quite near the intersection of the I-84 and I-205 freeways. To visit this Portland climbing crag, take exit #5 eastbound off I-84 (or exit #23 from I-205 at Sandy Blvd). Once you are on NE 82nd Avenue, drive to the point where it intersects with NE Fremont Street. Turn east and drive approximately ½ mile until the road curves north to become 91st Avenue. Shortly the road curves east again and becomes NE Rocky Butte Way. The quarry cliff is accessed on your immediate left or northeast side of the road across from the City Bible Church domes. Parking is available for 0.3 mile along the road shoulder from the last house (Breakfast Cracks area) to the stone retaining wall (Video Bluff area) at the eastern end of this short stretch of road. Do NOT park in the Bible College parking area.

To reach the bouldering areas, continue on Rocky Butte Way as it loops up clockwise to the top of the butte. The views of the City of Roses and the surrounding mountains from the butte are exceptional.

POODLE ROCK

A. Poodle with a Mohawk 5.11a

Pro to 2½"

A good climb located by itself along the eastern perimeter trail. Hike approximately 300' along the trail. Above the trail is a face with an easy start, a crack and an outside arête. Lead this to a tree and rappel.

TRIVIAL WALL

Hike east on the Rocky Butte Perimeter Trail to the tunnel under the roadway. Continue a few feet on the trail further and then angle north toward the cliff.

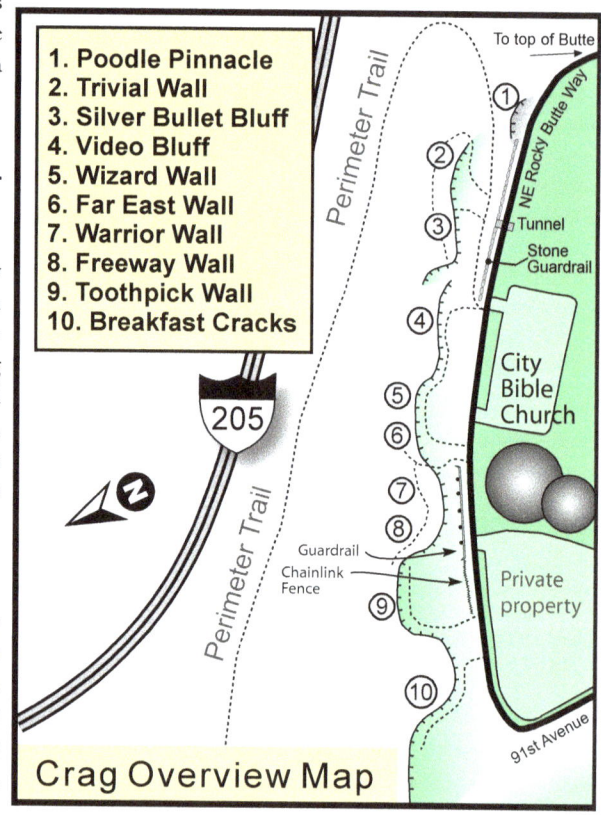

1. Poodle Pinnacle
2. Trivial Wall
3. Silver Bullet Bluff
4. Video Bluff
5. Wizard Wall
6. Far East Wall
7. Warrior Wall
8. Freeway Wall
9. Toothpick Wall
10. Breakfast Cracks

Crag Overview Map

There are belay anchors at the lip of the small outcrop. The base of Trivial Wall can be accessed on foot by a narrow steep path just to the east.

1. **Harlequin 5.10b** ★
   Pro to 1½"
   Good climb. Commence up an easy slab and follow a curved crack up right (25') until it eases near the top. *Note*: A variant trends off left midway up Harlequin via a thin seam/crack (**Bane 5.10b**).
2. **Trivial Pursuit 5.10b**
   Pro to 1½"
   A minor face climb.
3. **The Joker 5.8**

SILVER BULLET WALL

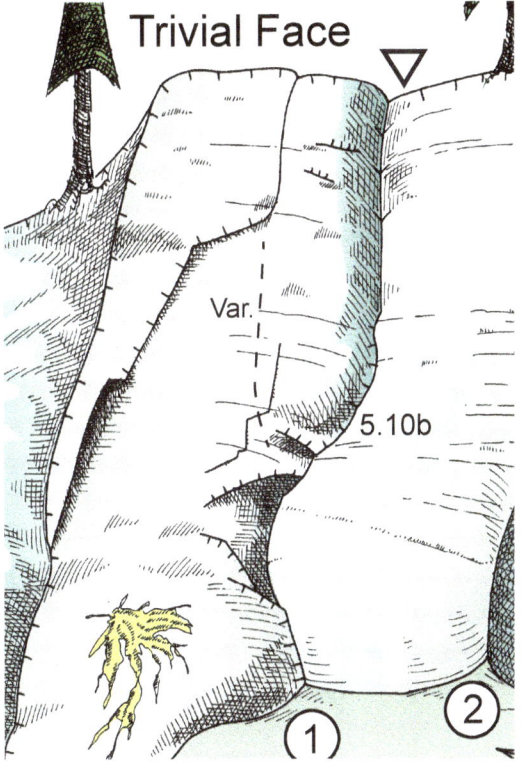

Aptly named because of all the bullet scars dotting the face of this crag. Approach by hiking east along the perimeter trail to the tunnel under the roadway. Aim north to the crag and step 20' down to a large ledge. Belay at the ledge for the routes on the main wall below. The height is approximately 40' (12m).

4. **Captain She's Breaking Up 5.8 R**
   Pro to 2"
5. _____
6. **Sundance Kid 5.10a** ★
   Neat shallow corner climb on upper left corner of Silver Bullet Bluff.
7. **Panama Red 5.9+**
   Climb the smooth face broken with small ledges and cracks immediately right of Sundance Kid.
8. **Miss Kitty 5.7**
9. **Gunsmoke 5.9** ★★
   An excellent easy face climb just left of Bite the Bullet.
10. **Bite the Bullet 5.11a R** ★★★
    Length: 40', Pro: 5 QD's and minor gear to 1"
    One of the best routes on Silver Bullet Bluff. Start up left of a tree and on a face with good but angled edges. From a good stance 15' up angle left onto a bullet-scarred face and climb desperately to a sloping ledge, then move up right to join with the last move on Jack of Hearts. Bite the Bullet has 5 bolts and gear to 1" if you are inclined to lead the route.

ROCKY BUTTE QUARRY 85

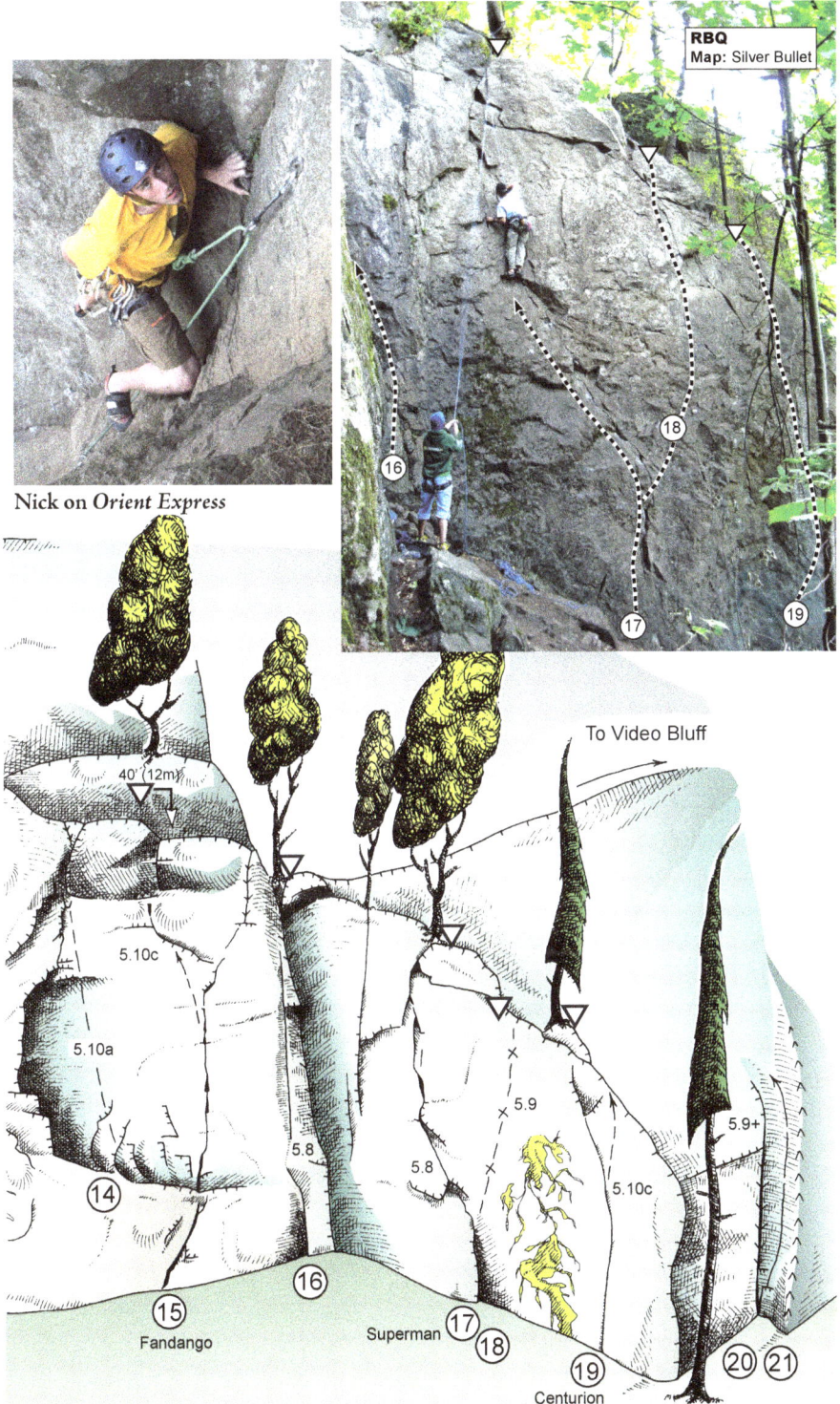

Nick on *Orient Express*

86 CHAPTER 1 ✧ ORC

11. Jack of Hearts   5.9+   ★★★
Length: 40', Pro to 1"
An exciting thin crack climb. Start up a short right facing corner to a stance, and then up a thin crack to a sloping ledge. Finish up a last vertical step to the belay ledge.

12. Silver Bullet   5.9 R   ★
A good route that starts up the face, then enters a dihedral that is lacking a crack. Smear up the corner to join with Jack of Hearts.

13. Urban Cowboy   5.8 R

14. Last Tango   5.10a

15. Fandango   5.10c R   ★★★
A superb route of only moderate difficulty. Start up a crack on a slab left of a main corner. From an easy stance continue up the crack on the vertical face, follow the left crack and pull a mantle (crux). Move up further via a corner to a ledge. Belay from the large tree.

16. Midnight Warrior   5.8   ★
Pro to 2"
The main corner on this side of the wall.

17. Superman   5.8   ★★
Pro to 1"
A fun problem on good edges and sloping smears.

18. Glenn's Route   5.8   ★
Pro is 3 QD's
Starts at the same crack as Superman but aim straight up the face to a bolt anchor at the

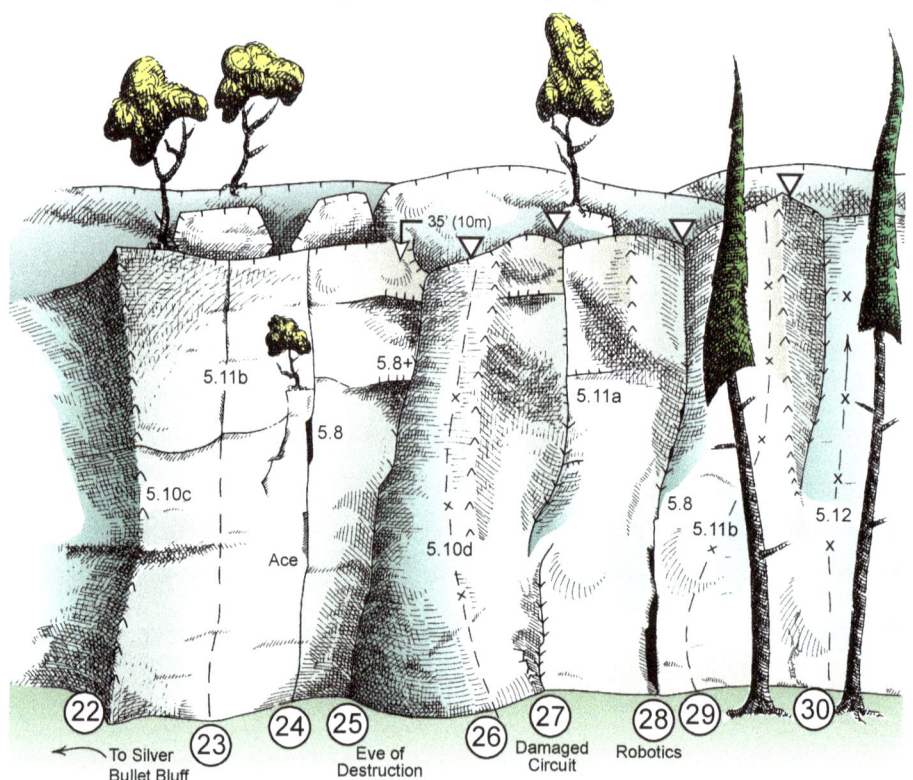

edge of the cliff.

19. Centurion 5.10d ★
A unique short vertical crack problem on the lower right corner of this wall. Climb the crack until you can reach over right (crux) and up to easy steps and tree belay.

20. Invisible Man 5.9+

21. Temporary Arête 5.10a

VIDEO BLUFF

One of the most popular walls at Rocky Butte. Excellent place to top-rope and learn technique. Approach Video Bluff by parking at the easternmost pullout just before the stone retaining wall and walk north a short distance to the crag. A well established trail meanders along the top of the precipice above Video Bluff. It loops along at the top of this crag and continues to the west to emerge onto the roadway at the guardrail descent trail. This trail gives excellent and quick access to setting up TR on virtually all the climbs from Video Bluff to the Warrior Wall. Cliff height is approximately 35′ (10m).

22. Body Language 5.10c R
The overhanging arête with a horizontal crack halfway up.

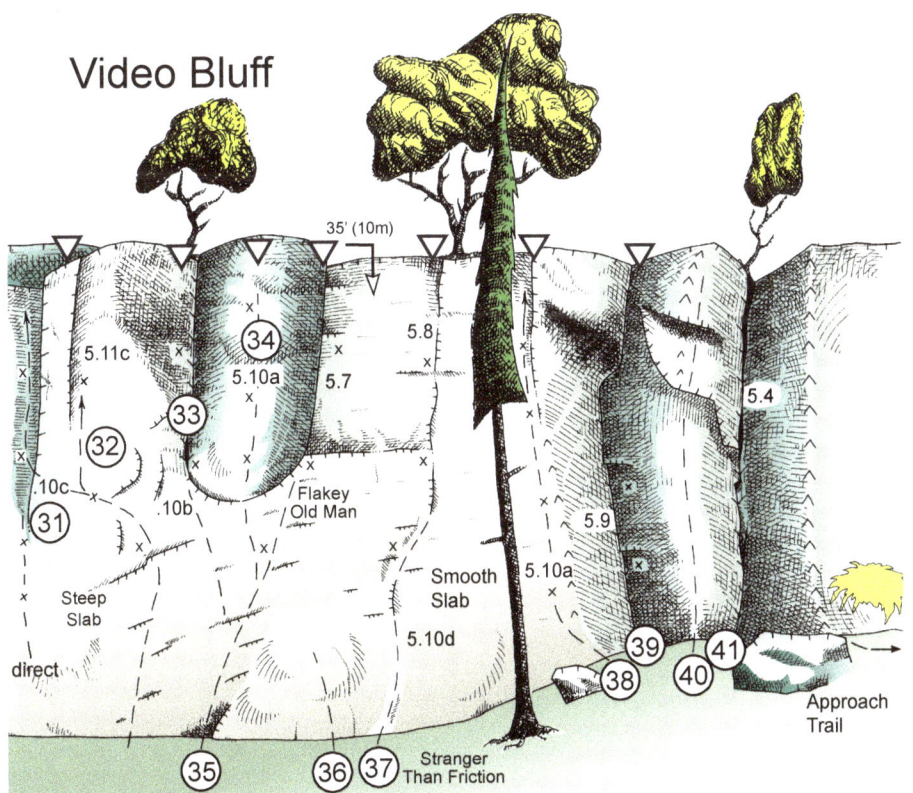

23. **Body Bionics   5.11b R**
24. **Ace   5.8   ★**
25. **Eve of Destruction   5.8+   ★★**
    A slabby dihedral problem. A good practice climb.
26. **Live Wire   5.10d   ★**
    Length: 35', 4 QD's
    Difficult face climb on the round outside corner to the right of Eve of Destruction.
27. **Damaged Circuit   5.11a   ★★**
    Challenging stem problem up a shallow scoop. Begin up a shattered start, pull a thin move to an awkward stance, then smear, stem up a face using strange finger holds in the seam.
28. **Robotics   5.8**
29. **Edge of Might   5.11b   ★★**
    Fantastic climb. Begin up the face immediately right of Robotics and angle up onto the arête. Thin holds and pinches on the arête are the crux.
30. **Hard Contact   5.12**
31. **Lever or Leaver   5.10c**
    Length: 40', 4 QD's
    Can be climbed using a difficult direct start.
32. **Persistence of Time   5.11c   ★**
    Length: 40', 4 QD's
33. **Zeeva   5.10b   ★**
    3 QD's
    An interesting steep corner climb with balancy moves.
34. **Bikini   5.10a   ★★**
    Length: 40', 4 QD's
    A popular face climb on a minor rounded buttress immediately left of Flakey Old Man.
35. **Flakey Old Man   5.7   ★★★**
    Length: 40', 4 QD's
    The flake has long since fallen away but the popularity of this and other nearby routes continue to be a favorite for everyone to climb or top-rope.
36. **MTV   5.10a (V1)**
    Minor boulder problem variation following the left seam at the ground.
37. **Stranger Than Friction   5.10+   ★★★**
    In the center of the slab is a pocketed boulder start and slap move leading upward to a seam. The local classic on this wall and certainly worth it. The initial boulder move is a very long height dependent reach from a pocket to a small edge. Once you get past the initial bouldery crux start off the ground the remainder of the climb is a mere 5.8.
38. **Panes of Reality   5.10a   ★**
    Length: 40', 4 QD's
    Step left and up onto the face immediately left of Stained Glass. A neat problem on a rounded bulge.
39. **Stained Glass   5.9   ★**
    Length: 40', QD's and pro to 2"
    The obvious fun dihedral corner.

40. Toxic Waltz   5.11d
4 QD's
Vertical face to the right of the dihedral.

41. E-Z Corner   5.4

Bill's Buttress is a buttress-like formation about 70' to the west of Video Bluff that provides several rock climbs developed by Bill Coe. The climbs here are approximately 90' (27m) in length and have good anchors at the top of the crag for ease of access. A 60-meter rope is wise. There are presently five routes ranging from 5.8 to 5.10 and three possible variations in-between. Beware of the broken glass along the top and the base of this section of cliff.

A. Corona Glass Houses   5.10a/b
Length: about 100', Pro to 1" (includes cams and small nuts)
The far left route. Starts up 4th class terrain then up an obvious crack system to the top of cliff. *Note:* Pro is small cams to 1" and wired nuts; a single 60-meter rope is helpful.

B. Labrador   5.5 / 5.9
Length: about 100', Pro: small cams to 1" and wired nuts
Starts just LEFT of a fir tree, and begins a bit further downhill of the leftmost (Corona) route. At about halfway up the route, it splits into two variants (left via a wide crack, and right variant straight up the obvious crack). A single 70-meter rope is useful.

C. The Plum   5.9
Length: about 100', Pro: small cams to 1" and wired nuts
Located immediately RIGHT of a big fir tree at the ground. Ascend an intermittent crack up past a crux section, moving up and slightly right. The difficulty eases the higher you climb the route. A single 70-meter rope is useful.

D. _____ 5.8 / 5.9
Pro: __"
This is the rightmost crack on Bill's Buttress (the route starting stance is the same starting point as Dream Weaver route, and this particular route starts 5' left of Dream Weaver.). From a maple tree about 25' above the ground the route ascends a crack system.

DREAM WEAVER WALL

This is a narrow section of wall located between Video Bluff and Wizard Wall. These climbs are good though infrequently ascended. Height is approximately 65' (19m).

42. Dream Weaver   5.9   ★
Length: 60', Pro to 2"
Begin on a stance near a small tree, and climb a crack through a small overhanging lip, then up the crack as it trends slightly left-ish and becomes a right-facing corner crack system. It gradually trends up rightward for the last brief section and then lands on a small ledge stance just below the top of the cliff.

43. Tarzan   5.10a
Length: 60', Pro to 1½"

44. Tiger Pause   5.9   ★
Length: 60', Pro to 2"
Begin near a small tree, and climb up right in a right trending crack till it hits a small overhung lip. Power through the lip and continue up a rightward trending crack, then power

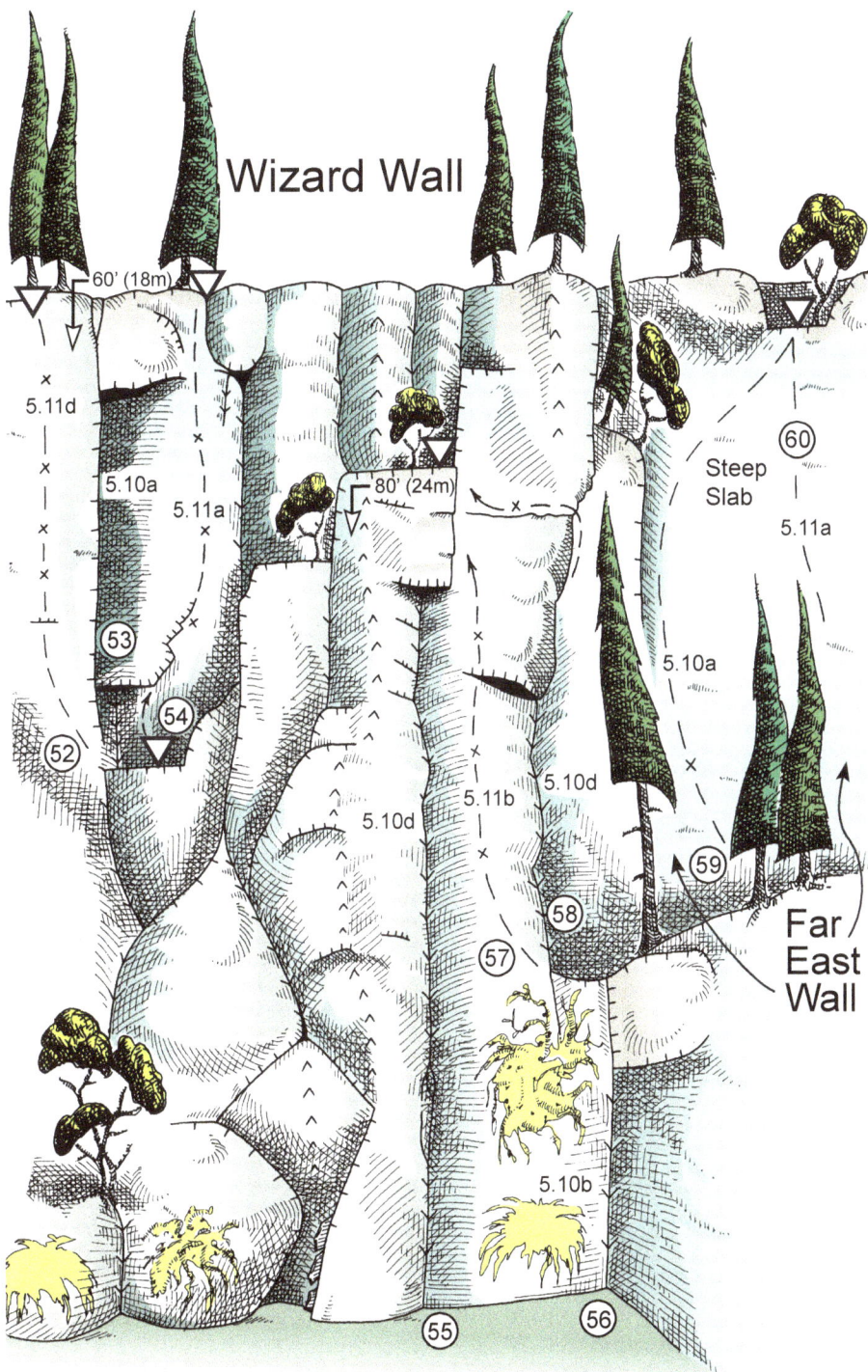

through a second overhanging lip, then up the final brief crack to the top of the cliff.

45. Kleen Korner   5.9

WIZARD WALL

One of the finest long vertical sections of rock at the Butte. All of the routes are located on the upper half of the wall. Either set up a TR belay from the trees at the top of the cliff or rappel down approximately 70' (21m) to bolt anchors on the lower ledges and then lead climb back up. This wall is of superb quality, yielding some of the finest high angle face climbs at Rocky Butte.

46. Naked Savage   5.10a
47. Lord of the Jungle   5.9+
48. Slavemaker   5.10b
49. Grub   5.10c
   Pro to 3" Cams suggested
50. Eye in the Sky   5.10c R   ★★
   Pro to 1"
   Start at the Phylynx belay, but stay just to the left of the route on an outside corner after the bulge crux.

David Boekelheide on *Joy Ride* 5.11a

51. Phylynx   5.11b   ★★★
   Pro to 1½"
   One of the finest routes at Rocky Butte. Rappel to a hidden anchor 80' down on the left, then lead up right (bolts), pull through bulge (crux) then directly up the crack on the face.

52. Walk on Water   5.11d   ★★
   QD's and pro to 1"
   An impressive and extreme face route to the right of Phylynx.

53. Mind Games   5.10a   ★
   Offwidth Chimney.

54. Wizard   5.11a   ★★
   QD's and pro to 1"
   A dynamic and unusual climb.

FAR EAST WALL

This hidden section of wall is the westerly extension of the Wizard Wall. Approach by rappeling in from the tree at the top of Seventh Moon or scramble up a 3rd class trail from the bottom. The height is 40' (12m) to the

ROCKY BUTTE QUARRY 93

halfway terrace, and approximately 100' (30m) total cliff height.

- 55. **The Wanderer   5.10d** ★★
- 56. **Great Wall of China   5.10b** ★
- 57. **High Road to China   5.11b** ★
- 58. **Chinese Finger Torture   5.10d** ★★
- 59. **Ghost Rider   5.10a**
- 60. **Flight of the Seventh Moon   5.11a** ★★★
   Length: 40', Pro: 4-5 QD's
   A cool challenging face climb that goes up just left of the Orient Express dihedral and ends at the tree belay.

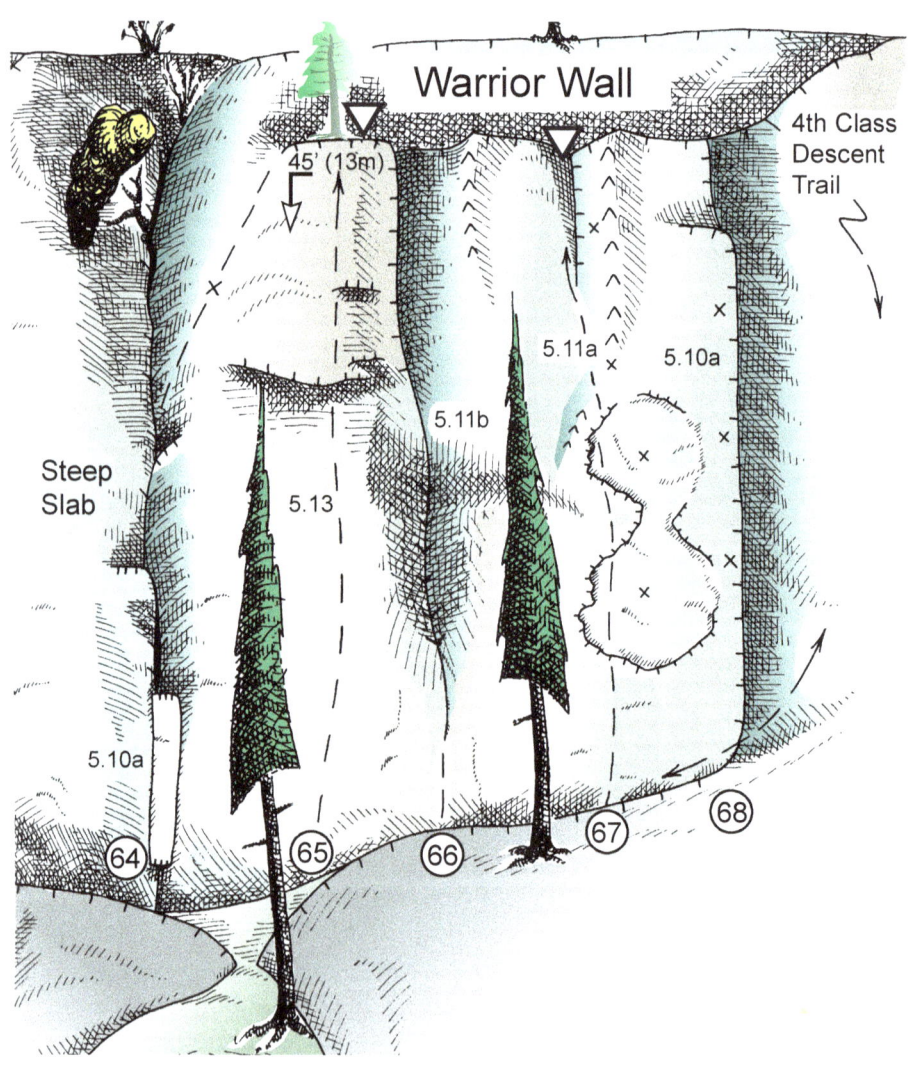

61. Orient Express 5.8 ★★
Length: 40' Pro: fixed bolts
Popular thin face/seam and corner system located at the center of this wall.

62. Secret Maze 5.11b ★
Length: 40' Pro: 6 QD's
A difficult face climb. Start to the right of O.E. and climb up (crux) to a stance, then meander up the face using holds that seem to be in all the wrong places.

63. Tiger's Eye 5.10b
Length: 40', Pro to 3" (smallest is .4" nuts)
Fun direct start leading to the terraced ledges below Orient Express.

WARRIOR WALL

An extension of the Far East Wall it was coined because of the favorite difficult corner problem here. Also called the "Bug Wall". Access by a steep scramble descent via the standard guardrail descent trail next to the chain link fence. Approximate height ranges from 45' (13m) on the left to 100' (30m) on the right.

64. Smears for Fears 5.10a
Length: 45', Pro to 2"
A good crack climb further right of Secret Maze. Ends at the large fir tree on a ledge.

65. _____ 5.13a (TR)
The extreme face climb just left of Crack Warrior.
66. **Crack Warrior   5.11b R   ★★★**
Length: 45', Pro to 1½"
A great climb with a nasty crux. Silverfish frequent here. Climb the corner stem problem up to a bulge (crux). Pull through and move up an easier right facing corner to the large fir tree.
67. **You'll Dance to Anything   5.11c   ★★**
Length: 45', Pro: 4 QD's
Beautiful face climb that makes use of a broken section of smooth rock. The exit is the crux due to numerous sloping finger edges.
68. **Sheer Madness   5.10a   ★**
Length: 45', Pro: 3 QD's
69. **Quarry Cracker   5.6**
70. **Lathe of heaven   5.11a**
71. **Arch Nemesis   5.11a   ★★**

Mike on *Blackberry Jam 5.10b*

Length: 80', Pro to 1½" including pitons
A major dihedral on this face. Climb up the vertical corner until possible to step out right and up a flake that leads to a large fir tree.
72. **Boy Sage   5.10+ (variation)**
Length: 80', Pro to 1½" including pitons
Take the direct up a crack to the tree.
73. **Jealous Rage   5.11c R**
Length: 80', Pro to 1"
Leads up an indistinct face (bolts) left to join with Arch Nemesis.
74. **Emotional Rescue   5.10b   ★★★**
Length: 80', QD's and gear to 2"
One of the finest classics at the Butte. Very popular. Climb the steep bolt and pin protected face to exit up a crack and a bolt anchor hidden around corner.

FREEWAY WALL

Approximate height of this wall ranges from 20-40 ft (6m-12m).

75. **Simple Twist   5.11   ★**
76. **Hyper Twist   5.11   ★**
77. **Passing Lane   5.6   ★**
78. **Speeding Down South   5.8**
79. **Ranger Danger   5.9   ★**
80. **Telegraph Road   5.11a   ★★**
    Length: 35', Pro: 3 QD's
81. **Highway Star   5.10c   ★★**
    Length: 35', Pro to 1½"
    A good crack climb with a strenuous exit move.
82. **Dead Man's Curve   5.9**

MEAN STREET

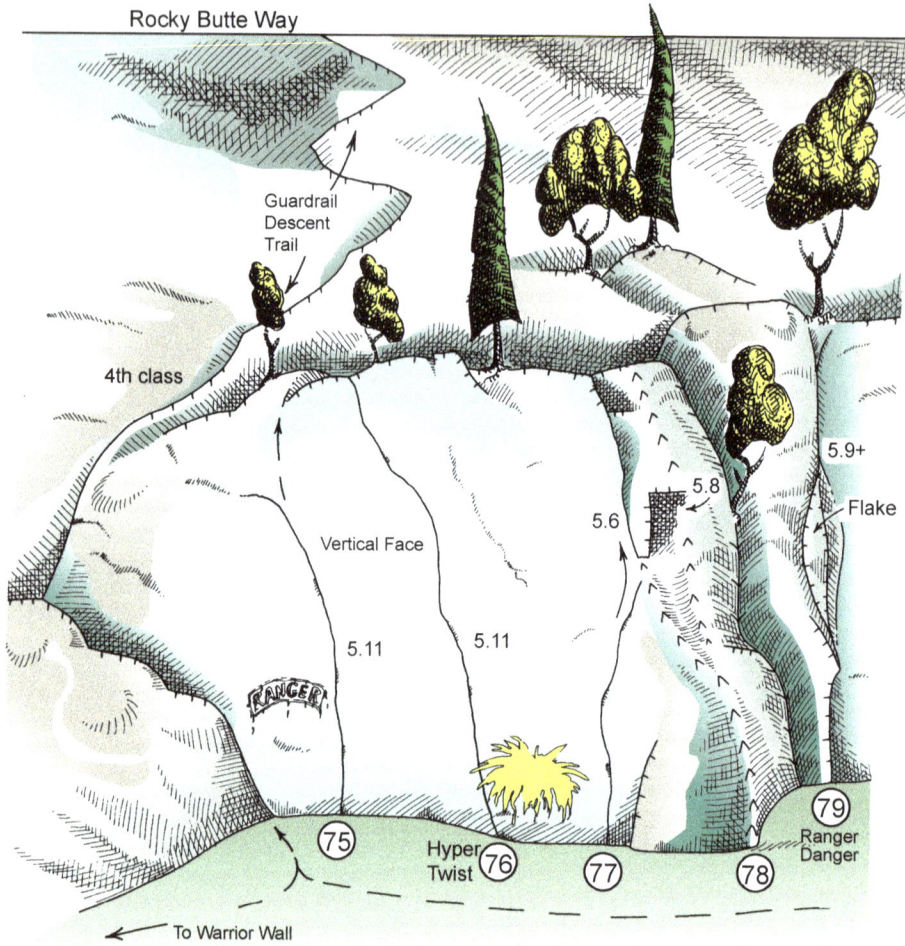

This steep wall is situated directly below the guardrail adjacent to the road. The routes are characterized by difficult, hard to protect and usually dust-covered rock. Height approximately 100' (30m).

83. Thunder Road   5.10a
84. Lethal Ethics   5.10d R
   Poorly protected face climb intersected by a ledge halfway up.
85. Spiritual Journey   5.10d
   Ascend the face just left of a minor arête and continue up an inside corner leading to the top.
86. Little Arête   5.9 R
87. Seamingly Endless   5.11b   ★
   Pro to 1"
   Start on right side of the arête and zig zag up discontinuous cracks and corners to the top.

ROCKY BUTTE QUARRY 99

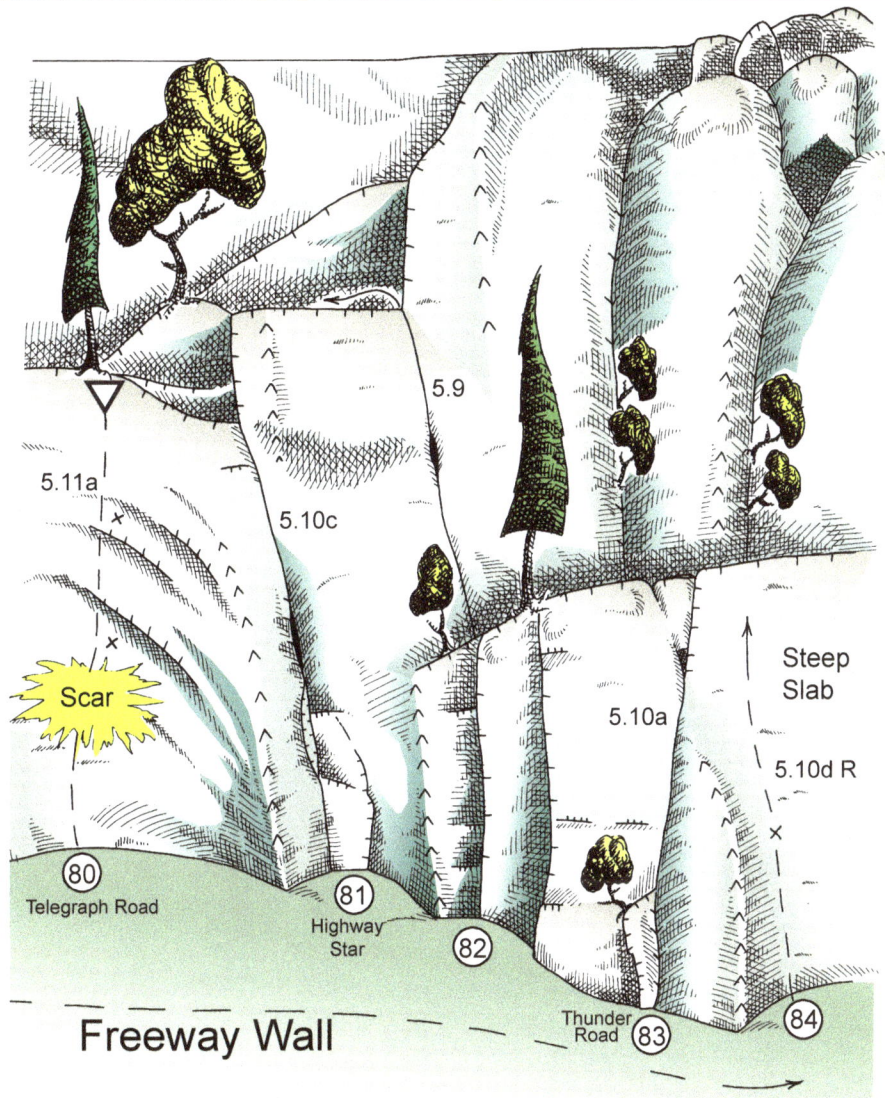

Freeway Wall

88. Holy Bubbles   5.11b   ★
   Start to right of the arête, ascend up and over a roof, then up an inside corner to a belay.
89. Pluto   5.12b
   A bolted face left of the "nose". A bit runout, strenuous, a little dusty. Yet to see a free ascent.
90. Stump the Jock   5.11+
   The crack and inside corner just left of the prominent "nose" of rock. Begin up and angle left up an overhang corner until it is possible to turn the crux and continue up a steep wall above. Pull another small roof and rappel from trees just above. The climb is dirty.
91. Packin' Heat   5.13a
   Length: 40', Pro: 6-7 QD's
   A prominent [infamous] overhung bolted arête rock "nose". One of the stoutest RBQ

100 CHAPTER 1 ✦ ORC

routes.

92. No Leverage   5.11c
Could be a good climb, but the new drainage ditch pours down immediately to the right. Begin up a bolt and pin protected face to a corner and traverse directly left just below a large detached flake of rock to a bolt belay. Rappel.

93. Be Bold or Not To Be   5.11c
A true blue water course now.

94. Claymation   5.10c
A crack corner system to the right of the water course. May be dusty, but still feasible to climb.

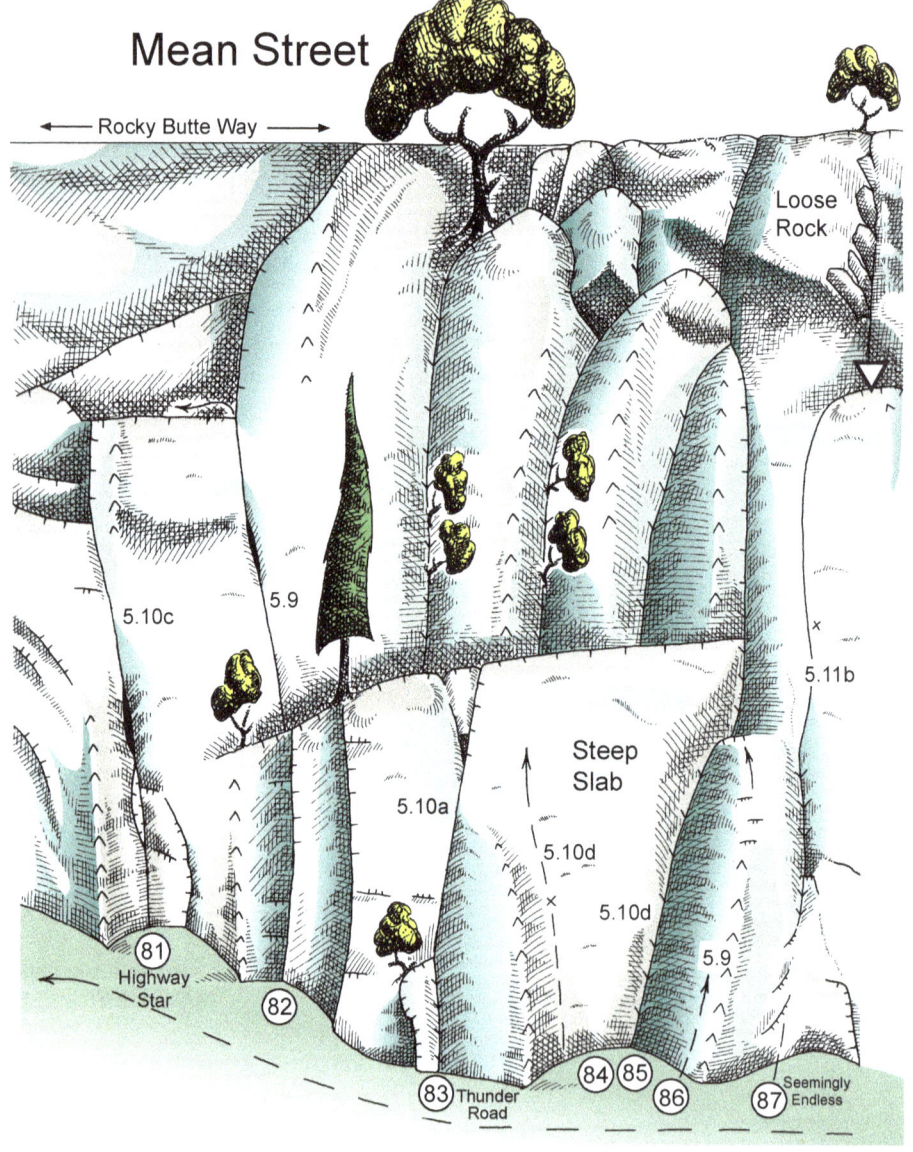

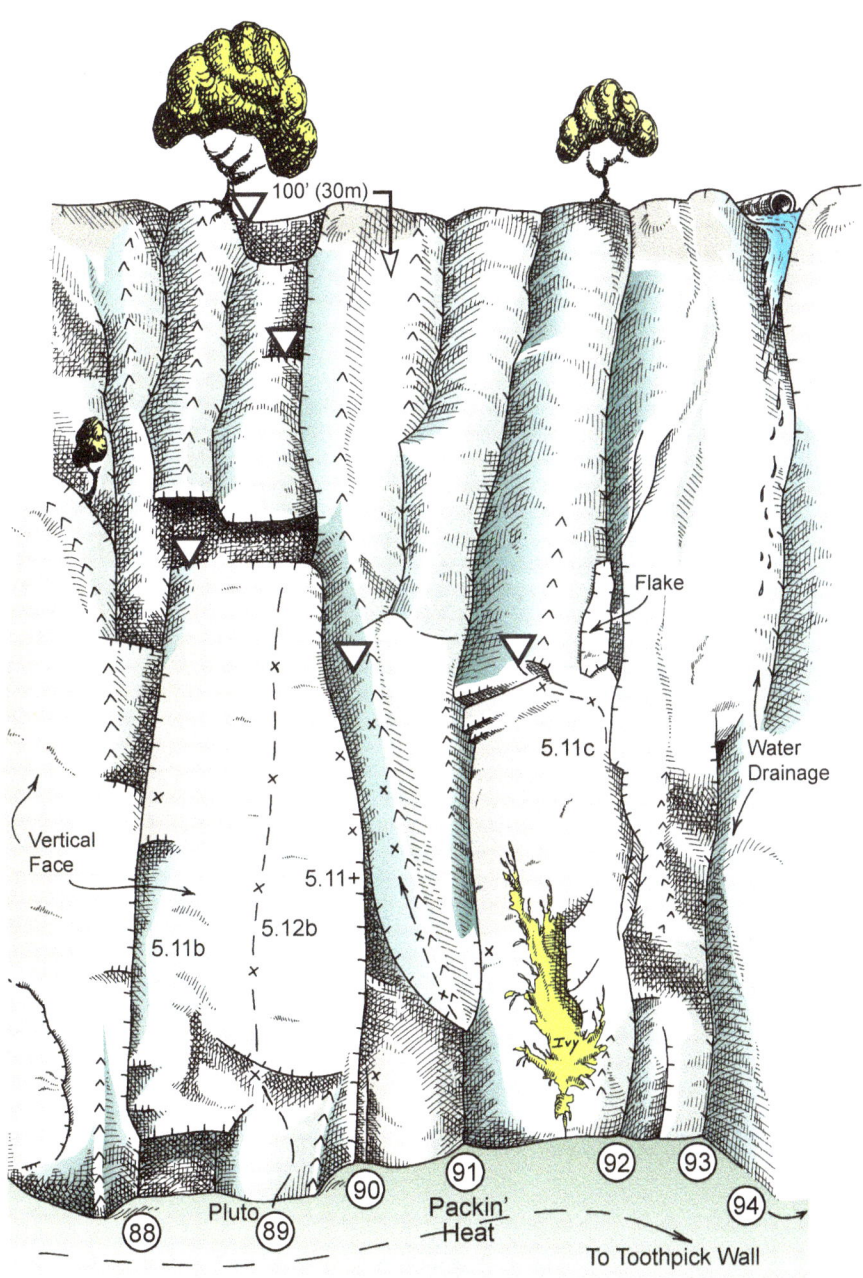

94b. Vaudeville   5.7
   A crack corner system to the right of the culvert water course.

EASY STREET

A good practice wall; approximate height is 35'.

A. Hand Crack   5.7
   An interesting minor hand crack with a horizontal break ⅓ way up the route.
B. Short Stack Face   5.3
   A brief short face climb (with minor cracks) immediately left of the next route.
C. Chimney Route   5th class
   A short fat chimney route.
D. Face 'n Finger Route   5.9
   A short face that goes through a small overhang (at the ⅓ point).
E. Chimney Route   5.2
   A short wide chimney route.

TOOTHPICK WALL

A beautiful, colorful wall. Characterized by clean, steep rock and several incredible thin crack routes. Approximate height 50' (15m).

94c. Peach Cobbler   5.9   ★
   The start is located on a higher ledge around the corner to the left of Blueberry Jam. Climb a face just to the left of 'Reach for the Sky' route.

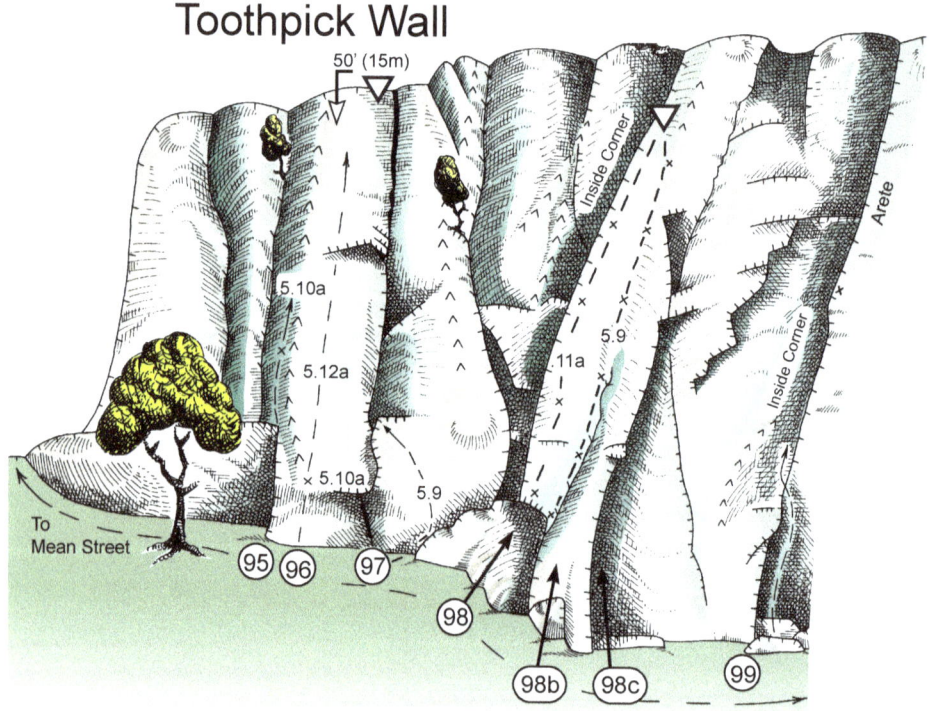

95. Reach for the Sky 5.10a ★
Pro to 2"
A fun climb. Ascend via a crack start then an outside corner until possible to move to the right side of the arête (1 pin - 1 bolt) and top out.

96. Zenith 5.12a ★★
Climb the prow left of Blueberry Jam.

97. Blueberry Jam 5.9 (5.10a boulder start) ★★★
Length: 50', Pro to 3"
A very popular climb. Start to the right or do the direct boulder start (5.10a), then ascend to the top using a broken crack system and large holds.

98. Joy Ride 5.11a
Length: 45', Pro: 4 QD's
Bolted face climb to the right of Blueberry Jam that has a large roof at the first bolt. Muscle over the overhang (crux) to a stance, then carefully balance up the remainder of the outside arête to the anchor.

98b. Hot Donna 5.9 ★
Start same as Joy Ride and bust up through the roof going up right (5 bolts).

98c. Social Distancing 5.11a ★
Immediately right of the previous route is a corner crack. Climb the outside blocky crack and face.

99. Leading Edge 5.10d
A corner to face arête system to the left of Close to the Edge.

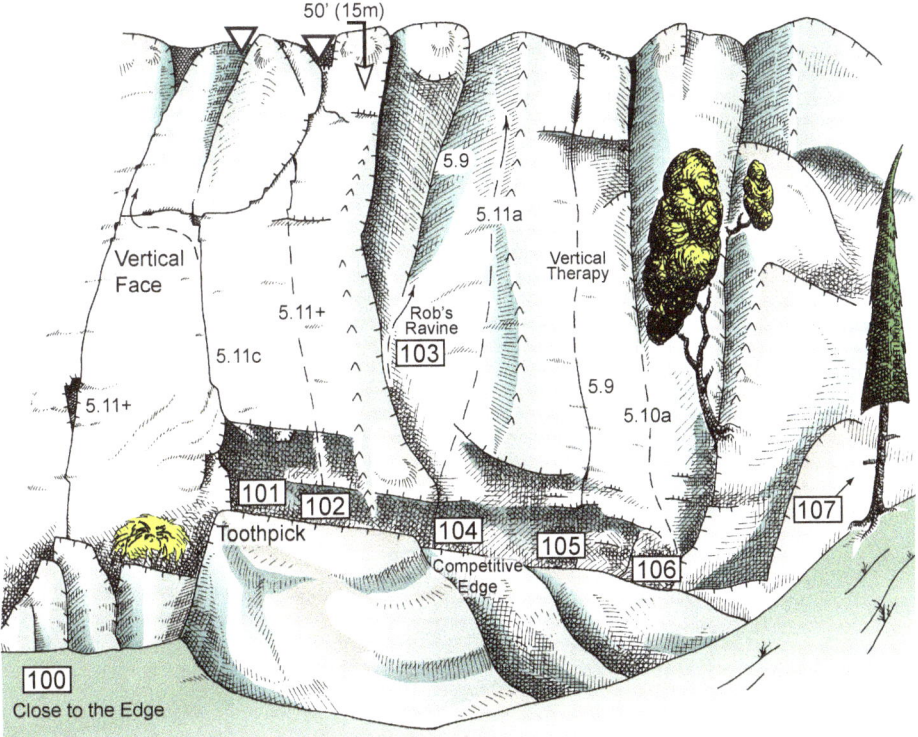

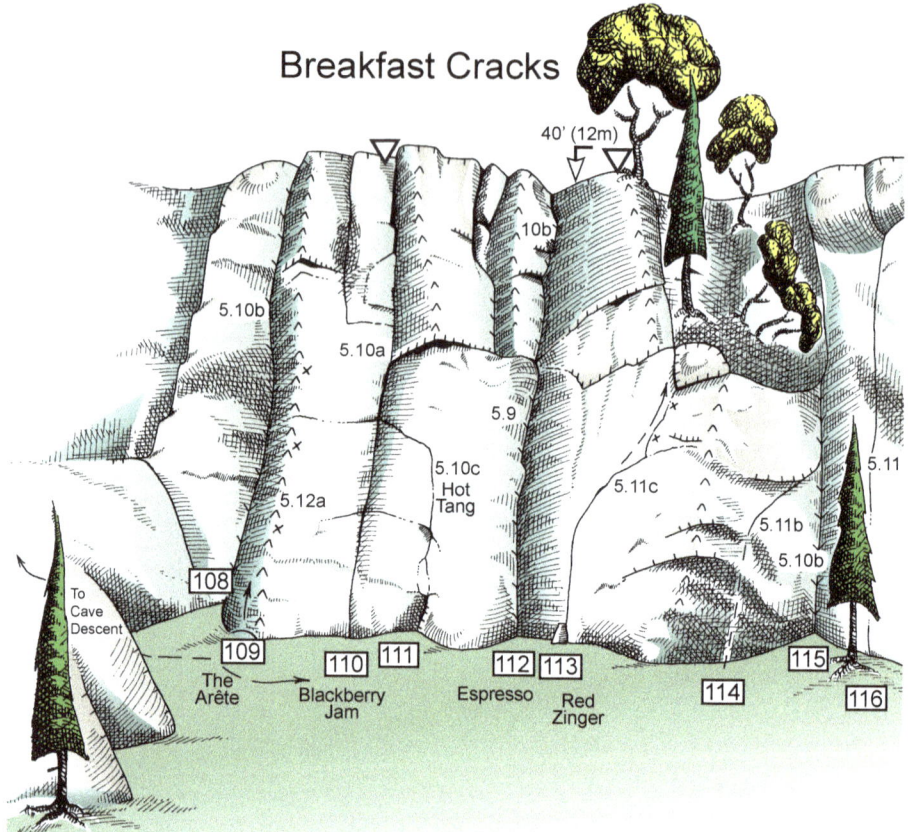

Breakfast Cracks

100. **Close to the Edge   5.11c/d**   ★ ★ ★
    Excellent climb on superb rock involving strenuous technique. Climb a thin crack that diagonals up rightward.
101. **Toothpick   5.11c**   ★ ★ ★
    Length: 50', Pro to ___" including thin nuts and cams
    Local classic, one of Rocky Butte's finest. Start on a ledge, step up left onto the vertical face via awkward holds. Either traverse left on a horizontal crack to finish up 'Close to the Edge' (the standard method) or climb straight up a crack-seam to the top (harder).
102. **Far from the Edge   5.11c/d**   ★
103. **Rob's Ravine   5.9**
    Length: 50', Pro to 3"
    A deep dihedral to the right of Toothpick.
104. **Competitive Edge   5.11a**   ★
    An interesting route that is a series of compression and balance moves on an arête.
105. **Vertical Therapy   5.9**   ★ ★
    Length: 50', Pro to 3"
    Ascend up a crack leading to a face, then finish up a crack near the top. Excellent climb and a must for everyone.

◆ ROCKY BUTTE QUARRY 105

106. Power Surge 5.10a
Length: 50', Pro: .5" to 1"

107. Stiff Fingers 5.9
Obscure route 30' right of the above climb.

BREAKFAST CRACKS

This small historical amphitheater offers several of the finest 5.10 cracks at RBQ.

108. "D" and Rising 5.10b

109. The Arête 5.12a ★
3 QD's and 2" cam
A bolted arête at the left end of this little amphitheater.

110. **Blackberry Jam 5.10b ★★★**
Length: 40', Pro to 2"
A very popular route at RBQ. A steep vertical jam crack system ending with powerful slightly overhung crux exit moves.

111. **Hot Tang 5.10c (variation) ★**
A quick fingertips start to Blackberry Jam. Interesting climb. Possibly 5.11?

112. **Espresso 5.9 ★★**
Length: 40', Pro to 2" (plus small cams and nuts)
An obvious dihedral corner with a dirty exit move. Fun and quite popular. Climb the right facing corner.

113. **Red Zinger 5.11c ★★**
Length: 40', Pro to 1"
An excellent and difficult undercling smear problem. Frequently top-roped and good for a quick pump. Start as per Espresso, but attack the seam that diagonals up right to a brushy slope.

114. **Orange Spice 5.11b ★**
A top-rope face problem that ascends vertical rock diagonally to join with Lemon Twist. A good but short climb.

115. **Lemon Twist (Direct Start) 5.10b**
Length: 40', Pro ___"
The obvious (usually brushy) corner climb.

116. **You Lunge You Plunge 5.11b/c ★**
Length: 40', Pro: 5-6 QD's

117. **White Rabbit 5.10b ★★★**
Length: 40', Pro to 1"
One of the original all time favorites at RBQ. Commence up right to a crack, then follow this up leftward then directly to the top of the cliff. Eases at about two-thirds height to sloping steps then a final vertical move.

118. **White Rabbit Buttress 5.12c ★★**
Length: 40', Pro: 2 bolts (and 1 fixed piton)
An exciting climb ascending the outside face just to the right of White Rabbit. Start up thin holds just to the right of White Rabbit to several good large holds, then move up on side pulls and clings until possible to move up left onto the slabs above. Continue to the top.

119. **Unknown 5.12c (TR)**

120. **Harder Than Life 5.11d (TR)**
A powerful crimp climb. Just after the midway point it enters into a slight crack corner system.

121. **Birds of Paradise 5.10d ★★★**
Length: 40', Pro to 2"
A very popular, well deserving classic at Rocky Butte. One of the best climbs at the

◆ ROCKY BUTTE QUARRY 107

RBQ
Map: Breakfast Cracks

Quarry. Start by angling up easy steps to a stance next to a small fir tree. Then continue to climb up the crack on the left of the tree. Undercling through the crux and jam upward to the top of the crag.

Direct #1: Lower direct start exists about 20' below the small tree by climbing directly up a crack corner till you merge with the regular part of the 'B of P' route at the tree.

Direct #2: Another optional 3-bolt low direct start face route exists down to the right below the tree (to the immediate right of #1 direct start).

122. _____ 5.12 (TR)
123. **Wisdom Tooth** 5.11b ★
124. _____ 5.10

Prominent 100' long dihedral that diagonals up leftward to the summit.

125. **Trix are for Kids** 5.11+ (TR)

A beautiful, difficult overhang seam face climb partway up the same prominent dihedral. Step onto the right face at ½ height to ascend.

Jacqueline climbing on Stranger Than Friction

126. **Time of Your Life** 5.11a (TR) ★

An excellent arête problem that starts up the aforementioned dihedral. Traverse to the arête near a patch of bright yellow lichen. Ascend via the left then right side of the arête.

127. **Swiss Miss** 5.10b

Pro to 2½" TCU's recommended

A crack that leads to the right side of the same arête. Use the natural pocket for protection. Crux is a minor bulge 25' up and may need pins.

CARVER BRIDGE CLIFF

WELCOME TO THE FABULOUS Carver Bridge Cliff, a rare and unusual, privately owned sport crag that was unknown to rock climbers until 1987. The crag now features excellent climbs—as well as a series of superb bouldering problems in the forest below the crag.

Overlooking a beautiful Clackamas River near the community of Carver, this forested, private property continues to offer one of the region's best opportunities to experience the sport of rock climbing. Hopefully, this small Carver cliff will continue to be a valuable asset to Portland area rock climbers for many generations to come.

BRIEF HISTORY OF THE CRAG

Though nearly unreachable, early "pioneers" did venture to Carver to climb on this hidden crag. The occasional fixed piton attested to this fact. Even on the Yellow Wall (on Angular Motion) there was an old fixed 10-foot rope hanging from a "bashie." A portion of this route on the Yellow Wall was ascended in 1975 by Jeff Alzner and Terry Jenkins.

Late in the summer of 1987, several climbers visited here and immediately realized its vast potential for free climbing routes. In a few short years these climbers transformed this place into a quality sport crag that now offers several fine classic climbs on excellent rock.

The Carver Bridge Cliff formation faces north and extends generally along an east-west axis for several hundred yards. A few minor outcrops exist beyond the main sections described herein, but these are not developed for climbing. The highest section of the cliff (Rockgarden Wall) is approximately 130 feet. The topographic maps have been separated into two sections. They are as follows: the Rockgarden Wall and the Yellow Wall. The majority of the routes are rated between 5.9 and 5.12. The lower-rated climbs tend to be mixed natural protection and bolts, while the higher-rated climbs (5.11 and above) tend to be more heavily bolted. The natural protection climbs offer good equipment placements, so you may have to look hard to find an "R" rated climb at Carver.

Greg Lyon, Mike Pajunas, Robert McGown, Gary Rall, Wayne Wallace, Tim Olson, and many others were highly instrumental in the development of this crag.

Here are several astounding classics that will test your ability: Smerk (5.11a), Angular Motion (5.12a), Uncola (5.11c), Notorious (5.11b), Sea of Holes (5.12a), and Rites of Passage (5.10b). These and a host of other great climbs put Carver on many a rock climber's map.

There are also many classic bouldering problems located in the woods below the main crag. A number of climbs have a rather healthy re-growth of moss and are generally not climbed anymore, including the small section of wall between the two main crags. Yet, all of the best climbs are very accessible and always

Ian Goss climbing *Angular Motion 5.12a*

challenging.

ACCESS ISSUES

The following guidelines apply to all visitors who come to Carver Bridge Cliff to rock climb. This unique environment is privately owned, and access is granted only to members of the Carver Climbing Club.

Club members are expected to respect the property owner's privacy and to give due diligence to how the property is used. Do not litter, or vandalize, or cause excessive noise, and be vigilant when others trespass or cause problems that could jeopardize access privileges. Continued freedom to climb at this crag ultimately depends upon your willingness to obey the rules.

Limited provisional access is granted to each climber for a one-time membership fee. This membership requires signing a liability release waiver, obtainable at the website *carverclimbingclub.org*. Apply on this website for a number which will be emailed to you. Print the liability release form, fill it out, and take it to one of several local indoor sport climbing gyms in Portland, and pay a cash membership fee to attain a numbered CCC card. The card should be

---

CARVER RULES AND OBLIGATIONS

Do your part to preserve our access by observing the following rules:
- You must be a signed member of the Carver Climbing Club to climb or boulder on Stone Cliff property and/or property owned by the Rosenbaum family.
- You may bring guests who are 18 years of age or older, but they may not boulder or climb. They may only observe, which does not include handling of any rope or other equipment.
- Only canned beverages are allowed. No glass of any kind.
- Dogs are not permitted.
- Each climber or boulderer is responsible for picking up their own garbage or garbage left by others. This is a joint effort.
- No new trails or paths or routes will be allowed. Use only those which are already in place.
- People must stay on the trails at all times. People walking off the trails can cause damage to the flora and fauna.
- Each person, whether a member or guest, must have picture ID on their person at all times and be able to present it to anyone acting on behalf of the Stone Cliff Inn to verify membership or identity.
- The Stone Cliff Inn parking lot may be used all days except holidays and Friday and Saturday evenings from 5pm on. During holidays or Friday and Saturday evenings, members may park at the intersection of Hattan and Gronlund Roads and come in through that trail starting on Stone Cliff Lane.
- Radios or other music players are not allowed.
- No rock wall climbing is allowed unless you are an experienced climber with skills suitable to the rock terrain.
- No removal of rock, moss, wood, or any other item from the site unless it has already been removed for climbing purposes.
- Be respectful of property and others. You are here at the discretion of the owners. Your right to boulder or climb here is subject to revocation at any time.

visible on your harness or pack when you access the property to climb or boulder.

Greg climbing *Digital* 5.12d

You must be 18 or older to rock climb or to practice on the rock boulders at this site. When visiting the crag you must carry photo ID. All bouldering activists are required to sign a liability release waver before entry onto the land. All persons under 18 are NOT allowed to rock climb at this site nor play on the rock boulders.

CARVER CLIMBING CLUB

The Carver Climbing Club (*www.carverclimbingclub.org*) was originally formed as a grassroots effort to keep a scarce and valuable resource available. The fact that this land is still being utilized as a climbing area is a testament to the efforts of many individuals, but mostly to the generosity of the owner. Signs are posted at the entrances to the Carver climbing areas.

The website *carverclimbingclub.org* allows an effective means of communication between the landowner and club members. Every member of the club must take an active role in making sure that the restaurant, the owners property in general, and their family and staff specifically, are treated with the respect and courtesy they deserve.

Everyone who climbs at Carver must treat the cliff, the boulders, and the property as they would their own, with the full knowledge that we are there only through the generosity of the owners family.

Work together as a community to help protect this valuable resource and allow climbing at Carver to continue. This can only be achieved through adherence to the following list of guidelines by all users of the property. Our presence at Carver Bridge Cliff as climbers is a privilege. Take an active role in maintaining the climbing at Carver, the property, and the privilege of access.

Continued access is by no means guaranteed, and depends wholly upon our ability as a community to police and maintain this area.

The Carver Climbing Club and the landowner have identified a number of guidelines that every user of this recreational resource will need to both personally follow, disseminate, and enforce if any of us are to continue to climb at Carver. Read the access guidelines. Attain the road directions, parking requirements and trail information when you sign the liability waver.

VISUAL BIO

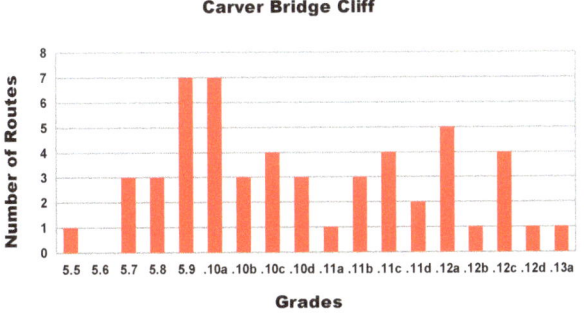

These emblems represent all of Carver Bridge Cliff climbing site. Carver is generally a sport climbing site, although there is some opportunity for gear leads.

ROCKGARDEN WALL

1. **Crack in the Mirror 5.9** ★★
   30' (9m) in length, Pro to 1½"
   At the far left side of the wall and just uphill is a unique looking 'broken' flake start. Ascend this and exit right to an anchor at a ledge.

2. **Variation 5.10a**
   30' (9m) in length, several QD's
   Short bolted face route.

3. **Notorious 5.11c/d** ★★★
   35' (10m) in length, 5 QD's
   One of the great Carver classics. A very good climb! Climb the arête using large holds to a ledge and finish up left to an anchor.

4. **Marqueritaville 5.10d**
   40' (12m) in length, Pro to 2"
   The deep overhung dihedral. A stiff crux and joins with Uncola.

5. **Cherry Cola 5.11d** ★★
   45' (13m) in length, 4 QD's
   This difficult variation problem that begins off the top of a large boulder. Crimp thin holds up the face, then join Uncola as it cruises through it final ending difficult moves. Waltz up left on small holds and smears to a belay anchor.

Chris Alexander leading *Smerk*

6. **Uncola 5.11c** ★★★
   45' (13m) in length, 5 QD's
   One of the ten great Carver classics. Located just left of a large chimney. Start next to a large boulder and ascend up right onto a steep face. Bust up leftward through a crux section on a slightly overhung series of powerful moves. Waltz up left on small holds to a belay anchor.

7. **Neptune 5.9** ★★
   40' (12m) in length, Pro to 1½"
   The obvious wide offwidth. A fun climb. Stem, jam and body climb up to a bolt belay. A minor crack on the right face of the chimney offers good small pro.

8. **Smooth Torquer 5.12d** ★★
   45' (13m) in length, 4 QD's
   An excellent, desperate, physical "tips" climb just to the left of Smerk. Eases to a smooth slab after the crux. Rap from anchor.

9. **Smerk 5.11a** ★★★
   120' (36m) in length, (40' 1ˢᵗ pitch) 5-6 QD's [P1]
   One of the finest classic routes at Carver Cliff. Very popular! Route was coined from an old friends nickname. Ascend a bolted face left of New Generation past a crux (5.11a) exiting to the belay on the right (or up left to Smooth Torquer belay). The second pitch (4 bolts) ascends directly up the head wall (5.10c) to another bolt anchor. The third pitch finishes straight up a smooth face (3 bolts) using a diagonal seam start. Rap from belay.

10. New Generation 5.8 (1st pitch) ★★★
120' (36m) in length, (40' 1st pitch) Pro to 1½"
A popular climb. Begin up an awkward start to a small corner and climb a sweet finger crack (5.8) to a bolt belay. Angle up left via a low angle ramp to another bolted face. Continue up this (5.9) to a ledge, then finish up an arête (5.9) to a belay. Rappel.

11. Free Ride 5.12a
20' (6m) in length, 2 QD's
A bolted variation direct start to Scotch and Soda.

12. Scotch and Soda 5.10d ★★★
40' (12m) in length, QD's and pro to 1½"
Fantastic crack and face climb. Start at a ledge beneath the Red Dihedral. Ascend a harsh finger crack until possible to maneuver left onto a small pedestal. Finish up a bolted face to an anchor.

13. Tequila Sunrise 5.10c
120' (36m) in length, Pro to 2"
Start as for Scotch and Soda, but traverse right to Red Dihedral, then up left around a minor corner to the New Generation anchor. Continue up easy ramps to the left then up and right (1 bolt) through a 5.10 A crux to a ledge. Move up a 5.8 crack and offwidth to the summit. Rap from belay anchor.

14. Red Dihedral 5.10a ★★
60' (18m) in length, Pro to 1½" TCU's recommended
Interesting dihedral. Originally named due to the red lichen on the rock. Pull up a crux start into the corner and ascend this up and then right to a stubby maple tree. Move past this and up a tight crux corner to a large ledge and bolt anchor on the right.

15. _____ 5.12+
60' (18m) in length (TR)

16. Jungle Safari 5.10a ★★
120' (36m) in length, Pro to 3"
An excellent LONG dihedral climb. Begin just left of the offwidth (Combination Block) and stem, jam your way up an awkward corner. The crux is a narrow crack corner section about 80' up the climb. Finish up a steep but easy (5.8) fist crack to a tree belay.

17. Night Vision 5.11b ★★
120' (36m) in length (65' 1st pitch), Pro to 1½"
Not often climbed because it requires some pro, but is a superb route nonetheless. Commence up the offwidth crack on the left side of Combination Block. Follow a minor corner up and over a wild bulge then up a stiff face (crux) to a bolt anchor. The next pitch ascends a 5.9 crack up right to the top of the cliff.

18. Sanity Assassin 5.7 to 5.10
20' (6m) in length, 2 QD's

19. Sea of Holes 5.12a ★★★
75' (22m) in length, 7 QD's
One of the best climbs at Carver. Begin from off the top of Combination Block and ascend the rounded buttress (crux) on unique pocketed face holds and edges. Enter a shallow dihedral where the route eas-

Leading 1st pitch of *Smerk*

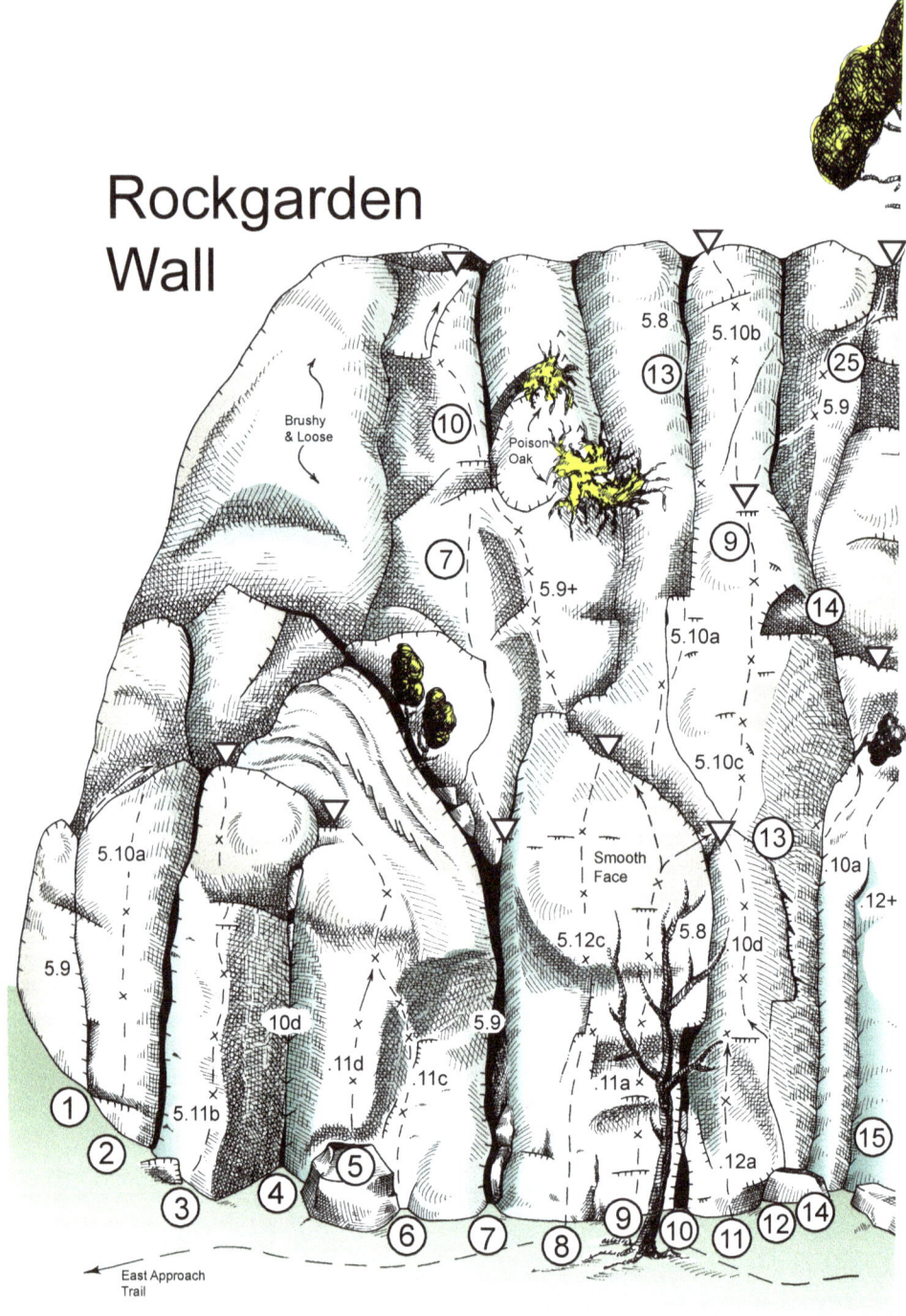

CARVER BRIDGE CLIFF

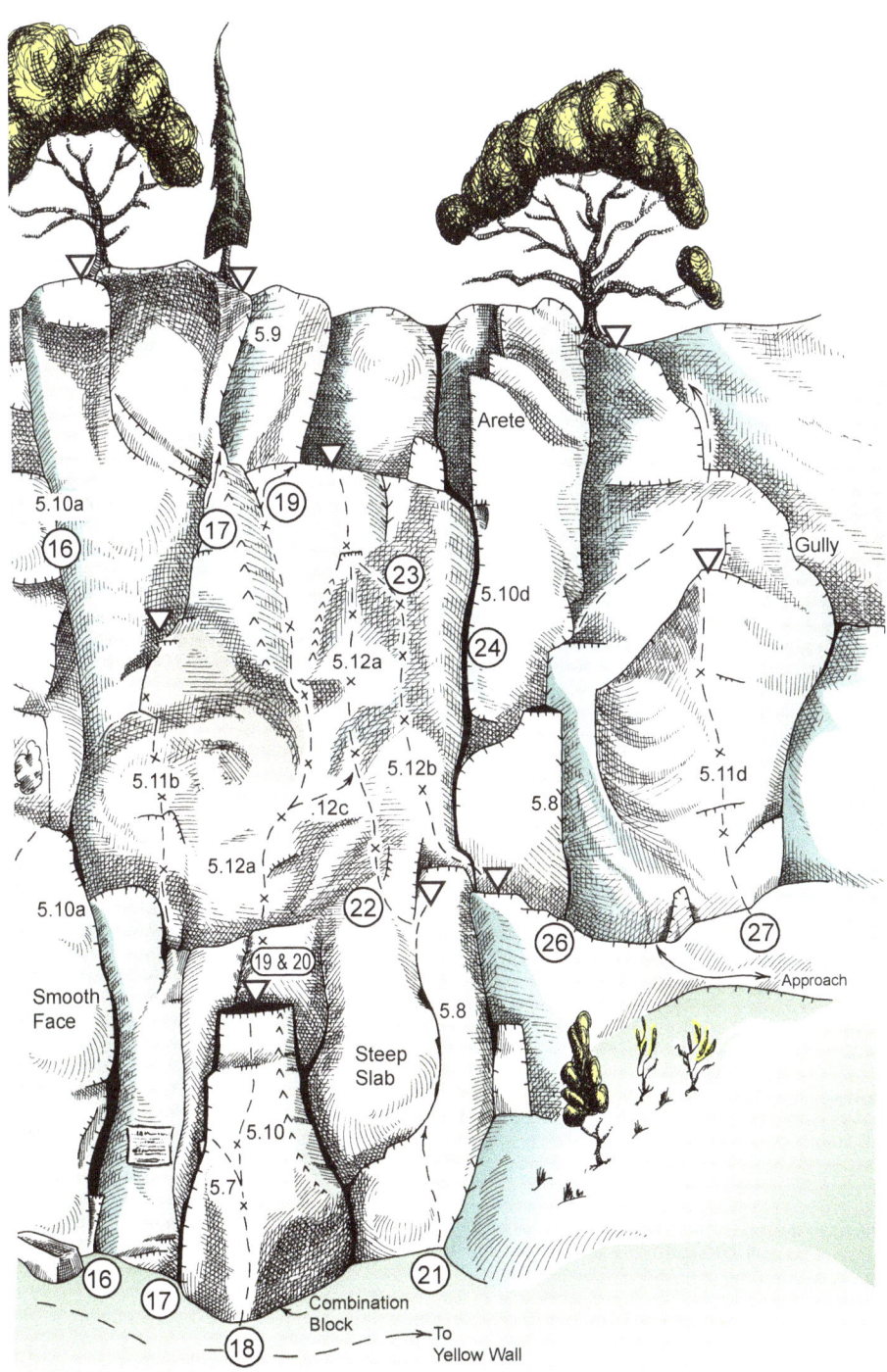

es. Exit up right to a bolt belay anchor.

20. Sport Court 5.12c ★ ★ ★
75' (22m) in length, 8 QD's
This exciting superior route exists by connecting the lower half of Sea of Holes with the upper half of Wally Street.

21. Shadow Fox 5.8
25' (7m) in length, Pro to ¾"
A short crack climb on a smooth slab. A good approach to the upper face climbs. Mostly bolts now.

Bri Stekly on *Edges & Ledges*, Broughton Bluff

22. Wally Street 5.12a ★ ★ ★
70' (21m) in length, 5 QD's and minor pro to ¾"
Start as for Shadowfox but enter up left onto a stiff, vertical face climb of quality proportion.

23. Wally Wedding 5.12b
20' (6m) in length, 4 QD's

24. Sweat and the Flies 5.10d PG
20' (6m) in length, Pro to 3"
This bold flared offwidth is a surprising lead. Short and nasty.

25. Battleship Arête 5.9 (variation)
20' (6m) in length, 2 QD's

The next six routes are located on the In-Between Wall, but are inaccessible due to overgrowth of brush and vines on the routes and along the base of the wall. For exact locations of these routes refer to one of the older PRC guides.

26. Passport to Insanity 5.8
35' (10m) in length, Pro to 2"
Ascend a perfect corner, mantle to a ledge, then mantle again, continuing up right, then left to an oak tree belay.

27. Burning From the Inside 5.11d ★ ★
20' (6m) in length, 3 QD's
This exhilarating problem dances up an overhung rounded face to a bolt belay. A great climb.

28. Hinge of Fate 5.10c
25' (7m) in length, 3 QD's and optional pro to ¾"
At the top of a dirt gully you will find a dark, water streaked face. Ascend this past a crux, then lay back and smear your way up a flared seam (the hinge).

29. Eyes of a Stranger 5.10a
40' (12m) in length, Pro to ¾"

30. Shady Personality 5.10b
65' (19m) in length, Pro to 1½" Cams recommended
A unique climb that can be done in two short pitches. Move up a smooth slab (5.9) and

up easy steps to a belay on a ledge. Continue up a slightly overhung crack that begins as a mantle into an offwidth pea-pod. Bolt belay.

31. Rats in the Jungle 5.10a
20' (6m) in length, Wide pro to 6"
The large chimney problem immediately right of Shady Personality.

YELLOW WALL

32. Call to Greatness 5.10c ★★
60' (18m) in length, Pro to 2"
An impressive route. Classic thin hand jamming. Begin up a large brushing corner at the left edge of the Yellow Wall. Embark from a stance up the overhung crack system. Boldly climb around three small bulges, the toughest one being the last bulge.

33. Plastic Monkey 5.13a
60' (18m) in length, 7 QD's
A very difficult problem and one of the most difficult at Carver. Ascend the vertical bolted face on the left corner of the Yellow Wall.

34. Rites of Passage 5.10b ★★★
80' (24m) in length, 10 QD's
One of the best routes at the crag. Commence up a face (1 bolt) and move right (or start up a jam crack to this point), then up a bolted face (5.10b) until possible to move right to an anchor above Angular Motion. Move hard left and continue up via a shallow corner (5.10b) then up right to a flake that ends at a belay anchor just under an overhang. Rappel. The thin crack above (1 bolt and pro to 1") is seldom done (dirt/moss) and is 5.11c to the top of the bluff.

35. Digital 5.12d ★★ (Dry)
20' (12m) in length, 4 QD's
A unique, yet difficult balance problem.

36. Angular Motion 5.12a ★★★ (Dry)
40' (12m) in length, 5 QD's
One of the most popular climbs here. Super classic! To the left of Chemistry Slab is an overhung face. Power your way up this until you must make a long reach to a jug then up right on tenuous holds to a ledge and a bolt belay. An exciting route with dynamic moves.

37. Out on a Limb 5.10a ★ (Dry)
60' (18m) in length, QD's and pro to 1½"
A good route. Start up the left side of Chemistry Slab alcove. Exit out left along a narrow ramp (crux) and up to a bolt anchor. Belay, then continue up a face (1 bolt) that leads to a dihedral above. Rappel from a bolt anchor under the final overhang.

Tyler leading a Video Bluff favorite

The next six climbs are reasonably easy short slab climbs that are located on the Chemistry Slab. This section of rock is protected from the occasional rain shower during the summer months, making this a good practice slab for learning the basics of rope handling. There is an anchor on the upper right side, and the upper left side of the slab.

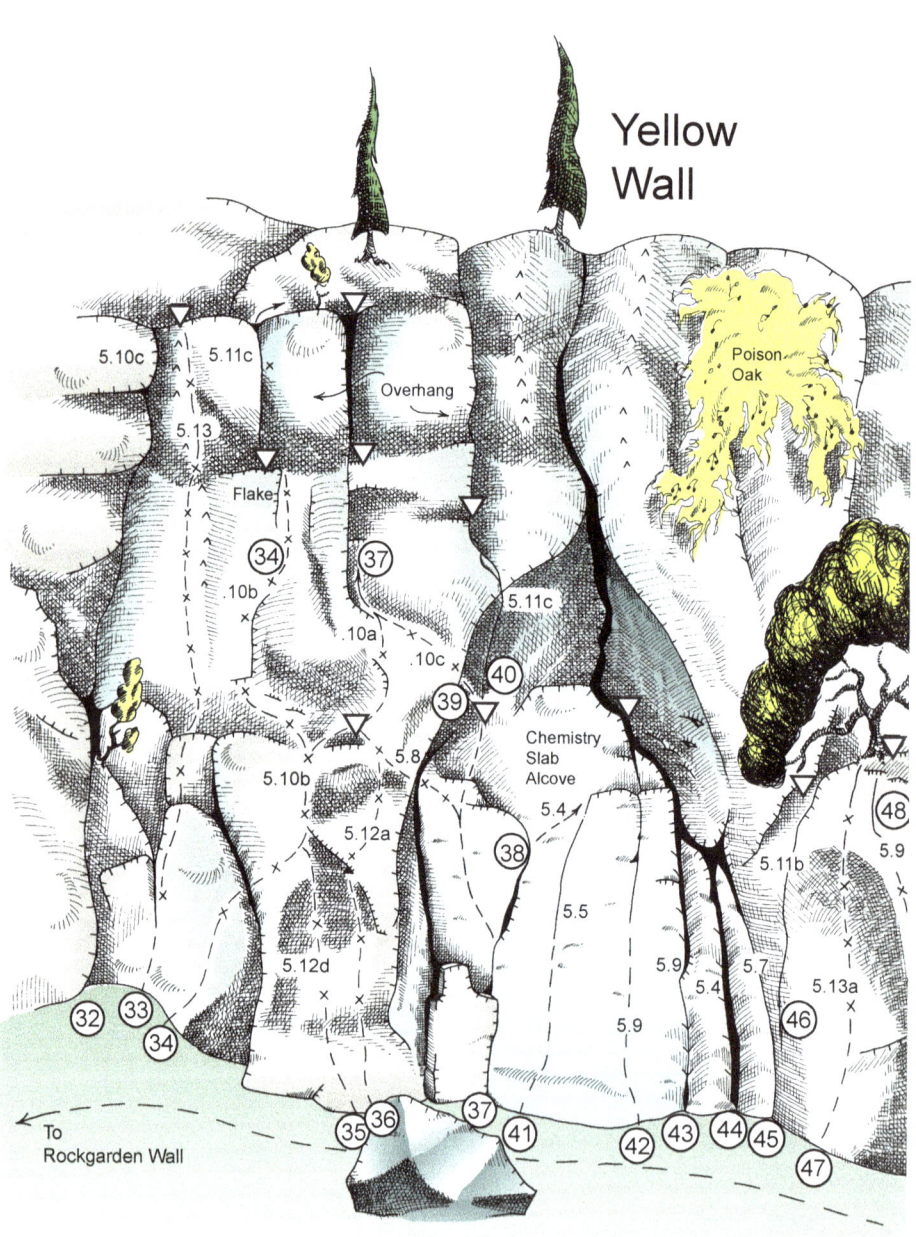

CARVER BRIDGE CLIFF 119

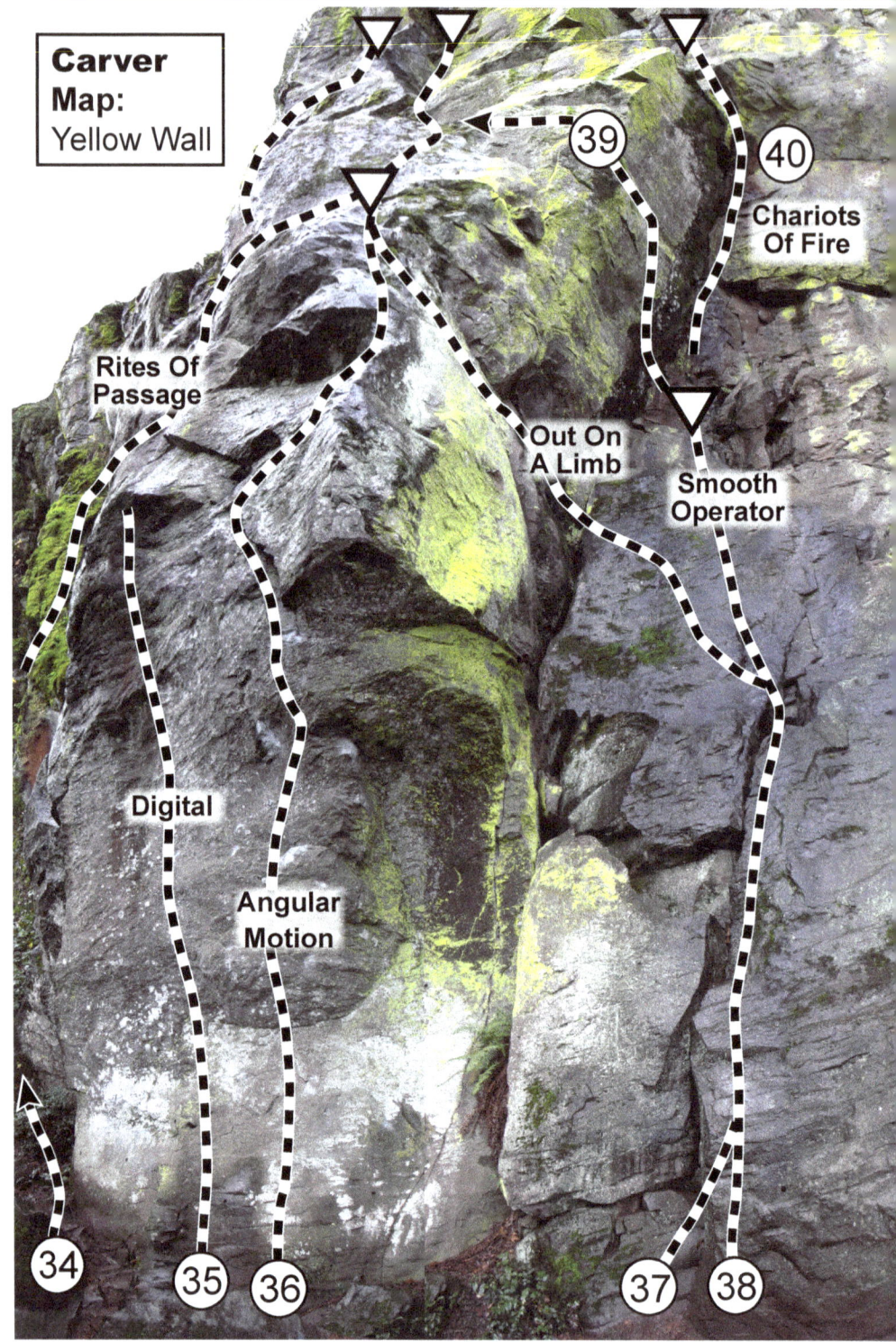

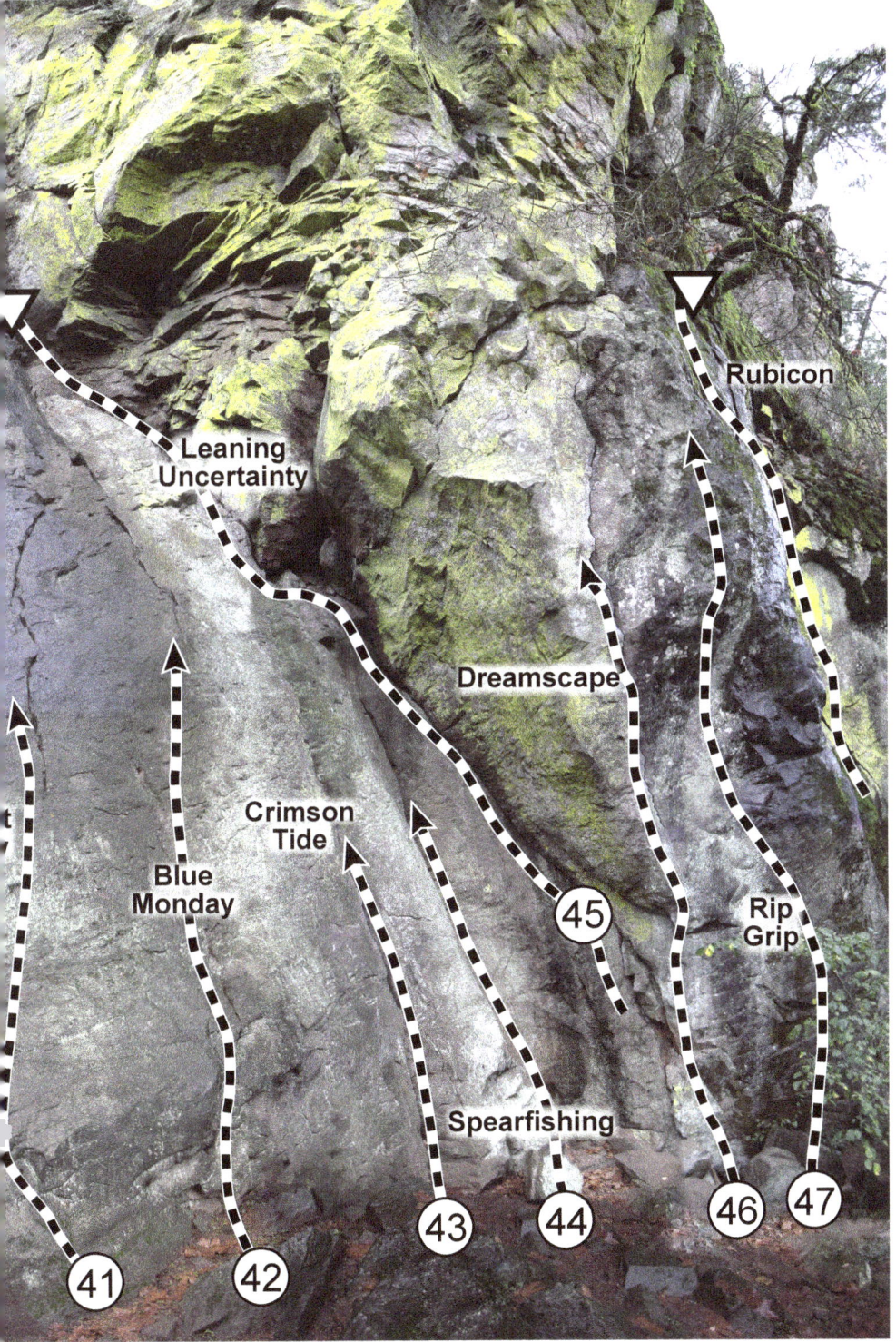

38. **Smooth Operator 5.4** ★ 🌂
30' (9m) in length, Pro to 1 ½"

39. **King Rat 5.10c** 🌂
60' (9m) in length, Pro to 1½"

40. **Chariots of Fire 5.11c** ★★★ 🌂
55' (16m) in length, Pro to 2"
An incredibly physical classic climb. Race up easy slabs passing a bolt anchor. Enter a hand jam crack leading directly up a desperately overhung wall. Exit past a block to a bolt anchor on a small ledge.

> **TEN GREAT 5.12 SPORT ROUTES (NO GEAR)**
> For the extreme climber already firm with the upper numbers, here is a cool list of select 5.12 sport routes (no gear-just QD's).
> 1. Road Face, 5.12a, French's Dome
> 2. Jackie Chan, 5.12b, French's Dome
> 3. Angular Motion, 5.12a, Carver
> 4. Dracula, 5.12a, Broughton Bluff
> 5. Bad Omen, 5.12b, Broughton Bluff
> 6. Bloodline, 5.12b, Broughton Bluff
> 7. Kashmir, 5.12a, Broughton Bluff
> 8. Closet Nazi, 5.12a, Broughton Bluff
> 9. Grace, 5.12b, Ozone
> 10. Scott Free, 5.12b, Madrone

For The Extreme Climber

41. **Talent Show 5.5** 🌂
30' (9m) in length, Pro to ¾" TCU's and small wires
Left side of Chemistry Slab.

42. **Blue Monday 5.9** 🌂
30' (9m) in length (TR)
A steep face climb on Chemistry Slab.

43. **Crimson Tide 5.9** 🌂
30' (9m) in length, Pro to 2"
A steep face climb on Chemistry Slab.

44. **Spear Fishing in Bermuda 5.4** 🌂
30' (9m) in length, Large pro
Right side of Chemistry Slab.

45. **Leaning Uncertainty 5.7** 🌂
30' (9m) in length, Pro to 2"
Right side of Chemistry Slab.

46. **Dreamscape 5.11b** ★★ 🌂
30' (9m) in length, Pro to 1½"
A difficult vertical tips crack that powers up the right outer face of Chemistry alcove. Rap from a fixed belay anchor left of the large maple tree.

> **TEN GREAT TRAD ROUTES UNDER 5.10**
> For those who relish the challenge of placing pro while on lead, here is a great selection of stellar gear routes under 5.10.
> 1. Gandalf's Grip, 5.9, Broughton
> 2. The Sickle, 5.8, Broughton
> 3. Loose Block O., 5.9, Broughton
> 4. Classic Crack, 5.9, Broughton
> 5. Free For All, 5.8, Beacon Rock
> 6. Jill's Thrill, 5.9, Beacon Rock
> 7. SE Face Route, 5.7, Beacon Rock
> 8. Cruisin', 5.7, Beacon Rock
> 9. New Generation, 5.8 P1, Carver
> 10. Cornicks Corner, 5.9, Madrone

Starting Point

◆ CARVER BRIDGE CLIFF   123

47. Rip Grip   5.13a   ★★
30' (9m) in length, 4 QD's
A difficult bolted face immediately right of Dreamscape.

48. Rubicon   5.9   ★★★
30' (9m) in length, 4 bolts, minor pro to ¾"
A very popular easy climb for everyone. Ascend the outside corner to easy edges, then up a steep face (crux) until you can grab the base edge of a thin crack. Rap from chains at a tree belay.

49. Edge of the Reef   5.10b   ★★
45' (13m) in length, Pro to 1" TCU's recommended
A really good climb. Challenging but not extreme. Move up the curved starting crack (numerous edges) then straight up a crack past a face crux with 1 bolt. Finish up a thin crack that rounds to a slab and bolt anchor.

50. Great Barrier Reef   5.7 R
30' (9m) in length, Pro unknown

51. Penguins in Heat   5.12a
30' (9m) in length, 4 QD's
A difficult problem located above the first pitch of Edge of the Reef.

52. Challenger   5.11b/c   ★★
30' (9m) in length, 3 QD's   TCU's optional
The name describes the route very well. This quality climb begins up easy steps until you must enter a smooth face broken with unusual edges. Finish up and left to exit to a small stance with a bolt anchor.

53. Last of the Mohicans   5.9   ★
40' (12m) in length, Pro to 2½"
A good, enjoyable climb to learn the basics. Ascend a broken crack system with a bulge on the right side just short of the anchor. The upper section of this far right section of wall is not available due to a luxurious growth of moss and dirt.

54. Riders of the Purple Sage   5.10b
40' (12m) in length, QD's and pro to 1"
Step up easy rock terrain to a considerably overhung corner (1 bolt). Stem and lay back up right through the crux, then up left to the bolted belay. P2: power up right on crux face moves, over a small lip, then up right on edges to a high belay. Pitch 2 has a notable regrowth of moss and is not presently climbed. Rappel from midway belay.

> **TEN GOOD SPORT ROUTES**
> **UNDER 5.10**
> Every extreme climber started on reasonable ground somewhere, so here is our choice of local bolted sport routes.
> 1. Kung Fu, 5.9, Ozone
> 2. Dirty Jugs, 5.9, Ozone
> 3. Standing Ovation, 5.9, Ozone
> 4. Helm's Deep, 5.9, Ozone
> 5. Alpha, 5.8, French's Dome
> 6. Straw man, 5.8, French's Dome
> 7. Tin Tangle, 5.8, French's Dome
> 8. Orient Express, 5.8, RB Quarry
> 9. Flakey Old Man, 5.7, RB Quarry
> 10. Route Crafters, 5.8, Madrone Wall

A GREAT PLACE TO BE

"...we have ceased to be slaves and have really been men. It is hard to return to servitude."
~Lionel Terray

CARVER BRIDGE CLIFF

Madrone Wall

THIS BEAUTIFUL AND UNIQUE FOREST CRAG is considered by many local rock climbers to be one of the best multi-season climbing sites in the Portland metro area. This southwest oriented cliff scarp provides excellent rock climbing opportunities for all levels of rock climbers from beginner to advanced.

The Madrone Wall Park was opened on Oct 21, 2017. Rock climbers can once again enjoy climbing at a site that sports an extensive list of over 100 rock climbs from 5.4 to 5.12.

The Madrone Wall Park concept was brought to fruition by the long-term efforts of a core group of pro-active citizens such as Keith Daellenbach and Kellie Rice, including substantial influence from organizations such as the Mazamas, American Alpine Club, the Access Fund, various climbing gyms, and outdoor retail stores. Through a 20-year interaction with county commissioners and (from 2009 onward) with the county planning department, these various citizens (via Keith's preservation committee) were central in bringing the Madrone Wall Park forward to completion so all recreation enthusiasts could once again enjoy visiting this unique county treasure. Thank you Clackamas County!

BRIEF HISTORY OF THE CRAG

The crag received sparse attention by rock climbers as long ago as the mid 1970's. Yet the difficulty and overhung nature of the crag precluded extreme vertical development of the crag.

In the continual quest for the perfect climb, route exploration took hold of the Madrone Wall late in 1986. Through the special efforts of Chuck Buzzard, John Jackson, Scott Smith and other friends, they pioneered numerous excellent super classics such as Beam Me Up Mr. Scott (5.11c), Mr. Noodle Arms (5.11b), Ant Abuse (5.10a), Catharsis (5.11c) and Sheesh (5.10c).

The area remained a well kept secret until October of 1988. In just a few years nearly 100 routes were established. Chuck Buzzard, Wayne Wallace, Robert McGown, Greg Lyon, Dave Sowerby, Mr Olson, and many others were instrumental in creating great classics like Where the Wild Things Roam (5.11d), Scott Free (5.12b), Full Spank Mode (5.12a), Shining Wall (5.12a), Nouveau Riche (5.10c) and Divine Wind (5.11c).

Geographically, the Madrone Wall complex is just one long crag, but is subdivided into six sections. From left to right: Left Corner Wall, Orange Wall, Fourth Class Wall, the main section of the Madrone, the Shining Wall and the south end is Hardscrabble.

VISUAL BIO

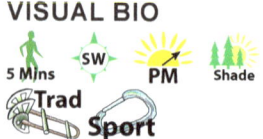

These emblems represent virtually all of Madrone Wall climbing site, except for the Shining Wall which receives a fair amount of direct sunshine in the afternoon hours.

HOW TO GET THERE

To reach this wonderland of rock, drive east on Highway 212 from the I-205 Clackamas exit #12. Drive east 3 miles to the Rock Creek Corner intersection. Turn south at the signal light onto Highway 224 that leads to Estacada. Drive one mile to the small community of Carver. Continue on Highway 224 for approximately 2¼ miles east of Carver. Entrance to the Madrone Wall County Park is located on the east side of the road at a large metal gate at street address 19485 SE Highway 224, Damascus, Oregon. This county

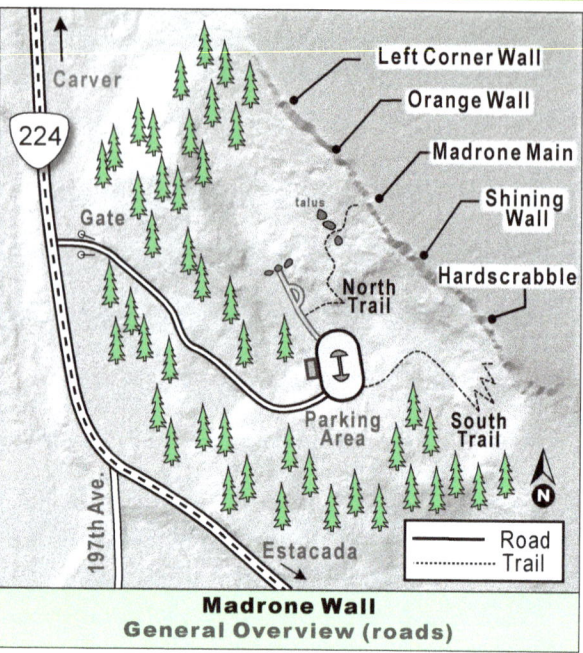

park has fee-based parking (daily, 6-month, 1-year, or 2-year). See the Clackamas county website for park regulations and other info.

APPROACH

The North Trail begins at the Kiosk on a wide path, then takes a sharp turn off the wide path at a sign pointing to the right. This path lands near the route Superstings. The South Trail proceeds from the south edge of the parking spot, and marches up east on a path for about 100' then continues right (south) a short distance, then ascends a series of steep switchbacks on a steeply angled rocky slope. The south path reaches the cliff near the route Divine Wind.

LEFT CORNER WALL

Immediately left of Jackson's Daring Deeds are several more new climbs. **Urushiol** (5.10+) cuts left under an overhang (two bolts) then up into a 90° dihedral with an overhanging hand crack. **Tecnu** (5.9) angles right from the same starting overhang through two juggy

◆ MADRONE WALL 127

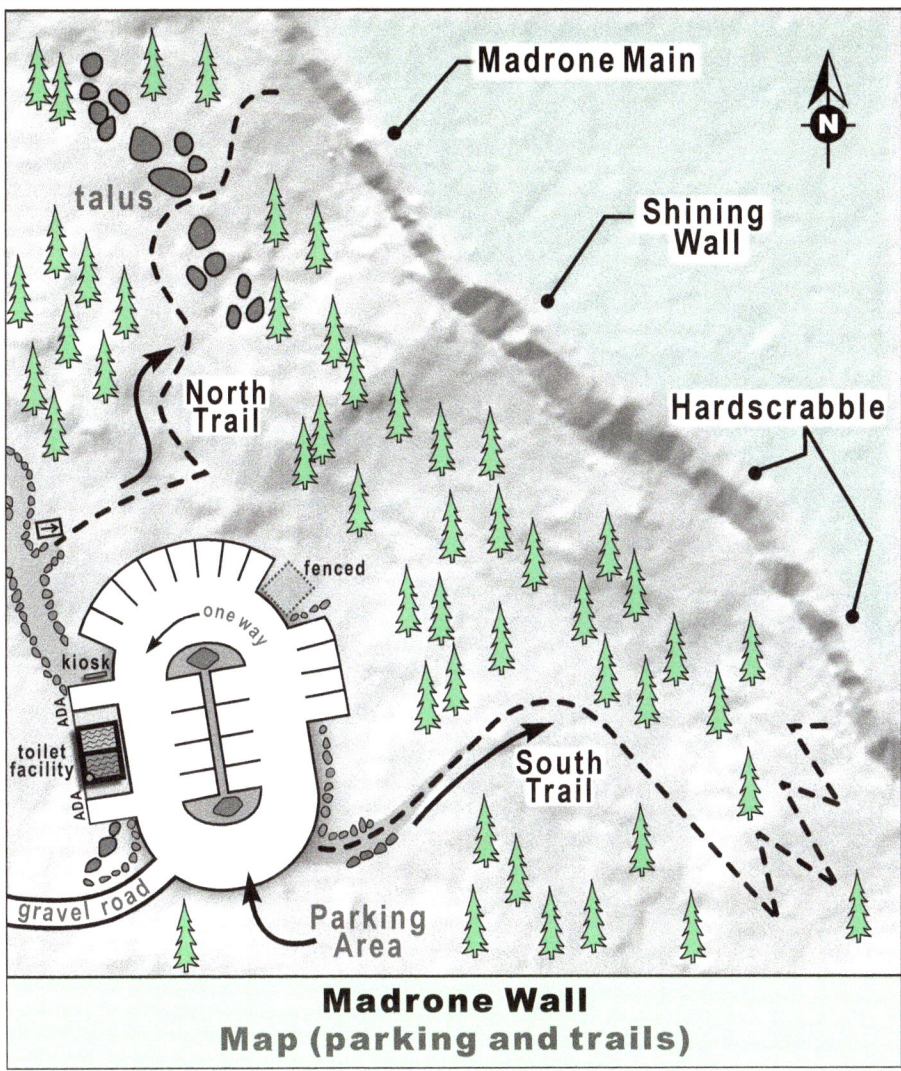

Madrone Wall
Map (parking and trails)

bulges to a ledge.
1. **Jackson's Daring Deeds   5.10a**
   45' (13m) in length, Pro to 2"
   This dihedral is located at the far left recesses of the wall.
2. **Patrick's Dihedral   5.9**   ★★
   35' (10m) in length, Pro to 1½"
   A large dihedral that begins as an offwidth and climbs up past a narrow crux section to a Madrone tree belay. Located to the right of a small rounded buttress.
3. **Sheesh   5.10c PG**   ★★★
   35' (10m) in length, Pro to 1" including RP's
   Excellent climb. Sheesh is the clean, smooth dihedral with a small half-moon imprint on the left face. Thin crux.

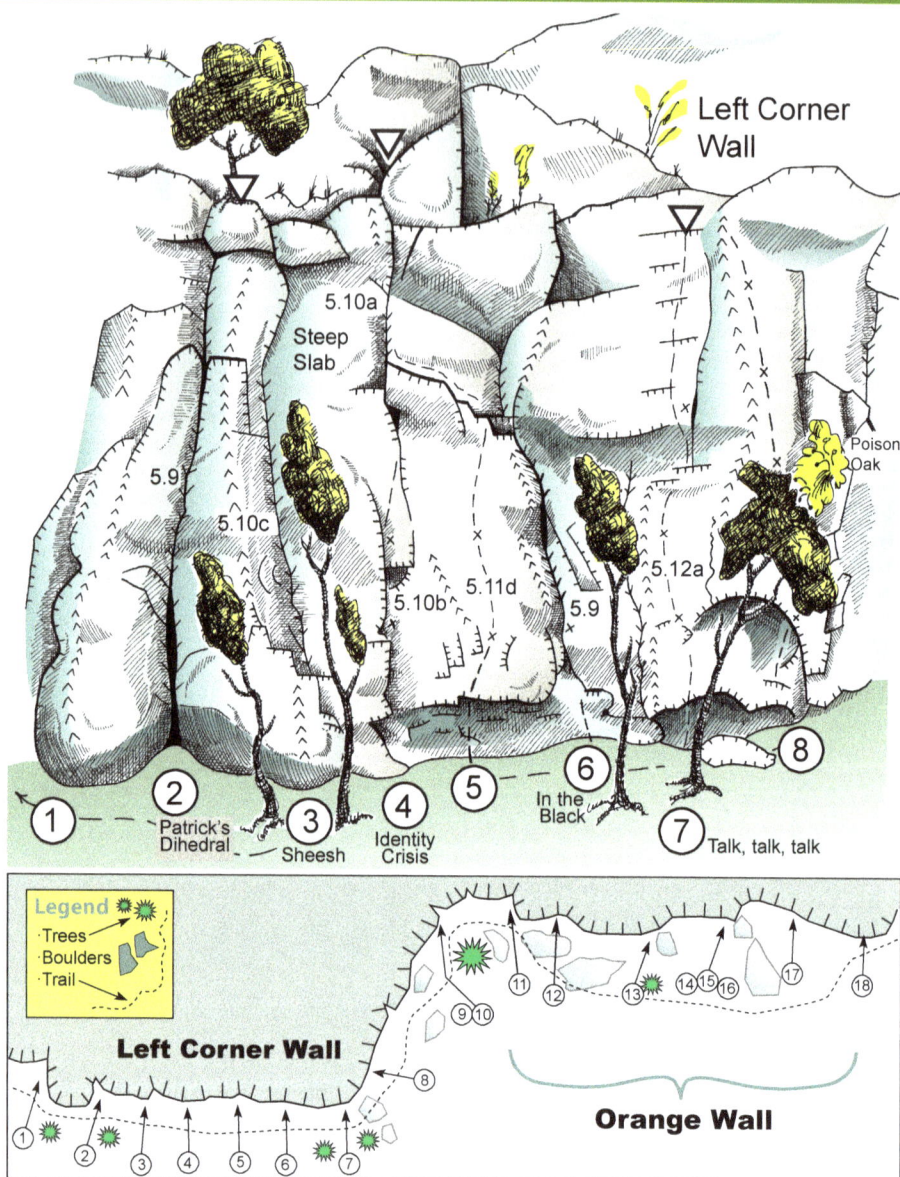

4. **Identity Crisis   5.10b R   ★★**
   35' (10m) in length, Pro to 1" including #4 Rock
   A great climb. Commence up the outside face to the right of Sheesh passing 2 bolts to an easy slab. Surmount a final bulge and move up left to a bolt belay.

5. **Mental Crisis   5.11d   ★**
   35' (10m) in length, QD's and minor pro to 1"
   A good, short, difficult problem. Face climb over a substantial bulge past 2 bolts to join with Identity Crisis.

6. **In The Black 5.9** ★★
   35' (10m) in length, Pro to 2"
   A dark, contorted left-leaning crack system that joins with Identity Crisis.

7. **Talk Talk Talk 5.12a** ★★
   30' (9m) in length, 3 QD's
   A definite must on your list of climbs. This short, power packed line ascends up a rounded outside corner to a bolt belay. A harsh finger crux.

8. **Verbal 5.11a** ★
   30' (9m) in length, 4 QD's
   This climb starts 5' to the right of the main outside corner just to the right of the previous route.

9. **Back in 'Nam 5.10b PG**
   50' (15m) in length, Pro to 1½"
   This route is near the large tree at the left side of the Orange Wall. Follow a left leaning corner crack over a small roof about 30' up the cliff, then continue up left again. Angle up left to a madrone tree and rappel from there.

10. **Feat of Clay 5.10-**
    30' (9m) in length, Pro to 3" including long slings
    Starts the same at 'Back in 'Nam' but cut up right at 15' beneath the large roof until you reach a large ledge, then move back to the left to an anchor. Rappel. Several lead variations exist for this route.

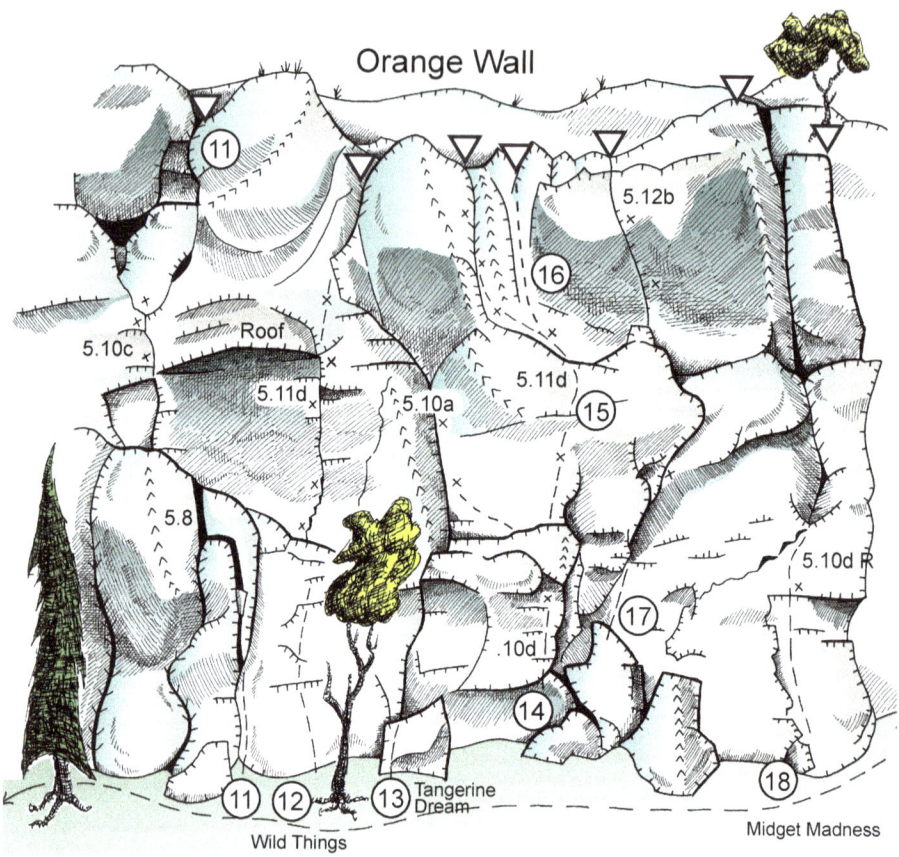

ORANGE WALL

11. Wild Blue Yonder 5.10c ★★ (Dry)

45' (13m) in length, Pro to 2"

An interesting route with plenty of variety. Start next to a large boulder. Begin up a sickle shaped offwidth crack to a small ramp. Step left, then proceed directly up the broken face (3 pitons) just left of the large roof. From an alcove pull over an awkward bulge to a bolt belay.

12. Where the Wild Things Roam (aka Wild Things) 5.11d ★★★ (Dry)

45' (13m) in length, 5 QD's and minor pro to ¾"

One of the ten great classics at the Madrone Wall. Exhilarating problem ascending up a brilliant orange face. Begin up an easy slab to the first bolt, then up a continuously overhanging face using numerous in cut edges. Turn to the right side of the large roof and move up a reasonable dihedral to a bolt belay. This is an excellent rainy day climb.

13. Tangerine Dream 5.10a PG ★ (Dry)

45' (13m) in length, Pro to 1"

A popular route. Start off a boulder and mantle over a crux bulge move, then continue up a dihedral (bolts) until able to angle up left to a bolt anchor.

14. Direct Start to Tangerine Dream 5.10d ★
   15' (4m) in length, QD's and pro to 1"

15. Agent Orange 5.11d ★★
   45' (13m) in length, Pro to ¾" including TCU's
   A superb, demanding climb! Ascend TD Direct Start to a ledge then face climb up (1 bolt) past a horizontal crack, then up left to an overhung tight corner dihedral (3 bolts) to a bolt anchor.

16. O.J. 5.12a ★
   50' (15m) in length, Bolts on Agent Orange, then small nuts and #0 TCU
   Climb the lower portion of Agent Orange, except finish up the square cut flaring groove near the top.

17. Comfortizer 5.12b (5.11 to mid belay)
   45' (13m) in length, QD's
   A difficult line punching out a large overhang at the top. An upper left variation exists.

132   CHAPTER 1   ◆   ORC

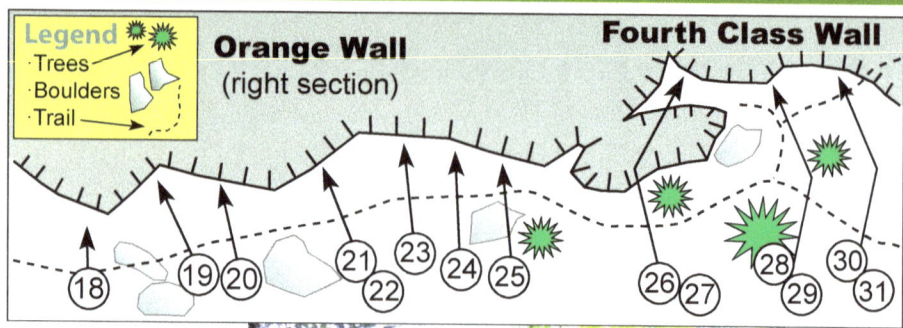

18. Midget Madness 5.10d

45' (13m) in length, Pro to 2" including TCU's

A tantalizing problem. Move up easy ground just left of an arête using a right-leaning seam and pull an awkward mantle into a crack corner, then continue to climb straight up to the top of the pillar to a belay.

19. Graduation 5.9

40' (12m) in length, Pro to 1½"

A left-leaning dihedral with one fixed pin. Step up on large holds then make a quick crux move to easier ground up left. A little dirty near the tree belay, but still a fun climb.

20. Orangotang 5.10b

A vertical direct option that starts between Graduation and Route Crafters.

21. Route Crafters 5.8 ★★

40' (12m) in length, 5 QD's

A very popular and well-bolted route that wanders up steep ground via many ledges, then up a short dihedral to a bolt anchor.

22. Chop the Monkey 5.8+

20' (6m) in length, 5 QD's

A pin protected corner up left from the 3rd bolt on Route Crafters.

23. _____ 5.10d (TR)

40' (12m) in length

TR up easy edges to a stance under a roof. Surmount a crux getting past the roof.

✦ MADRONE WALL   133

Madrone
Map: Orange 3

24. Cornick's Corner   5.9   ★★
40' (12m) in length, Pro to 1½"
An interesting route that ascends the obvious deep dihedral just to the right of a large roof. Bolt anchor.

25. Surfing with the Alien   5.10d R   ★★
40' (12m) in length, Pro to 1" RP's, TCU's recommended
This technically demanding route is well worth the blast. Begin up the seam (immediately right of the large dihedral) that angles right to a vertical crack. Continue up a steep face and crack, then bail out left to the dihedral or proceed up through another crux via a thin seam to a bolt anchor.

FOURTH CLASS WALL

26. Cut and Dried   5.10c
40' (12m) in length, Pro to 2"
On the left side of this tiny section of cliff is a large dihedral. Climb up past a hard move until it eases. The quality deteriorates as the vegetation increases near the top.

27. Severed Heads   5.12b   ★
30' (9m) in length, 3 QD's
Difficult arête climb.

28. Short But Sweet   5.10d   ★
40' (12m) in length, Pro to 1½"
An excellent climb. Proceed up the dihedral corner, moving past several small lips, step up

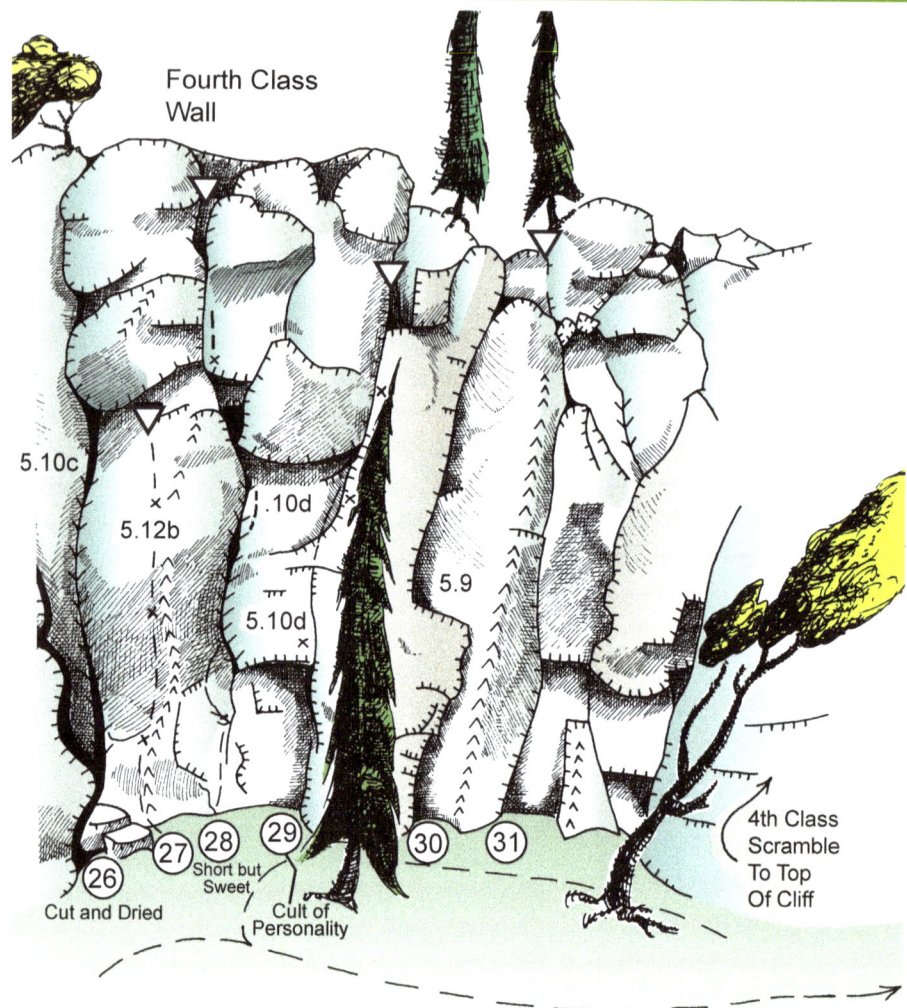

left (1 bolt) and continue up easier vertical ground to a unique belay.

29. Cult of Personality   5.10d   ★

40' (12m) in length, QD's

Step up and surmount a vicious move past a small bulge, then move up right and into a right-facing dirty corner. Rappel from belay anchor.

30. Wolf of the Steppes   5.9

35' (10m) in length, Pro unknown

31. Slippery Sage   5.8

30' (9m) in length, Pro unknown

MAIN WALL - SCOTT FREE AREA

MADRONE WALL 135

32. **Save the Whales   5.10a**
30' (9m) in length, Pro to 3"

33. **Hungry for Duress   5.10a**
30' (9m) in length, Pro to 3"
Located 5' left of Beam Me Up, Mr. Scott. A quick pump.

34. **Beam Me Up Mr. Scott   5.11c PG   ★ ★ ★**
65' (19m) in length, Pro to 1½" including TCU's
One of the 10 super classics at the Madrone Wall. A fantastic, bold route of superior quality. Proceed up an overhanging face via in cut edges (2 bolts) to a small stance. Desperately continue straight up the crack above (bolt) to a small ledge, and bolt belay anchor.

35. **Scott Free   5.12a /.12b   ★ ★ ★**
60' (18m) in length, 5 QD's and minor pro to 3"
Another excellent super classic. This one involves a fierce lunge! Start at the inside corner and move up right to a stance. Step up and left onto the central face and climb straight up. Lunge to a jug, then finish up an easy right facing corner to a bolt anchor on the right.

36. **Rising Desperation   5.10a   ★ ★**
60' (18m) in length, Pro to 2"
Interesting, fun, jagged crack system that ascends the vertical blocky section immediately right of Scott Free.

37. **Direct Finish   5.10a   (variation)**
15' (4m) in length, Pro to 2½"

38. **Dr. Opus Goes Power Lunging   5.11c   ★**
60' (18m) in length, Pro to 1½"
An impressive climb with much variety. Begin up a smooth, clean 3 bolt face until possible to step out left onto a short (5.9) arête mantle move. From the upper ledge, power lunge your way up a very thin seam to the summit.

39. **Spectrum   5.10b   ★**
20' (6m) in length, Pro to ¾" including TCU's
Excellent short problem. Start in a roof capped dihedral, then under cling out left and up the face to a fixed anchor on a ledge. A short 2 bolt 5.8 lead continues above Spectrum to another belay station.

40. **Aerial Display   5.11b   ★ ★**
100' (30m) in length, Pro to 1½"
One of the few exciting roof climbs at the Madrone Wall. Start to the right of the deep corner (Spectrum) and move up an odd but easy (5.8) groove to ledges. Step left and embark up easy ground to the huge slanting roof broken by an under cling crack. Cling desperately out (1 bolt) and up to the ramps above. Continue up left to a tree belay.

41. **Mixing It Up   5.10b**
100' (30m) in length, Pro to 2"

42. **Catharsis (5.9+ 1ˢᵗ pitch) 5.11d R   ★ ★ ★**
100' (30m) in length, Pro to 1½" TCU's, RP's required
Mentally challenging and a serious lead. Begin up a vertical outside corner (5.9) that has numerous small edges (2 bolts) until you reach a ledge and belay. Step right and proceed onto desperate ground above, then angle up a difficult left seam (bolt) exiting to the top.

43. **True Catharsis   5.11c PG**
25' (7m) in length, Pro to 1½" TCU's, RP's required
Where Catharsis takes a left on the second pitch, this route goes straight up the crack

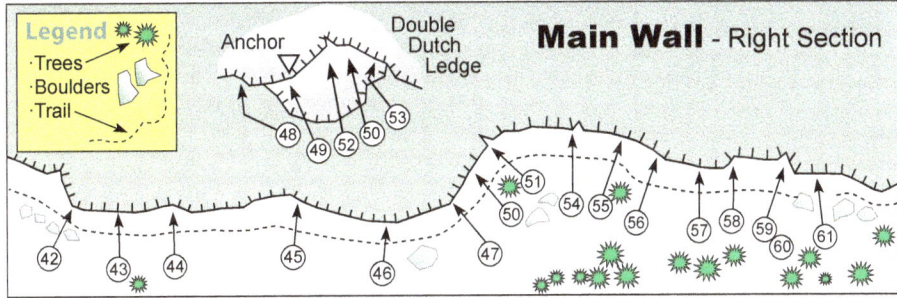

system above. The rating is unconfirmed.

44. Superstrings 5.10c ★
30' (9m) in length, 3 QD's and optional pro to 1"
A frequently climbed shallow dihedral that ends on good ledges.

45. Lost in the Delta Neighborhood 5.10a
100' (30m) in length, Pro to 2"
Ascend a vertical corner crack system until you must pull over a semi-detached set of blocks split with a crack. Wander up another dihedral and vertical ground to the summit.

46. Sultans of Swing 5.9
30' (9m) in length, 3 QD's and minor pro to 1½""

47. Double Dutch Left 5.7 ★★
25' (7m) in length, QD's and pro to 1"
Popular, easy dihedral with numerous ledges.

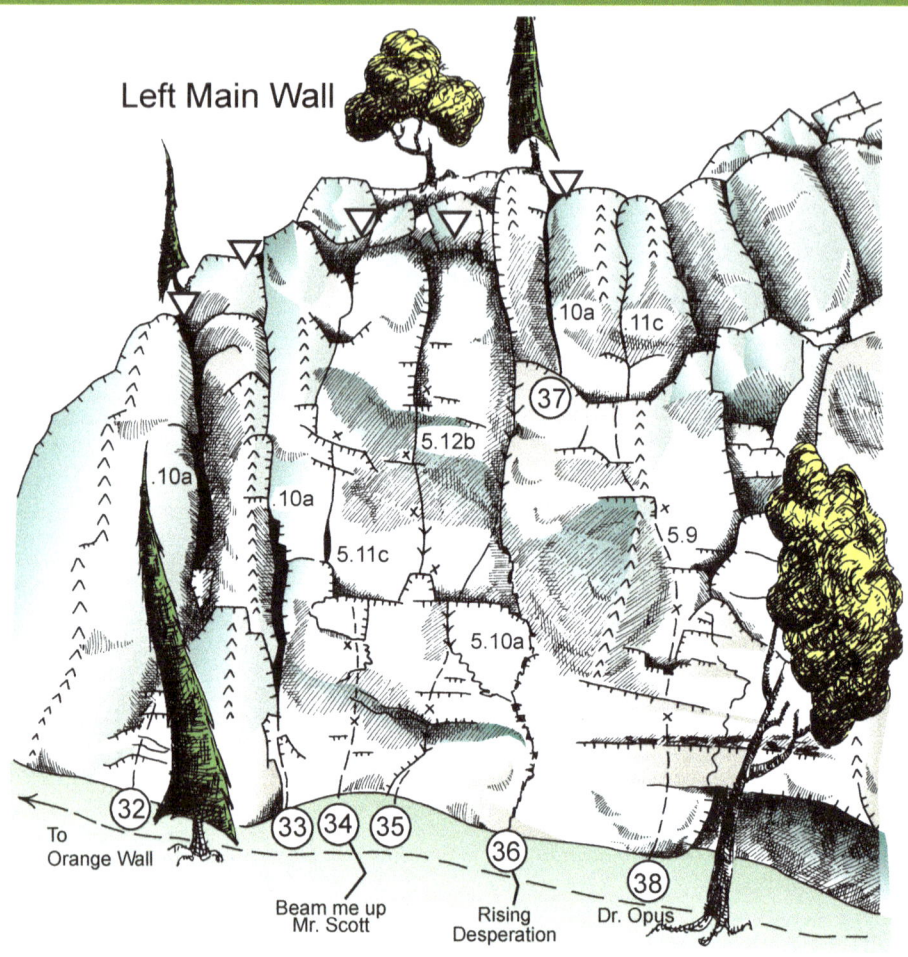

48. Scotty Hits the Warp Drive   5.10c
100' (30m) in length, Pro to 1½"
Start at the Double Dutch belay ledge, step left and ascend a short dihedral to another ledge, then up a slightly overhung crack to the top.

49. Subway to Venus   5.12a   ★★
18' (5m) in length, 3 QD's
Just above the Double Dutch belay ledge is a unique but short arête problem. Bolt anchor.

50. Trauma Center   5.11b   ★★★
100' (30m) in length, Pro to 1½"
This route has an excellent second pitch. The first pitch (5.11a) climbs up a face (2 bolts) between the two Double Dutch routes. From the belay ledge, step right and finish up an orange dihedral (1 bolt) leading to (5.11b) the top. The second pitch is stellar!

51. Double Dutch Right   5.6   ★
20' (6m) in length, Pro to 4"
The obvious large offwidth corner.

✦ **MADRONE WALL** 139

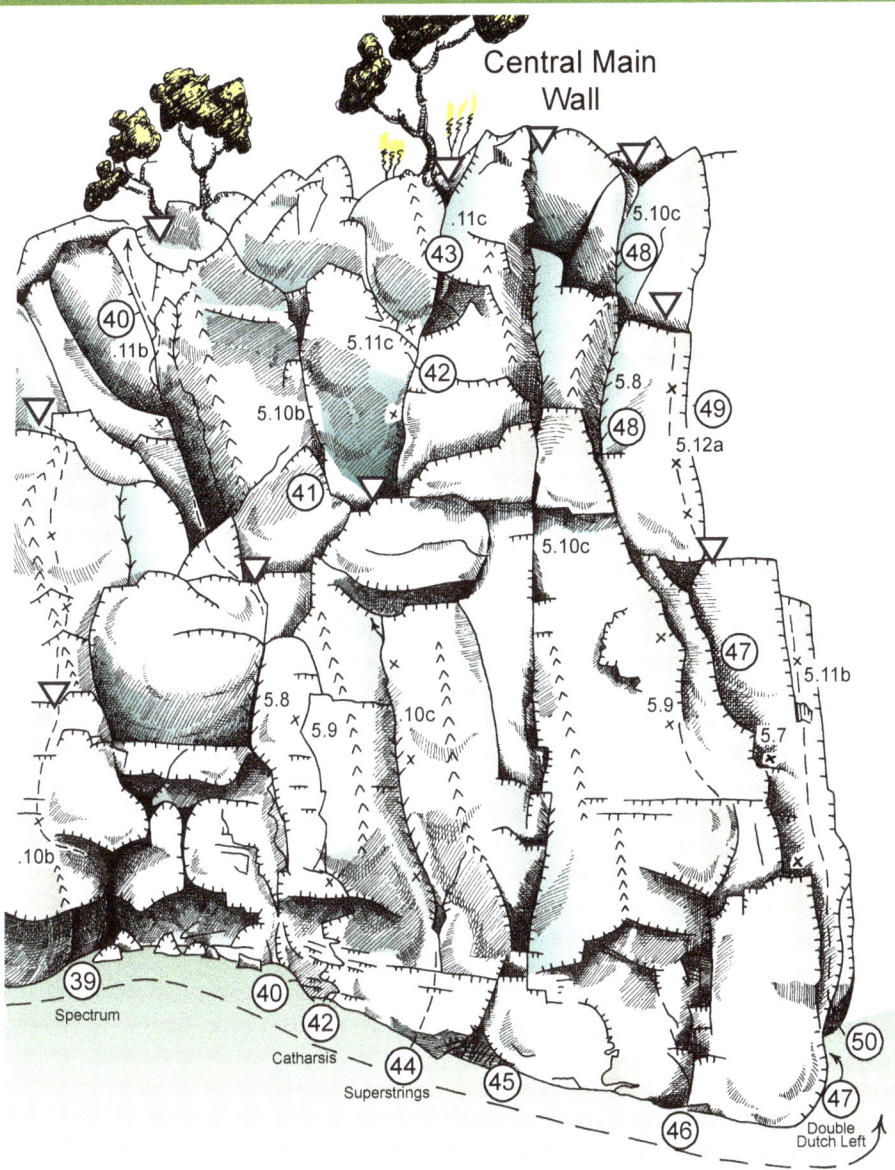

52. **Primary Gobbler   5.10c**
    20' (6m) in length, Pro to 6"
    The second half of this large offwidth.
53. **Never Mind   5.12a**
    25' (7m) in length, Pro is QD's
    This line ascends up a short arête face to the right of the last portion of Trauma Center.
54. **Whatever Blows Your Skirt Up   5.10b PG**
    65' (19m) in length, Pro to 1½"
    Ascends up easy rock left of Pillow Talk to a smooth face (1 bolt), then up a shallow

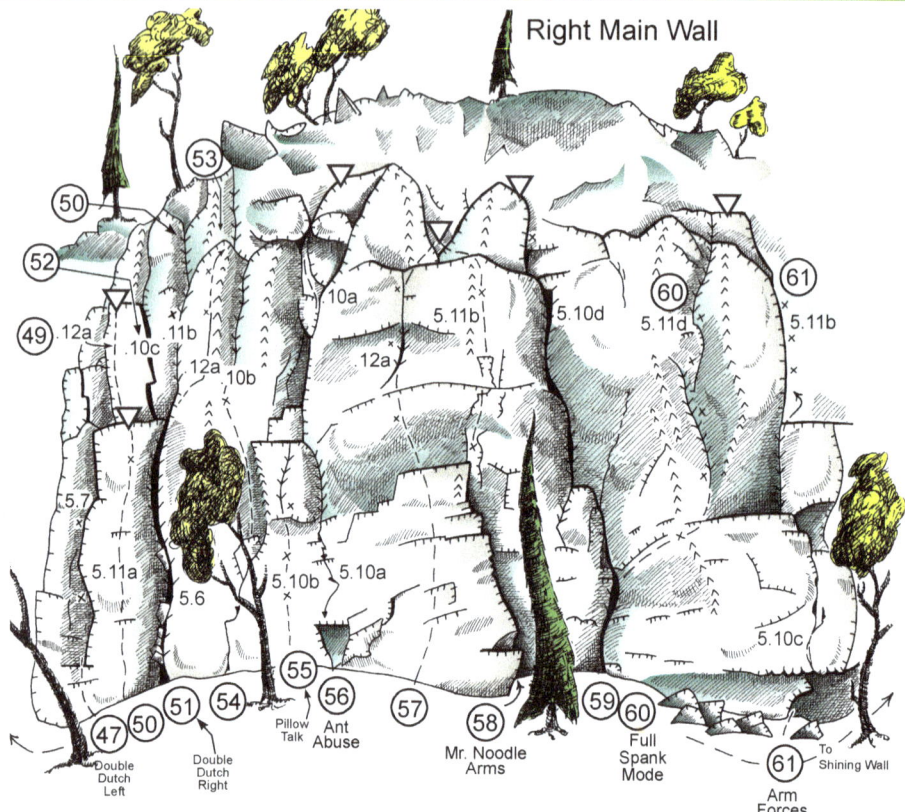

dihedral capped by a small bulge.

55. Pillow Talk 5.10b (variation) ★★
20' (6m) in length, 3 QD's and pro to 1½"

A popular trade route, though it is much more interesting when combined with Ant Abuse.

56. Ant Abuse 5.10a PG ★★★
60' (18m) in length, Pro to 1½" Cams recommended

This fun, clean route begins up the thin cracks immediately right of Pillow Talk. Pull up to the ledge, then move up a large open dihedral and step left to crank over an overhang (crux). Bolt belay.

57. Time To Kill 5.12a ★★
50' (15m) in length, QD's

An enticing and quality face climb with a short but unusually difficult crux at a minor overhang. Rap from belay anchor.

58. Mr. Noodle Arm (Goes Limp) 5.11b PG ★★★
50' (15m) in length, Mostly QD's, minor pro to 1" (TCU's or small nuts)

A route of stellar proportion. A very quality route and a must for everyone. Begin near a tall, thin fir tree. Climb a vertical broken arête (crux) to a stance, then move up left to a bolt anchor.

MADRONE WALL

59. Sisters of the Road   5.10d   ★★
60' (18m) in length, Pro to 1½"
Highly recommended. Move up easy ground in a dihedral. The climb increases in difficulty with height until you encounter a deceiving crux in a pea-pod flare. From a small stance, pull through a mantle (piton) and finish up easy ground to a bolt anchor.

60. Full Spank Mode   5.11d   ★★★
65' (19m) in length, 5 QD's and minor pro to ½"
One of the ten super classics. Start as for Sisters of the Road, but step right, lean out around on jug holds to a stance. Then embark up the difficult and slightly overhung face above. Eases to several ledges and a bolt belay. A variation (**Full Wank Mode** 5.12a) exists at the 4th bolt that powers up right (1 bolt) onto rounded feature to finish at same belay.

61. Arm Forces   5.11b   ★★★
65' (19m) in length, Pro to 1" including TCU's
A superior climb and one of the ten famous classics. This bold and demanding route begins up a thin (5.10d) vertical seam to a large ledge. Boldly march onto the sustained, overhung, rounded dihedral (bolts) leading to several ledges and a bolt belay.

SHINING WALL SECTION
One of the best places to be during the winter months is climbing here at the Shining Wall in a T-shirt.

62. Cold Hand of Technology   5.10c
70' (21m) in length, Pro to 1½"
Unique. Start at the large halfway ledge on Arm Forces. Step up right and ascend a dihedral until you can launch into a left leaning crack that turns a corner. Transverse left to the Arm Forces belay.

63. Red Scare   5.10c
25' (7m) in length, Pro to ¾"
Step off a large boulder and ascend a thin seam (3-bolts) to the large ledge. Finish by climbing up one of several route choices above the ledge. Thin pro [RP's/nuts] for trad leading initial section (the original method).

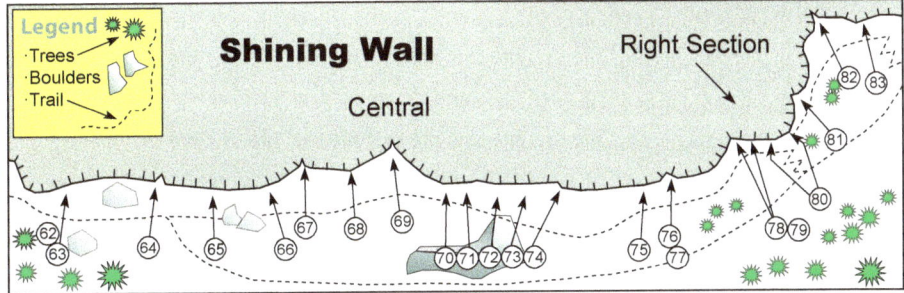

64. Domino Effect 5.9 R
   25' (7m) in length, Pro to 1"

65. Dirty Dancing 5.9 R
   80' (24m) in length, Pro to 2½"
   Start at an overhang. Climb a corner up to the halfway ledges and step right to ascend a dirty meandering (5.7) corner system up a near vertical cliff. Bolt anchor at top.

66. Firing Line 5.11b
   80' (24m) in length, QD's and pro to 1"
   An interesting bullet-scarred face. Pull through a flared overhung slot, move up a smooth

◆ MADRONE WALL 143

face, over a short vertical crux to a stance, then go up a series of good edges to power through an overhang with jugs and finger crack. The midway belay is available if only doing lower part.

67. Lord of the Rings 5.9
25' (7m) in length, Pro to 3" Cams suggested
A short flare problem that angles up to join Dancing in the Lion's Jaw at the bolt anchor on a ledge.

68. The Gift of Time 5.11b (variation)
15' (4m) in length, 2 QD's and minor pro to 1"

69. Dancing in the Lion's Jaw 5.11c PG
80' (24m) in length, Pro to 1 1/2" including TCU's

A bold lead for the serious climber. Start up a central dihedral on the Shining Wall (5.10a) to a ledge and bolt belay. Commence up the prominent dihedral through two significant crux (5.11c) roofs. Pull wildly over the last bulge to the belay.

70. Paleontologist 5.10b ★★
60' (18m) in length, Pro to 2"

A popular climb, and rightly so. Start by stepping up onto a large rock platform. Move up left over a bulge (2 bolts) to a ledge and bolt anchor. Continue up left via a face then a crack to a large ledge with a bolt anchor on the right and above Rainman.

71. Extinction 5.10d PG
60' (18m) in length, Pro is QD's

This variation starts on Paleontologist using the first two bolts to the small ledge stance, then branches over left, and up to the roof, then moves right to the anchor ledge. Runout between the bolts and a risky fall.

72. Rainman 5.11b ★★
25' (7m) in length, Pro to 1"

Outrageous, gripping climb. From the first belay on Paleontologist, step up right and climb a steep face to an easy vertical crack. Bolt anchor.

73. Playing with Fire 5.11b ★
60' (18m) in length, Pro to 1"

Good route. From the large platform, move up a deep dihedral (1 bolt) to a ledge. Continue up a fun curving finger crack system (1 piton) ending at an upper ledge. Step right and belay at anchor above the Shining Wall route. It is a 5.10a if topping out above here.

74. Shining Wall 5.11d ★★★
60' (18m) in length, 9 QD's

A super classic. Climbs the obvious bolted orange face. A physically difficult route using many sloping small edges that gets thinner near the exit move.

75. Cloudwalker 5.11c ★
60' (18m) in length, Pro to 1" TCU's recom-

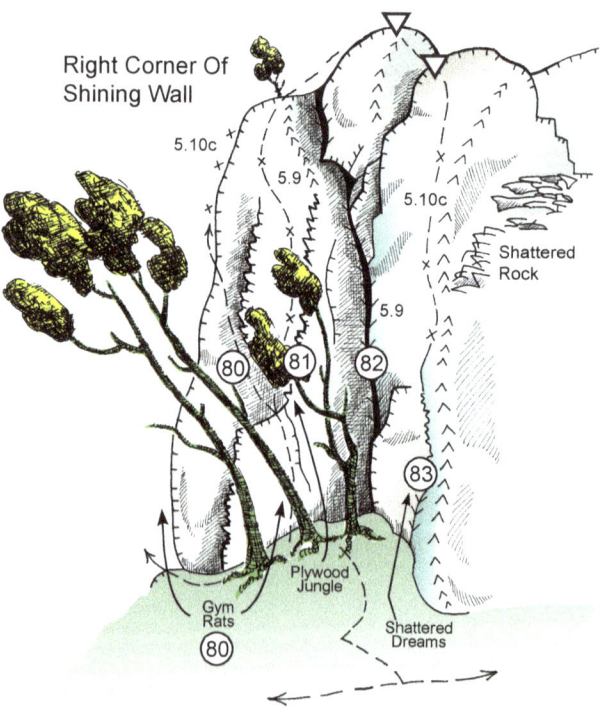
Right Corner Of Shining Wall

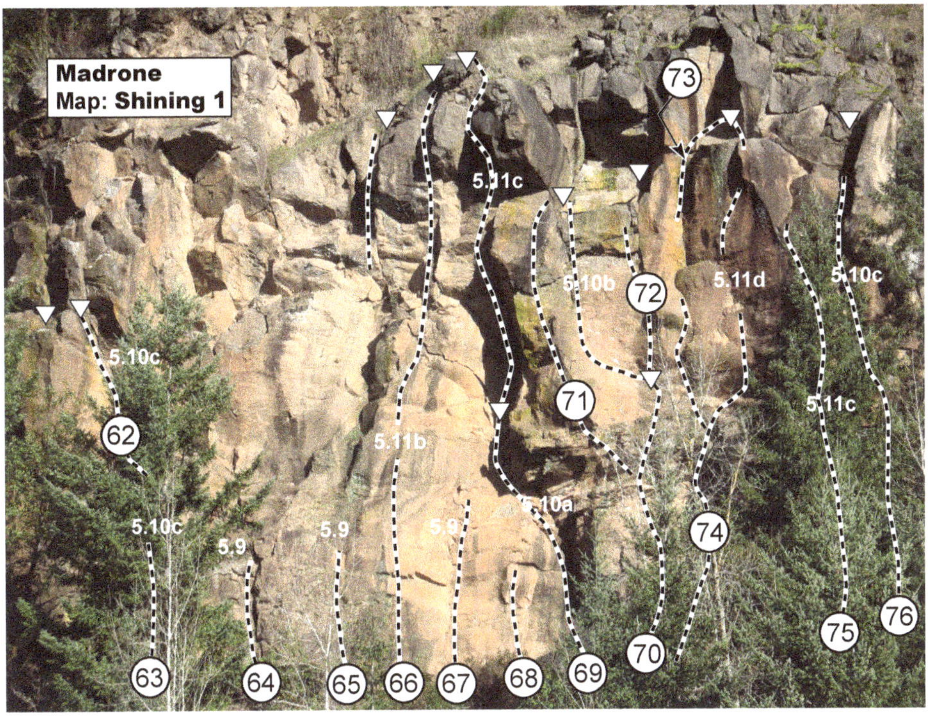

Madrone
Map: Shining 1
73
5.11c
5.10b
72
5.11d
5.10c
5.10c
62
5.11b
71
5.11c
5.10a
74
5.10c
5.9
5.9
5.9
63
64
65
66
67
68
69
70
75
76

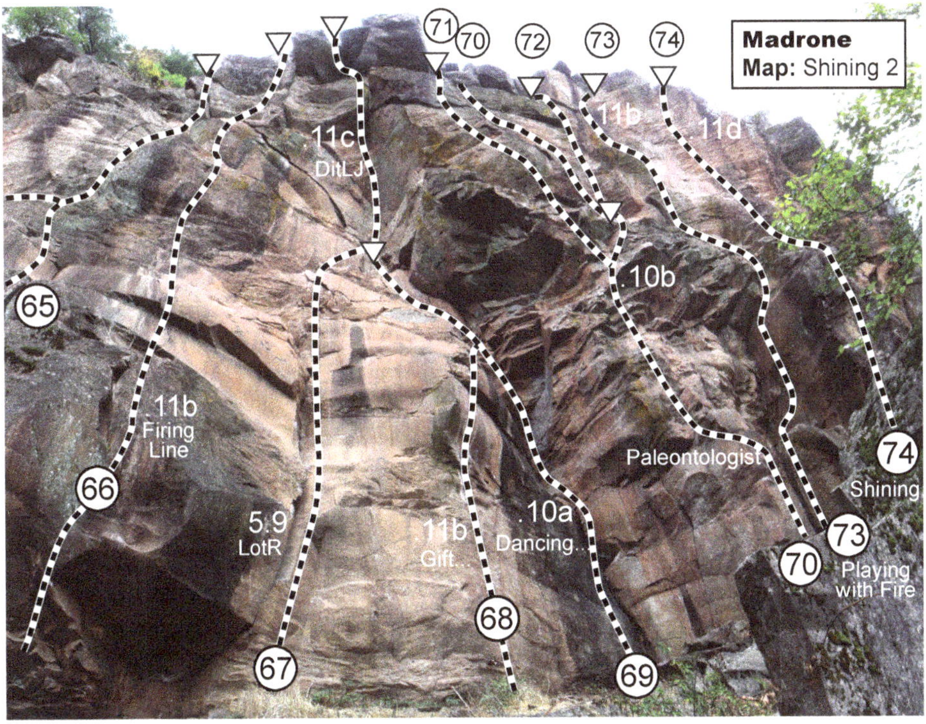

71
70
72
73
74
Madrone
Map: Shining 2
11b
11d
11c
DitLJ
.10b
65
.11b
Firing
Line
Paleontologist
74
Shining
66
5.9
LotR
11b
Gift
.10a
Dancing...
73
70
Playing
with Fire
68
67
69

mended
The first 15' is the crux. Start near a group of madrone trees on the right side of the wall. Surmount a difficult start, step up left to a steep but reasonable crack with one hard move (5.10b) at a bulge. Struggle over this to an easy dihedral and a bolt belay.

76. Banana Belt   5.10c R
60' (18m) in length, Pro to 1½" Needs bolts
An inconspicuous prow that would make a fine climb were it bolted. Climb an easy offwidth to a ledge, then up a vertical prow broken with numerous edges. Belay at Cloudwalker anchor.

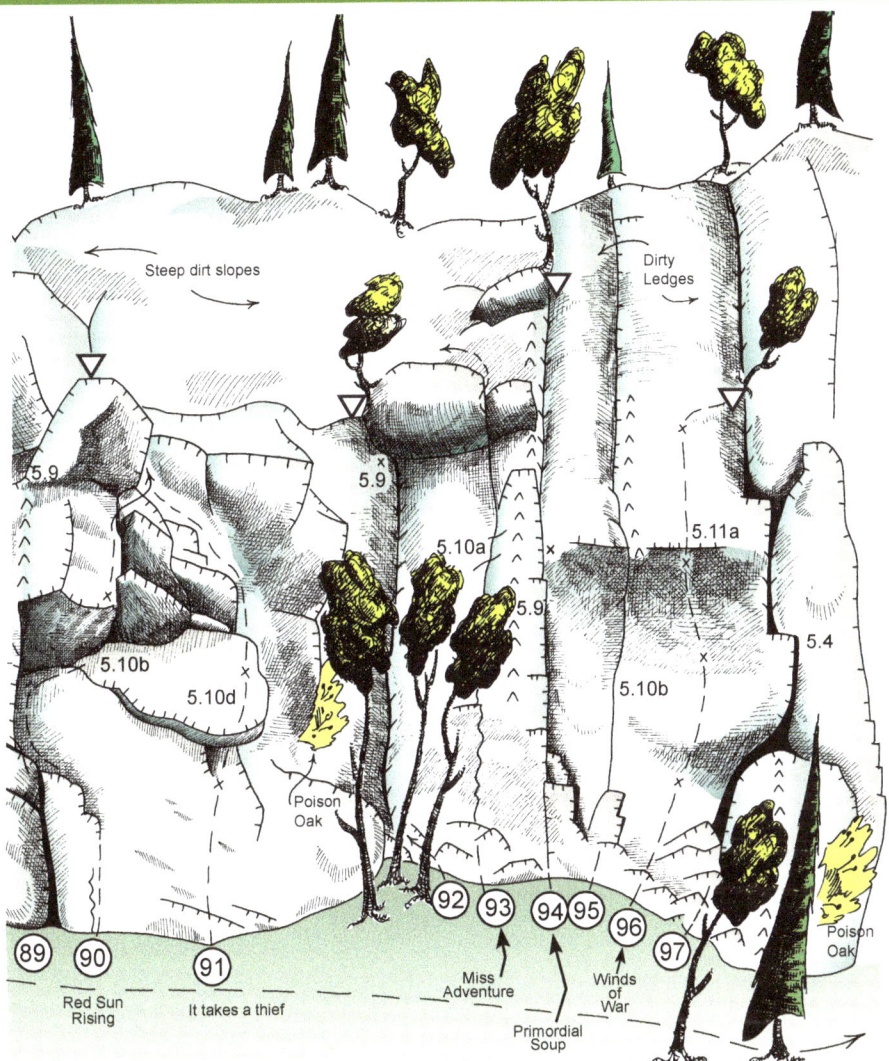

77. Fits and Starts   5.10a
30' (9m) in length, Pro to 1 ½"

78. Beginner's Luck   5.5
60' (18m) in length, Pro to 1½"
You can't miss it. Obvious wide chimney corner behind several madrone trees.

79. Yeoman's Work   5.10+
45' (13m) in length, Pro to 2"
Start up Beginners Route, then climb a hand crack behind a flake (1 bolt) to a cruxy face move finish.

80. Gym Rats From Hell   5.10c PG   ★★
40' (12m) in length, Pro to 2"
A unique climb. A nice top-rope area because of its easy access from one anchor. This climb has two starts. The left start is a steep crack (PG), while the right is an easy ap-

proach via shattered flakes. From a halfway stance crank up a smooth face (bolts) and mantle using numerous sloping edges.

81. Plywood Jungle   5.9 ★★

40' (12m) in length, 3 QD's
Fun lead. Do it!

82. Dihedral of Despair 5.9 (TR)

40' (12m) in length
The large yet somewhat loose dihedral. Top-rope only!

83. Shattered Dreams 5.10c

40' (12m) in length, Pro to 1"
A bit dusty, but otherwise a fun route. Start just to the right of Dihedral of Despair and ascend a short, jagged finger crack to a smooth face. A few tricky moves (bolts) and then traverse left to the bolt anchor.

HARDSCRABBLE WALL

84. Sacrifice   5.10a

40' (12m) in length, Pro to 1"

85. Inner Vision   5.11a

40' (12m) in length, Pro to 1" including TCU's
A bolted overhang left of Mind Games.

86. Mind Games   5.11b   ★★★

40' (12m) in length, Pro to 1" including TCU's
One of the ten classics and a fun roof problem at that. Step up an easy slab, then ape your way out to the overhang (2 bolts) and straight up to easier ground. A final 5.8 move brings you to a bolt belay.

87. Chicken   5.7 left (5.9 going right)

25' (7m) in length, Pro to 1" including TCU's
A minor easy variation to get around Mind Games. The left original route is 5.7. The bolted variation is 5.9.

Hardscrabble Left
Map: It Takes A Thief

◆ MADRONE WALL   149

88. **Gym Droid** 5.9
    25' (7m) in length, Pro to 1"
89. **Life As We Know It** 5.8
    30' (9m) in length, Pro to 1"
    Thirty feet to the right of Mind Games is a beautiful red-orange face broken by an overhang halfway up. The left variation is the easiest.
90. **Red Sun Rising** 5.10b PG ★ ★ ★
    30' (9m) in length, Pro to 1½"
    A great climb and very popular. Begin up an unprotected seam immediately right of the offwidth. At the roof, under cling out and surmount the overhang (1 bolt) via large jugs. Continue up and left to a bolt belay.
91. **It Takes a Thief** 5.10d PG ★ ★
    30' (9m) in length, QD's and pro to 1"
    A tantalizing route. Ascend the steep red face (bolts) past a hard move, then angle up and left to the anchor.
92. **American Girl** 5.9
    30' (9m) in length, Pro to 1"
93. **Miss Adventure** 5.10a
    35' (10m) in length, Pro to 1½"
    An interesting thin finger crack immediately right of the dihedral and behind several madrone trees.

Madrone
Map: Hardscrabble 2

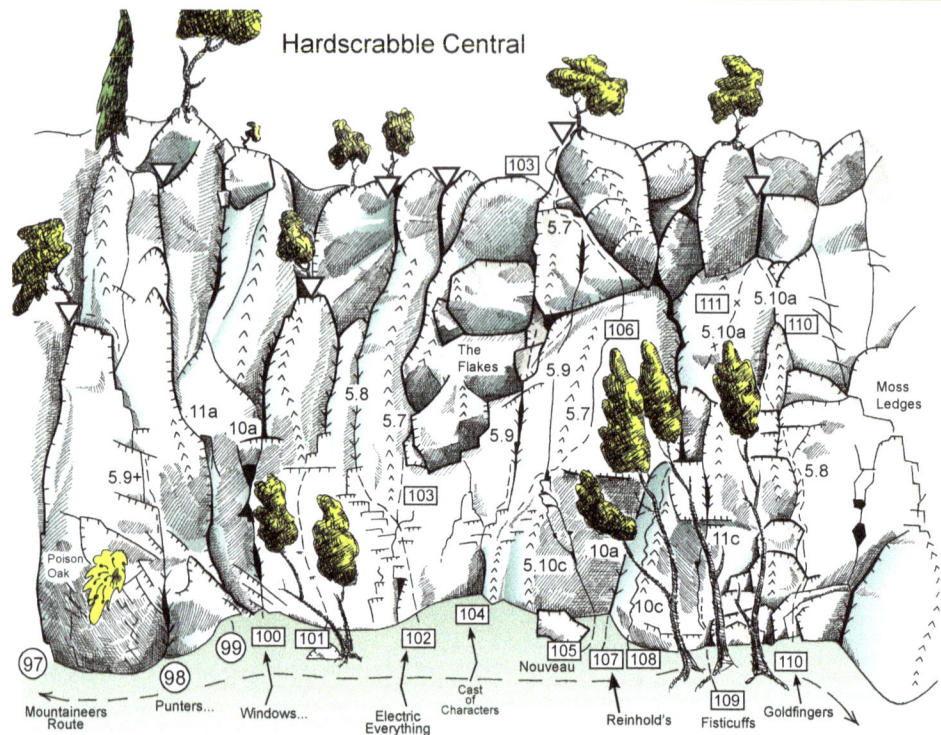

Hardscrabble Central

94. Primordial Soup 5.9
40' (12m) in length, Pro to 1"
A nice climb that is actually better than it appears to be.

95. Crystal Hunters 5.10b
40' (12m) in length, Pro to 1"

96. Winds of War 5.10d ★★
30' (9m) in length, 4 QD's
Quality face climb. Begin up just left of the Mountaineer's Route. Ascend a steep face and pull through a thin crux, then step right to a tree belay. The cracks on both sides detract slightly from the aesthetics of the route.

97. Mountaineer's Route 5.4
30' (9m) in length, Pro unknown

98. Punters in Paradise 5.9+
50' (15m) in length, Pro to 2"
Proceed up the slightly overhung buttress via a crack just to the right of a poison oak bush. Angle up left and finish up an easy hand crack to a large fir tree near the summit.

99. Red Fox 5.11a PG
50' (15m) in length, Pro to 1½"
An interesting climb with a nasty crux. Ascend a beautiful right-facing dihedral (has poison oak) and exit up left (crux) to easy slabs. Continue up a hand crack to the top.

100. Windows of Your Mind 5.10a ★★
40' (12m) in length, Pro to 1½" optional pro to 3"
This great climb starts up a vertical crack broken with several large triangular "win-

dows." Pull through a thin crux and finish up an easy offwidth. Bolt belay.

101. PC 5.11b (TR)
40' (12m) in length

102. Screensaver 5.6
40' (12m) in length, Pro to 2 ½"

103. Electric Everything 5.7 ★
40' (12m) in length, Pro to 2½"
Climbs up around the left side of the Guillotine Flakes topping out via an offwidth.

104. Cast of Characters 5.9
20' (6m) in length, Pro to 1"
Start in a minor corner below Guillotine Flakes to a crux 5.9 move as you get near the flakes. Then continue up steep ground to where the flakes overhang, and angle over right to join Nouveau Riche for the last steep but easy bulge section that leads to an easier slab just under a left-sloping roof. Move around a block then up to a tree belay.

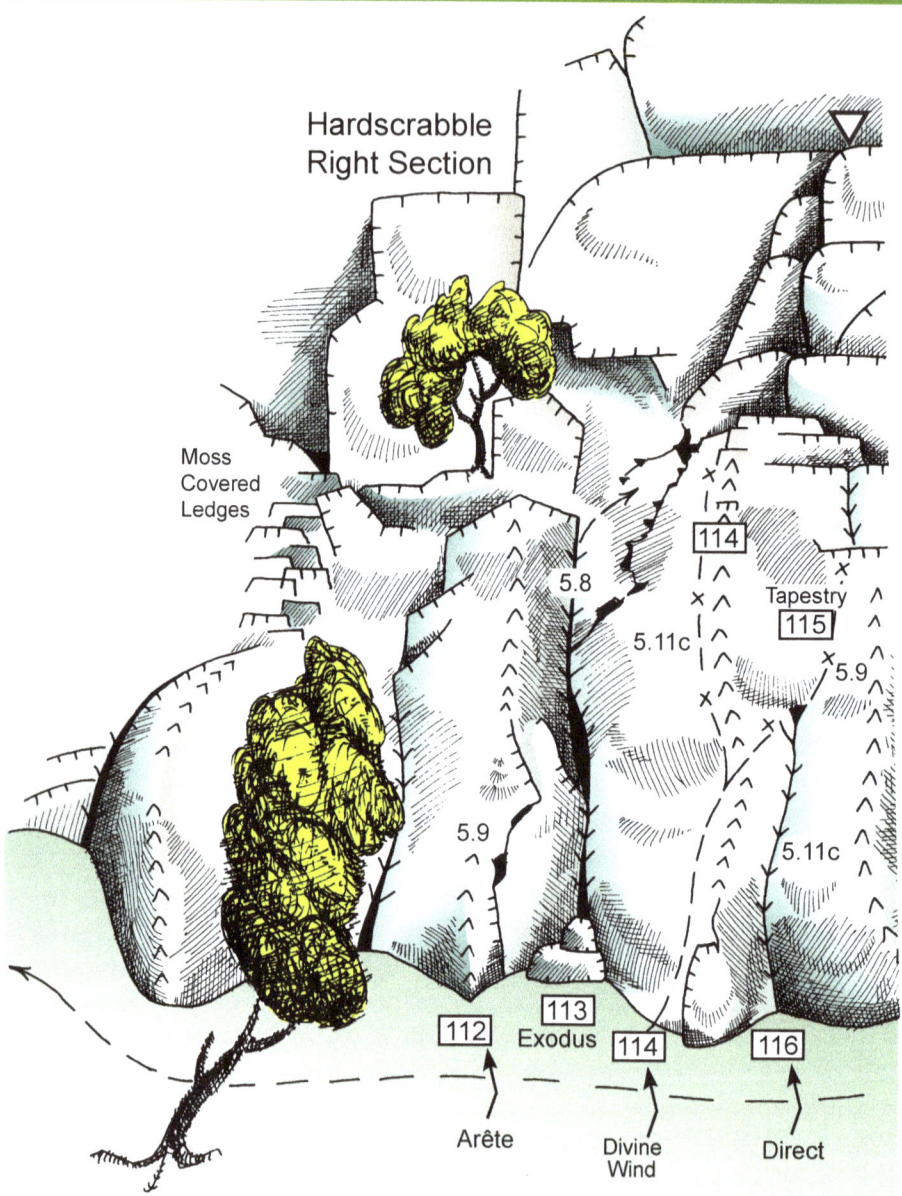

105. Nouveau Riche (New Wealth)   5.10c   ★★★
70' (21m) in length, Pro to 1½"   TCU's suggested
A super classic and well worth it. Superb, fun climbing. Begin at a large boulder near the head of the approach trail. Dance up a steep left-leaning crack (5.10c) to a stance, then up a 5.9 crack splitting a smooth face. Step right, surmount an easy bulge. Wander up easy slabs just under a left-sloping roof, and move around a block then up to a tree belay.

◆ MADRONE WALL   153

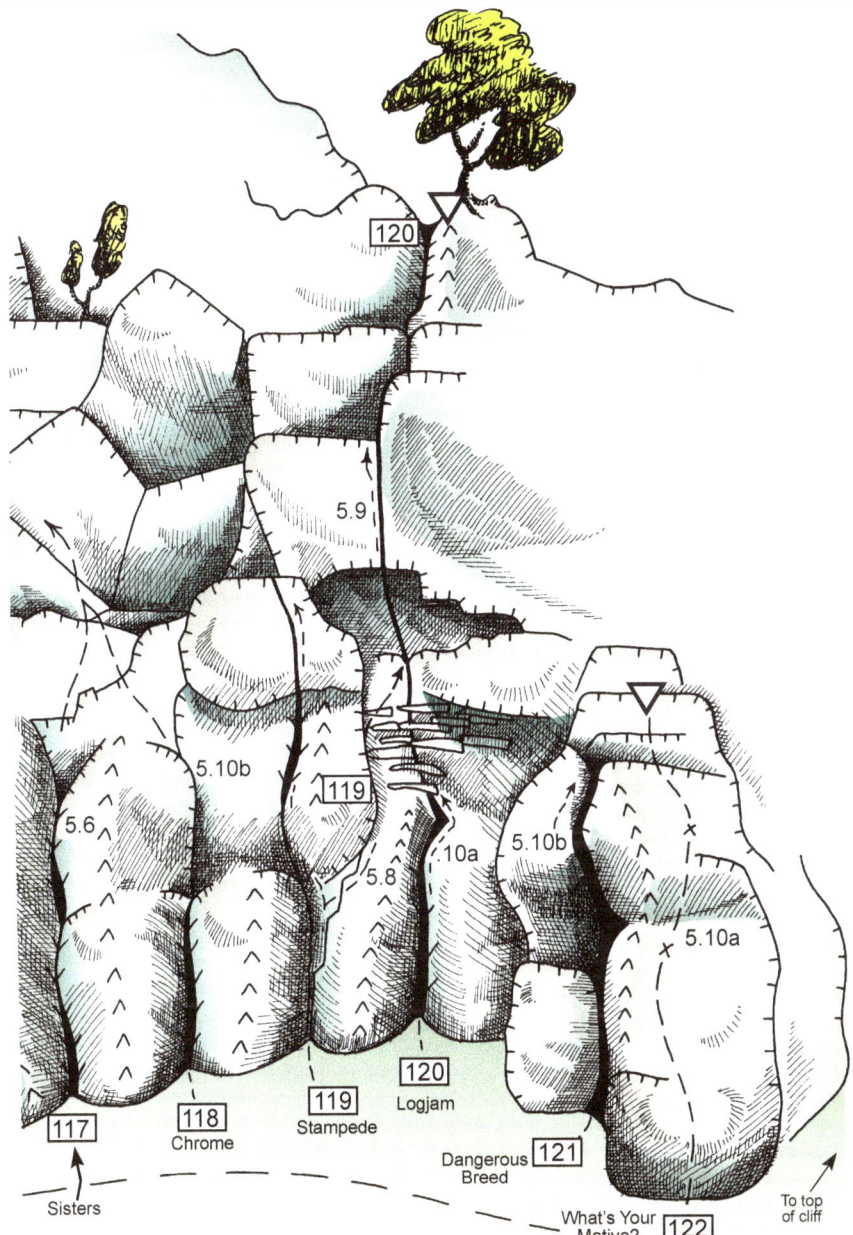

106. **Stamina 5.7 R (variation)**
20' (6m) in length, Pro to 3" Cams recommended
Starts same as for Cast of Characters, but angles across Nouveau Riche up rightward following a minor crack. A bit runout for a lead, and should have a fixed bolt.

107. **Reinhold's Dihedral 5.10a**
30' (9m) in length, Pro to 1½"
A short right leaning dihedral, followed by several ledges leading to a bolt belay.

108. **Eye of the Tiger 5.10c PG** ★

    15' (4m) in length, Pro to ¾"

    The dull arête just to the right of 'Reinhold's.' A thin seam protects the moves.

109. **Fisticuffs 5.11c** ★

    20' (6m) in length

    A short but physically demanding top-rope problem that ascends a smooth overhang split by a flared crux move.

110. **Goldfingers 5.10a** ★★★

    60' (18m) in length, Pro to 1½" TCU's recommended

    A fabulous and popular route. A must for all. Begin up an odd corner near four madrone trees. Move past a thinly protected seam (5.7) to a series of ledges. Proceed up a clean flared crack until able to step left to an offwidth. Pull up to a ledge and bolt belay.

111. **Girl Crazy 5.10a**

    15' (4m) in length, 2 QD's and minor pro to 1"

    An interesting variation that joins Reinhold's Dihedral with the Goldfingers offwidth section.

HARDSCRABBLE - SOUTH END

112. **The Arete 5.9 [TR]**

    25' (7m) in length

113. **Exodus 5.8** ★

    40' (12m) in length, Pro to 1½"

    A deep dihedral with a unique large jagged crack on the right face. Climb the dihedral until possible to exit up right to easy ledges. Step up to a bolt belay above Divine Wind.

114. Divine Wind 5.11c ★★★

40' (12m) in length, QD's and minor pro to ¾"

One of the ten super classics. Begin on the left side of a minor outside corner. Move up to and ascend the bolted smooth arête, past a crux move to easier ledges. A very popular route. Bolt anchor.

115. Tapestry 5.9 ★

40' (12m) in length, QD's and minor pro to ¾"

Start up Divine Wind but step right and venture up a separate line of bolts passing a bulge to easy ledges. Bolt belay.

116. Direct Start to Divine Wind 5.11c

15' (4m) in length, Pro to ¾" TCU's and RP's

An odd but demanding problem. Originally led on-sight.

117. Sisters 5.6 ★★★

40' (12m) in length, Pro to 1"

A good quality climb for beginners. Ascend the obvious corner to the right of Tapestry.

118. Chrome 5.10b

40' (12m) in length, Pro to 1"

Starts as an offwidth but involves a slightly overhung thin crack crux move.

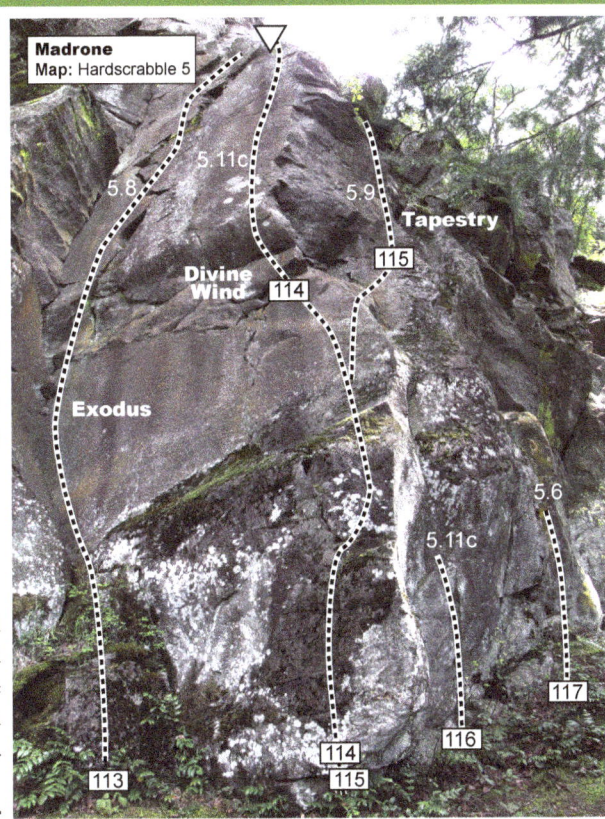

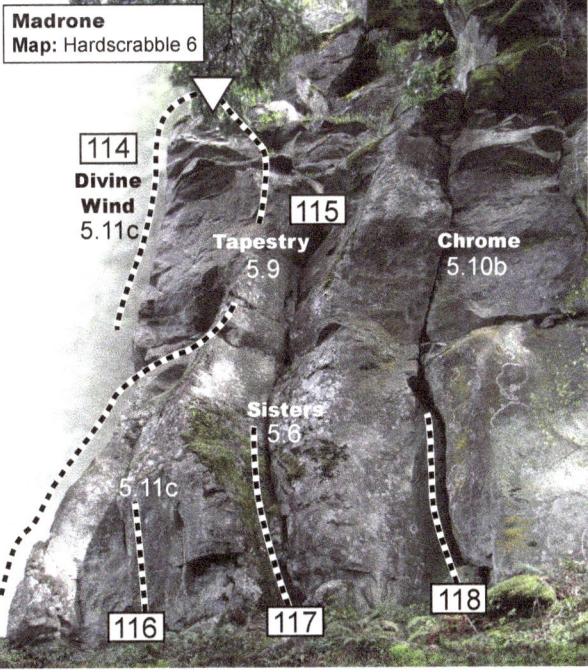

119. **Stampede 5.9**
    40' (12m) in length, Pro to 1½" Cams suggested
120. **Logjam 5.10a**
    40' (12m) in length, Pro to 3" Cams suggested
    This fun, wide crack is located immediately left of a dirty gully. Ascend this and angle up left to a stance below a steep upper section. Several quick jam moves lead to good ledges and a madrone tree belay.
121. **Dangerous Breed 5.10b** *
    30' (12m) in length, Pro to 4"
    The next two climbs are located on the last climbable buttress at the southern end of the Hardscrabble Wall. Dangerous Breed is the 'enjoyable' offwidth. Rap from belay.
122. **What's Your Motive? 5.10a** ★★
    30' (9m) in length, 2 QD's and optional pro to ½"
    The last climb at the bluff, but a great one at that! Climb up the outside face of the buttress to a belay anchor.

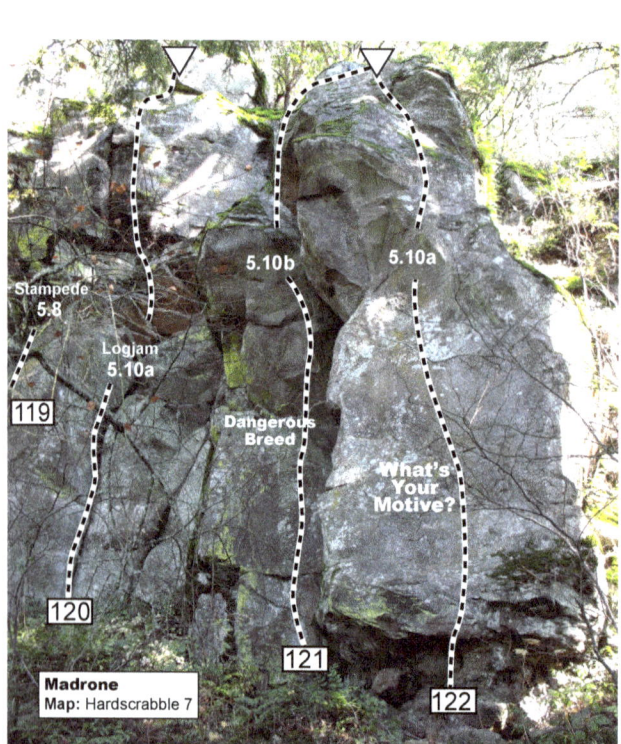

MADRONE WALL

2

COLUMBIA GORGE CRAGS

This lengthy chapter provides an in-depth research treatise concerning the natural value and historical aspect of rock climbing in the Columbia River Gorge.

The first primary section provides an inquiry about rock climbing at three common crags (Ozone Wall, Far Side Crag, and Beacon Rock).

The remainder of this extensive chapter is split into two sub-sections capturing all the other climbing options (the south side, and the north side of the Gorge).

The first sub-section details climbing sites on the south side of the Columbia River beginning near Rooster Rock State Park, and ending with the Apocalypse Needles formation east of The Dalles. The second sub-section details historical beta concerning places of interest starting near Cape Horn on the north side of the Gorge, then proceeds eastward to Horsethief Butte at Columbia Hills State Park.

Ozone Wall

It's not often that an outstanding climbing crag just outside a major metropolitan area sits undeveloped for very long. But Ozone, an 800-foot-long andesitic-basalt cliff full of classic cracks and heavenly jugs less than 20 miles from Portland, managed to remain relatively hidden — and essentially untouched — for nearly 25 years after it was originally stumbled upon and climbed back in 1984.

Today, thanks to the efforts of a handful of dedicated and hardworking climbers, Ozone has been transformed from an illegal roadside dump into not only a splendid mass of topnotch climbs, but a valuable recreational resource as well. The more than 75 routes that have been put up primarily since 2004 range in difficulty from 5.6 to 5.12c, with the majority falling somewhere between 5.8 and 5.10. There are single and multi-pitch climbs, pure trad routes that only take gear, fully-bolted sport climbs, and routes that employ both gear and bolts.

Hidden among the evergreens just north of the Columbia River in Washington, Ozone also affords sweeping and unique views of the Columbia River Gorge. And the cliff, which is now fully developed, provides an alternative venue for climbers during Beacon Rock's seasonal closure.

HISTORY AND DEVELOPMENT

Heading east on I-84 toward the Eagle Creek trailhead back in 1984, Jim Opdycke caught a glimpse of something across the Columbia River that intrigued him.

Contrasted against the darkened evergreens that blanket the steep walls of the Washington side of the Columbia River Gorge was a narrow band of gray rock. He saw it only briefly, but Opdycke, a veteran climber who by then had been climbing at Beacon Rock, Yosemite, and elsewhere for almost a decade, knew it was something worth seeing again.

Soon after this first sighting, Opdycke paid a visit to that narrow band of rock. He found it just a few miles east of Washougal despite the absence of a trail or any other sign that someone had been there before. Opdycke bushwhacked through the trees, dropped down a steep hillside, and found himself at the base of an imposing andesite-basalt cliff that looked out to the Columbia River through an evergreen thicket. The wall, about 800 feet long and 200 feet tall at its highest point, was overgrown with moss and trees and thick shrubs of poison oak. There were a couple dead deer and the scattered remnants of illegal trash dumping. But all that wasn't enough to hide the snaking cracks, the textured faces, the clean lines running up the face.

Opdycke and his friend Mike Jackson returned to the unknown cliff that same year and worked their way up a few of the more natural cracks on the face. Those first few

Misako on *The Humbling 5.12a*

routes are now known as the Opdycke Crack (5.9+) and Eight is Enough (5.8).

They also decided to name the wall Ozone because, like the invisible layer of stratosphere miles above the earth, so too was this Ozone invisible.

At the time, however, Opdycke and his friends were more into climbing and developing new routes at Beacon Rock than they were in taking on Ozone. So they focused their attention on the 850-foot monolith up the road and left Ozone for another day.

Over the ensuing years, Ozone sat relatively untouched and unknown, though a few local climbers like Dave Dick spent some time at the wall climbing and putting up a handful of routes. Then, around 2003, Opdycke clued several folks in on Ozone, including Bryan Smith, Kevin Evansen, Glen Hartman, and Mark Deffenbaugh. Though various parties paid various visits to the wall — eyeballing prospective routes among the tangle of trees,

Alison climbing May Day 5.10b

moss, loose rocks, and massive growths of poison oak — it would be another year before serious development began at Ozone.

In late December 2004, Kevin Rauch, having heard about Ozone from Deffenbaugh, ventured out to Ozone with Smith and a borrowed drill for a little reconnaissance. In a meticulously-kept climbing journal, Rauch mentions Ozone for the first time on Dec. 18, 2004: "Fixed 2 lines; installed 1 anchor bolt prior to darkness . . ." A new wave of development had begun at Ozone.

By very early 2005, full-on development of new routes, as well as work on cleaning up the

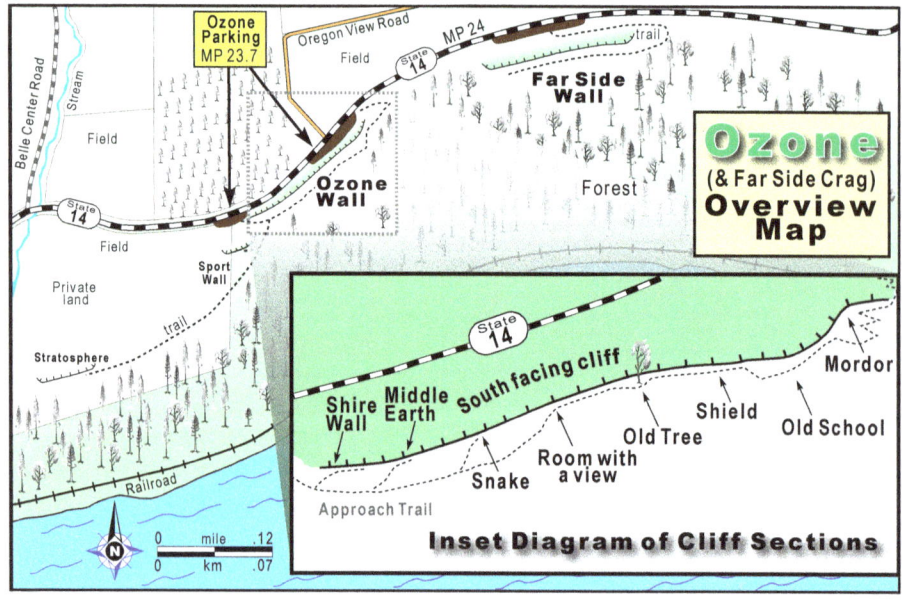

area and establishing a better trail system, had set in at the crag, driven primarily by climbers like Rauch, Jon Stewart, Kevin Evansen, Deffenbaugh, Smith, and Glen Hartman.

Though the intent of some of the original developers — many of whom had never done any route development before— was to put up all trad climbs, or at least to utilize natural protection wherever possible, and though the first few routes put up were done without the use of bolts, differing development styles and approaches emerged.

Some routes were put in from the ground up without any bolts; some were established by rappelling from above and installing bolts the entire length of the climb; some ended up being protected by a mix of gear and bolts. Whatever the style, all routes along the overgrown wall had to be painstakingly cleaned of moss, dirt, grass, trees, loose rocks and boulders, and poison oak.

Throughout this early development phase, Ozone remained unknown to all but the handful of tight-lipped climbers focused on cleaning up the wall and putting up routes. But, as can happen within the climbing community, grist began grinding through the rumor

Map #1: Shire Wall

Ozone Wall

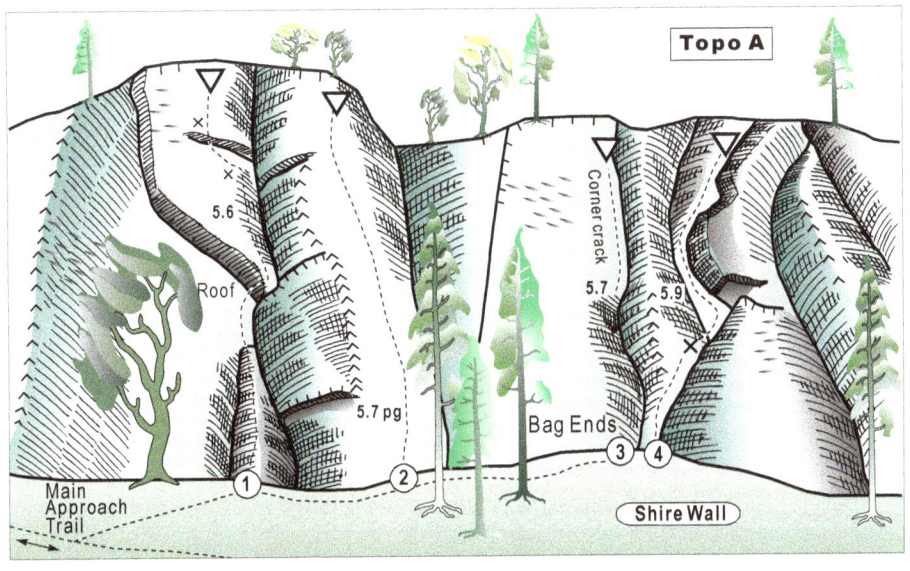

Topo A

mill, and within a year, more and more cars started to make their way to a random pullout just off Washington State Route 14. This led not only to more people climbing at Ozone, but to further development of the wall until the final few routes were established in an area on the east end of the crag known as Mordor in May 2008.

GEOLOGY

Ozone lies within the Grande Ronde Basalt, a formation of basaltic andesite within the Columbia River Basalt Group. The CRBG comprises immense outpourings of lava that erupted from vents in central and northeast Oregon during the Miocene period of 6 million to 17.5 million years ago. These eruptions created one of the largest flood basalt provinces in the world, with an outpouring of lava that would have been immense enough to construct a wall one mile wide and two miles high around the earth.

The ancestral Columbia River provided a natural conduit for these lavas as they made their way to the Pacific Ocean, and the river successively moved north as it cut new channels through the hardened lavas. The basalt cliffs of Ozone were likely exposed during the Missoula Floods, cataclysmic floods of the last Ice Age 13,000 to 15,000 years ago. The floods were the result of periodic ice dam failures of Glacial Lake Missoula in what is now northwestern Montana. Floodwaters racing through the Columbia River Gorge at speeds of up to 80 miles per hour carried away debris and steepened the walls of the Gorge, exposing the more resistant basalt cliffs and paving the way for modern-day climbing enjoyment.

OZONE BETA

Ratings: All the climbs at Ozone are rated based on the Yosemite Decimal System, e.g. (5.10a/b = 10-) (5.10b/c = 10) (5.10c/d = 10+). The crux of each climb is identified by its rating on the corresponding topo maps.

Gear: Fixed protection should always be considered suspect and when possible backed up with protection you place yourself. Many routes are mixed sport and traditional.

Do not assume that there is adequate protection available higher up. Make use of all available protection until you become familiar with the route. An extensive gear rack allows you to take advantage of all climbs listed below.

It should be noted that as of July 2008, the USDA Forest Service, Columbia River Gorge National Scenic Area, has proposed a recreation and management plan for the Cape Horn planning area in Skamania County, which covers the land where Ozone sits. The purpose of this planning effort is to identify and locate preferred recreational assets, such as hiking trails and scenic overlooks, on the contiguous federal land parcels near Cape Horn. Again, it is not clear how or if Ozone will be affected by this planning effort, but because the crag falls within the planning area's boundaries, it will be important to remain informed of this process.

For more information, visit www.fs.fed.us/r6/columbia/projects/ and look under "Current Projects" for "Cape Horn Recreation Management Plan."

Ownership: Ozone sits on public land owned by the federal government as part of the Columbia River Gorge National Scenic Area. People were climbing at Ozone before the establishment of the CRGNSA in 1986, though the land does fall within the boundaries of the scenic area, which is managed under the auspices of the Columbia River

Gorge Commission: In order to preserve and maintain unfettered access to Ozone, please respect and take care of the land and the crag.

VISUAL BIO

◆ OZONE WALL 163

These emblems represent virtually all of Ozone. The entire wall can be accessed by either the *Westside Trail* or the *Eastside Trail* in five minutes or less. The upper portion of many climbing routes are in the full sunshine, especially from about 70'-120' and just when you are getting pumped a few moves short of the belay anchor. The Mordor Wall, which is heavily shaded receives a very limited mid-afternoon sunlight, and it is so steep it can be climbed for 12-months of the year. The cold windy Gorge temperatures tend to dissuade most climbers from using this site during the heart of Winter. The site offers considerable sport route opportunities, but also a variety of partly bolted gear leads. Ozone offers some less-traveled quality crack climbs.

DIRECTIONS FROM PORTLAND

The Ozone crag is in southwest Washington, roughly 7½ miles east of the town of Washougal on State Route 14. From Interstate 205 in Portland or Vancouver, head east on SR 14 for approximately 18¼ miles to a small pullout on the south side of the highway, just about three-tenths of a mile east of Belle Center Road in between mile markers 23 and 24. (See note below about parking.) Hop on the rugged trail hidden in the trees and walk to the base of the crag in just a few minutes. There is also a second pullout a few hundred feet east of the first pullout on the south side of the road. The east end of the trail is accessible from this pullout as well.

Parking: As of this publication, only the two pullouts mentioned above are available for parking. As those areas are extremely limited in capacity, it is absolutely imperative that climbers carpool to the crag. And please, park at an angle, not parallel to the road.

The west side climbers path descends from the roadside down eastward to the base of the wall. The initial cliff section is short, but quickly lengthens as you continue to descend to the base near Masterpiece Theater.

The Ozone Wall introduction was written by Jon Bell.

SHIRE WALL

The Shire Wall (Map 1, Topo A) encompasses a selection of four short/moderate rock climbs at the first side trail as you descend the main trail.

1. **Bearded Lady 5.6** *Dry*
   40' (12m) in length, Pro to 2" and QD's
   Ascends a broken corner system that heads up left past two bolts to an anchor.

2. **Old Toby 5.7 PG** *Dry*
   40' (12m) in length, Pro to 2",

Map #2: Middle Earth

cams and wires

3. **Bag Ends 5.7** ★

   40' (12m) in length, Pro to 1", cams

   From the level belay platform ascend straight up to a left facing open corner by stemming or face climbing. Has a tough move to get to the anchor.

4. **Brandywine 5.9** ★

   40' (12m) in length, Pro to 3½"

   From the ground aim up right into a deep corner system past one bolt to a small roof (crux). Pull up right over the roof to a short slab that leads to the anchor.

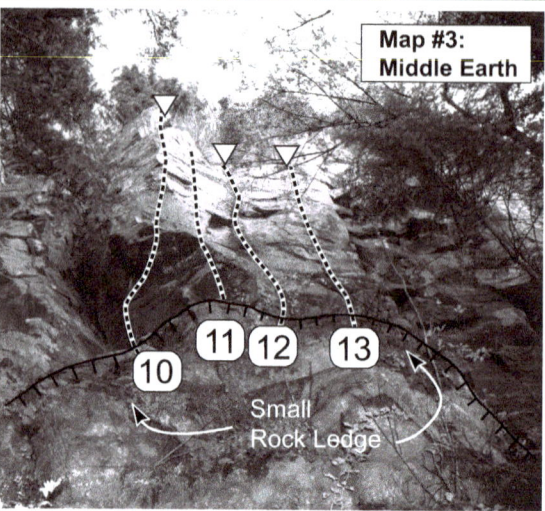

Map #3: Middle Earth

MIDDLE EARTH

Middle Earth (Map 2, Map 3 and Topo B): A short side trail angles up to this section onto the top of a small rock tower with a large flat ledge on it. These next six climbs are on the wall left and above the small rock tower.

5. **Rude Boy 5.8**

   80' (24m) in length, Pro to 4"

   Ascends moss covered ledges up left to a crack system. Follow it over a bulge (crux) to a wider crack and boulders leading to an anchor. Loose rock near the top of the climb.

6. **Why Must I Cry 5.10a** ★

   80' (24m) in length, Pro to 1" and QD's

   Ascend up the face, and aim left under a small fir tree in the wall, and up to a ledge. Continue up left to the Rude Boys anchor.

7. **Night Owl 5.6**

   80' (24m) in length, Pro to 5"

   Climbs the gully to the right of the previous route.

8. **Leisure Time 5.9**

   90' (27m) in length, Pro to 1"

   Ascends a shallow corner system past a small roof. Use slings to rap from a tree on the upper right near the top of the bluff.

9. **Variety 5.10**

   100' (30m) in length, Pro to 5"

   Long steep hands-to-offwidth crack corner system that takes lot of pro. Rap from same tree on Leisure Time.

Kevin Evansen on *Chain Mail*

10. **House of Pain   5.11a**
★ ★

50' (15m) in length, QD's
From the large belay ledge on top of the rock tower head up a corner, then right and over the roof (crux), then continue up an arête to an anchor.

11. **Grab 'n Go   5.10c**

50' (15m) in length, 5 QD's
Climb up and out a small roof (crux) and continue up a fairly sustained face above. Use House of Pain belay.

12. **Redhorn Gate   5.9** ★

50' (15m) in length, Pro to 4"
Ascend up the smooth face to the flake, then follow crack system up to the left (crux). Use larger gear in the upper part of the crack.

13. **Helm's Deep   5.9**
★ ★ ★

Map #4: Snake Crack

80' (24m) in length, Pro to 2" and QD's
From the very lip of the small tower step across the gap onto the face to the first bolt. Continue up the bolted route powering up incut holds. Gear protects a runout in between the 4th and 5th bolt.

SNAKE WALL

Snake Wall (Map 4 and Topo B): Just past a prominent rock tower another short trail heads up to the cliff. Two large roofs identify this section of wall. These climbs start below and right of the small rock tower.

14. **Before the Storm   5.9**

95' (28m) in length, Pro to 2" including small cams & wires
Ascends a steep corner crack immediately left of Snake Face route. Good rest stances with an optional early exit off right to attain the Snake Face anchor. A 60-meter rope is needed for the rappel from the cliff top anchor.

15. **Snake Face   5.9** ★ ★ ★

70' (21m) in length, Pro to 1" and QD's
Just to the east of the rock tower ascend a bolted route up the face. Small gear protects between the 2nd and 3rd bolt. A slight crux bulge in the upper crack system quickly eases to a gear crack. Angle up right to bolt anchor.
A top-rope problem (5.11+) exists by aiming up right through the roof after the last bolt.

TR only; detached blocks.

16. Snake Roof 5.10a ★★

70' (21m) in length, Pro to 2½" including cams and wires

This route climbs through the large double large roof. Ascend the deep corner crack system to the first large roof. Move left on small edges around the first roof, then up right to the second roof (bolt). Surmount this section and angle up easy steps left to the same anchor as the previous route.

The next 4 climbs can be accessed by a short 4th class scramble up to a large ledge immediately right of Snake Face. Reference Map 4 and Topo B for clarity.

17. Vicious 5.11a ★

70' (21m) in length, Pro to 3" and QD's

From a belay ledge ascend up left and follow the bolts on an arête. Pull a difficult boulder problem then use gear (small cams) to continue up left onto the Snake Roof route. Or angle up right into the Opdyke Crack route using large gear to finish on that line.

18. Opdycke Crack 5.9+

70' (21m) in length, Pro to 3"

Ascends a large crack corner system, traversing under a detached block, then up right in a wide corner system to an anchor.

19. Party at the Moon Tower 5.10a ★★

65' (19m) in length, QD's

Start up the previous route, then aim up right onto the arête. Follow this directly up to an anchor.

20. Eight is Enough 5.8 ★★★

65' (19m) in length, Pro to 2"

From a ledge aim up right, and stem past a sustained corner that gets steeper. A series of runout jugs lead to an anchor.

MASTERPIECE

Bennett on *Masterpiece Theater*

Masterpiece / Gold Wall (Map 5 and Topo B): The access trail lands at a wide stance immediately below this tall vertical section of the wall at the Masterpiece Theater route.

Map #6: Kung Fu

21. Chaos 5.8 ★★★

80' (24m) in length, Pro to 1" and cams

This partially bolted climb begins where the trail initially meets the main wall. Follow up the right facing corner, and pull up left under the roof and up to a stance. The climb continues by ascending up a steep arête to the anchor.

22. Siddartha 5.8

40' (12m) in length, Pro to 3" and long slings

Starts same as for Chaos up the right facing corner, past the roof, and then traverses up right along the obvious ledge to the broken crack system. Ascend up the nice left facing open book corner system. When the crack ends pull up right to the anchor.

23. Masterpiece Theater 5.11c ★★★

95' (28m) in length, QD's and a ¾" to 1" cam

This line is certainly one of the testpiece classics at Ozone! Ascend up an initial short slab clipping several bolts as the climb steepens into an overhang. The cam protects a critical moves between the 3rd and 4th bolt immediately above the crux. Continue to climb the long vertical sustained arête up to an anchor.

24. Beyond the Glory 5.11d ★★★

90' (27m) in length, QD's

Ascends a thin seam through an overhang using large underclings and thin edges to a no hands stance, then continue up a steep face on runout but good edges to join with the last bolt on Masterpiece Theater.

25. Screaming For Change 5.10c ★

90' (27m) in length, Pro to ¾" including cams

Ascend past a bolt to a chimney move that leads to a block stance. From the top of the block lean out left and then climb up left using face edges. Sustained climbing leads up a cliff section of mixed bolts and gear to an anchor.

Kung Fu (Map #6): A consistently steep non-

Tim Pitz leading *Carrots*

Map #7: Old Tree

descript section of cliff with several popular climbs.

26. Afternoon Delight   5.7 - 5.10   ★★

100' (30m) in length, Gear to 2", Small cams and optional 3½" cam

Start as for Kung Fu, but move up left into the obvious vertical crack in a shallow dihedral corner system. At approximately 80', exit left to the Sreaming For Change (5.7) belay anchor. Or...continue up one of three crack options to the top which involves climbing over a block and past a deep overhung section. Reach around to the left to surmount the gaping maw overhang (use the large cam here).

27. Kung Fu   5.9   ★★

80' (24m) in length, QD's, and 1" cams

Start up vertical terrain on positive holds. Clip the first bolt (avoid the crack system on the left) and aim up right onto a minor steep arête. The quality of the rock and the climb-

✧ OZONE WALL 169

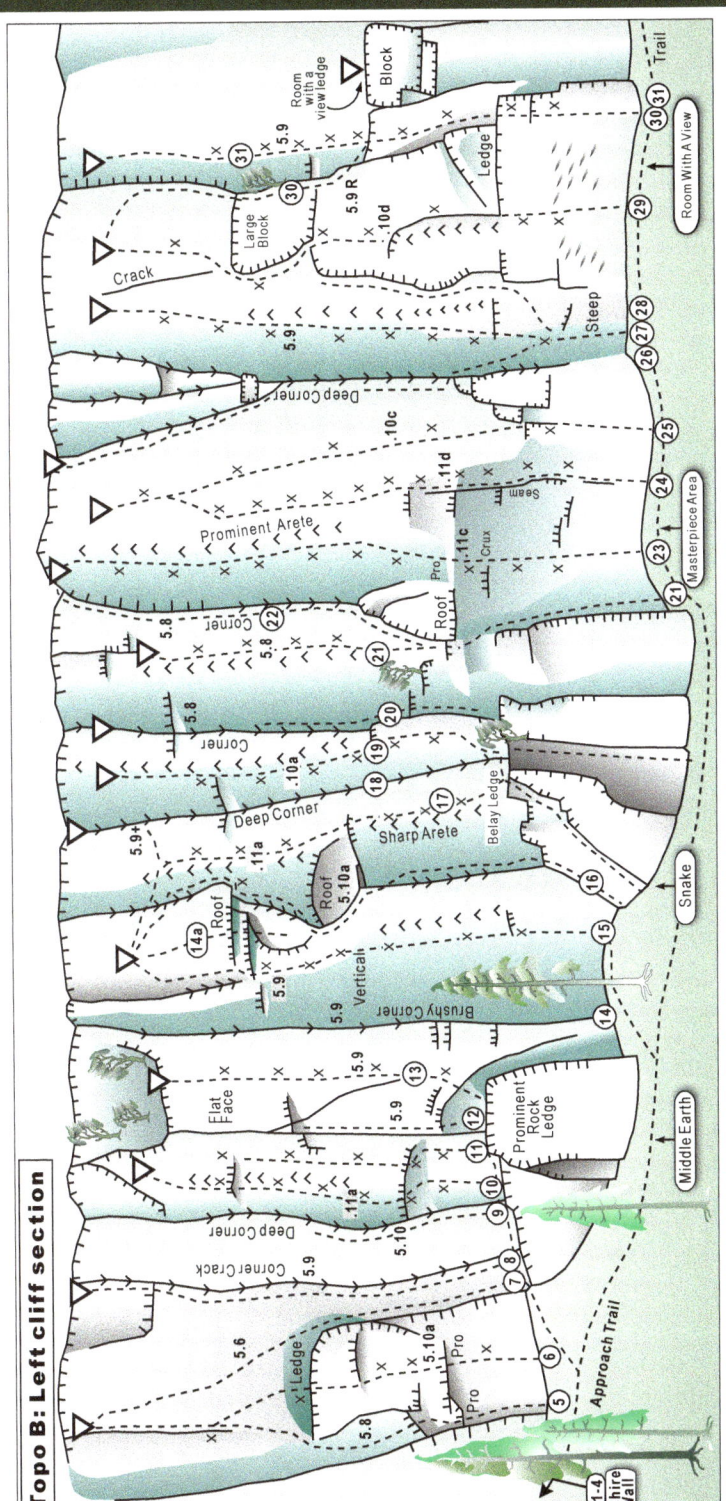

Topo B: Left Main Aspect of Ozone Wall

ing improve considerably as you climb further up onto this quality arête.

28. **Bitterroot 5.9**
80' (24m) in length, Pro to 2" [?]
Start on Kung Fu (clip first bolt), then move right and climb a minor crack till it merges with Whine and Cheese just before the belay anchor.

29. **Whine and Cheese   5.10c**
80' (24m) in length, QD's [upgraded from gear to bolts]
Ascend up past two bolts to a ledge. Aim up the corner system past a face climbing sec-

tion (crux) to the next ledge. Traverse left around a large boulder, then aim up the face until you reach the anchor.

30. **Ganesh 5.9 R**
90' (27m) in length, Pro to 3"
A dirty left facing corner system which currently shares the same start as for Dirty Jugs. Runout sections. Beware of the large chockstone on the route.

31. **Dirty Jugs 5.9 ★★★**
90' (27m) in length, QD's
Look for a huge suspended boulder about 30' up the cliff face. This route ascends a face on the left side past some awkward moves to a '**Room with a View**' ledge. Continue directly up following dirty jug holds that are protected with bolts.

32. **Sweeping Beauty 5.10b ★★★**
100' (30m) in length, Pro to 3" and QD's

Brad Jarrett leading *Chain Mail*

Begin by climbing up steep terrain on the right side of the huge suspended boulder that is situated 30' above the ground. **Room With A View** ledge is the top of this massive block. Belay here or continue up and right, following a crack system to a steep headwall. A 60-meter rope will marginally get you back down from the top anchor.

OLD TREE AREA

Old Tree Area (Map #7 & Topo B): A crooked old tree grows next to the base of this section of cliff. See cliff photo map for clarification.

33. **Carrots For Everyone** 5.10a ★★★
60' (18m) in length, QD's (optional ¾" cam for start)
A very popular first class Ozone route! From the belay anchor on **Room With A View** ledge climb up the left face, and then pull past nice jug hand holds up to the chain anchor.

34. **Trinity Crack** 5.9 ★★★
100' (30m) in length, Pro to 3" and QD's
Immediately to the left of the 'old tree', ascend steep terrain up to the top of the large suspended block. Climb numerous steep steps and hand edges (inobvious pro) till you are even with Room With A View ledge. Aim for a short corner crack system up on the right, then climb up the broken corner system (protected with some bolts) passing a fir tree. Continue up a hand crack to a fascinating finish to the anchor.

35. **Deep State** 5.10b/c
90' (27m) in length
A face climb *squeezed* in next to the famous 'Carrots' route.

36. **Kamikaze** 5.10a ★★

Marcus D. on *Carrots*

90' (27m) in length, QD's and optional small cams
A stellar climb. From the 'old tree' aim up the slab into a squeeze chimney. From the ledge above the chimney move, aim up left into the corner system, and then back onto the arête. This route has a difficult crux getting established onto the arête, but a nice finish near the anchor.

37. **SOS (variation)** 5.11+
Top-rope only. Do not bolt.

38. **May Day** 5.10b ★★★
80' (24m) in length, Pro is QD's (can also merge with Trinity Crack but will need 3" pro and 60-meter rope)
To the right of the 'old tree' is a corner. Stem up this past solid flakes and pull up left onto a ledge. Aim up right, then past several sustained moves at a bulge, and then climb up left to the arête to merge with Kamikaze. Shares belay anchors with Kamikaze, but can be extended by traversing left to climb the last portion of Trinity Crack (3" gear).

39. **There and Back Again** 5.10c/d ★★
90' (27m) in length, Pro to 3" including cams
Climb up the outer face of a pyramid shaped pedestal of tock past one bolt, and then move over to the right. The climb quickly becomes steep below the obvious large roof. Pull this roof to a ledge and step up left onto a face climbing section as you get nearer to the anchor.

THE SHIELD

Andrew Blake on *Rauch Factor*

OZONE WALL 173

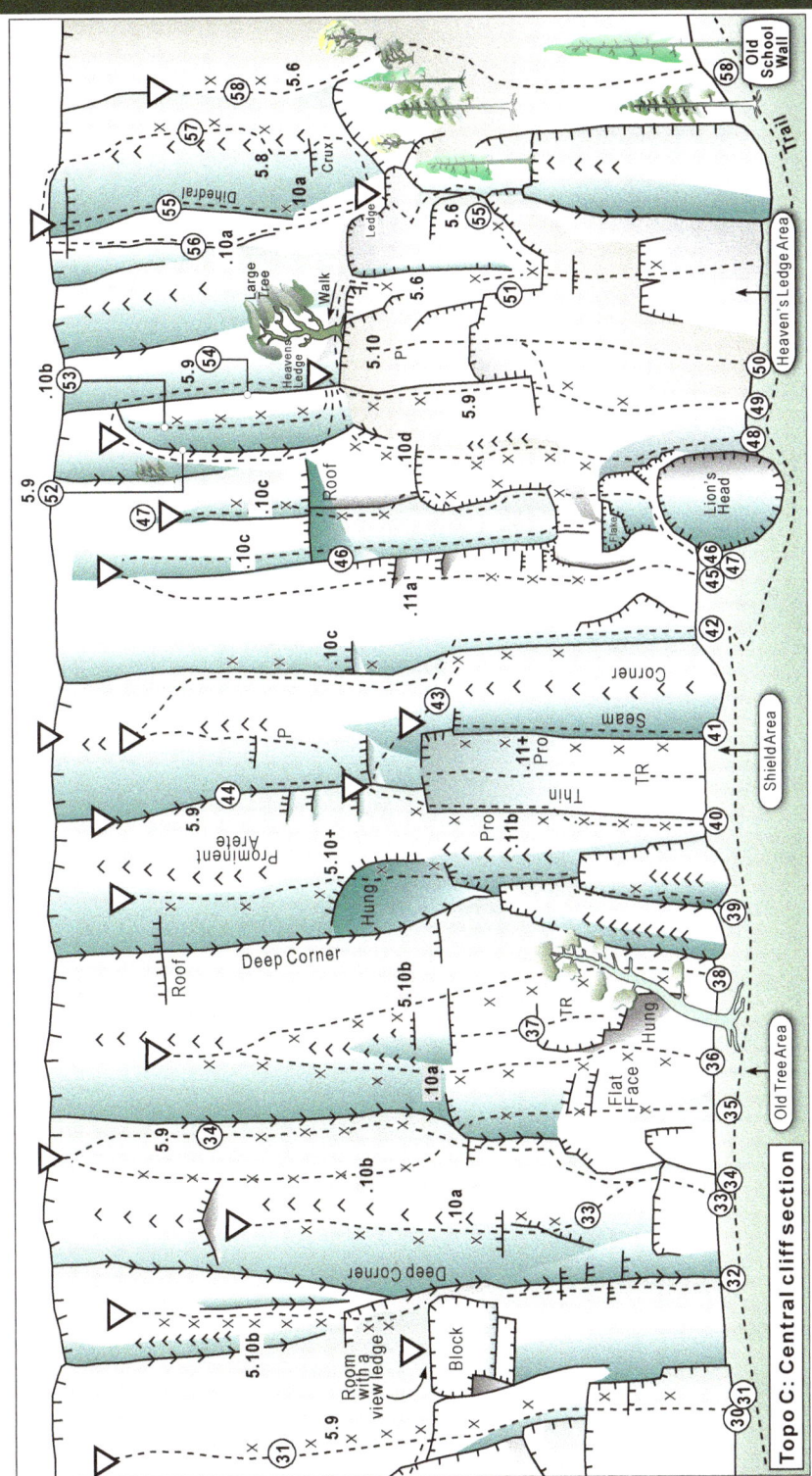

Topo C: Right Main Aspect of Ozone Wall

174 CHAPTER 2 ✦ ORC

Map #10: Stairway

The Shield (Map #8 & Topo C): A very steep, slightly overhung section of cliff with a popular selection of very difficult routes.

40. Chain Mail   5.11b   ★ ★ ★
50' (15m) in length, Pro is mixed, including QD's and #3 BD Camelot.
This is certainly one of the Ozone classics! Ascend the left bolt line using the path of least resistance, and then step up right into a crux section. Gear protects the obvious wide crack. After you pull through the roof the rock climbing will ease up.
Chopped Suey is a top-rope between Chain Mail and MD Route that goes free at 5.11. TR only; please do not bolt.

41. MD Route   5.11c/d   ★ ★
45' (13m) in length, QD's and minor cams to 2" (TCU)
A difficult free climb on the central portion of this clean wall.

42. Rauch Factor   5.10c   ★ ★ ★
50' (15m) in length, Pro to 1" and QD's
A great Ozone climb on steep pumpy edges. Ascend up a deep right-facing corner system

(bolts). Cut out left for several moves, then up right onto a steep face climbing with mixed gear. Continue up a slightly overhung sustained crack using positive hand holds.

43. Back in the Saddle   5.9   ★   Dry
50' (15m) in length, Pro to 1"

Begin up route Rauch Factor, then traverse up left to the anchor for Chain Mail. Move up onto the face climb section then up to a crack system on the right past a small roof.

44. Little Rauch That Could   5.9
110' in length, Pro to 1¼" (plus long slings)

Minor crack corner above MD Route. Climb lower half of Rauch Factor to reach this route.

45. Short Straw   5.11a   ★ ★ ★
100' (30m) in length, Pro to 1½" and QD's, cams suggested

Climb the 3-bolt start on a slightly overhung smooth face to a rest stance on a small ledge. From the small stance continue climbing up a very sustained steep crack through small bulges to an anchor.

46. Meat Grinder   5.10c   ★ ★
100' (30m) in length, Pro to 4" and long slings

From the top of the 'razorblade flake' place gear, and then free climb up to the next ledge (runout or clip a bolt). Aim up left in a right-facing corner system, then jam your way up the crack (crux) past a belay anchor and continue to the top of the cliff.

47. High Plains Drifter   5.10c   ★ ★ ★   Dry
80' (24m) in length, QD's

An Ozone classic and very popular to lead! From the 'razorblade flake' climb up past a bolt to a large stance. Pull past a rounded buldge to another small stance, then embarkc onto an overhaning power climb usin large incut edges. The crux is the smooth face using small edges just before the anchor.

HEAVEN'S LEDGE

Heaven's Ledge (Map #9, Map #10 and Topo C): This section of cliff is open to the sunlight since most of the trees are not next to the base of the cliff.

48. Rolling Thunder   5.10d   ★
70' (21m) in length, QD's

Begin on top of the Lion's Head large boulder. Ascend a steep face to a minor prow (bolts). Balance up a delicate slightly overhung section to a stance. Then up balancy thin face move on a smooth face, then exit up right to a belay anchor on a large ledge.

To lengthen the climb merge into the Tip Top route [bring gear] and continue to the next anchor.

49. Jacob's Ladder   5.9   ★ ★ ★
70' (21m) in length, Pro to 2" and QD's

Begin on the right side of the Lion's Head large boulder, and ascend up good edges (two bolts)

Nick leading *Chain Mail*

to a large ledge at the base of a scooped out overhang. Carefully move up into the scoop and place some pro, then surmount the hang (crux). Continue up easier edges to the Heaven's Ledge belay anchor.

50. **For Heaven Sake   5.10b/c**   ★
70' (21m) in length, Pro to 1" and cams
Ascend good edges (gear placements are inobvious and small) till you encounter a thin crack (fixed piton) splitting a minor overhang. Surmount the overhang using face edges and continue to the main ledge above to belay.

51. **Stairway to Heaven   5.6**   ★
70' (21m) in length, Pro to 1" and QD's
A basic climb on easy ledges. Ascend a series of large ledges (bolts) and angle up left in a corner (bolts), then past some bushes to a ledge. Continue up a few moves then traverse hard left to the Heaven's Ledge (belay anchor) with a big fir tree growing on it.

The next three rock climbs begin at the roomy Heaven's Ledge. All three routes end at the upper belay anchor on a slab.

52. **Tipp Topp   5.9**   ★★
25' (7m) in length, Pro to 2½"
From the Heaven's Ledge belay anchor step directly left past the Burrito Killa arête into a crack corner. Stem up this corner past a crux move onto the slab and belay anchor. Anticipate rope drag on this climb.

53. **Burrito Killa   5.10b**   ★★
25' (7m) in length, QD's
This terrific climb ascends directly up the arête immediately left of the bolt anchor from the Heaven's Ledge. A good line to connect with Jacob's Ladder which ascends up to this route from below.

54. **There Yare   5.9**
25' (7m) in length, Pro to 3
This is the obvious steep hand crack corner system immediately right of the bolt anchor on the this large ledge. The belay anchor for this route is on a slab above the crack.

55. **Love Supreme   5.6 1st pitch (5.10a on 2nd pitch)**   ★★
150' (45m) in length, Pro to 2", cams and QD's
Pitch 1: This first pitch is quite popular. Begin as you would for the route Stairway to Heaven, but at the second bolt angle up right past a bolt (5.6), then directly up a minor corner to a bolt belay anchor at Cloud 9 ledge.
Pitch 2: This section is 5.10a and ascends up a steep slab using small gear in a seam. Clip the bolt, and make several face moves to the right and gain a ledge at the bottom of the corner system. Continue up the corner past the roof and follow more ledges to an anchor.

56. **Bitches Brew   5.10a**   ★★
60' (18m) in length, Pro to 1"
From the Cloud 9 belay anchor climb up the same steep slab up left (gear), place a long sling on the bolt around the corner, and then continue up to the top of the large boulder. Continue up the face (gear) and climb up over a fascinating roof, then finish climbing up some ledges to the bolt anchor.

57. **Hang Up Your Hang Ups   5.8**   ★★★
60' (18m) in length, Pro to 1" and QD's
From the Cloud 9 belay traverse around a corner to another small ledge. Directly above is

OZONE WALL

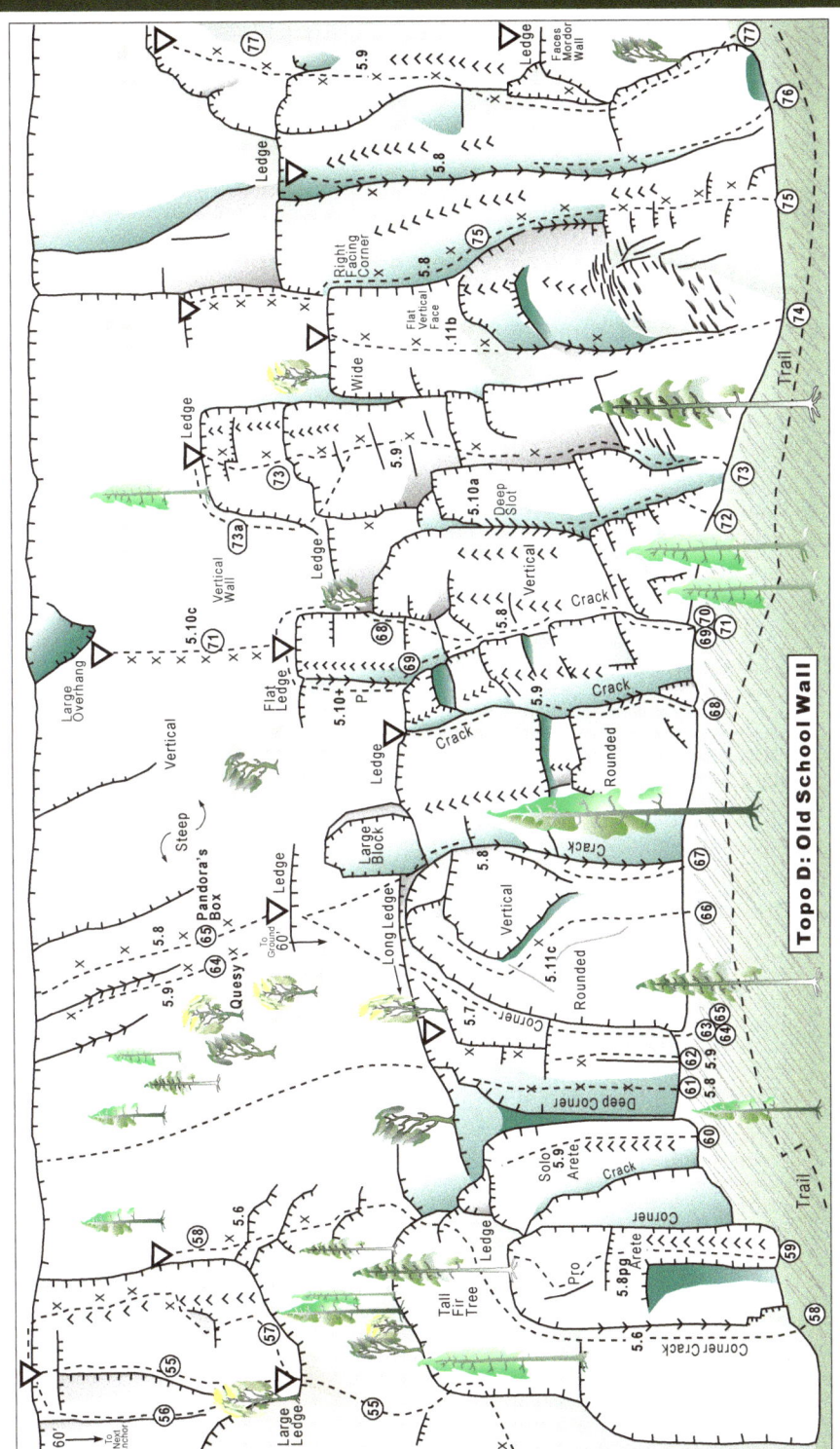

Topo D: Old School Wall

a slightly overhung face with a crack in it. Place pro in the crack and surmount the bulge using large holds. At a tiny stance clip the bolt, then move up right on tiny holds to easier terrain. March up good large edges another 30' to a fir tree. Traverse left about 20' to a bolt anchor above Love Supreme and rappel.

OLD SCHOOL WALL

Old School Wall (Topo D): Follow the trail as it gradually ascends up into the dense forest again. This section has some older climbs established during the late '80s and '90s, but now sports some newer rock climbs, as well.

58. Mountaineer's Route   5.6 ★★
190' (57m) in length, Pro to 2" and QD's
Ascend a deep corner system to the top of a crack, past a block and continue to climb up and to the right. Continue up 30' to a tree, and then proceed up onto a nice section of face climbing (2 bolts) to a small tree and an anchor just beyond. Rappel from here, or continue up past a minor bulge to the top of the Ozone cliff. Walk off to descend.

59. Ivans Arête   5.8 PG
30' (9m) in length, Pro to 1" and QD's
This is a direct start for the Mountaineer's Route which climbs a short clean arête. Place pro in a small crack 15' above the ground. Merge with the previous route on the large ledge system.

60. Rasta Arete   5.9
30' (9m) in length, No pro
Uphill and to the right of Ivan's is another short steep arête. Solo.

61. Outshined   5.8
Pro to 2"
Climb 3-bolt face, then traverse up left (mixed gear/bolts) to top of cliff. Rap w/70m rope.

62. Rusty Cage   5.9
Pro to ___"
Climb thin crack (bolt) up left to steep jugs, then up onto a ledge, and continue up rightward (more bolts) to reach a belay. Rappel.

63. Flayel Bop   5.7
60' (18m) in length, Pro to 3"
A short corner system which can be climbed to a ledge system. Rappel from a nearby tree, or continue up and right to join with the route Stigmata.

64. Quesy   5.9
___' in length, Pro to 2"
Climb Flayel Bop to its ledge belay. Then climb about 50' (bolts & 2" cam) to cliff top.

65. Pandora's Box   5.8
___' in length, Pro to 3"
Climb Flayel Bop to its ledge belay. Then climb this face route to cliff top.

66. The Bulge   5.11c
60' (18m) in length, Pro to 3"
A very short difficult section (or brief 5.12a variant) moving up left across a bulge face to latch onto the left edge of a block, but eases quickly enough. Jaunt higher to a belay.

67. Stigmata 5.8 ★★
60' (18m) in length, Pro to 3"

This good route ascends an obvious clean crack to a slight overhang, then up the crack to a large ledge system. Continue another 40' to a chain bolt anchor. Two rappels will take you to the ground with one 60m rope.

68. Ripper 5.9 ★★★ Dry
35' (10m) in length, Pro to 2"

Ascend a very nice finger crack through a slight overhang then up to a chain bolt anchor.

69. Little Dipper 5.8 ★★
60' (18m) in length, Pro to 3"

Ascend a left leaning crack corner system to a ledge, then aim up right into a crack system which will lead to an anchor on the left at Flat Ledge belay.

A top-rope climb called **Star Gazer** is located on the arete immediately right of Little Dipper. The first half is .12a and the upper half is .11b.

70. Piton Variation 5.10c/d ★
60' (18m) in length, Pro to 2"

Climb either Little Dipper or Ripper to the ledge, then traverse left to a corner crack

system with one piton fixed in it. Climb the corner crack to the Flat Ledge belay.

71. Orion 5.10c ★★
35' (10m) in length, QD's
Use any of the previous two climbs and climb up to the Flat Ledge belay. From that ledge climb up the bolted face past a bulge to the anchor and rappel.

72. Big Dipper 5.10a PG
40' (18m) in length, Pro to 4"
Start as you would for Standing Ovation, but aim up into an offwidth slot. After you exit

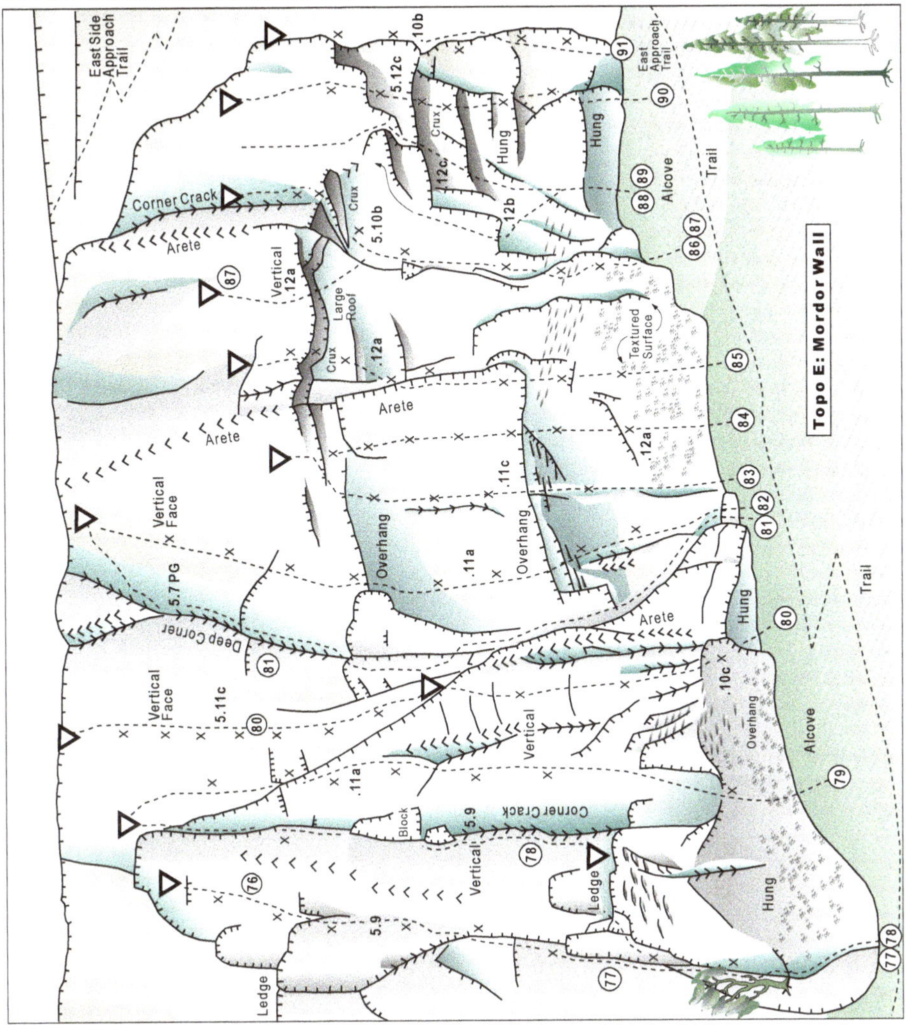

♦ OZONE WALL   181

the peapod slot, continue up and left to the Flat Ledge belay.

73. **Standing Ovation   5.9   ★★★**
80' (24m) in length, Optional cam pro to 3" or 4" but mostly QD's
A stellar Ozone climb with small leftward-sloping edges that will surely keep you on edge! Start by climbing up next to a large flake which can be protected with a very large cam. Step up over right and ascend a vertical face (5 bolts) using small left slanting edges. From a nice stance move up and surmount the small roof overhang (2 bolts) then march up to a tree ledge and bolt belay anchor. Rappel.

Standing Variation: An alternate variation exists which follows the original ascentionists line. Instead of using the last three bolts step left to a large ledge, then climb up right using a short crack corner. Ends at the same belay anchor.

MORDOR WALL

Mordor Wall (Map #11, Map #12 and Topo E): At the far right end of the Ozone Wall is a dark cliff section capped by large overhangs on the right and a long steep slice of vertical wall on the left.

74. Gophers Gone Wild   5.11b
80' (24m) in length, 7 QD's
Ascend a corner to a steep vertical face that commits you to crux move up right to a flat stance. Dance up a short face to a belay anchor on a large ledge. Rap or continue up Numb Nuts.

75. Numb Nuts   5.8   ★★
80' (24m) in length, 14 QD's
On a prominent clean buttress of rock just prior to the main Mordor alcove are two long climbs. This is the left bolted line which ascends a steep corner system with ample good edges and steps. The last several moves short of the belay anchor are pumpy. It is possible to climb portions of this route on natural gear.

76. Small Nuts   5.8
60' (18m) in length, Pro to 1½" and QD's
At the lowest point on the foot trail are two climbs on a long steep section of cliff buttress. This is the crack corner system on the right that sports one bolt near the top and one near the bottom of the climb. Beware of the sparse protection near the central crux section of the climb.

77. No Nuts   5.9   ★★
80' (24m) in length, QD's
Begin on the right side of a prominent mossy buttress. Ascend knobby rock and a corner to a ledge. Climb a steep corner till it is possible to move up right onto a section of face climbing. Continue up this nice section to a bolt anchor.

78. Dad's Nuts   5.9   ★★★   ☂Dry
80' (24m) in length, Pro to 3½"
A superb crack climb on a slightly overhung wall. Begin as you would for No Nuts, but step up right on a large ledge to a bolt belay anchor. Climb the very steep but quality crack corner system past several blocks. Surprisingly sustained lead but the difficulties ease near the top.

79. Getting Your Kicks   5.11a   ★★   ☂Dry
100' (30m) in length, QD's and optional pro to 1"
A stellar long face climb immediately right of a steep corner crack. Start where the bluff leans out in a knobby bulge. Clip the bolt and balance over the bulge to easier terrain. Move up right the climb a fun series of continuously overhanging positive holds and balancy moves to the top. There are two crux sections between the third and sixth bolt.

80. Route 66   5.11c   ★★★   ☂Dry
100' (30m) in length, QD's
A classic long sport route on the left side of the Mordor alcove.
Pitch 1: Clip the first bolt to protect your moves (5.10c) off the deck. Scamper up to a small ledge and bolt anchor. **Pitch 2:** Launch onto the fabulous slightly overhung long face climb above (7 bolts). Climbs the steep face to a sequential move to attain a ledge, then more sustained climbing to a bolt anchor.

81. Meth Rage   5.7 PG
80' (24m) in length, Pro to 4"
Climb easy terrain to a midway belay (used by Route 66). From the midway belay anchor on Route 66 launch up right into an obvious challenging and loose corner system. Rappel

from bolt anchor at the top of the cliff above The Crumbling.

The following climbs ascend consistently steep terrain through a series of unusually difficult roof sections on the Mordor Wall.

82. Tofutti Cutie   5.11a
95' (28m) in length, 8 QD's"
Power up a series of sidepulls and edges, crank a trick jutting roof move with a mantle and good rest point. Then casual climbing over a bulge, another rest, and a final steep demanding section just below the belay anchor. Optional roof cam (#1).

83. Mrs. Norris   5.11c
60' (18m) in length, QD's and optional small wire or RP pro to ½"
Climb a slightly overhung face, then power through the roof using positive holds to a sit-down rest above the first roof. Place optional pro at the top of the shield (8' above the rest spot), then ascend sustained ground through another overhanging roof section and move up right to the same anchor as The Crumbling.

84. The Crumbling   5.12a   ★ ★ ★
60' (18m) in length, QD's
A stellar route! Stick-clip the first bolt, then boulder through a series of difficult pumpy moves all the way to the rappel anchor.

85. The Humbling   5.12a   ★ ★ ★
60' (18m) in length, A superb climb! This line powers through a large roof that makes you feel as if you are wrestling upside-down with huge overhanging blocks, and then culminates with several sloper moves to finish.

86. Stepchild   5.10a   ★ ★ ★
50' (15m) in length, QD's and optional pro to 2"
An excellent route! Ascend up moderately steep terrain on good edges to a stance, then up a short crack. Angle up to the right under the great ceiling, then pull around the roof on balancy holds to a bolt anchor.

87. Hell Boy   5.12a
60' (18m) in length, 3 QD's
A difficult variation that branches up left from Stepchild at the large roof.

88. Grace   5.12b   ★ ★ ★
40' (12m) in length, 7 QD's
Ascends the prominent overhang by traversing up left through a series of tight moves to a thin face section. Continue up the face rightward to merge with Dark Lord to the belay anchor. A powerful link-up variation called **Slackface** (.12d) connects the first two bolts of Grace, then merges with the upside-down foot jam slot crux on Dark Lord. Like Dave said, "It ain't over till it's over."

89. Dark Lord   5.12c   ★
40' (12m) in length, 8 QD's
Power up through a prominent overhang past a very difficult foot lock reach problem. From a tiny stance continue up the 5.11 face to the belay anchor.

Matt leading *MD Route*

90. **Angle of the Dangle 5.12c** ★
   40' (12m) in length, QD's
   Last climb on the Ozone Wall. Begin from the right side of a small cave to a large roof crack. Power your way out past this crux lip move, then ascend more difficult overhung moves to the anchor.

91. **The Tumbling 5.10b**
   40' in length, ___ QD's
   The very last climb at the east end of the crag. Steep, slightly hung and entertaining.

SPORT SCHOOL WALL

And though listed last, this next tiny section (Sport School Wall) is actually located immediately downhill from the west parking spot. To reach this spot, hike the west access trail for about 2 minutes, then branch off back west on a brief wide trail to reach the Sport School Wall. Beta is Right to Left (E to W).

1. **Playing Hooky 5.7**
   30' on length, Pro QD's
   First (easternmost) route on this outcrop. Short but good route for beginners. The small overhang offers variations (the overhang is rated 5.8).

2. **1st Grade Problems 5.8**
   30' on length, Pro 4 QD's
   Climbs up to (and over) a small roof using crimps and mantle.

Walk about 25' west to another section of this same outcrop formation. Two more short routes exist here.

3. **_____ 5.7**
   30' on length, Pro 3 QD's
   The right of two routes on a very small outcrop.

4. **_____ 5.5**
   30' on length, Pro 3 QD's
   The westernmost (and last) route.

OZONE WALL 185

Steve Wolford on Carrots For Everyone

Dave leading Grace 5.12b

Matt climbing Dark Lord on the Mordor Wall

"Going to the mountains is going home."
-John Muir

OZONE WALL

FAR SIDE CRAG

The Far Side introduction written by Jon Bell

Like Ozone Wall (its neighbor about a quarter-mile to the west) the Far Side crag is a hidden wall of andesitic basalt high above the Columbia River in southwest Washington. Also like Ozone, the Far Side was discovered by local climber Jim Opdycke in the early 1980s, then left relatively untouched for more than twenty years. The Far Side later became a unique climbing area much the way Ozone did as well, when dedicated climbers took the time and energy to explore the area, establish routes, and otherwise transform an abandoned roadside dump into a one-of-a-kind crag just an hour outside of downtown Portland.

Tucked in a deep canopied forest of maple trees the Far Side crag enjoys considerably more sunlight during the winter months than its neighboring Ozone crag, while Douglas fir trees at the cliff top help shield the wall during light rain showers. At about a hundred feet tall, the Far Side crag is a bit shorter than Ozone, and where Ozone has a higher percentage of sport routes, the Far Side has a greater percentage of traditional gear lead routes (and only a tiny handful of sport or nearly all-bolt routes). But that's where most of the similarities between the Far Side crag and the Ozone Wall end.

Many of the routes at the Far Side crag are quite gear-tech savvy traditional lead routes utilizing plenty of specific natural protection, and though rock climbs range from 5.5 up to 5.11- the routes will challenge even the most ardent on-sight lead climber. A few select routes do not see much activity, so anticipate cobwebs and plant growth if you plan to tackle one of those routes. As a whole the crag remains a much less traveled crag where you might encounter 1-2 teams of rock climbers on a typical weekend summer day.

HOW TO GET THERE

The Far Side crag is in southwest Washington, about 8 miles east of the town of Washougal on State Route 14 near milepost 24. From Portland or Vancouver, drive east on SR 14 for roughly 18.5 miles. Beyond the two pullouts for Ozone, look for two long pullouts on the south side of the road that are just barely separated. Park at the second pullout. Trails to either the east or west end of the crag begin at opposite ends of the pullout.

Gear: Though there are a few bolts, pitons, and bolted anchors at the Far Side, traditional gear and knowledge of its placement is essential for climbing here. Many routes have belay anchors, though bring gear for those route that have none. Some of the cracks used for protection are thin seams ideally suited for micro nuts, Lowe Balls, or micro cams.

Special Considerations: The Far Side sits on public land within the Columbia River Gorge National Scenic Area. Please respect the area and keep it clean to help preserve access.

VISUAL BIO

These emblems represent the Far Side, a gorge climbing site with southern exposure, shaded with deciduous trees and a quick five-minute approach.

EAST END FORMATION

A small rocky formation at the utter east most end of the bluff.

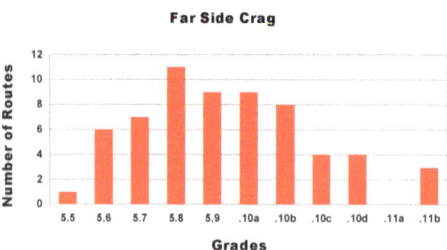

1. **Silverdyke 5.7**
   Pro: several nuts & small cams
   Start on the 3'x 6' flat ledge and ascend past a bulge to an interesting 25' short thin crack. Uttermost east end of cliff formation.

2. **Monkey Moves 5.9+**
   Pro: nuts and cams to 3"
   Start in an alcove at the east end of the cliff. Monkey pull through two mini roofs up discontinuous cracks. Getting off the ground and out of the alcove over the first roof is the crux.

3. **The Pin 5.10**
   Pro: several nuts and cams
   Immediately to the left of Silverdyke is this good, but short route that starts off the Silverdyke platform. A one-move 5.10 crux. Located at the eastmost end of the cliff formation.

4. **The Trembling 5.9**
   Pro: wired nuts, one optional 3" cam
   Climb a steep lumpy rock formation past a fixed pin and a bolt to where the rock radically changes character, then up a broken dihedral to the top to the fixed anchor.

5. **Introductory Offer 5.8 to 5.9**
   Pro: small nuts and cams to 1½"
   A nice route at the east most edge of the cliff formation. Step on the Lizard Locks starting blocks, move straight up veering right, then climb the dihedral (harder) or wander to the right and up to easier ground then up left to the Lizard Locks rappel tree.

6. **The Arête 5.11 TR**
   This squeeze job between 'Lizard Locks' and 'Introductory Offer' was intentionally left as a top-rope. It is an excellent top-rope route.

7. **Lizard Locks 5.10b**
   Pro: nuts and cams to 1½", including large cams to 3½"
   The obvious crack near the far eastern end of the wall shared by Introductory Offer has three stacked blocks between two shallow caves. Attack the highball moves direct from the ground to the crack placing 3½" cams. Opt #2: Or boulder through the lumpy blocks for 12' and step left 7' and up until 20' off the deck and place first pro at the base of the obvious crack with a 3" cam. Continue up a thin crack utilizing small cams to 1". Say "Hi" to the Northern Alligator Lizard if he hasn't moved on yet. Climb past a small tree growing in the crack; finish up slightly to the right of the buttress on easy moves to a huge fir with the rappel sling.

INDIAN HEAD

A minor rock formation with a steep broken flat face on its west aspect.

8. **MJ08 5.6**
   Pro: small cams to 1½"
   Climb the buttress following one of several lines (the line of least resistance) to the top.

9. **Birthday Surprise 5.6**
   Pro: small to medium cams
   Climb the face to the right of Wounded Knee using pro in marginal horizontal cracks. J.O. turned 65 today, but missed out on this ascent.
10. **Wounded Knee 5.6**
    Pro: small nuts, including a 3" cam
    Climb the shallow chimney using face holds, and rappel off the tree. Expect creative pro.
11. **Dulcinea 5.5**
    Pro: large nuts, medium sized chocks and cams
    On the east aspect of Indian Head buttress climb a short 12" wide crack to a capstone (near a dihedral). Rappel from a rock horn.
12. **Sheep Skinners Delight 5.10**
    Pro: several small nuts and small cams to 1½"
    Climb the obvious varicose cracks on the west side aspect of the Indian Head buttress and rappel from a rock horn.

GIANT FIR TREE

The landmark Bare Buttress section is immediately to the right of White Lightning. A huge fir tree with large blocks of rock located next to the base of this part of the wall provides shade as well as protection from the wind and occasional sprinkle of rain. The bluff forms a wide open ravine offering several climbing alternatives at a nice fat landing platform. Several routes on it were inspired and named due to the clothes-free style of the first ascent.

13. **Scary As… 5.7**
    Pro to 3" including a large cam, long slings
    Start in the offwidth under a big tree and climb the easy edges (no pro) to a sloping dirt ledge above. At this point the climb crosses lines with Sweet Surprise. Continue up into a small gully immediately to the left of the open book. Once through the gully look right for the hand-to-fist sized cracks described in Sweet Surprise. Expect some loose rock in the gully.
14. **Sweet Surprise 5.7*ish***
    Pro to 3" including a large cam, long slings
    Begin at the shared start of the Right Cheek; ascend till you are above the lower face, then traverse right ten feet and climb up good edges to an easy open book with nice hand and fist jam moves, and then exit this to a fir tree. Rappel or walk off.
15. **Right Cheek 5.8**
    Pro: small nuts and cams to 1½", small cams & nuts are crucial
    The right cheek sits directly to the right of Adam's crack and shares the start with Sweet Surprise and Scary. Climb the crack 9' to the left of the large fir tree growing out of the cliff. Rappel from the same tree anchor as Adam's crack.
16. **Adams Crack 5.8**
    Pro: small nuts and cams to 1½"
    Ascend the crack and large face holds to a small obvious maple tree where the route eases. Aim up to a large Douglas fir and rappel off. Good gear route for aspiring leader.

17. **Left Cheek 5.7**
Pro: small nuts and cams to 2"
This fun route is situated directly to the left of Adam's crack and stays closer to the left side of the buttress and uses the same belay anchor at the top.

18. **Bill's Thrill 5.7**
Pro: small cams up to 2", small to medium wires, long slings
Shares same start as White Lightning but at the ½ way point stay slightly right and up the obvious crack past a small tree to the shared belay anchor.

19. **White Lightning 5.8**
Pro: nuts and cams to 3"
Next to the giant fir tree is a flat roomy platform surrounded by a wide low angle bluff. Ascend up a wide finger crack or thin hand crack that eases to the right and leads to some large face holds to an obvious move left. Pull over a bulge then race straight up to a belay anchor.

20. **Snake 5.8**
Pro: small rack and a 3" cam for the top
Start up the White lighting gully and follow the Snake like crack that wanders up and right. Finish at the fir tree 20' from the top, or finish off on Happy Crack.

21. **Snake Buttress 5.8**
Several starting points of varying degrees of hardness. Start on the left in Happy Crack, or start on the right, or higher up on the right in the Snake route. Finish up Snake or Happy Crack. Nice climb with nice ledges to work laps on. This is now bolted.

22. **Happy Crack 5.8**
Pro: Medium and large wired nuts, several small cams to 1½"
A five star classic climb like a well designed staircase. Ascend easy shallow dihedral straight up to the top using face holds interspersed along a crack. A nice left-hand variation uses under clings and face moves. The easier right-hand variation aims right about ½ way up the route by dancing up small ledges before rejoining the route. Sling a small fir tree en route, and then finish straight up 20' to a rappel point at a large fir tree.

23. **2Trad4U 5.9**
Pro: Quick Draws
A 'non-sport' sport climb that starts at a flat landing site near two tall Maple trees. A fun little route that dances up moderate terrain using ample edges to a slight bulge crux power move.

24. **Ur Baby's Daddy 5.10a**
Pro to 3" and Lowe Ball Nuts
Start up the moderate dihedral to a seam in the face to the anchor.

25. **Freak Freely 5.10b/c**
Pro to 1"
Right of the above route is an interesting line ascending natural cracks and features using small gear. A boulder start traverses 5' right into the obvious crack, then follows up through various features to a dihedral groove crux with a thin crack. It bypasses the belay anchor of TLW by aiming to the top of the bluff via three possible endings. Rap from a tree or walk off.

26. **The Lonesome Winner 5.10a/b**
Pro: Thin nuts and cams to 2"
Has three fixed bolts and a piton on lower portion of face. Begin up steep terrain (bolts

& piton) using small cams aiming up rightward to a stance under a large roof. Move up a thin crack on the right side of the roof, and power up the sustained tricky thin crack moves to an anchor. The alternative is to follow the crack above the roof up leftward to the Oracle anchor.

27. Wushu Roof   5.10+ / .11-
Pro to 5" cams mandatory
Start on Lonesome Winner and then head slightly left and up using features interspersed with small cracks. Turn the lower feature to the left to gain the Bombay roof visible from the ground, and high step up right through the chimney/wide crack to the anchor.

28. Oracle   5.10c
Pro to 6"
Moderate face/crack climbing leads to rest below first roof. Long reaches over the roof will get you to a stance. From the stance expect sustained and steep climbing to the anchor.

29. Solid Gold   5.10-
Pro: Nuts to 1", and an optional 3" cam, extra small cams
To the right of Hollow Victory is an obvious long slightly golden corner that angles up toward the left. Start below the Sword of Damocles feature on a shallow crack and aim right up a corner avoiding the hanging block. Continue up the corner where it eases to a steep face. Power up several moves (small cams helpful) and tuck back into the corner before you finish to the top to the Hollow Victories belay anchor.

30. Hollow Victories   5.10+/5.11-
Pro: Nuts and cams to 2", mostly very small cams
In the center of a tall flat section of bluff, ascend a very thin crack below and slightly left of a wedged block hanging like the Sword of Damocles. Climb the thin crack to a small ledge till you are standing on the wedged hanging block. Then cruise up interesting and challenging features past a single bolt using strangely hollow but secure holds on the face.

THE LANDING

A common roomy meeting area where climbers will usually first arrive to socialize and become oriented at the site.

31. Day of Atonement   5.10a
Pro to 3" including Lowe Ball Nuts, small TCU's or other cams
The first official route established at the crag. Climb a steep short hand crack to a series of edges to the base of a smooth vertical face split by a thin crack. **Opt #1:** Power up the spicy moves on thin holds (small nuts, Ball nuts, or tiny cams), and balance carefully directly up a minor corner till it eases near an anchor. **Opt #2:** at the smooth face traverse left to Lion of Judah finish. **Opt #3:** or move further left to a small stance [above Naughty and Nice] then balance up an awkward steep short dihedral crux to a belay anchor.

32. Lion of Judah   5.10a PG13
Pro to 3" including small cams
Start just left of Day of Atonement and head up a shattered left-facing shallow corner crack. Continue directly up a minor corner/chimney feature until you can traverse left under an overhanging block to gain the anchor on top. The second official route established here.

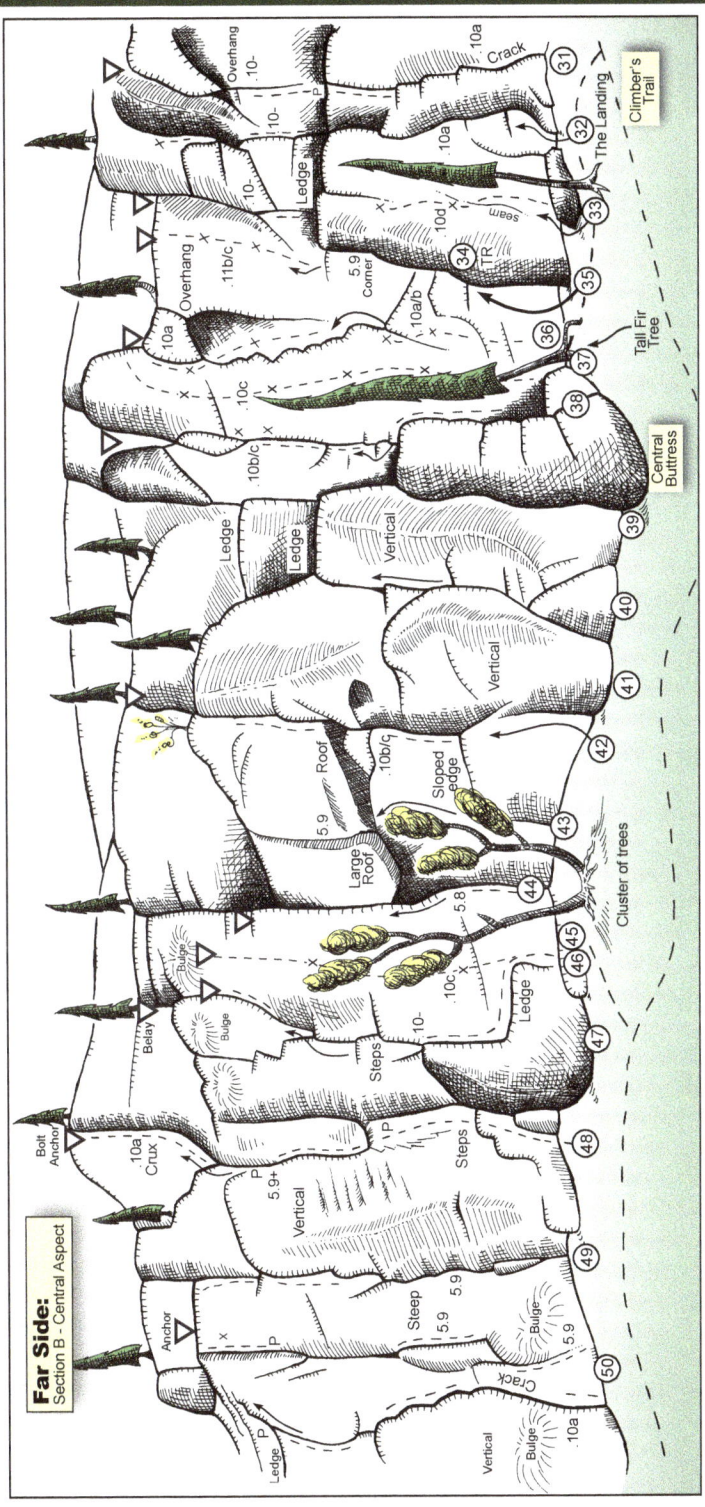

33. Naughty and Nice   5.10d

Pro: 3 QD's and gear to 3"

A great climb involving a series of steep technical face moves. Start up the shattered left-facing corner, then traverse left to the first bolt. Pass two more bolts to gain a flat ledge, step up left, and then climb the overhanging right-facing dihedral and exit left to a belay anchor.

34. Squeeze Play   5.10C

A top-rope that utilizes the entire arête immediately right of Tunnel Vision.

35. Tunnel Vision   5.11b

Pro to 1" (optional 3" cam) and bolts

Start up dark left-facing dihedral, then continue up the nice corner above to reach first of three bolts. Commit to steep face climbing by pulling over a stout overhang to an anchor.

The next three routes start at a flat landing next to a very large fir tree.

36. The Darkhorse   5.10a

Pro: Minor cams and nuts to 2"

A quality route that begins at a large fir tree. Boulder up a steep hung face (just left of a corner crack) to a small stance and continue straight up (natural pro) on small ledges and blocks using in-cut holds and a thin seam past a bolt. Clip another bolt at a small overhang, and then power over the roof on the left angling up right to the anchor.

37. Thin Line   5.10c

Pro: Thin gear to 2" [?]

Climb a face (bolts) just left of a large fir tree, and punch past a brief upper overhang.

38. Center Squeeze   5.10b/c

Pro: Small gear rack, small cams, Lowe Ball Nuts, optional cam to 4"

Start next to a large fir tree on a rock stance, make a boulder move start up to a stem past the outside of the obvious 40' squeeze chimney that you face climb to avoid the 'squeeze', then up easy climbing to a couple of small staggered ledges mid-pitch. Clip two bolts and climb over a detached pillar and aim up an easier 20' finish to a rap anchor on top.

CENTRAL BUTTRESS

39. Hidden Treasure   5.8

Pro: Nuts and cams to 4"

On left side of a central buttress is this wide crack and ledge system. Climb it to the top.

40. Boo Coup   5.10- PG

Pro: Nuts and (offset) cams to 2"

Start on a small pedestal of broken square blocks, place an offset cam for the initial flaring crack semi-mantle at the ground. Use face holds and intermittent cracks moving up left, then up right along the walls natural features to gain the upper ledges just below the very top. Traverse left a short distance to the Good Vibrations belay anchor.

41. Sharpen your Teeth   5.10+

Pro to 2" has two fixed bolts

This is the mixed gear route on the face to the right of an obvious corner 12' left of Boo Coup. Climb up to the obvious ledge with the chain belay shared with Good Vibrations.

42. Good vibrations   5.10b/c

Pro to 2"

Head up the right side of the large roof to same anchor as Boo Coup

FAR SIDE CRAG 195

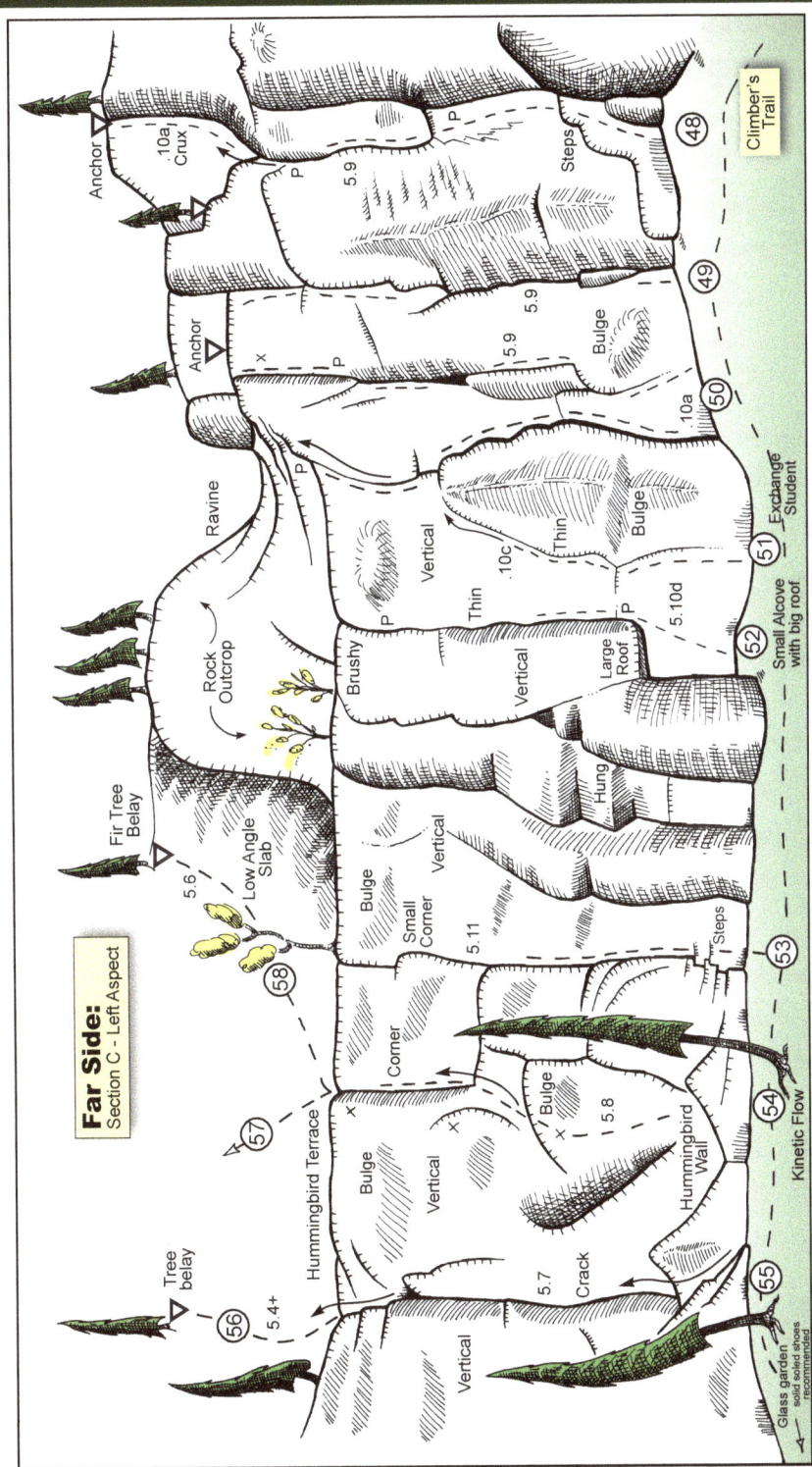

43. Closeout 5.9
Pro to 2"
Same start as Good Vibrations. Traverse left under the roof, then clip the bolt and pull over and up a seam to the anchor.

44. The Martyr 5.8
Pro to 1.5"
Follow the crack up left side of large roof to a two bolt anchor and rappel.

45. Step and Fetch It 5.10c
Pro to 1", triples in .5" range
Starts same as the Head Wall, but instead of traversing left, go directly up via a crux hard step move, then up the middle of the upper slab trending right and over the top of the buttress and then left. Can exit left early to Head Wall route.

MAPLE TREE ZONE

46. The Head Wall 5.10-
Pro to 2" especially ¾" to 1" nuts for crux
Start by the Maple tree cluster, and make a few face moves up to a small ledge, then traverse to the left a few feet. Ascend the broken buttress with a crack in parts of it up to a stance 20' below the top to a fixed belay anchor.

47. Shoulder Hop TR
Located right of the above route on the outer scarp.

48. Sweet _____ 5.10a
Pro: Small nuts and cams (TCU's) to 2", Lowe Ball Nuts, slings
One of the better routes here in terms of mental and physical focus. This route is located at the right section of the short Hummingbird Wall just before the path descends down around the central formation. To start the climb: Ascend up several initial steps to a steep corner like face with some pods and small intermittent cracks (two pitons) requiring some small TCU placements between the pins. Once you move up beyond the tricky section at the pitons, you will pass a small fir tree that is located on your left. Aim up right over a tree root to a steep headwall crack, and then power up this crack to a fixed anchor.

49. 'Je' Mapel Jon Phillip 5.9
Pro: Nuts and cams to 3"
An initial muscular boulder move ascends quickly up past the bulge, and then continues up an offwidth and face climbing (piton & bolt) to an anchor.

50. French Intern 5.9 to 5.10a
Pro: Nuts and cams to 2"
A minor crack weakness in the wall located between Exchange Student and 'Je Mapel'. The line has two variations.

51. Exchange Student 5.10c
Pro: Thin nuts and cams to 2"
A powerful quality climb that shares the same start as Stewart's Ladder and then immediately moves right on a right arching seam.

52. Stewart's Ladder 5.10d
Pro: Small wires and cams to 1"
Start at an obvious right facing large roof next to the ground. Power up thin holds past the roof to the steep shallow corner (pitons) passing a midpoint crux, then finish via Well Hung in a single pitch lead or aim for another rap anchor at the top.

Hummingbird Wall: Located towards the west end of the main cliff, just east of the broken glass debris drop zone. Various local residents scavenge for glass bottles here. Refrain from placing bolts or fixed pitons on this section. The ledge area has no fixed belay anchors so ascend to the top and walk off. A single 60-meter rope is sufficient to rappel from the trees at the bluff top. The lower routes are described first, then the upper routes on the Hummingbird Terrace.

53. The Warm Up   5.11
Pro: small cams, nuts and Lowe Balls
Still dirty but with additional cleaning would be easier. Climb some relatively easy steps using gear for 35' to a crux directly below a rotting old Maple tree at the edge of a ledge. Continue up Northern Passage or Well Hung to the top or rappel from trees.

54. Kinetic Flow   5.8
Pro to 2½" including cams
Ascend three bolts to the left of the Warm Up route, sling a tree root and aim up left. Finish to the top by one of the upper routes. Bring gear for upper route.

55. Northern Passage Lower   5.7
Pro: Minor nuts and cams to 1¼", including Lowe Ball Nuts
West of the Maple tree cluster 15' is an obvious crack. Ascend this to Hummingbird Ledge, and then follow the steep rocky steps left to the large fir tree.

The Upper Routes on Hummingbird Terrace

56. Northern Passage Upper   5.4+
Pro: small nuts and cams to 1" (6" optional), slings
Northern Passage Upper starts from the left side of the Hummingbird terrace. A large short 6" crack at top can be climbed or bypassed by heading left to the large fir tree and up the short face above to top out. Tread gingerly across the dirt ledges.

57. Senior Moment
Thrash through the 4th class brush off Hummingbird Ledge ascending dirt slopes in the center-right of the upper area to get to the top; dirty and no protection.

58. Well Hung   5.6
Pro: Nuts and Cams to 1½"
Starts from the right hand side of the terrace off Hummingbird Ledge. A nice climb with subtle gear placements on nice stances, and an easy upper portion.

59. _____   5.7
Pro: Small nuts and cams to 1"
Limited gear options protect this line between Tribal Therapy and Northern Passage. Bring long slings for the large tree. Traverse in from easy ledges that go to the left or climb the poorly protected difficult direct start straight up to it. Pass the fir tree on Hummingbird Ledge on the left side and finish up Northern Passage upper or via the top of Tribal Therapy.

Dropzone area: Just west of the glass garden the bluff provides a tall sweep of broken corners and cracks. The following climbs start jus a few feet west of the Maple Tree Cluster on the trail.

60. Tribal Therapy 5.9
Pro: small nuts to 1", small cams to 2½"
A good route that starts at 20' left of a four Maple tree cluster on the trail. Scramble up a broken pillar section to the obvious perfect finger crack. Climb up to an obvious traverse left gains a horizontal ledge below a thin hand crack that widens near the top into the Far Side perfect hand jams and an anchor at the top.

61. Dwarf Toss 5.8 PG
Pro: Minor set of small nuts, cams to 2½"
Located 30'+ west of the four Maple trees cluster, it passes Hummingbird Ledge on the far left side about 20' left of a large fir tree. Start to the right of the Far Side or 13' to the left of Tribal Therapy. Climb ledges straight up past a fixed horizontal pin just below the right facing dihedral at the ½ way point. Finish on the Far Side hand crack.

62. The Far Side 5.8 PG
Pro to 2½"
Start up to the left of Dwarf Toss. Traverse right at the ½ way point and finish up a dihedral, traverse right onto the face slab at the ¾ mark to the obvious sweet hand crack below the top. The PG encompasses moves from the dihedral to the hand crack on easy terrain.

63. Gas Station Fashion A1
Unfinished aid line up the center of the face.

64. Fall From Grace 5.10b R or A2
An initial roped solo attempt in February '09, but finally went free a year later.

65. Fool's Rush In 5.9
Pro: Gear to 3"
Start up the thin seam located to the right of the large off width. At the crux climb around the detached block then onto easier rock. Step left below a slab and finish up the low angled ramp to the right.

66. Mark it Eight Dude 5.9+
Pro: Variable gear to large cams
Start with some bold boulder moves on thin gear to gain a very wide crack which slightly diagonals to the right to two bolts. Pitch two extension is called 'Smokey' at 5.10- and continues up and right and up past a single bolt up a crack to the top.

67. Child Abuse 5.8
Pro: need ¾" to 1" cams, small-med Nuts, 5" or 6" cam on last 10'
Ascend a short finger crack up and slightly left, then up right slightly to a gully of easy broken flakes to a ledge with a fixed rap anchor. Utilize all various placement options.

68. Happy Ending 5.10
Pro to 1"
Stem up the dihedral just left of 'Child Abuse' using small and funky gear then transition onto a uniquely featured but cryptic face past two bolts. Mantle onto a ledge, then battle through a steep crack section before escaping right to the anchor.

Arena of Pleasure area: A minor outcrop located to the west of the main cliff.

69. Kiddy Litter 5.2+
Ascend an easy ramp 50' and rap off a large fir tree. Second ascent was followed by Wes' 4 year old daughter.

70. Wet and Dirty 5.7
Pro: minor nut and cams to 2"
Climb up to a left slanting ramp just right of the preceding route to a shared anchor at 30'.

71. 31 Feet of Pleasure 5.6
Pro: Minor small gear, minimal large gear
Start in the middle of the arena and head up to a wide crack that slants slightly to the left. Duck under the horizontal fir tree to get to the sling on the tree anchor.

72. 41 Feet of Pain 5.6
Pro: Mixed gear rack
Start to the right of Thirty-one feet of Pleasure.

BEACON ROCK

THIS MAGNIFICENT GEOLOGIC MONOLITH of the Columbia River Gorge is the centerpiece to an extensive Washington State Park system. The park provides a multitude of activities including camping, boating, hiking, horseback riding, as well as fabulous rock climbing.

Captivating scenic views of the very heart of the Columbia River Gorge are part of the unique experience you will find when climbing here!

Portland area climbers could not have asked for a finer big wall crag than Beacon Rock. Technically sustained and demanding rock climbing of the finest degree can be found here on the huge 400-foot vertical south face aspect.

BRIEF HISTORY OF THE AREA

Beacon has enchanted and hauntingly enticed generations of adventurers even before the first ascent of the SE Face in April of 1952 by John Ohrenschall and Gene Todd. This historical monument was named Beacon Rock by Lewis and Clark while on their expedition of 1805–1806 to the Pacific Ocean. Later, in 1811, it attained the name "Inshoack Castle" but was generally known as "Castle Rock" until 1916 when the U.S. Board of Geographic Names reestablished the original name. The rock's first ascent was recorded on August 24, 1901 by Frank Smith, George Purcell, and Charles Church. They ascended a series of brush covered ledges on the west side. Several old fixed 1" thick by 12" long metal bars can still be seen on the 3rd pitch of the "spike" route.

In 1915 Henry J. Biddle initiated the building of the present-day trail leading to the summit of the rock. In 1935 Beacon Rock became part of the Washington State Parks system so that all could enjoy the beauty and wonder of this majestic monolith.

In 1961 the early roots of rock climbing at Beacon had begun. The spectacular efforts

Southwest face of Beacon Rock

of Eugene Dod, Bob Martin, and Earl Levin came to fruition when they succeeded in ascending a prominent crack and offwidth system to Big Ledge. To this day, Dod's Jam (5.10c) stands as a remarkable and classic example of early route pioneering achievement.

Throughout the latter half of the 1960s a core of climbers broke major barriers via mixed free and aid climbing technique. They developed excellent climbs like Flying Swallow (5.10d), Right and Left Gull (5.10a), Jensen's Ridge (5.11b), culminating with an ascent of Blownout (5.10a) in January 1969 by Steve Strauch and Danny Gates. Dean Caldwell, Dave Jensen, Steve Strauch, Kim Schmitz, Bob Martin, and others involved in the climbing scene will long be admired and remembered for their efforts.

Jim Toon, Dod's Jam (5.8 first pitch)

The next decade provided an even wider variety of mixed free and aid ascents. Two such notable feats certainly would have to be Les Nugent's ascent of Steppenwolf (5.10d) and Free For All (5.8) in 1973 by Dean Fry and Steve Lyford. The mid-1970s brought a new group of climbers to the crag as they ascended superb routes like Flight Time (5.11c); Pipeline (5.11a); Blood, Sweat, and Smears (5.10c); and Free For Some (5.11a). Jeff Thomas, Mark Cartier, Ted Johnson, Avery Tichner, Alan Kearney, Jim Olson, Mike Smelsar, Robert McGown, and others frequently turned toward the countless old aid lines, discovering that these routes produced excellent free climbs. Free climbing was now in vogue.

Subsequent decades brought an even wider spectrum of climbers to Beacon. From this new generation came quality routes like Cruisin' (5.7), Fear of Flying (5.10b), Bladerunner (5.10c), Winter Delight (5.10b), Borderline (5.11b), Excalibur (5.12b), Flying Dutchman (5.10b), and Windsurfer (5.10b). Those who continued to test the edge in the 1980s and 1990s were mainly Ron Allen, Scott Tracy, Mark Cartier, Darryl Nakahira, Robert McGown, Wayne Wallace, Nathan Charleton, Jim Opdyke, and Jim Yoder. Uncountable tales will be told in the years to come, as time will attest. So stay tuned to Beacon Rock.

REGULATIONS

Beacon Rock is a part of the Washington State Park system. This state park has a Climbing Management Plan in effect, which regulates all rock climbing activity at Beacon Rock. The following Washington State Park rules are to be respectfully observed while climbing here.

- Climbing is presently limited to the south face, the northwest face, and west face. The south face is closed from about Feb-

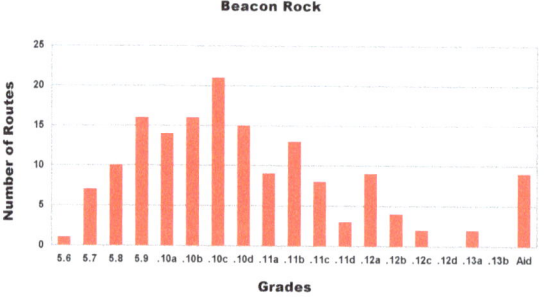

ruary 1 until approximately July 15 in order to facilitate and encourage the nesting habitat of the resident peregrine falcon. The south face occasionally opens early each year, but this is dependant upon the falcon chicks having fledged and the Park Rangers' approval to open the south face.
+ The east face is closed to all climbing. At the present time that section of the monolith will remain as a species habitat zone.
+ The northwest section of Beacon Rock is open year-round and presently offers a selection of rock climbs. This area is located in the forest to the right of the north side water spigot and ends just before reaching the west side hiking trail as it zigzags back left to meet the cliff. This portion is marked with state park signs.
+ Rock climbers must use the east side approach trail to reach the south face. Do not park at the boat ramp and camping area west of Beacon Rock to approach the cliff. (The amount of space for automobiles is limited and the railroad company does not appreciate seeing people walk along the tracks.).

Kyle Lehman leading *YW* **(5.8, P4)**

Please review all the rules and safety regulations posted on the bulletin board at the parking lot before climbing at Beacon Rock. Any violation of the rules would jeopardize the privilege of climbing on Beacon Rock. Review the State Park Internet web site, the bulletin board near the climbers trail, or check with the park manager if you are seeking more detailed information concerning the State Park rules. In keeping with these regulations, climb safely and enjoy your adventure while visiting Beacon Rock.

PRECAUTIONS

There are some distinct dangers at the south face of Beacon Rock: poison oak and rockfall. The rockfall is often generated near the west side hiking trail at a point above the third tunnel where sightseers gather. Another point of rockfall concern is above the Southeast Face route where rock climbers occasionally stir up trouble when dragging the rope through loose rocks on the Grassy Ledges route.

Some incidents due to stone fall have occurred. Because there is a risk of encountering rockfall while at the base of the cliff, climbing helmets are highly recommended. If others are known to be climbing above you on the Southeast Face or Right Gull, take extra precaution when moving about on the lower sections of the cliff and while standing around at the base of

Mark Retzlaff on the *SE Face*

the wall.

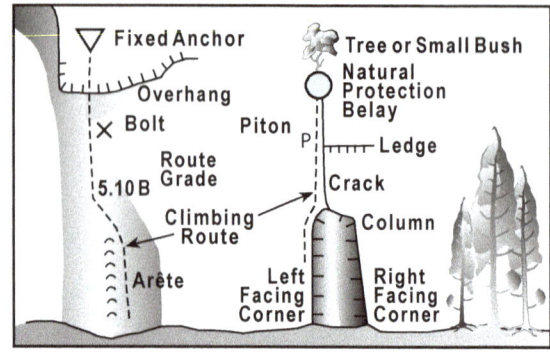

The other problem, poison oak, is seasonal. Long pants may suffice in protecting most climbers who visit Beacon, but persons whose skin is more susceptible to poison oak need to take greater precautions. Learn to recognize the shiny green three-leaf shape, the season, and the habitat where poison oak flourishes to limit your risk of infection. Some climbing routes up left of the Arena of Terror on the West Face are virtually unclimbable because of the poison oak.

In addition, excellent knowledge-based rock climbing skills are highly recommended when climbing at Beacon Rock. The activity of rock climbing here is neither for beginners nor for learning basic skills. Many of the routes are multi-pitch, bold leads that offer many difficult variables from steep, thin crack climbs to overhung offwidth corner systems. Some climbers visit Beacon Rock to just experience the climb. Take some time to relax on a ledge with a snack and water where you will surely develop a deeper appreciation for the vast beauty of the tremendously scenic Columbia River Gorge.

VISUAL BIO - SOUTH FACE

South Face: **Month** **5 Mins** **S** **All Day**
Regs **Trad**

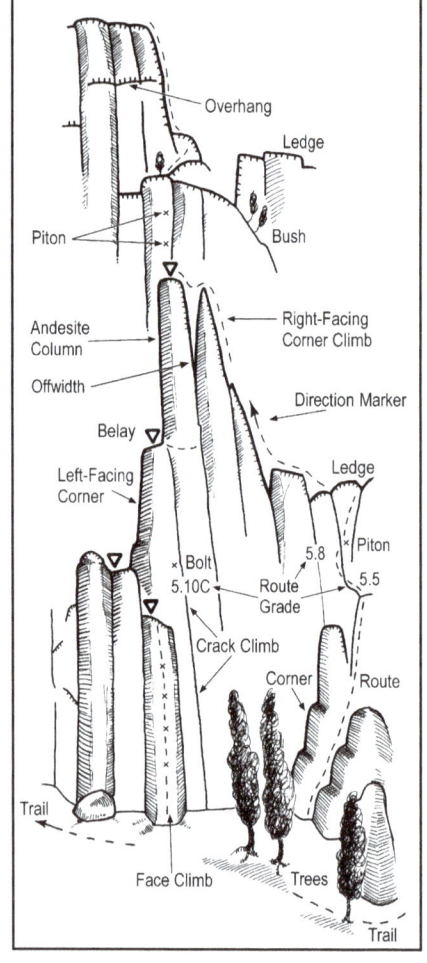

These emblems represent most of the south face of Beacon Rock. The south face offers some limited shade for the belayer, but not for the climber. You can escape some of the heat on a summer day by climbing on any southeasterly facing routes #1 to #26 after 3pm. Beacon is a traditional climbing site with plenty of gear leading up virtually endless steep crack systems.

🧗 HOW TO GET THERE

From I-205 (in Washington) drive east on State Route 14 for 28.8 miles to Beacon Rock. Or (in Oregon) drive east on I-84 to Cascade Locks. Cross the Bridge of the Gods, then drive 7 miles west on SR 14 past Bonneville Dam to this famous andesitic monolith of the Columbia River Gorge. Park at the east end of the parking lot near the rest facility.

🥾 APPROACH

The east side climber's trail gently zigzags downhill beneath the great east face overhangs and meets the southeasterly facing cliff aspect near Boardwalk. The trail wraps around and continues west along the entire base of the monolith. Along the base of the south face are three man-made tunnels; once there, you can pinpoint your location using the topographical maps herein to find your next climb.

The climbing routes at Beacon Rock are described from right to left (east-to-west). The first section details climbs from Boardwalk to the SE Corner and is immediately followed by details about all of the

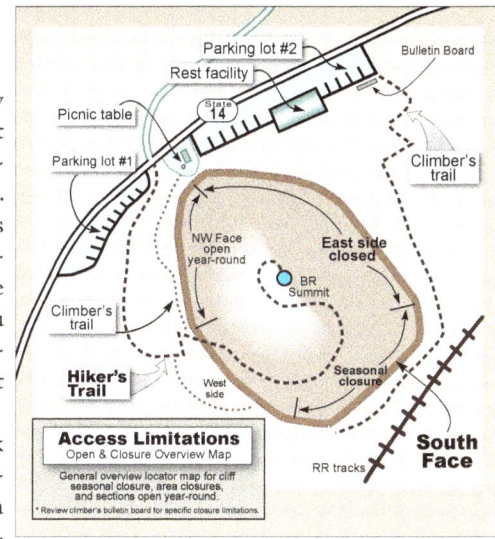

upper routes on or near the Grassy Ledges. The next section details climbs from just left of the SE Corner and ends with Jensen's Ridge. The next section details climbs on the upper west face of Beacon that are accessed by way of Jensen's Ridge.

1. **Pacific Rim   II 5.10c   ★**
   60' (18m) in length, QD's and minor pro to 1"
   A route that keeps you on the edge all the way. Begin below an overhang thirty feet downhill and left of an alcove. Commence up a shallow corner then face climb (bolts) up right along the virtual edge of the abyss directly below. Belay at anchor, then rappel 60'.

2. **Rhythm Method   5.7   ★★**
   80' (24m) in length, Pro is 6 QD' (for RM P1)
   This is the bolted line immediately to the right of Boardwalk. A nice clean face climb that is definitely worth doing! An 80' (24m) rappel from the belay. This route has more bold leads above the first belay station. The next pitches are called **Menopause**. P2 (5.10+) goes up a right facing corner ramp system through several small roofs to a belay. P3 (5.12+ **R/X**) climbs up to and through an A-framed overhung roof. Rappel with two ropes.

3. **Boardwalk   5.6**
   120' (36m) in length, Two rope rappel, Pro to 2"
   A long, obvious right facing corner system approximately 40' uphill from the trail. Climb the corner up to a roof, step right then up to a bolt anchor. Technically, this climb is the official boundary route.

4. **Young Warriors   III 5.9   ★★**
   Multi-pitch, Pro to 2½" including cams
   This 6-pitch route begins left of Boardwalk a short distance, and ascends in a fairly direct line via crack corner systems passing Tree Ledge on the right.

Pete G. on *YW* (5.8, P3)

Beacon Rock reference map 1: *South Face Aspect*

BEACON ROCK 207

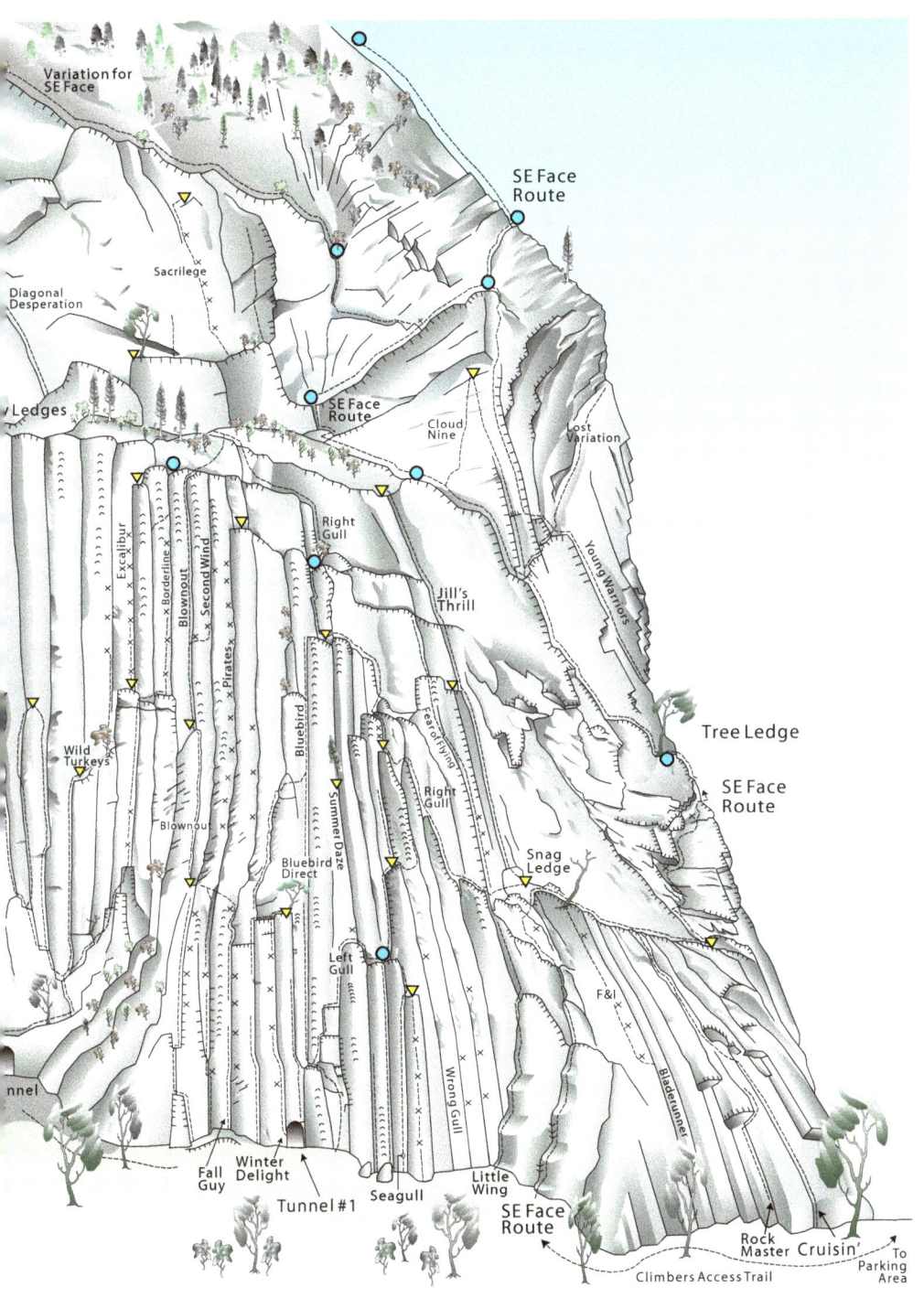

Beacon Rock reference map 2: Ink illustration of the South Face Aspect

Beacon Rock 15"x20" map: www.portlandrockclimbs.com

Beacon Rock reference map 3: *Photograph of the South Face Aspect*

Pitch 1 (5.8) : Climb a nice long face with mixed bolts and pro to a bolt anchor at 110'.
Pitch 2 (5.9): Move left and climb up through an overhanging 'A' shaped feature (5.9) to merge into SE Face route. Step to the right to a stance at a bolt anchor just short of Tree Ledge.
Pitch 3 (5.9): Continue straight up a minor but long corner system to a large slab and ledge. Angle up left into a small alcove with some old fixed gear nearby.
Pitch 4 (5.9): Move up out to the left onto the obvious arête. Stay on this rounded arête, then go up a short slab and a shallow corner system to an airy belay stance. The upper SE Face route also uses this airy belay stance. You can finish up the regular last upper portion of the SE Face route, or you can move up right via a short ramp and corners for short 5.10ish move.

A seldom repeated route **Lost Warriors** (5.11+) takes off at the P1 belay climbing up and slightly right. Multi-pitch. If it ever becomes popular we'll include beta.

5. **Stone Rodeo   5.12a** ★★★
   65' (19m) in length, QD's and minor pro to 3" and cams recommended
   A powerful punch of physical endurance. As the trail meets the cliff beneath Cruisin', look to the right 25' past an oak tree. Beyond is a bolted overhung face that leads up through a roof split with a crack. Excellent climb. Protection will be needed for the roof move.

Jim Meyer, 1ˢᵗ pitch of *SE Face*

6. **Rock Police   II 5.10c**
   Multi-pitch, QD's and pro to 1" and TCU's required, Poor hangers
   To the right of the same oak tree 15' is a bolted face that follows a right leaning arête. An unusual climb that is still fun, but presently has poor hangers. Climb up a short face (immediately right of Return To The Sky) to a bulge crux move (bolt). Angle up right on a steep slab while staying near the outer right edge (crux) till the climbing eases to a ledge and bolt anchor. Rappel 65' or angle up left to the second belay on the SE Face route. From there step up right (5.9) onto the outer edge of a steep slab, until it rejoins with the SE Face route near the top of this slab.

Jim Toon on *Cruisin'*

Cruisin'

The route *Cruisin'* is an excellent high quality and challenging 5.7 alternative start to getting onto the *Southeast Face* route. This route merges with the traverse pitch to belay at the 2nd anchor of the *Southeast Face*. Be sure to bring some thin pro.

7. **Return to the Sky   5.10a**
   65' (19m) in length, Pro to 1½"
   A seldom climbed route that angles over several dihedrals then up a corner. Start behind the oak tree and climb up right past a bolt (crux) then upward to a bolt belay. Rappel.

8. **Sky Pilot   5.11a**
   95' (28m) in length, Pro to 2"
   Start as for Return To The Sky except storm through a weakness in the overhang above. Obscure climb.

9. **Couch Master   5.9**
   100' (30m) in length, Pro to 1½"
   Start up slab behind oak tree, step left and turn corner stemming up (crux) to join with Cruisin'.

10. **Jingus Jam   5.9 (variation)**
    35' (10m) in length, Pro to 2"

11. **Cruisin' Direct Finish   5.11c (variation)**
    25' (7m) in length, Pro to ¾" and pitons

12. **Cosmic Dust   5.10b (variation)**
    25' (7m) in length, Pro to 1"

13. **Cruisin' (aka Cruise Master)   5.7   ★ ★ ★**
    100' (30m) in length, Pro to 2"
    An excellent local favorite, and rightly so. Start up a fun slab 15' left of the large oak tree. Follow a thin crack (crux) to an overhang. Move left to sidestep the roof, the continue up a dihedral to easy ledges. Belay at the established anchors on the SE Face. Reference Topo Diagram A.

14. **Stardust   5.8   ★**
    100' (30m) in length, Pro to 1½"
    Start up a left facing corner to a small roof. Turn this by sidestepping around to the right and continue up until it joins Cruisin'.

15. **Rock Master   5.11c PG   ★ ★**
    100' (30m) in length, Pro to 2" TCU's required
    Technically very bold. Stem up a left facing corner (crux) using very unorthodox maneuvers to succeed (#0 TCU). Pull through a difficult roof move and continue up a crack system that eases and joins with the SE Face route.

Topo A: *Cruise Master*

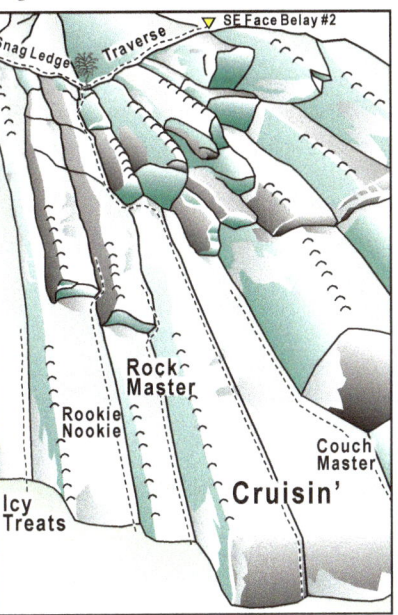

SE Face Route

The *Southeast Face Route* is the premier climb at Beacon Rock and rightly so. The SE Face route (5.7) is the most frequently climbed technical route on the river face at Beacon. This favorite climb is certainly worth sending on your first visit here. It offers 600' of multi-pitch rock climbing on variable terrain ranging from long ramps, a tour across the *Grassy Ledges*, to the famous high angle crux pitch face climb, all with good cracks. A great climb for skilled crack protection climbers.

16. Rookie Nookie 5.10c PG ★★

100' (30m) in length, Pro to 2"
Slightly uphill and left of Rock Master is a prominent left-facing dihedral with one fixed piton. A great climb. Joins with the SE Face route.

17. Icy Treats (aka Frozen Treats) 5.10d R

100' (30m) in length, Pro to 1½"
Look for a shallow corner with two bolts near the start. A difficult stem problem with hard to place pro and a little run out in places. Climb up past the bolts to a halfway stance. More awkward, desperate smears lead to the top where it joins the SE Face route.

18. Switchblade 5.11a PG

110' (33m) in length, Pro unknown

19. Bladerunner 5.10c ★★

110' (33m) in length, Pro to 2"
An incredible route and an excellent prize. Begin up and pull through (1 bolt) a loose section of rock to a stance. Angle up left then straight up a seam (2 bolts and crux) until the crack widens and eases in difficulty. Belay at bolts just below Snag Ledge tree.

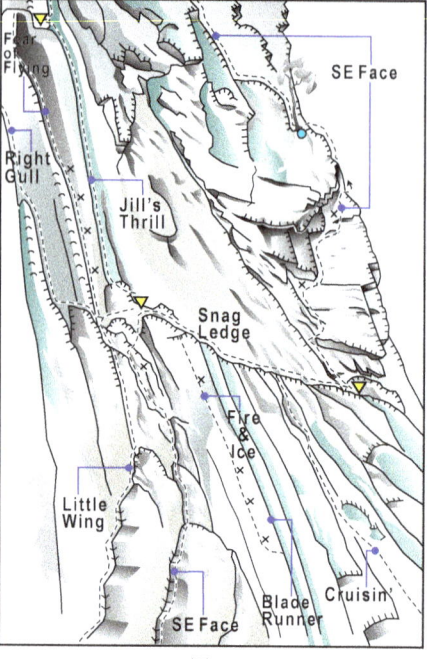

Topo B: *Southeast Face*

20. Fire and Ice 5.11b ★★

110' (33m) in length, QD's, small wires, and TCU's to 1"
A high quality route. Ascends a smooth, rounded arête slab left of Bladerunner. Climb up Bladerunner to the second bolt, traverse left onto the face and go straight up the bolt line. From a stance above the halfway crux, step left to finish up a thin seam (pitons) which ends at the snag Ledge tree.

21. M B T N 5.11b R

50' (15m) in length, Thin pro to 1"
A thin crack system that is infrequently climbed immediately left of Fire & Ice.

22. N B N F 5.11a

50' (15m) in length, QD's and pro to "
A thin crack system that is infrequently climbed. Just left of previous route.

EXIT OPTIONS FOR UPPER SE FACE

Two possible exits are available from the 'good stance' at the top of pitch 5; you can climb the *Upper West Ramp* or the *Standard SE Exit* to the steep rock rib.

To climb the *Upper West Ramp*:
Exit left at the ¼" bolt (P6) by traversing left along small grassy steps, then up bushy ramps and 4th class ground westward until it eases and lands on the hikers trail. Or you can access the *Upper West Ramp* by climbing a short 5.6 slab crack directly above the belay at the 'good stance' at the top of pitch 5.

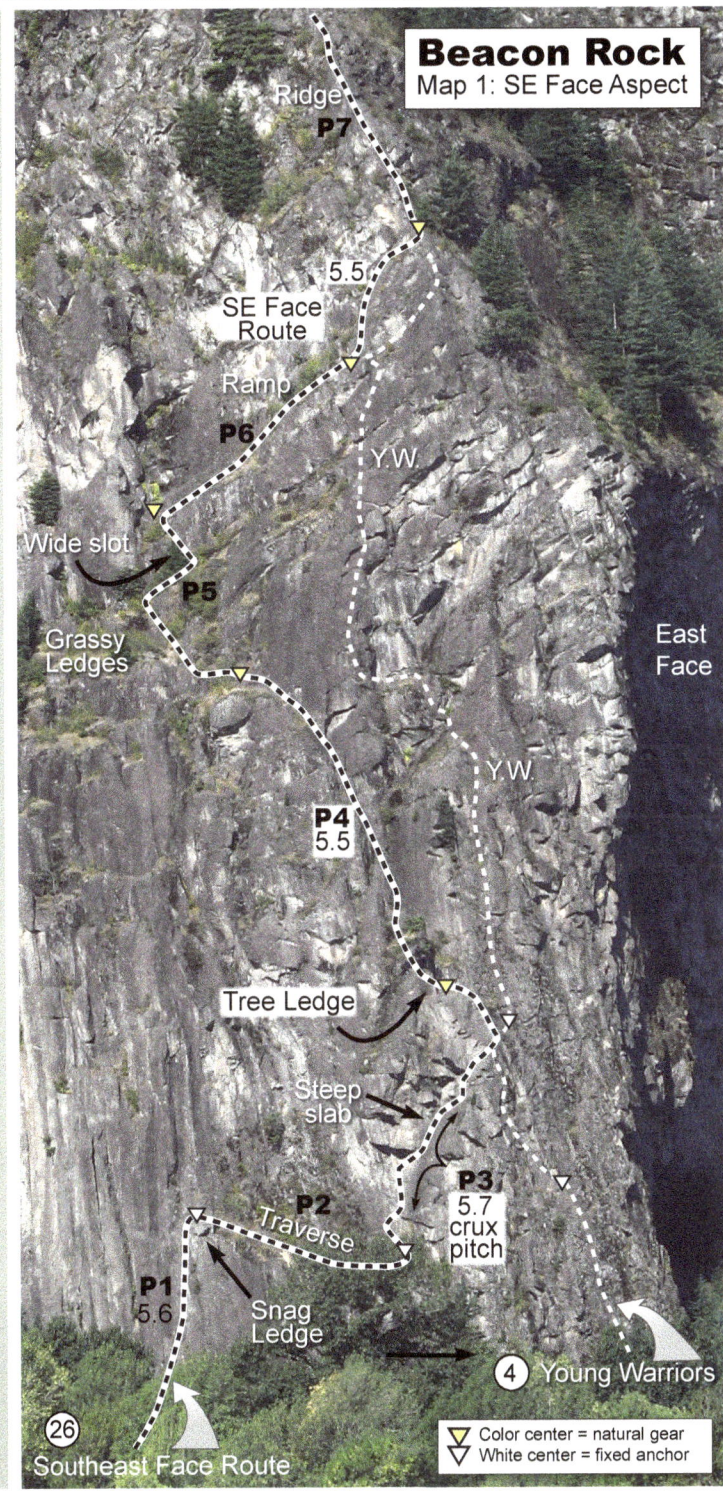

23. Levitation Blues 5.10d
50' (15m) in length, QD's and pro to 1"
Another thin crack system that is seldom climbed. Left of previous route.

24. Repo Man 5.10c
40' (12m) in length, Pro to 1"
A thin crack system that is infrequently climbed.

25. Lethal Ejection 5.9
60' (18m) in length, Pro to 2"
A crack climb located above MBTN and ends at Snag Ledge.

SE FACE AREA

26. SOUTHEAST FACE III 5.7 ★★★
Multi-pitch, Pro to 2"
This is THE Beacon Rock classic route, and was the first established rock climb here. It is an enjoyable multi-pitch route that meanders up 600' of rock to the west side hikers' trail. Begin west and uphill about 30' of a prominent corner near the railroad tracks.
Pitch 1: Climb easy steps on clean rock 80' to a bolt belay at Snag Ledge.
Pitch 2: Traverse horizontally right (NE) along ledges 70' to another bolt anchor.
Pitch 3: Move up a slab to the left 12', then move right (crux) over a slight bulge to a small stance under a roof. Move up right along a steep right-facing slab corner system for 40'. When possible work up to the right to turn an exposed corner, then up to the Tree Ledge belay (bypassing the Young Warriors bolt anchor on the SE Buttress face).
Pitch 4: Follow a left leaning dihedral ramp system 160' to Grassy Ledges and set a belay.
Pitch 5: Wander up and left past a small fir tree through a short offwidth 'slot' move to a good stance and set a belay.
The Standard Exit for the Southeast Face (the popular method) is as follows:
Pitch 6: From the good stance continue up a right-facing low angle ramp system (¼" bolt at top of ramp) as it angles up right to an airy stance.
From the airy stance climb straight up 30'

Map 2: Upper West Ramp exit variation

to a notch and set up another belay.

Pitch 7: Continue up the steep rock rib for 160' and belay for the last time at a tree. A short scramble from here up in the forest ends at the paved summit hikers trail. Descend the hikers trail back to the car.

Note: Some of the pitches of the SE Face described above can be combined with use of a 60-meter or 70-meter rope. Also, the first two pitches have fixed belay stations, while on the remainder of the climb you will need to set up your own natural belay anchors. Reference photo Map #1, Inset Map #2 and Topo Map B for a closeup visual analysis of this route.

3rd pitch slab SE Face

Note: Be vigilant when traversing across Grassy Ledges. Handle your rope with caution, because loose rock is easily disturbed by foot or rope. Dislodged rocks are a hazard to the rock climbers below. The belay anchors for the SE Face route above Grassy Ledges are not fixed and you will need to use natural protection at each belay stance.

6th pitch SE Face

27. **Variation   5.9**
    25' (7m) in length, Pro to 2"
28. **Desdichado   5.10c**
    40' (12m) in length, QD's and pro to 1½"
    A unique short climb with poor hangers. Located about ⅓ of the way up the crux pitch of the Southeast Face on a slightly overhung corner.
29. **Dynaflux   5.11b**
    50' (15m) in length, QD's and pro to 1½"
    Up left from the second belay on the Southeast Face is a bulging face with a vertical crack in it. Two bolts protect the hardest moves. Rappel from bolt anchor.
30. **Jill's Thrill   5.9   ★ ★ ★**
    190' (58m) in length, Pro to 2"
    A fun route, especially the second half. Start at Snag Ledge belay. Climb a long corner up right with 2 fixed pitons. Belay at anchor on a ledge to the left at 80'. Step back to the right and continue 60' up a steeply angled flared crack system past a minor stance up another crack to a large ledge at a belay anchor. A 50' third pitch powers up a thin crack and ends on another ledge on Grassy Ledges.

Jill's Thrill is a common rappel on Beacon Rock that many climbers use to exit down from Grassy Ledges. There are other rope rappel options, but this one is conveniently oriented near the SE Face, and it can be done with a single 60-meter rope.

31. **Tooth Faerie   5.10a**
    70' (21m) in length, Pro to 2" and #0 TCU recommended
    Ascend a clean crack directly above belay anchor. At the overhanging flake, face climb up the left side of crack to join with Jill's Thrill.

32. To the Edge and Beyond 5.11b
70' (21m) in length, Pro to 2" including TCU's
Somewhat contrived, but challenging.

33. Fear of Flying 5.10b ★ ★ ★
160' (48m) in length, Pro to 1½"
A superb Beacon Rock climb. Step left from the Snag Ledge belay as if you are heading to Right Gull. Just before stepping onto a sloping wide stance, commence up a steep corner dihedral protected with 4 fixed pins (5.10a). As it eases slightly, power up another short crack to a flat ledge (65') and belay at Jill's Thrill anchor on right. Continue up a 5.10b thin crack (fixed pin) to a minor ledge and step right to join the remaining portion of Jill's Thrill.

34. Desperado 5.10d R
160' (48m) in length, Thin pro to 1½" and pitons

34b. Crazy Horse
Pro: Nuts to 1" and cams to 4"
Start on Right Gull P2 and pull past the crux to a ledge, but avoid the next wide 5.8 part of Right Gull. Look for another wide crack and ascend up this crack corner (5.8ish) to a ledge, then up a face with a crack on the left. Climb over a minor bulge and step right and up to a large ledge where it lands on a gravelly bench low on Grassy Ledges. Expect some moss and friable rock in this area.

35. Right Gull III 5.10a (or 5.7 A0) ★ ★ ★
Multi-pitch, Pro to 3"
A very popular route with plenty of variety.

Pitch 1: From the Snag Ledge belay step left around a corner and enter a large right-facing corner. Climb this until it tops out on a pedestal, then gingerly move left to a bolt anchor.

Pitch 2: Either A0 or free climb (5.10a crux) past 2 fixed pitons to a ledge. Above are several options. On the right is an offwidth (4"); in the center, a slightly dirty left leaning crack (5.8); or on your left is a 3" hand/fist crack (5.8). At the top of these options, step left to a bolt anchor on a comfortable ledge. Bluebird and several other routes end here as well.

Pitch 3: Continue up a wide crack pulling through an awkward bulge (5.8) to a rocky ledge with a small oak tree.

Pitch 4: Wander up behind the tree and leftward via a series of steps and belay on Grassy Ledges at a tree. Reference Topo C.

36. Vulcan's Variation 5.8
12' (3m) in length, Pro to ¾"
A rather convenient way to bypass the crux on Right Gull. Climb a thin crack to the right of the second belay and above a sharp ear of rock.

37. Muriel's Memoir 5.9
25' (7m) in length, Pro to 1½"
When Right Gull eases to the rocky ledge near a small oak tree, look to your left. This is the good looking clean corner crack. Rejoins with regular route.

The following 13 routes are located above Grassy Ledges beginning near Tree Ledge and ending at the top out point for Flying Swallow.

38. Synapse 5.10c
35' (10m) in length, Pro to 1"

39. Death and Taxes 5.12c ★
45' (13m) in length, QD's and minor pro to 1"
This short, premium quality face climb utilizes a series of incipient seams and edges. A very unusual climb to be found here at Beacon. It is located approximately 40' up and left of Tree Ledge (SE Face route).

40. Lost Variation II 5.8
Pro unknown
An indisputable route so named because numerous parties were unable to find it, yet it is rumored to be an interesting climb.

41. Elusive Element 5.10d R ★
80' (24m) in length, Pro to 1½" including TCU's
A fabulous yet easily missed route roughly 100' up left from Tree Ledge. Lead up a right facing corner (crux) past 2 bolts to an easy slab. Continue up the crack to a short steep section (crux) and reach a bolt anchor just beyond. A really good climb except for the weird hangers and run out sections.

42. Cloud Nine 5.9
80' (24m) in length, Pro to 2"
A bit mossy, but still a neat crack climb on a long slab. Located immediately uphill and left of Elusive Element. No fixed belay at present.

43. High and Mighty 5.11b ★
80' (24m) in length, TCU's and wires to 1½" Needs bolts or fixed pins
An excellent route high above Grassy Ledges. Located up left from the easy 5th class offwidth move on Grassy Ledges (SE Face route). Climb a wandering set of seams on a steep smooth face until possible to turn a corner leftward then up a crack on a slab. No fixed belay anchor.

44. Sacrilege 5.10d ★★★
80' (24m) in length, QD's and minor pro to 1"
A fantastic face climb on very steep terrain. Incredible lead and one of the better upper wall Beacon classics. To the right of Diagonal Desperation is a large hidden terrace with an oak tree on it. Sacrilege is the route on the right side of this terraced ledge.

45. _____ 5.12+
80' (24m) in length (TR immediately left of the above climb)

46. Diagonal Desperation 5.11c R
160' (48m) in length, Pro to 2" & very small pro
Located just to the right of the upper pitches of Smooth Dancer. This free climb ascends a long left-leaning crack system, then branches up right under a small overhang. Surmount the overhang to easier terrain. Merges onto the upper west exit of SE Face.

47. _____

48. Riverside 5.10b
Multi-pitch, [P1 80' (24m)], Pro to 2½"
Steep sustained crack climbing that utilizes odd pods (half-body jams) up a left-leaning crack system located near the left end of Grassy Ledges. Rappel after 80' or continue up to the west side trail.

First Tunnel

A great selection of stout short climbs are available at the First Tunnel, such as Spring Fever, Winter Delight and Sufficiently Breathless. These tricky leads are a must for any solid 5.10 lead climber.

49. _____ **5.11+**
   80' (24m) in length (TR)

50. _____ **5.12+**
   80' (24m) in length (TR)

The following routes are described right to left beginning immediately left of the SE Face route.

51. Little Wing 5.8 ★★★
   80' (24m) in length, Pro to 2"
   Immediately left of the SE Face route is a fun little classic climb that begins up several reasonable slab steps. Follow this corner to a stance on a detached pedestal, then finish up a shallow well-protected crack until it is possible to step right at the Snag Ledge belay.

52. Broken Arrow 5.10a
   60' (18m) in length, Pro to 1"

53. Unknown 5.12a
   120' (36m) in length, QD's and pro to 1"
   Uphill and left of the SE Face is a smooth face that offers several thin steep rock climbs. Climb (the right one) a very difficult steep face that has fixed bolts and pitons for 40' until you can reach over and use the outside corner of Right Gull. Lay back up this (2 bolts) until it is necessary to join the Right Gull route.

54. Magic Fingers 5.12c
   110' (33m) in length, Pro to 2½"
   Magic Fingers is the left climb, a serious and demanding 2 bolt seam on this steep face. The climbs eventually opens up to a crack and becomes the large wide chimney section on the last 20 ft. of Left Gull.

55. Wrong Gull II 5.10c ★★
   110' (33m) in length, Pro to 2½"
   No two ways about it, a terrific climb with excellent protection. Start in the minor corner near an old tree stump. Stem up 80' to a bolt anchor on a ledge. Then, if you're very bold, jam up the left side

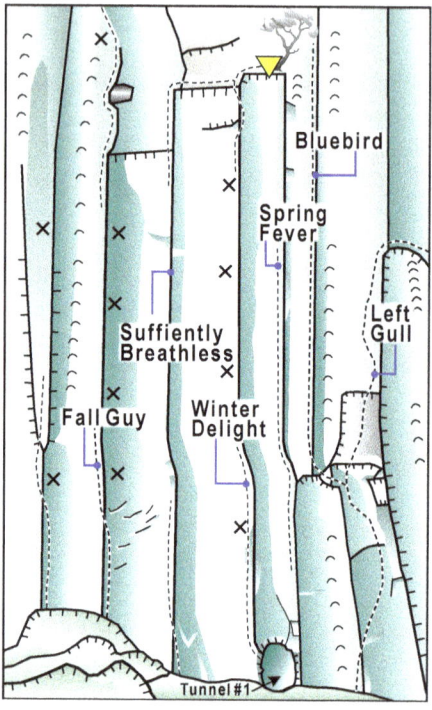

Topo D: *Winter Delight*

Kyle leading Sufficiently Breathless

of a detached free standing pillar. Joins Right Gull.

56. Sorcerer's Apprentice 5.10c
40' (12m) in length, Pro to 1"
A thin seam crack immediately left of Wrong Gull.

57. Old Warriors Never Die 5.12b ★
80' (24m) in length, QD's and minor pro to 1"
A great bolted climb located on the outside of a minor rounded corner. Climb 45' up the steep face and short dirty corner to a ledge. Belay at anchor. Rappel or continue up right (bolts) via dubious cracks to join with Wrong Gull at the bolt belay. Rappel.

The following three routes are great climbs that define what Beacon is all about... steep powerful stemming up thin crack corners. Hopefully there is a fixed belay anchor, but if not just wrap a long sling around the blocks and rappel.

58. Seagull II 5.10c ★★★
45' (13m) in length for P1, Pro to 1½" and cams suggested
This and the following two climbs are superb classics. They accurately portray Beacon stem climbing at its finest. The route ascends a double cornered crack system (5.10c) just to the right of a large boulder. Bolt belay on ledge (45'). Rappel or climb a thin crack above (5.10d) to join with Right Gull.

59. Ten-A-Cee Stemming 5.10c PG ★★★
45' (13m) in length, Thin wires and pro to 1½"
An excellent thin crack and corner stemming problem.

60. Av's Route 5.10d ★★
45' (13m) in length, Thin wires and pro to 2½"
A good stemming climb on thin but good protection. Ascends the corner system just to the left of the large boulder. Beware of minor poison oak near the top of the climb.

61. Too Close for Comfort 5.12a
This is the outside corner next to Av's Route.

62. Left Gull III 5.10a or 5.8 A0
Multi-pitch, Pro to 3"
An unusual but fun climb. Some chimney climbing to contend with. Starts up broken corners and ledges immediately right of the first tunnel and joins with Right Gull at its second belay on the pedestal. Reference Topo E.

63. Summer Daze 5.11c or C3 ★★
95' (28m) in length, Thin wires and TCU's to 2½"
Great climb with a desperate thin start. From the belay ledge at the top of Av's Route / Seagull step left then proceed up the seam (piton). The crack widens and passes a fir tree halfway up before it joins with Right Gull at a ledge belay.

64. Unknown 5.12
130' (39m) in length (TR)
An outside arête and face between Summer Daze and Bluebird.

65. Bluebird Direct 5.10d R ★
160' (48m) in length, Pro to 2½"
Directly above the first tunnel is a long dihedral. Commence

up a thin seam on the tunnel's right side to a ledge 20' up. Stem up a poorly protected dihedral to where it joins with the standard Bluebird route. A good climb but a little run out.

FIRST TUNNEL

The following five routes offer high quality and moderately difficult climbing with callenging characteristics.. Reference Topo D. These climbs are located at the First Tunnel.

66. Spring Fever   5.10a   ★★

55' (16m) in length, Pro to 1½"
Ascend the thin seam just to the right of the first tunnel. At the small ledge 20' up step left and continue up a weird crack to a bolt anchor belay. Rappel.

67. Winter Delight   5.10b PG   ★★★

55' (16m) in length, Pro to 1½" (#2 TCU required)
A prize worth attaining and a delight to climb. Climbs a partly bolted seam immediately left of the first tunnel. Rappel from the bolt anchor.

68. Sufficiently Breathless   5.10a   ★★★

55' (16m) in length, Pro to 1½" Doubles at ¾"
Superb route with excellent protection. Ascend via a minor crack and corner system just left of Winter Delight. Several fixed pitons. Exit right to the belay anchor.

69. Fall Guy   5.10d   ★★

65' (19m) in length, 5 QD's and optional pro to ¾"
An exciting definitive face climb. Climb a shallow vertical corner to a sloping stance (loose rock just above) stepping up left and around corner to join with Aging Fags. Rappel from bolt belay.

70. Aging Fags   5.10d PG   ★

65' (19m) in length, RP's, small wires and TCU's to 1"
A wide dihedral that is quite bold to lead. Starts off from a ledge 15' left of the tunnel.

71. Blownout Direct   5.10b

65' (19m) in length, Pro to 1½"
Climbs a free-standing thin flake, then pulls into a corner stance before ascending a piton protected seam. Rappel from bolt anchor.

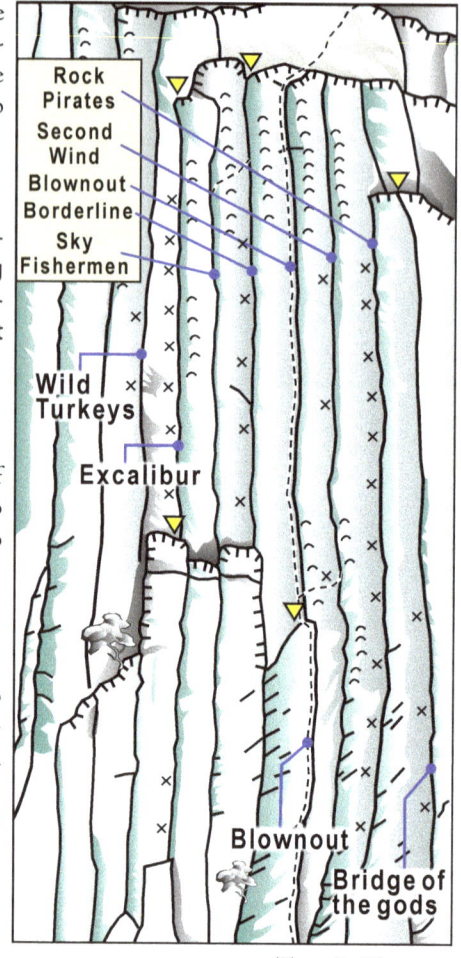

Topo F: Blownout

BEACON ROCK 223

Shane leading Excalibur 5.12b

Nate leading Borderline 5.11b

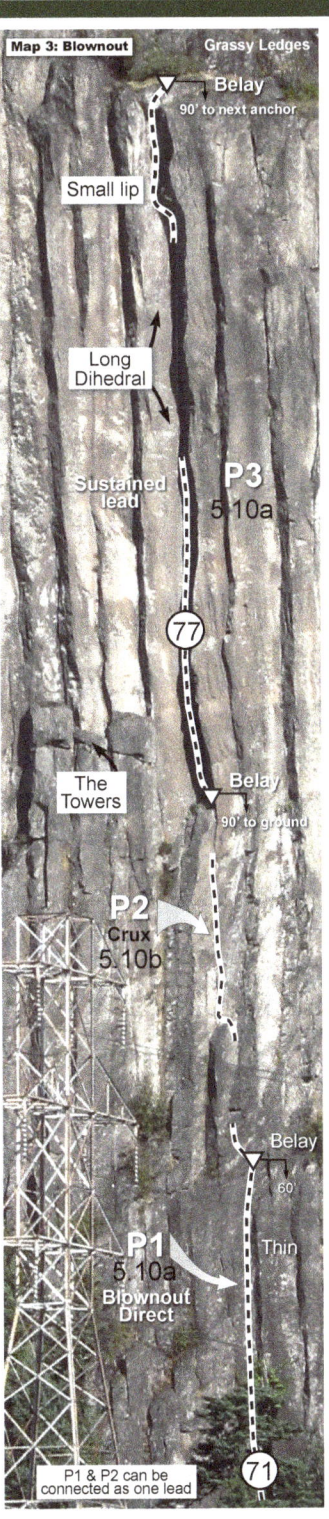

72. Tombstone Territory   5.7
25' (7m) in length, Pro to 2½"

73. Bluebird   II 5.10a ★
Multi-pitch, Pro to 4"
One of the original Beacon favorites with an excellent crux pitch. The old starting point was located at a fir tree next to the base of Wild Turkeys. From there it traversed rightward via brushy, sloping ledges and minor down steps. Otherwise climb one of a number of routes near the first tunnel to approach.

74. Variation   5.9
40' (12m) in length, Pro to 3"
Halfway up the crux pitch of Bluebird, step left onto a good ledge and finish up a deep dihedral choked with

bushes.

75. **Bridge of the Gods   5.12b**
110' (33m) in length, Pro to 4"
High above the first tunnel is an impressive shallow corner system that eventually widens to an off-width crack splitting an arête. Two rope rappel. Approach via one of the lower variations.

76. **Pirates (aka Rock Pirates) 5.12a R**
110' (33m) in length, Pro to 2" and run out
An unusually demanding climb on balancy holds. A very long lead with many fixed pitons. Approach via one of the lower variations. Two rope rappel.

77. **Blownout II 5.10b   ★★★**
Multi-pitch, Pro to 2½" Doubles recommended
One of the ten supreme classics. Commence up Blownout Direct (or another nearby option) to a bolt belay. Move up left, then straight up a jagged hand crack to a belay in a protected corner beneath the great upper dihedral. Step forth and climb the obvious corner 120' (crux) until possible to exit right onto a gravelly ledge. Reference Photo Map #3 (Topo F).

78. **Second Wind   5.11d   ★★**
100' (30m) in length, Pro to 2" and TCU's recommended
Twenty feet up the last pitch of Blownout (¼" bolt), traverse right around the arête and finish up a strenuous thin finger crack.

79. **Borderline II 5.11b   ★★★**
80' (24m) in length, QD's and pro to 1½"
The second pitch is an impressively powerful climb. **Pitch 1:** Begin at the lone fir tree immediately right of the Wild Turkeys start. Climb up right onto a detached flake and

climb (pitons) 40' up (5.10+) to a belay on the 'Beacon Towers' ledge. **Pitch 2:** Step right and embark up the beautiful second pitch (bolts and gear) via face climbing and lay back to the top. Pitch two is the primary portion that most hard core climbers aim to lead so avoid the first pitch by climbing Blownout Direct or a nearby alternative route.

80. **Sky Fishermen   5.13a PG**
80' (24m) in length, 4 bolts, pro to 1½"
The pitch left of Borderline is now free. Technical, thin, healthy flight time, with quality and power packed in one little route utilizing the crack/seam all the way.

81. **Excalibur   5.12b   ★ ★ ★**
80' (24m) in length, QD's, small wires, TCU's, and Cams to 2½"
Incredible! An extreme line and one of the more difficult established free climbs at Beacon Rock. Start on the 'Beacon Towers' immediately right of Wild Turkeys. Face climb straight up until it eases and widens gradually near the top.

82. **Crankenstein   5.11a**
35' (10m) in length (TR)
Immediately right of the start for Wild Turkeys is this minor dihedral corner.

83. **Wild Turkeys   5.13a R**
Multi-pitch, pro to 1½"
A powerful sustained free climb with demanding small gear placements on a beautifully unique climb. P1/P2 is 5.10c and P3 is 5.13a. Ascend a corner, then angle up right 25' to a sloped ledge belay. Continue up right via easy steps to the 'Beacon Towers'. Climb the seam left of Excalibur. WT is one of the original Beacon aid routes 5.10c A2.

84. **Unknown   5.12+**
120' (36m) in length (TR)
From the first belay on Wild Turkeys commence directly up a shallow dihedral. It soon straightens to a vertical seam on a perfect smooth face.

SECOND TUNNEL

The following climbs are above the Second Tunnel.

85. **Psychic Wound   5.10b**
80' (24m) in length, Pro to 1½"
This climb and the following several routes are located above the second tunnel. From a stance at a thin oak tree step up right and climb a left facing corner (piton) to a stance. Finish up a weaving corner system until possible to exit left to the Flying Dutchman bolt belay. The upper portion of this crack system is 5.12 TR.

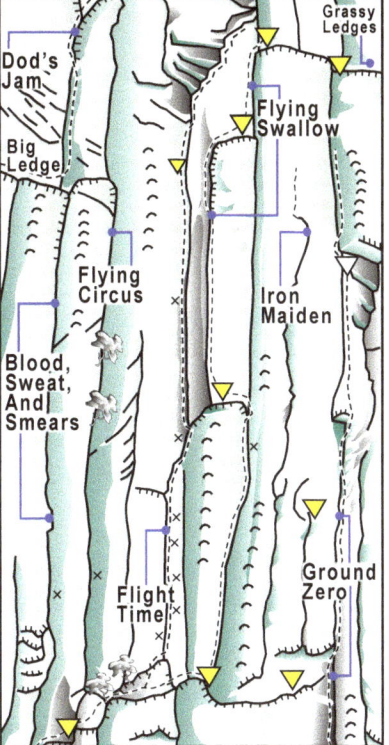

Topo G: *Flight Time*

86. Flying Dutchman 5.10b (P2 5.11b/c) ★★

80' (24m) in length for P1, Pro to 1½" Small wires and TCU's suggested

An enjoyable route. Excellent rock. Begin at the thin oak tree and climb up past two pitons to a stance. Continue straight up a left facing dihedral to the bolt anchor. The upper pitch has been free climbed at 5.11b/c to Grassy Ledges.

87. Bears in Heat II 5.11b ★★

80' (24m) for P1, Pro to 2½" and cams suggested

A great climb. The name describes accurately the second pitch bear hug. Start as for Flying Dutchman past the pitons to a stance. Step left, then ascend an unusual crack system to a crux move just short of the anchor. Rappel or continue up (35') the second pitch bear hugging and jamming to reach a final belay. Rappel.

88. Dirty Double Overhang III 5.7 A3

Multi-pitch, Pitons and pro to 1½"

A long, multi-pitch aid route immediately right of the great roofs in the center of the wall. The two pitches above Grassy Ledges offer good free climbing.

89. Smooth Dancer   P1: 5.11c, P2: 5.12b

Multi-pitch, set of stoppers to 1", cams to 6", P1 has 4 bolts, P2 has 6 bolts

A quality two-pitch route on the central face. Pitch 1 goes free at 5.11c, while the second pitch goes free at 5.12b. The climb is still a spicey and commiting free route requiring a full rack of gear.

89b. Crack To Nowhere 5.8 C1 or A2

Pro: Nuts to 1", Cams to 3" including doubles, brass aid nuts, hook, Pecker or birdbeak, KB's

Located immediately right of Take Fist is a crack breaking through a roof which contin-

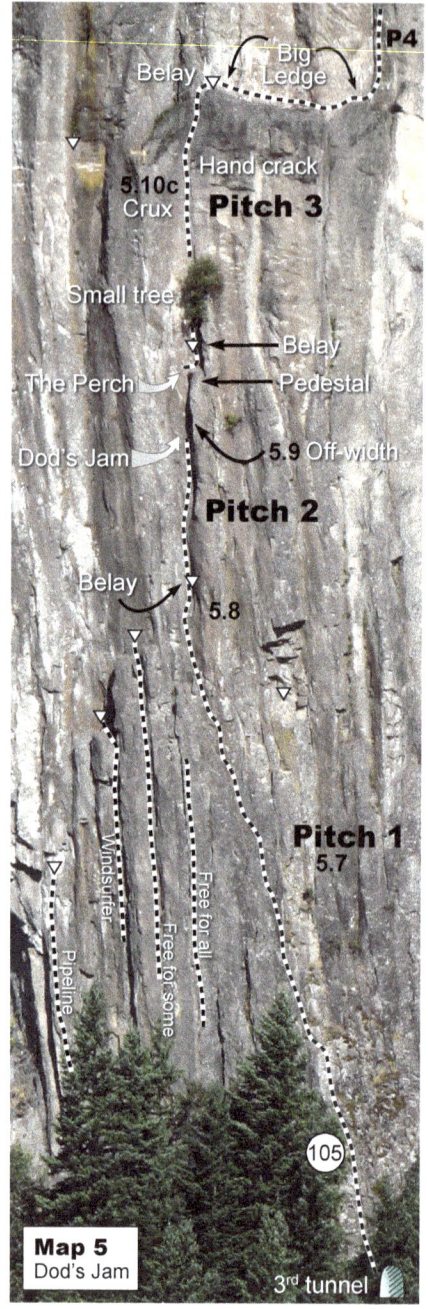

Map 5
Dod's Jam

THIRD TUNNEL

A stellar list of high quality climbs is available immediately past the Third Tunnel. Classics such as Dod's Jam, Free For All, Free For Some, Windsurfer, and Pipeline should always be on your hit list when visiting Beacon.

ues a short distance then stops. This climb ascends to that point, but a possible free extension could exist with the addition of bolts on the arête above the crack. Ascend Take Fist P1 and jump over right onto the crack system to punch through the large roof till the crack ends.

90. Take Fist   III 5.10d
Multi-pitch, Pro to 3"
This wild climb leads through a fist crack in the 'great roof' area. A little brushy on the first pitch. Start near the twin oak trees angling up right to a vegetated dihedral. Commence upward and through the overhang to the top. Rappel via another established safer rappel on Grassy Ledges.

A series of overhangs exist about halfway up the vertical wall starting with Dirty Double Overhang and proceeding up leftward to Ground Zero. The crux for Ground Zero is turning the left side of the large overhang.

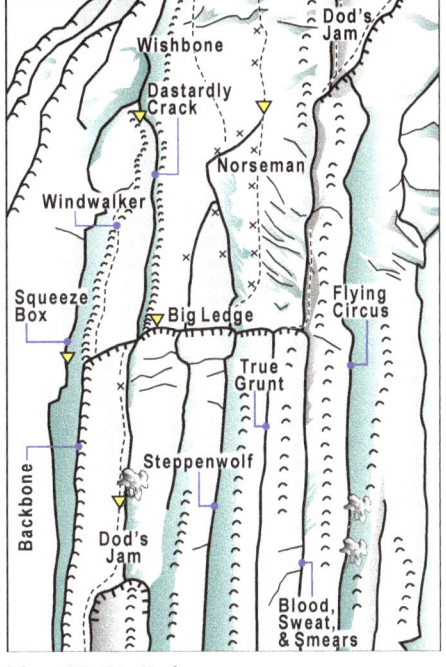

Topo H: *Big Ledge*

91. Ground Zero   III 5.11d ★★
Multi-pitch, Small wires, TCU's and double sizes to 2½"
Seldom climbed in its entirety but one of the more challenging and unusually physical leads. Each pitch is more extreme than the previous culminating with a crux at the roof. Start near the twin oak trees up easy 5.9 slabs to a piton belay 80'. Continue up to a small lip (5.10c) and some difficult climbing to a bolt anchor on the left 80'. Another 25' lead to an anchor underneath the roof. Smear left (crux) around the corner, then finish up a very steep crack to the top 50'.

92. Nuke-U-Later   5.10c R
120' (36m) in length, Pro to 1½"
Start as for Ground Zero but a thin crack that leads up through flaky, hollow rock. Anchor just below a small overhang. Rappel.

93. Iron Maiden   III 5.11 A4
KB, LA, Baby Angles and Pro to ¾"
Step left from the Nuke-U-Later belay and nail up a seam on a blank face.

94. Flying Swallow   III 5.10d PG   ★★★
Multi-pitch, Pro to 3", Extra thin-to-medium wires and very small cams
One of the better Beacon Rock classics.
Pitch 1: The present route starts up the 5.6 section of Dod's Jam, then traverses rightward across to the top of Black Maria, Reasonable Richard and Local Access. But it is much more direct and fun to climb one of these three options mentioned above.
Pitch 2: From that bolt anchor traverse up right to the base of a 60' dihedral. Belay, then have at it.
Pitch 3: This lead is unusually strenuous and involves difficult protection placements.

Stem upward (crux) to a sloping ledge and bolt anchor.

Pitch 4: Above is a slightly overhung finger crack that opens to an offwidth. Climb this to another ledge and belay.

Pitch 5: Then continue up a nice left-facing corner 20' to a belay anchor on Grassy Ledges.

95. Variation 5.10b ★

60' (18m) in length, Pro to 2½" Extra wires

96. Direct Start to Flying Swallow 5.11a

100' (30m) in length (TR)

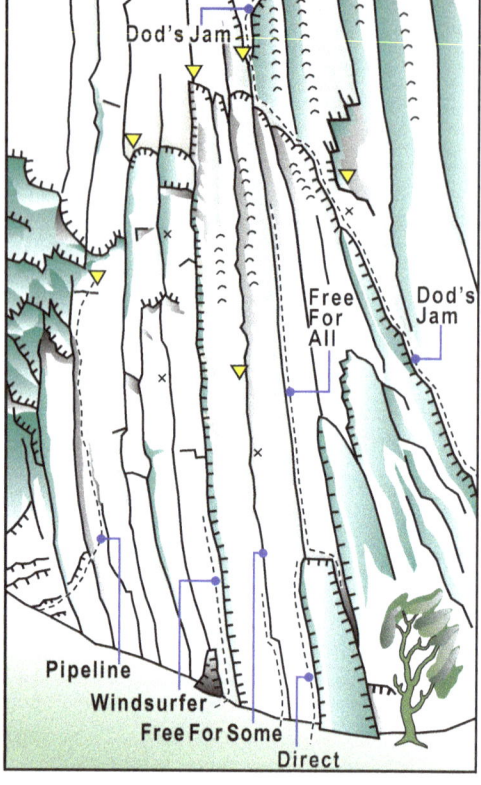

Topo I: *Free For All*

The following three climbs are viable direct start options to Flying Swallow, Flight Time and Blood, Sweat and Smears.

97. Local Access Only 5.10a

110' (33m) in length, Pro to 1"

Wander up an unprotected slab to a small corner dihedral. A viable option for accessing the upper routes such as Flight Time. Another route called Third Rail (5.10-) is located immediately to the right of LAO. Third Rail ascends minor corners and tiny stances then angles left to end at the same belay anchor.

98. Reasonable Richard 5.9 PG

110' (33m) in length, Pro to 1½" and TCU's recommended

Commence up an unprotected slab to a stance, then embark up a minor crack (1 bolt) on a rounded face leading to a bolt anchor. A good climb but a bit bold [*unreasonable?*] to lead.

99. Maria 5.9+ PG

110' (33m) in length, Small wires, TCU's and cams to 3"

A minor corner directly below True Grunt and just left of Reasonable Richard. Start up easy slabs but work left from a stance into a dihedral. Continue up this until you can exit right to the anchor.

100. Flight Time II 5.11c ★★

Multi-pitch, Pro to 1½"

For the climber with strong wings here is a terrific and well-protected route. Move up right (from the belay at Reasonable Richard) along dirty ledges to a mostly fixed crack. This is the wild one. Desperately climb up using the right crack when necessary to a sloping ledge and belay. Step back left and continue up a stiff dihedral to a hanging belay. Rappel or continue up and exit out right under a roof to join with Flying Swallow just above the west edge of Grassy Ledges. See Topo G.

101. Flying Circus III 5.10c R

Multi-pitch, Pro to 4" Extra set of wires

Above Reasonable Richard is a crack (with a small bush growing from it) that opens up to an offwidth. A long 50-meter lead. Joins Dod's Jam route in the great amphitheater.

102. Blood, Sweat, & Smears II 5.10c ★★★

165' (50m) in length, Pro to 3" Double set of wires

A most excellent route and one of Beacon Rock's finest. Traverse up left from Reasonable Richard belay. Enter and climb the dihedral passing through several small overhangs and thin sections. Belay on Big Ledge.

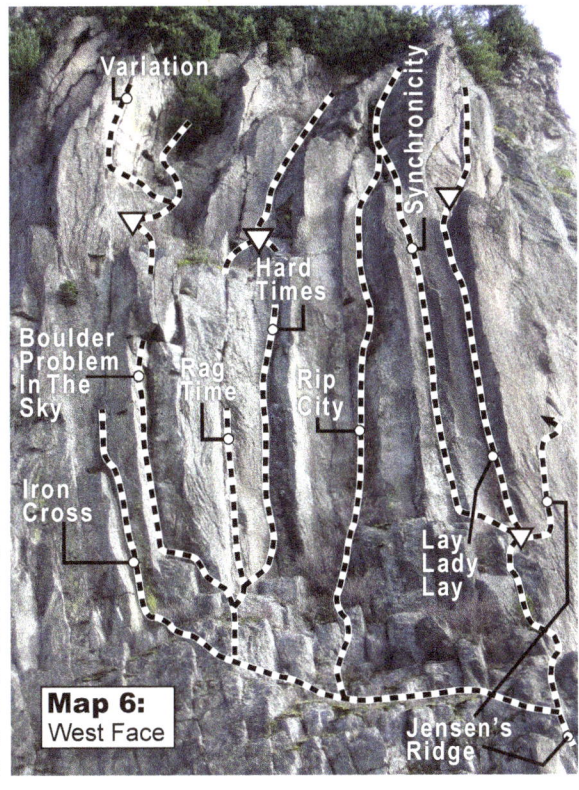

Map 6: West Face

103. True Grunt II 5.11a PG

165' (50m) in length, Pro to 2" Extra wires

A difficult and technical crux. Unique but seldom ascended. A very long lead.

104. Steppenwolf IV 5.11+ A0 (5.10d to Big Ledge) ★★★

165' (50m) in length for the 1st pitch, Pro to 2" Extra wires

This route is one of the best prizes at Beacon Rock. Start at the third tunnel up steep corners and steps on the lower 5.7 section of the Dod's Jam route. When possible, angle up right to a bolt belay under a roof. Step up right around the roof and climb a long exhilarating dihedral. Pull through a final overhung jam crack to Big Ledge. Above are two clean cracks that join halfway up and then angle to the right. The right crack is Steppenwolf, while the left is a continuation of Journey to the East (now Wishbone). Free climb up the right crack (5.11d/.12a) for 60' to a bolt anchor. Above are several more pitches of mixed free and aid climbing up the main headwall to the west side hikers trail.

THIRD TUNNEL

Dod's Jam begins at the Third Tunnel.

105. Dod's Jam III 5.10c ★★★

Multi-pitch, Pro to 3"

One of the all time Beacon classics. Very popular, especially the lower portions. **Pitch**

1: Start up easy slabs (at the 3rd tunnel to the right of the large oak tree) leftward along a series of corners and small ledges. When you reach the base of the main dihedral (Free For All joins here) step up to the birds nest belay.

Pitch 2: Climb a crack that quickly becomes an offwidth (5.9) to a ledge aptly called 'The Perch'

Pitch 3: Climb up past a small tree via a crux (5.10c) jam crack to the famous Big Ledge belay.

Pitch 4: To continue the next pitch, step to the far right end of the ledge and into a deep corner system. Move up a series of wide cracks and offwidth chimneys (5.7 - 5.9) then angle up right along slabs to a sling belay about 40' directly above the west edge of Grassy Ledges. The original route bailed down to Grassy Ledges.

Pitch 5: To continue up, surmount a small bulge which leads up past some small ledges and short 5.8 sections before exiting onto the rocky slope near the west side trail. The upper portion has route finding challenges that require experience and diligence on steep, seldom climbed terrain.

Most climbers rappel from Big Ledge or climb Dastardly Crack because it offers a quality finish to the trail above.

Dod's Direct Finish: A good alternative climbing route is a direct finish located at the immediate right edge of the main upper headwall. Although seldom climbed it offers an unusually wide man-eating, overhanging (5.9) wide crack system that ends near the trail overlook. Reference Photo Map #5 (Topo H) for a visual detail.

106. Dod's Deviation   5.9 (variation)   ★
45' (13m) in length, Pro to 3"

107. Wishbone   III 5.12
Multi-pitch, Pro to 3½"

This line is the original **Journey To The East** IV 5.11 A4 aid line, but now established as a free climb. From a large oak tree follow a series of large flakes (5.9) and minor cracks. Cross over Dod's Jam to access a crack on the right side of Dod's Deviation. Climb this crack/face (5.12-) to Big Ledge. From the ledge climb a thin crack (5.12-) directly off the ledge till it merges with Steppenwolf at the tiny roof, then angle up left via a seam and lead (5.12) to the final belay. The original aid line continued to the hiker's trail, but the free version does not top out.

108. Devil's Backbone   5.12a   ★★
80' (24m) in length, Pro to 1½"

Probably the finest example at Beacon of a crack that splits an arête. Approximately 20' above the first belay on Dod's Jam move left via under clings to an arête. Climb straight up to Big Ledge. An incredible climb!

109. The Norseman   5.12b   ★★
60' (18m) in length, 5 QD's and minor pro to 1½"

This is the bolted route on the headwall buttress. From Big Ledge climb up Steppenwolf a few feet until possible to move right to a bolted rounded buttress. Ascend this to a bolt anchor. Excellent climb.

110. Dastardly Crack   5.9   ★★
165' (50m) in length, Pro to 2"

Directly above Dod's Jam from Big Ledge is a large dihedral. Climb the obvious tight corner, then angle up left (passing the Windwalker belay anchor) on good edges to a bushy corner that leads to the west side hikers' trail.

111. **Squeeze Box   5.10b PG ★**
165' (50m) in length, Pro to 2"
An interesting fist crack through a roof. From Big Ledge angle down left until possible to turn a corner. Climb a dihedral and overhangs to rejoin with Dastardly Crack.

112. **Windwalker   5.11d ★★**
90' (27m) in length, Pro to 3"
This is the arête immediately left of Dastardly Crack. Traverse left off from Big Ledge to the arête, then ascend directly up till you merge with Dastardly at a belay anchor.

Starting with the route Free For All and moving leftward to Pipeline you will find a superb selection of long challenging leads. This area is a popular destination for Beacon climbers. Depending on your skill level there are stellar rock climbs here for all expert levels from 5.8 to 5.11+.

113. **Free For All   5.8   ★★★**
150' (45m) in length, Pro to 2"
Excellent route. A must for everyone! Just left of a large oak tree (left of the 3rd tunnel) is a detached free standing 25' pillar. The left side is the Direct Start (5.10a), while the right side is 5.8. Climb either. From the top of the pillar continue up the obvious crooked hand crack until it joins with Dod's Jam at the first belay. Reference Topo Diagram I for a visual detail.

114. **Free For Some   5.11a PG   ★★★**
140' (42m) in length, Pro to 2" TCU's recommended
A remarkable and demanding lead with excellent protection. Immediately left of Free For All is a thin seam. Climb this to a bolt anchor at 65' then ascend the second half (5.10c) or rappel.

115. **Windsurfer   5.10b   ★★★**
120' (36m) in length, Pro to 3" Double set of wires
A popular and exciting climb. To find this good route look for a left-facing dihedral with three small roofs. Begin up a wide crack that ends at a ledge and bolt belay.

116. **Fresh Squeeze (aka Squeeze Box Direct) II 5.11c/d ★**
120' (36m) in length for the 1st pitch, Pro to 2" and pins (P2 140')
On a face between Pipeline and Windsurfer are two crack systems. The right is Fresh Squeeze. Ascend the first pitch (5.11c) to a ledge and belay. The second pitch steps up above the anchor, moves right and climbs a vertical face broken by a seam. Eventually enters a dihedral and eases (5.10) until it joins with Squeeze Box.

117. **Rise Up   5.10c**
90' (27m) in length, Pro to 3"
This route begins immediately right of Pipeline and ascends a long discontinuous crack using gear till you pass a single bolt near a crux face section. Continue up a finger/hand crack to a large ledge

Tyler Kamm on *Free For Some*

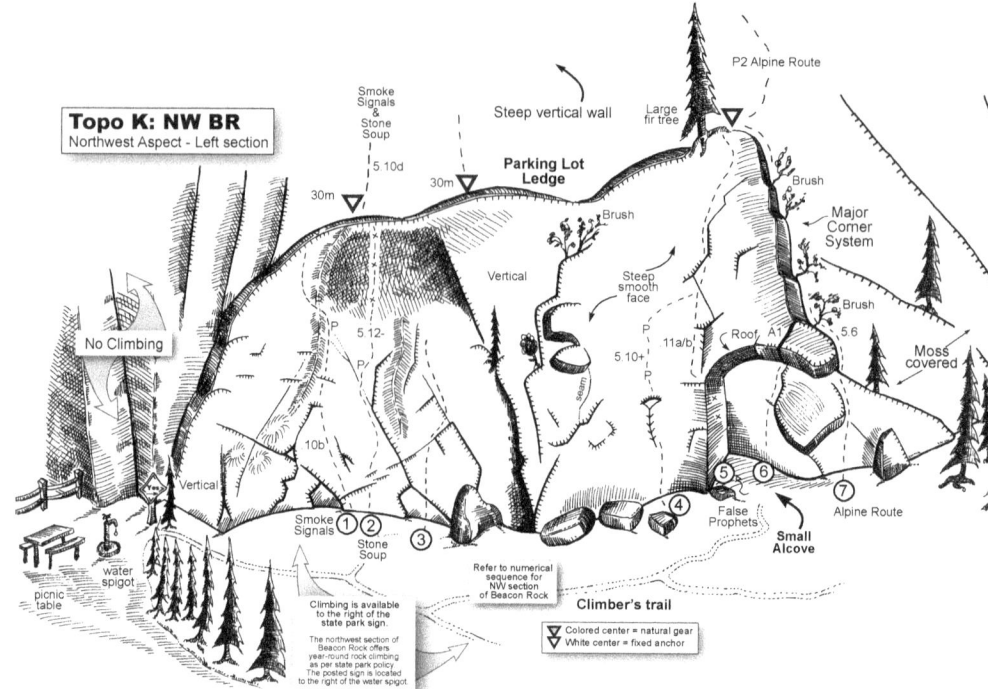

where the Windsurfer belay anchor is also located. Rappel.

118. **Pipeline 5.11b** ★★★
     60' (18m) in length, Pro to 1½"
     Superb classic route. On the right side of the Arena of Terror is a thin, difficult layback finger crack that ends at a bolt anchor next to several small overhangs. A barndoor crux.

119. **Pipe Dream 5.12a** ★
     160' (50m) in length for the 1st pitch, Pro to 3" and extra set of wires
     Little is known about the quality of this route, but it looks incredible! The route has been free climbed in very bold style (ground-up). From the belay ledge for Fresh Squeeze (1st pitch) step left and ascend a remarkable crack on a smooth face to an anchor at the base of an easy dihedral. Rappel with 2 ropes or continue up and join with Dastardly Crack.

120. **Pipeline Headwall III 5.11b**
     Multi-pitch, Pro to 2"

121. **Silver Crow IV 5.10d A3 (or 5.10c free)**
     KB, LA, Rurps and pro to 4"

122. **Axe of Karma IV 5.10c A3**
     Multi-pitch, KB, LA and pro to 4"

The following six climbs are located left of the Arena of Terror. The left most is the regular (5.7) approach arête to Jensen's Ridge and the other west side routes.

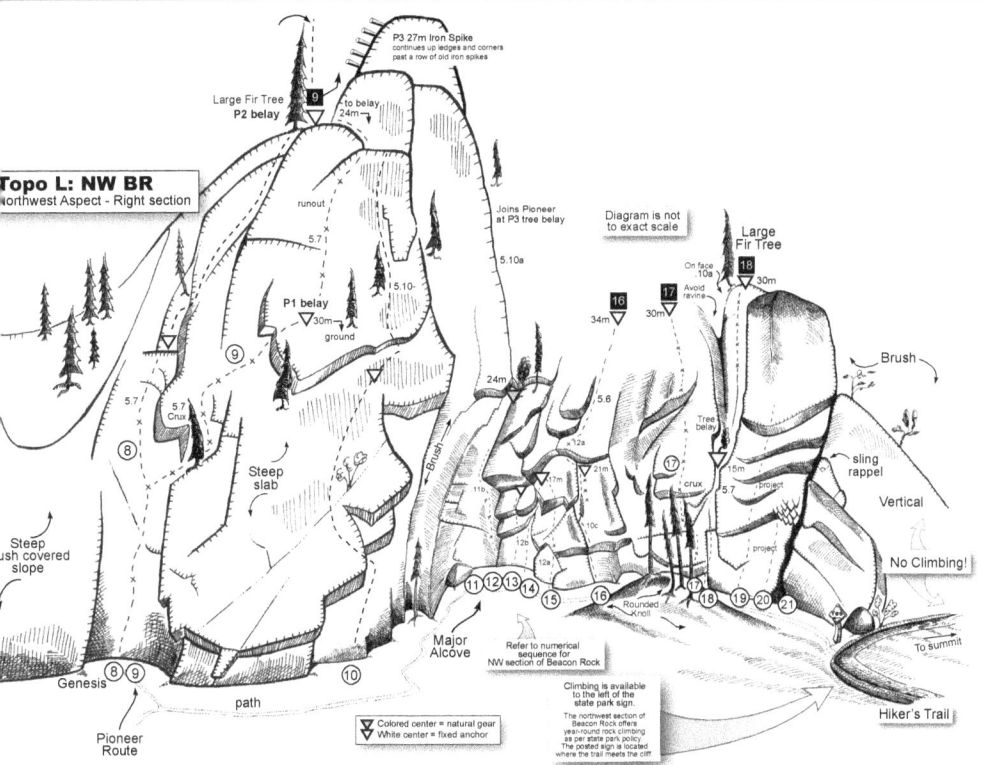

123. **Red Ice   5.10d** ★
145' (44m) in length, Pro to 2½"
Just left of the Arena of Terror. Ascend easy ground to a loose, hollow section. Move up left and finish up a beautiful finger to hand crack in a dihedral. Bolt Anchor. Rappel with two ropes or ascend one of the upper climbs on the west face.

124. **Doubting Thomas   5.10c**
145' (44m) in length, Pro to 1½"
This climb (and the next three) are seldom ascended, but could provide a variable approach to climbs on the west face or an alternate to Jensen's Ridge upper pitches.

125. **Boys of Summer   5.10b**
145' (44m) in length, Pro to 2"

126. **Fingers of a Fisherman   5.10b**
145' (44m) in length, Pitons and pro to 2"

127. **Crack of Dawn   5.9**
145' (44m) in length, Pro to 2"
A short climb near the outer edge of the Jensen's Ridge approach buttress.

128. **Jensen's Ridge   III 5.11a** ★★
Multi-pitch, Pro to 4" including TCU's and big pro for OW
The physical crux is a thin tips crack on the second pitch, while the offwidth just beyond is certainly the psychological mind bender. Commence up an easy ridge (loose) to a bolt belay. Step right (nearly off the platform) and ascend the desperate thin crack 20' to a ledge. Enter into a deep dihedral that opens to a wide offwidth. Belay at bolts just

where Lay Lady Lay joins. Continue to the hikers' trail via two options. Both are 5.9+.

128b. Jensen's Rimjob   III A2+
Pro: Birdbeak or KB's, Hook, Double set of Nuts to 1", and Cams to 6"
From the top of Pipeline Headwall/Silver Crow launch onto vertical terrain via a crack corner system immediately right of the upper part of Jensen's Ridge route. Can reduce cam size to 5" if utilizing the upper section of standard Jensen's route.

129. Updraft to Heaven   III 5.10d R A1
160' (48m) in length, KB and pro to 6"

130. Mostly Air   5.10b PG
160' (48m) in length, Pro to 2½" (poorly protected)

Reference the West Face (photo map #6) for an analysis of the following routes

131. Lay Lady Lay   II 5.10b   ★ ★ ★
100' (30m) in length, Pro to 2½"
Excellent quality route. Poison oak plagues the start of this (and the next several) routes.

132. Synchronicity   II 5.8 A2
Multi-pitch, KB, LA and pro to 4"
The next crack corner (left of LLL route). Long thin crack corner lead.

133. Rip City   II 5.10a   ★ ★
80' (24m) in length, Pro to 1¾"
An excellent climb, but poison oak impacts accessibility of the route.

134. Hard Times   II 5.10c
80' (24m) in length, Pro to 2½"
Plenty of steep stemming.

135. Rag Time   II 5.10c
80' (24m) in length, Pro to 2½"
Excellent route.

136. Boulder Problem in the Sky   II 5.10d   ★ ★
Multi-pitch, Pro to 2½"
P1: Excellent stem problem corner crack with an exciting powerful roof crack exit. P2: from a ledge belay, climb a double hand crack up the face of the left buttress.

137. Iron Cross (aka On the Move)   II 5.11b PG   ★
Multi-pitch, Pro to 4"
The leftmost route (accessed via Jensen's).

Is It The Best Multi-pitch 5.10 At Beacon?

Try this route combination, and perhaps you will consider it to be one of the best multi-pitch 5.10 rock climbing routes at Beacon Rock.
Climb up **Free For All** using the direct start .10a on the left side of the pedestal. Continue up a long stellar 5.8 jam crack and merge with the 1st belay on **Dod's Jam**. Climb **Dod's** up to the perch, then past the small bush and up the precarious .10c jam to Big Ledge. Then launch up left onto a high quality 5.9 stem corner crack system called **Dastardly Crack**. Once you are past the initial 80' it eases to moderate 5.7 terrain that ends at the tree belay next to the hikers trail. Wow, is that a wild line! .

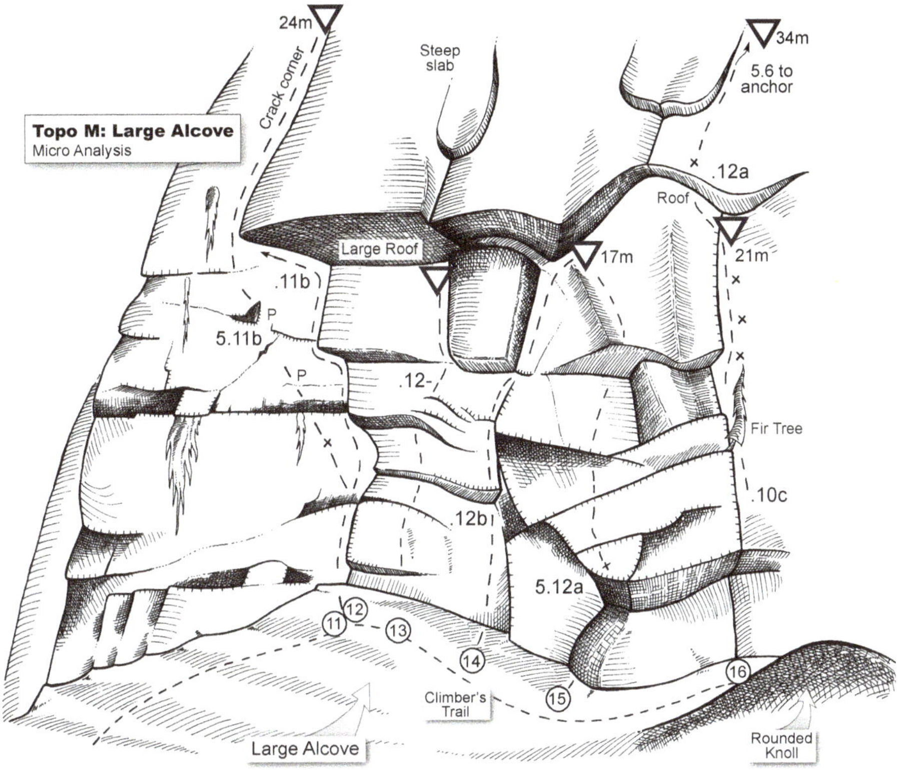

BEACON ROCK 235

Topo M: Large Alcove
Micro Analysis

138. Variation 5.9
___' in length, Pro to 2½"
From top of BPITS (at belay ledge) climb a dirty slab and corner up to the trail.

NORTHWEST FACE

VISUAL BIO NW Section only: **Month** 1 **Min** **NW** **Shade** **PM** **Regs** **Trad**

These emblems represent most of the Northwest section of Beacon Rock. This area offers a shaded environment with limited afternoon sunshine. The right-most routes (such as Siege Tactics) are approximately a 3-minute approach.

This section is an analysis of the Northwest section of Beacon Rock which is accessible for year-round rock climbing. The Northwest Section starts from the posted sign near a water spigot and picnic table at the north side near State Route 14. It extends rightward to another posted sign along the summit hiking trail as it encounters the main west wall of Beacon Rock before proceeding uphill on a paved walkway. The topos (Topo K, L & M) detail two main sections which are separated by a zone of low angled brush covered slope. The upper portion of the two main diagrams are not to exact scale. The illustrations visually detail mainly the intitial ground pitch(es) of most routes (not the upper multi-pitch leads visual details).

1. Smoke Signals   P1 5.10b, P2 5.10d
100' (30m) in length P1, Pro to 1½" including cams
P1: Climb a face past criss-crossing seams and cracks, exiting left around a corner, then

up a slab to a belay anchor. P2: Ascend a shallow corner right of the belay, pass a small tree on its left side. When you reach a small roof traverse left below this roof, then continue up a short bolted wall (past a small tree on your left) landing on the 3-Tree Ledge.

2. **Stone Soup IV 5.9 C1**
Multi-pitch, Pro: Double set of offset Nuts to 1", some Aliens, large cams to 5" (Two 3" cams), a Hook, small cams down to #00, and thin aid Nuts.

This route ascends mixed nailing and free terrain on the less-traveled northwest section of Beacon. Both the aid and alternate free version are detailed below.

P1 30m 5.7 C1: Begin just right of Smoke Signals route.

P2 32m C1: Climb the second pitch of Smoke Signals.

P3 25m 5.8: Starts at 3-Tree ledge and ends at the Alice-In-Wonderland Ledge.

P4 15m C0: Bolt ladder (7-bolts). Ends at a large platform called Swiss Family Ledge.

P5 30m 5.6 C1: Slabby terrain (fixed gear) to anchor at a tree, then up (bolts) past a small roof and eventually move right to a hanging belay anchor.

P6 25m 5.8 C1: Up then briefly right, then climb a short 5.6 section, more C0 (bolts) terrain. End at bolt belay at small (phone booth) stance near a small tree.

P7 30m (3rd, 4th and minor 5th class): Basic terrain navigating to reach the top.

Steamboat Captain's Dream:

The free climbing version combines both Smoke Signals and Stone Soup routes. The free route beta (and gear) is:

QD's, slings, nuts to 1", cams to 3" (doubles below ½"), set of offset nuts to 3/8"

P1 5.10b (28m): Ascend edges up to a left leaning ramp, zigzagging up discountinous cracks to a stance (pin), then a crux (pin), then exit left & cruise easier features to a belay.

P2 5.10d (32m): Ascend a shallow corner right of the belay, pass a small tree on its left side. When you reach a small roof traverse left below this roof, then continue up a short bolted wall (pass another small tree on its right) and up to a final crux headwall. Move belay 25' up above trees to a comfortable ledge belay.

P3 5.10c (25m): Climb right facing corner, short cracks, and a series of ledges. Weave up a series of ledges, move left to a stance at a tree, then further left, then up the ramp. Layback a big flake (bolts) and traverse up right across face to a belay.

P4 5.10a (18m): Climb low angle left leaning crack (piton), use Stone Soup's last bolt [bolt ladder] if need. Belay on a face to the left after exiting onto the comfy ledge.

P5 5.6 (20m): At a 6' corner, climb low angle ledges (2 bolts) to a belay below a steep arête (behind tree).

P6 5.10c (30m): Go up arête (line of bolts) to a small roof. Step right, through the roof, continue up ridge past a short crack to a belay above a small ledge on the face.

P7 5.9 (30m): From belay move right, up crack-corner system (bolt & piton). Climb discontinuous crack to a shallow roof. Step right at the roof and continue up (several bolts) as the terrain eases. A final belay exists at a comfortable stance. Be careful – some loose blocks.

P8 3rd – 4th class (30m): Rocky steps, easy terrain on crest (100') to the Beacon Rock trail.

3. _____
   100' (30m) in length, Pro to __" [?]
   This face climb starts immediately left of a large boulder at the bottom of the pit. Sends a steep face using thin cracks and seams for protection. Likely one of Andrew's routes.

4. _____ **5.10+ R**
   80' (24m) in length, Pro to 3" [?]
   Climb the face on the outer left side of the prow of the little alcove. This route is mostly a natural gear lead. Climb past two fixed pitons and angle up right to merge into route #5.

5. **False Prophet   5.11a/b   ★**
   80' (24m) in length, Pro to 3"
   This line begins on the inside left face (2 bolts) of the tiny alcove. Power up several nice holds, then use hard smears and desperate side clings to gain a small edge above the roof at the beginning of a crack. Race up nice 5.10a broken cracks angling up right to the fir tree belay on a large ledge.

6. **Alcove Overhang   5.11 [?] or A2**
   35' (10m) in length, Pro ?
   This line ascends the very short but fiercely overhung crack in the roof of this tiny alcove.

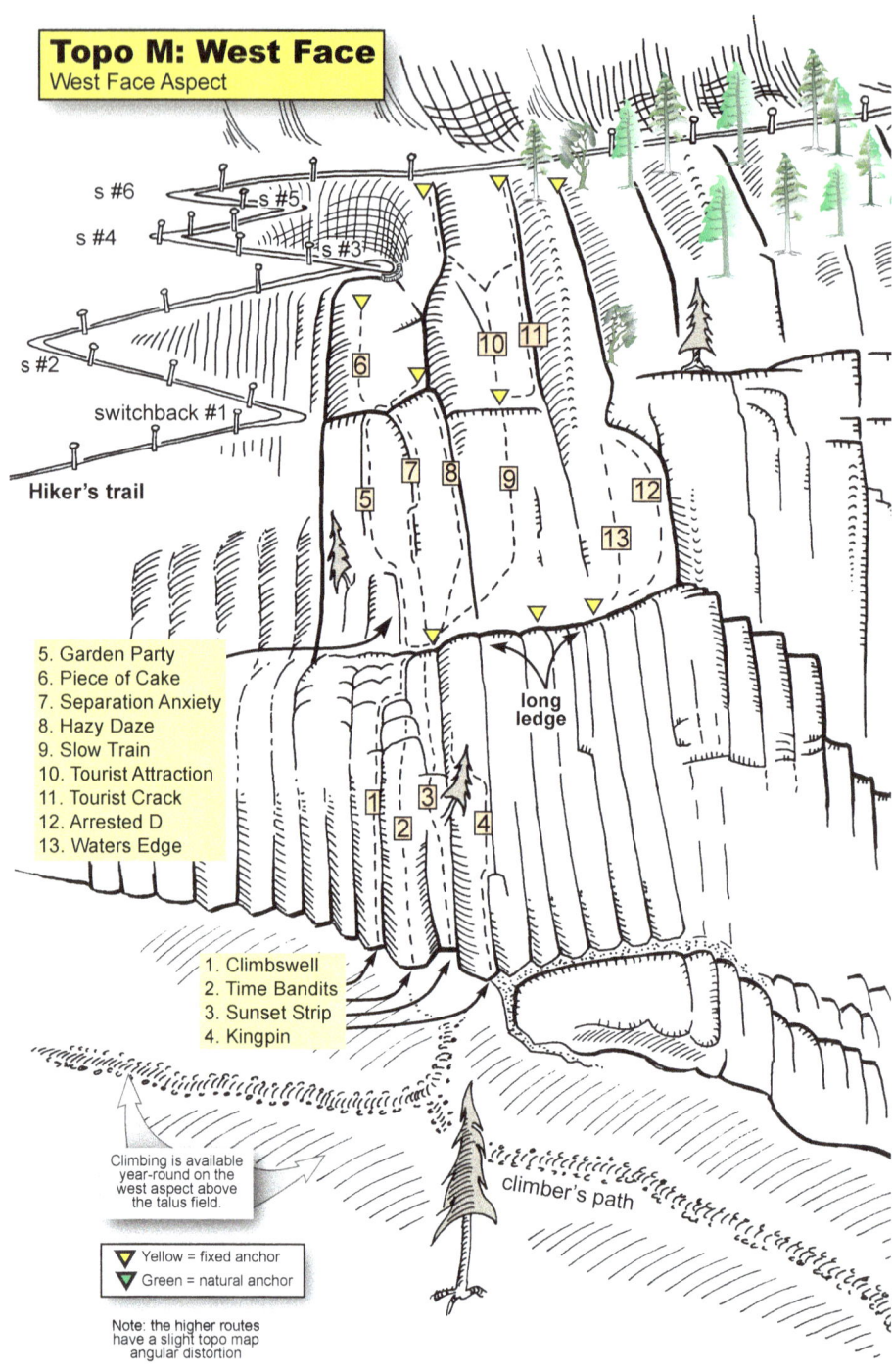

7. **Alpine Route   5.6**
   75' (23m) in length, Pro 3" [?]
   A major corner system that ends at a giant fir on a ledge. P2 continues up various ledges, steps, and corners to land at '3-Tree Ledge' system on Stone Soup route.

8. **Genesis   5.8**
   80' (24m) in length, Pro to __" [?]
   This route branches directly up left (from 2nd bolt of Pioneer) using a minor slab corner and ends abruptly at a belay. P2: moves up right from the belay then up a corner system.

9. **Pioneer Route   P1 5.7, P2 5.7, P3 5.7   ★★**
   Multi-pitch, Pro to 3" including cams
   This is a great route worth climbing...at least the first three leads. A bit mossy in places due to lack of use, but hopefully you will be encouraged to make the ascent regardless. This is a fairly long multi-pitch route where the first two pitches are well fixed with bolts requiring the occasional gear placement along the way.
   P1 90' lead (5.7): Commence up a steep slab with edges placing gear when needed. At the second bolt traverse directly right to a thin fir tree, and then climb a tight vertical crux section (bolts) using small edges. Continue up right on smears past another bulge to a belay anchor at a stance.
   P2 80' lead (5.7): Climb a steep slab using smears and edges with some runout sections. Ends on a nice ample ledge and a fixed anchor near a large fir tree.
   P3 85' lead (5.7): Scramble upward into a dirty corner of brush and trees. At about 40' you will encounter the Iron Spike ladder. Ascend this (5.7) by slinging the 1" thick metal spikes or placing large cams in the crack corner. Ends at a large fir tree belay.
   P4, P5 & P6 (5.5 etc): Traverse south along a narrow path ledge system (poison oak) and up to a ledge at 60-meters. From a fir tree climb variable terrain (5.5) for several more leads ascending up various ledges.

10. **Forbidden Fruit   5.10-**
    Multi-pitch, Pro to __"
    A multi-pitch slab route that ascends the slab just south of the Pioneer Route.

See Topo M for a closeup detail of the Large Alcove. Headcase and Siege Tactics are located in this well-protected overhanging nook.

11. **Head Case   5.11b   ★**
    80' (24m) in length, Pro to 3½" including cams (has a fixed pin/bolt)
    Starts in the very corner of a major alcove, but quickly launches out onto the face to exit up around the lip of the roof (crux) to a long dihedral crack corner system. Belay at a tree at 24-meters. Continue climbing a steep crack corner (P2) 5.10a for another lead.

12. **Spiny Fish   5.11b**
    80' (24m) in length, Pro to 3½"
    Also starts the same as for Headcase but literally stays in the very corner of this major alcove using the crack, then turns the lip crux rejoining there with Headcase. Continue up a crack system to a tree anchor. The climb takes mostly 2" pro except for the large stuff needed to surmount the roof.

13. **_____   5.12 [?]**
    60' (18m) in length, Pro to ?
    An unfinished 5.12 project that ascends the face immediately right of Headcase and ends at the giant roof.

14. **Siege Tactics   5.12a**
    55' (17m) in length, Pro to 2½" (wires and cams)
    This is the power line that ascends up through very steep ground on the right inner section of the alcove. At a large block move around it to the right, then up to the last main roof. A few moves up right is the anchor. Rappel.
15. **_____   5.12b project**
    55' (17m) in length, Pro to ?
    Unfinished project. This line sends the outside of the nose next to Siege Tactics by surmounting the overhang straight on. Continue up dicey face edges till it merges again with Siege Tactics anchor.
16. **Dorian's Dilemma   5.10c 1st pitch   ★**
    55' (17m) in length 1st pitch to anchor under large roof
    Pro: 2" wires and cams, small wires are useful
    This climb ascends a crack, breaks through a small crux overhang and continues up past a small fir tree using a minor right facing corner (bolts) to a belay-rappel anchor immediately under the upper large roof. Crux is pulling roof; 2 bolts on upper face (10a or so) just below rap anchors.
    Pitch two of Dorian's Dilemma is 5.12a. This second part powers through the crux large overhang (2 bolts) and then waltzes up an easy corner crack to an anchor at 24m. Rappel.
17. **Gitmo Love Machine   5.12a   ★**
    100' (30m) in length, Pro ?
    Pro: QD's, small TCU's and wires to 1"
    This is a stellar face climb on tenuous holds. Stick clip the first bolt. Powerful .10+ climbing to get off the ground then you hit a solid .12a crux immediately to pass the first bolt. Some hard face moves then surmount the second roof (TCU) which is a tricky .11d move. A long 15' run out above the second roof with several bolts and a single large midway jug. At the third roof (place small cam) power over this at .11c to another runout 5.8 slab to the anchor, and then rappel if you still have any energy.
18. **Fireballs   (P1) 5.7 to small tree, (P2) 5.10c**
    50' (15m) in length to small tree
    100' (30m) in length when done as one full lead
    Pro: gear to 1½" including cams (especially small cams)
    This line ascends a corner crack to a tight slot in a roof where you must squeeze behind the constriction to end at the small tree belay. Avoid the upper ravine. Rappel or continue up right onto pitch 2 of Fireballs.
    Pitch 2 continues past the small tree up right on a very steep angled crack that avoids the ravine. Ascend a steep vertical face via a 4-bolt line to a fixed anchor at 30 meters next to a large fir tree. Rappel.
19. **_____**
    100' (24m) in length
    A project?
20. **_____**
    80' (24m) in length
    Another project?
21. **_____   5.9 [?]**
    40' (12m) in length, pro to [?]
    A wide offwidth crack system that smears up steep terrain past a slight overhang and ends

◆ BEACON ROCK 241

Map 8: West Face Upper Section

Map 7: West Face Left Section

on a minor sloped ramp at a sling rappel around a rock horn of a detached flake. Rappel. The summit-bound hikers trail meets the west face of Beacon Rock at this point.

WEST FACE

Below the hikers trail (and above the talus field) is a section of the West Face of Beacon Rock that has seen renewed climber interest. Routes continue to be developed on this aspect of Beacon Rock.

1. **Climbswell Butterflakes   5.9**
   90' (27m) in length, 10 QD's, optional ½" cam
   Start just left of the large vertical 15' friable flake. The route climbs well, but her flakes! The route ends at the same belay as Time Bandits/King Pin.

2. **Time Bandits   5.10b PG**
   90' (27m) in length, 7 bolts, optional cams to 1"
   A bolted route on a minor outside prow immediately left of Sunset Strip.
   Climb a gradually fading thin crack utilizing stemming and face holds. A final stretch of thin face holds bring you to a midway ledge that has some flakiness. Two finish options (left or right) exist. The left offers bolted & flakey (+cam pro) moves. The right option (more solid) is a short crack on a face with runout final ending moves to reach the belay.

3. **Sunset Strip   5.10**
   40' (12m) in length, pro to _"
   A double inside corner system with a small tree at mid-height. Hollow is spots; unappealing.

4. **Kingpin   5.9 PG**
   90' (27m) in length, minor pro to _"
   Interesting route with some fixed gear. From talus, climb up onto a landing, then commence up the right side (bolts) of a finger jam flake. At the top of this small column (piton) traverse left a few feet to a small corner and arete. Climb the arete (3 bolts, some gear) finishing with a bold move to attain the main choss ledge system and several belay stations. Note: the first bolt can be pre-clipped on the left before starting the climb.

5. **Garden Party 5.10a**
   90' (27m) in length, pro: nuts to 1", cams to 3"
   From King Pin belay move left to a fractured area, then climb a crack up to a ledge. Climb up the crack and slabby overlaps (some bolts). After the crack ends at the top move right across a gap on easy ledges to reach the belay. Rappel.

6. **Piece of Cake   5.10a**
   110' (33m) in length, pro: nuts to 1", cams to 3"
   This is an extension of Garden Party P2. This is mostly bolted (gear is needed for the Garden Party portion of the route.

7. **Separation Anxiety   5.10a**
   90' (27m) in length, bolted, optional pro to ½" (cams or nuts)
   Start at the Kingpin/Time Bandit belay. Climb a minor right-facing corner above the belay. Halfway up you encounter a left-facing crux corner (bolt). The final portion of climbing becomes right-facing and slabby (optional pro). Move right for the final few moves to a belay. Rappel.

◆ BEACON ROCK 243

8. Hazy Daze 5.8
90' (27m) in length, bolted, optional pro to ½" (cams or nuts)
Start at the Kingpin/Time Bandit belay. Climb up to the right (bolts) to reach a nice ledge. Move left briefly, and ascend a slight crack corner-ish feature (bolts). Route ends at same belay as previous route.

9. Slow Train 5.8 PG
90' (27m) in length, bolted
Start at the Kingpin/Time Bandit belay. Angle up right on a face (bolt) using the initial moves of Hazy Daze, but continue angling up right then climb directly up a nice series of edges on a face (bolts) to a belay. Rappel, or tackle one of the next two routes.

10. Tourist Attraction 5.9
60' (18m) in length, bolted, minor cam pro to 1"
This starts on the ledge where Slow Train route ends. Climb directly up a long slab (L-C-R variations exist) and exit left, then up a brief minor corner to a Metolius rap station. Rap down to the hikers trail, and hike down when your done. A right variation blends into Tourist Crack route to finish on its last few moves.

11. Tourist Crack 5.7
70' (21m) in length, pro to ___"
This starts on the ledge where Slo Train route ends. Traverse right on the ledge, then climb a prominent left-facing crack corner system to the top. Belay just below the hikers trail.

12. Waters Edge 5.9
110' (30m) in length, pro: nuts to 1", cams to 3"
Start at Sunset Strip belay and traverse far to the right on a long ledge sytem (use other belays if need). Commence up right to a prominent left facing corner. Climb the corner crack (and briefly on left face) up past a tree (which you will sling). When you reach the base of an arête, then climb cracks just right of the outside corner. The last portion utilizes both the left outer arête and the crack on your right. Ends just beneath the hikers trail.

13. _____ 5.9
110' (30m) in length, pro: nuts to 1", cams to ½"
Start at Kingpin belay, traverse along a ledge system and belay again near Waters Edge. Climb directly up using double cracks, surmount a small roof, and go up a crack to a stance below an arête. Move right, ascend a thin crack on a face, then left (bolt) onto the arete (2 more bolts) continuing up to the belay. Merges into Waters Edge ½ way up route. Note: 60-m rope is fine if you walk off when done.

14. Labyrinth 5.8 R
Multi-pitch, QD's and pro to 2"
Located further down the talus field closer to Jensen's Ridge area. Route not shown on the diagram. A mostly bolted face (with some runout). This is a good option for accessing the other West Face routes (such as Iron Cross to Hard Times routes). The 120' route ends on a ledge at a fixed belay below the start of Hard Times.

The Legend of Beacon Rock

Chances are, if you've climbed at Beacon Rock over the past three decades or so, you've met, talked to, heard about, or even tied in with one of the giants of Northwest climbing, Jim Opdycke. Born April 25, 1944, Opdycke first made it to the top of Beacon Rock when he was just five months old. Literally. A picture from the fall of 1944 shows baby Opdycke and his family atop the monolith after hiking all the way up the trail. But it wasn't until forty years later that Opdycke really began to make his mark at Beacon Rock.

In the interim, Opdycke grew up in Vancouver. In 1967, he hit the road, thumbing his way around the country for three years before returning home and joining the workaday world. An inveterate adventurer, Opdycke needed more, so in 1972 he started climbing mountains. Over the next four years, he embarked on some hardcore mountaineering, heading to the hills in the harshest of conditions to sharpen his skills and learn how to survive.

And then in 1976, Opdycke's friend, Jay Kerr, introduced him to rock climbing, first at Broughton Bluff near Troutdale and then at Beacon Rock. At Beacon, the two climbed all the way to the top via a wet, dirty 5.10c known as Seagull. Opdycke was hooked.

Though he continually climbed all around the west — Yosemite, Devil's Tower, Colorado, Arizona, Alaska, Oregon, Idaho, and Washington — Opdycke eventually found his true calling at Beacon Rock. After being injured in a fall in 1984, Opdycke headed out to Beacon to find the rock dirty, overgrown, and largely silent. Many of the pioneers from earlier decades had backed off by then, but Opdycke saw that there was still plenty of trail to blaze at Beacon. He began solo aiding up some of the lines he'd always wanted to do, cleaning them all the way up, adding solid bases down below. He would take friends out to Beacon and turn them on to his routes; he'd also listen to what other climbers had to say about his routes, whether they were any good or not.

Over the ensuing years, Opdycke put up some of the most classic routes at Beacon Rock: Young Warriors, Little Wing, Jill's Thrill, Ground Zero, Stardust, and Cruisin' to name a few. In total, he has put up close to 4,000 feet of new routes at Beacon Rock.

Yet beyond just his climbing at Beacon, Opdycke is known as well for his stewardship of the place. Always friendly and encouraging to up-and-coming climbers — a mentor even — he has logged countless hours cleaning and tending to routes at Beacon. On opening day every year, he's almost always the one who cleans the Southeast Corner and gets it in shape for the season to come. And even if he's not climbing when he's at Beacon, Opdycke's likely doing something to make it better: battling poison oak, picking up trash, shoring up a base. It's what he loves to do, not only because he reveres Beacon Rock, but because he wants other people to be able to have the same adventures out there that he's had.

So the next time you head out to Beacon, keep your eyes and ears open for a wiry, mustachioed man with the hands of a climber and an easy, enthusiastic smile. He's part of the reason you're there.

Written by Jon Bell

BEACON ROCK

ALL OTHER GORGE CRAGS

ROOSTER ROCK

Rooster Rock is a popular tooth shaped basalt pinnacle on the south side of the Columbia River Gorge located immediately west of the boat launch area at Rooster Rock State Park. Drive east on I-84 from Portland and take exit #25 at the State Park. Pay the daily user fee and park your vehicle at the State Park, then walk around the south side of the small boat moorage lagoon to access the rock pinnacle which is located on the west side of the lagoon. From the freeway walk north along a nice dirt path that soon angles directly over to the start of the popular South Face route. Just before you reach the base of the cliff another steep dirt path wanders directly up to the seldom climbed East Face area.

Crediting the first ascent of this pinnacle is rather dubious but yields an interesting history. As recorded in 'A Climber's Guide to the Columbia River Gorge' by Carl A. Neuberger, "...about 1910, a sailor from a Swedish ship undertook the climbing of the rock when challenged by other members of the crew. When nearing the summit he lost his nerve and would neither go further or back down. However, he was finally persuaded by companions from below to go on to the summit. He was too frightened by the experience to descend and it was necessary to shoot a line to him before he could be brought down." And so perhaps it is possible for those Swedes to climb just about anything.

1. South Face 5.4
Pro: Nuts and Hex's to 3" and two 60m ropes for rappel
Vertical Height of Route: 165'
A popular and enjoyable rock climb. The ap-

Hugh near the top of *Rabbit Ears*

proach trail leads directly to the base of the pinnacle and up to a small level dirt stance next to a large fir on the SW shoulder of the pinnacle. Lead up easy 4th class steps on the SW shoulder and after you surmount several steep spots belay (2-bolt belay anchor) at a small stance below a slight overhang (60' lead). Traverse right 15' to the base of the obvious diagonal ascending corner system. Ascend this corner system (crux) for 70' till you attain the southeast ridge. Scramble up the exposed ridge crest 30' to the summit. Rappel with two ropes down the south face (165' vertical).

2. **East Face Route 5.6 R**

To approach the East Face route scramble up the steep dirt path to the east face of the pinnacle. Begin by leading up rightward on steep dirty steps 30' to a sling belay in the top of a large fir tree that leans up against the pinnacle. Climb to a shelf above the snag tree then continue directly to the summit using nailing gear by means of direct aid. Alternative B: Another route option is to angle leftward from the snag tree sling belay on poorly protected, and steep moss-covered terrain up to a point where it joins with the South Face route at the southeast ridge. Scramble up 30' to the summit.

Mike & Hugh at 1st belay on *West Chimney, Crown Point*

3. **North Face II 5.6 A3 (or 5.8 R)**

The route is reached by starting at the base of the east face, then dropping down 25' to a ledge. Follow this west till you can belay at one of several trees. Climb diagonally up left 25' and continue straight up through a notch in the first overhang. Ascend over the second overhang to a vertical slab, then up grass slopes to the top. It is ninety feet from the original tree belay up past the vertical slab, and then 45' up the grass slope to the summit.

4. **Southwest Face II 5.6**

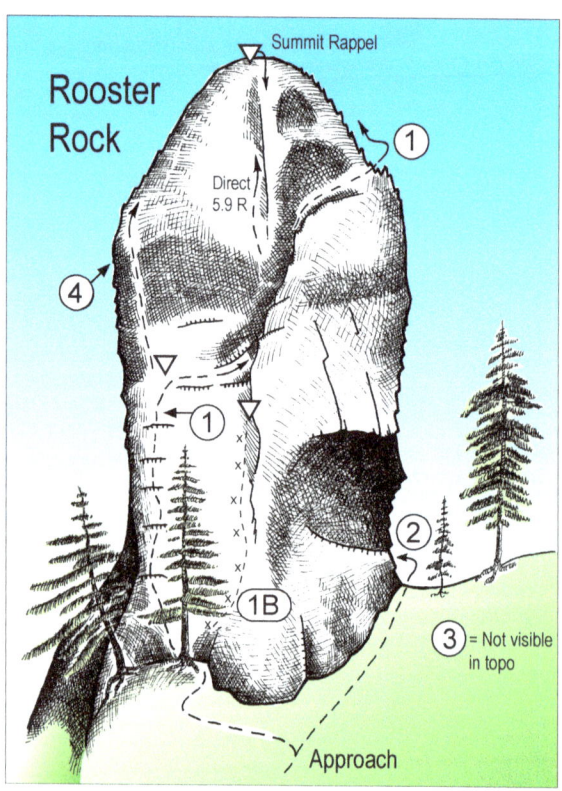

A2 (or 5.9 R)

Ascends directly up the vertical rock on the SW shoulder above the first belay on the South Face route.

Note: All climbing routes other than the regular South Face route on Rooster Rock are infrequently climbed friable, mossy adventures.

CROWN POINT

Crown Point is the prominent 500' north-facing scarp immediately south of Rooster Rock. The historic and panoramic Vista House is situated upon its summit. There are several known routes located on the north face, but expect to find difficult climbing on well vegetated steep friable rock. The climbs on this historical scarp are seldom ascended.

1. **Zucchini Route (NE Face)   III 5.6 A2 or 5.10a R**

   Multi-pitch climb, Pro: Nuts and cams to 3" including pitons

   To reach the Zucchini Route scramble up the talus slope to the base of the face directly below Vista House. Ascend up leftward on easy 5th class moss ledges 60' to a belay on a ledge system. Traverse east 30' to the base of a steep crack system and belay. Climb up the crack for 165' but do expect friable rock on the second half of this lead. Continue up right on poor rock to a left leaning diagonal system, follow-

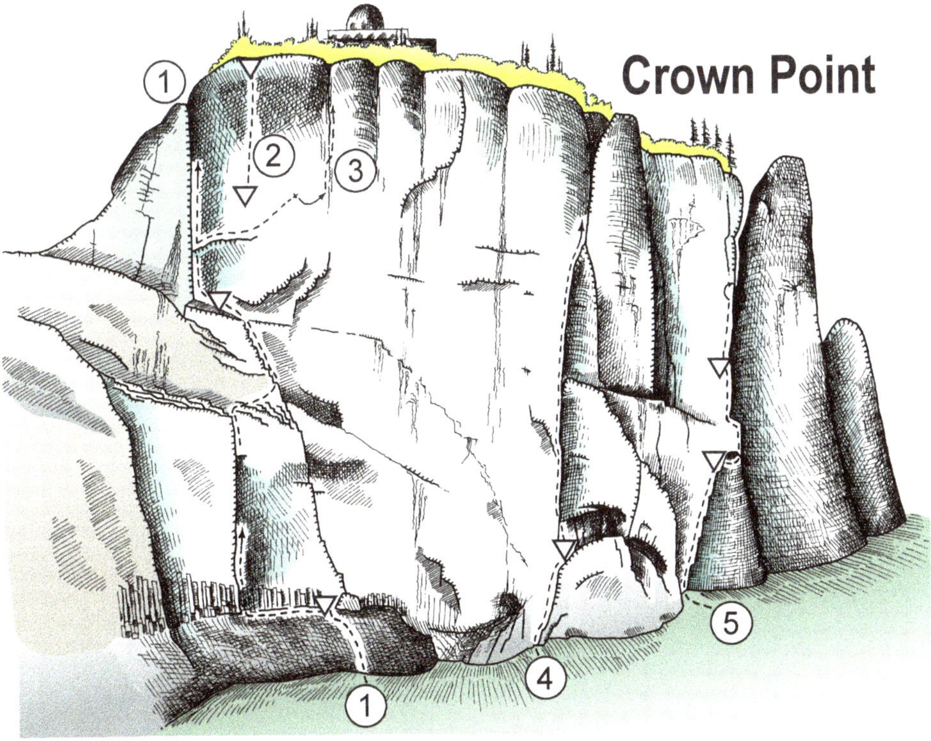

Deep in the West Chimney

Crown Point

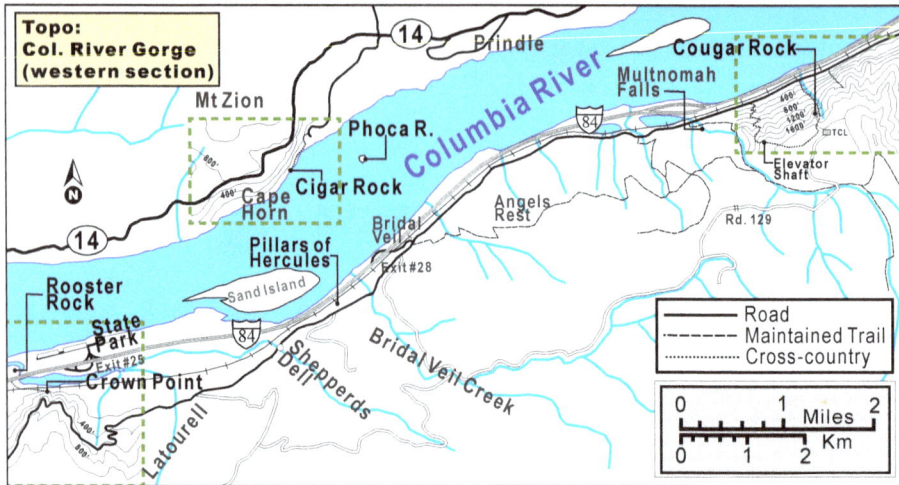

ing this up left 90' to the 'zucchini ledge'. This ledge is a small triangular ledge beneath the major chimney system at the upper east portion of the northeast face. If you are hungry and it is mid summer you can survive on wild zucchini for lunch. Climb 40' of corner crack into the chimney, and then squeeze up the chimney 50' to a notch belay. Walk up to the road and descend by scrambling down a steep western gully past the Alpenjager. There may be other variations on the first part of this route.

2. **Jewel in the Crown 5.12a**
3. **RURP Traverse III 5.10 A2+ X**
4. **Unknown**
5. **West Chimney II 5.4**

Multi-pitch climb, Pro: Nuts and cams to 3"

On the far right side of Crown Point a dark gash separates the main massif from a cigar-shaped dome of rock called **Alpenjager** in Nick Dodge's book. The deeply sliced corner system is called West Chimney. Although seldom climbed it is an impressive feature and a unique Gorge chimney route. To approach ascend a ravine in a forested slope just beyond the western edge of Crown Point wall. When you are level with the base of the wall scramble left through thick brush to the base of the route. Look for a diagonally rightward leaning brush corner system with grass steps (some fixed pins) that leads up into the main chimney far above.

P1: The first pitch is a 150' lead up easy 5th class grass and moss steps to a fixed pin belay on a good grassy stance. Expect lots of grass hummock climbing on this lead.

P2: Traverse right 12' on steep thin edges (fixed piton) to attain a prominent corner system. Work up and left around a slight bulge, then stem up a vertical crux section avoiding the loose rock. The climbing difficulties quickly ease as you enter into the main *deeeeeeeep* chimney system. Belay at 90' at a good fixed piton belay just below

Crux pitch on West Chimney

a large rock wedged in the chimney.

P3: The next 150' is a classic slightly smaller than shoulder-width chimney squeeze. You are certain to hear burly yet festive pig-like grunting sounds while in the depth of this great chimney. The adventure will take you literally right through the darkness of this rock wall chasm, and out the other side into the sunlight. Descend the west side of Alpenjager in a ravine.

6. Alpenjager 5.4 R

The summit of **Alpenjager** is a harrowing feat, because steep dirt and friable rock make this a rather challenging undertaking. It can be ascended by a small ledge system on the south side near a tree. Or...halfway through the third pitch (P3) on the **West Chimney** you can ascend directly up vertically following several old fixed pitons. Expect runout sections on dubious rock to attain the top of **Alpenjager**.

PILLARS OF HERCULES

Although the pillars (aka Speelyei's Columns) are readily accessible and technically reasonable to climb, this formation is seldom ascended because the rock is mossy and friable. The West Arête, the Northwest Face and its variation, and the North Face Traverse are not climbed these days. This cobblestone basalt formation is located approximately 3 miles east of Rooster Rock State Park on the south side of the freeway, but west of Bridal Veil exit #28 about ½ mile. If the Pillar is your goal consider parking at a dirt pullout immediately west of Shepperds Dell State Park

Topo: Pillars of Hercules

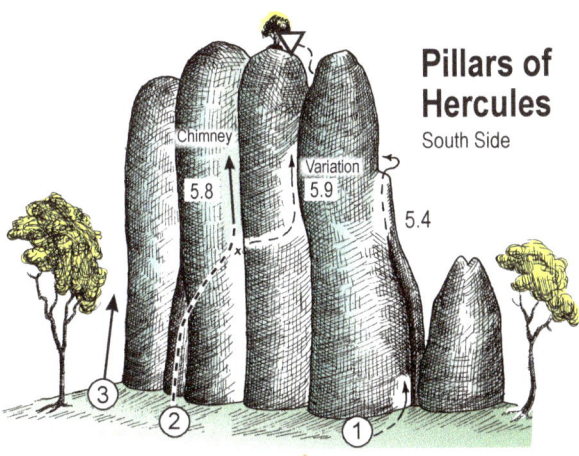

Pillars of Hercules
South Side

rest facility on old U.S. Hwy 30 and cross-country over to the south side of the pillar. Bring a helmet.

1. **East Route 5.4**
   Length: 120', Pro to 3½"
   The standard East Route begins on the *south side* of the pillar. Step up under a prominent notch and climb up left in a crack system for 60'. Traverse fifteen feet right on a minor ledge around to the north face. A tree is growing at the base of a wide corner crack. Climb the wide crack up to the notch, then to the top where a cable is wrapped around a large bush. Two ropes are needed for the rappel.

2. **South Face 5.8 R**
   Length: 120', Pro to 3" and pitons
   The **South Face** route ascends a vertical cobblestone face for 30', then traverses right 10' to climb a wide vertical chimney to the summit. Dirty and loose in places.

THE RAT CAVE

The Rat Cave is one of Northwest Oregon's rare little gems in that it sports the highest concentration of difficult rock climbs within a reasonable proximity to Portland metro area.

The Cave is an unusual basalt rock feature with a wildly overhung 30' horizontal cave roof surrounded with a 50' steep overhanging outer face. The routes provide an intense oppor-

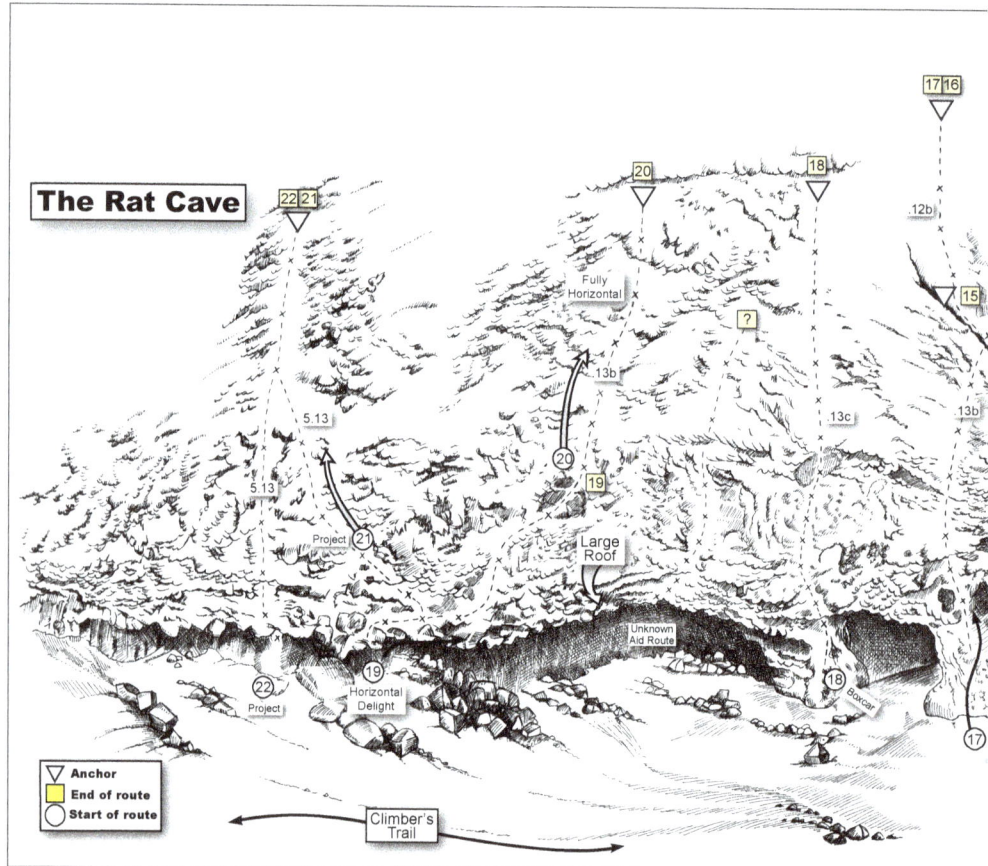

tunity to experience beta-intensive rock climbing requiring endurance, power and movement. The routes are beta intensive, because every single knob looks like a hold. An initial foray might leave you with a sense of being sandbagged but local climbers who know the routes very well can provide great guidance to each climb. The grades are based on a red-point lead, not an on-sight lead, because of the difficulty to identify which is a real hold and which is not. The listed ratings are 2-3 letter grades harder based on this red-point method. Beta was compiled by Tymun Abbott.

Seasonal variables

Climbing at the Cave is feasible for 12 months of the year, but the best time to climb here is generally from September till February. March and April bring considerable rain showers and warmer temperatures that allow steady seeps to occur along portions of the walls of the Cave, hindering access

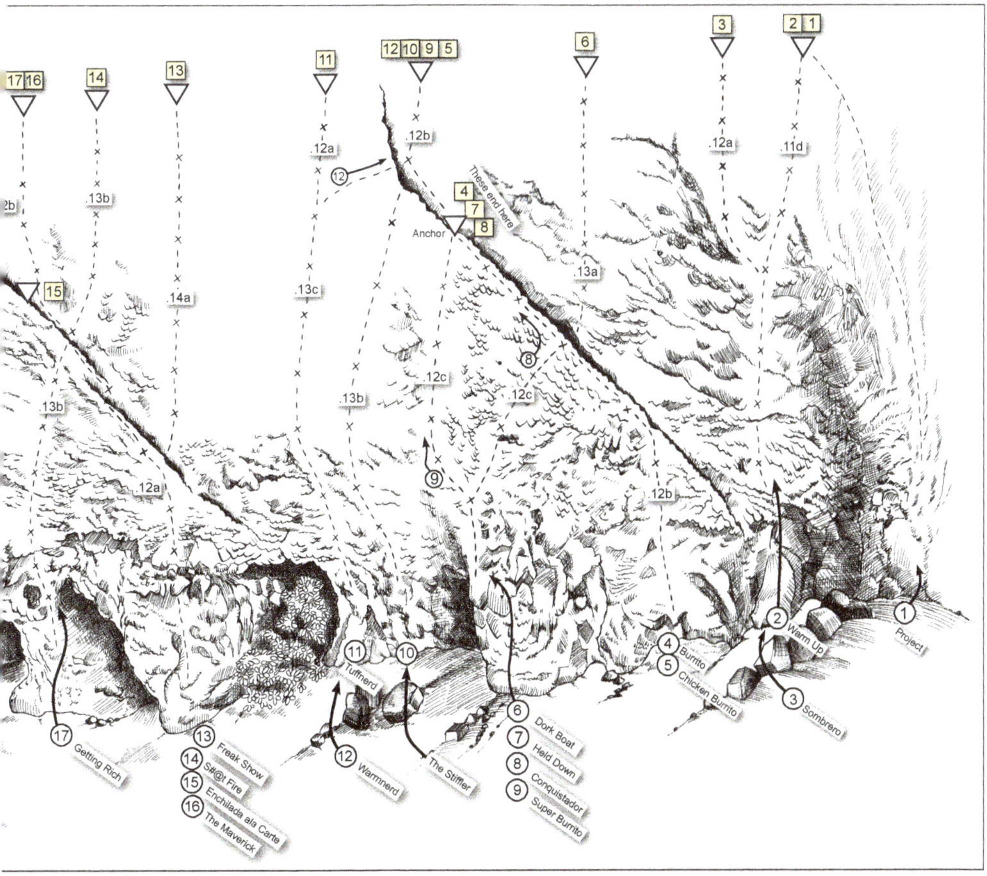

Dave leading *Dork Boat*, *The Cave*

to certain climbs. June through August is typically humid (not like the east coast) and can lower your ability to effectively cling to pinches and tiny grips. Yet even during the long sultry days of summer you can find many days where climbing at the Cave is great and summer lighting colorfully photogenic. For climbers who already know where the Cave is...have fun! The Rat Cave is located about ¼ mile west of the Multnomah Falls parking lot directly across from Benson Lake at a small gravel pullout.

Wolfgang leading *Horizontal Delight*

1. **Project**
   Starts on the outside wall of minor buttress and merges with the next route at anchor.

2. **Pissfire (aka Warm Up) 5.11d** ★
   Length: 50', Pro: 8 QD's
   This route has been cleaned up considerably and is a viable initial route to warm-up lead. Start on the far right side of the cave. Climb through a hard move to start then continue on big holds to a rest. Climb past a second hard section to reach the anchor.

3. **Sombrero 5.12a**
   Length: 60', Pro: 7 QD's
   Clip first 3 bolts of warm-up route, then aim up left (4 more bolts) in a groove to the anchor.

4. **Burrito (aka Warm Up) 5.12b** ★★
   Pro: 7 QD's, Usually fixed draws on the second half
   This route is still considered to be the original 'Warm Up' route at the Rat Cave. The crux comes at the beginning which is a long lock-off utilizing an under cling pinch to another pinch which continues up left through more pumpy climbing. The route follows a small left leaning channel to the first set of anchors in the middle of the face.

5. **Chicken Burrito 5.12d** ★★
   Start on Burrito and end at the top of the wall on Super Burrito.

6. **Dorkboat 5.13a** ★★
   Length: 70', Pro: 9 QD's
   This route starts just left of Burrito on the same start as Held Down, and climbs straight to the top of the wall. Punch through an early crux move after the first bolt, which involves a tricky sequence of pinches utilizing a well placed drop knee. Hard moves continue until the 4th bolt where the Warm Up route crosses at the good pinch jug rest. Continue straight up using decent pinches and under clings passing through a crux at mid-height. A small Gaston at the 7th bolt lets you get just enough strength back to push through the next two clips. Endurance is the key to sending this line.

7. **Held Down 5.12c** ★★★
   Pro: QD's
   Held Down is the next logical route to climb after the Warm Up route. It starts the same as Dorkboat moving left at the first bolt to finish at the anchor in the middle of the wall. Begin up a small pillar to the face. Punch through a couple of long moves to set up the crux, which is a long lock-off to the second bolt followed by a reach to a small triangle and undercling requiring a back-step and lock-off. Expect another under-cling lock-off

before you reach the anchor.

8. **Conquistador 5.12c** ★

   Start on Dorkboat and end on Held Down.

9. **Super Burrito 5.12d** ★★★

   Length: 65', Pro: __ QD's

   Start on Held Down. After clipping the anchor for Held Down continue on up the top of the wall with a surprise waiting at the end.

10. **The Stiffler 5.13b** ★

    Pro: QD's

    The business begins early on this route. Start just left of Held Down. Climb through a small roof past a horn which entails a knee-bar followed by tenuous lockoffs. Continue through a series of sloped holds, lockoffs and pinches to the anchor.

11. **Tuffnerd 5.13c** ★★★

    Length: 70', Pro: QD's

    Start just left of The Stiffler under a small roof. Begin with double hands and double heels on a hanging block-shaped rock feature followed by a series of side pulls using reasonable edges. The crux is moving off of two sloped holds at midway to a reasonable under-cling, followed by a series of lockoff Gaston moves. The climbing remains very sustained all the way to the anchor. You can find several useful knee-bar placements on this route. Some have the guns to make it to the end…some don't.

10. **Warmnerd 5.13d** ★★★

    Length: 70', Pro: 8 QD's, mostly fixed Quick-Draws

    This route starts on Tuffnerd and finishes on the Chicken / Super Burrito anchor. Pull the first three cruxes of Tuffnerd which take you to the 7th bolt. At the 7th bolt bust hard right by traversing through a series of sloped holds till you reach the last few bolts on the next route to the right. Make a powerful transition onto the under-cling to clip, then fire through a powerful pinch to sloped side pull crux and finish to the anchor.

13. **Freak Show 5.14a**

    Length: 65', Pro: QD's. There is a midway anchor at the 5th

    Start up Enchilada ala Carte for the first three bolts (.12-), the head straight up instead of following the left leaning weakness. The first few moves off the seam involve a tough sequence of powerful crimper lockoffs to a desperate toss to a marginal sloped hold (V7ish). Make a clip off an OK under cling, and then enter the crux. A series of desperate pulls off sloped holds on a 30° overhang. This follows for two bolts (roughly V8). Unlike Tuffnerd this route lacks a decent rest before its pumpy headwall. Finish on sustained 5.12 for the last 5 bolts. This follows the second left leaning weakness from the right.

14. **S#@t Fire 5.13c** ★★

    Length: 70', Pro: Some QD's. The second half has fixed quick-draws on it

    Begin up Enchilada ala Carte and climb along the left leaning ramp/channel. At the 5th bolt transition to the upper wall. The climb kicks back dramatically here involving intense power climbing through three consecutive bulge sections. Expect long reaches in spots to marginal holds; however the occasional good pinch or crimp appears just when you need them most.

15. **Enchilada ala Carte 5.12a** ★

    Length: 50', Pro: QD's

    This route provides access to one of the rat caves finest routes (S#@t Fire). Start just left of Tuffnerd and climb out a short but powerful overhang crux section, and then angle up left along a left-leaning ramp/channel. The climb is roughly 5.11- climbing for the last part to the RC mid-height anchor.

15b. Kings of Rat 5.13b

Length: __; Pro: __ QD's (fixed)

From the Enchilada belay, reach right and clip a bolt, then climb directly up a series of underclings and steep dynamic climbing till you reach a belay jug.

16. The Maverick 5.12b ★★

Length: 65', Pro: 10 QD's

Start just left of Tuffnerd using the same start as for Enchilada ala Carte. Climb out the roof and follow a left-leaning ramp/channel to the 6th bolt where the climbing eases near the anchor at mid-height. Continue past this anchor by making a long high clip, and then engage in a series of powerful pinches (2 bolts total) to the upper anchor.

17. Getting Rich Watching Porn 5.13c

This line punches out of the right edge of the main overhanging roof of the cave.

18. Boxcar 5.13c ★★★

Length: 45', Pro: Sports long fixed draws

Boxcar is a wildly overhanging route that begins at the very back of the cave. Move up on hanging blocks of rock using marginal pinches, and then climb horizontally for 30' out the roof using a variety of crucial opposition hand holds and knee-bars. Power past a 'pod' at the lip of the cave roof, then finish by climbing up the outer upper wall without getting too pumped.

18b. Boxtop 5.13d ★★

Length: 70', Pro: 16 QD's

Start on Boxcar and climb out to the lip, then continue directly up after pulling the lip ending at a new set of belay anchors (left of Maverick belay).

Note: An unknown aid bolt line exists just left of Boxcar in the very back portion of the cave, but it is generally not used for free climbing purposes. Boxcar is the right bolt line.

19. Horizontal Delight 5.12d ★★★

Pro: 6 QD's, two bolt rap anchor

A stellar route that begins on the far left side of the cave. Climb out horizontally toward the center of the cave using a variety of oppositional counter pressure and knee-bars to finish in a 'pod'. Lower off here for just the .12d portion. Bolts have fixed chains and carabiners for the first 6 bolts to facilitate efficient climbing. The upper portion ascending the outer wall to the upper anchor is 5.13+.

20. Fully Horizontal 5.13b ★★★

This is the continuation of Horizontal Delight and it ascends the outer face past six more bolts with a crux at the upper bolt anchor. Has one reasonable rest point on the upper wall, but beware when clipping the anchor, especially if you line up backward for it.

21. Project 5.13?

This project branches directly up from the third bolt on Horizontal Delight.

22. Project 5.13?

A project located at the very left edge of the cave.

LITTLE COUGAR ROCK

Little Cougar Rock (Winema Pinnacles) protrudes from the south wall of the gorge one mile east of Multnomah Falls at the 1683' level. This rocky promontory juts out against the green forest and can be seen from the Multnomah parking area when looking east. Located immediately above it is the forested Big Cougar Rock. Though Cougar Rock is a seldom traveled summit for the off-trail gorge rock climbing hound this is a great objective.

The origin of the name of this pinnacle is mentioned in the Crown Point Country Historical Society's 2006 newsletter as follows. "An early settler in the area in the 1890's named George Pau was trying to climb to the viewpoint of the Columbia River Gorge. He found a tree lodged against the rock which afforded him handholds to do so. As he neared the summit, he spotted three cougar kittens in a den in the rocks. The kittens' mother came out of the trees at him trapping him at the top. The cougar slashed at him and finally lunged for him. Pau used the cougar's momentum to fling it off the cliff. Bleeding from several wounds, he was able to climb down and make his way back to help. The next day, he and some fellow loggers went back, rescued the kittens which were taken to the Portland zoo. After this, it was named Cougar Rock."

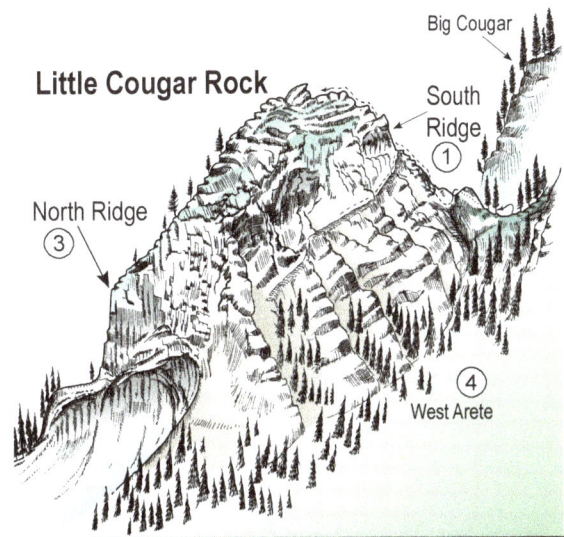

Three different approaches are available.

Option #1: Park at Multnomah Falls and ascend the Larch Mountain trail. Then hike the Multnomah Basin trail to the Trails Club's Nesika Lodge, then descend a trail immediately west of the lodge down to Big Cougar. Descend down east under BC to access LC.

Option #2: Park in a small pullout ½ mile east of Multnomah creek and ascend the Elevator Shaft trail which zigzags up a long talus field east of the falls, then cross-country to the main trail, then follow the same descending trail toward Big Cougar. Descend east off from the ridge, skirting the base of Big Cougar to access the saddle between BC and LC.

Option #3: Take the 2½ hour grunt directly up the stream drainage immediately east of the pinnacle. This drainage is exactly 1 mile east of Multnomah creek and is best when you park on the shoulder of the I-84 freeway. Ascend the stream gully till a small vertical waterfall forces you to the right. Ascend the dirt and talus slopes

St Peters Dome from the west

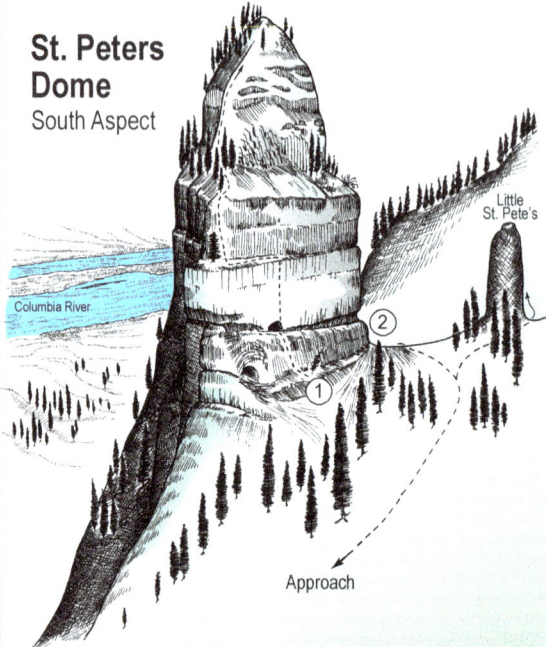

St. Peters Dome
South Aspect

St. Peters Dome
Map A: Darr detail

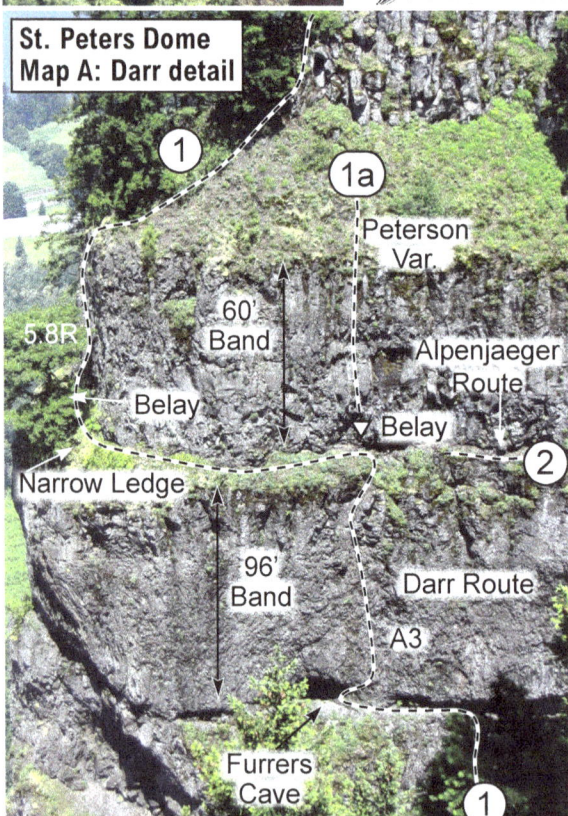

to the right of the creek and aim for the upper saddle of Little Cougar, which is below Big Cougar.

1. South Ridge Lower 5th class

Multi-pitch climb, Pro: Minor gear to 2"

This is the standard route. Ascend from the saddle out onto the South Ridge of Little Cougar over a minor hump. Traverse left and up loose scree, then back over to the right side of the ridge to a good corner crack. Ascend the short corner, then cross a jumble of blocks over to a notch for the final rather delicate balance move to get up onto the airy summit. Expect about 200' of technically easy but occasionally loose 4th and easy 5th class rock climbing.

St. Peters Dome
south face aspect

2. East Arête 5.4 R

Start near a prominent tree and ascend the crest until vertical rock forces you onto the north side. Climb a large tilted steep slab section on aid, then continue to the top on easier ground.

3. North Arête 5.8 A2+

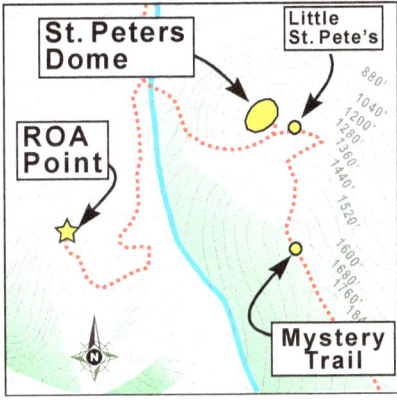

An unfinished climb that starts next to a tree on the east side of the north ridge, and ascends a leaning 5.4 crack system to a single 5.8 move onto a broad ledge and belay at 80'. Step over to the arête and aid climb the vertical face. This lead is about 80' long till it eases onto a ledge and continues up steep ledges to the summit. Incomplete ascent.

4. West Arête Lower 5th class

This ascends the jumbled west face until it merges with the main wall. Traverse right on steep rock and continue climbing diagonally upward until you can gain the south ridge.

ST. PETERS DOME

Southeast from Ainsworth State Park is a historical and prominent feature of the Columbia Gorge. St. Peters Dome (1525'), a decomposing monolith of volcanic rock that was fairly popular up till the 1960s but now relatively few climbers set their sights on this serious endeavor. An ascent of the Dome by *any* route is a very technical endeavor involving considerable risk. St. Peters Dome is a piton-required nailing aid climb on a vertical wall of cobblestone chunks of friable rock. It is the site of a fatal climbing accident so beware of the hazards.

This beta is included for historical purposes. For additional information on the Dome ascents reference the article by Don Baars & Jeff Thomas called *Dodging Peter: A Climbing History of St. Peters Dome,* **Mazama Annual Vol. LXXXIX, No. 13,** year 2007. For additional analysis browse the website www.summitpost.com for Rakek Chalupa's early 2008 ascent of the Dome, which will provide you with a strong taste of the characteristic nature of the Dome's friable rock quality.

At I-84 freeway exit #35 park along the shoulder of the secondary road, and hike up the creek drainage described for the Mystery Pillars. Walk up the creek drainage ½ mile south, but angle up left at the beginning of a deep ravine and scramble up a steep boulder field slope to the Dome. If the main dome is too wild for your taste ascend **Little St. Pete's pinnacle** which is a great alternative backwoods tiny summit that provides a nice view of its immediate big brother.

1. **Darr Route (the south face)   III 5.6 A3**
   Length: 250', Pro to 1", KB and LA pitons
   Involves some risk climbing on friable rock. Distance to the Dome from the road is 1¼ miles with an elevation gain of 1525'. Expect 1½ hours to reach the south side of the rock dome.

   How to find the Darr Route: From the main saddle between big St. Peter massif and Little St. Peter contour west on a ledge system then proceed up a short loose 5th class rotten rock section directly to Furrer's Cave. From the east end of the cave nail straight up about 76' of aid, then traverse left slightly to a point just below a crack corner. Ascend the corner about 20' (5.8) to the steep dirt ledge above the 96-foot band and set a belay. From a belay move left to a tree on the outer corner of the Dome. Find a weakness in the wall on the prow, then ascend 60' up loose rock (5.8) to the top of the 60-foot band. Regain the ridge crest and continue up a steep slope of dangerous loose stacked moss-covered rock (low 5th class) to the top. Use considerable caution on this climb. Long thin KB & LA pitons are recommended for this ascent.

2. **Alpenjaeger Route (from the saddle)   III A3**
   Length: 250', Pro: KB & LA pitons and nuts
   The Alpenjaeger route ascends on aid from the main saddle up bad rock to 8' of 5.6 moves near a bolt belay just below the 96-foot band. Aid up left and then traverse left along the narrow 96-foot band west to join with the Darr Route where it must ascend the 60-foot band on the prow near the trees.

3. **Kirkpatrick Route (from the saddle direct to top)   III A3**
   Length: 250', Pro: KB & LA pitons and nuts
   The Kirkpatrick Route ascends the Alpenjaeger route, but at the top of the 96-foot band it continues directly up the 60-foot band to a 5.6 exit mantle onto steep dirt slopes. The climb proceeds across the steep moss slopes westward to the last part of the upper Darr Route.

4. **Pearly Gates Route   III A3**
   Length: 250', Pro: KB & LA pitons and nuts
   To climb the Pearly Gates Route, traverse from the saddle along exposed grassy ledges right (east side) to a rock shoulder, and then continue traversing to a point directly below the northeast face cave. Ascend a short distance up a fourth class section to the cave. Traverse east on a narrow ledge for fifteen feet, then climb up ninety feet vertically to a sloping grassy ledge and establish a belay. Then continue right 50'+ on a grass ledges,

✦ GORGE ROCK CLIMBS 259

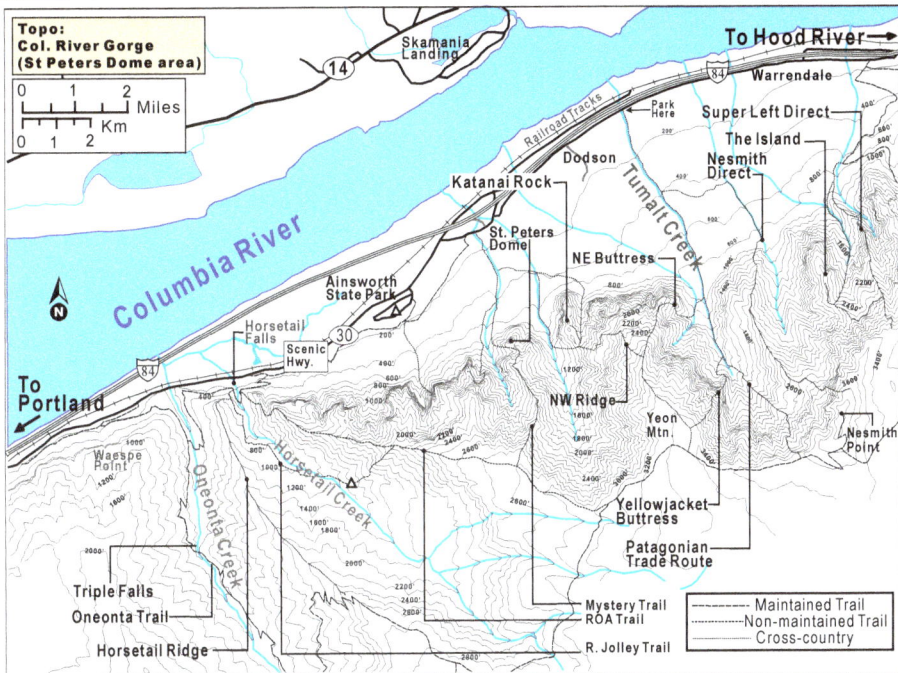

then continue up 80' on steep rock and moss. Another 80' will bring you to the trees near the summit.

LITTLE ST. PETE'S

5. **Standard Route 5.7 R**
    Length: 60', Pro to 2" and a few thin pitons
    Little St. Pete's pinnacle is a great objective. This 60' tall pinnacle composed of cobblestone-like basalt rock yields a commanding view of the Dome and the surrounding area, while offering a somewhat more pleasant summit experience. Rappel from anchor.

KATANAI ROCK

Katanai Rock (1500') is located ¼ mile directly east of St. Peters Dome. Katanai is connected by a saddle to the northwest ridge of Yeon Mountain. The top of Katanai Rock is a series of tiered basalt cliff faces capped by a forested summit that requires exposed scrambling along narrow ledges and steep gullies.

1. **North Couloir**
    Pro: Pitons and minor gear to 1"
    This is a cross-country endeavor with route finding challenges. The approach distance from the old Dodson school is 1¼ miles, 3 hours

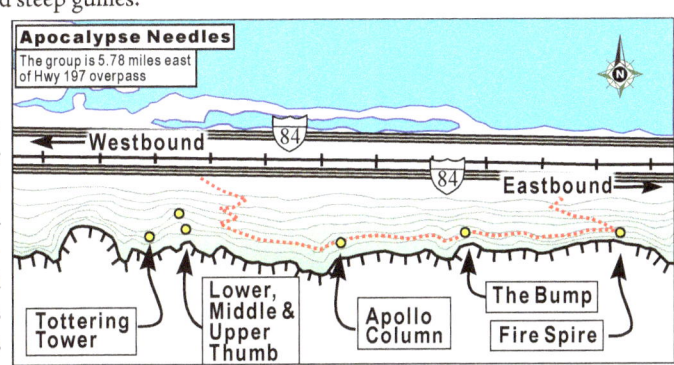

of hiking one-way, and mostly exposed 3rd class scrambling. Start this adventure by located some limited parking near the old Dodson school property at the tiny community of Dodson. Hike on an approximate bearing of 180° directly south through open forest to access a prominent couloir located immediately *east* of Katanai Rock and *west* of Yeon. Ascend the coulior, and before you arrive at the saddle scramble right along a narrow ledge to access a gully that ascends to a notch between the two summits of Katanai. Ascend north from the saddle up 60' of low 5th class dirt covered rock steps (pitons fixed) to a knoll. Descend 200' to the very northern tip of Katanai to the summit register. A rare place indeed that was first climbed by early 20th century photographers.

Fire Spire
South Aspect

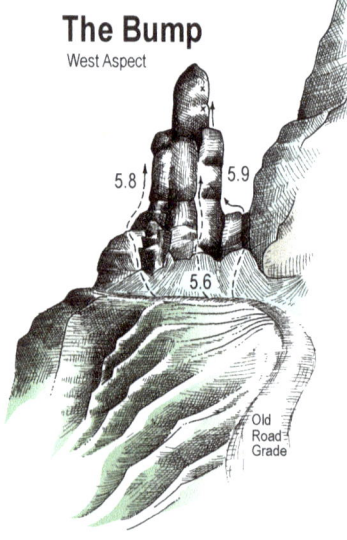

Apocalypse Needles
Map 1: Three Sore Thumbs

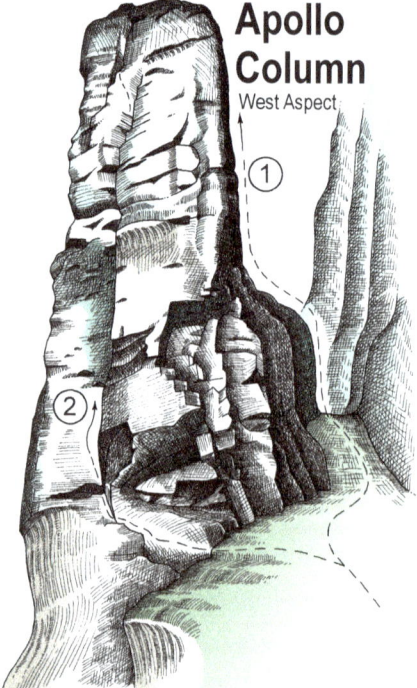

Apollo Column
West Aspect

The Bump
West Aspect

APOCALYPSE NEEDLES

This cluster of small spires is located on the south side of I-84 about 5¾ miles east of Highway 197 overpass (east end of The Dalles). The Apocalypse Needles are difficult to see because they tend to blend into the band of cliffs behind them. These pinnacles are quite challenging due in part to the friable nature of the rock. Best to climb here during cool weather (such as winter) because it is generally free of ticks and rattlesnakes at that time of year. Historically, this area has attracted climbers since the 1950s and possibly earlier. Park on the south shoulder of the freeway at a railroad access pullout ½ mile prior to the Tottering Tower, or at another pullout ½ mile beyond Firespire. Hike up the steep sandy slope to the pinnacle of your choice. The pinnacles are described from west to east. Some likely gear you may need for an ascent of these pinnacles will be a rope, pitons (KB, LA), nuts, cams to 3" and a helmet.

1. **Tottering Tower**
   The western most pinnacle is the Tottering Tower, a thin pencil of rock that swayed when the first party of climbers Tyrolean traversed across on a rope tied to the wall above. It probably still sways even today. Best to leave this absurd thin finger of rock to the credit of the very bold first ascent party (Eugene Dod & Bob Martin) who climbed it in 1963.

2. **Upper, Middle & Lower Sore Thumb**
   Immediately east of a well scoured rocky gully and west of Apollo Column is the Upper, Middle and Lower Sore Thumbs. These rock piles offer generally lower 5th class climbing (minor pro to 3" on the lower thumb). The Upper Sore Thumb is accessed from the top of the bluff. The Middle Sore Thumb (5.2R) can be accessed by rappeling to the notch from above, but may be accessed via a very steep ravine east of the pinnacle. The Lower Sore Thumb (5.4R) is readily accessed from the east to the notch where a short steep crux awaits.

Jim on *Rabbit Ears in the Gorge*

3. **Apollo Column 5.4 R A2+ (or 5.9 X)**
   Pro: LA, KB, thin nuts and cams to 1½"
   First climbed in 1963 Apollo Column this large pinnacle is vertical on all sides and is generally ascended by nailing the south side crack from the notch. Located immediately east of the Sore Thumbs, this pinnacle is approximately 70' tall on the shorter side. The route is generally aided due to the moss and detachable holds. The west face **Schmitz Route** (II A2) is a prominent crack on the west side of the column.

4. **The Bump 5.8 or A1**
   This pinnacle is located east of Apollo Column on a flat rocky promontory. There are several climbs available on this 60' pinnacle. The **Golden Spike** route (5.8) on the north side is a good thin crack and ledge climb. The **South Crack** (5.8) climbs a short steep crack from the saddle to a stance, then up a short section of face climbing (bolts) to the top.

5. **Fire Spire 5.7 or A1**
   Pro: Pitons, nuts and cams to 2"
   Located ¼ mile east of the Bump is this unique 50' precariously pointed pinnacle. There are two routes, both of which start near the saddle behind the spire. One route is a left facing corner, and the other is a steep crack on the far right side. Both merge near the top again. Approach the pinnacle using the open slopes immediately west of the spire.

NORTH SIDE OF THE COLUMBIA GORGE

The north section provides an historical analysis of climbing sites from Cape Horn eastward to Horsethief Butte.

CAPE HORN

Cigar Rock is a seldom touched small pinnacle located near the east entrance of the railroad tracks tunnel on Cape Horn. The pillar is composed of friable cobblestone sized basalt chunks of rock that tend to make an ascent quite difficult. Yet for those hardy individuals here are the logistics.

A possible access point is by using the Cape Horn Trail. Drive east on State Route 14 and park at mile post 24½ where the Cape Horn trail crosses the road. Follow the trail as it zigzags down below the initial scarp and then follows the precipice eastward. You can see the pinnacle from a viewpoint along the trail so do get a specific bearing on it if you are planning to rappel into the saddle. The trail continues to descend to the Cape Horn Road, but local land owners in the area do not appreciate people parking along the road, even though the road is county owned and maintained. The pinnacle protrudes from the southeasterly facing main wall on a wide rocky beach at river level about 500' west of the east entrance railroad tunnel.

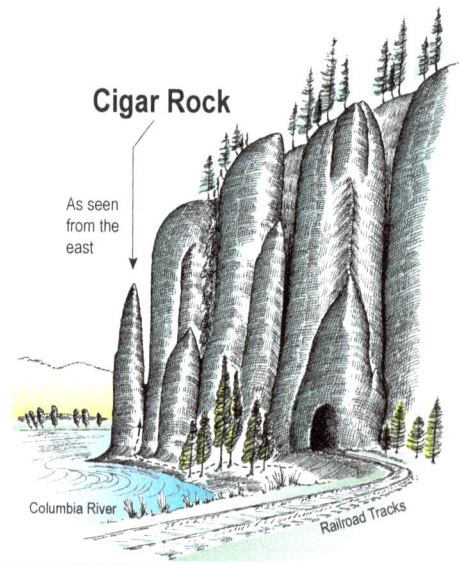

1. **East Couloir II 5.3 A2+ (5.7 X)**

The East Couloir is accessed from the rocky shoreline by climbing a short chimney and then scrambling up a debris gully to a fixed belay at the notch that separates Cigar Rock from the main massif. Climb up a short corner to an airy stance then ascend very rotten rock 30' to the

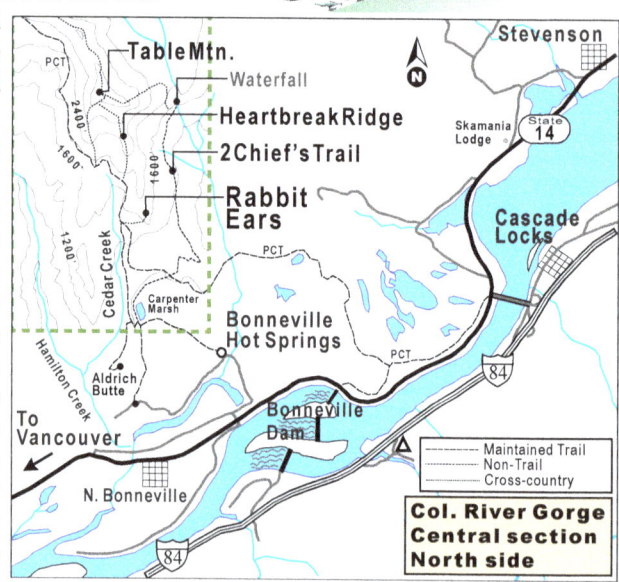

top. Beware of friable rock. Pitons required.

2. **North Face Direct II 5.3 A2**
Climb the 50' friable crack on the inside wall starting near the notch.

Another generally avoided summit along this scarp is the **Tyrolean Spire** (II 5.4 A1), a 230' high pinnacle that is approached using the escarpment above the cliff. Original party rapped to the notch between the parent cliff and the spire, then proceeded to climb the north face directly to the summit using direct piton aid.

RABBIT EARS

Pro: A few LA, KB pitons, minor gear to 3", helmet

Deep in the heart of the scenic Columbia River Gorge, and north of Bridge of the Gods is a unique hike leading to the summit of Table Mountain. Low along the southern exposure of this mountain is the Rabbit Ears. The local Indians called the place Ka'nax and To'iha, while other residents refer to it as Sacajawea and Papoose. An afternoon sun will sometimes rivet these two small ears against an ethereal blue sky.

Rabbit Ears involves cross-country forested terrain of about 2½ miles one way, with an elevation gain of 1600'. Expect about 2 hours to approach and 1 hour to climb the pinnacle.

Least you might think this to be a casual tour hold onto your camel. For those who wish to proceed do so with the enthusiasm of a hunt, because the Rabbit Ears are indeed a remarkable summit for the adventurer. The quality may be less than desirable so don't expect great

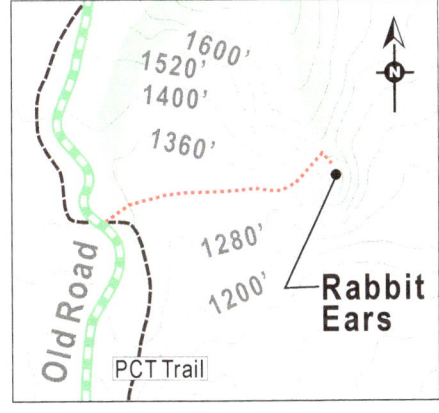

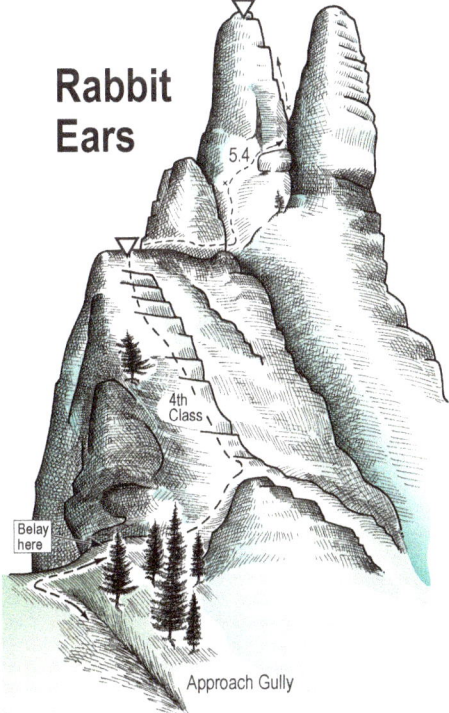

South side of Rabbit Ears

rock, but rather a challenging climb with a captivating view.

Turn off Washington State 14 at Bonneville, and drive north through the small community to the Bonneville Hot Springs resort. Continue driving 1½ miles west of the resort till you cross a small bridge at the end of the paved road. Park nearby and hike an old logging road directly north to Carpenter Marsh. The old logging road splits at the marsh. The left road branch leads to Table Mtn., and the right branch leads to Two Chief's Trail. Go left and as you turn the initial bend in the old road another left branch leads up to Aldrich Butte. Walk up the main road northward along Cedar creek and when you intersect with PCT #2000 at 1200' proceed eastward cross-country through an alder tree forest and ascend a very steep dirt gully on the SW side of the pinnacle.

Rope up on a narrow spit of soil separating two cataclysmic gullies (one of them you just came up). Eighty-five feet of 4th class scrambling leads to a belay anchor on a narrow point. Traverse right 30' on a small ledge around a corner, and then aim up toward (5.4) the notch between the ears. Belay at the notch or continue to the summit anchor. From the top of the ears the entire beauty of the Gorge can be seen and photographed.

Alternative access: Start at the Bonneville Hot Springs resort parking lot and walk southwest uphill to a trail (past a sign nailed on a tree) that enters the woods just beyond. Ascend trail to the southeast edge of Carpenter Marsh to junction with the old logging road at that marsh.

JIMMY CLIFF (TWILIGHT ZONE)

Route beta compiled by Bill Coe

This south facing crag might just be the place for your next adventure. Discovered by Jim O. and friends they quickly established a small selection of rock climbs on this wall. The southern exposure lends well to multi-season climbing potential, though due to the 2800' elevation can be snow covered at various times in the winter months (N 45.67926 / W 122.05244).

The andesite bluff formation likely formed by block slippage releasing along its base when softer terrain slid downhill exposing the cliff structure. Its less than vertical cliff face makes route cleaning a vigorous task. Wear a helmet while belaying and climbing here. Beware of yellow jacket bees that may nest on the wall. Be mindful of hunters in the fall out searching for the next deer or bear dinner. A year-round pure spring exists on the east end of the boulder field near the third clump of maple trees. Though the site lacks poison oak, scorpions are quite prevalent under rocks (just like the scorpions at Beacon Rock). Expect friable rock so beware what you are climbing on, whether an established route or a new project.

Directions:

From State 14 highway at Beacon Rock State Park, drive north on Kueffler road. Set your odometer and drive exactly 5.1 miles. This road goes past the equestrian trail head, then at 2 miles turns to gravel on FS CG-1400 road. Stay on the main gravel road. At 5.1 miles the road veers left abruptly, but you will turn right into a small pullout onto an old logging skid road. Park here or drive a short distance along the skid road and park at its end.

The trail initially drops down to the east but becomes very apparent on a nice path that walks mostly horizontally east to the bluff in ¼ mile. The climbing routes are listed left to right, the first route being on the western end of the bluff. The routes start out at about 50' and increase to 300' tall by the center of the wall.

1. **The Short Bus 5.10b/5.10c**

   Pro (in sequence): long sling for fir tree root, several small/med nuts, .75-1" cams, me-

dium cams, some Aliens, #7 or #8 Hex, 3" cam

Scramble leftward up a steep slope from the trail to a big dead snag, passing it, then cut over right on a minor ledge to the route. This route is the left crack and when cleaner may be 5.10b. Climb to the Fixe carabiner style rappel station.

2. **Bride of Wyde 5.10a**

   This is a wide crack which leans to the right and appears steeper up close than from afar. Climb the ever widening feature as it goes from #4 cam to #6 cam size then for a short section at the top to near body width size. Two Valley Giant cams (#9 and #12) were used but not critical. The climb involves adroit use of laybacking and arm bars with an odd face smear. A single bolt at the base for belayer. Shares rap anchor with The Move.

3. **The Move 5.8**

   Pro: ____

   Just right of 'The Short Bus' is a small pinnacle and a short route. Starting from the shared belay bolt of 'Bride of Wyde' ease up and right of the pinnacle, clip the bolt at the ¾ way point and make 'The Move' with the bolt right near your chest.

4. **Kyles Big Adventure Gear 5.7+**

   Pro: small selection of nuts up to 3" cams

   Climb pitch one of Mr Denton to Scorpion Ledge and traverse to the left 25' to a shallow dihedral above a rotting tree stump. Clip a lone bolt which can be backed up with a nut behind a flake for the belay.

5. **Mr. Denton on Doomsday 5.9 R (or 5.10a R)**

   Pro: small HB brass nuts, a screamer, 3", 3-½", 4" and/or 5" cams for upper crack

   Scramble up 4th-5th class above and right of the big dead snag to a 2-bolt belay on Scorpion Ledge. Climb up 15' and left about 10' to a bolt, then straight up following thin cracks and tricky pro past a small tree to a larger crack ending at a 2-bolt anchor on top.

6. **Jimmy's Favorite 5.10a**

   Pro: QD's only

   Completed and name in honor of Jim (who was unavailable). Climb easy low angle 4th-5th class to the Mr Denton belay on Scorpion Ledge. Step right 8' and climb up (9 bolts) the face just right of (and then inside) the obvious shallow chimney to a belay anchor stance 8' from the cliff top. A single 60m rope rappel back to Scorpion Ledge.

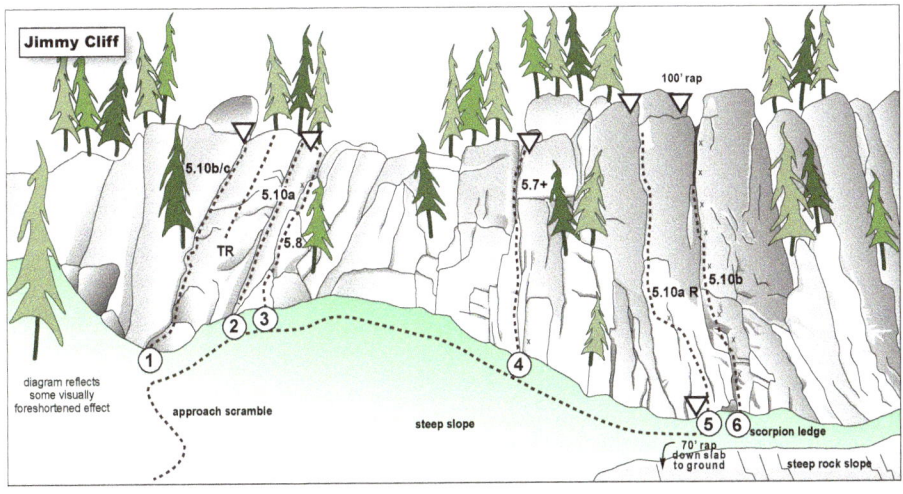

7. **Beekeeper Magic**
Project unfinished as Bill was stung 200+ times while on an inspection rappel of the line.

RUMBA RIDGE

The next climbs are on a 300' long ridge buttress on the far eastern end of the cliff scarp wrapped in a cluster of trees. Walk along the base of the bluff eastward, then up a 3rd class narrow low angle bedrock ravine scoured by water runoff. Walk east on a grassy tier covered with trees to the base of the ridge. The ground up routes are still raw; climb diligently; expect friable rock. Avoid leaving excrement here as the pure water spring is directly below.

8. **Conga Line 5.7**
Pro: nuts, small cams, 1", 2" and opt 3" cam, 9-10 full length slings
Likely five-star route eventually once clean. From east side of a buttress move up a gully to the first break in a rock wall. P1: Climb up a crack and face holds 15'-20' to the crux (bolt) then step left onto the ridge proper. Dance up the ridge on easier terrain using various trees that offer monkey hangs (the highlight of the route). Belay at a 9' long ledge at 110'. P2: traverse leftward up 15' to the base of a hidden rock pitch (a wide shallow gully). P3: aim up 100' and leftward, over a short final bouldery move, and past another 25' of spruce trees to the top of the ridge. Use a tree with rappel runners and ring to descend. Single 60m gets you down.

9. **Conga Variation**
At the end of Conga line P1 instead of using the leftward traverse on P2, head straight up a thin crack and some face holds. Avoid the obvious loose flake in the corner. Move left across the buttress past a tree, and up trending rightward till Conga Line is rejoined.

10. **Couchmaster Shuffle 5.10+ (X-rated for now)**
Pro: set of cams to 2", ¾" nut, doubles on ½" to 1" cams, long slings
Starts directly at the foot of the buttress. Climb up a few feet, step left to a small ledge, and up an easy 12' ramp, then up left to the aesthetic Couchmaster Shuffle crack. Aim straight up the obvious crack in a shallow dihedral for 70' until forced to wander out right on the face. Ascend up past a fir tree on easy ground to gain the ridge and belay at a tree. Finish via the standard P2 of Rumba Ridge.

ROCK CREEK CRAG

This small yet quality west-facing climbing crag (aka Clif's Crag) is great for afternoon warm sunny climbing in early Spring or late Fall seasons. Though limited in scope this site is an idyllic example of back woods cragging on a 40' to 65' tall cliff that has both trad and sport climbs.

Directions:

Drive north from Stevenson, WA on Red Bluff Road at the upper west end of town. It quickly turns to gravel. Shortly ahead the road splits (go right) on CG-2000 forest road. This road follows alongside the Rock Creek stream. Cross a small bridge at six miles with a pretty waterfall on the left. At 8½ miles the road turns sharply left to cross another small bridge. Instead you will go right just before the bridge on road CG-2060 and park in a wide area below the crag. Way uphill perched like a castle overlooking the valley is this tiny little west facing andesitic crag. A steep narrow path starts just past the flat open area and angles up right into the forest to the right of the landslide. The steep climbers path ascends directly uphill till it is

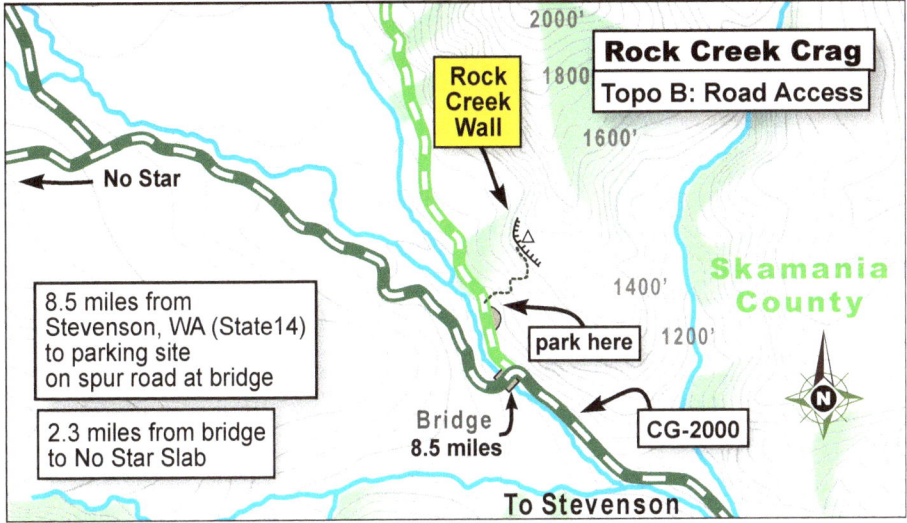

even with the upper tier of rock and then walks leftward to the base of the upper tier.

1. **Northern Pearl 5.8 R** ★

   Pro to 4"; length 45'

   A continuous crack that varies in size from fingers to fist. The crux is near the top; don't be tempted to bail left into the easy but loose blocks.

2. **Pearl's Jam 5.9 R** ★

   Pro to 4"; length 45'

   Start on the same jam crack as Slow Dance. When the crack ends, traverse left four feet and finish via the top half of Northern Pearl. Detached, but seemingly stable blocks form the left side of the crack on the top half of this and the following climb; because of this, all gear placements through this section are suspect. SS chain/ring anchor.

3. **Slow Dance 5.10a** ★★★

   Pro: 3 QD's & #1, #2, #3 Cam

   Jam up the sweet hand-crack located in a shallow dihedral. A small pedestal allows for

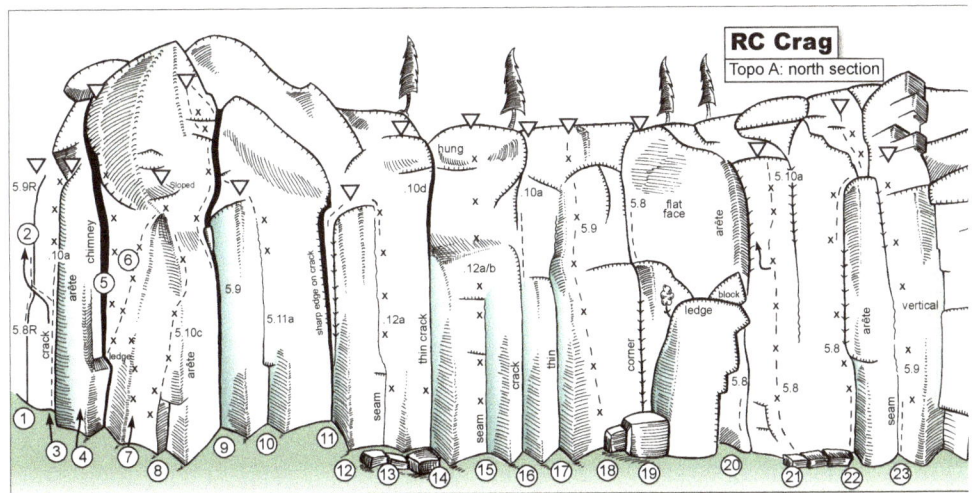

a rest once the crack ends. Angling slightly right onto the face via a sequential blend of side-pulls, smearing, and crimps will get you near the top. If you've made it this far, a mantel move below the anchor won't throw you for a loop.

4. Bearhug 5.11-
Pro: QD's

A "double arête bearhug" climb with problematic stance positions. Falls are going to be *de rigueur* on lead. Ends at an anchor with Metolius rap hangers (shared by **Slow Dance**).

5. Inner Sanctum 5.10c ★★

Pro: 5 QD's and a #2 Camalot for the beginning; length 60'

The obvious off-width/chimney with several lead bolts lining the right side. Start by scrambling up a couple small ledges to the start of the off-width. Employ whatever trickery necessary to work your way up to several rests in the widening crack. Wiggle up the final 15' fully immersed in the bowels of the climb. SS chain/ring anchor. Could use some more cleaning.

6. Bottle Rocket 5.10c ★★

Pro: 4 QD's and a #2 Camalot for the beginning

This climb shares the start and first bolt with Inner Sanctum but avoids the off-width by angling right onto a fun and exciting face. A final perplexing move will put you at the anchor which is shared by The Watchman.

7. Mists of Time 5.12a

Pro: 6 QD's

A face with a thin seam running up it. A stout direct start that merges into the Bottle Rocket route. Shares the anchor with The Watchman.

8. The Watchman 5.10c ★★★

Pro: 6 QD's

A stellar arête climb. This is the first route encountered immediately after turning the corner on the north end of the cliff. Look for the first bolt under a light-brown mini-roof on the left side of the arête. A deceptive and tricky climb that won't let you off the hook until rounding the arête near the top. After you finesse the balancy crux switch to the right side of the arête then finish with a sloped mantle to the anchor Perhaps the best, moderate sport climb on the cliff. Carabiners installed at anchor.

9. **Motional Turmoil 5.9** ★★★

   Pro: 4 QD's, nuts to 1", cams to 5" (4" feasible); length 60'

   The standard and classic warmup at the crag with a bit of ye ol' punch to it. Place good pro in the initial moves then power through the steep crux till it eases at a large wedged block. The remainder of the crack widens to 18' (and fatter) but is pre-fixed with several bolts on the upper part for your convenience and pleasure.

10. **Butterfinger 5.10d** ★★

    Pro: 2 QD's and pro to 1", and small TCU's recommended; length 45'

    Quality climb that starts vertical and packs a healthy punch to it. Start climbing up a narrowing crack until it disappears. Continue on up the face making use of the arête to the left. A finishing mantel brings you to a sloped ledge where the climb moves left and continues up the final moves of Motional Turmoil. A variant exists on the upper right face has been lead.

Chad Ellers leading *Bottle Rocket*

11. **Wyde Syde 5.10a** ★

    Pro to 2" including two C3 #00. A 12" Valley Giant is optional

    A wonderful off-width that is a great introduction to the world of wide. The seam to the right takes small TCU's. SS chain/ring anchor.

12. **Electric Blue 5.12a** ★★★

    Pro: 5 QD's

    An arête to the right of the off-width that offers tricky sidepulls and crimper holds. Shares the same anchor with the next & previous route.

13. **Sands of Time 5.11d** ★★

    Pro: 5 QD's

    Unusual opening moves lead to a very powerful crux section. This is the clean face with the seam in the center. Shares the same anchor as Electric Blue.

14. **Naked 5.10d** ★★★

    Pro: Thin nuts and TCU's, and cams to 4"

    A stellar crack climb with powerful opening moves on a steep relentless thin corner seam that lands on a sloped slab at midway. A few moves up a fat crack ends with a wild ride up a sharp edged layback overhang crux to finish. This is a proud test of endurance and ingenuity. Stays wet longer than most of the climbs at Rock Creek because the crack corner faces left

Chad Ellers leading *The Watchman*

on the lower portion of the climb.

15. Blue Highway 5.12a
Pro: 6 QD's
Powerful line with several technical bulges to surmount.

16. Mighty Mite 5.10a ★
Pro to 2" including small TCU's, doubles on #0.4, #0.5, & #0.75 Camalots optional
Begin in a small dihedral directly in front of the large fir tree. A tricky starting sequence is harder yet for those on the short side. After a good rest at the mid-point, the top half keeps you working right up to the (tree) anchor. Could use some more cleaning.

17. _____

18. Airtime 5.9
Pro: 6 QD's
The buttress on the right side of a blunt arête with numerous edges. A quality climb with tricky crux and a surprise crux ending.

19. Niceline 5.8 ★
Pro to 2"
This crack is never too difficult and consistently fun. Start by climbing up several large steps to get into the corner. SS carabiner anchor. Could use some more cleaning.

20. Plaidtastic 5.8 ★
Pro to 3"
Start in a blocky alcove with numerous edges. Halfway up, a small roof needs to be negotiated before gaining a pleasant crack that will take you to the anchor.

21. Committed Convenience 5.8 (crack finish) ★★
Pro for crack finish: 4 QD's, nuts and cams to 2"
Rating is 5.9 if staying on the face and using just the 6 bolts
Tricky opening moves combine pzazz with punch to make a worthy climb. Fairly fun but

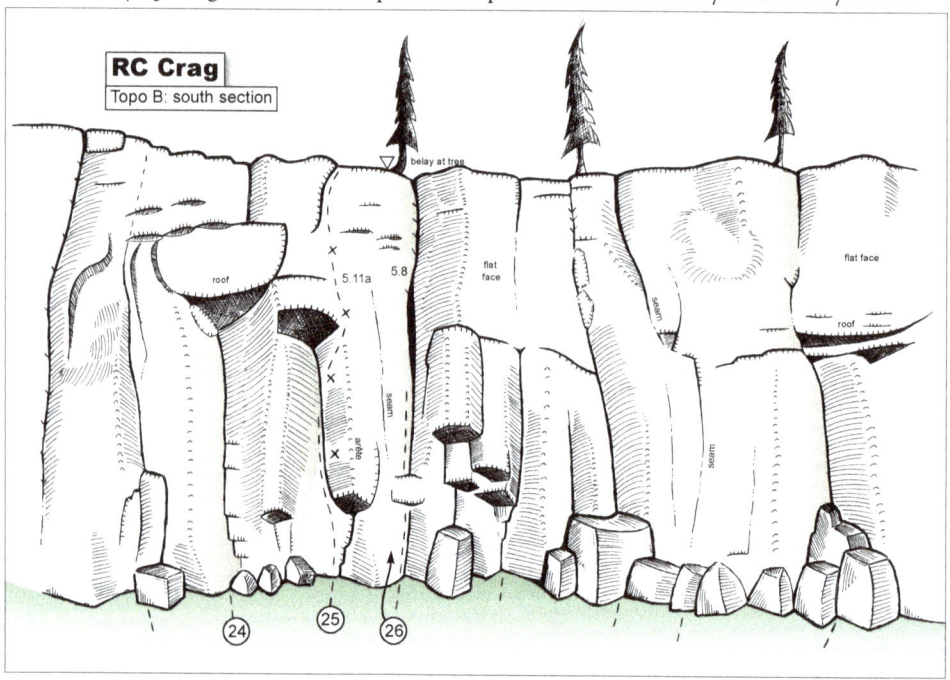

the face needs to cleaned better. Anchor is shared by this climb and the Plaidtastic crack.

22. Progressive Climax 5.8 ★ ★ ★
Pro: 7 QD's, length 55'
Awesome climb that ascends a large dihedral sporting numerous small horizontal edges. At the fifth bolt, step right (or move up to the jug then right) onto the airy arête and finish on easy jugs. Great warm-up. Webbing anchor. A high quality steep face climb that seems to put a smile of satisfaction on the face of every climber.

23. Scorpio 5.8+ ★ ★
Pro: 5 QD's
A fun romp up an open book loaded with edges. The difficulty starts early but quickly gives way to easier climbing. There are two possible ways to finish Scorpio: The harder option is going straight up to the obvious ring anchor. Alternately, one can clip the last bolt on Scorpio with a runner and step left of the rock fin to finish on Progressive Climax (two more bolts).

Note: About 100 feet separate the previous two climbs from the next climbs.

24. _____

25. Black Ribbon 5.11a ★ ★
Pro: 4 QD's and a #3 Camalot for the finish, length 40'
Directly in front of a leaning snag is a clean dihedral with a large roof at mid-height. After two intense cruxes, moving up the dihedral and clearing the roof, scamper up the relatively easy face to the tree anchor (shared with Bungee's Crack). Consider clipping the 2nd bolt with a single carabiner.

26. Bungee's Crack 5.8 ★ ★
Pro to 3", length 40'
The southern most climb at Rock Creek is this enjoyable well protected crack climb. Stemming on the numerous edges allows for several rests and casual gear placements. A crux near the top needs to be surmounted before reaching the (tree/chain) anchor. Could use some more cleaning.

NO STAR SLAB

A boorish tilted pocketed landscape straight from the moon this little angled friction slab with dimpled hand holds just might entertain you for an hour. The formation is a rotting siltstone erosional remnant from pyroclastic flows. Drive over the small bridge on Rock Creek road (CG-2000) at 8½ miles, then continue another 2¼ miles further up the main gravel Rock Creek road. GPS coordinates for this slab are 45°45.341'N by 122°02.833'W. Located on the immediate shoulder of the gravel road a short distance east of the pass.

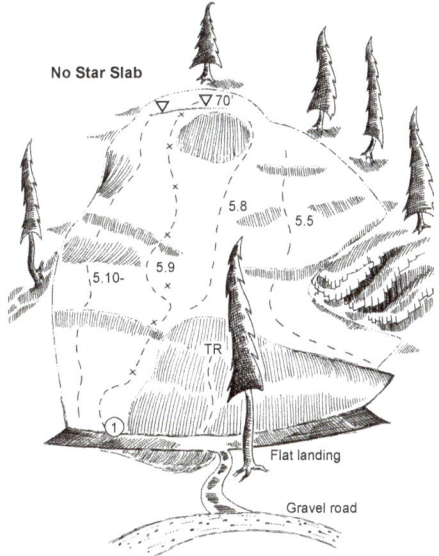

1. Lunar Dreams 5.9 ★
Pro: 7 QD's
A little example of friction slab climbing on mere rounded dimples. Probably not

worth the drive up here just for this, but if you happen to be in the area.

SKOOKUM PINNACLE

A minor plug of steep rock tucked below another rotten plug of rock on a steep hill slope overlooking the upper Rock Creek valley above a clearcut logged area in the upper valley. The pinnacle is about 60'+ tall on the uphill side and is quite elusive, hidden from view except in a few places along the gravel road.

The route is 5.7 and fixed (8 bolts), but expect some hollow flaky, loose rock in places. Rap anchor in place. Typical gorge rock climb with plenty of off-trail adventure thrashing and route finding skills. Not a destination site, but an odd-ball plug vertical on all sides. A climb not for the weak minded due to the good navigational off-trail skills and semi-dubious nature of the friable terrain.

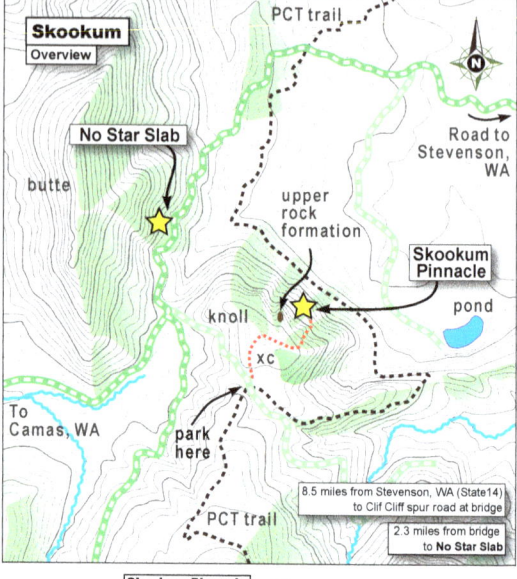

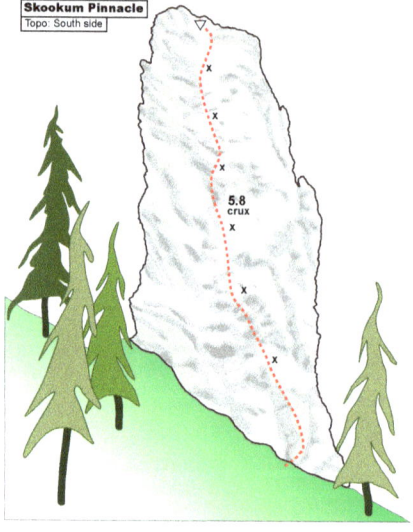

Directions:

Drive north from Stevenson, WA on Red Bluff Road at the upper west end of town. It quickly turns to gravel. Shortly ahead the road splits (go right) on CG-2000 forest road. Continue on CG-2000 all the way up to the pass to a 4-way intersection. Take CG-2090 uphill for about ¾ mile to where the PCT trail crosses. Park here.

Approach:

Walk north on an old skid road (well obscured) to a wooded knoll, then descend a mild sloped ridge east, then down very steep slippery slope (ice axe) in forest about 300'. You will pass the Rotte Plug, the upper rotten plug of rock with a 5.7x minor boulder move to get to its top, so skip this garbage pile by descending down below it, angling left under its base till you see the Skookum Pinnacle. Car to pinnacle time is about 20 minutes, but the destination is instinct-based since neither rock outcrop is visible in the thick forest when approaching them. To depart, continue descending down the forested slope for another 400' to land on the PCT trail. From there just walk back up the PCT trail to the vehicle. Otherwise retrace your path uphill to the car on the steep slopes past the upper rotten plug.

WIND MOUNTAIN

The 500' tall west face of Wind Mountain is a rather imposing massif located ¾ mile east of Home Valley, Washington. This west facing aspect is certainly a visually appealing objective when viewed from the highway. The cliff scarp has notable sections of friable rock with challenging exposed leads. If you are considering climbing here expect difficult route finding assessment, friable rock, exposed scrambling, ticks, and dirt covered ledges. Bring a sixth sense of knowledge for route finding because each prospective climb is tough with no sharp distinction between 'R' and 'X' climb ratings. Wear a helmet. Definitely not a place to have a climbing accident. Park on the shoulder of State Route 14 at the west side of Wind Mountain and ascend the boulder talus field to the base of the main wall.

Both images: Matt Carter climbing on *Wind Mtn*

1. **West Face Crack 5.9 R/X**
   Pro: Pitons, nuts and cams to 3"
   This route is one reason why climbers might choke up the energy to venture up Wind Mtn. But don't be lulled into thinking its a breeze. There is considerable friable rock on the approach gully, as well as friable rock on several of the lead pitches that will tend to keep most climber's away. The route is the prominent crack system that faces south into the main amphitheater. The top portion of the climb becomes a left leaning, west facing ramp. The west side boulder field ends at a short cliff. Lead up this (5.4) into the main long exposed 4th class approach gully. There are several belay anchors in this gully on the right face, the upper one being at the upper most platform in the gully on the main wall. Step across the main gully and climb up the left face on 5th class rock aiming for the crack system above, avoiding the other huge loose deep chimney corner system to the right. Belay at a stance. Lead past the crux vertical rock corner crack system till it eases onto the left facing corner and ascend this till you can exit to the trees near the top. Descend by walking off to the north slightly through steep forests and cliff bands using game trails.

2. **Utopia 5.8 R/X**
   Pro: Pitons, nuts and cams to 3"
   This is the deep corner system immediately right of West Face Crack climbed by Jim Nieland. Climb a very short cliff (5.4) into a long steep exposed 4th class gully. Belay at the upper most platform in the gully at the main wall. Climb up into a low angle deep corner system (friable rock) that gradually steepens and aims up right. Expect some short sections of chimney, but otherwise 3-pitches of mostly variable sized cracks and wide sections.

3. **Lost Wages 5.8 R**
   Pro: Pitons, nuts and cams to 3"
   A prominent corner system on the west face that starts up a steep, brush filled 5.8 corner system. Belay at 80' on a small ledge at the bolt and piton. Continue up left in the 5.6 brushy corner 80' till it eases onto a scree slope where you will find a large fir tree (WC merges here). Belay. This huge fir tree is at the base of the prominent west side gully and is visible from the road. Scramble up the broad gully 100' and belay near an oak tree. Step

up to the main steep corner system and climb on the right face on small holds (fixed pitons) until forced to stem the vertical corner past a 5.5 crux (piton). Scramble up a loose scree gully and belay at the large sling festooned block. Scramble into the prominent 3' wide vertical sided corner system and step up into a cavernous ledge to belay. This ledge is capped by a large overhang. Free climb (5.8 or A0) by stemming or aiding the main wall and mantle out the top past the overhang. Scramble up left for 30' to a fixed belay. The next pitch is unfinished. Rappel the route.

4. Workman's Comp 5.4 R

Pro: Pitons, nuts and cams to 3"

This is perhaps slightly easier to get to the giant fir tree belay. It will still tweak your tail feathers, but the lower two-thirds of the first lead is on large relative steps in a wide corner system. From behind a large tree angle up left into a steep but easy series of steps in a corner. At about 120' the climbing abruptly veers directly upward crossing some friable rock. The lead is 180' long to reach the large fir tree mentioned in Lost Wages. Follow the remainder of Lost Wages from the huge fir tree at the base of the prominent gully. Rappelling down LW is feasible with a single 60m rope.

5. Termination 5.6 X

Pro: Pitons, nuts and cams to 3"

This route takes on the main lower west face directly, but does involve some meandering sections that provide a ton of rope drag. Beware of substantial friable rock on the final lead along the exposed x-rated ridgecrest just before the route merges with the main gully of Lost Wages/Workmans Comp.

Mike climbing at *Windy Slab*

GORGE ROCK CLIMBS 275

WINDY SLAB

This crag is located along State Route 14 at the base of the south side of Wind Mountain. Windy Slab is a south-facing low angle 40' tall slab. The rock is reminiscent to granite friction climbing and is a perfect late Spring, Summer and Fall place to visit while traveling east to other objectives. Routes range from 5.4 to 5.10+. The crag was originally developed by the late Jeff Walker of Willard, Washington. He and friends climbed many of the original routes, but today most of the climbs have fixed gear.

Don Gonthier at Windy Slab

Directions

Drive east of Home Valley 1 mile and park on the north side of the road in a large gravel pullout west of the Borrow Pit at milepost 51¼. Scramble up the scree slope for 200' to a comfortable, sunny platform at the base of the crag.

Windy Slab is a unique little site that attracts a small selection of rock climbers who are interested in low angle slab climbing. Stop by and enjoy the simple beauty of this delightful small rock slab, so be considerate of others and use the site wisely.

1. **The Steppes 5.3**
   Pro: Minor gear to 2"
2. **Dare 5.5**
   Pro: Minor gear to 2"
3. **Night Music 5.6** ★ ★ ★
   Pro: 5 QD's
   The most popular climbing route here and it is usually the first route everyone leads.
4. **Icon 5.7** ★ ★ ★
   Pro: 4 QD's
   This great route has two variations at the small roof. Break left to #3 route, or stay right of

the roof and finish on easy ground to an anchor.

5. **East Wind 5.10a** ★★★

   Pro: 5 QD's

   A stellar line with great smears and balance, but not in an extreme sense. Tenuous opening cruxy moves, balancy mid-section and a reasonable ending on jug holds. Quite possibly the best rock climb at Windy Slab. Go for it!

6. **Dark Apron 5.10a TR** ★★

   A top-rope problem that kisses the left corner of the dark apron. Technical balance smears and odd counter pulls to hold the friction. The route stays left of the bolt line of #7 and right of #5 on the upper prow clear to the anchor.

7. **Apron 5.10a** ★★

   Pro: 4 QD's and minor 1" gear for the crack

   A great line that rides on thin smears up the dark apron to the large roof, then follows the splitter finger crack to the anchor.

8. **Heatwave 5.10d TR** ★

   Squeezes between the two routes but has a combination of powerful moves with dicey smears up high. Exit right under the large roof to the anchor.

9. **Braille 5.10a** ★

   Pro: 3 QD's

   A quality climb that acsends the right most part of the dark apron. Start at a small outcrop rib of rock. The crux is between the second and third bolt.

10. **West Wind 5.9**

    Pro: Nuts and cams to 2"

    A typical natural pro climb that pumps through a series of small overhanging roofs, then finishes up a steeply angled crack to a stance.

Winter snow ascent of the Dog Spine

DOG SPINE

On the southern flank of the famous Dog Mountain there is a super cool jagged backbone arête of rotten rock rising for 1900' directly from the roadside. Worthy? Absolutely—in fact for those who are looking for a daring alpine-like challenge **totally in a league of its own**, then this is the one for you! The highly exposed ravines and ridges along this backbone arête and the deep forest scramble for another 1000' to the summit of Dog Mountain is an extraordinary and historic Gorge classic.

The Dog Spine arête route is mostly 3rd class scrambling with some highly exposed 5th class sections. Depending on which variation you will be taking park in a pullout ¼ mile to the east or west of the 'toe' of a long rocky buttress along SR 14. This buttress is located ¾ mile east of the regular hikers trail head for Dog and Augspurger Mountain.

There are several different standard start variations: the **West Direct**, and the **Traditional** approach. Scrambling variations are practically unlimited on this mountain scarp. The Dog Spine spur can be ascended through out the year, but it is more difficult and serious when covered with snow and when the Gorge winds are blowing heavily across the Spine. Beware of

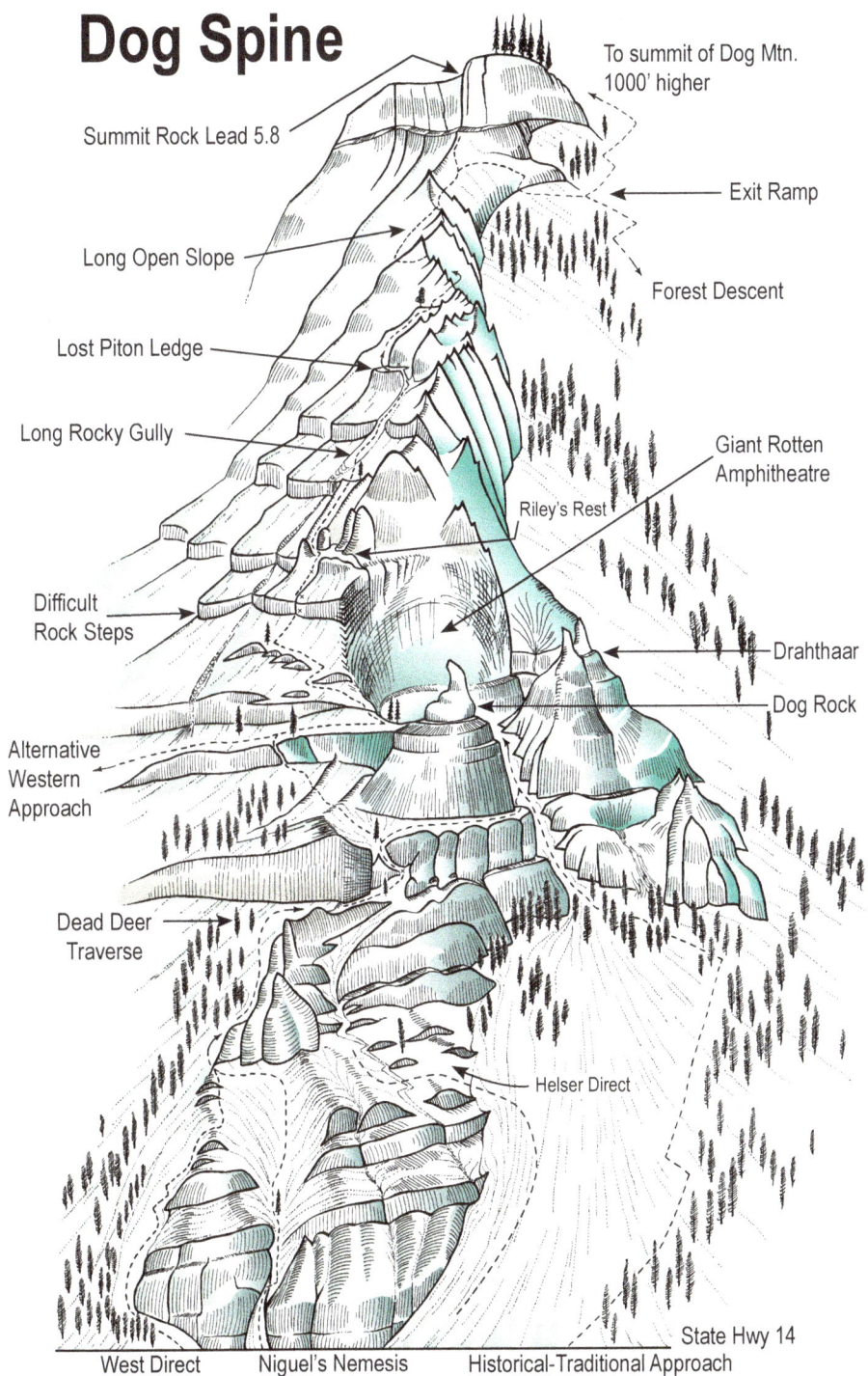

ticks and loose rock. Average time one way approximately 2½ to 3 hours to the 1900' level. Gear might include an ice axe, 9mm rope, a few carabiners, slings, and several nuts or pitons to 1".

The **Traditional Approach** ascends the long scree slope on the east side of the Dog Spine Arête near the forest edge. Then, angle up leftward through a sparsely tree covered slope into a large gully (elev. 640') immediately east of Dog Rock. This gully leads directly to the east side of the saddle next to Dog Rock (elev. 1100').

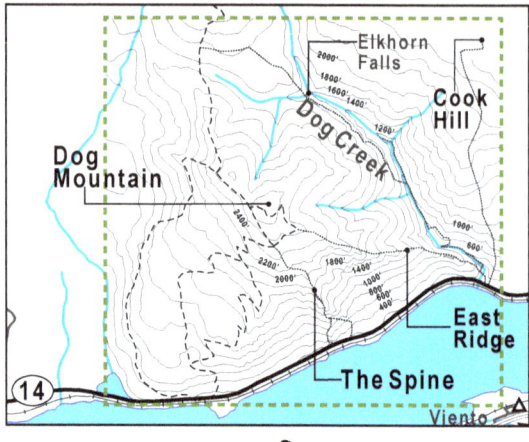

The best start is the West Direct, which is accessed up the slope to the west side of the main buttress. This will allow you to bypass the gully difficulties so you can proceed quickly up the ridges and ravines leading to the 'dead deer traverse'.

Scramble up leftward, and then rightward around a prominent buttress until you come to the base of a 100' vertical wall that covers the full breadth of the arête. Step right (east) over the ridge, and gingerly cross an exposed 4th class 30' long catwalk known as 'dead deer traverse'. The traverse is thin and loose and a belay rope is recommended. Wander up slope past a wide groove to a deceptive cul-de-sac. From here step left on small edges then

Dog Rock

continue up a steep leftward leaning 5th class ramp onto easier terrain above. Belay at a tree 120' up from the cul-de-sac. Either exit right to join the Traditional Route in the main gully, or...wander up left, then up a very steep 4th class moss corner onto the main deer track immediately west of the obvious pinnacle, which is Dog Rock.

The **Helser Direct** ascends the long scree slope immediately right of the toe of the buttress and merges on the immediate right side of the Dead Deer Traverse.

To climb the 5th class 40' high Dog Rock Pinnacle you need a rope and pro to 1", otherwise the climb is mostly fixed. Just across the ravine is a flaky point of rock called Drahthaar. Both the **Direct Variation** and the **Traditional Variation** meet here at this saddle next to Dog Rock.

From the saddle at the Dog Rock pinnacle angle up left steeply to a small tree. Keep to the left of the massive amphitheater directly behind Dog Rock and right of a smaller westward sloping ravine. From the tree belay go up through an exposed 5th class place (fixed pitons) that allows passage to a terrace above. Belay at a fixed anchor at 160' on a terrace called Riley's Rest. Step left, and then scramble up some 4th class terrain for 150' to another tree belay. Waltz up an easy scree ravine for several hundred feet, then grunt up to the left by a short step onto Lost Piton Ledge (elev. 1400'). Move left (4th class) around the corner then up the slopes till you are on the very crest of the spine.

Continue to follow the spine directly or on either side where necessary for approximately the next 300'. At the toe of the final 40' headwall you can either climb the 5th class crack or take the standard exit off to the right into the forests when the spine ends at 1900' elevation. At this point either continue up through the forest to the summit of Dog Mountain for the supreme finale, or descend down forested slopes to the east while staying clear of the cliffs.

THE BYPASS

A little site that sports a surprisingly stout string of hard routes. When you're done climbing all the short pumpy sport routes, toss your dog a bone. The climbing is ultra short but a viable spot to get a summer evening fix after work. Indians and fisherman have been wandering across this land for a thousand years.

1. **Old Geezer Teaser 5.8**
   Pro: 4 QD's
   The standard line aims up right to the anchor. Another variation angles up left to join the same easy route.

2. **Barnyard Boogie 5.10b/c** ★
   Pro: 5 QD's
   Jaunts up hard right and merges at last bolt of next climb.

3. **Haiku 5.10b** ★
   Pro: 3 QD's
   This route starts off a stack of two large blocks and angles up left to a bolt anchor.

4. **Conundrum 5.11c** ★
   Pro: 4 QD's
   This face route ascends up slightly overhanging terrain past an obvious pocket.

5. **Yellow Bellied Sap Sucker 5.11b/c** ★★
   Pro: 5 QD's
   Excellent route and much harder than it looks from the ground. Power your way up overhanging terrain up to a hidden anchor on the left. An alternate exists: Climb first 2 bolts, then cruise a crack to the left.

6. **Aesthetic Anesthetic 5.11b** ★★★
   Pro: 4 QD's
   A quality power climb that does not give you anything easy. Starts up a minor corner utilizing face hold and pockets. The route aims up right to the small prow. Bolt

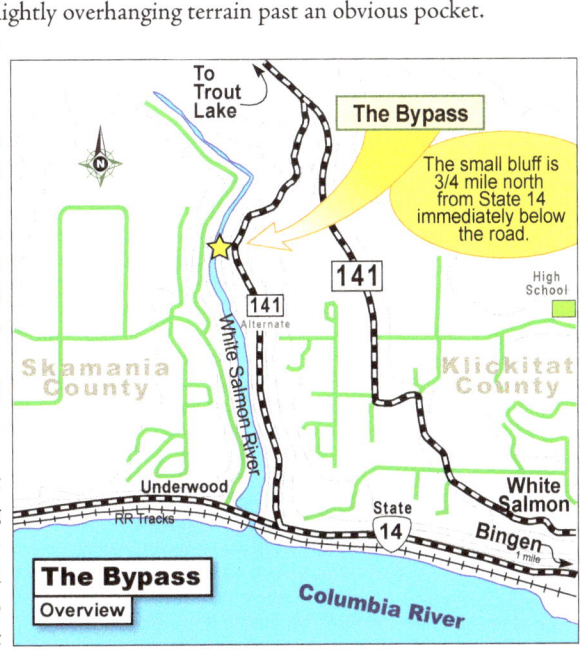

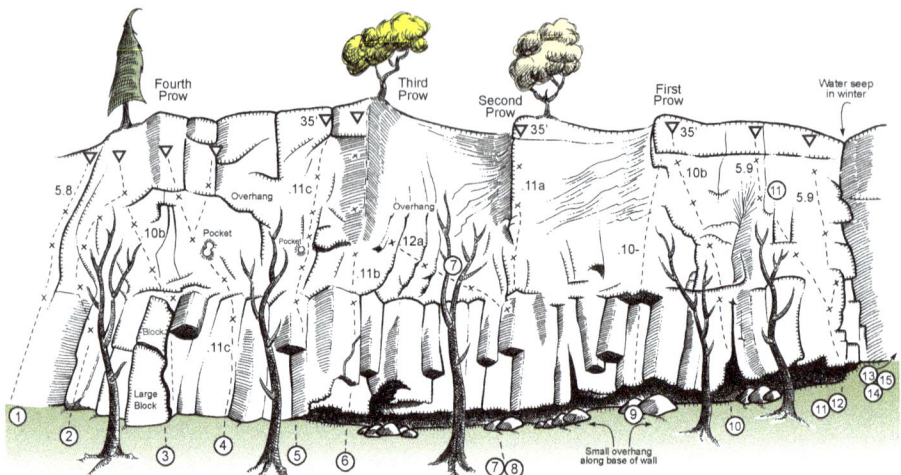

anchor is visible at the lip, but take a small carabiner to get it through the link.

7. **Smirk 5.12a** ★

   Pro: 6 QD's

   This is a long pumpy left-ward angling traverse that ends at the previous routes belay anchor.

8. **Girlilla Pillar 5.10+** ★★

   Pro: 4 QD's

   A great powerful face climb that aims for a prow near the top. The 5.11+ traverse route starts here also.

9. **Stealhead 5.10-** ★★★

   Pro: 4 QD's

   Some holds are long reaches which make it possibly harder for short people. If you can stick with the final prow to the anchor...great. Otherwise most step off right slightly near the belay anchor.

10. **Coho 5.10b/c**

    Pro: _ QD's

    A variation just left of Stealhead using the same belay.

11. **Daft Dogs 5.9**

    Pro: 4 QD's

    Nice basic route for starters. Both #9 and #10 routes start at the same initial point.

12. **Fish from a Friend 5.9**

    Pro: 4 QD's

    This is the dark colored water groove.

To the right of a groove are these extra shorty's at the south end of the crag.

13. **Cat Nip 5.10+**

    Pro: 3 QD's

    Just left of 'The Shark'. Tricky route seldom climbed. Same belay as Cat Nap.

14. **Cat Nap 5.9**

    Pro: 3 QD's

    Easier route sharing belay with Cat Nip.

15. **The Shark 5.6**
    Pro: 2 QD's
    The farthest route at the south end. An easy route put up for kids to climb.

WANKERS COLUMNS

This quality 50' tall basalt bluff is situated on a prominent south facing syncline immediately west of Rowland Lake. This syncline (aka Syncline Wall) overlooking the Columbia River is a scenic region to visit whether you are rock climbing, biking or hiking.

Wankers Columns offers distinctively steep columnar crack climbing opportunities good for Fall, Winter, or Spring climbing, especially when the west side of the state is too rainy. The columns have a southwesterly facing orientation which takes advantage of the sunshine on wintery days.

Fixed anchors exist along the rimtop above most of the popular climbs making it well suited for setting up a quick top-rope although some routes are leadable. The easiest climb is a stout 5.7 so the site may not be conducive to beginner climbing. The routes are seldom lead, although the classic 5.7 Hanz Crack on the far left is definitely worth the blast either as a top-rope or lead.

Certain rock climbs start easy and then steepen to roughly 80°. In some cases, the routes start surprisingly easy on the lower half only to end ridiculously thin on the upper half. The basalt bluff has a right leaning two-directional tilt with slightly weathered cracks.

Flora & Pests

Ticks are active in the Spring season. Anticipate rattlesnakes during the warm season. If you are susceptible to getting the itch from poison oak it's best to avoid climbing here. Consider bringing a ground cloth to protect your rope.

Directions

Drive east from Bingen, Washington on State 14 for three miles. Convenient roadside parking is available at the old Highway 8 turnoff next to Rowland Lake, or at a popular mountain biking trail next to Locke Lake alongside Courtney Road. The approach will take about 20 minutes. Follow the narrow hiker/biking trail uphill as it follows alongside a small stream. When the trail crosses the stream, a prominent rock bluff is located directly uphill on the east slope of the stream.

SOUTH END (RATTLER AREA)

Common zone to begin climbing as it's where the rough climbers path first meets the cliff.

1. ____ 5.12- [?]

    Three very closely spaced narrow columns yield one difficult route. Hard TR on steep thin narrow columns. Starts just north of an oak tree.

2. **Buried Treasure 5.9**

    Tall box corner chimney system.

3. **Seven Eleven TR 5.11+**

    A thin jam crack that starts easy but closes tight on the upper part of the route increasing the difficulty the higher you go.

4. _____ 5.__ [?]

    Potential corner system.

5. _____ 5.12- [?]

    The infamous detached column chimney is gone. Now its a powerful thin seam cruising up an orange colored face of a slight boxed corner. Top-rope.

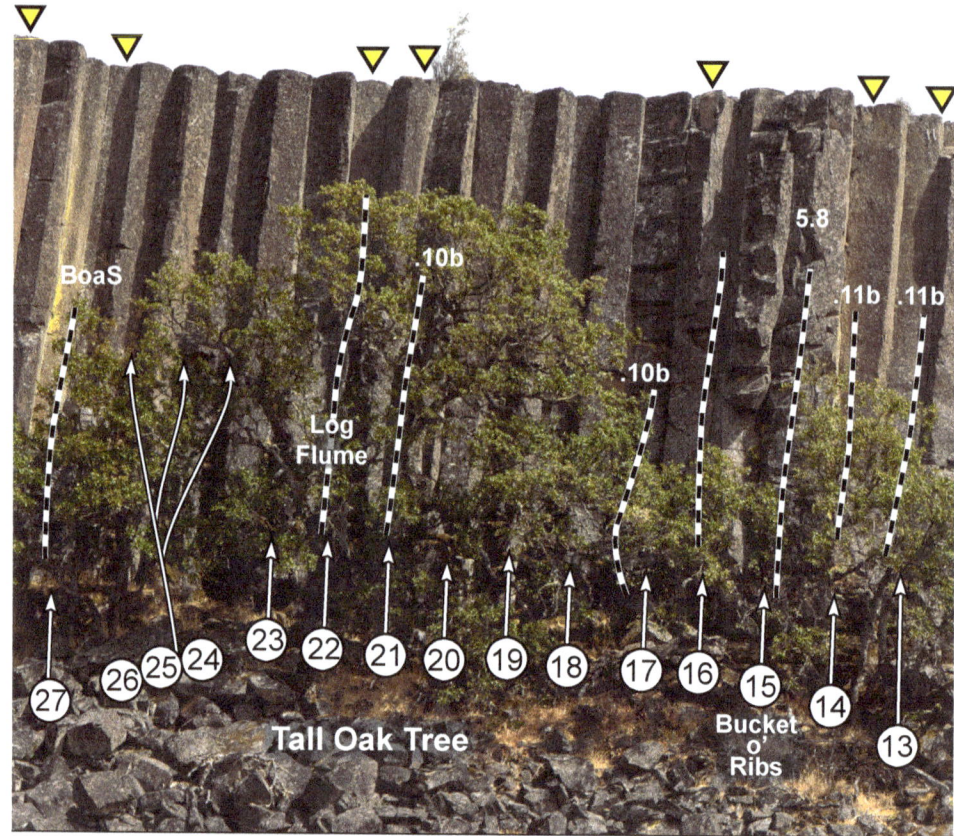

6. **Rattler 5.11+ [?]**
   Climb the initial corner system (of the above route), then move fully into a vertical left seam about 12' up the route.
7. **Measure of Pleasure 5.8** ★★★
   Located on the outside of the buttress immediately left of the detached chimney column. Clamber up past a stubby tree at the start, and cruise up a long steep crack corner. This long consistent hand jam crack is a stellar little climb.
8. **Wendell's Big Mistake TR 5.10+**
   Near the middle of the crag, about 15' left of Measure of Pleasure.
9. **_____ 5.9+ (?)**
   A tall boxed corner system.
10. **Nuggets 5.7** ★
    Climb a low angle slab and edges, then at mid-height, step left and continue up an obvious crack to top up. Use Sluice Box belay.
11. **Sluice Box 5.9** ★★
    Climb low angle steps, and when the crack steepens stay in the crack corner. Tight opposition stemming smears to finish the upper crux part.
12. **_____ 5.10 c/d**
    Lower slabby climbing to upper tricky balancy face climbing. If you can't figure out the upper part don't be surprised.

South End

13. _____ 5.11b
    A thin seam in a slight corner.
14. _____ 5.11b ★
    Stay in the thin seam in a tight corner the entire way using an occasional left jug.
15. **Bucket o' Ribs 5.8**
    A dirty rib with jug holds and edges on the outside of a column. Avoid the crack on left.

TALL OAK TREE AREA

This section has a large oak tree at the base of the wall next to the popular Log Flume route.

16. _____ 5.8 ★★
    Quality crack corner system (2-bolts). Gear to 3".
17. _____ 5.10b
    Starts up a steep slightly mossy face, then punch past a tiny lip midway up the route.

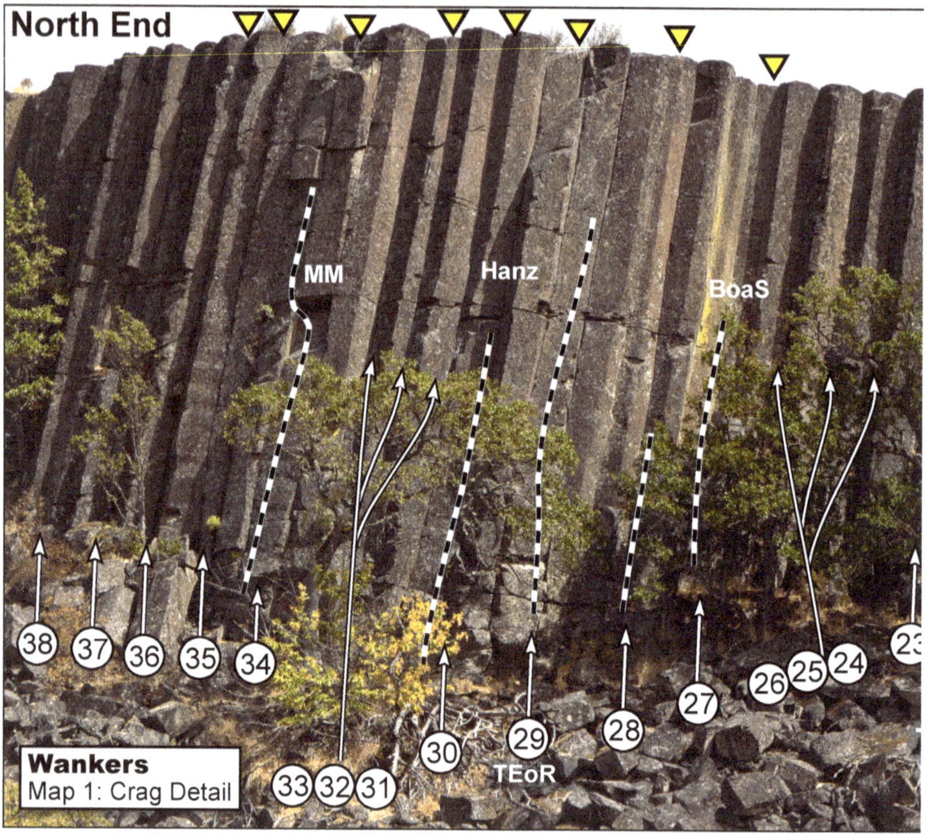

284 CHAPTER 2 ✧ ORC

North End

Wankers Map 1: Crag Detail

18. _____ 5.__ [?]
19. _____ 5.__ [?]
20. _____ 5.__ [?]
21. _____ 5.10b

Climb a corner system immediately right of Log Flume (which ends at same belay anchor).

22. **Log Flume 5.10a** ★★

Start in a steep double corner behind the large oak tree. At the mid-point small edges launch into a series of tight oppositions stemming smears to finish the upper crux part.

NORTH END

23. _____ 5.11-

The upper half is a thin clean corner-*ish* seam.

Wankers Map 2

24. _____ 5.__
25. _____ 5.__
26. _____ 5.__
27. **Birds on a Shelf 5.10+ (TR)**
    A wide stem box corner above a mossy shelf.
28. ___ **5.11+**
    A very thin crack with a slight right lean to it.
29. **Thin Edge of Reality 5.11+ ★★**
    A top-rope that uses a combination of two tight seams on a steep face. Merges into Hanz crack for the last move.
30. **Hanz Crack 5.7 ★★★**
    A stellar jam crack worth leading or top-rope.
31. _____ **5.11**
    Immediately left of Hanz Crack are three thin cracks on a steep face. This is the right and shortest corner seam.
32. **Ptero 5.11 ★**
    Middle thin corner seam.
33. **Latent Genes 5.11+ ★**
    The leftmost of three thin seam crack corner.
34. **Mouse in a Microwave 5.10a**
    Climb easy crack to a stance capped by a small lip. Surmount lip and climb a jam crack to top.
35. _____ **5.11- (?) ★**
    Long thin tips crack corner with quality climbing.
36. _____ 5.__ (?)
37. _____ 5.__ (?)
38. _____ 5.__ (?)

OH8

Beta written by Kucera / Cousar

OH8 is a minor but conveniently situated road side crag along old highway 8 on the northeast side of Rowland Lake located at the extreme west end of the Catherine Creek syncline. Though easy to drive right past the fractured cliff, upon closer inspection you will find an interesting little treasure of rock climbs scattered along this fairly lengthy flood basalt rock formation. The crag faces west making maximum use of the afternoon sunshine suitable for a fast workout in the

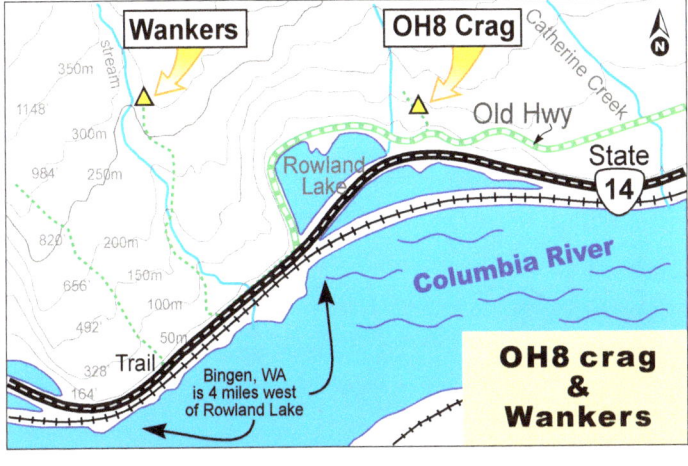

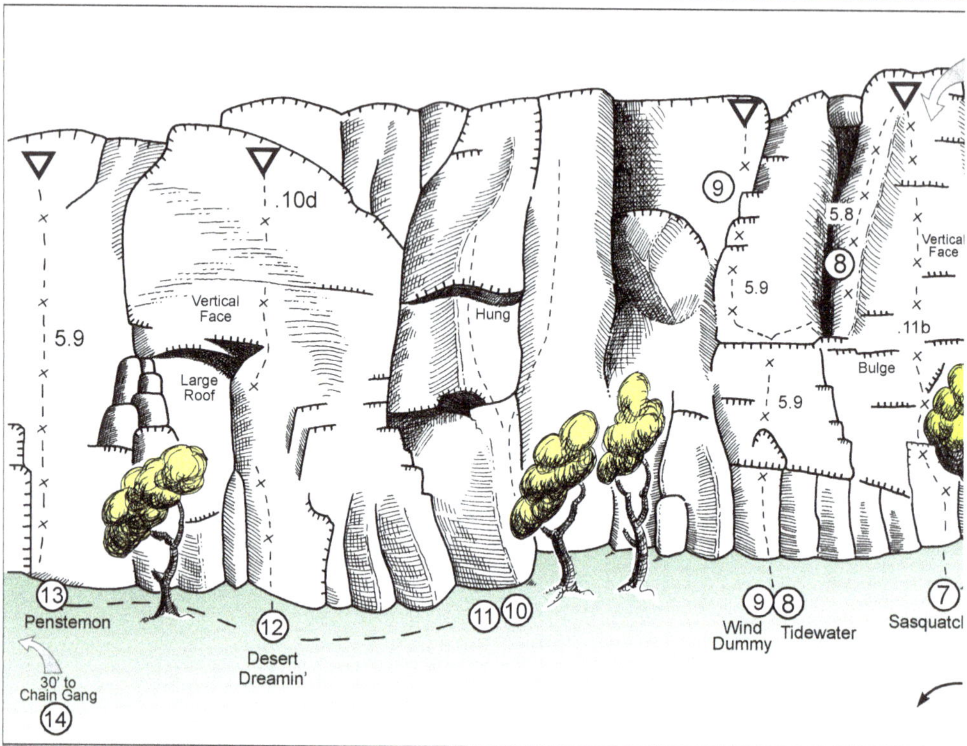
.10d
9
5.8
8
Vertical Face
5.9
Vertical Face
5.9
Hung
.11b
Large Roof
Bulge
5.9
13
Penstemon
12
Desert Dreamin'
11
10
9
8
Wind Dummy
Tidewater
7
Sasquatcl
30' to Chain Gang
14

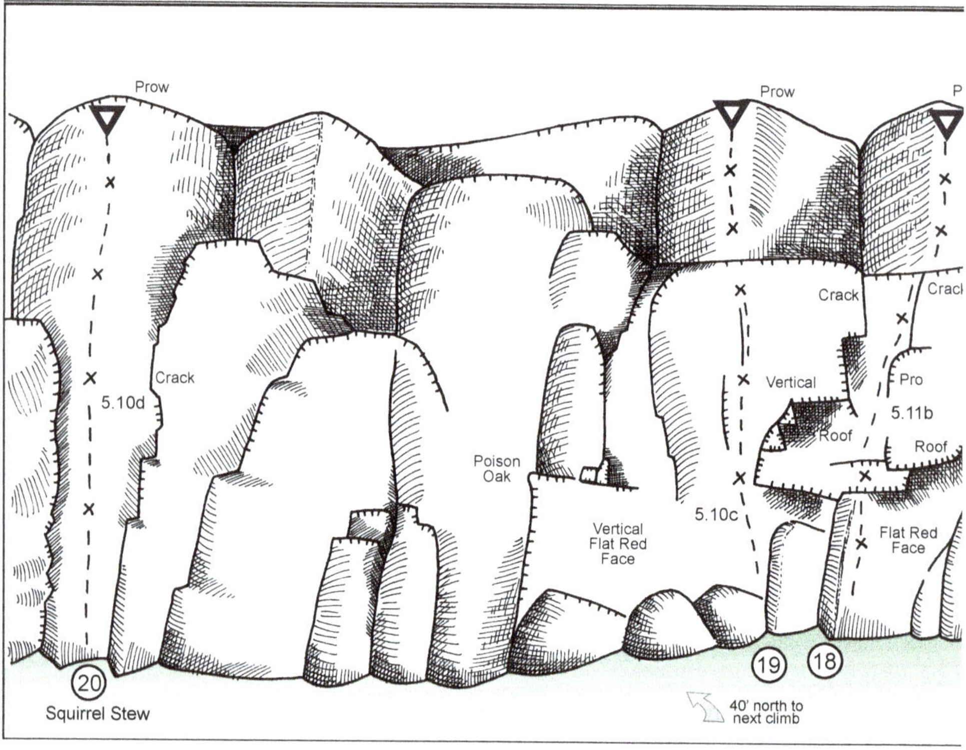
Prow
Prow
P
Crack
Crac
Crack
Vertical
Pro
5.10d
5.11b
Roof
Roof
Poison Oak
Vertical Flat Red Face
5.10c
Flat Red Face
20
Squirrel Stew
19
18
40' north to next climb

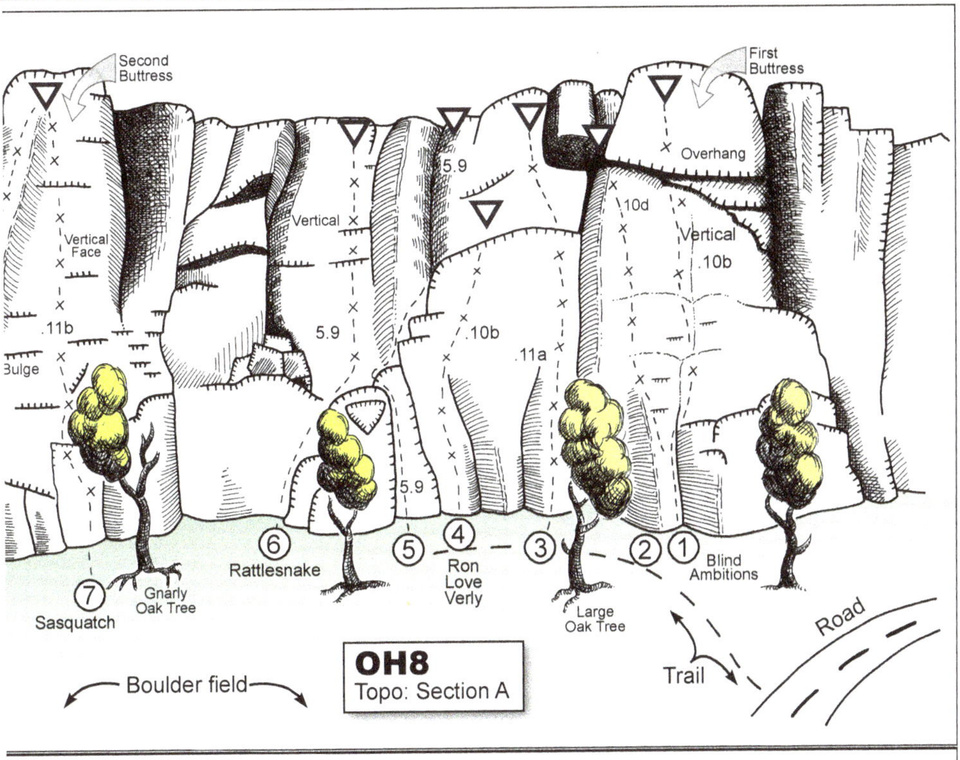

GORGE ROCK CLIMBS 287

OH8 Topo: Section A

- ⑦ Sasquatch
- ⑥ Rattlesnake
- ⑤
- ④ Ron Love Verly
- ③
- ②
- ① Blind Ambitions

Second Buttress, First Buttress, Overhang, Vertical Face, Bulge, 11b, Vertical, 5.9, 10b, 11a, 10d, Vertical 10b, Gnarly Oak Tree, Large Oak Tree, Trail, Road, Boulder field

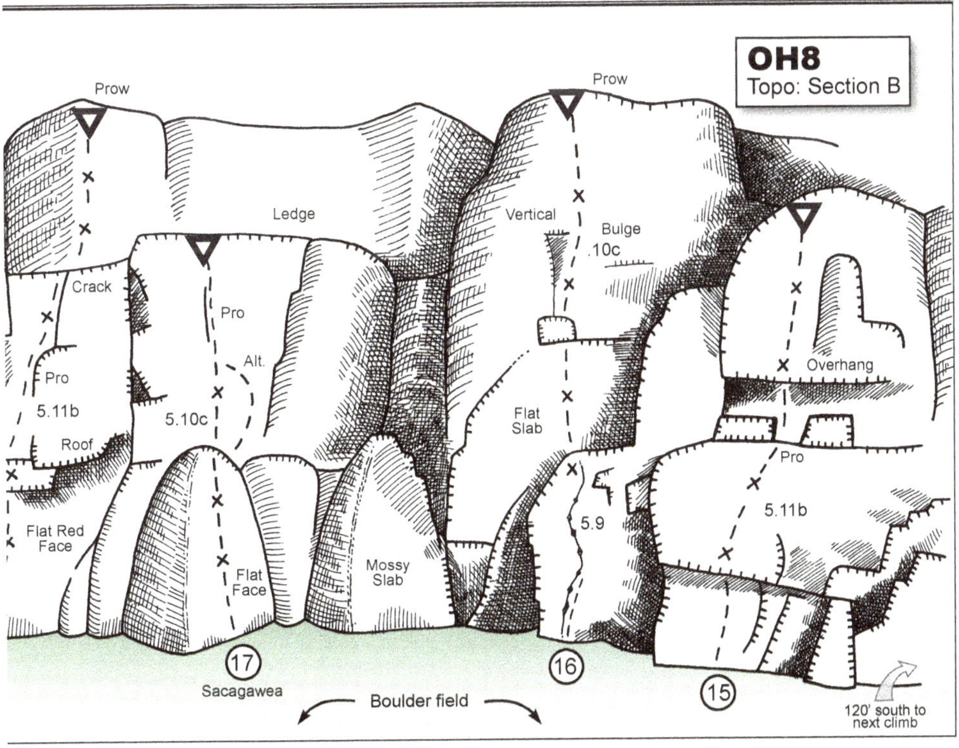

OH8 Topo: Section B

- ⑰ Sacagawea
- ⑯
- ⑮

Prow, Ledge, Pro, Alt., Crack, Pro, 5.11b, Roof, 5.10c, Flat Red Face, Flat Face, Mossy Slab, Prow, Vertical, Bulge 10c, Flat Slab, 5.9, Overhang, Pro, 5.11b, Boulder field, 120' south to next climb

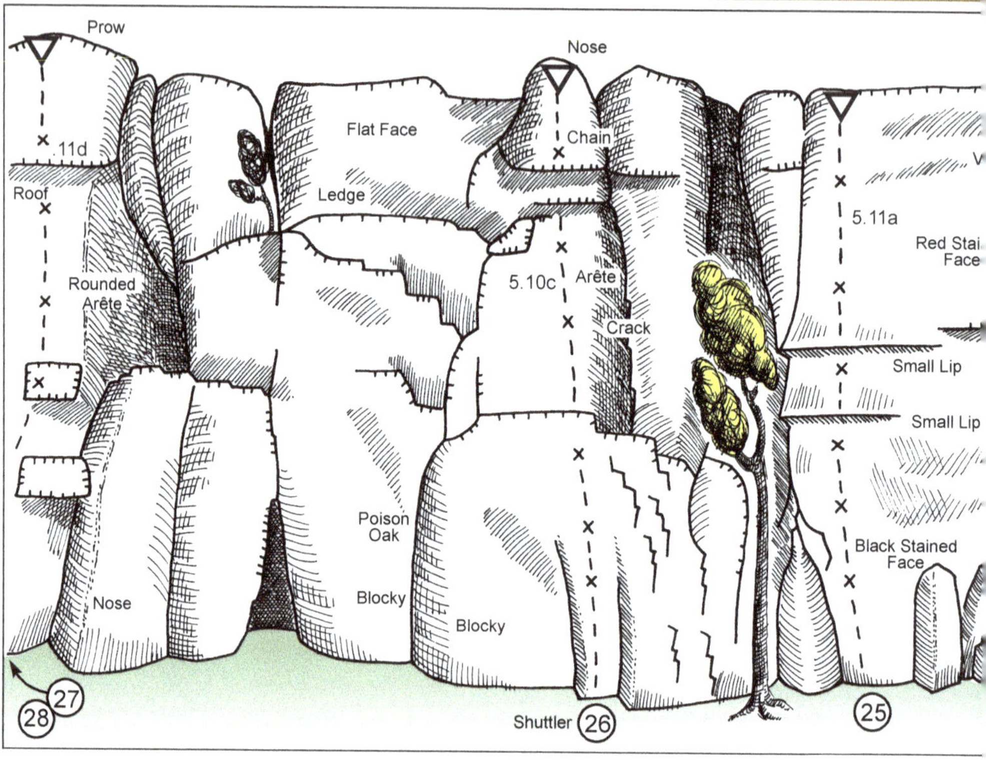
Prow
.11d
Roof
Rounded Arête
Nose
Flat Face
Ledge
Poison Oak
Blocky
Blocky
Nose
Chain
5.10c
Arête
Crack
5.11a
Red Stai
Face
Small Lip
Small Lip
Black Stained Face
27
28
Shuttler 26
25

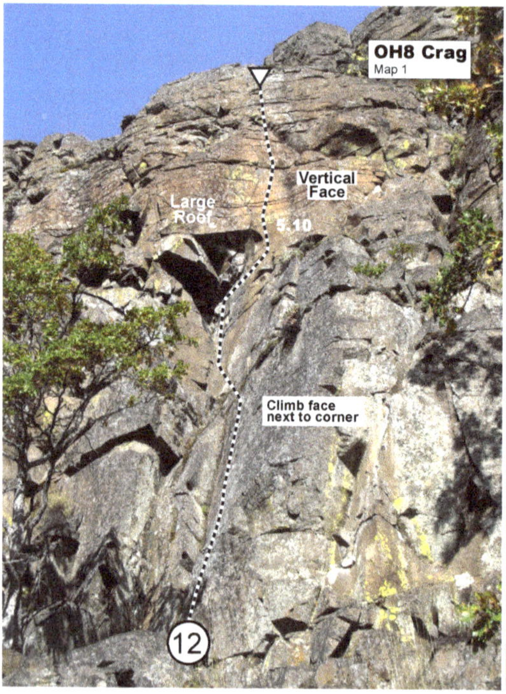
OH8 Crag
Map 1
Large Roof
Vertical Face
5.10
Climb face next to corner
12

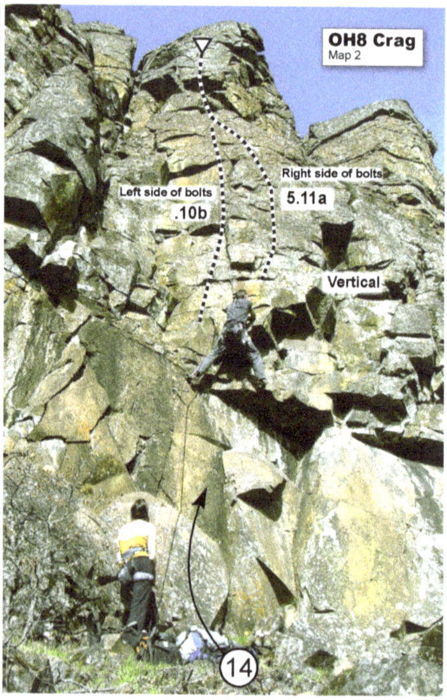
OH8 Crag
Map 2
Left side of bolts
.10b
Right side of bolts
5.11a
Vertical
14

Prow
.10c
ertical
Corner
ned
Roof
Ledge
Corner
5.8
Block
Steps
.11a
Roof
Sharp Arête
Lip
Nook
Vertical
.11c
Crux
Ledge
Crack
Corner
Sharp Arête
24
23
22
Risky Sex
21
Shorty
OH8
Topo: Section C

5.11c
5.11d
Bat Stupor
Forest Circus Fiasco
30
29
OH8
Map 5: Two Roofs

OH8
Topo: Section D
Prow
Prow
5.11c
5.11d
Roof
Roof
Round Arête
Poison Oak
Block
Blocky
Nose
Bat Stupor
28
27
FCF

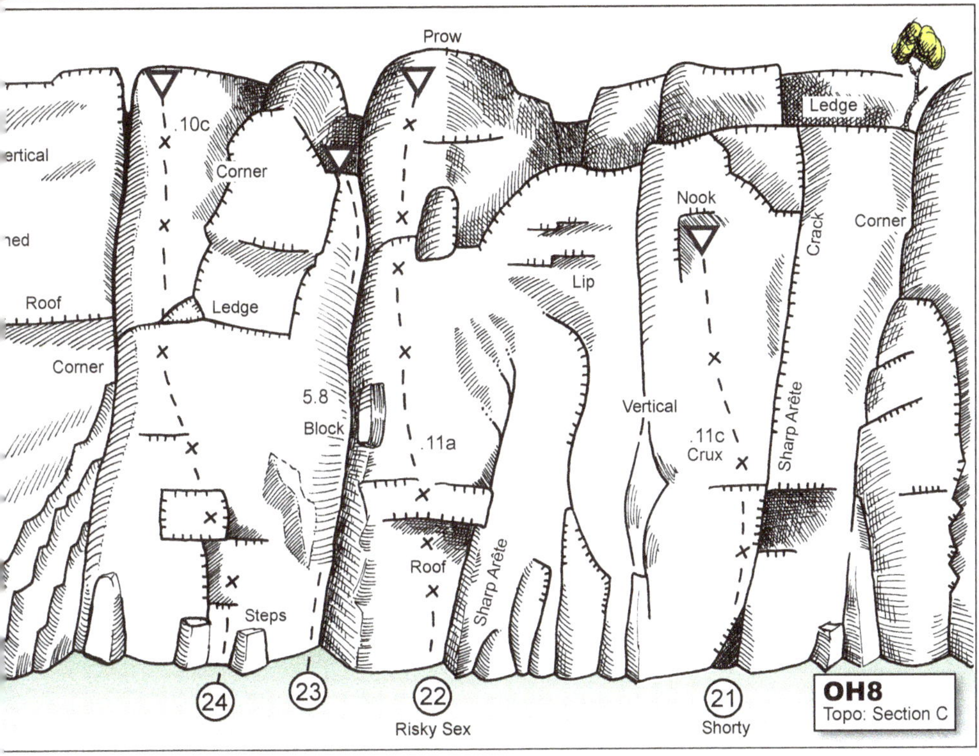

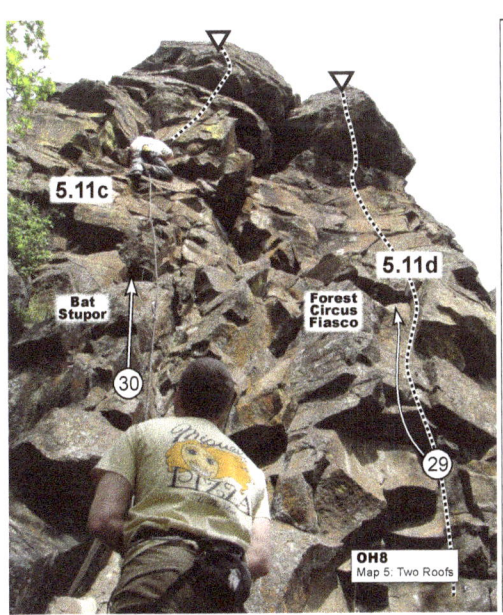

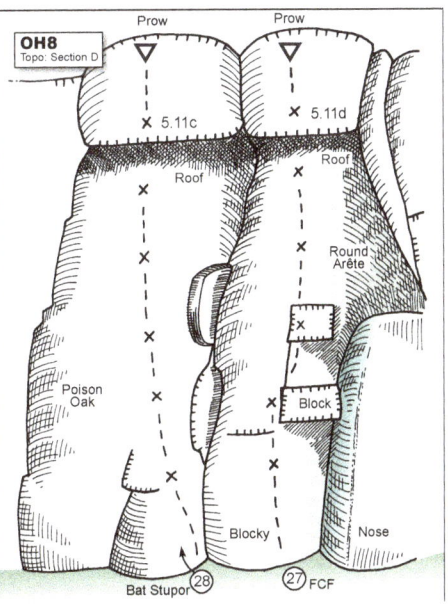

early Spring and Fall seasons. The basalt is a slightly grainy textured surface to which rock shoes readily stick, but the routes are deceptive; what appears easy and lower angled is actually surprisingly steep and difficult.

Accessibility and Concerns

Virtually all the rock climbs require some trad gear. Don't climb here if you don't have various cams, stoppers or hex's. The rock is a bit chossy so a helmet is advisable. Avoid walking along the rimtop as this will damage various ecological plants. The Barretts Penstemon is an endemic cliff-dwelling wildflower of colorful purple clustered blooms that makes its home here. Removing cliff dwelling plants and moving talus is prohibited. Most fixed belay anchors are not accessible from above so you must be a competent lead climber to use this place. Owners should keep their dogs leashed or leave them at home. Expect ticks, rattlesnakes, wasps, friable rock and plenty of poison oak along the cliff base. If you are susceptible to poison oak it is best to avoid this site. The rock climbs are listed from right to left as you are walking uphill.

Sam Elmore leading *Molly's Route*
Dave leading *Carl's Route* 5.11b

1. **Blind Ambition 5.10b**
   Pro: 6 QD's, two ½" cams, one each 2" cam, ½" nut
   Thin cracks lead to a pumpy face.
2. **Buckwheat 5.10c**
   Pro: 9 QD's
   Same start as above. Two bolts to ledge, (runout) then left up smooth face. Contrived finish left over roof.
3. **Just a Freakin' Rock Climber 5.11a**
   Pro: 7 QD's and one each 1", 1½" cam
   Two roofs, one low and one high with a crack.
4. **Ron Love Verly 5.10a**
   Pro: 6 QD's
   Technical move in corner, easier climbing above.
5. **Hostile Old Hikers 5.9+**
   Pro: 3 QD's, and two each 1", 2", 2 ½", 3 ½" cams
   Follows beautiful hand crack in corner onto ledge; finish up slabby ramp to crack in corner.
6. **Rattlesnake 5.9**
   Pro: 6 QD's, two 1", one each 1 ½", 3", & 4" cams
   Wide crack start, hard past first bolt then easier above.
7. **Sasquatch 5.11c**
   Pro: 8 QD's, and one each ½", 1", 1 ½" cams
   Technical, long, and pumpy. Lots of fun!
8. **Tidewater 5.9**
   Pro: 8 QD's, and one each ½", 1" cam
   Cruise past small roof to ledge, then up and right.

9. **Wind Dummy 5.9**
   Pro: 8 QD's and one 1" cam
   Same start as Tidewater but climb straight up off ledge.

10. **[Decommissioned]**

11. **OCD 5.11d**
    Pro: 4 QD's, and one each ¾", 2", 3" cams
    Same start as Grass Widow then left up bulging arête.

12. **Desert Dreaming 5.10d**
    Pro: 4 QD's, one ¾", and two 1" cams
    Gray slab at start morphs into faux sandstone at finish. Easier if you traverse right before the last bolt, and then up to the anchor.

13. **Penstemon 5.9+**
    Pro: 5 QD's
    Start on gray face, do a tricky mantle, then climb past the penstemon at mid-height to more red rock.

14. **The Chain Gang 5.10c**
    Pro: 4 QD's, one each 1", 2", 3" cams
    Chain on second bolt at roof; super fun.

15. **Carl's Route 5.11b**
    Pro: 5 QD's and cams to 1"
    Start up the left half of a flat gold face, then surmount steep bulge above.

16. **Molly's Route 5.10b**
    Pro: 4 QD's and gear to 1"
    Start up crack on front face to a ledge, then up a slab to a bulging crux face.

17. **Sacagawea's Route 5.10b**
    Pro: 3 QD's, one each 2", 3" cams
    Start on smooth protruding face with fractures. Avoiding flowers, romp to top.

18. **Paul's Route 5.11b**
    Pro: 4 QD's, one each 1", 1 ½" cams
    Thin crack to bulge, finish high on prominent prow.

19. **Reed's Route 5.10c**
    Pro: 6 QD's
    Unusual movement on angular terrain.

20. **Squirrel's Stew 5.10c**
    Pro: 4 QD's, one each ¾", 1", 1½" cams
    Increasingly difficult to bulgy prow.

21. **Get It, Shorty 5.11a**
    Pro: 3 QD's
    A crux for each bolt, excellent movement on this tiny test-piece.

22. **Risky Sex 5.11a**
    Pro: 7 QD's, one ½" cam or nut
    Two bolts to roof; crux is the final bulge.

23. **Butt Shiner 5.8**
    Pro: lots of cams, some small nuts
    Discontinuous cracks in a dirty corner.

24. **Itchy & Scratchy 5.10c**
    Pro: 6 QD's, one ¾" cam
    Wander up and left to bolted arête finish.
25. **Open Space Plan 5.11a**
    Pro: 6 QD's
    Initial moves on black rock, pumpfest above in red.
26. **The Shuttler 5.10b**
    Pro: 6 QD's
    Shattered columns to smooth face, wild arête finish.
27. **Forest Circus Fiasco 5.11d**
    Pro: 6 QD's
    Thoughtful moves below, footless mantle to gain right hand roof.
28. **Bat Stupor 5.11c**
    Pro: 6 QD's
    Easy climbing past questionable blocks, crimpy crux guards anchor above the left hand roof.
29. **Spring Breezes 5.10d**
    Pro: __ QD's
    About 50' left of Bat Stupor. Initial bulge with crimps, then eases to 5.6 climbing.
30. **The Gap 5.11d**
    Pro: 3 QD's
    Short face, surmount large steep faceted block to anchor.
31. **Columbina 5.10a**
    Pro: __ QD's
    About 10' left of The Gap is this short face line.
32. **End of the Line 5.9**
    Pro: __ QD's (optional gear to 1")
    Very short climb just left of Columbina; last route at crag.

LYLE WEST CRAG

This crag is located about ⅓ mile east of the state highway rest facility near Lyle. This miniature site offers road side access to some brief rock climbs on a small 40' tall bluff of vertical basalt.

Park at a small dirt pullout on the north side of State 14 at the west end of a small enclosed pond called Chamberlain Lake. Most of the rock climbs are bolted and have good fixed belay anchors although several are mixed traditional crack

Lyle West
Map 1: Left section

leads. Though the site was infrequently used in the past with several newer fixed routes it provides a viable stop over site while you are en route eastward to greater destinations.

WEST SECTION

1. _____ **5.9**
   Pro: 7 QD's
   Climb west arête passing a roof on the left then finish on a flat face.
2. _____ **5.10-**
   Pro: 7 QD's
   Climb face to a roof, then exit left and up left to merge with previous route.
3. _____ **5.10-**
   Pro: 6 QD's
   Climb a corner crack to a ledge, then bust up left onto a flat face to finish.
4. **Prow 5.9** ★
   Pro: 4 QD's
   Climbs the outside of the basalt column then angles off right to route #2 anchor.
5. **Corner / face 5.8** ★★
   Pro: 5 QD's
   A quality face climb utilizing the thin inside corner seam.
6. **Winter Roast 5.10+** ★★
   Pro: 4 QD's
   A powerful thin face climb with positive incut crimper face edges.
7. _____ **5.11- (TR)**
   Climb up to a ledge, then up to a roof, and surmount it leftward finishing on face crimps.

The Middle Section
8. **Half Seed 5.10- (TR)**
A TR starting as a thin crack and face edges on upper part.
9. **Wide Crack 5.9** ★
Pro to 4" (3 bolts on upper part of wide crack)
Ascend the crack corner that quickly widens. Great route, and when the off-width size of the crack gets too big for casual pro several bolts ease your trip to the anchor.
10. **_____ 5.9 to 5.10+ (TR)**
Climb a crack to a ledge, then a short crack, then climb past a roof.

EAST SECTION
11. **_____ 5.__ (?)**
Pro: _ QD's
Thin seam passing a roof, to finish on face crimps to a belay. Project.
12. **_____ 5.11 (?)**
Pro: 6 QD's
Climb up passing two small lips, then crimps on face to the top.
13. **_____ 5.11 (?)**
Pro: 4 QD's
An outer column and arête, then face crimps to the top.
14. **Crack 5.9**
Pro to 3"
A crack climb on the right end of this small crag.

LYLE TUNNEL CRAG

The LTC is a minor rock formation viable as a climbing stop over if you are on your way to greater destinations for the day or if you are on a Gorge marathon climbing tour. An hour or two and you can ascend virtually all the rock climbs at this crag. LTC is a quaint tiny slice of bluff situated immediately west of the State 14 highway tunnel at the east end of the small community of Lyle, WA. The bluff faces directly south and tends to be a warm sunny site from mid-morning onward and is conducive to year-round climbing. The small 40' tall rock bluff is a vesiculated (pockets) old flood basalt

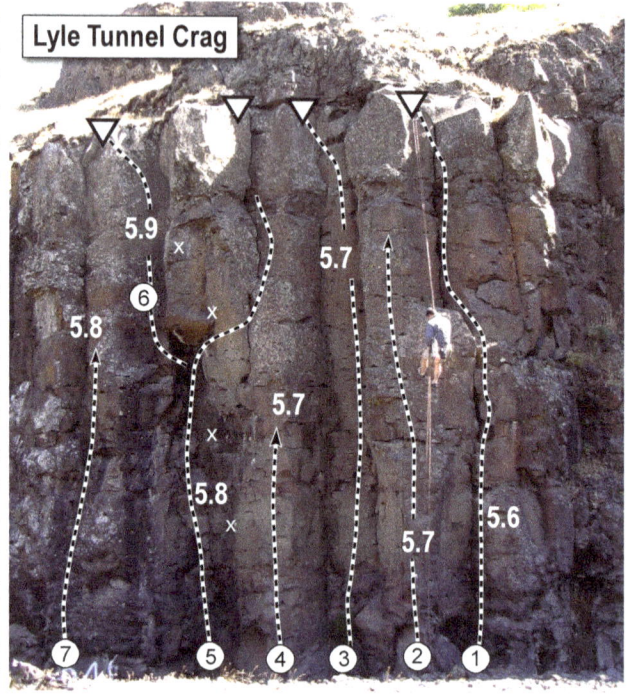

formation. The well featured pockets provide good hand and foot holds as well as pro placements. Typical lead gear ranges from nuts and cams to 4". All routes have fixed belay anchors at the top. A history of rock climbing has taken place here and access is encompassed by WSDOT right-of-way.

1. _____ 5.6 ★★
   Pro to 3"
   Common initial foray that starts vertical to a ledge with plenty of holds/edges to the top.

2. **Arête 5.7 TR**
   The right arête.

3. _____ 5.7+ ★★★
   Pro to 4"
   Climb the deep double-duty crack corner system. A stellar fun and steep route.

4. **Arête 5.7+ TR** ★
   This climbs the left arête.

5. _____ 5.8 ★★
   Pro to 2" and QD's
   Climb up the deep corner (bolts) and launch out right at the roof and up a thin crack.

6. **Roof Left Exit 5.9-**
   Pro to 2" and cams
   A boorish awkward left exit steals the quality of the show.

7. _____ 5.8 TR
   A road show that would be nice to see it fixed for leading.

HORSETHIEF BUTTE

The popular Horsethief Butte offers an ideal respite from the liberal amounts of western Oregon rain where you can often find sunny weather crag climbing by the Columbia River.

For rock climbers it offers a tremendous variety of short boulder problems within a series of corridors in the inner portion of the butte. This site offers an effective means to practice and enhance the basic concepts of rock climbing and rappeling. The natural open atmosphere of the inner butte offers easy communication from instructor to climber.

Brief History of the Area

The Butte is a prominent feature within the Columbia Hills State Park and is a popular site for climbing as well as hiking. The nearby lake was formed when The Dalles Dam was built.

For centuries local American Indians lived near the Butte. The ease of access to the river also provided excellent opportunity for them to catch some of the seasonal migration of salmon for food and for barter. Celilo Falls was the heart of a long established trading region

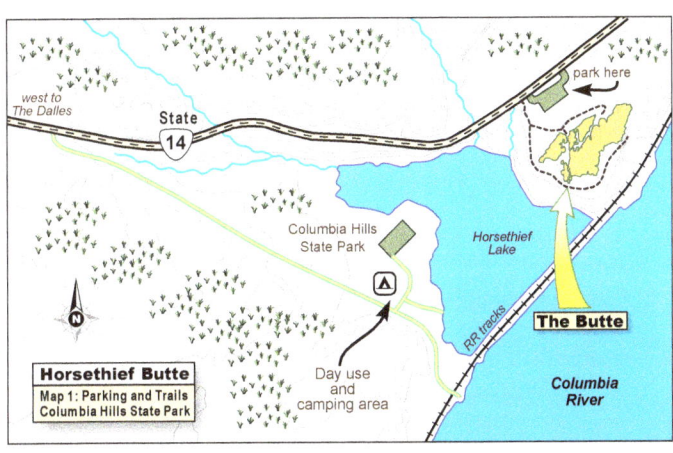
Horsethief Butte
Map 1: Parking and Trails
Columbia Hills State Park

that sustained a thriving community of native Indians from the Wisham, Cloud and Lishkam tribes. The Lewis and Clark expedition camped at a village during their journey west in 1805-1806. Salmon caught near the Celilo Falls provided an important source for trade and barter with other indigenous native tribes of the region. Excellent remnants of native Indian petroglyphs such as *'she who watches'* provide visitors with archeological insight of ancient tribal customs.

Visitor considerations and state park regulations

- Horsethief Butte has several areas signed as 'no climbing' for cultural resource protection. Columbia Hills State Park has archeological sites including Horsethief Butte which are protected by State and Federal laws. Disturbance and/or removal of any artifact, pictograph, or petroglyph is prohibited.
- Expect windy conditions.
- Beware of the occasional rattlesnake. Frequent visitor foot traffic tends to keep most rattlesnakes at a distance.
- Poison Oak grows along the base of several walls. This thick short shrub has seasonal glossy leaves which grow in groups of three per branch and have small white berries.
- Ticks are common in the Spring and Fall seasons. Ticks are quite small so be certain to inspect frequently for ticks if you visit here. There is a plethora of bouldering problems far beyond what this section could possibly convey, but this in-depth treatise strives to detail the greater portion of the well traveled climbs found at the Butte.

Directions

Directions from Oregon: From exit #87 at The Dalles drive north across the Columbia River bridge on U.S. 197 for 3½ miles, then east on Washington State 14 for 2¾ miles to Columbia Hills State Park. The Butte is located east of the lake at Mile Post 85. Hike on the path south to the butte and enter either via the west side trail or at the 'Entrance Cracks' gap in the wall. Camping (closed from Nov. thru March) is available at the developed facility on the west side of the 90-acre Horsethief lake. Climb safely and enjoy your visit!

ENTRANCE CRACKS

1. **OW & Hand Crack 5.9** ★★
Left of the left prow are several climbs in the shaded portion of the bluff. Both begin up the same crack using edges and steps. From the midway stance, embark up *left* in a wide offwidth crack using a small hidden edge in the offwidth which leads to better edges at the top. The *right* jam crack is closer to the arête. Ascend the lower crack to the midway stance, then embark up right into a jam crack which forces you to use the arête more than the crack. There are several more thin optional climbs just to the left of these two climbs that are fairly difficult.

2. **Jam Crack 5.9** ★★
Great hand and fist jam climb. Start initially in the Left Entrance Crack and punch out left to a short vertical jam crack.

3. **Left Entrance Crack 5.10c/d** ★★★
This is the left major corner system. Ascend the steep tricky corner by smearing delicately on smooth sloped holds using the thin crack where possible. No such thing as a free lunch.

4. **Arête 5.12**
Between the two Entrance Crack routes is a technical minor arête top-rope.

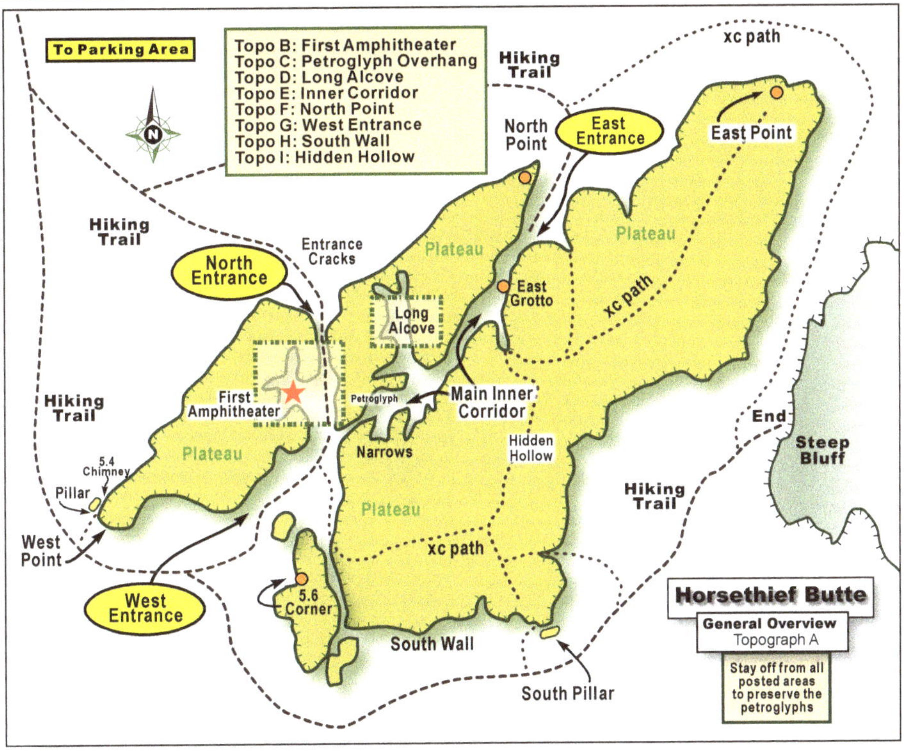

To Parking Area
Topo B: First Amphitheater
Topo C: Petroglyph Overhang
Topo D: Long Alcove
Topo E: Inner Corridor
Topo F: North Point
Topo G: West Entrance
Topo H: South Wall
Topo I: Hidden Hollow
N
Hiking Trail
xc path
North Point
East Entrance
East Point
Hiking Trail
North Entrance
Entrance Cracks
Plateau
Plateau
East Grotto
xc path
Long Alcove
First Amphitheater
Petroglyph
Main Inner Corridor
Hiking Trail
Narrows
Hidden Hollow
End
Steep Bluff
Plateau
5.4 Chimney
Pillar
Plateau
Hiking Trail
West Point
xc path
West Entrance
5.6 Corner
South Wall
Horsethief Butte
General Overview
Topograph A
Stay off from all posted areas to preserve the petroglyphs
South Pillar

5.9
5.9
5.9
5.12 Arête
5.10c
VB
2
5.8
Var.
North entrance to first amphitheater
4
VB
V5
5
1
3
V1
Horsethief
Map 1: Entrance Cracks
VB
VB
This section faces northwest

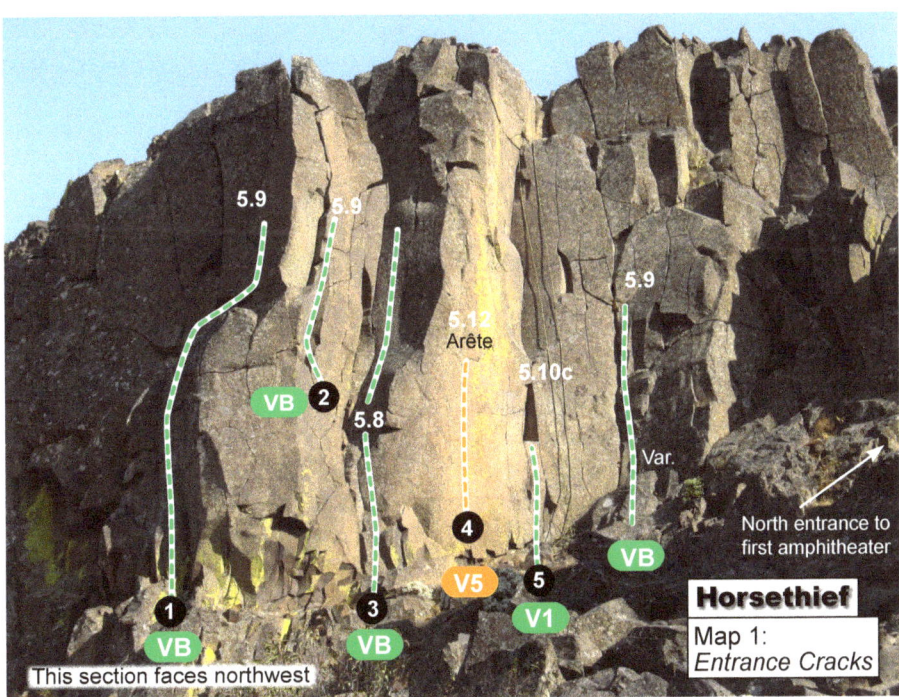

5. Right Entrance Crack 5.10b ★★★

This is the right most (and best) of two classic corner systems known as the Entrance Cracks. Involves long reaches, technical smears, and powerful layback moves using a jam crack. On the right face of this entrance crack is another minor seam that branches up right at about 5.9.

THE PASSAGEWAY

These two under-age minors are together on the east wall of the Passageway just as it opens into the First Amphitheater.

6. Face V0 (5.10-)

A short smooth face ending on a ledge.

7. Arête V1 (5.10+)

Another short problem.

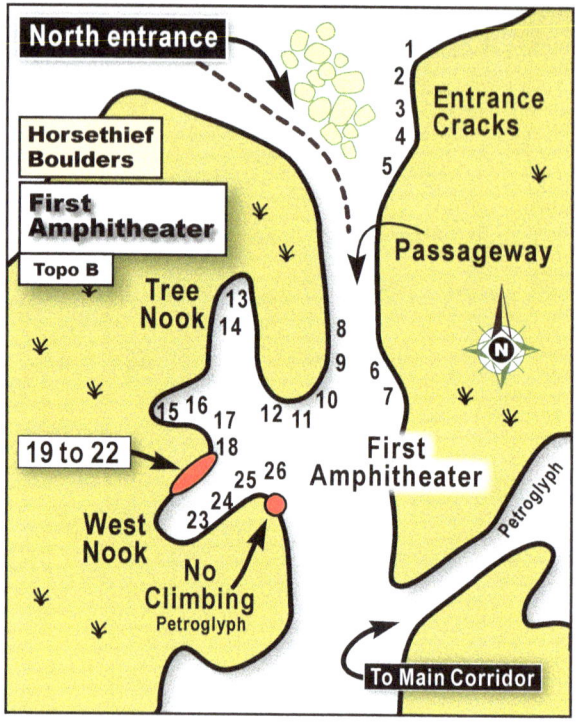

The next two steep lines are found on the west wall of The Passageway.

8. Corner 5.8 ★

Layback up the pillar and then stem the corner.

9. Corner 5.7 ★

Climb up a crack to finish in a corner with a long reach to finish.

FIRST AMPHITHEATER

The following string begins on the west side of the Passageway and curls around the initial buttress counter-clockwise into the First Main Amphitheater. Two nooks (north tree nook and west nook) provide a great series of problems.

Wide Buttress

10. Groove V0

Right side of the buttress.

11. Smooth Dihedral 5.7

In the middle of the buttress climb up a dihedral corner using jams and stemming.

12. Discontinuous Cracks V0

Broken cracks on left most side of buttress.

Tree Nook

A tiny nook with a small tree tucked in the corner.

GORGE ROCK CLIMBS

13. Face 5.9 ★

Deep in the Tree Nook on the left side before the small tree is a tall face. Climb up the well-featured and cracked patina face to a tricky finish.

14. Crack-Prow V1 (5.10+)

In the same Tree Nook left of the tall face is a crack/prow. You can jam or bear hug this.

Half Nook

15. Thin Crack V1 (5.10+)

A stubby. Use the right diagonal crack on a smooth slab.

16. Green Slab VB

This is the outermost nose of a low angle slab.

17. Prow V1 (5.10+)

Climb the left side of the prow to a mantle.

18. Overhang V1 (5.10+)

Start on a left trending seam. Climb up to a jug and mantle.

West Nook - routes on the right

West Nook offers a great punchy thin traverse all the way to Half Nook.

19. Flake VB

A great warm up flake climb.

20. Crack Seam V1 (5.10+) ★★★

This classic line (and the next one) are the central feature of the West Nook. They offer complexity, steepness, and quality great for bouldering or for a top-rope.

21. Corner V2 to V4 ★★★

A stellar V2 thin crack corner that is much harder than it looks. Using rules staying in the crack will make it V3. Traversing in from the far left then up the central corner crack is V4.

22. Face V7 (5.13-)

Climb the thin face left of the corner using just the small holds on the face.

West Nook - Left routes

Jerad working a V4 in the Narrows

23. Low Angle Face VB
This is on the south side of the West Nook. Climb up on jug holds.

24. Face V0 (5.10-)
Climb up through the missing block.

25. Crack System V2 (5.11-)
Start on the jug and climb up the shallow crack to a flake.

26. Arête (CLOSED)
This is the outer buttress with posted off-limits signs informing visitors of the aboriginal petroglyph graffiti.

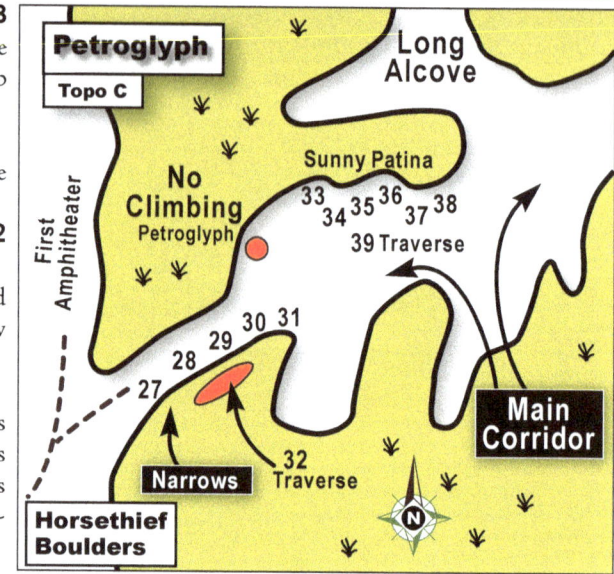

INNER CORRIDOR

From the First Main Amphitheater walk through a small opening in the cliff scarp (The Narrows). This quickly opens up into the Main Inner Corridor or Grotto. On your immediate left is the Petroglyph Overhang and just beyond (also on the left) is the Sunny Patina. A smidge beyond on the left is the Long Alcove. If you continue walking directly east all the way through this Main Inner Corridor you will pass the Long Wall and exit out the East Entrance to the North Point.

THE NARROWS & PETROGLYPH OVERHANG (TOPO C)

The first five problems are located on the right (south) wall in The Narrows just as you are entering the Main Corridor across from the 'off-limits' sign on the opposite side of the corridor.

27. Thin Crack V1 (5.11-)
Jam the crack in the corner.

28. Steep Face V0 (5.10+)
Climb up on fractured jugs.

29. Bulging Prow V2 (5.11-)
A minor prow.

30. Tall Face V3 (5.11+) ★
A very committing tall boulder problem.

31. Tall Arête V4 (5.12a) ★★
A difficult line with tenuous pinches and smears on the lower half of a tall arête. Lock into each sequence, hold the balance, then slap for the rounded

GORGE ROCK CLIMBS 301

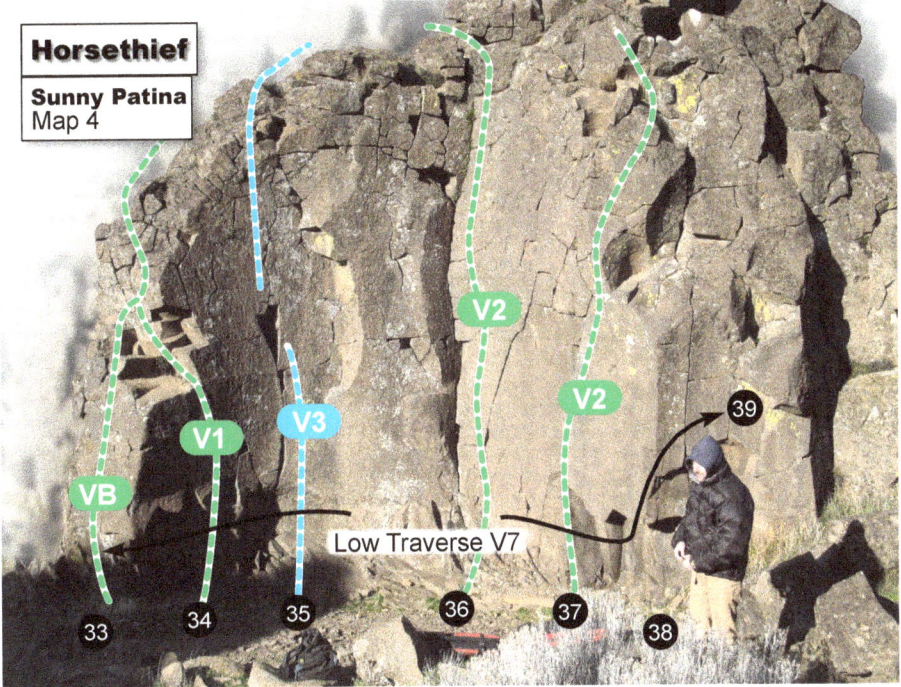

sloper.

Traverse Challenge
32. Narrows Traverse V3 (5.11+)
Traverse from before #27 passing the tall arête #31.

Petroglyph Overhang (CLOSED)

This is an overhanging inner scoop on the north side of the inner corridor at the narrows. There are posted off-limits signs informing visitors of the aboriginal petroglyphs.

SUNNY PATINA
After you admire the off-limits petroglyphs wander a few yards east to a great little sunny kink where this fine selection of favorites can be found. Definitely fire up the triangular shaped pocket climb called Arrow Point. In the distant past this line had a small block wedged in the triangle pocket with two ¼" bolts and a slice of metal holding it in place. Now days we all just enjoy the nature of the line without all that old hardware.

33. Arête VB
Short and juggy and a little loose on top.
34. Face V1 (5.10+) ★
A bump problem over a slight hang on a nose. A bit loose at top.
35. Arrowhead V2 ★★★
Certainly one of the best line face climbs at the Butte. Start left of the corner and balance up using the triangular arrow-like feature with your left hand. Power through a series of wild face crimper

Low Traverse at the *Sunny Patina*

moves past the triangle, and to slightly loose jug holds at the top. Eliminates are possible also.

36. Cool Corner V0 ★★★
A classic stemming problem in the corner.

37. Thin Crack V1-V2 ★
Two thin cracks power up away from the corner. Using both thin cracks work up rightward and trick your way carefully onto the slopers above. Eliminates possible.

38. Arête V3 (5.11-)
Sit start at hidden undercling and ends with a mantle finish.
The **Triangle of Pain V5** rules on this same arête: sit start to jug undercling, left crimp, triangle crimp in middle of face, left arête, mono-pocket right of the arête, and top to a mantle.

Traverse Challenge

39. Low Traverse V7 (5.13-)
Start on #33 and traverse right staying low to finish on top block 6' right of route #38. It is about V4 if you start and end high, and V7 if you start and end low.

THE LONG ALCOVE (TOPO D)

Walking east along the Main Inner Corridor (or Grotto) past the Petroglyph Overhang you will find a Long Alcove running left (north). This long alcove splits into two directions; the longer portion continuing north while the Veranda cuts back hard west to a very popular cul-de-sac.

The Veranda

The Veranda is a stellar slice on the immediate left in the Long Alcove. This north facing and very flat smooth face has become one of the most popular spots to power up. The tick-list of problems here and the quality of the rock (smooth and slippery) combine to provide a string of favorites that will keep you jumping. The first problem starts on the very nose while the remainder is on the flat, steep, north-facing shaded aspect.

40. Outer Buttress V1 (5.10+) ★
Crimps and stemming lead to jugs and a nice finish. Variations (V2-V3) exist.

41. Arête to Corner V1 (5.10+) ★
Smear up ramp using a seam, palm the minor arête onto a tiny perch, then finish up a small inside corner.

42. Thin Crack V2 ★★★
Classic boulder problem, and polished from plenty of use. One of the most well-known Horsethief problems.

43. Thin Face V3 (5.11-) ★★★
Start on the lowest holds 5' up for V3. A Horsethief test-piece.

44. Face V3 (5.11-) ★
Avoid the good jug on the right or it will be easier still.

45. Face V0 (5.10-)
Right most very short problem. The finishing block seems kind of sketchy.

Traverse Challenge

46. Long Traverse V6+
Start on Arête (#41) and traverse low for the full length of wall, ending on the top of down climb rocks after Face (#45) and ends at the bush.

Dave leading *North Point Arête*

47. Short Traverse V6 (5.12+)

Start on Thin Crack (#41) and traverse right to Face (#43) and finish up to the top on that route.

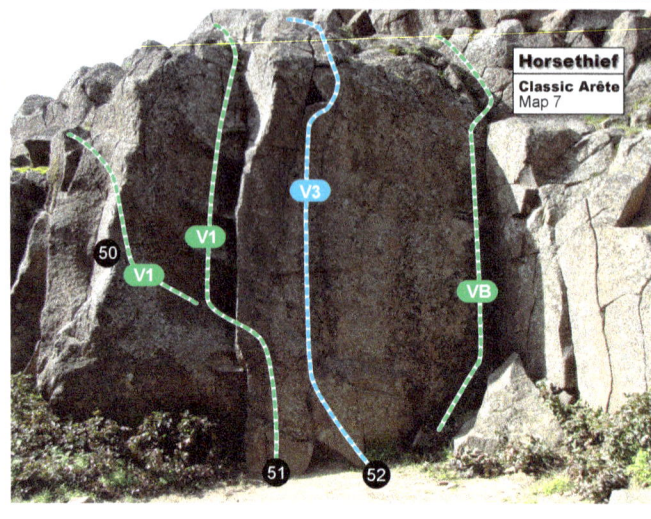

Sunshine Face on left side of Long Alcove

In the Long Alcove is this sunny slice of rock which faces southeast and offers several top-rope problems of moderate difficulty on a nice wide and tall section of wall.

48. Main Face 5.6 to 5.9 ★

Plenty of variables on a steep face quite suitable for top-rope climbing. Even has a few V2-V4 eliminate problems if it catches your eye just right.

East Face of Long Alcove

Walk deeper into this Long Alcove until you are surrounded by poison oak bushes. On your left (west) side of the long alcove is a viable narrow minor arête with a thin left crack and edge-like features. On the right (east) side of the long alcove several fine long lead or top-rope climbs are available with plenty of variations, so do not feel limited to the only over-aged hillbilly listed below.

49. Crack Corner 5.7 ★

The obvious tall crack and corner climb (multiple exits) on east wall of the Long Alcove.

EAST HALF OF INNER CORRIDOR

Walk further east along the Main Corridor beyond the Long Alcove. The Classic Arête is located on the sunny north side at a kink, while the ever popular Long Wall is on the shaded south side of the Corridor. At the far east end of the Main Corridor you will see the East Grotto Face, while beyond is the East Exit/entrance that quickly leads over to the North Point.

The Classic Arête

The next three problems are on a stellar sunny steep flat face with a prominent crisp short arête. Working the arête is one of the finest problems at the Butte. I never knew that V1 could be so fun till I tried this one. Nice sandy landing.

50. Dull Prow V1

A minor round prow as a left exit.

51. Sharp Arête V1 ★★★

Use the sharp arête and gingerly slide up left into the inside corner, and then dance up on intricate small edges to the large incut hold at the top. Classic Horsethief boulder problem.

52. Seam Only V3 (5.11+) ★★

Avoid arête on the left at this grade. Involves a long lock-off to a mono-pocket, and then to a jug hold (wobbles but still there).

LONG WALL (TOPO E)

The Long Wall is one of the most popular sections of wall at the Butte for top-rope climbing. This portion of wall faces north and on hot days stays shaded while offering a plethora of fine problems, including one of the best traverses at the Butte.

Many of the rock climbs along the Long Wall offer numerous variables, so rather than attempting to solve every idiosyncratic nuance…just get the rope out and set up a top-rope and have at it.

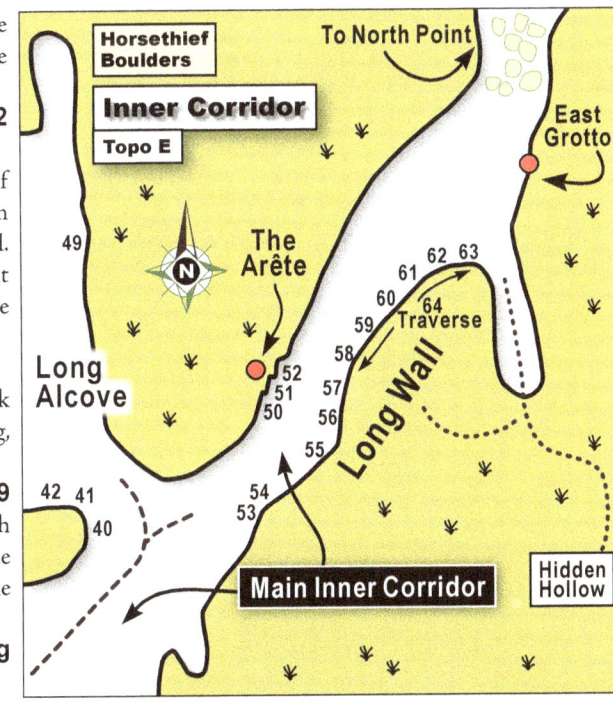

53. Face to Mantle V2 (5.10+)

Immediately south of the Long Alcove on the shaded Long Wall. Down climb off right immediately after the mantle.

54. Thin Crack 5.8 ★

The striking thin crack with good pure jamming, but is short lived.

55. Green Slab 5.6 - 5.9

A long green slab with many variations; some are harder while some are easier.

56. Short Overhang

V2-3

Start sitting and end on ledge...or stand and make it V1 fun.

57. Corner to Ledge 5.7 ★

Climb the shallow inside corner to an awkward move getting on the big flat ledge, then waltz up the right face to top out.

58. Face to Groove 5.8 ★★

Great line! Climb the steep face on good holds to finish up a lower angled groove.

59. Steep Face 5.10- ★★★

Super classic line. Start at the thin crack and climb up an awkward face past missing blocks.

60. Face to Groove 5.7 ★★

Climb up the enjoyable well-feature face that has lots of cracks and holds until it eases in difficulty in the groove to the top. Beware of a loose thin flake up high.

61. Face 5.8 ★

Steep face with sequential holds.

62. Thin Block 5.7 ★

Grab the thin block and climb up to a big edge and finish on the lower angle rock.

63. Groove 5.5

A moderate groove on good rock at the far left end of Long Wall prior to the uphill scramble.

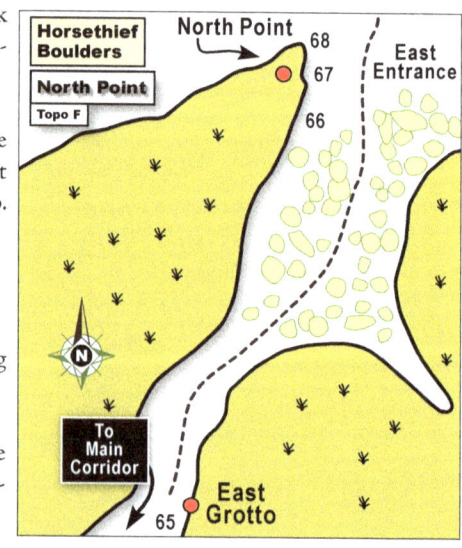

Traverse Challenge
64. Long Wall Traverse V3-V4 ★★★
A totally stellar boulder traverse can be done along the Long Wall in either direction. Start just west of Corner to Ledge #57 and continue to Groove #63. Likely V6 if staying low for the entire traverse.

East Grotto Face

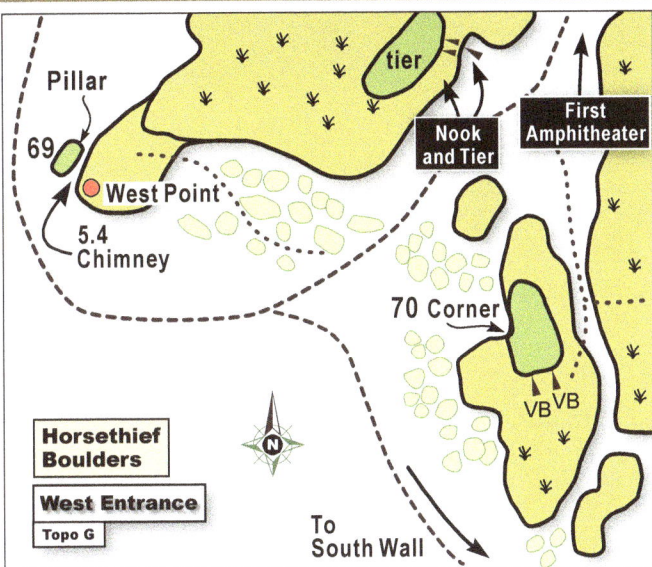

A good location for top-rope climbing. The rounded slab formation is less than vertical and has many cracks and seams crisscrossing the face at angles.

65. Face 5.7 to 5.10- ★
Nice blocky climbing on a wide rounded face with a corner in the middle of the wall.

NORTH POINT (TOPO F)
The following routes are quite tall and are on the North Point which is a sharp prow of rock facing out over the East Entrance. Most climbers reach this locale by walking through the entire inner main corridor. A large boulder field is located at this East Entrance.

66. Old Bolt 5.10
Cruises up a smooth vertical face (several old ¼" bolts studs) past an upside down triangle roof feature on a flat patina face. Once you power past the triangle into the thin jam crack to a stance, continue up easy steps in a corner to the top. Somewhat loose at the top. About 30' left of this line is a nice short VB (5.9) jug haul boulder problem on a flat face.

67. North Point Crack 5.10b ★
Climb a steep crack to a stance, and then climb a smear move into a corner system immediately left of the arête.

68. North Point Arête 5.11c ★
Start at the North Crack and launch up right (2 bolts) on a smooth face, and then power out (3 bolts) the severely overhung arête to the top.

WEST ENTRANCE (TOPO G)

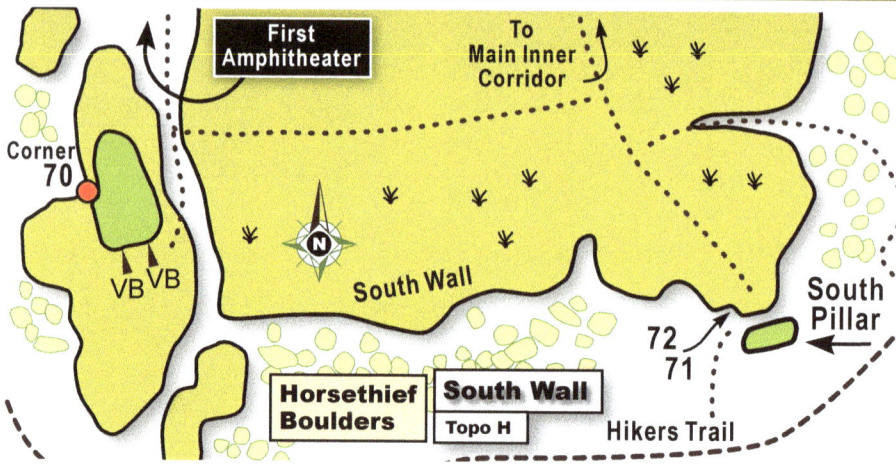

There are several options near the West Entrance that are good for learning technique.

69. West Chimney 5.4

The West Chimney is found at the very tip of the West Point, and is a nice chimney smack between the main wall and a large obvious isolated pillar. Stem the chimney to the top of the pillar, and then launch up the nice series of steps and ledges to the tip of West Point. Once you top out on the tip you can easily descend southward down a boulder field slope. Or you can continue up another short steep step onto the main upper plateau and walk east to descend into the First Amphitheater.

70. Tall Corner 5.6

A fairly well-used corner climb is available to your immediate south as you are hiking up the slope of the West Entrance.

SOUTH WALL (TOPO H)

To reach the South Wall river face hike past the Western Entrance south eastward around the Butte until you can see an obvious isolated pillar separate from the main massif. Scramble up a boulder slope to the base of the west-facing slot formed by this isolated pillar. These two climbs are on the main wall just to the left of the slot.

To set up a top-rope anchor walk east past the pillar to a steep ravine to access the top of this bluff. Or walk south across the plateau from the Main Inner Corridor to the top of the formation above the isolated Pillar.

71. Corner and Roof 5.10a

A good long climb and best done as a top-rope. Climb a steep corner and power out the overhang directly to the top.

72. Face and Prow 5.9

Begin by powering up left using the prow and nearby features and continue to the top.

HIDDEN HOLLOW (TOPO I, J, K)

A quality string of short problems on a rock plateau south of the inner corridor. To reach it, ascend up a big stepped slot from the Inner Corridor at the Long Wall that land on a scenic plateau, then drop down into another low grassy dell.

North side - Hidden Hollow

The beta details for the north side problems, L to R (West to East).

Vbss High nose
Begin on low horizontal, then power up over high nose.
V0ss Crack
Climb crack.
Vbss OW arête
Climb face with right hand on the arête. The arête has a deep off width crack behind it.
V4ss Outer point
Climb the outer point starting low.
V6ss Arête
A slightly overhung tall flat-face with a sharp outer edge on the lower left. Sit start on crimps with left initially low on outer edge. Crimps mid-face, yet hs better exits holds up high. A V4 exists to its immediate right.
V3ss Low bulge
At east end of Hidden Hollow. Sit start a short low bulging overhang using just the round arête.
V2ss Crack/face
A short crack corner that is overhung. Climb mostly the deep V-shaped crack corner.
V0ss Shorty
Shorty round bulge with crimps.

South side - Hidden Hollow

The beta details for the south side problems, L to R (East to West).
V1 Outer Arête
Climb the left-leaning arête of wide flat face. Left hand is on arête, right on crimps.
V0 Face
Numerous thin cracks and edges crisscross at angles on a nice wide flat face.
V0ss Jugs
Jugs on a short face.

A gap of about 30' to the next problems.
VBss Jugs
Jugs on a short flat face.
V2ss crimps
Short low 'ss' using crimps and left prow, but marginal smears for feet.

HH Plus
This is an extension of the Hidden Hollow (Part 1 & Part 2). This "plus more" zone extends as a northward deep long trough that eventually dumps out onto the north slope talus field. Here you will find select string of unique boulder problems to spark the quest. A series

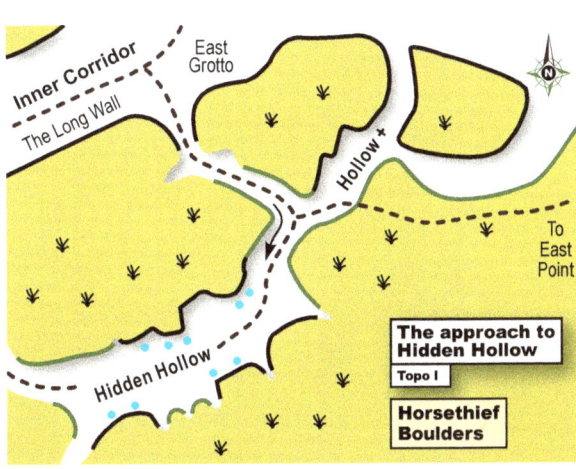

The approach to Hidden Hollow
Topo I
Horsethief Boulders

of short crimp lines and/or juggy highball power lines beckon (see topo).

The HH+ Part 1 first deep low grassy zone has a brief pack of VB-V0 problems.

The HH+ Part 2 yields about 3-4 problems, some a bit tall.

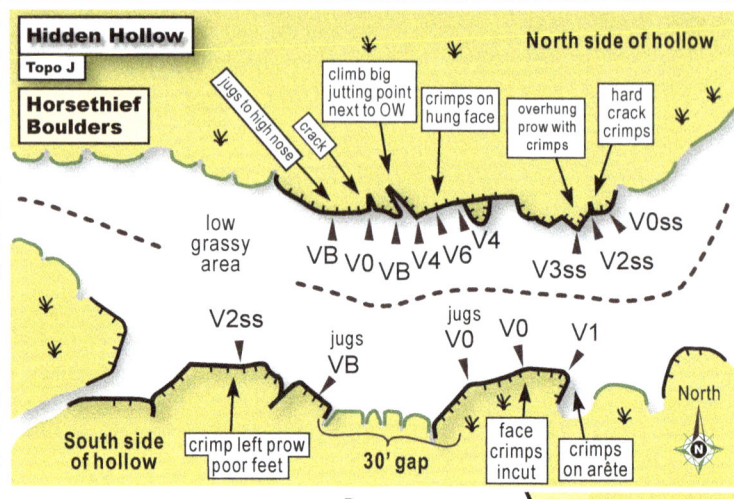

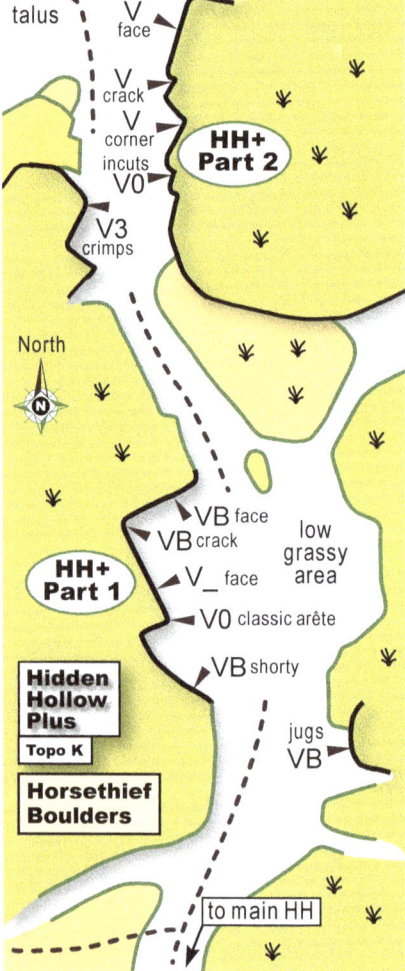

MONTE CRISTO SLAB

    The MCS is an impressive diorite slab tucked along the west slope of a minor forested ridge crest overlooking a broad sweeping panoramic plateau of the fir tree covered South Prairie region near Trout Lake. The rock slab is a good example of the kind of granitic slab rock climbing you typically find at places like Leavenworth, Washington, but this crag is just a few hours from Portland.

    Though not nearly as steep as you typically find at most major granite climbing sites, the MCS none-the-less is a quality destination for locals who relish low angle slab climbing. The steeper sections of the slab vary from 40°-55° overall angle (with a few near vertical steps). Considering its mid-Cascades Range locale, as expected the crag does have some minor moss and lichen, yet the slab does gets thoroughly scoured each winter by the snow pack buildup as it avalanches off the low angle slab. The west-facing aspect of the slab receives considerable hot summer sunshine, while the dioritic rock structure lacks micro-sized pockets between the crystalline matrix, thus tending to minimize moss growth. The crag is encapsulated in a forest of Douglas fir, cottonwood, alder, and willow brush thickets, yet the slab offers broad sweeping scenic view of the entire region to the west from the top of the wall.

    The core emphasis for route grade ratings on this slab commonly range from 5.3 to 5.9 (the fun range), though a few short sections of several routes have slightly higher ratings.

    One of the prime benefits about the MCS is to start warm-up leading on the short 100' climbs, then bust into a series of long 200' leads on the main wall of the South Dome. These long routes provide lead climbers with a distinctly unique opportunity to hone calf-burner

Hugh leading *Superchron*

sharp-end of the rope long slab leading skills, sending you home at the end of the day with a smile of satisfaction.

MCS is suitable for a certain general skill level of rock climber. Considering all factors, from the 4th class descent runnels, to good rappel stations, to the 9'-25' runout sections between lead bolts, to the large array of entry level routes, the MCS is quite suitable as a beginner to moderate climbing area. Most of the beginner routes (5.2-5.6) are well bolted. The youngest person to climb here was 3 years of age (little Davey). The site is especially well suited to the old-timer (and the young) generation climber who have no desire to climb much beyond the 5.9 range. The slab is <u>not</u> a hardman climbing site for dedicated 5.11/.12 (and higher) climbers pushing the 'number' game. Thus, a .12+ climber here is like a fish out of water burdened by a subtle incongruency [like an intentional under achiever].

In addition, the crags numerative square-foot usability factor is quite small, yielding about sixty rock climbs maximum (considerably less than Broughton Bluff), while 50% of the visible slab is simply too low angle for any 5th class climbing purposes. The MCS distance from the city, its general isolated locale on back-country gravel roads may naturally limit overall user interest.

Directions

From Portland, Oregon drive east on I-84 freeway to Cascade Locks. Cross the Bridge of the Gods bridge. Continue east of Washington State Route 14 (through Stevenson, WA) for 14.5 miles (passing Dog Mtn Trailhead). Turn north onto Cook-Underwood Road (CR86) and drive 5.1 miles (through Mill A community). Turn left (north) onto Willard Road and drive 2.1 miles (passing through Willard). Willard Road becomes Oklahoma Road at Willard. Just north of the community of Willard turn left onto NF 66 road (South Prairie Rd). Drive north on paved road NF 66 for 12.7 miles (becomes gravel), then east on gravel road NF 6610 for 2.2 miles. Turn right on NF 6610-030 and drive 1/10 mile, then left on NF 717 a narrow old logging grade for 2/10 mile. Park at a circular loop turn-around sizable enough to hold perhaps 6-8 cars. Driving time from east Portland is about 1¾ hours (from Hood River about

50 minutes).

Several alternate driving directions to MCS for non-AWD vehicles.

From South Prairie Pond (for 2WD vehicles): Continue north on NF 66 past South Prairie Pond for several miles, then cut east on a rough road NF 8820 for 1.5 miles, then south on NF 070 for 1 mile, then west on NF 6610 for .5 mile, then south on NF 030 for .1 mile, then on final narrow decomm road NF 717 for .2 miles to loop parking spot.

From White Salmon (for 2WD vehicles): At highway SR14 at the White Salmon River (where it meets the Columbia River) drive north on SR 141 (the Bypass) 2.1 miles to a junction. Continue north on SR 141 for 19 miles to Trout Lake, then go through town and west on SR 141 for 4 miles, then turn left (southwest) on NF 86 (gravel) and drive 1.8 miles. At a 'Y' go right on NF 8620 (Cave Creek Road) and drive 4.9 miles west uphill to a 'T' intersection.

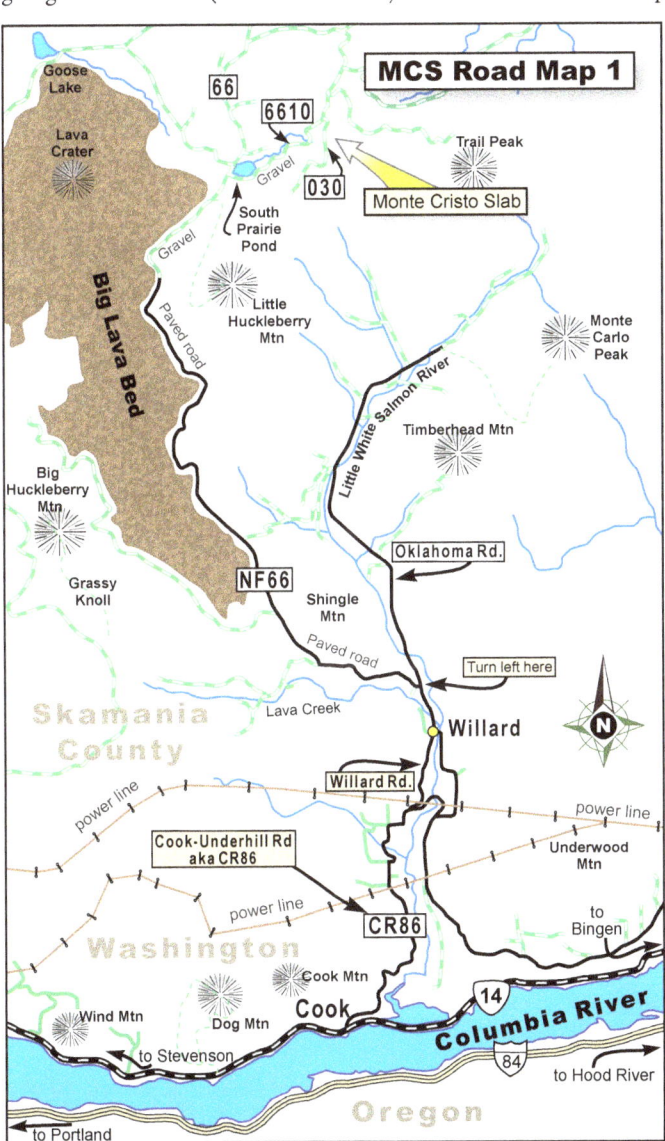

Drive south from the T on NF 070 for .5 mile to a 'Y', then drive west on NF 6610 for .5 miles. Turn left (south) on NF 030 for .1 mile, then on final narrow decomm road NF 717 for .2 miles to loop parking spot.

Path Info

Two paths exist to reach the crag (the north path and the main path). Both start the same, but split in about 40' from the parking spot.

North Path: At the northeast end of the parking spot the primary foot path cuts northward. In about 60' you will reach a dry creek drainage. Cross the dry creek drainage, then gently gain elevation for several hundred feet, then cut directly sideways along the base of a minor rock outcrop to reach the North Nook Landing, a nice sunny gravel landing with a fat string of quality climbs. From the north nook walk south a few yards along the base of the 2nd rock lobe, then up onto a wooded minor ridge crest. Follow up this wooded ridge crest for about 200' (at 100' a brief short path cuts over to the base of the 1st rock lobe to access a string of rock climbs there) to reach the Middle Landing. This landing has a plethora of easier routes conducive for basic and beginner type rock climbing on a low angle slab environment. You can reach this section of the crag easily by taking either the north path or the main path.

Main Path: At the northeast end of the parking spot the primary foot path cuts northward. In about 40' just **before** reaching the dry creek drainage, the main path cuts directly eastward and cruises uphill to the cliff, landing just below the main south dome headwall section.

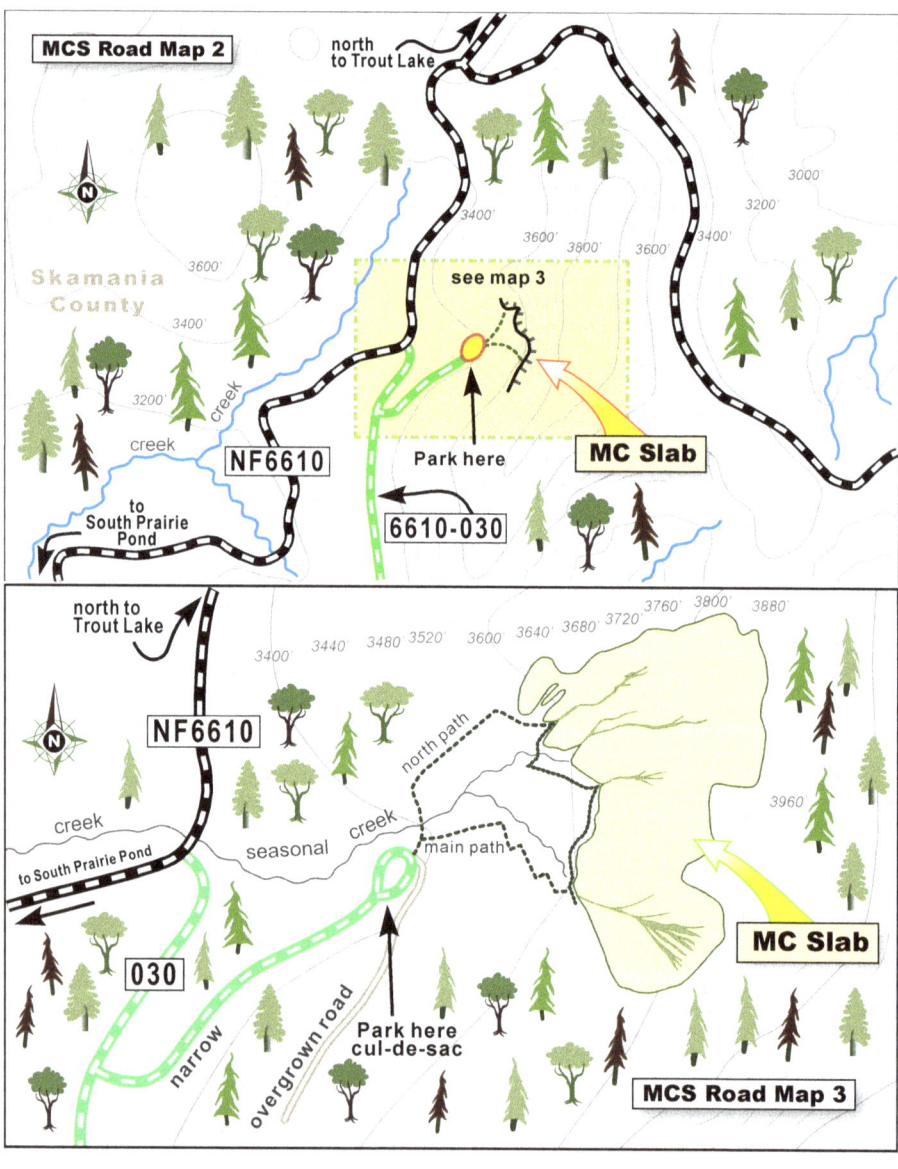

A connector path exists along the entire base of the wall from the south end to the north end.

Rock Surface Nuances

Textural nuances of the rock vary from low angle to moderate angle slab, mostly flared rounded pockets (1"-5"), various water grooved runnels, delicate techy smears, and lots of undulating wave-like terrain offering rounded palm friction surfaces. The site is basically un-like any other Northwest Oregon or southwest Washington climbing site, so be prepared to re-learn your footwork technique, especially if you are not accustomed to a slab climbing environment. The crystalline mineral surface friction is excellent (light to medium grade sandpaper) giving an ease for smearing on all surfaces.

Descent Options

About 80% of the routes are setup as 90'-100' lead climbs and all those routes are frequently ascended on lead or top-rope, and rappeled.

The steep solo descent runnels are mostly 3rd or 4th class, but you still may not like solo descending a steep slope of rock. Alongside the Dark Water Streak at the south end is a series of assistance or emergency rappel (ER) stations that you are welcome to use for rapping down that runnel. If you are really hard pressed, its possible to walk into the forest at the north end of the crag and descend a midst the trees.

South Dome Main Wall: Avoid rappeling down the long 200' routes on the steep main south dome headwall. Why not? **1.)** Because other climbers will likely be climbing on a route directly below or next to you, or perhaps even starting on the route you just finished (you cannot see them from above). **2.)** When you rappel your knot will get snagged on a bolt hanger on the upper part of the wall and you will have a hernia trying to unsnag it. **3.)** To pull down 200' of rope on a rounded slab lets the rope snag every little pebble. **4.)** The rope may get entangled with another nearby climber and cause an incident. **5.)** Its very difficult to pull two ropes across 200' of rounded slab. **6.)** Its much faster to walk off.

So, coil up your rope and walk off south (or north) to the 4th class descent water runnels. Both walk-off options are steep yet fairly basic (provided you don't slide). Or, use one of the specifically arranged 100' rappel stations descent methods explained in the beta section.

Lisa Rust climbing *Uluru*

Gear Needs, and Other Site Awareness Factors

Bring just quick-draws (or expandable loop quick-draws) because there are no cracks on the entire wall (leave all your stoppers and cam devices at home).

A 60-meter rope works for most routes, but the lead length of two routes require a 70-meter rope. A few routes are a bit over 60-meters in length (about 204' long), but can still be done with a 60-m rope provided the leader knows that when reaching the belay anchor they should tie in with a sling or daisy chain. The first six routes on the South Dome area are best ascended with a 70-meter rope.

If it begins to rain heavily while you are rock climbing, stop immediately and lower off from the nearest bolt hanger (or from the nearest belay station). The diorite slab can become slick very quickly during rainstorms, and the common 4th class walk-off descent methods may not be an option, so when need use the ER's near the Dark Streak.

Karl leading *Retro Cognition*

If you are unfamiliar with slab climbing technique and its your first 1-3 visits, try not to get too bold on lead. Learn some foot smearing methodology on high-angle friction first before tackling a bold lead. If we all lived in the land of granite this would not be a lesson to relearn.

If you skate or grease off a slab while on lead you will slide and scrape your way down below your previously clipped bolt so perhaps long pants might be beneficial in this instance. Since bolts are 9' to 25' apart its best to build up your smear leading confidence gradually.

Technically speaking, there are no R/X rated lead climbs at MCS, though this parameter is based entirely on logical anticipatory preparation factors and skill level in dealing with slab climbing technique, which is all foot technique and not finger crimping. Some routes may still feel bold, but most crux sections are well protected. When the terrain angle eases on the upper portions of many longer routes, the bolt spacing increases to usually 15'-25' apart as the grade difficulty eases.

There are several sections (see diagram) at the top of the slab with some square-ish flat stones (2"-6") in diameter lay scattered along the edge of the forest. Do not drag the rope through these areas. A helmet may be beneficial when leading or belaying. If you accidentally dislodge any rocks while at the top of the crag, let us know you did something dumb, and yell loudly to any persons at the base of the slab. Due to the rounded curvature of the steep slab a tumbling stone may take perhaps 3-5 seconds to reach the bottom of the cliff, hopefully enough time for others to react quickly. Much of the slab is generally void of loose material, though the slab has some loose 1" flat rock chips that exfoliate a bit seasonally (typical of granitic rock).

The black lichen (mostly at the top of the slab) and the minor areas of moss can become very slick during rainstorms, and on cold Oc-

Laila climbing *Bronze Whale*

tober days (when the humidity is high), so use caution.

Etiquette

Friendly climber social interaction is indispensable here at MCS, primarily because communication helps each climbing team to coordinate its next climbing route goal, especially if a plethora of teams are actively climbing on the same day.

There is no poison oak, no ticks, no nearby water source (the ravine dries out quickly), and no cell phone reception. Car camping exists along NF 66 road at several fee based campgrounds with water and toilets. There are plenty of pullouts along various nearby gravel roads for free overnight car camping. Avoid car camping at the turn-around loop (limited space for vehicles). Refrain from setting up campfires at this site, because it's a fire risk with no nearby emergency water to put it out.

Parking space is limited, so plan to carpool. Park your vehicle so as to allow enough space for other vehicles to use the turn-around loop, too. There is minimal space for about 7-9 vehicles at the turn-around loop. Consider limiting your total group team size to 1-15 persons. Instructional guiding, commercial, clubs, and organization activities in this Forest Service district are permit regulated. Some advisory recommendations within the stewardship framework promote effectual continuity goals.

At present, the open square footage maneuvering space along the cliff base is narrow due to the encroaching brush thicket. There are 3-4 common spots along the cliff base where climber's tend to congregate and most of those are quite small (its more like rubbing shoulders in an escalator). The entire length of the cliff base is mostly a thicket of dense brush which makes it difficult for human or dog to step off the path to go potty pooh. So, the answer should be obvious (i.e. not on the path). Walk away from the cliff base a fair distance if you need to find a pooh spot. Consider leaving your pet at home. If you bring it here keep it fully controlled (e.g. leashed). Do not leave non-

Steve, Hugh, and friends climbing at *MCS*

degradable trash strewn along the base of the crag.

Seasonal Factors

The MCS is generally accessible from late-May through late-October. Hot mid-summer temperatures can be a challenge, especially when the temperature reaches 90°F (or higher) in Portland, which is about 80°F at MCS. During July and August, when there is little or no breeze, its best to get there early and climb until it gets too hot. On hot summer days (1-4pm) when the afternoon sun is directly facing the slab it can be unbearably sultry along the base of the crag. Some tall trees and minor shrubs grow along various parts of the slab base providing some shade (not at the North Landing or Middle Landing). During the summer months most west side rain systems forecasting 40% rain simply do not effect the crag much, primarily because of its slightly easterly locale in the high Cascades Range.

In early May and late October the slab can be damp with morning dew, or it may be damp with narrow water seeps all day, especially when the weather remains cool and cloudy, or had recent rainfall, or is well below 60°F at the slab. Shaded portions of the rock slab tend to remain damp during this part of the season making certain routes unclimbable. In summation, heavy rains in Spring or Fall season, excessive dew, and high humidity will effect the climbing options.

Limitations

Leave the power drill at home; all the hard work

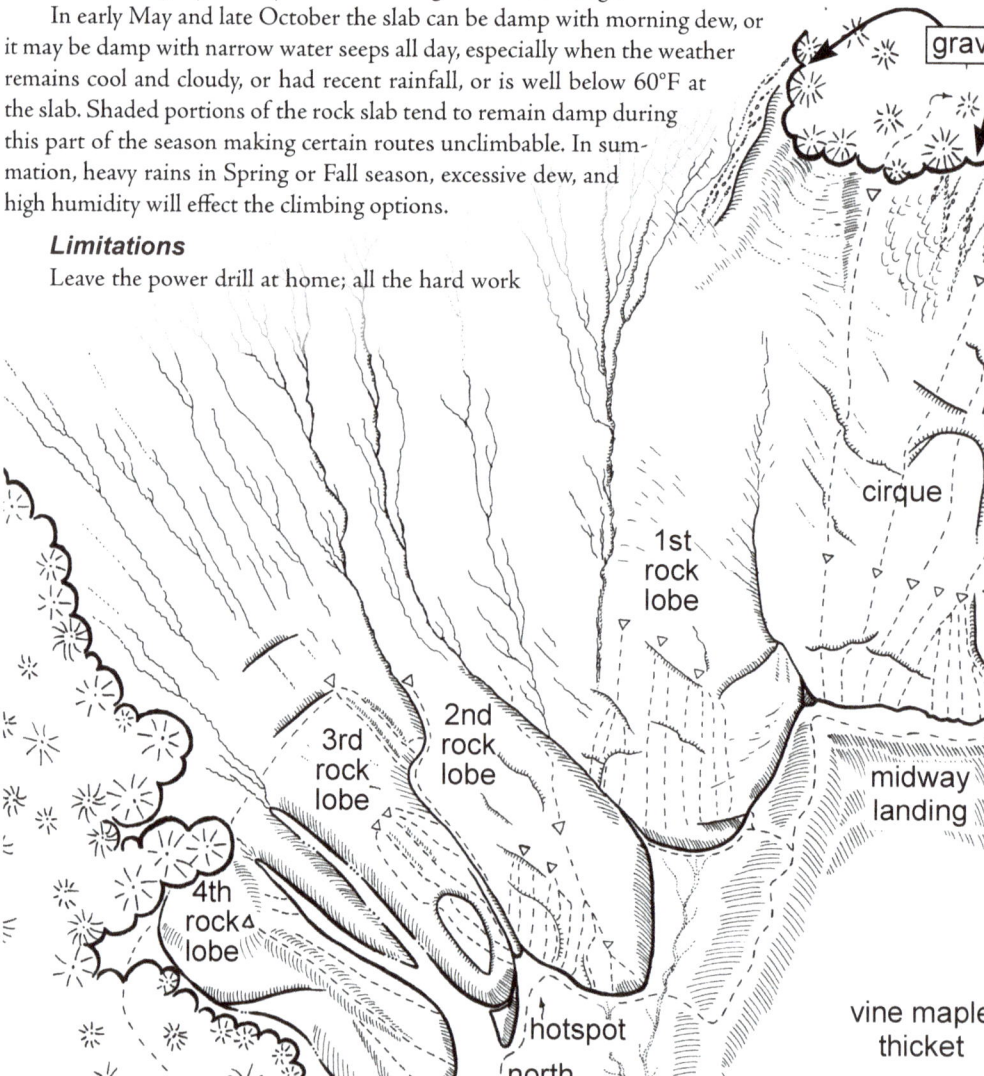

is done, and all the routes are developed. Do not strive to 'squeeze job' climbs between the existing climbs. The present routes are identifiable as lead routes, because of the slight separation (a factor lost through further condensing).

Though some of the routes may start a bit wider at the base of the slab, when a set of climbs reach the top of the slab they tend to get much closer together, primarily because the climbable portions of the slab have a dome-shaped aspect (like the top of an egg). Even smaller

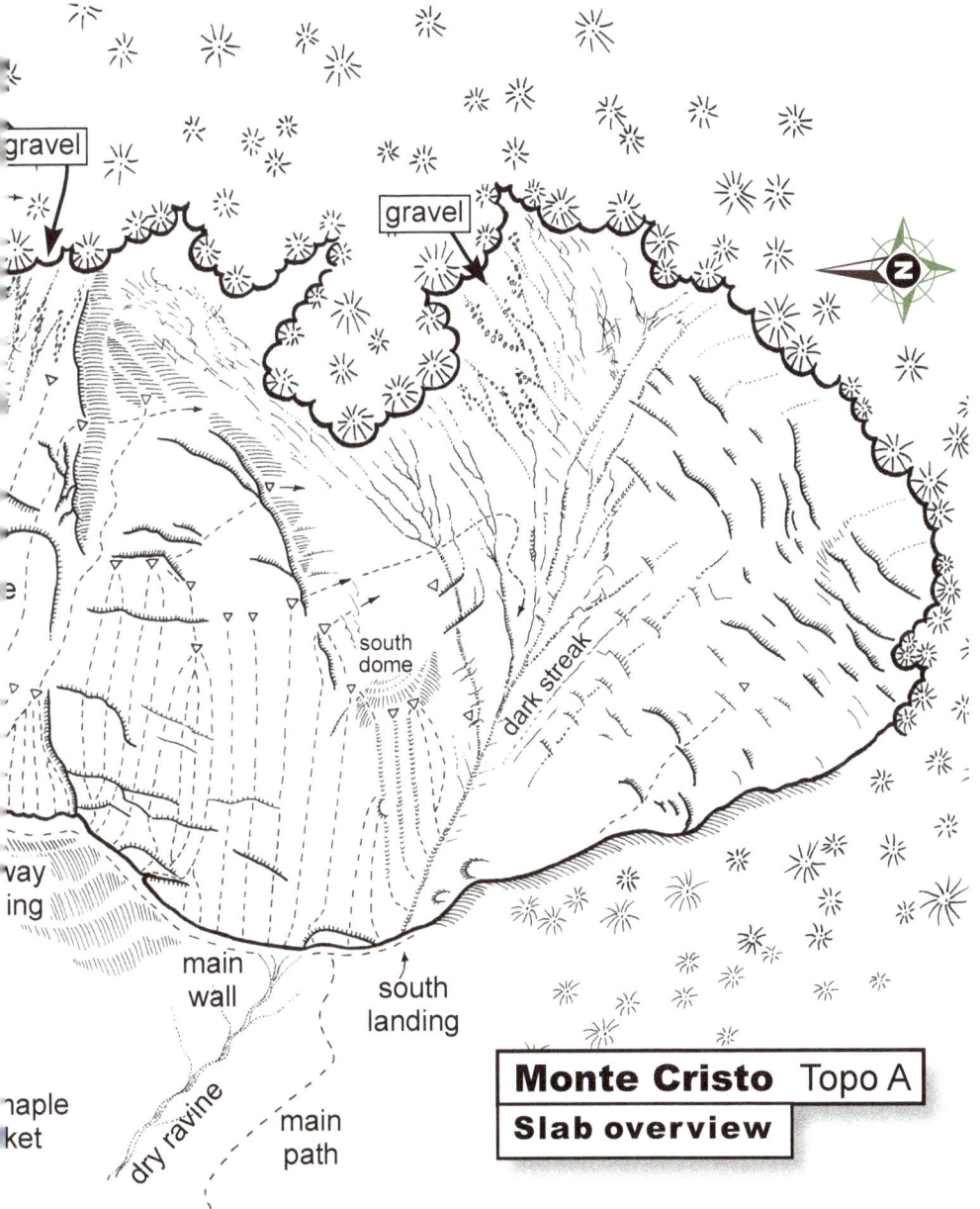

portions of the slab have additional mini dome-shaped curvatures, such as the first ½ dozen routes at the south end, and the string of routes on the 2nd, 3rd and 4th rock lobe at the north end. Some routes meet at the same belay station (varies from 1-4 routes per belay).

Most of the routes follow some form of natural nuance, be it a series of natural pockets, a fat rib, or a skinny water runnel. These characteristics give the route its sense of natural flow and intrinsic value. This goal enhances the leading experience without a potential tangle of grid pattern bolt lines that loose the essence of each routes characteristic qualities.

Stewardship at MCS

The view from atop the slab provides a stellar captivating scene of distant Lemei Rock in Indian Heaven, the South Prairie Pond, the Big Lava Bed, Huckleberry Mtn., and (on a lucky day) very compelling peaceful silence, all wrapped in an extensive fir forest. Its thoroughly rewarding just to rock climb up to the top of the slab to sit and partake of the vast scenic beauty. Visit and enjoy the rock climbing here and experience the unique qualities and value of this Washington state natural resource.

Stewardship ideals emphasize user group diversification options, site maintenance needs through organized efforts, anchor program, and other practical site recreation goals.

MCS site stewardship ethical continuity ideals are coordinated through an advisory committee that works with various regional entities. MCS primary development phase is through the efforts of Mr O & Mr B (plus positive effort by friends). See the MCS CCA page for stewardship and general climbing info. Ethically based stewardship brings value, incentive and inherent harmonious quality toward use of this crag. Enjoy the serene experience and enjoy the climbing.

Rock Structural Characteristics

MCS is geologically known as Miocene Intrusive Diorite (Mid) of a granitic stock family with medium-grained dark minerals (1-5mm), lacking quartz minerals, roughly a porphyritic pyroxene diorite. The entire structure is likely the top exposed portion of intrusive diorite stock, formed originally as a subsurface congealed marginal portion of magma stock from a larger, deeper diorite mass. The west-facing exposure of the slab likely reached its present visibility when the upper layers of softer detritus materials eroded away, or possibly when the surrounding slopes abruptly sloughed off downhill westward sometime in the past millennium.

The northern portion (with the lowest angle) of MCS shows very distinct heavy snow loading and avalanche impaction features, mainly long scratch lines (top down), a total lack of moss, and sections of unusually smooth surface rock where the natural rock curves were partially scoured for 200'+ down the slab. These factors match similar characteristics as those found on worn rock surfaces below various glaciers.

Several basic geographical observations for the MCS site are: elevation at the lowest point (3rd lobe) 3518'; elevation at the highest point (upper northeast end) 3818'; vertical height of slab: 300'; length (south to north): 815'; width at angle (top to bottom): about 510'.

The GPS (via GE *[see Introduction]*) geographical quadrangle coordinates are: UTM 10T 603653 5086444.

MC SLAB BETA

Beta is described from right (South End) to left (North End).

Dark Water Streak 4th **class, descent groove, length: 250'**

The standard 4th class descent route. This is a dark water stained runnel at the south end of the slab. This water stained groove can be quite slick in early or late season, and after rainstorms. At those times it may be unnegotiable or tricky to descend. A series of three 100'

GORGE ROCK CLIMBS 321

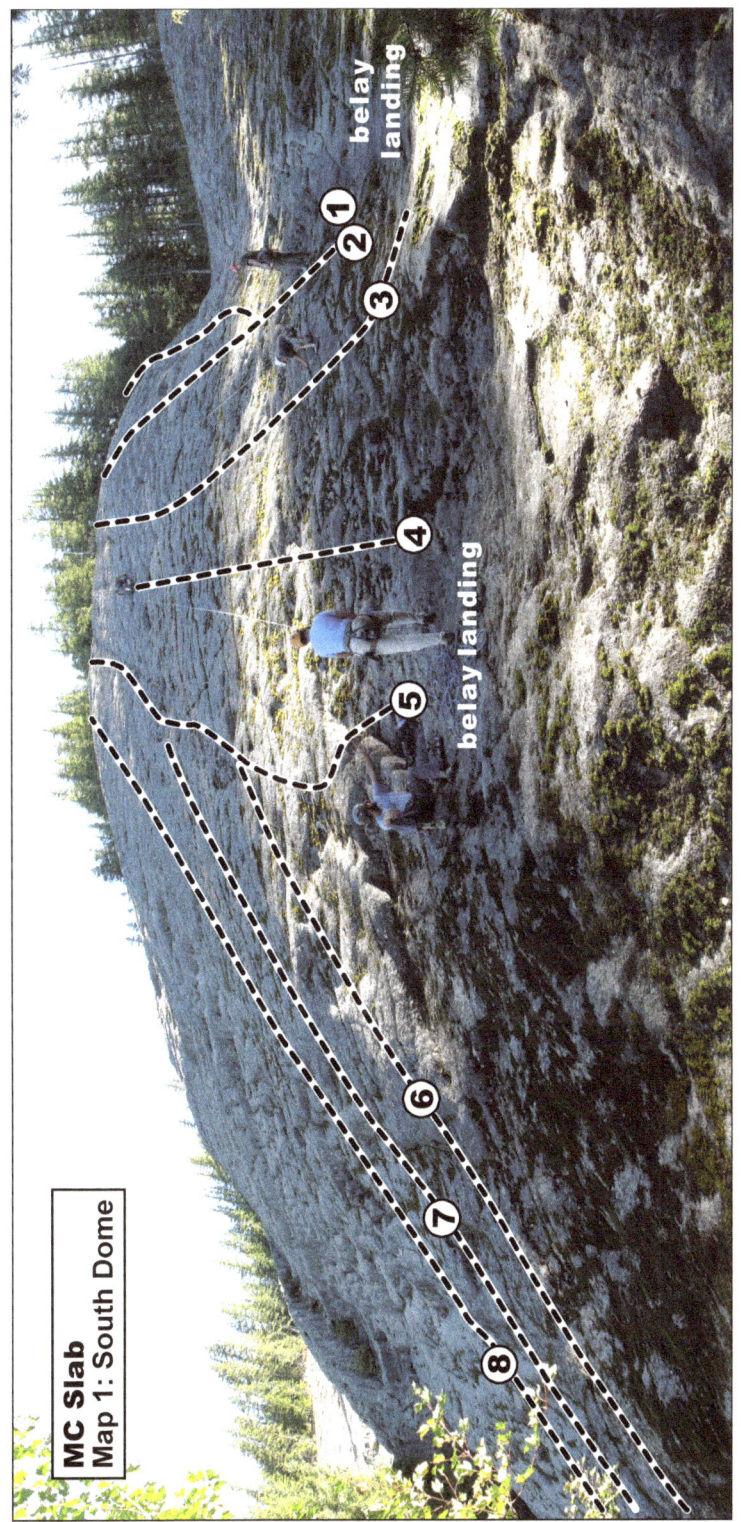

MC Slab
Map 1: South Dome

long assistance or emergency rappel (ER) stations exist on the immediate left side of this dark stained water streak, just in case you get caught up topside in a rain shower, or if you are uncomfortable with steep 4th class down smearing descents. To the far right of the Dark Water Streak is a basic **Beginner's Route** on a very low angle slab (5.0-*ish*) that has one 100' lead.

SOUTH DOME

To the left of the Dark Water Streak is a subtle yet broadly rounded dome shaped rock formation with three subtle and slightly darkened water streak grooves trending down its west aspect. The following routes ascend this rounded dome formation. A 70-meter rope is recommended for these routes, but a 60-meter rope is feasible in a pinch if you tie an end knot.

1. **My DNA 5.4**

   Pro: 9 QD's, Length: 110' (70-meter rope recommended)'

   A fun variation next to the dark water streak. Start up the initial part of Outback BBQ, then angle up right at the third bolt to climb up a set of giant steps (6 more bolts) to a belay station.

2. **Outback BBQ 5.4**

   Pro: 8 QD's, Length: 105' (70-meter rope recommended)

   This route is the first primary route left of the Dark Streak. It is a low angle smear run that steepens on its upper portion as it ascends a set of large rounded steps.

   ### Three Narrow Water Streak Grooves

   Each of the next three routes cruise up a set of three narrow water streak grooves all in a row.

3. **Tor the Hairy One 5.5 ★★**

   Pro: 9 QD's, Length: 105' (70-meter rope recommended)

   This is the right thin water groove. Initially ascend a low angle slab that steepens for its upper portion, generally utilizing the right edge of the groove. Mostly rounded sloping edges.

4. **Blind Deaf Old Goat (aka BDOG) 5.5 ★★**

   Pro: 9 QD's, Length: 105' (70-meter rope recommended)

   This is the center thin water groove. From a big fat natural bowl smear up low angle terrain passing a minor crux on the steeper upper portion. Mostly rounded sloping edges, but with good characteristics and quality.

5. **Count of Monte Cristo 5.6 ★★**

   Pro: 8 QD's, Length: 110' (70-meter rope recommended)

   A good quality climb ascending the leftmost of three water grooves. From a big fat natural scoop step left to a bolt, then climb directly up on low angle smears. A large round natural bowl at mid-height is the transition point where the low angle smears end and the

Bob Murphy leading *Uluru*

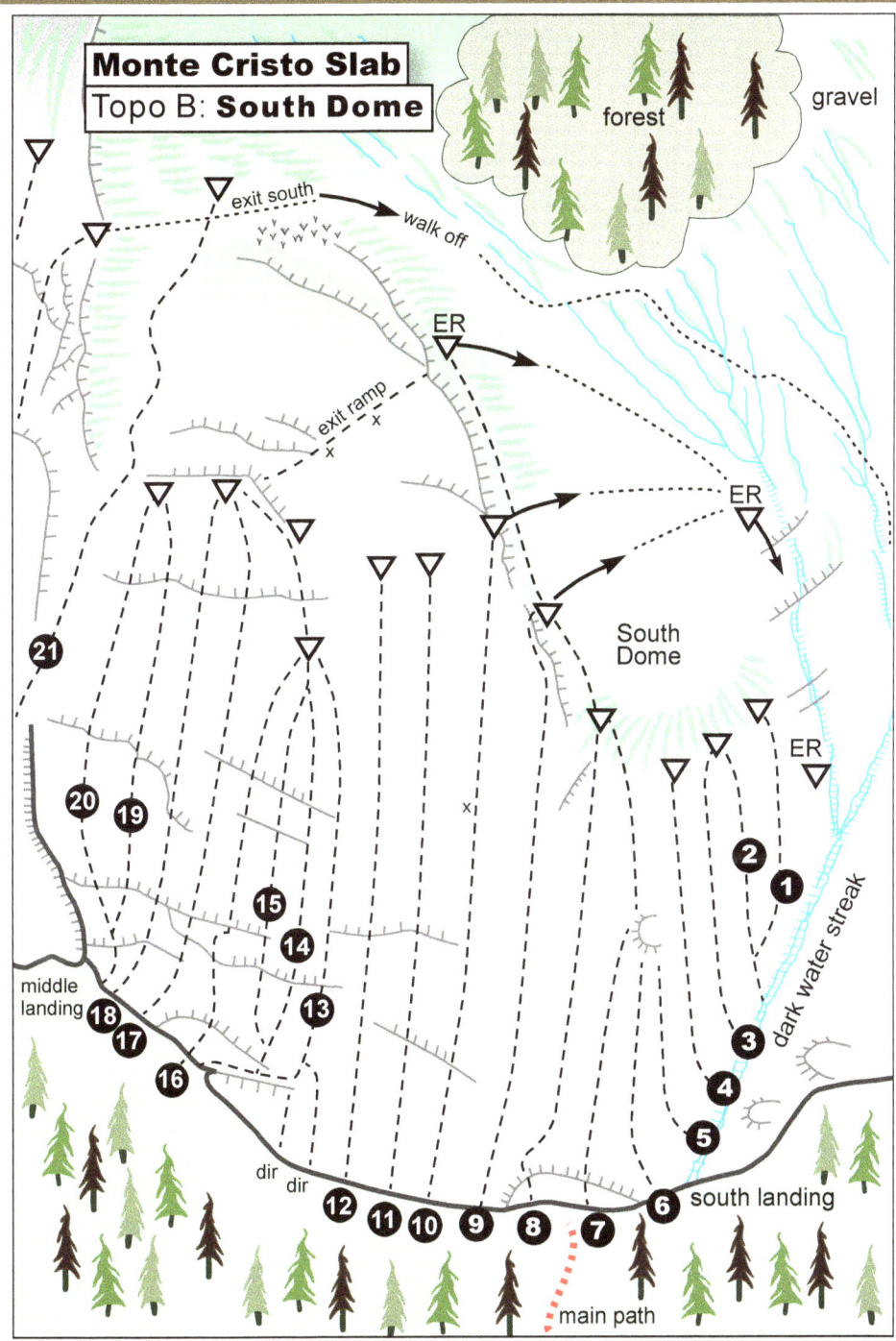

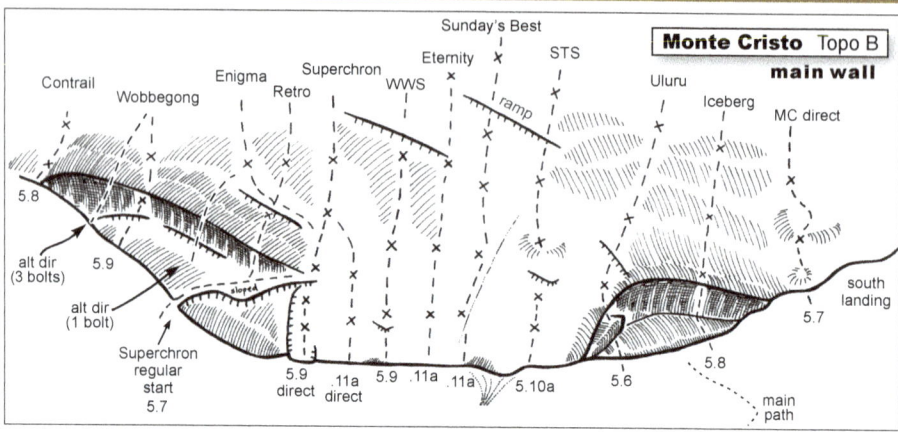

high angle dancing smears (crux) begin on rounded slopers.

6. MC Direct 5.7
Pro: 10 QD's, Length: 135'
A brief tricky direct start initial crux move using steeply sloped rounded pockets and smears. A high step puts you onto a round stance, then dash up easier terrain following a string of bolts. This direct start route merges at the large round natural bowl at mid-height into the Count of Monte Cristo.

MAIN WALL OF SOUTH DOME
From the little nook northward is a 40' wide, near vertical sweep of slab that offers a good string of powerful direct starts to all the long routes on the headwall.

Little Nook
A slightly overhung section of rock creates a minor 15' wide nook with a narrow gravel landing. The left side has a sloped step start (Uluru), and the overhung bulge to the right is the route Iceberg In A Sauna. The main climber's path from the parking spot to the crag lands here, too.

7. Iceberg in a Sauna 5.8 ★
Pro: 11 QD's, Length: 145'
Surmount up out of the little nook over a slightly hung odd crux bulge, then dance up a low angle slab. The route merges rightward into Monte Cristo at mid-height.

8. Uluru 5.6 ★★★
Pro: 14 QD's, Length: 145'
A superb climb. Though it has no specific crux move, the climb is a long series of sloping smears lacking prominent jugs. Begin at the left side of the overhung nook by stepping up a sloped step (bolt), reach over the lip to a jug, then from the second bolt continue straight up, past another minor rounded step, then up a long long flat face with thin techy sloped smears (160' to first belay). **Pitch 2:** Climb up (5.0) another 30' to another belay station then walk off south to the 4th class Dark Streak descent water runnel to descend.

9. Silence the Serenity 5.10a [5.6] ★★★
Specs: 5.10a (crux start), max 5.6 on upper ¾ route
Pro: 17 QD's, Length: 200'
Immediately left of the small nook a few feet is a very steep slab. The start dances up thin crux (5.10a) smears past a rounded bulge before easing at the 3rd bolt. The remainder of

the route is a great little fun run traveling directly up the wall. Climbs various prominent ramps, scoops, small dishes, a brief thin smear-fest, then as the terrain eases it travels up easy 5.0 terrain to a belay anchor. Walk southward to the Dark Streak to descend.

10. Sunday's Best 5.11a [5.6] ★★
Specs: 5.11a (crux start) and max 5.6 upper ¾ route
Pro: 16 QD's, Length 200'
A thin tricky crux start smear problem that eases to a sloped ramp. Continue past a series of four closely spaced bolts, then cruise on high angle terrain using smears and rounded pockets. The terrain eases as you reach the upper belay anchor at a rounded low angle crest. Though a mid-belay exists on this particular route it is far more enjoyable to do the entire climb in one very long lead. Walk south to the Dark Streak to descend.

11. Eternity 5.11a [5.8] ★
Specs: 5.11a (crux start), max 5.8 on upper ¾ route
Pro: 17 QD's, Length: 210' (70m rope required)
Power up a technical thin face (crux). As the terrain eases, dash up a short ways till the face steepens again. Continue up a long run of moderate (5.7-ish) smears, small scoops, and face climbing. When the terrain eases, dash up to an independent belay station. Belay here, then climb rightward to another belay anchor on a rounded crest, then walk off south to the Dark Streak water runnel.

12. Walk on the Wild Side 5.9 ★★★
Pro: 17 QD's, Length 210' (70m rope required)
A fun initial steep crux start using an incut crimp, then the angle eases briefly. When it steepens again continue up a long steep portion (5.7-ish) using smears and edges. The upper part of the route eases and ends at an independent belay station (at same level as Eternity belay). Belay here, then climb rightward to another belay anchor on a rounded crest, then walk off south to the Dark Streak water runnel.

TRIPLE BELAY STATION LEDGE SYSTEM
Several options for topping out from the broad triple belay ledge system. **1.)** Exit horizontally right (2 bolts, 5.0, 30') to another belay station, then walk south down Dark Water Streak. **2.)** Or...from the leftmost belay, ascend 50' uphill (5.0 terrain) to another belay anchor, then walk south to the Dark Water Streak. **3.)** Or...rappel from the leftmost belay station, down exactly 95' (tie the ends) to another rappel station (next to the Midway Landing belays), then rappel from there to the ground (95'). See introduction notes for why its best not to rappel down the 200' long routes. Most of the routes that land at the triple belay stations are a rope stretcher, in that a 60-meter rope will barely work.

Multiple Route Belay
The following four routes all land at the same 190' belay station. From this belay the route continues briefly upward to the Triple Belay Station ledge system.

13. Superchron 5.7 ★★★
Pro: 13 QD's standard sloped ramp start,

Family day at MCS South Dome

Length: 190'
A very good route. **Pitch 1:** Begin by traversing rightward out a sloped ramp for 15' to a narrow stance (bolt), then make a delicate crux smear move and dash up easier slab smears till the wall steepens, then ascend a series of steep wavy undulations. As the terrain eases on the last part of the lead expect healthy runout on 5.0-*ish* terrain till you reach a multi-route belay station. **Pitch 2:** From this belay continue up leftward on low angle 5.0-*ish* terrain (1 bolt) till you reach a flat broad ledge system with three belay stations.

Superchron Direct Start #1: Minor 2-bolt 5.9 direct start exists for this climb which powers up a brief round nose of rock merging into the standard route at a small stance. You will need 2 extra QD's for this variation.

Superchron Direct Start #2: A minor 2-bolt 5.11a direct start exists for this same route. Initial technical crux moves that quickly morphs left into the standard route at the small stance. You will need 2 extra QD's for this variation.

14. Retro Cognition 5.7 ★★★
Pro: 11 QD's, Length: 190'
A superb route! Begin at a sloped ramp (same as Superchron). Surmount a vertical crux step (thin flake crimp), then smear up easy slab. The route steepens again as it travels up various sloped edges and holds. As the route eases to a lower angle, it surmounts one last short step, then eases to 5.0-*ish* terrain (spaced out bolts) ending at a multi-route belay station. **Pitch 2:** continue up left (1 bolt) on easy 5.0-*ish* terrain 30' to another belay anchor. This is the triple belay anchor ledge system.

15. Enigma 5.9 ★
Pro: 11 QD's, Length: 190'
The starting point is the same as the previous route. After the initial flake move, smear left, then up easy slab smear terrain to a near vertical face. Climb this near vertical face and at the upper lip (5.9 crux) slide sideways to the right (odd moves). Once past that continue up easier terrain till you dance up a long smooth slab (5.8). A final 3' high rounded lip is surmounted, then continue up easier runout sections till you reach a belay station at 190' (multi-route belay station). **Pitch 2:** continue up left (1 bolt) till you reach the triple belay anchors on a broad ledge system.

16. Wobbegong 5.9 ★★★
Pro: 13 QD's: Length: 190'
One of the classic routes at the crag with variety and techy movement. Commence the journey by surmounting an initial vertical 5' tall step (5.6), then dash up a long low angle slab to a steep near vertical cliff face. Ascend a crux section of technical movement using various rounded crimps, slopers and thin rounded finger pockets. Move right under a big lip, and surmount this at a big fat rounded pocket (crux). Then smear up a long flat steep face (5.8) till this eases to lower angle terrain. Dash up rightward slightly on healthy runout easy terrain to a multi-route belay station. **Pitch 2:** continue up left (1 bolt) till you reach the triple belay anchors on a broad ledge system.

17. Contrail Conspiracy 5.8 ★★★
Pro: 14 QD's, Length: 202'
A superb classic route with plenty of unique variety, certainly one of the best routes here. Start at an initial steep move (or skip the first bolt) then dash up an easy low angle slab till the cliff steepens to near vertical. Ascend steep delicate movement (crux section) passing a brief lip landing on a stance. Then up a long steep smooth smear slab (crux) which

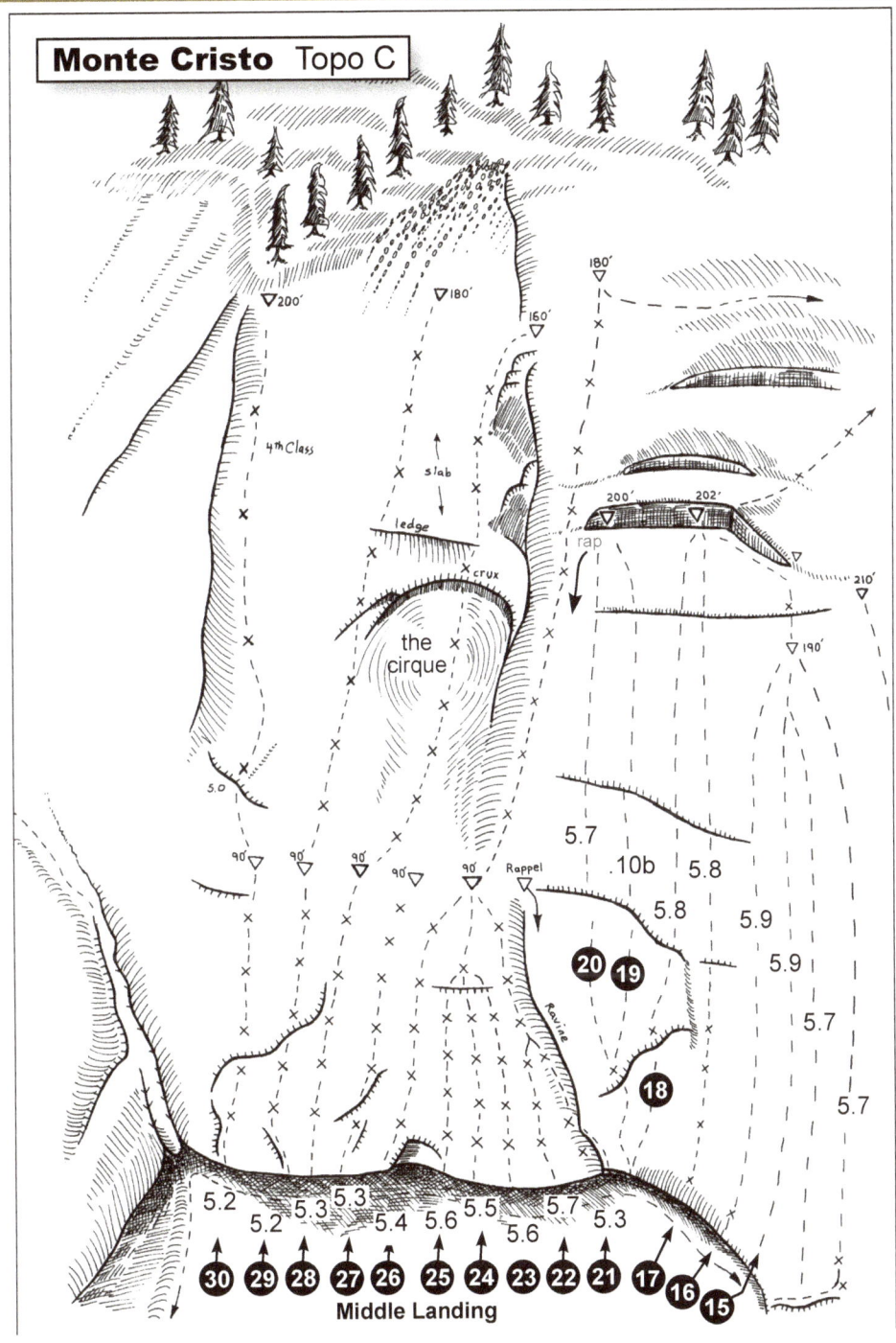

eases quickly when you get past the next minor rounded lip. Continue to dash up considerable low angle slab terrain till you reach the triple belay station on a broad flat ledge system.

18. **Indian Summer 5.8** ★★

    Pro: 11 QD's, Length: 202' (a stretch for 60m)
    Cruise up a low angle slab, surmount a step, then ascend a tall crux section utilizing various sloped edges. At about 100' the terrain eases to low 5th class ending at the triple belay station ledge system.

19. **Sky's the Limit 5.10b**

    Pro: 11 QD's, Length: 202' (a stretch for 60m)
    This climb is located where the base trail levels off just below a prominent ravine system. Two climbs utilize the same initial crux bolt at a short lip bulge. Dash up low angle terrain, surmount a minor lip bulge, and dash up more low angle terrain to the rightmost set of bolts on a vertical section of rock. Surmount this dicey vertical crux lip, then ascend a fun steep slab section to a second dicey vertical foot smear lip crux. The slab terrain eases for many meters eventually landing at the triple belay station on a broad flat ledge system.

20. **Griddle Cakes 5.7** ★

    Pro: 11 QD's, Length: 202' (a stretch for 60m)
    Same starting point as the previous route. Commence up low angle terrain, surmount a minor lip bulge, and dash up more low angle terrain to the leftmost set of bolts on a vertical section of rock. Surmount the vertical crux, then continue up a fun run slab to a second easier rock step. The slab terrain eases for many meters eventually landing at the triple belay station on a broad flat ledge system.

Center Ravine Rappel

A prominent 100' tall deeply cut stepped ravine (rated 5.3) slices the central portion of this wall. To the right of it lay the steep main wall of the south dome. To the left of this ravine is an initial nose-shaped prow, then a long swath of friendly easy low angle slab climbs all situated at the flat sunny Middle Landing.

It is fairly common to rappel from the left belay anchor on the triple belay station ledge system, down 100' to another specifically setup rappel station on a terrace (next to the five other belays that serve the Middle Landing lower routes). From there, rappel again down the ravine 100' to the ground. Beware of climber's below. The rightmost rappel is designed to send you conveniently down the ravine system. Use the rightmost specific rappel whenever the other popular belays to the left are being used.

MIDDLE LANDING (AKA PLAY PALACE)

This wide flat terraced area offers qualitative variety, plenty of 90'-100' leads at a low angle slab with ratings ranging from 5.3 to 5.8 difficulty with some long second pitch leads. This section has some fine thrills that fit a virtual novice lead or top-rope repertoire. Even the old guys enjoy these climbs. There are five belay stations at the 90' mark to allow convenient top-roping for beginner level climbers.

21. Cosmic Journey 5.3 ★★
Pro/length: P1 6 QD's (100' 5.3), P2 9 QD's (140' 5.3)

A prominent quality prow route. **Pitch 1:** Commence up an obvious steep prow using various steps and edges. The prow rounds off to an easier angle for the last 25' to the belay station. **Pitch 2:** Let the fun continue by climbing directly above the belay on a subtle rounded buttress (20' runouts) for 180' (passing by the famous triple belay station on your right). The last 40' crosses easy 4th class terrain. From the last belay anchor, walk south and descend the Dark Streak water runnel.

22. Inukshuk 5.7
Pro: 7 QD's , Length: 95'

The opening move is the crux, then some minor smears up near vertical terrain till it merges onto the prow. Finish dancing up the arête to the belay station (same as the previous route).

23. Global Warming 5.6
Pro: 6 QD's, 95'

A nice moderately steep slab route that eases onto flat terrain near the belay station.

24. Raging Sea 5.5 ★
Pro: 6 QD's, Length: 95'

Climb steep steps on a slab passing a crux section (easier on the right side of crux bolt). The fifth bolt is shared with the route to the left. After passing that bolt you land on a

MC Slab
Map 2: Midway Landing

wide low angle ledge system (bolt). Continue 30' more to a belay station used by the previous route.

25. Hammerhead Shark 5.6 ★★
Pro: 6 QD's, Length: 90'
A great climb. Start on a steep section of face, smear past a brief crux section, continue up moderate angled slopers till it merges at the fifth bolt, then lands on a wide ledge system (bolt). Continue 30' more to a belay station used by the previous route.

26. Bronze Whale 5.4 ★★★
Pro: 5 QD's, Length: 90'
A superb easy climb. Start at a slight vertical nook using smears on the left. Continue up a long series of sloped smears till the route eases onto the wide ledge system (bolt). Continue 30' more to a belay station used by the previous route.

27. Black Raven 5.3 ★★
Pro: 6 QD's, Length: 90'
Start up a minor left facing corner on a very low angle slab, then up a series of steep giant steps. When it eases onto a fat wide ledge system, continue up easier slab (bolt) terrain to a belay station.

28. Crooked Finger 5.3 (P2 5.7) ★
Pro/length: P1 5 QD's (90'), P2 9 QD's (160')
A fun run for beginner climbers on the first pitch. The unique second pitch ascends up into a broad rounded scooped out vertical sided rock cirque, but that lead is best for a climber who can deal with an odd crux lip bulge mantle.
Pitch 1: Begin up a very low angle slab, power through a brief steeper section (crux), then up easier low angle terrain to a belay station. **Pitch 2:** Continue up slightly right (bolts) aiming into the center of the rock cirque. When you reach the center bulge in the cirque, surmount the stout lip (5.7 crux) and move up to a flat landing. Continue up a nice low angle clean slab and when the terrain becomes a series of steps angle right to a belay station. Walk off south to the Dark Streak descent runnel.

Bob M. leading *Seasonal Anxiety*

29. Broken Hand 5.2 (P2 5.1) ★
Pro/length: P1 5 QD's (90'), P2 9 QD's (180')

A fun basic climb reasonable for virtual beginners. **Pitch 1:** Climb up a short very low angle slab until it steepens (crux), moving up slightly right, then continue directly up to a belay station at 90'. **Pitch 2:** Continue up from the belay on a low angle slab until you reach the left edge of the broad scooped out rock cirque. Continue up past its left edge to a brief flat landing, then dance up a nice smooth slab till the terrain eases near a belay station just below the forest. **Note:** Scattered gravel lay just above this upper belay station so its best not to climb up beyond this anchor station, but to either exit directly right south onto the rounded crest, and continue south to the Dark Streak Streak runnel to descend.

30. Tour de France 5.2 (P2 5.0)
Pro/length: P1 5 QD's (90'), P2 4 QD's (200')

A good beginner climb for the first pitch. The second pitch involves 25' runout sections. **Pitch 1:** Dance up the initial low angle slab to a minor vertical step (crux), then continue up more low angle slab to a belay station. **Pitch 2:** Continue up over a minor small step, and up easier terrain with well spaced 40' runout bolts on 4th class terrain. The final belay station exists just below a prominent single tree on a small black flat ledge. The upper portion of this climb follows a subtle slightly rounded rock knoll.

Note: There are several brief clusters of rock debris scattered along the cliff top (see diagram) just below the forest. Avoid disturbing both clusters of debris if possible. If there are other persons climbing at the Middle Landing it might help to communicate to each other in advance.

FOUR ROCK LOBES

Looking to the north from the end of the Middle Landing you will see four rock prominence's or rounded rock lobes. This entire remaining northern end of MCS abruptly drops downhill for about 200'. Each rock lobe has a steeper aspect at the lower end of each lobe. Its these steeper aspects that yield a small selection of worthy rock climbs. From the Middle Landing zone walk the forested ridge crest path down hill to reach the next climbable sections. The lobes are described from south to north; the first lobe, the second, a third and then a fourth rock lobe.

FIRST ROCK LOBE

To access the climbs located at the base of the First Rock Lobe descend the trail about 100' then cut in along the base of the lobe. The last three climbs are tucked in a small rock ravine on the left steeper side of the rock lobe. This slab has numerous basic fun routes great for beginner's. Described from right to left:

31. Conscious Haze 5.5 ★★
Pro: 6 QD's, Length: 90'

A quality low angle friction slab ending with a series of large edges in a right-facing corner groove.

32. American Eagle 5.4
Pro: 7 QD's, Length: 90'

A low angle friction slab to a ledge, then delicate smears followed by easier terrain.

33. September Morn 5.3 ★
Pro: 7 QD's, Length: 90'

A series of thin smear moves up into a left-facing corner, then step up right onto easier terrain.

34. Raven's of Odin 5.4 ★★
Pro: 8 QD's, Length: 90'
A nice brief string of thin techy smears on a flat smooth section of the face.

35. Don't Tread On Me 5.2
Pro: 9 QD's, Length: 90'
A fun string of smears and sloped edges, then a steep rounded bulge crux section, which quickly eases as you near the anchor.

36. Live Free or Die 5.2 ★
Pro: 9 QD's, Length: 90'
A few moves up a slab, a big step, then a brief smooth section, and a series of nice rounded edges on a minor rounded rock nose formation that eases near the belay anchor. Title is the New Hampshire state motto.

37. Raven's Revolt 5.4
Pro: 5 QD's, Length: 90'
Climb up a minor slab with smears and small edges, then surmount a 4' tall lip, and

Karl leading at MCS

cruise easier terrain to a flat stance. Then continue up a narrow dark water stained groove another 25' to a belay station. Rappel.

38. Crows Feet 5.5 ★
Pro: 5 QD's, Length: 90'
Ascend smears and friction along a minor rock rib, then up easier terrain to a flat landing. Then continue up a narrow dark water stained groove another 25' to a belay station. Rappel.

39. Little Crow 5.8
Pro: 4 QD's, Length: 90'
The crux is a briefly entertaining three pocket smear challenge. After the crux it merges into the route to the right at the flat landing and continues up a steep slab to the belay.

4TH Class Runnel Descent
Between the First Rock Lobe and the Second Rock Lobe a low angled 4th class rock groove provides an optional down scramble method to walk down off from certain nearby rock climbs.

SECOND ROCK LOBE
This lobe is the next prominence which juts down slope another 100' lower than the First Lobe and lands in an alder thicket. At the base of the lobes steeper aspect is a nice sandy alcove called the Hotspot or North Nook. A fascinating string of high quality power climbs exist here. Walk a forested ridge crest downhill to the base of this lobe and over to the Hotspot landing. This landing area is often sunny and warm, beneficial on cold October days, but a bit extreme if you are there on a sultry hot day in July. The routes are described from right to left

GORGE ROCK CLIMBS 333

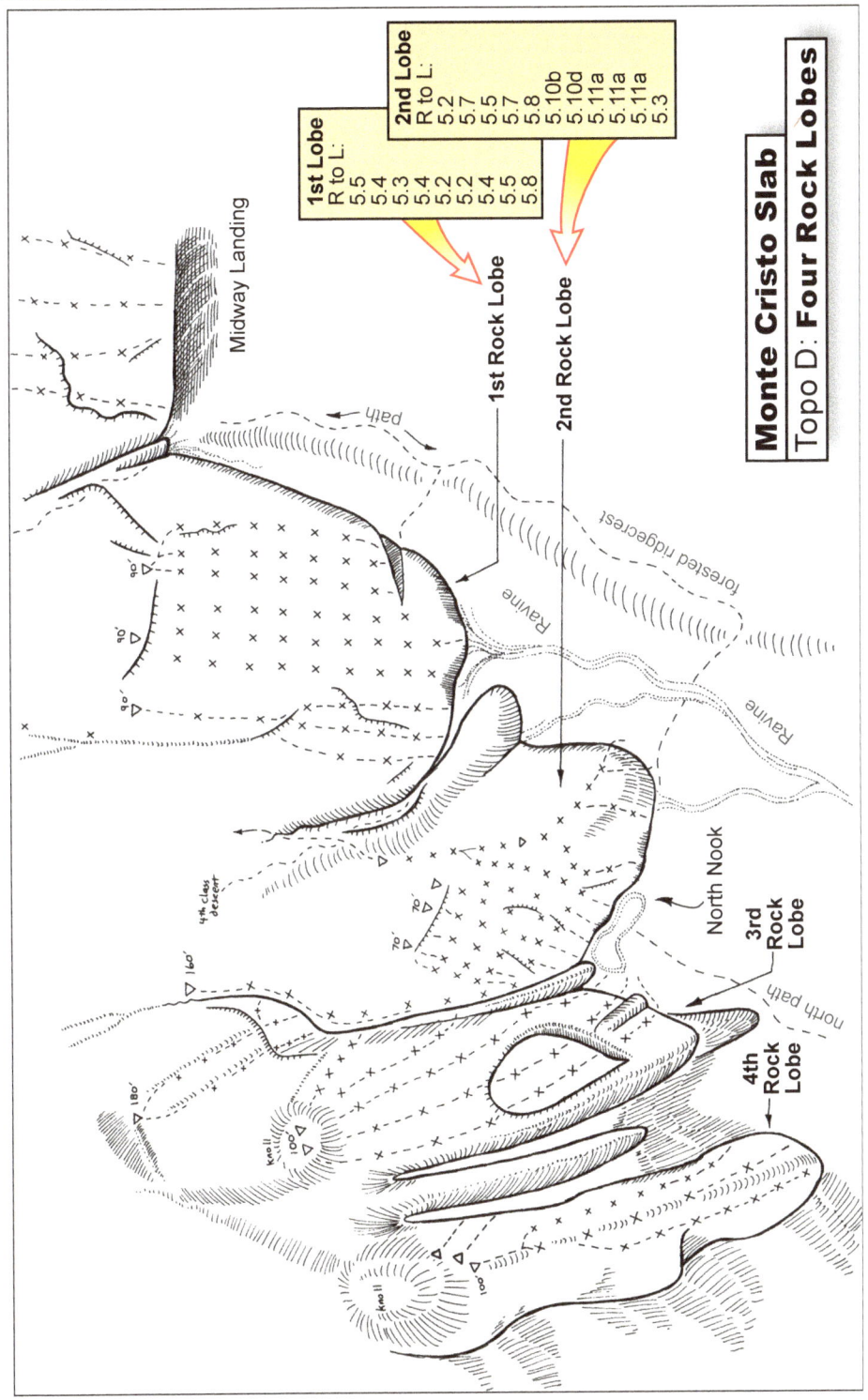

Monte Cristo Slab
Topo D: Four Rock Lobes

1st Lobe
R to L:
5.5
5.4
5.3
5.4
5.2
5.2
5.4
5.5
5.8

2nd Lobe
R to L:
5.2
5.7
5.5
5.7
5.8
5.10b
5.10d
5.11a
5.11a
5.11a
5.3

for this lobe.

40. Beginner's Route 5.2 ★

Pro: 7-8 QD's (max per lead), Length: about 90' to each belay (multi-pitch)
A viable beginner's first time lead route. Well bolted, and provides a grand tour of the wall for a beginner. Literally starts at the lowest point at the crag, and ends at the top. For **Pitch 1** (5QD's) 5.3, for **Pitch 2** (5 QD's) 5.0, etc. A very brief 12' long 5.5 direct start is feasible via a smear move to reach the standard 5.2 start.

41. Quasar 5.7 ★

Pro: 5 QD's, Length: 90'
Two prominent small pockets on a steep flat face offer a brief technical climb. The route joins into the first pitch of Beginner's Route.

42. Redneck Knuckle Draggers 5.5

Pro: 5 QD's, Length: 90'
Waltz up a very low angle left trending groove, then dance up rightward on various shaped small edges and sloped pockets, dance through a thin crux smear move, then join into Beginner's Route at its first belay.

43. Bullah Bullah 5.7 ★

Pro: 10 QD's, Length: 100'
A long slab route utilizing one obvious initial large rounded pocket at the start. Get to the pocket, then move up right to a stance, then up left to a sloped stance and make a skinny crux sequence move. A few more thin easier moves lands you at a nice step. Then continue directly up the face using a variety of smears and sloped stances till it merges with the 3rd bolt on P2 of the Beginner's Route. Bullah Bullah is Australian the aboriginal name for Butterfly.

44. Silk Road 5.8 ★★

Pro: 4 QD's, Length: 60'
Superb route. Smear past several scoops, then smear holdless terrain using slight nuances, then at the final crux make a tricky move up right (or up left) to merge into either next route.

45. Autumn Gold 5.10b ★★★

Pro: 4 QD's, Length: 60'
This is a superb quality friction smear climb with some sequential techy movement. Commence up into a minor left-facing sickle shaped corner. At the top end of the corner the holds disappear, and the technical smear kicks in (crux) on high angled terrain. Dance your way through the tight moves until you reach easier

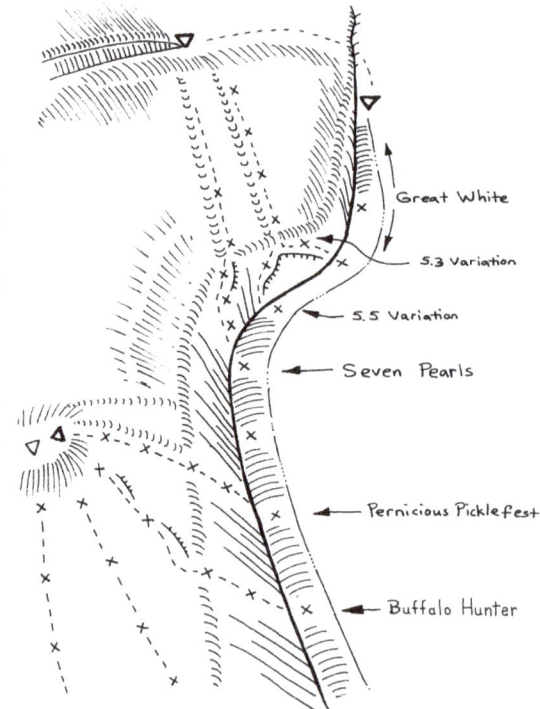

terrain ending at a belay station.

46. Seasonal Anxiety 5.10d ★★★
Pro: 5 QD's, Length: 60'
The ultra classic gem at the north end of the MCS. High angle friction smears, lacking holds, sustained, mentally energetic, with fascinating yet committing sequential movement.

47. Autumn Joy 5.11a ★★
Pro: 4 QD's, Length: 60'
Another uniquely difficult high angle smear climb. Smear up a brief subtle corner 10', then commit to several very sequential moves. Exit the locked in crux moves carefully.

48. Manic Madness 5.11a ★
Pro: 4 QD's, Length: 60'
A shorter smear climb that begins a few yards up the great white dihedral.

49. Altered State 5.11a
Pro: 3 QD's, Length: 60'
A brief technical smear-fest on steep terrain.

50. Great White Book 5.3 ★★★
Pro: 8-9 QD's, Length: 160'
A very prominent, light toned, deep cut corner ramp system that launches upward from a sandy landing zone. Ascend the dihedral passing a minor crumbly section at mid-height. When the left wall of the dihedral meets a steep cove, it angles up right and becomes a nice light colored fat clean ramp system. To descend: **1.)** climb up leftward to another belay station 30' and walk off around the 3rd lobe in the forest; or... **2.)** rappel (single rope) down to one of several anchors near the top of Autumn Joy.

THIRD ROCK LOBE

The third lobe is a large rounded buttress immediately north of the deeply cut great white dihedral system. The sunny south aspect of this lobe offers steep techy starts that land on a rounded upper slab. A surprisingly extensive string of superb climbs exist on this lobe (some being way up in the main dihedral). The following routes are described from LEFT to RIGHT (lowest to highest) going up the dihedral as if you are facing this lobe while standing at the sandy landing zone.

51. Forest Fright 5.7 ★
Pro: 7 QD's, Length: 100'
Start on the far left next to a large tree trunk. Step up onto a brief steep face (crux) with sloped holds. You quickly land on a narrow flat ledge facing a big circular donut-shaped amphitheater. Smear up the

A busy day on *Seasonal Anxiety*

low angled face to a vertical rock step, surmount the 4' tall step onto a flat landing. Then smear up easier low angled slab to a belay station.

52. **Squatch's Travesty 5.8** ★★★
Pro: 7 QD's, Length 100'
An entertaining climb. Ascend a briefly steep face next to a minor rock column. You will land on a narrow flat ledge facing a big circular donut-shaped amphitheater. Smear up the right portion of the slab, angling rightward. Surmount a minor vertical 4' step onto a flat landing. Smear up a holdless long dark water stained groove to a belay station.

Chuck on Contrail Conspiracy

53. **Barramundi in a Billabong 5.9** ★★★
Pro: 8 QD's (9 QD's if doing the direct), Length: 100'
An ultra quality gem. The great dihedral is initially divided into two grooves at the base in the North Nook. This route has 2 starts (the left direct start is 5.9-*ish* while the right start is a tad easier). *Option 1:* The direct variation start climbs a vertical flat face then merges into the regular route at the 4th bolt. *Option 2:* Climb up the left groove past a brief odd move. Just before a bush step up left onto a steep vertical face, and make a high step exit left onto a stance. Two rounded bulges create two crux friction smear sections. After these bulges proceed up a long dark stained subtle water runnel on a steep hold-less friction slab. The route ends on a broad rounded clean rock knoll with several belay stations.

54. **Buffalo Hunter 5.10c**
Pro: 7 QD's, Length: 100'
Not your casual affair, certainly bizarre, but if you like this kind of stuff, get 'er done. Climb up the dihedral about 30', then step left to the vertical face (bolt). A vertical face has a minor left leaning rail 1" wide. Use a vertical outer fin of a column, layback up, grab an incut (and clip the chain 'biner). Then, a delicate smear kissing moving to stand fully up (use a locking carabiner here). Move left, make the technical crux exit move up onto a steeply sloped stance. Gingerly ascend a series of steeply sloped steps to the belay station on the rounded rock knoll. *Note:* use a locking carabiner on the crux bolt hanger (not on the chain), and don't blow the clip (or you might kiss the slab).

Karl on Contrail Conspiracy

55. **Pernicious Picklefest 5.10a**
Pro: 8 QD's, Length: 100'
Another odd climb. Dash up the easy dihedral about 40', then step left to the vertical face (bolt). You will be standing below a vertical dark corner system. Layback up to catch an incut, muscle onto a tight stance in the corner, then exit up right to catch an

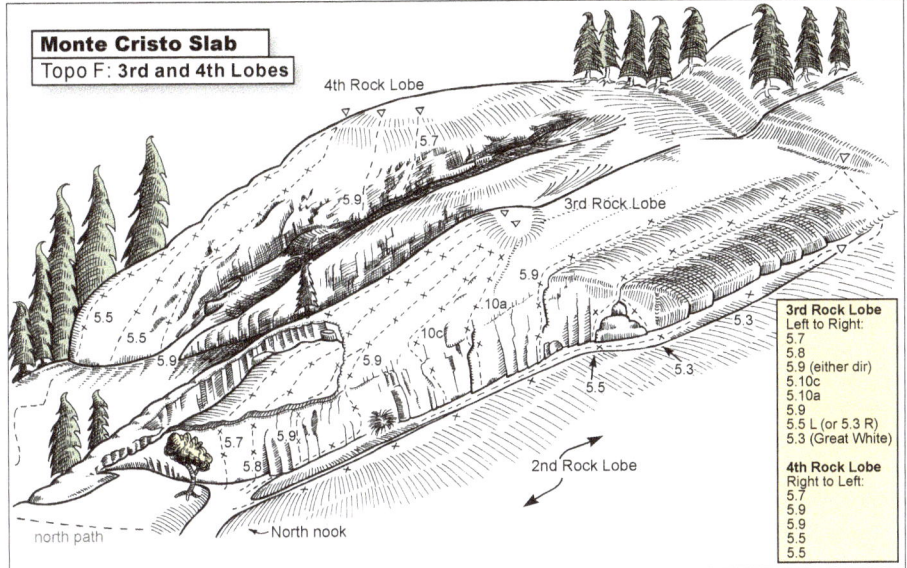

incut wedged block (quite hollow). Another very steep cruxy move to a stance, then more steep, sloped terrain that keeps you focused all the way to the rounded rock knoll belay station. Rappel. (Note: pull downward, not outward on the hollow block).

56. Seven Pearls 5.9 ★
Pro: 11 QD's, Length: 180'

An intriguing climb situated at the dark vertical headwall about ⅔ way up the dihedral. Dash up the dihedral to the ⅔ point, then layback up the incut angled ledges (crux) till the angle rounds off into a long low angle water channel. Dash up this runnel (bolts) to a shared belay station. Rappel with two ropes, or just walk off to the northwest, or to the south (see diagram).

Note: Be sure to have available 5 QD's for the brief vertical section and beyond, using about six QD's for the lower dihedral. Shares belay with next route.

57. Bookmark 5.5 [L] 5.3 [R]
Pro: 9 QD's, Length: 180'

This route jumps up left out of the dihedral at about ⅔ way up the great white dihedral. Two ways to start this variation (5.5 Left & 5.3 Right) at the crux steep section; both merge after a few moves, then continue up a low angle water runnel (bolts). Rappel over to Great White Book belay, then rappel again. Or walk off to the northwest.

FOURTH ROCK LOBE

This is the final large rounded rock buttress at the far north end of MCS. There are several entertaining climbs on this rock lobe. To reach this fourth lobe, you need to walk along the North Path for about 50' then cut uphill to the base of this lobe. The routes are described right to left.

58. Slim Pickins 5.7 ★
Pro: 3 QD's, Length: 35'

Unique route. Can be climbed on either the left or right side of the bolts. Just steep enough to keep you feeling on the dicey edge all the way.

59. Norwegian Queen 5.9 ★★
Pro: 4 QD's, Length: 35'
Techy movement with gently sloped holds yet uniquely beautiful in its own special way.

60. Toveline's Travesty 5.9
Pro: 8 QD's, Length: 90'
An odd diagonal traverse climb where most of the holds are steeply sloped to yield a tenuous experience. Start on the right side of lobe. Climb a right trending string of bolts (skipping the last bolt if desired) to a belay station. Rap or walk off.

61. Crowds of Solitude 5.5 ★★
Pro: 5 QD's, Length: 90'
This is the commonly climbed route on the fourth lobe. It starts near the toe of the buttress but on the sunnier aspect, and climbs fairly steep, sloped smears and edges, gradually easing to a long rounded low angle ridge ending at a belay station. Rappel or walk off.

62. Lonely Climax 5.5
Pro: 7 QD's, Length: 90'
The uttermost northern leftmost climb and a variation with a fair amount of moss on it. This starts at the utter lower leftmost portion of the buttress toe. It merges with the previous route on the final 30' of terrain (near the second to last bolt) to the belay station. Rappel or walk off.

THE BEST SLAB CLIMBING

3

SW WASHINGTON CRAGS

In a region known for its great hiking trails beside swift flowing streams that carve canyons through lush forested hills, you might not think southwest Washington has much to offer for rock climbing. Yet climbing sites in close proximity to the metro area have been explored such as the well known pluton-granitic formations of Chimney Rocks, and even further afield at places like Tower Rock, Pinto Rock and the Dark Divide area.

Though some destinations are isolated from the convenience of mainstream rock climbing, places like Chimney Rock offer adventurous sub-alpine rock climbing opportunities on a variety of spires both large and small. Avid rock climbers will relish the unmatched beauty and photographic grandeur while climbing at some of these places.

CHIMNEY ROCKS

Chimney Rocks is a semi-isolated, inspiring cluster of pinnacles scattered along a sub-ridge extending southeast from Silver Star Mountain. If the crag were located in Portland it would surely be a very popular climbing area. The outcrop though, is nicely situated on a wind swept ridge with breathtaking views of nearby mountains and the Columbia Gorge.

The crag is an intrusive (plutonic) lava formation part of the Silver Star dike and is composed of Aplite mantled diorite, which is granitic related stock that became exposed along the ridge crest after the surrounding terrain had eroded away. The spire offers great quality rock climbing. Numerous crack climbing opportunities exist ranging in difficulty from 5.6 to 5.11 and involve mostly natural gear protected leads. You could not ask for a better alpine environment near Portland than this. Never overrun with crowds, crisp mountain air, plenty of sun, plenty of climbing, easy two-mile hiking access along a gated road, and superb scenery. All we need is better access via a shorter hike in to the Chimney Rock spires.

Directions

To explore this climbing area drive east on State Route 14 to Washougal, Washington. Take the 15th street exit which is State Route 140 for 6½ miles and turn left onto NE Hughes Road (Vernon Road Bridge is just beyond on the right). Follow this winding uphill road for 3¼ miles up onto Bear Prairie to its junction with the Skamania Mines Road (412th street & Skye road). Follow this road 1½ miles downhill to the bridge at the West Fork of the Washougal River. Continue one mile uphill past the river to the 3-way intersection at W-1200 road. Drive north (left) for a few hundred feet then take the right branching dirt road. The left split leads to Yacolt/Silver Star Mountain. Continue on the right fork road for 1¼ miles and park at gated road #1250. Walk up this road 1 mile to the 2600' level, then walk north on another heavily rutted and brushy dirt road for 1½ miles to the pinnacles. Access to this pinnacle crosses private land. Hiking is the standard accepted method of approach to access this outcrop of rock so please park your vehicle at the bottom of the hill and hike to the crag.

The following routes are described clockwise around Chimney Rocks, starting with the standard summit scramble. Most of the common routes have been lead or top-roped.

1. Summit Scramble 5.0 ★★★

Scramble 100' up the east side along a ridge crest to the top of Chimney Rocks.

2. SE Arête 5.10b TR ★

A huge cavernous slot separates the main massif from the South Pillar. This cavernous slot has several large jammed blocks perched partway up the wall. A convenient walkway leads through this slot to the popular South Face Chimney.

At the east end of this slot on the immediate right is an arête. The arête is a fine top-rope, but a bit challenging to set up protection at the top for a belay.

Brian on lead at *Chimney Rocks*

3. **Wedged Block 5.4 R** ★

This is an alternative means for getting onto the summit of the South Pillar. Climb up the main wall on the right side under the massive block and squeeze around the block. Wander across the top of the massive block over to the South Pillar. Rappel from a horn with a sling or rap from the tree.

4. **Wedged Block Right Exit 5.4 R**

Climb the right same again passing the massive block. From the top of the block continue up onto the main Chimney Rock and aim for the summit.

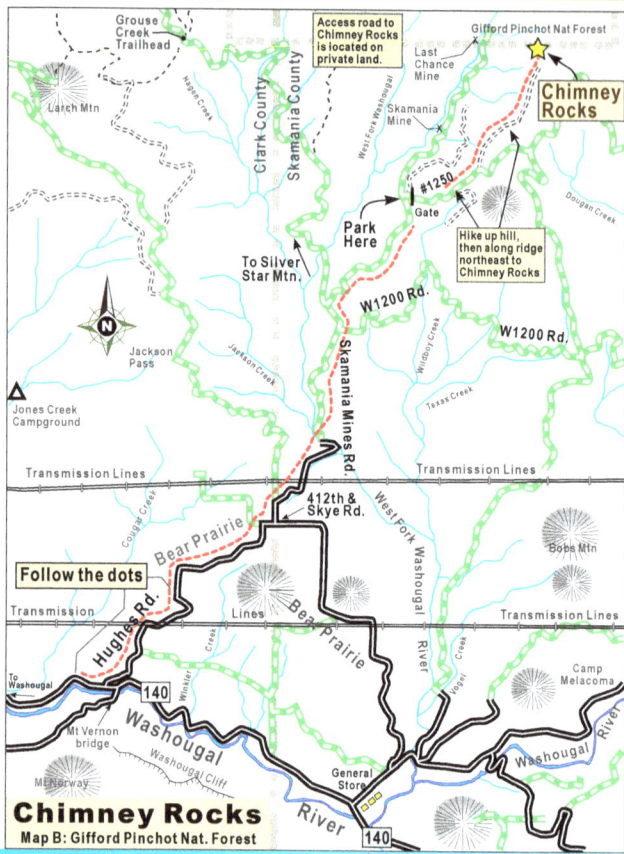

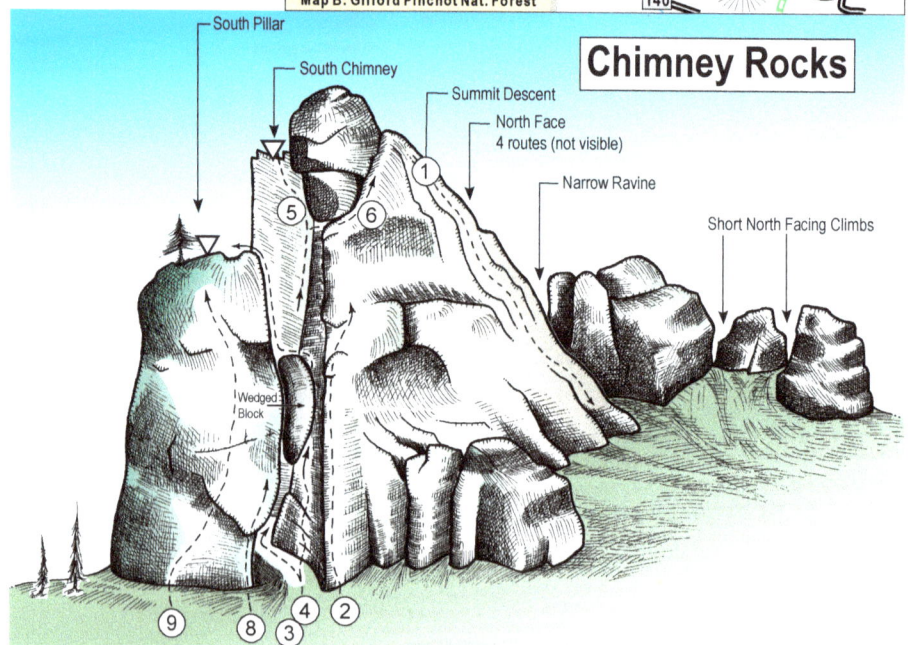

SW WASHINGTON 343

Descend down the standard scramble route.

5. **South Chimney 5.8 (or 5.9 direct start)** ★★★

Pro to 4"

The standard climb everyone aims for when visiting this site because the prominent dihedral chimney system is readily visible on the hike in. Walk through the cavernous slot. The high trail bypasses the 5.9 crux start. The lower trail lets you tackle the friable 5.9 crux start. The remainder of the climb is 5.8. Start by climbing the obvious wide chimney corner system. As you near the capstone, angle up left into another crack which also

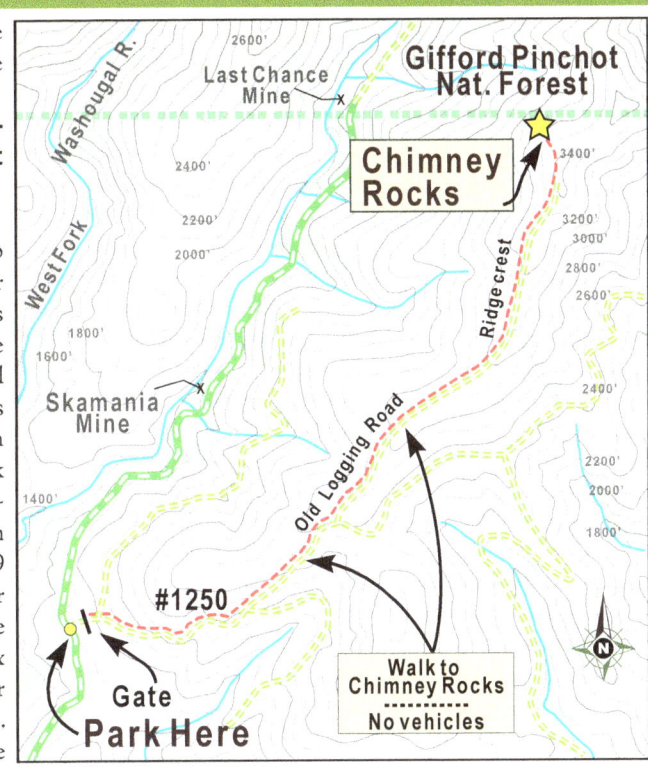

steepens to a small roof. Before you reach the small roof (at a bush) traverse right on face holds and exit through a notch to a large fat ledge to belay. Scramble 25' to the summit and descend route #1.

6. **Right Roof Exit 5.8**
Pro to 4"
Climb the South Face Chimney, but aim for the capstone, then traverse *right* under the roof and exit around the far end of it. Scramble to the top and belay, but be mindful of rope drag.

SOUTH TOWER

This is the 80' tall pillar on the immediate left side of the cavernous slot that stands separate from the main massif.

7. _____ **5.12- TR**
An extreme top-rope exists on the overhanging northeast side of the South Pillar next to the bivi site.

8. **East Face South Tower 5.6**
Pro: Mostly slings for rock horns
A nice method to attain the top of the South Tower. Fun climbing using mostly natural horns for sling protection. This starts just a few feet left of the bivi site.

9. **South Face South Tower 5.7**
Pro: Nuts and cams to 2"
Start a few feet left of the East Face route on steep terrain where you can power up to a

central scoop on the face, then traverse up left using edges and dance gingerly up to the top.

WEST FACE OF CHIMNEY ROCKS
The west side of this spire has a very long 200' tall scarp.

10. Southwest Crack 5.9 R
Pro to 3"

A cool looking line, but very steep in places. Don't be lulled into thinking its a cruise. Located immediately left of the South Face Dihedral is a very tall noble fir tree. A few feet left of the tree you can access the mid point of this route on some easy steps, and then get right to it at the vertical crux. This method will shorten the overall lead.

If you want the full blown deal, descend down slope to the top of a massive block. An overhanging wide crack (crux) starts up the wall then eases to steps. It walks up right (mid-point merges here) then launches into the vertical 5.9 thin jam and finger crack.

11. West Arete 5.10b ★★★

*Pro is 14 QD's, length 170'
(some longer sling draws, and a
few small cams)*

A quality steep arête with plenty of exposure. Descend thru the slot downhill to Tree Frog, then climb a fat 15' tall slot between a monster block on the lower west face.

Climb past a crux and several bolts continuing on 5.8 terrain on the left side of the buttress. Move up an easy broken slab, then step around to the right side of prow, for some vertical exposed (crux) climbing, and finish with another 40' or so of easy climbing to attain a belay anchor near the summit.

12. Tree Frog 5.8 R

Pro to 3" and may need pitons, length 170'

On the immediate lower west side of Chimney Rocks is another fir tree. From the top of a large block immediately right of the fir tree diligently dance 60' up small edges (5.8R) to easier ground. Wander up steps and ledges leftward to the north side till you merge with the north face crack system. The upper west side has a slightly overhanging section which commits to angle up left. Limited pro

options.

NORTH FACE OF CHIMNEYROCKS

There are three prominent crack corner climbs on the north face, as well as one bolt route. The crack climbs are nearly 200' long leads and are popular challenging climbs for visitors. The north side has a narrow squeeze slot for convenient access to all these routes.

13. Southern Cross 5.9 ★★

Pro to 5" if you have it
This is the lower of three major crack climbs on the north side. Start a few feet left of the west side fir tree and climb a consistently steep and dark stained wide crack corner. When you encounter a small capstone bust up right onto easy ground. Climb up left 30' and merge with the next crack system. This climb is best when broken into two pitches.

14. Orions Belt 5.8+ ★★★

Pro to 5" if you have it
A well-traveled route because it has small stances and it is not quite as sustained. But it has a 'poison pill' crux move mid-way up the route where you move past a large wedged chockstone that leans out at you. Still a cool route and worth the venture. A 200' lead.

15. Northern Lights 5.9 ★★★

Pro to 3½"
The upper left most route, but it is a stellar crack line as well. The climb is shorter than the other two, but has a definite overhanging crux bulge to surmount past. The climb eases significantly the remainder of the way to the top.

16. _____ 5.11+ ★

Pro: QD's
The north side has a narrow squeeze slot for convenient access. This route is on the vertical face left of the three cracks. An extreme face climb. No fixed belay anchor.

17. The Point 5.11+

On the opposite side of the squeeze slot is well over-hung overhang to put it lightly. The Point powers up

Brian leading *South Chimney*

a bolt line on the upside down chin of this pointless point.

NORTH BLUFF

Immediately northeast of Chimney Rocks is a north facing bluff about 40' tall. It can be accessed through the narrow squeeze slot that leads down to the north face. After you get thru the slot, walk around the bluff end to this short steep flat wall. Most of the routes have been lead although most visitors these days generally just top-rope the climbs. To set up a top-rope (see diagram) aim to either notch at the top of the northeast bluff. Plenty of horns and cracks allow easy anchor placements.

18. First Crack 5.7
Starts as slightly overhung moves, angling up leftward using a crack.
19. Second Crack 5.7 ★
Starts as overhung move, then a straight forward jam crack to top.
20. Corner Crack 5.6
A nice basic corner crack climb.
21. Left Arête 5.9 TR ★
The outside arête is a quality bit of arête pinching and face climbing.

You can also top-rope face sections between some of these routes if desired.

NW PINNACLE

The large inobvious pinnacle downhill on the northwest side of Chimney Rocks. To get there, descend through the slot, and cut downhill across the talus to it.

NW Buttress 5.8+
Pro: cams to 4", nuts to 1", Length 200'+ (2-pitches)
Begin just right of the toe of the lower northwest end of the pinnacle.

Climbing the north side cracks at *Chimney Rocks*

P1 (120', 5.8): Climb 5.5 face (2-bolts) past a short crux diagonal finger crack to a large ledge. Climb sustained 5.8 dihedral above, then up a series of easy ledges to large belay ledge (with a belay tree). **P2 (80', 5.8+):** Climb up a short left-facing OW corner (protects with #4 cam) and trend to the right. Angle eases, then trend up left via an easy section till you reach several large chockstones. Traverse right (bolt) on 5.6 terrain to gain a ledge, then up left to a tree belay (near a bolt).

SW Buttress 5.9

Pro: cams to 3", nuts to 1", Length 220'+ (2-pitches)

Begin at the toe of the southwest end of this pinnacle. Mostly 5.6 climbing with a minor section of 5.9.

P1 (110', 5.9): Climb a crack to a small roof (bolt), do crux 5.9 move, then continue up crest of ridge, using thin cracks for gear, and utilizing various ledges to reach a large belay ledge (bolt belay). **P2 (110' 5.6):** Continue up past some small

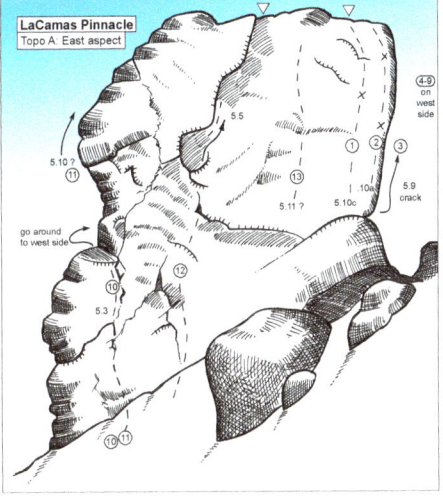

trees, then aim generally up to the left, making some exposed moves around a corner to attain a large ledge. Several final summit block cracks provide the last bit of entertainment. Belay at the summit belay at a minor notch.

LACAMAS PLUG

A rather minor plug-*ish* stump of rock in outer suburbia northeast of Camas, WA. Though partially developed, once it is well refined it may yield about 15 routes ranging from 5.5 to 5.11 (see diagram) for 360° around the plug, the shortest being 15' and the longest about 40' tall.

The short two-minute walk to the outcrop may make it viable for group climbing. The rock plug has a circumference width of about 40' max and is suitable for lower grades climbing (5.7 to 5.10+) and TR practice with a wide, flat summit. Maintain good etiquette here; the land is a mix of state DNR and timber company domain. The Lacamas Plug is granodiorite rock that is good for climbing on…even though this plug is desperately small. GPS 45°41.000'N / 122°16.000'W.

There are 3 possible country roads that will get you to the outcrop, and the following is one option. From I-205 bridge drive east on State 14 highway to Camas, WA. At the main light in front of the Safeway store, drive northeast of Camas of state 500 road passed Lacamas Lake. Turn right at NE 19th at Fern Prairie store and drive east 1 mile, and take a left at the "Y" and drive north uphill on 272nd. This winds north and east for 2 miles to a 3-way stop intersection. Turn north (left) on 292nd and drive one-half mile. Turn right on Ireland road, then 'Y' left onto Lessard road. Follow the signs to Jones Creek motocross parking area. The L-1610 gravel road continues past this parking site and winds its way uphill to junction with L-1510 road. Go left (uphill) on L-1500 for ¾ mile, then take a left onto an unmarked well graveled road, and follow this downhill for about ¾ mile. The LaCamas Plug is apparent on the uphill side of the road in a recently logged out clearing. The last 4 miles are on forest gravel roads but this particularly gravel road is better maintained. Distance from I-205 bridge is 50 minutes on gravel roads (23 miles).

TOWER ROCK

Tower Rock is an imposing 1100' tall north facing diorite massif with vertical and slightly hung sections of wall. Though the impressive cliff scarp size might beckon you here to climb it, the combination of low altitude rainy climate, and northern mossy aspect seem to create ideal exfoliating conditions that frequently send voluminous quantities of stone tumbling down its steep face. Even the FA party found the stacked rubble piles en route to be a bit intimidating and yearned for a happy ending to their multi-day rock climb with an unanticipated bivouac due to a late start.

To reach Tower Rock, drive north on I-5, then take exit #68 and drive east 46½ miles on US 12 to Randle, Washington. Go south from Randle and cross the Cowlitz River. Drive south one mile, then turn east on NF 23 and continue southeast for 8 miles. Turn right (south) onto NF 28 and drive 9/10 mile (crossing the Cispus River). Turn west on Cispus River Road (aka NF 76) and drive for 1¾ miles. Park near an old closed dirt road NF 075 which can be used to access the lower slopes of Tower Rock. Walk up this old dirt road about 45 minutes to reach the base of the wall.

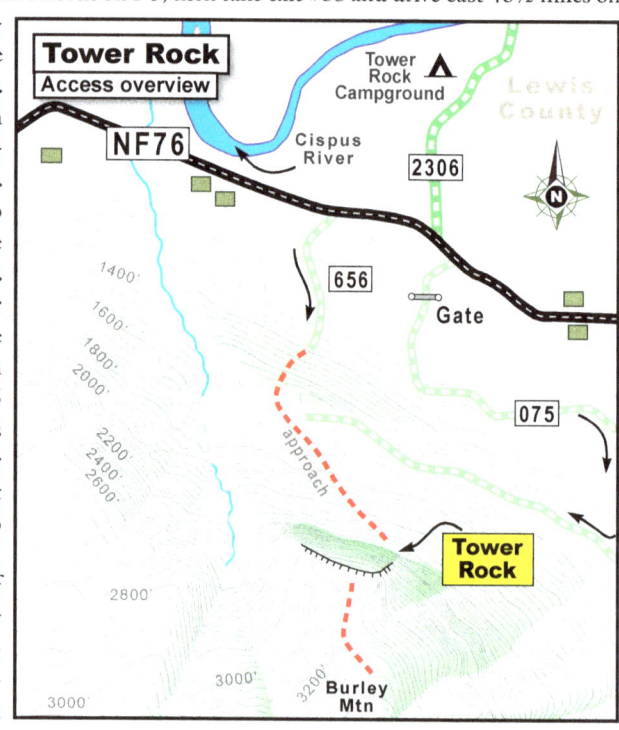

This north facing cliff scarp is located immediately north of Burley Mtn. overlooking the Cispus River valley. The wall is vertical, north

◆ SW WASHINGTON   351

Tower Rock
Map 1: North Face

facing, and at a fairly low elevation so anticipate gravel, loose rock, and moss on ledges. The GPS coordinates is N 46.432000, W -121.869000 with a high point at 3,160'.

Camping Options:
The Tower Rock U-fish RV campground is an ideal place to stay when planning to climb this rock wall. When you turn onto Cispus River Road drive a total of 2.6 miles to reach this campground. This locale also has a excellent farmland open zone to view and photograph the wall.

NW Face (Nieland-Valenzuela route)
Pro: nuts, hexes, and pitons

Begin left of a large cleft on the left side of this broad cliff scarp (see photo), and 4th class up a ramp to a sloping ledge. Climb up right for 3 pitches (5.7) (some loose rock and some mixed aid). P4 acsends up for 60' and rightward for 30' landing at a large central nook on the wall with overhung cliff above. P5 and P6 ascend up right along a series of ledges on a steep ramp system. P7 moves up right and ascends a corner system (5.6) landing on a big ledge on the west ridge. P8 continues up a steep face (5.6) on the crest for one lead till you reach the final headwall. P9 move directly right onto the west side and face climb (5.8) upward on low angled small mossy ledges to the top of the cliff. Per Jim Nieland: expect some poorly protected sections, considerable moss, grassy sections, and loose rock. Descend down the ravine on the west side.

Rapunzel's Back in Rehab Grade V, 5.9 C1, 1100' tall

FA: 7-2017, Eric Linthwaite, Bill Coe, Geoff Silverman.

Gear suggestions: Up to 30+ trad-style draws (if clipping all bolts) which is full length slings, 2 bathooks, 60'-meter rope (2 if you plan on rapping down), cheater stick perhaps, lower off webbing or quick-links/biners (for the follower when traversing), helmet. A hand drill is suggested (and a few bolts). A 70-m rope is optional.

Note: the above is not a free rating—but an aid rating. Rumor is some free sections are a bit difficult (aka 5.9+ -ish).

Note: the tower exfoliates random rockfall at times, but the route itself is generally cleaned up.

Note: the P1 first bolt is about 5' above the ground near a clump of trees about 50' above a huge lounge-like boulder (viable safe observation spot). The mid-pitches [P4-P5] and the upper pitches are tricky reverse rappels (be prepared for that challenge). The entire route is fixed with a ton of bolts/hangers, and numerous bolt holes for hooking. It's possible this route will eventually be free climbed.

The Rapunzel's route is 14-pitches total.

Lower Wall

P1 (35m long): "P1 (35-m long): Low angle moss lead fest straight up and then ease left where it changes from aid to free 5/8 of the way up"

P2 (40m): This a steeper tier of mossy rock to the next prominent ledge. Many hooks.

P3 (55m): The very steep vertical lower wall begins. Many hooks.

P4: Climb leftward under a huge corner roof system under a massive hanging detached block. One hook used.

P5 (55m): Continues up vertical mossless rock angling up left slightly. Many hooks.

P6 (20m): Fixed rope. Start up on the left side of the ledge you are standing on.

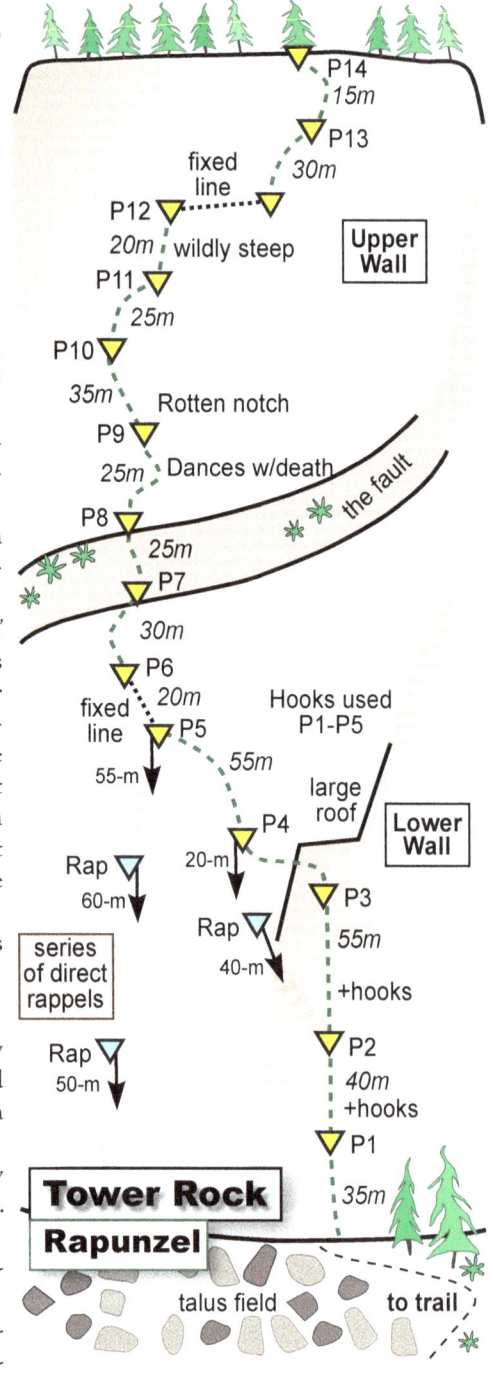

P7 (30m): lower angled mossy rock where the terrain eases as you reach the edge of 'the fault', a broad ramp system to the base of the upper wall.

Upper Wall

P8 (25m long): Move across 'the fault' which is a lesser angled mossy ramp system between the lower vertical wall and the upper vertical wall. This is also where the Nieland-Valenzuela route criss-crosses the Rapunzel route.

P9 (25m): The infamous 'Dances with Death' pitch which looks terrifying but is more solid than it appears. Long reaches, have the tall climber (if you have one) lead this pitch.

P10 (35m): Combining P10-11 together suggested. Takes off out of a cozy notch, and goes up just left of a vertical corner system. The first bolt is a long reach high.

P11 (25m): Belay from an uncomfortable corner position, free moves off the belay gets you the bolts which are to the right of the major corner.

P12 (30m): Climb the radically overhanging headwall above.

Belay on the small stance or use a fixed line traverse right about 25' to a better belay.

P13 (30m) goes up and then rightward up mossy corners and steep ramps.

P14 (15m): climb some 50' approximately to reach the summit saddle flop. Belay off of the trees. Success!

Descent:

Three options. A 2-car shuttle walk off is easiest (may scout in advance in case you top out in the dark).

Option #1: walk trail on top to the east, then down to a saddle. Then go right and bushwack down straight down a steep forest to the base where you started.

Option #2: follow the flagged hiking trail back ¼ mile as it turns right, then descends on a nice trail downhill to the trailhead. Parking spot is N 46.43017 W 121.87833 for that shuttle.

Option #3: follow hiking trail south, then uphill to intersect with Burley Mtn trail to your shuttle car N 46.42227 W 121.87108 for that shuttle.

SUNSET BLUFFS

Deep along a forested backcountry gravel road about 30 minutes from Yacolt, WA are several tiny roadside rock formations that provide minor entertainment for beer swillin' gun shooting Yacolter's who have made the most of limited stone in their valley. So, if you're not driven by selfish ideological perfection then these tiny crags may beckon. Each site is well situated with a WSW facing aspect to catch the early Spring and late Fall sunshine (sometimes even T-shirt climbing in Dec-Feb).

The first site is **Dalle de Cristal (Crystallin Slab)** at 1900' elevation. It's a slightly fractured rather puggish short 35' tall basaltic bluff which offers some fun slab climbs and some moderately desperate leads (including a smattering of TR's and projects).

The **Thunder Wall** (the second minor roadside site) is just a mere roadcut (made totally by machinery) composed of granite rock (the elusive stuff that keeps its little munchsky hidden around Silver Star Mtn).

The **Top O' The Bluff** (the third minor roadside outcrop) is a low angle outcrop of granodioritic peripheral complexity, but showing signs of metamorphic crystallin adjustment. It is loaded with edges, pockets (1" - 12"), and several cracks, and plenty of crimps (and 4 fixed TR belays).

Season:

Seasonal access is from May through mid-November typically, but often accessible even in the winter (at the first and second site). The NF41 road south of Sunset Campground is gravelled and generally maintained every 1-4 years. From there the road is occasionally maintained (when USFS has logging goals in the area). The last recent road re-grade was in 2018.

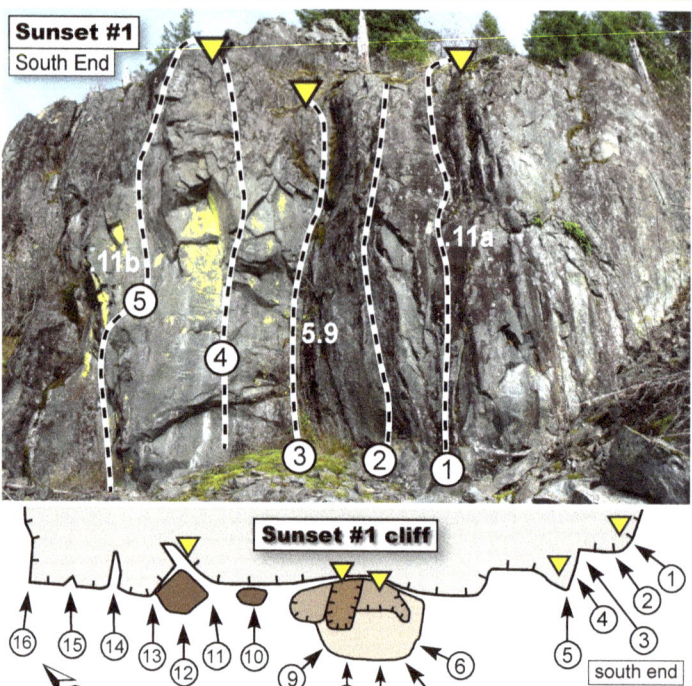

History:
Mr M and Mr O were the primary route developers (cleaning, bolting, naming, leading) of the first two sites (while Mr M developed the third site). General development phase occurred from about 2011-2016.

Directions:
From Battleground, WA drive north on SR500, then east on Lucia Falls Road. When you reach Moulton Falls county park, turn east on Sunset Fall road and drive 7¼ miles. When you reach the campground called Sunset Falls Campground, turn south and cross a bridge. The Sunset Hemlock Road (aka NF Rd 41) is gravel and continues uphill from the bridge. Drive a total of 4 miles and park in a wide spot near an old gate (used by a dead-end road that descends to some mining claims along the creek). Walk the main gravel road uphill south about 100', then cut up a long talus field slope for 550' to reach the rock climbing slab (Crystallin Slab).

DALLE DE CRISTAL (THE CRYSTALLIN SLAB)
The Crystallin Slab is a nice but minor little crag situated at about 1900' elevation (lowest of the three Sunset Bluffs). The main slab is the prime objective and it hosts several fine quality routes. Beta is described right to left (south to north).

1. **Dreamcatcher 5.11a** ★
   Pro: 4 QD's, 30' tall
   Very short uniquely stout route with closely space bolts; cruxy crimps on a flat face.
2. **_____ 5.11+ (TR)**
   Untested but possible, yet desperately short.
3. **Double Trouble 5.9**
   Gear to 3", 30' tall
   Double jam crack in a corner. Crux is getting off the ground.

4. _____ 5.11+ TR
35' tall
Tall flat slightly hung gold face with thin crimps power climbing potential. This is the right side of the tall prow.

5. **Viper's Nest 5.11b (TR)** ★
35' tall
This route is on the left side of the tall prow. Crux is first 15', then eases to 5.8. Not bolted.

A gap of about 20' to the next climbs which are on the main west facing slab.

MAIN SLAB

6. **Coucher du Soleil (aka Sunset) 5.10a** ★★★

Sunset #1
Sunset Slab

7 QD's, 40' in length
A superb route with steep, techy unique quality movement (smears and small edges), then up a brief prominent jam crack on the prow, then move left, clip main anchor and lower down.

7. **Le' Premie're (aka The First) 5.7** ★★★

7 QD's, , 40' in length
The classic route. Start at the toe of the slab and dance up a long series of enjoyable face crimps, edges, and smears passing a crux, then onto a pedestal and a final step. At last bolt move left and use the belay anchor on the route to the left.

8. **Zabo's Enchanteur (aka Zabo's Delight) 5.9** ★★

7 QD's, 35' in length
Start as low as possible on low left part of the slab, move up left past a thin crux, then easy terrain to midway stance. Surmount the final vertical step to the nice belay anchor (merely clip and

lower down).

9. **Choix des Dames 5.10b ★★**
   7 QD's, , 35' in length
   On left part of Crystallin Slab. Closely spaced initial bolts set you up for the initial tricky crux. A set of easier edges, then a second steep face section (can bypass on big left ledges). Then finish up left facing crack corner. **Note:** lowest start yields crux variant at 5.10b while the upper left step-in yields 5.9.

Most of the following are mere short TR's and are on the left portion of the crag ending at a short prow.

10. **_____ 5.11- (TR)**
    Potential short vertical face.
11. **Double Eagle 5.8**
    Fat 18" wide chimney with odd fat movement. Belay anchor is used for this and the next two routes.
12. **Lousy Putter 5.10- (TR)**
    Awkward face between both cracks.
12. **Reckless Rookie 5.8 (TR)**
    Crack cruising up then right onto same landing for previous two routes.

◆ SW WASHINGTON 357

13. _____ **5.10- (TR)**
A short groove slot-ish weakness.
14. _____ **5.10+ (TR)**
Minor short face.
15. **Charlatan Salesman 5.11+ (TR)**
The north end short prow. Awkward crux makes it a candidate for early retirement.

THUNDER WALL

Thunder Wall is a minor granite roadside roadcut phenomenon with a series of ultra short rock climbs on steeply angled rock. Definitely not a destination crag, but if you happen to live in the general area…. The site holds the rare distinction of being the closest developed rock climbing real granite crag to Portland. Some people refuse to climb here; after all its just a literal roadcut—they're convinced its not 'real' climbing (yet they'll go practice at a bloody indoor sport gym and somehow call that 'climbing'!?).

1. _____ **5.8 [?]**
Left Crack Corner system. A mixture of ledge, face, crack and corners. Needs extensive leverage yet.
2. _____ **5.10+ [?]**
A possible minor flat face with some thin holds that might yield a tricky hard line.
3. **Twister 5.10c** ★★
Pro: 9 QD's, Length 40'
Steep slightly leftward leaning prominent face route with a provocking leg-wrap block crux.
4. **Typhoon 5.10b** ★★★
Pro 9 QD's, Length 40'
See a large obvious drilled blast hole high on the face. Climb up the first part of #3 route, split up right but stay left of drilled hole on thin crimp holds. Classic? (well…its got quality).
5. **Tsunami 5.10a** ★★★
Pro: 8 QD's, Length 40'
Dance up easy terrain to mid ledge. At the drilled mega blast-hole, climb a steep face just to the right of it on small crimps. At a thin stance, move right merging onto the ramp of the Squall route. Or….make a tricky left-*ish* maneuver up into the previous route (5.10b).
6. **Squall 5.9** ★★
Pro: 7 QD's, Length 40'
Numerous steep steps and ledges, then left up a nice

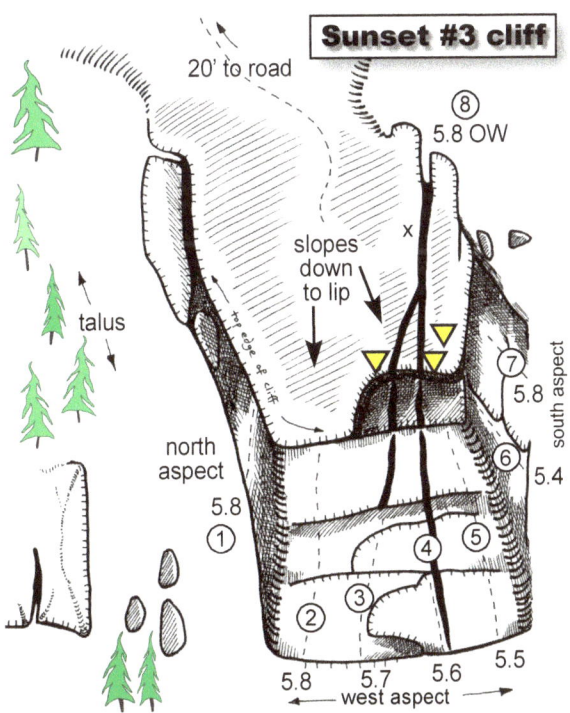

steep ramp, then a few tricky face moves to finish. An enjoyable route.

7. **Tornado 5.9 (TR)**
   Pro: __ QD's (just a top directional bolt)
   Climb a dirty face just right of "the squall" route, then at mid stance, smear up into a vertical slot, past a lip onto a flat thin face. Nice quality face but the best part is very short.

TOP O' THE BLUFF

The southernmost crag in this series along NF 41 road, is this roadside outcrop located where the road curls around the west end of a wooded ridge (see map). This site is generally used for top-roping purposes, and offers 4 fixed belay anchor stations to easily setup your sunny afternoon climbing session. Mr M was the primary route developer. This site is infrequently utilized by the Yacolt Search & Rescue team.

Beta is described north to south:

1. **North Face 5.9 (TR)**
   The north facing aspect, though mossy, yields several vertical face TR's.
2. **The Prow 5.8**
   A long steep arete that separates the vertical mossy north aspect from the easier west aspect.

The next climbs are on the tall sunny west facing aspect.

3. **The Roof 5.8**
   From a ledge surmount a roof then finish up an easy face.
4. **Luck of the Irish 5.7**
   On the main west face slab are TWO obvious cracks. This is the left one (facing the bluff) that surmounts a small roof above a ledge. Fixed anchor at the top of this climb.
5. **River Dance 5.6**
   The rightmost and easier of the two cracks in the middle (below a fixed anchor).
6. **Four Leaf Clover 5.5**
   Pro: 6 bolts, 35' tall
   Climb the lower part of the arete initially then mostly the face on the upper part.
7. **Blarney Stone 5.8**
   Climb immediately on the vertical south face next to the arete.
8. **One Half Shilling 5.4**
   Around on the shorter southern aspect and uphill is this short steep face climb.
9. **Pick Pocket 5.6**
   A very short face uphill of previous route.
10. **_____ 5.9**
    Way uphill on the south side of the outcrop is a short but 18" wide upside down off-width.

4

MT HOOD REGIONAL CLIMBS

Mt. Hood is a picture perfect jewel and a dominant feature of our northern Oregon Cascade mountain range. This mountain is the states highest summit, and also the states most frequently climbed peak.

Surrounding this majestic mountain is a forested landscape which provides local rock climbers with a multitude of opportunities from extreme precipitous pinnacles to quiet enjoyable wooded crags. The extensive variety of high altitude and sub-alpine climbing destinations along the Mt. Hood scenic highway corridor provides a virtual year-round source for exceptional outdoor adventure of inherent value. These rock climbing sites encompass a well-established core selection of regional favorites you are certain to find rewarding.

Your Gateway to Adventure

This chapter details a variety of fine rock climbing sites on the lower forested south and west side of Mt Hood, beginning near ZigZag, Oregon along the smaller tributary forks of the Sandy River, and Salmon River, with a culmination of wild routes on Illumination Rock.

FRENCH'S DOME

THOUGH TINY IN COMPARISON to many crags, the merits of French's Dome should not be overlooked. Many Portland area rock climbers have discovered that this miniature crag's rare qualities give it an enduring appeal. A visit to French's is sure to spark your enthusiasm, as well.

This unique and easily accessible dome of rock lies amongst a tall canopy of evergreen trees along the lower west side of Mt. Hood. There are about two dozen climbing routes available ranging from 5.6 to 5.12+. Most of the climbs are fixed with bolts, practically eliminating the need for natural protection. The overall height is 160 feet from the longest side and 80 feet on the road face.

The dome itself is not visible above the forests of Douglas fir trees, but it is just a short, one-minute walk to the crag. French's Dome is an interesting geological wonder of the Oregon woods and a perfect little area to escape from the city.

The Dome seemed to languish for years after the initial four original routes were established. In the 1980s local summer ski school coaches became enthralled by the place and sought to establish a string of new routes that has literally set the place on edge. Hermann Gollner, Vance Lemley, Pat Purcell, Tom Sell, John Rust, Joe Reis, Tymun Abbott and Dave Sowerby put considerable time into cleaning and establishing the 5.11/.12 grade at the Dome. Their route development energy helped tremen-

French's Dome
Map 1: Road & Parking
Approx 6¼ miles north on Lolo Pass road (NF18) to the Dome (from Zigzag).
The Dome
Sugarloaf Mtn
PB 44
NF1828
Sandy River
NF18
NF1825
MC NEIL
RILEY
Cape Horn
PB 45
To Zigzag
N

Perimeter Trail
Lolo Pass Road
NF18
Balloon Knot 22
Low Voltage 23
Psoriasis 24
Yellow Brick Road 25
26
27
28
GS Direct 20
19
Giant's Staircase 18
Do It Again 17
Tin Tangle 16
Oz 15
Alpha 14
Emerald City 13
12 Straw Man
11 Dirty Deeds
10 Crankenstein
9 Pumporama
8 The Dark Side
7 China Man
6
5
4
3
2 Road Face
1 High Voltage
Rappel
Summit of Dome
21 Static Cling
18 Giant's Staircase
Parking
Hiking Trail
Perimeter Trail
Aerial view of the French's Dome climbing routes

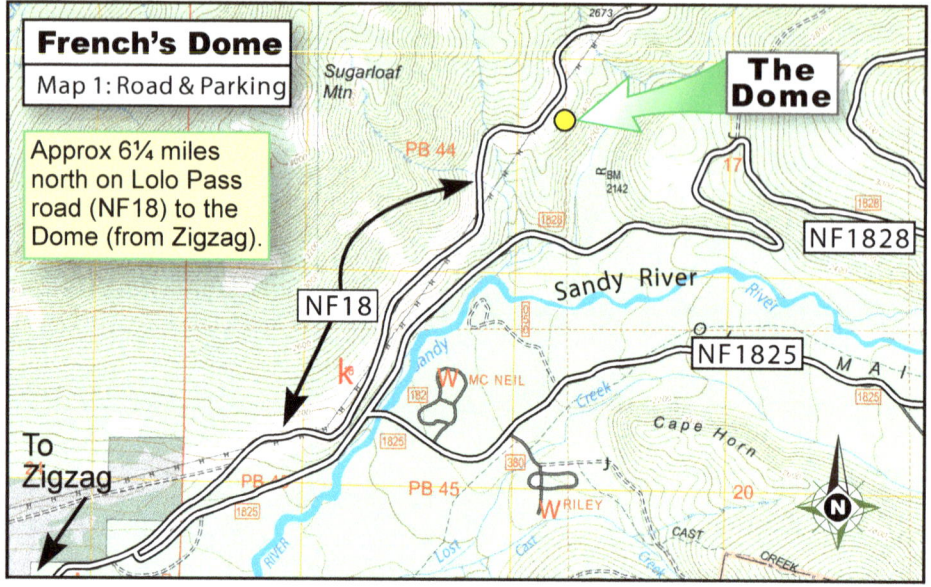

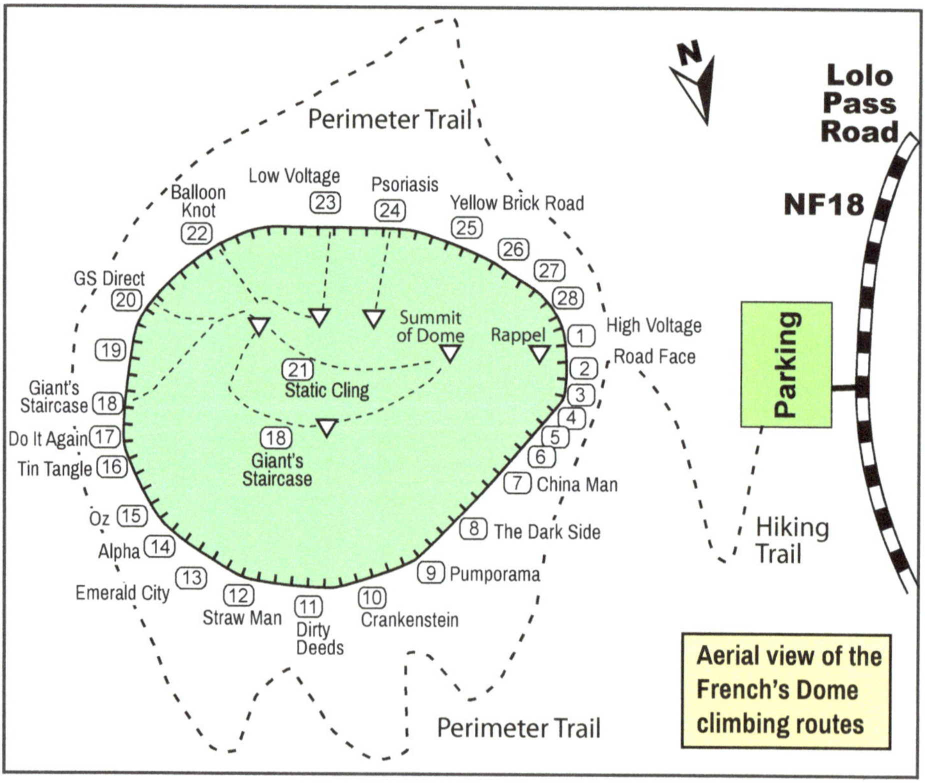

dously to make the Dome a premier climbing destination in the Mt. Hood National Forest.

Effective erosion control platforms have been built along the cliff base of French's Dome providing a long-term solution to a hillside that had been rapidly sliding away. With Forest Service trail building guidance and a volunteer workforce locals have built a legacy that will keep this place a perfect little Mt. Hood gem!

The routes at French's Dome are described symmetrically clock-wise, which you will find quite beneficial because the trail first encounters the crag at the routes facing the road. Beginning with the road face the list shown below details each rock climb as if you were to descend the perimeter trail around the crag to the left from the road face. Then from the lowest portion of the Dome the routes are described uphill past the Yellow Brick Road route.

French's Dome is a sport crag haven because the nature of the rock (crackless) lends itself to bolt protected climbing. If this is your first visit you are certain to enjoy the quality of this unique place, regardless of the climbing grade you typically send

French's Dome is composed of olivine basalt and is a tall remnant of an old volcanic neck core after the surrounding softer material eroded away exposing the rock knob.

Season: Accessible for approximately 6-7 months of the year from early May till late October (or early November). When the weather has been rainy and cool, the crag tends to remain slippery for a day, due mainly to its location within a thick tall canopy of Douglas fir trees.

HOW TO GET THERE

Drive east from Gresham/Portland on U.S. Hwy 26. Continue through Sandy, Oregon until you are near the small community of Zigzag at the base of Mt. Hood. Turn north on the Lolo Pass Road. The crag is located 6¼ miles up the Lolo Pass road (NF 18) from its junction with U.S. Hwy 26 at Zigzag. Look for an unobtrusive dirt pullout on the right and the NW Forest Pass sign. A vehicle parking pass is required for all users at this site. You can obtain a daily or annual Northwest Forest Pass parking permit at their office in the small community of Zigzag.

VISUAL BIO

7 Month | 1 Min | Shade | Trees | Regs | Sport

These emblems represent the French's Dome climbing site. French's is a giant round spherical dome encapsulated deep within a substantial green forest so there is generally no need for sunscreen lotion. French's Dome is a sport crag haven because the nature of the rock (crackless) lends itself to

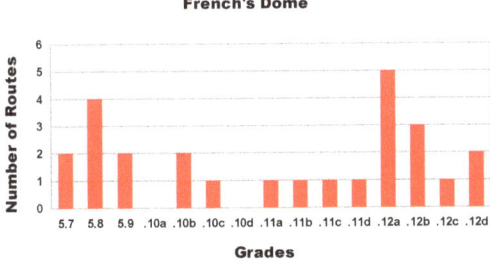

French's Dome

bolt protected climbing.

The following routes are numbered according to a descent made clockwise around the Dome from the road face area to the lowest portion and up the south trail.

1. **High Voltage (aka Rhoid Rage) 5.12 b ★★**
   60' (18m) in length, 5 QD's
   This rock climb starts a few feet immediately right of the Road Face climb, which is located at the crest of the slope where the trail meets the pinnacle. The steepest hung route at French's, with large edges and sidepulls, pumpy climbing that leads up to a big overhung bouldery crux bulge that ends on a final finishing jug. Very good climb, considered one of the best climbs for its grade at French's. High Voltage was named by Hermann, while some Portlander's called it **Rhoid Rage.**

2. **Road Face 5.12a ★★★**
   60' (18m) in length, 6 QD's
   The trail meets the crag at this point. This is the second climb from the right. This route, originally done as an aid line, is now a popular and difficult free climb. The climbing has a moderate variety of powerful thin crimp movement, offering a full shake hold out at mid-height, followed by some stout movement at a crux overhanging bulge section near the top just below the belay anchor.
   Note: For those of you who plan to ascend the Giant's Staircase (5.7) route to the top of the pinnacle, the summit rappel descends down to the base of the cliff here at the "road face".

3. **Road Kill 5.12a ★★**
   60' (18m) in length, 5 QD's
   Techy slightly overhung face climb. This is the upper direct finish from Road Rage that leads up to its own separate anchor. Where Road Rage moves left at the jug, Road Kill goes up and right slightly. Grade may be 5.12a/b.

4. **Road Rage 5.12a ★★**
   60' (18m) in length, 5 QD's
   Crimpy slightly overhung face climb. Climb the first 2 bolts of Road Kill to the rest jug, then move diagonally up left to a third bolt, then directly up the face to the anchor. Possibly 5.11d rating.

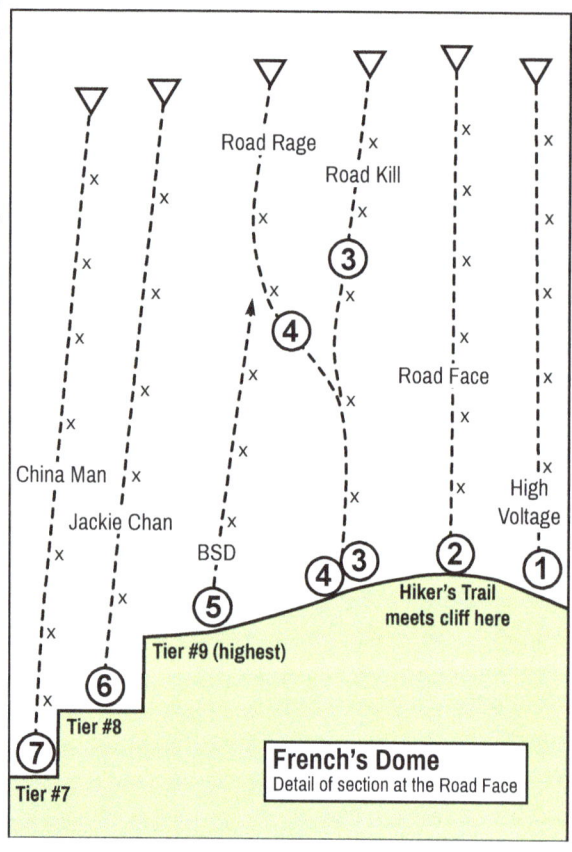

French's Dome
Detail of section at the Road Face

5. **BSD 5.12b** ★

   60' (18m) in length, 6 QD's (BSD merges into Road Rage at 3rd bolt)

   This route begins on the uppermost Tier #9 (see diagram). A three bolt direct start variation joining into Road Rage. Using the BSD direct start boosts the rating to 5.12b. Initial sequential movement on thin techy crimps (risky second bolt clip) with numerous holds for about 18' till it connects with RR at the fourth bolt.

6. **Jackie Chan   5.12b**   ★ ★ ★

   60' (18m) in length, 5 QD's

   This route begins on Tier #8. A steep thin crimp climb entailing considerable technical movement and endurance. The route starts with a series of initial tough crux opening boulder moves to get to the first bolt, then easier freedom of movement to an odd natural feature at mid-height, then finish with a series of moves on steep terrain to an anchor. Note: You can clip the first bolt from atop the upper tier, or you can bypass the initial opener moves entirely via an 5.11d variation by cutting in from off the upper edge of the top tier.

7. **China Man   5.11b**   ★ ★ ★

   60' (18m) in length, 7 QD's

   The route begins on Tier #7. An excellent climb on a slightly overhanging face with many small edges and finger holds. Powerful pumpy climbing on the lower section leads to a nice mid-height shake out rest point. More pumpy climbing on the upper section that ends with a good jug at the anchor.

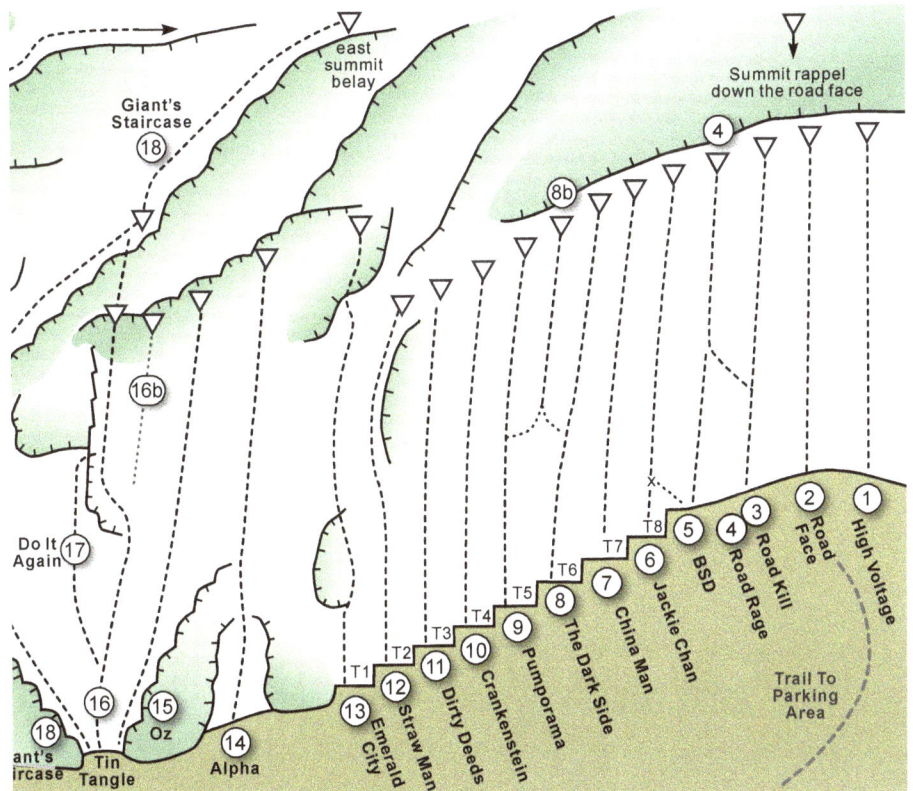

8. **The Dark Side (aka The Seige)   5.12b** ★
   60' (18m) in length,   6 QD's
   Initial moderate opening moves lead to a lower crux section, followed by a series of continuously pumpy climbing all the way to the anchor. This stout climb attracted a variety of interest in its development phase. It was bolted by Hermann Gollner, left untouched for several years, then further projected by Florian Jagodic (while strength training), but Hermann apparently completed an ascent before Florian could build endurance for the line. Dave Sowerby also found the climb of interest and began working the climb during this same brief period in hisbory and succeeded in an ascent.

8b **Philanthropy   5.12c**
   60' (18m) in length,   8 QD's
   A powerful variation that splits off from either POR or TDS. Climb first 4 bolts of Pump-o-rama, then veer right and climb a steep bulge (4 more bolts) to a fixed belay station. Via the POR start gets you 5.11+. If starting via The Dark Side clip first 2 bolts (or clip 3rd bolt with long sling to minimize risk), go through its crux, then move left onto the steep bulge (4 more bolts) and climb up to a belay. Via TDS start gets you 5.12c.

9. **Pump-o-rama   5.12a/b** ★ ★
   60' (18m) in length,   6 QD's
   An interesting, well named route that offers challenging sequential movement up steep overhanging and pumpy terrain that ascends along an obvious black water streak. A series of thin holds low on the climb lead to a difficult sequence of moves at the 4th and 5th bolts.

10. **Crankenstein   5.11c** ★ ★ ★
    60' (18m) in length,   5 QD's
    An excellent climb and considered to be one of the best routes at the Dome. The technical crux is low on the climb, but the bulge near the end of the climb is surprisingly formidable to most people.

11. **Dirty Deeds (aka Silver Streak)   5.10c** ★ ★ ★
    60' (18m) in length,   6 QD's
    Superb (and very popular) climb to help you quickly grasp the nature of steep edgy face climbing at the Dome. The route was developed and named (Dirty Deeds) by Pat Purcell, and to those climbers from the Hood River area it has been known by that name. And, for those climbers from Portland it was always referred to as Silverstreak. In any case, its a stellar climb and well worth sending.

12. **Straw Man   5.7** ★ ★ ★
    80' in length,   9 QD's
    A very popular and classic rock climb that starts up easy holds, then passes a steep crux section near the 5th bolt.

13. Emerald City 5.8 ★★
75' (23m) in length, 9 QD's
A steep enjoyable face climb located between Straw Man and Alpha. Surmount an initial bulge crux, then cruise up moderately easy terrain. The climbing steepens, then passes a pumpy lip section before the holds get bigger and difficulty eases near the belay station.

14. Alpha 5.8 ★★★
65' (20m) in length, 8 QD's
A great climb with a variety of small ledges, face climbing, and positive knobby hand holds near the crux. Climb up easy steps in a gully, then continue up a steep face to a short vertical crux section on a knobby face. The original left start has been carved into the new Oz route.

15. Oz 5.8 ★★
60' (18m) in length, 8 QD's
Ascends a ramp of large steps then embarks up and left on a steep face to a crux near the 4th bolt. and then large hand holds and edges on the upper portion near the bolt anchor.

16. Tin Tangle (aka Tin Man) 5.8 ★★★
60' (18m) in length, 5 QD's
This excellent and popular route climbs directly up a subtle blocky flat buttress starting at the lowest point of the east face of French's Dome (where **Giant's Staircase** begins). Ascend up the initial big holds till the face steepens. Gingerly work up just right of the vertical flat rib. The best holds are situated on the vertical blocky flat rib, but the first three

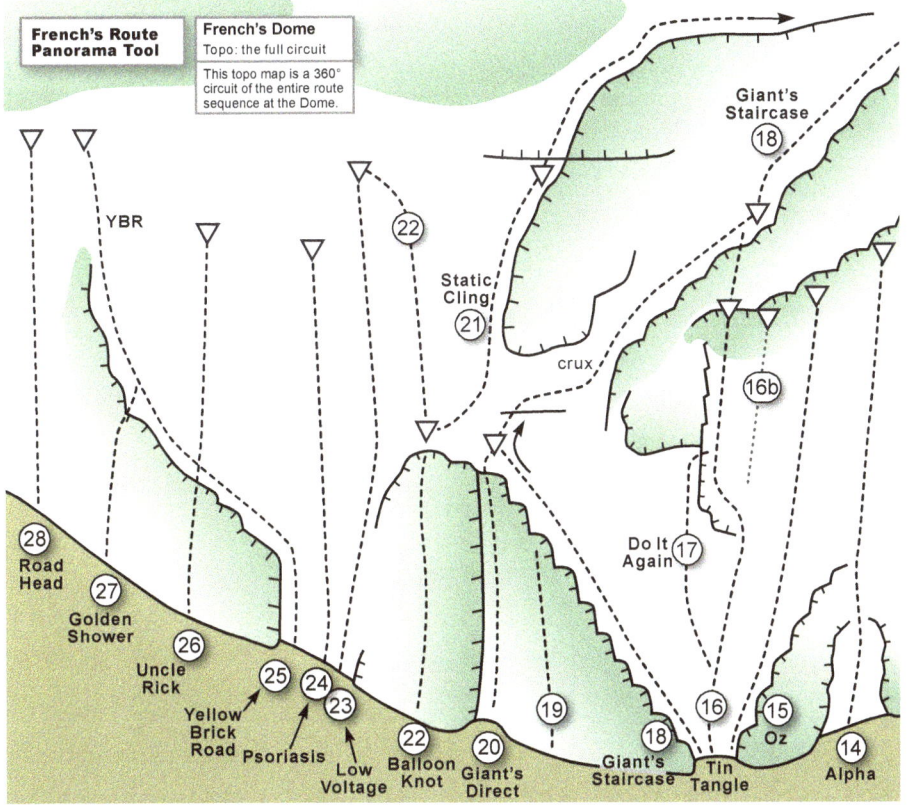

French's Dome
Map 1: Giant's Staircase

bolts are located a long reach out to the right. From about the third bolt angle slightly left onto the flat rib buttress then up easier terrain to the belay station.

Note: a recent 2-bolt extension (#16b) continues up right-ish (from the third bolt) into a weak corner ending at a belay station. You might use that variant but it's not the original route.

17. Do It Again   5.9   ★
50' (15m) in length, 8 QD's
This route travels up on the left side of the blocky flat ribbed buttress called **Tin Tangle**. Start at the same place as you would for **Giant's Staircase** at the lower eastside dirt landing but climb directly up to the first bolt, staying just to the left side of the inobvious flat ribbed buttress. At a small lip overhang, move abruptly right to merge in with **Tin Tangle**, then continue up easier terrain to the belay station. Rap or continue up to merge with **Giant's Staircase** route. This is a variation route left of Tin Tangle but is quite popular today.

18. Giant's Staircase   5.6   ★ ★ ★
Multi-pitch climb, and about 6 QD's per lead
This is a classic and original climb that as-

cends giant stone steps and ledges starting from the lower east side of the pinnacle. P1: Beginning at the lowest point on the east face, ascend up leftward on big easy steps (bolts) to a ledge and a belay anchor. P2: move up onto a thin stance immediately above the belay, then traverse rightward (bolts) to bypass (crux) a vertical section. A few brief steep moves quickly ease to large steps in a low angle ramp system and a belay anchor station. P3: Continue up the ramp system to the summit of the pinnacle and belay at the summit anchor. (Note: each pitch is roughly 60' per lead.)

Note: The Standard Rappel from the Summit begins here:

To rappel from the summit of French's Dome, descend a few yards west down slope toward the road face where you can locate a fixed double bolt (80-foot) rappel station. This rappel descends down the road face, a section of cliff that is substantially overhung, and lands a few yards from the French's Dome historical plaque.

19. Park Her Here 5.4
30' (9m) in length, 3 QD's
Something minor tucked just left of the famous Giant's Staircase route. This lil' minor route jogs up a pile of steps to its own belay (just a few yards from the Giant's Staircase first pitch belay. Bring more quickdraws if you're going above it.

20. Giant's Direct 5.7
30' (9m) in length, 5 QD's (for first short lead)
This is a short vertical bolted direct start alternative route that merges with Giant's Staircase at the first belay station. Bring more QD's if climbing another route above this.

21. Static Cling 5.10b ★
60' (18m) in length, 4-5 QD's (if doing two short leads)
Interesting route with a short steep crux right out of the gate. From the old westmost first belay anchor on the Giant's Staircase route, commence directly up right-ish into a vertical bolted scoop. Using the right side of the scoop will reduce the rating to 5.9. The climb eases quickly to another belay station, then climbs over a horizontal crumbly seam up a minor steep face to easier mossy terrain near to summit. The upper portion of the route is easier but a bit crumbly. Belay at the summit anchor.

22. Balloon Knot 5.9 ★
80' (23m) in length, 5 QD's (P1)
An initial steep section (5.9 crux) which soon lands at a belay ledge (used by Giant's Staircase). P2: climb airy 5.8 moves till it merges at the Low Voltage belay.

23. Low Voltage 5.11a ★
60' (18m) in length, 7-8 QD's
An interesting long climb which is a bit easier (.10-) if you are climbing on the big holds over to the right of the bolts.

24. Psoriasis 5.13a ★★★
60' (18m) in length, 5 QD's
This route (and the previous) share the same initial opening bolt. A true power-enduro route that lacks a comfort jug. The business begins at 3rd bolt so get your rests where you can find them. Crux between 4th and 5th bolt, but pumpy to the anchor.

25. Yellow Brick Road 5.10b PG ★
160' (50m) in length, QD's mostly, and minor pro to 1"
Less frequently climbed in the past, but with the addition of newer stainless bolts (and bolts added where there used to be odd gear placements) this route should certainly

gain in popularity in the years ahead. Brief minor runout exists near the top of the route. Located on the southwest side of the Dome on a surprisingly overhang aspect of the wall. Begin at a vertical right facing corner, clamber up, then traverse left on a slowly rising ramp that also narrows the further you go up it. As the ramp fades to a vertical corner, ascend up a steep slightly hung section of cliff face (bolts at the crux) till the terrain eases to a belay anchor. The route is one single lead. Rappel.

26. Uncle Rick   5.12d ★
60' (18m) in length,   7 QD's

Begin to the immediate left of the initial start of the Yellow Brick Road route. Climb a series of difficult steep moves, then cross over the ramp of the YBR route, and continue to climb up a powerful and crimpy substantial overhung cliff face. Somewhat pumpy .11+ climbing gets you to the second to last bolt.

27. Golden Shower 5.11a ★
60' (18m) in length,   6 QD's

A direct start variant to the renowned Yellow Brick Road route. Ascend up a slightly overhung cliff face (3 bolts at 5.11-) by going up right till it merges onto the narrow YBR ramp. Continue up left-ish as the YBR ramp steepens to a vertical corner (3 bolts) taking you to the high belay doing some laybacking and pumpy climbing (YBR 5.10- crux is just before the belay).

28. Road Head   5.11d
60' (18m) in length,   6 QD's

Road Head is actually immediately right of High Voltage route which faces west toward the parking lot. This route is a powerline involving long moves between good holds, and pumpy climbing on a substantial overhung section of wall. The climbing is slightly right of the bolt line.

Alan leading *Straw Man 5.7*

SALMON RIVER SLAB

SALMON RIVER SLAB is a steep slice of exposed rock face located at a small road side pullout just a few short miles south of the tiny community of Zigzag. The rock climbs here provide a brief compact cluster of well-bolted sport routes on smooth basaltic rock.

This small roadside rock bluff faces west and is shaded during the morning hours. Surprisingly, considering its limited scope the tiny SRS has become a fairly popular alternate climbing hangout spot in recent years partly because of its ultra roadside convenience. The steeply angled basaltic rock cliff is slightly flakey or hollow in spots, and the routes are quite short, but since the rock climbs do fit well into that 'easy-to-moderate' range the crag has gained a bit of popularity regardless of its personal drawbacks. The best season to visit here to rock climb is from May through October (on a sunny day!) so you can take advantage of the great Salmon River swimming hole just a few steps across the road from the rock climbs.

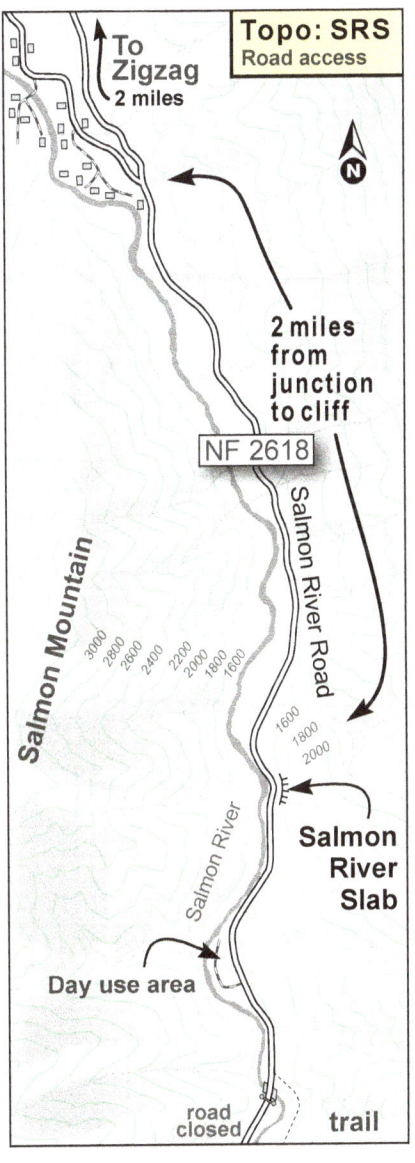

VISUAL BIO

6 Month   **1 Min**   **W**   **PM**   **Sport**

These emblems represent Salmon River Slab. Approach time is essentially just parking the car and stepping out. Don't forget to bring a swimsuit; a brisk splash in the river is refreshing! This steep slab of rock is good for ultra convenient sport climbing.

HOW TO GET THERE

Drive east from Sandy, Oregon on US Highway 26 to the tiny community of Zigzag. Turn south onto the Salmon River Road (NF 2618) and continue due south on this for 4 miles. The popular summer time swimming hole is on the west side of the road, while the tiny bluff is located on the left (east side) of the road at a small dirt pullout.

1. **Climbing Theme   5.6**
   45' (13m) in length, 6 QD's
   A basic minor rock climb, but it crosses several brief sections of hollow or slightly loose rock.

2. **Brown Rice   5.9**
   50' (15m) in length, 8 QD's
   Considered to be one of the better climbs here. The crux is at the small overhung lip a few moves below the belay anchor.

Salmon River Slab

3. **Camel Back 5.9**
   50' (15m) in length, 8 QD's
   A popular climb and an interesting lead on the long central part of the slab.

4. **Cave Man 5.7**
   Length: 50' (15m), 7 QD's
   Pull past a steep short bulge section for the initial opening moves, then cruise up a moderately easy steep slab using numerous edges to the belay anchor at the top of the cliff.

5. **Salmon 5.5**
   Length: 45' (13m), 6 QD's
   Start on the right side of the cliff. Power up an initial steep section while angling up leftward to easier ground. Route has numerous edges with some minor dirty sections to contend with.

South of the main cliff about 200' are several very short low angle slab routes.

A. **Spawning Sockeye 5.4**
   Length 30', 3 QD's
   The left shorty slab route.

B. **Moist Minnow 5.3**
   Length 30', 4 QD's
   The right shorty slab route.

ILLUMINATION ROCK

This challenging sharp profiled high altitude pinnacle is situated at the 9643' level on the SW slopes of Mt. Hood. Illumination Rock is deeply cut by glaciers on all sides yielding a three-sided sharp profiled fin of rock. This unusual rock formation represents some of the most difficult and committing alpine climbing in the entire State, and in recent years I-Rock has become the central scene of a whole new dimension in technically demanding alpine routes in Oregon.

During the summer months after the snow and rime melts off from the pinnacle, a somewhat reasonable ascent can be made on this wind-swept challenging pinnacle. All routes to the summit are 5th class rock climbs. After all of your hard effort to conquer I-Rock you will find that the summit block is a teetering boulder that few climbers will venture to stand upon.

Winter Alpine Ice Routes

During Oregon's long winter months, when Mt. Hood is covered in a mantle of ice and snow, Illumination Rock offers the totally honed alpine climber numerous exhilarating rime ice ridges and alpine ice gullies to ascend. This is the core attraction to Illumination Rock and provides quite possibly Oregon's only all-winter site for difficult rime ice ravine climbing of an extraordinaire degree. This type of steep ice climbing requires exceptional stamina, strength, and commitment, as well as proper equipment in order to succeed.

Beware of the hazards typical of high altitude climbing which are rapid changes in the weather, potential rock fall, and ledges that are covered with loose rock or debris. Protect yourself adequately by wearing a helmet and setting belays in a protected place. If you plan to climb here, face it; this is very bold climbing. For those who are mysteriously drawn to I-Rock, you are certain to find many challenges and rewards. The mountaineers who helped pioneer most of the original routes on I-Rock between 1913 - 1938 were Gary Leech, Bill Blanchard, and Ray Conway. Without doubt I-Rock, Steel Cliff, Eliot Glacier Headwall, and the Black Spider (east face of Mt. Hood) will put a spark in the wildest dreams of any local ice climber. Some original routes have changed radically over the years so the beta provided is consolidated from present day ascents.

The five-pitch route called **Castle Crag's Direct** route rides the crest of the rotten ridge immediately northeast of Illumination Rock. Rated at III 5.7X this notorious rock spine provides high-altitude precarious a summer time adventure for a well-seasoned climber. First climbed in 1994, the route proved surprisingly feasible given the overall odd nature of the rock. One must wonder why no one had crossed this wild ground before. The climbing has been reported as being stable for the 5th class sections, and rotten for the 3rd and 4th class sections.

To access Illumination Rock drive up to Timberline Lodge and park at the parking area. Fill out a wilderness day-use permit. The approach hike from Timberline Lodge to the base of the rock generally takes about 3 hours.

1. West Arête II 5.1 R *(summer rating)*

Ascend up a broad scree-dirt gully up onto the long west ridge. Continue up easy but loose 5th class terrain leading to the saddle of the West Gable. A plethora of routes top up at the West Gable. For the continuation of this route see the South Chamber route beta details.

2. **South West Ridge IV 5.9 AI2** *(5.9R summer)*
SW Ridge is climbed in early winter conditions usually when the route is generally exposed rock and feathers of rime ice intermixed. A difficult climb that is focused on or near the buttress ridge utilizing crack and corner features.

The South West Ridge is a six pitch route generally starting at a steep ravine and making use of the prominent buttress. Use a variety of dihedral corner crack systems at or near the ridge crest or utilize the main rib.

As you near the West Gable you can still use the left side of the main rib or venture over right to bypass some odd sections. Expect a liberal amount of loose rock as always.

Winter foray? Well…expect putting in some serious mega-power climbing like a bad dude on tenuous rime ice during the winter season. From West Gable the usual is to bail off down one of the rappel routes. *Summer Gear:* Nuts, pitons, hexes, and a few cams.

3. **April Insanity IV 5.9+ AI4 M4+**
An extreme winter climb that utilizes a prominent ravine on the south buttress wall left of Iron Maiden. The upper headwall just below the West Gable is difficult to get past.

4. **Iron Maiden III 5.7 AI2**
Iron Maiden starts the same as Rime Dog, but does not exit left at the stance. Iron Maiden stays in the deep corner system directly up staying near the general prow of the Standard Chamber Route. It parallels closely the summer route much of the way to West Gable while making ready use of the rime ice filled ravines.

5. **Rime Dog III 5.8 AI3 M5 200m+**
P1 165' (50m): Climb a mixed corner (5.7) for 80' to a stance, then move left to the next corner system. Ascend a right-leaning ramp to a belay at the top of the ramp at the base of a wide gully. **P2 150' (45m):** Ascend the wide gully on the right side, surmounting occasional ice steps till you reach the base of a headwall. **P3 165' (50m):** Ascend a wildly steep corner for 50' (5.8) and then traverse right to an exposed ramp and set a belay at the base of a corner. Note: Pitch 3 & 4 follow the same general area as the **South Chamber** (P2, P3, P4) route. **P4:** Ascend the short (20')tricky corner (5.7) and ascend open snow and rime slopes (80')to West Gable. Rappel into South Chamber to descend.

Note: Gary Leech's 7-1936 ascent of the **South Wall** likely follows a similar ravine as Rime Dog or Iron Maiden and merges onto the standard South Chamber route as it draws near to the

Hugh following P2, East Ridge South Chamber

West Gable.

6. **South Chamber   II 5.4 R (summer rating)**

This is the *'standard'* method by which climbers make an ascent of Illumination Rock. It is also the standard rappel route for getting your horse off this choss pile. The route climbs the inner left side of the South Chamber to the West Gable then along the upper West Arête to the summit. Its a bigger world than it looks from a book.

Crux on E. Rib South Chamber

P1 200' (60m): Scramble up into the South Chamber along the left side and locate an easy groove that wanders (5.4) up onto the ridge crest to a saddle. **P2 & P3 165' (50m):** From a sling belay at the saddle march (5.4) up steep slabs and steps to another belay. **P4 100' (30m):** Surmount a steep step and scramble up over loose debris to the West Gable. **P5 & P6:** From the Gable scramble up low 5th class steps and large blocks turning the left side of a short vertical prow and set a belay at 100'. Climb carefully along the ridge crest (200'+) passing the skylight to the summit block.

7. **East Ridge of South Chamber   III 5.6 R**

The East Ridge is a visually fascinating rib on the right side of the south chamber. The East Ridge offers wildly exposed climbing on moderately steep terrain and is a viable summer rock climb or a winter mixed climb (III 5.6 R AI3 M2). **P1 180' (54m):** Scramble into right side of the South Chamber onto (5.1 R) the ridge crest of the East Ridge. Waltz up easy but loose terrain to a belay stance. **P2 120' (36m):** Climb variable steep corners and steps (5.5) to a small belay ledge with steep-sided walls. **P3 180' (54m):** This lead starts immediately out of the gate with a punchy 5.6 crux. Stem a short vertical tight crack corner from the belay and then up basic steps and edges to a long scramble on low angle wide ledge along the crest to a belay.

P4 180' (54m): Step down to the notch, then ascend a broad flat face (5.4) with edges and breaks that is difficult to protect due to the nature of the rock. Delicately dance up this broad face, then exit up left onto the ridge line to a belay. **P5 40' (12m):** Scramble over easy terrain to the summit ridge.

8. **Abracadabra   5.10c**
9. **March Madness   II AI4 or WI4**

A difficult two pitch frozen waterfall when it fully forms. See diagram.

10. **Northeast Face (aka Northeast Ridge)   II 5.8 R**

From Illumination Rock saddle climb up along the ridgecrest over large boulders to

Summit ridge on Illumination Rock
Inset: I-Rock profile

the base of the main cliff. Climb up to a bolt anchor on a ledge. Traverse a short distance to the right and climb a crack corner system to the ridge crest.

11. **North Face II 5.5 R** *(summer)*

    From Illumination Rock saddle climb up along the ridgecrest over large boulders to the base of the main cliff. Climb up to a bolt anchor on a ledge. Traverse far to the right along a wide ledge till you are on the exposed north face above the Reid Glacier. Once you are directly under the skylight ascend steep ledges and cracks to the natural skylight on the summit ridge.

12. **Northern Skylight II AI3 M5+** *(winter)*

    Descend around to the north side of Illumination Rock on snow to the first buttress toe. Tackle the steep mixed terrain directly to the northern skylight. The two 60-meter pitches start about 250' left of the Southern Skylight route. The 2nd pitch offers some burly mixed climbing followed by half a pitch of mostly vertical rime ice.

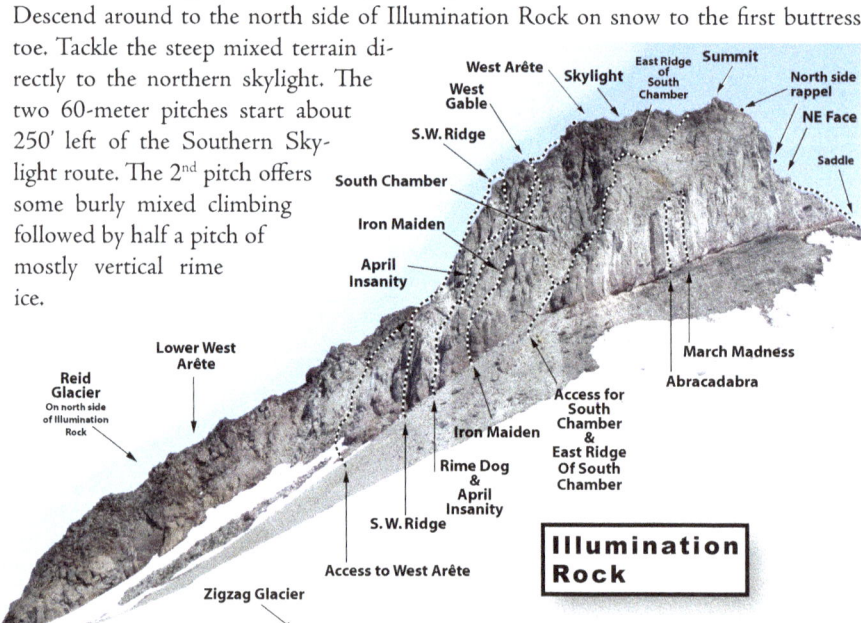

Illumination Rock
Topo G: Northwest Face

13. Southern Skylight II AI3 M5 *(winter)*

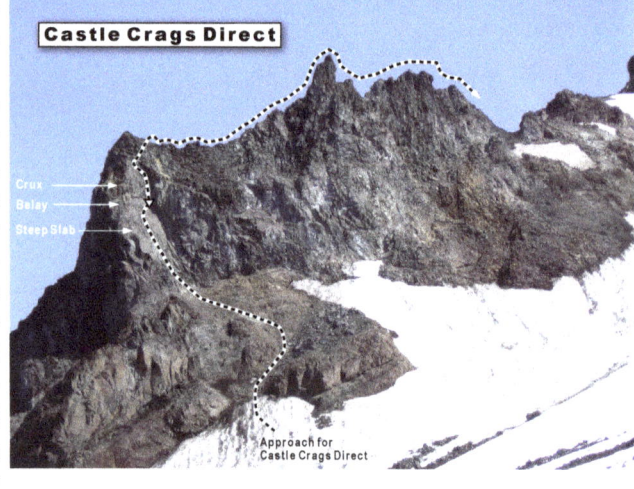

Descend around to the north side of Illumination Rock on snow past the first buttress toe to a snow slope at a minor ravine. This will place you directly under the southern natural skylight. Ascend minor crack corners and steep ledges aiming for the natural skylight along the ridgecrest. Expect a wild ride on rock covered rime and ice choked corners for two 60-meter pitches. Rappel the route or descend down the south side. A direct start variation (Skylight Direct M5) starts about 150' left of the regular start for Southern Skylight.

Illumination Rock rappel routes

The following is a brief analysis of the descent options on Illumination Rock. Only two descent routes are viable depending on your time commitment and the sweat collecting on your brow. The most commonly used rappel is also known as the South Chamber route. The other alternative is the NE Ridge descending down to Illumination Saddle. Neither is simple and both have inherent risks. Always bring a sufficient quantity of webbing for your planned descent. If in doubt about the safety of the rappel anchor consider bringing pitons or perhaps a bolt kit.

South Chamber rappel:

From the leaning summit block (highest point) follow the ridge crest southwest descending down around the massive gaping 'skylight' hole. Crawl back up onto the ridge crest and continue southwest to the very tip (200'+). Set up a sling belay/rappel point at the far west end of this ridge crest where it drops off into the void. The West Gable is visible from here.

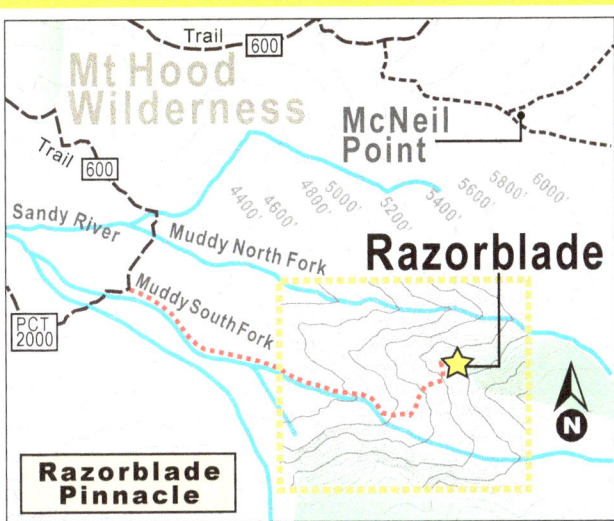

#1 Rappel 100': Rappel down toward West Gable, but initially aiming over toward the Reid Glacier side. Once around the very tip of the crest it will be quite apparent how easy it is to continue down direct to the West Gable. It is a 100' rappel down to the saddle at West Gable. **#2 Rappel 70':** Descend down toward the south chamber to a small stance at a rock horn. **#3 Rappel 70':** From the horn of rock rappel to a ledge with another sling festooned block. **#4 Rappel 80':** Descend down the ridge through a minor slot past a slab to a large ledge with a sling festooned block. **#5 Rappel 80':** Descend 80' to the inner left side of the South Chamber. Scramble down easy steps from here back to your packs at the base of the cliff. Or make another minor 80' rappel from blocks on the east side of the South Chamber.

NE Ridge rappel:

From the leaning summit block rappel or down scramble along the ridge crest toward Illumination saddle to an obvious sling festooned rock horn. Rappel onto the vertical Reid Glacier side (100') to a fixed bolt anchor on a ledge. Rappel again (150') along the ridge crest toward the saddle, down scrambling where feasible for the remaining portion.

RAZORBLADE PINNACLE

This superb isolated mountain jewel is a true alpine experience located at the 5700' level just below the Sandy Glacier. Separated by two deep river chasms, the profile of the Blade captivates all who tread near, while giving the climber a postcard perfect view of the stark west face of Mt. Hood.

Separated by two deep tributary chasms, the profile of the 'Blade' captivates all who tread near, while giving the climber a postcard perfect view of the stark west face of Mt. Hood. The first ascent was on 9-29-91 and the initial party was surprised to discover that this major summit deep in the heart of the Mt. Hood wilderness had never been climbed.

Directions

Approach by way of the Lolo Pass road (NF18). Take NF1828 near the McNeil-Riley campgrounds. The road winds uphill to a graveled side road leading to the Top Spur trailhead.

Hike the Top Spur trail, and then follow the Bald Mountain (Round the Mountain) trail south into the vast Sandy River basin. Take the southernmost drainage of the Muddy North Fork Sandy River. Follow the stream upward until the foreboding canyon walls steepen. Angle leftward up the steep hillside to the SW base of the Blade. To descend from the summit, rappel via an easy tree-to-tree descent on the south face of the crag (this can be done with a single 50m (165') rope. Expect a minimum of 3 hours to reach the base of the Razorblade Pinnacle.

1. Gillette Arête
5.10b ★★★

Pro to 2" including cams

Ascends the outer right corner of the western arête, and is a classic multi-pitch alpine climb. **P1 80':** Start by scrambling up a brushy leftward leaning ramp on the south face to a large fir tree, then step around tree 20' to the main notch that overlooks the north side chasm. **P2 90':** Embark straight up the prow following a crack system, and then surmount a slight overhanging bulge that has a good jam crack in it. Belay just above on a small ledge. **P3 100':** Step up right onto the next ledge, then up a slightly hung crack on a face (5.10b) then work up the outer edge of the arête, then on the right again to make the final

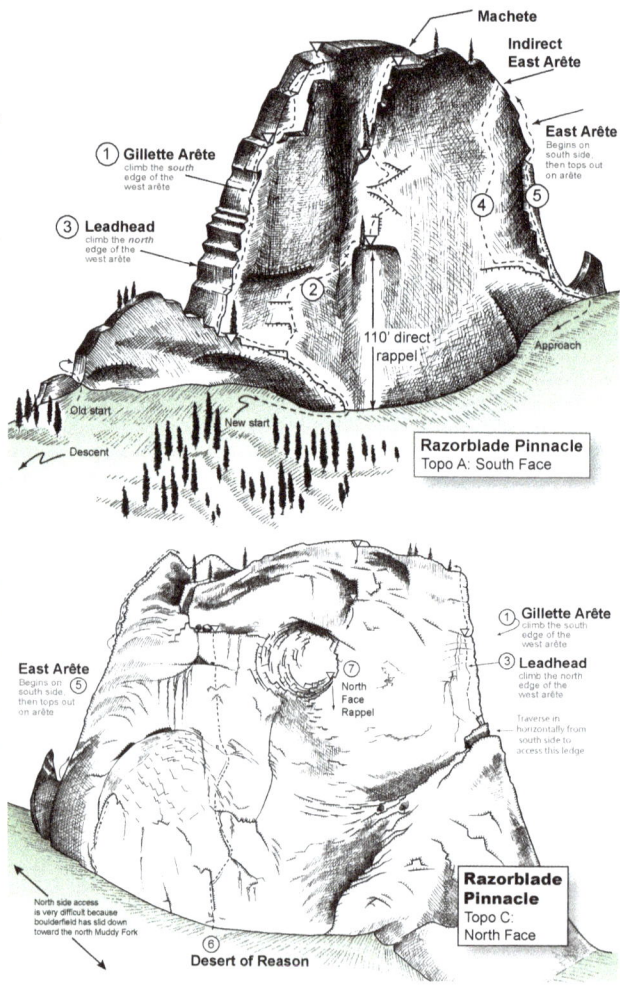

step onto a ledge. Belay from a small fir tree located near the edge of the north face up near the summit. Rappel down the south face by using the Machete route anchors.

2. **Machete 5.8** ★

Pro to 2" including cams

This is an interesting climb that ascends the sunny south side of the pinnacle and it is also the rappel route. **P1 80':** Start by scrambling up the obvious brushy ramp (mentioned above) to the large fir tree belay. **P2 70':** Step up right on steep ground (fixed pins) that quickly eases to a slab. Then angle up right ward, then smear directly right (crux) and up through some prickly bushes to the next belay just above a small cedar tree. **P3 40':** Zigzag directly up the wall above using a minor ramp to the next tree belay. **P4 30':** Then up an easy low angled chimney with steps in it that ends at the summit anchor.

3. **Leadhead 5.7 A3**

Pro: Pitons, nuts, and small cams

This is the outside left corner of the major west facing arête on the Razorblade. Begin at the notch on Gillette Arête, and step down and across an exposed traverse to a stance on a small pedestal. Belay here. Ascend the north face of this slightly overhanging out-

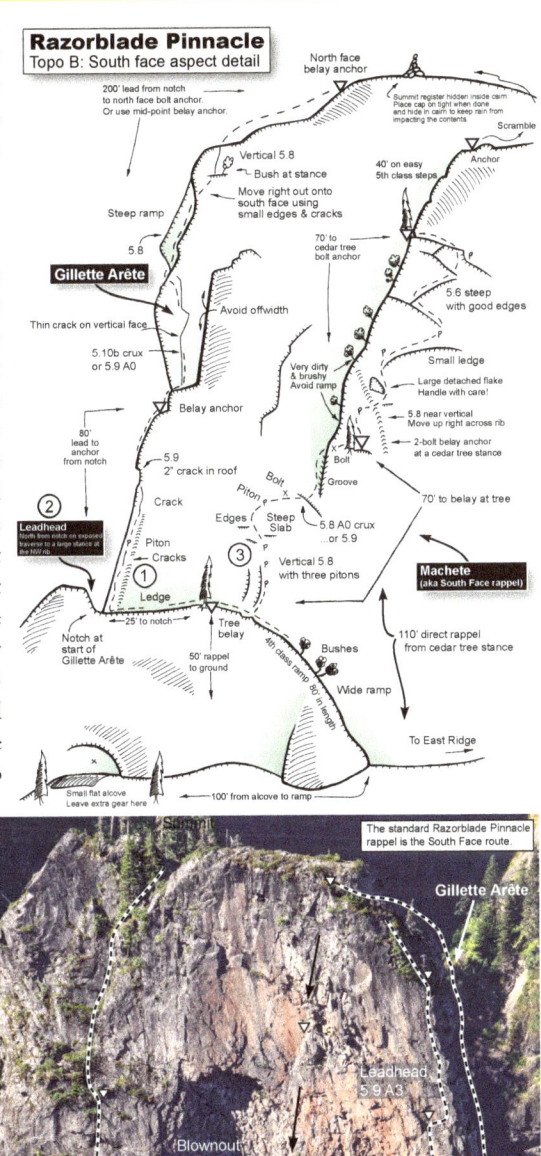

Top left: Pete G. on *Machete*
Top right: Base of *Gillette Arête*
Center: Kyle L. on *Machete*
Top center: Wayne on *Gillette Arête*
Lower Left: Steve on the *North Face*
Lower Right: Wayne on *Leadhead*

side corner via thin cracks and edges. Potential free route at 5.11.

4. **Indirect East Arête 5.8 R**

   An unappealing, exposed meandering line. An alternate option if you are desperate.

5. **East Arête 5.8 X**

   The lower ¼ portion of this route has loose rock.

6. **Desert of Reason IV 5.4 A4**

   Pro: Nuts to 1½", cams to 2", LA, KBs, Bugaboos, RURP's, hooks, and hangers
   This is an exhilarating, and fascinating ultra extreme nailing route that ascends the fabulous overhanging north face of the Blade. To the right of the route and high on the face is a blown out donut shaped rock scar. The Desert of Reason ascends the blank, overhung face to the left of this scar. The climb begins near the center of the north face in a short left leaning, left facing corner. Exit the corner onto a thin seam rightward that leads to a narrow left leaning ramp. Nail up left to the top of the ramp then upward to a hanging belay. The next lead continues up mostly blank sections of wall that offer hollow flakes, loose blocks, and incipient seams for nailing. Free the last 15' to the main ledge and rappel. Estimated height to the upper belay ledge is approximately 200'. The summit leans out from the base of the wall near the start of the route approximately 20'. The last 50' above the belay ledge is a steep unclimbed dirty corner system that leads to the summit.

Note: The extensive boulder field below the north face has slide downhill into the north Muddy Fork creek drainage. Expect difficult access to north side routes and expect the routes to be 25'+ longer.

HUNCHBACK WALL

The Hunchback Wall is an excellent rock climbers haven offering good climbs on a vertical 100' high wall composed of andesite rock. The technical nature of the rock climbing routes tend to make the place primarily suitable for experienced hard core face or crack climbers who are well honed at long, stout, sustained climbing. The site has a plethora of steep rock with powerful leads ranging from 5.10 to 5.13. The cracks luckily clock in at moderate ranges from 5.9 to 5.11 but are generally long and sustained in nature (and often very wide). The crag is convenient in its near proximity to Portland (1 hour drive) and has paved road access.

Hunchback Wall is nestled quietly in a tall wonderfully serene Douglas fir forest locale, sitting amongst tall 180' fir trees, never getting the direct blazing hot sunshine as other crags do. A gentle breeze generally keeps the place comfortable even on hot summer days (even when its 90°F) when other places are simply too muggy. This is a place where the sounds of nature predominate; no highway noise, and no boom box noise; instead you will find a quiet setting designed for those who relish quiet back woods climbing while still seeking high-end technical enduro rock climbs.

A Brief History

The site was initially explored by Don Gonthier, Craig Murk and friends in the early 90's. Craig and Don referred to the place as the Hunchback secret. Upon arrival during their first exploration of the crag they were impressed with the potential scope of the massive wall. They recruited several buddies, but kept the place in general secrecy. Some additional early partners were Clif and Justin. Don also invited several other folks to the cliff to join the adventure. Some of the friends in this original crew cut the original rough path all the way up to this wall, using a deer path for portions of the approach hike. They climbed a few routes, partly rap cleaned a few other lines, and rappeled down other sections of the bluff. The initial team though parted ways soon thereafter, and the place sat quiet until 2010 when a new generation of rock climbers found interest in the place. That crew found the Hunchback Wall to be a superb crag to fit their expectations of power climbing. Today another young generation of climbers have begun tackling HW anew.

Route Development

Route development requires patience because the cracks and face options are long and tend to be a bit mossy and dirty in places. Often the route project will be much harder than it appears, so if it seems like it might be a 5.10- anticipate it being a 5.10+. Fixed gear (bolts) are a common necessity if you plan to develop a new rock climb at Hunchback Wall.

Though the sloped terrace is quite grassy, there is some loose rock material which can jeopardize folks standing at the base of the wall. Most climbs are designed to end below the lip of the main cliff, thus avoiding the mossy, gravelly steep dirt slope of the midway terrace. By placing the belays on the steep face 10'-15' below the terrace it avoids displacing excessive amounts of dirt and moss and keeps the terrace in a virgin like state. Those persons hiking up to the midway sloped ledges to set up new projects will need to remain in close contact with their partners below. The vertical upper tier cliff is an impressive steep headwall buttress reaching an additional 80' higher above the lower 100' of main cliff that climbers use, but mixing the two tiers together (people on the ground and a person on the upper tier) is exposing everyone to potential rock fall risk problems. That upper tier has significant loose rock.

Directions

Drive east on U.S. 26 from Sandy, Oregon till you reach Welches. Turn south at the Subway store onto Salmon River Road (NF 2618). Continue about 9/10 mile south passing a guardrail on the right and a small rotten roadside bluff on the left, then a deeply cut water ravine exists also on the left. Park immediately on the west side of the road at a minor pullout. Step into the dry waterless ravine for a few yards, then angle up right onto the south slope into a grove of cedar trees. A faint path begins there and zigzags gently uphill, and gradually steepens for the remainder of the hike. The uphill hike is 25-minute approach time to reach the base of the wall so pace your hike well to avoid a sweaty over exuberant experience getting up there. The crag is split into two sections; the north Notre Dame Wall, and the Southern Wall (which has a classic amphitheater at the south end).

NOTRE DAME WALL

This very long main wall travels from the Central Ravine northward and gradually fades to low angle mossy sloped sections of minor bluff at the far north end of the main wall. The beta is described Left to Right (north to south):

1. **Critical Conundrum   5.10b/c**
★★★

Pro: 9 QD's, height 70'
Climb out an initial crux overhung bulge, up a brief short slab, then up

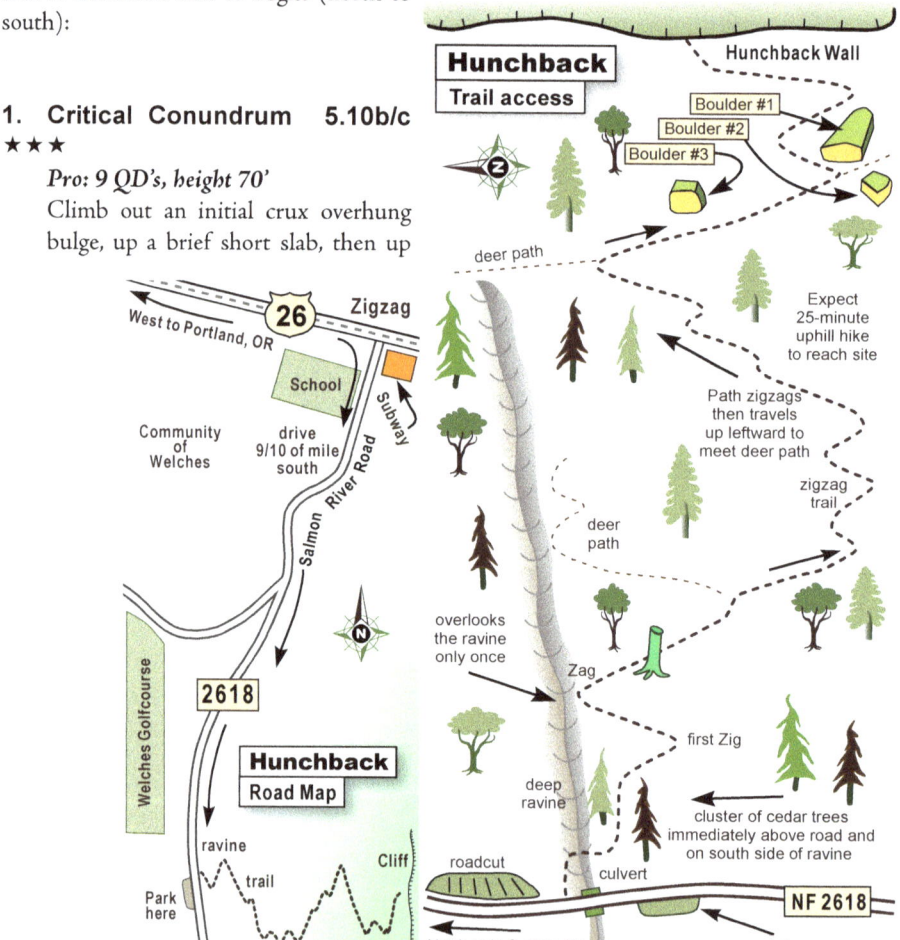

through a vertical second crux (bulge on your left), and up another brief short slab. At a slight overhung lip, power up onto a vertical final face on a minor prow that has incuts and positive holds all the way to the belay. Rap from belay.

2. **Tilting at Windmills 5.9**
   Pro: Nuts (to 1") and Cams (to 2.5"), height 70'
   Climb a prominent crack corner system (5.8) to a small midway stance (also used by next route), then bust out left over the crux bulge into the upper quality crack system.

3. **Metamorphosis 5.11c/d** ★
   Pro: 9 QD's, height 70'
   Start up initial easy small edges over the first bulge (5.8), then power over a second larger (crux 5.11d) overhung bulge. Continue up a rounded low angle prow (5.8) to a small flat stance (recompose your energy here), then power out a brief crux overhang (5.10c) up a vertical prow with incut edges to a high belay. Rappel. Note: 5-bolts on lower; 4-bolts on upper section.

4. **_____ P1 5.7, P2 5.8 [?]**
   Pro: __", height 40' (P1), height 70' (P1 & P2 total)
   Right angled crack system starting at the foot of a notable buttress. **P1**: Climb the crack to a very large midway ledge (belay). **P2**: Climb a short steep deep corner to another ledge belay. Rappel.

4b. **_____ 5.9 [?]**
   This is an alternate start leading up into the same double cracks.

5. **Mothership Supercell 5.11a/b** ★★
   Pro: 4 QD's, height 40'
   Step into first bolt from the right, then climb overhung face up past a giant gas pocket. Top half is delicate left handed side pulls, then easier exit moves to a large sloped ledge (belay).

6. **Meister Brau 5.6**
   Gear to 3.5" (or clip bolts), height 35' (P1), height 70' (P2 total from ground)
   Climb a short fun fat off width crack to a very big ledge and belay. Continue up the fat off width corner system to another higher belay. Rappel.

7. **Mirage 5.7** ★★
   Pro: gear to 2"
   Climb initial step, then (bolt) tricky right trending tiny ramp to stance (bolt), then up left via a thin face and crack to big ledge and belay.

8. **Oasis 5.10d** ★★
   Pro: 5 QD's, height 45'
   A thin techical face climb that stays sustained all the way to the ending on a small perched ledge. A quality route in a forested oasis. Shares same belay anchor with the next route..

9. **The Tallest Pygmy 5.11c** ★★★
   Pro: 4 QD's, height 45'
   The prominent and stellar overhung wild arête ending on a small perched ledge. Shares the same belay with the previous route.

10. **Lord Frollo 5.10a**
    Pro: .5" to 5" cams and nuts, height 65' (upper belay)
    Deep corner (5.9) crack off width system immediately behind the wild overhung arête. Climb up till it exits left at midway point to a belay. *The full length lead deal option*: continue up and power out a crumbly roof (5.10a) then up a short small crack to another

higher belay.

11. Axe with a Passion [aka AWAP] 5.8 ★★

Pro to 3" including cams, height: 65'

Start up onto a small stance, then climb up right on a thin jam crack passing a crux. At the first roof (bolts) the crack widens to a chimney. Finish up the chimney (bolts) to the belay anchor.

12. Abby Normal 5.9 ★

Pro: same gear as the Axe plus 3 more QD's

This extension launches off from the last bolt on AWAP and steps right out onto the vertical face and finishes to the anchor for the 5.12c.

13. Peloton 5.10c/d ★

Pro: gear same as Axe (plus QD's)

Climb AWAP, then at midway bust left (at 2nd AWAP bolt it's 5.11) and climb past a small lip up a vertical face. Note: If you move left at the 3rd AWAP bolt it's 5.10c/d.

14. The Magician 5.12+ ★★

Pro: 6 QD's, height 65'

A fascinating technical route with very thin crimps. This face route merges left onto the AWAP crack at mid height.

15. Magic 5.12c ★★

Pro: 9 QD's, height 75'

Prominent flat buttress formation near belay anchor. A powerful superb face route that begins on a broad face immediately left of S&E and launches up a flared crack on the vertical upper buttress face. Thin technical holds for a 10' crux section before easing slightly to better holds above a series of small lips, then up moderate terrain to the belay.

16. Slanted and Enchanted 5.10b ★★

Gear to 4" including cams (optional to 5"), (Singles up to .5 inch, triples 1 and 2 inch, otherwise doubles), height 65'

Climb up the leftward angling crack to a good rest stance. Power over a steep crux flared slot, and continue up past several more small lips to an anchor. Crux is wide, but the upper portions are nice hand jams to a technical face finish.

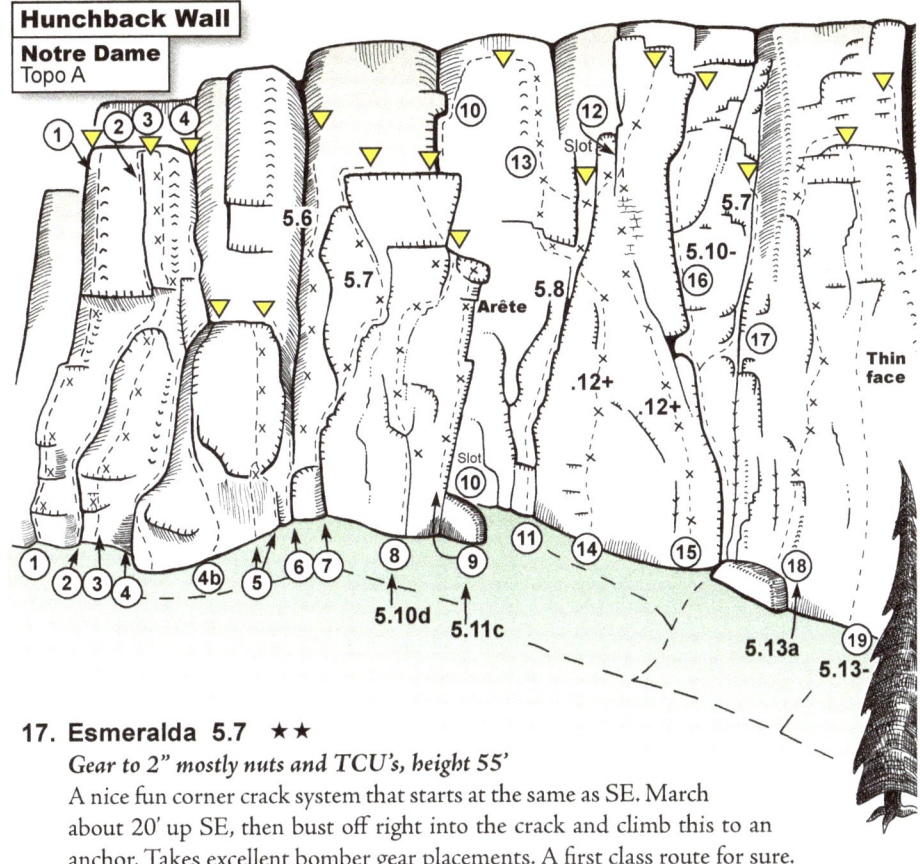

17. Esmeralda 5.7 ★★
Gear to 2" mostly nuts and TCU's, height 55'
A nice fun corner crack system that starts at the same as SE. March about 20' up SE, then bust off right into the crack and climb this to an anchor. Takes excellent bomber gear placements. A first class route for sure.

18. Quasimodo 5.12d ★★★
Pro: 8 QD's, height 60'
A burly techy thin face climb that starts with a stunning 4.5' long reach off a flake. Then very tricky balancy movement, followed by a snappy final crux at the lip where it is quite deceptive to line up for the final sequence.

19. _____ 5.13-
Another superb quality mega crimps power route.

20. Gypsy Dance 5.9 ★
Pro: .5" to 6" cams, Nuts to 1", height 90'
Nice long offwidth jam crack that angles up leftward on steep terrain. Good pro and mostly moderate 5.7 climbing except for a short crux section.

21. Archdeacon 5.10c
Pro: .5" to 7" cams, Nuts to 1", height 90'
Ascends a very wide vertical corner system. Eases at mid-height, then steepens again in a deep easy slot corner on the upper portion of the route. Rappel from a high belay.

22. _____ 5.12+ [?]
Potential face that goes over the upper large roof (well - maybe).

23. _____ 5.12+ ★★
Pro: 6 QD's, Height 60'
A superb technical power crimps face climb that goes through two large roofs.

24. Hangin' with the Hunch' 5.11b/c ★★
Pro: 7 QD's, height 60'
On the immediate right side of the double roof is a thin seem. A tough climb with powerful moves passing two roofs. The last portion eases but has a tricky exit to the anchor.

25. Murky Waters 5.10a ★★★
Pro: gear to 4" (includes cams), height 60'
One of the original routes established by the crew way back in the 1990s. A fine long technical and occassionally flared crack system with a belay at the mid-point on the cliff scarp. Rappel. The upper section is dirty (though its been led to the Zeno's belay).

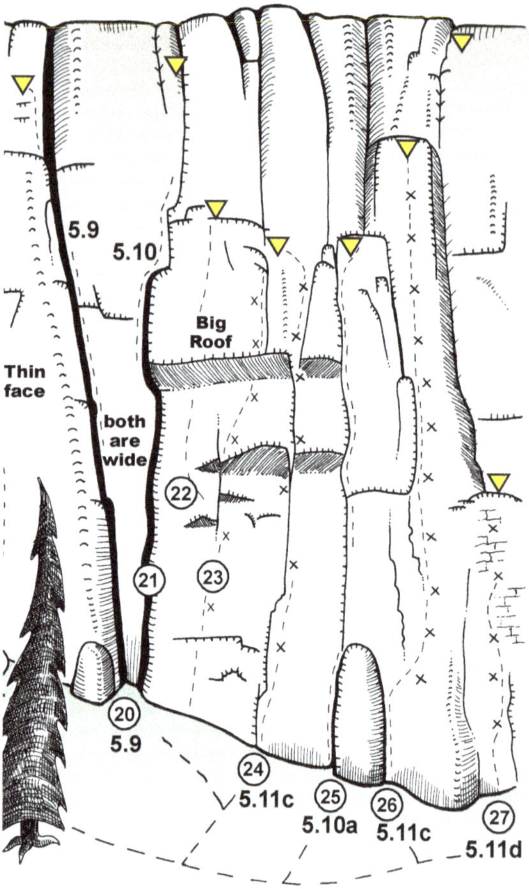

26. Zeno's Paradox 5.11c ★★
Pro: 11 QD's, Height 75'
A stellar technical climb. Start up the right side of a small pillar, then step onto the face and finesse through a very techy crux section till it eases at a flared crack. Prance up the flared crack using mostly nice edges and round features to a small perch below a minor lip (the Murky Waters route anchor immediately to the left). Step right (crux) onto a vertical face and send a double arete face that offers unique box-shaped flared seams for hand and foot holds.

27. Persistence Is Futile 5.11d ★
Pro: 5 QD's, height 40'
A short 40' very oddly techy climb on very flared box-shaped surface textured rock. Layback, then smear, layback then smear. Considered to be a unique challenge.

28. Plaid's Pantry 5.10b/c
Pro .5" to 6" cams, Nuts to 1", height 80'
A long crack with a prominent large ledge about 35' up, then continues up a long wide slot crack system to a belay near the top of the cliff. A midway belay and upper belay exist.

29. Phoebus 5.10- / 5.11a ★★
Pro: .5" to 6" cams, Nuts to 2", height 80'
Mixed gear/bolt free route. Climb initial part of the previous crack route to the ledge,

MT HOOD ROCK CLIMBS 389

then embark up right (bolts/gear) on a long face section with occasional gear placements..

30. Achilles 5.9 ★★
Pro: .5" to 6" cams, Nuts to 1", length 60'
A steep cool jam crack that punches over a small lip, and continues up a steep crack section on a high rounded rock pedestal ending at a belay anchor at 60'. Wide pro at top.

31. Djali 5.10b/c ★★
Pro: .5" to 4", Nuts to 1", length 60'
A excellent quality vertical jam crack ending at same belay as the previous route. An alternate direct boulder move face start is 5.11-.

32. Ho' Lotta Shakin' 5.11a ★★★
Pro: to 3.5" for main crack, then 4 QD's to finish, length 80'
Climb a cool right facing corner crack system that ends at a roof. Bust out right at the roof up past a stout crux at the first bolt, then continue up tricky face climbing (bolts) to the belay anchor.

33. Notre Dame 5.12b ★
Pro: 9 QD's, length 80'
A powerful crimps face climb immediately to the right of the previous jam crack.

34. _____ 5.9 (P1 & P2)
Pro: .5"to 6" cams (plus doubles large sizes), Nuts to 1", slings for blocks, length 100'
Climb a wide mossy corner that lands on a midway ledge (belay), then embarks up a second even wider chimney system to the top. Belay/rap using the Plaid's belay.

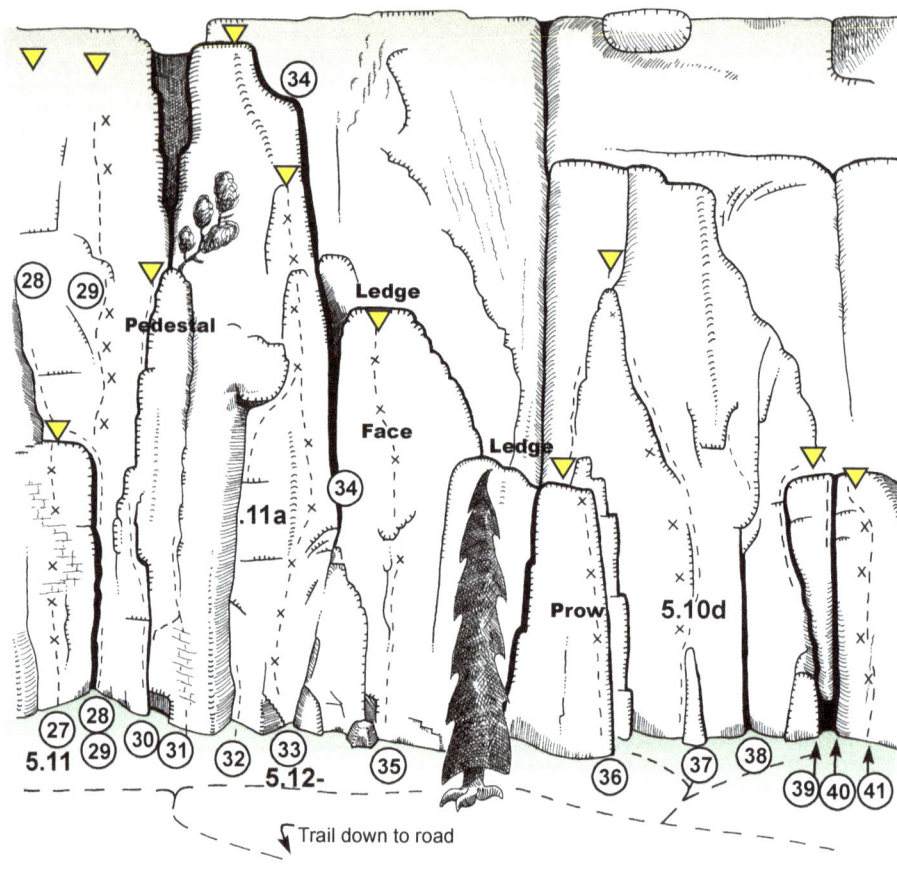

35. _____ 5.11+ [?]
Pro: 4 QD's, minor gear to .5", length 40'
Climb a short crack (use gear here), then move up right onto a face (bolts) as it ascends a slight overhung crimp featured scoop. Rappel from belay.

36. Three Martini Lunch 5.10d ★
Pro: 3 QD's, 35' length
A minor short arête that lands on a large belay ledge.

37. Cathedral 5.10d ★★
Pro: 5 QD's (plus minor 2" gear), length 50'
A quality route starting with a series of enjoyable face moves. The power crux climbing eases for a short bit at the short crack, then gets energetic for a final punchy ending near the belay.

38. _____ 5.__ [?]
Pro:
Short vertical jam crack that abruptly exits right and lands on a large belay ledge. An alternate second pitch will eventually embark up left onto a tall prominent face prow.

39. Victor 5.8 ★★
Pro: 2" to 6" cams, Nuts to 1", length 40'
This is the left deep flared groove (with aid bolts). The route ends on a large ledge with a

belay station.

40. Hugo 5.10c/d
Pro: 1" to 6" cams, Nuts to 1", length 40'
This is the right fat offwidth crack, of the two side-by-side flared offwidth cracks.

41. L a v e r n e 5.10b/c ★★
Pro: 4 QD's, length 40'
Power crimping on the flat vertical left aspect of a prominent tall rock outcrop formation with a large ledge. Rappel from belay.

42. _____ 5.__
Pro to 3", length 40'
Jam crack interspersed with minor steps and ledges. On right aspect of the same tall outcrop.

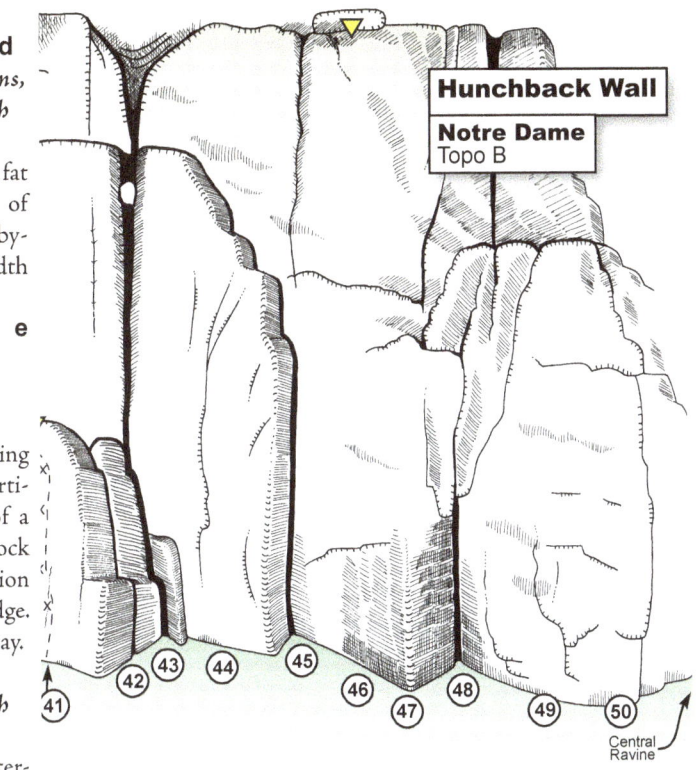

CENTRAL RAVINE
The Central Ravine gains access to several minor short lead routes scattered along the

inner aspects of the ravine system.

SOUTH WALL
From the Central Ravine southward is the grand South Wall, a very vertical formation with potential for single and multi-pitch lead routes, easy and stout.

SOUTH AMPHITHEATER
At the far south end of the South Wall you will find a superb major amphitheater for the grand finale. Some routes in this giant alcove lean in your face 5°- 10°, leaving a very naturally clean wall of hard core face, crack and incipient seam routes, perfect for a string of classic hardman climbs.

1. Hunch sack   5.10d / 5.11a   ★ ★ ★
Pro: 10-11 QD's
Superb climb on the left side of the stunning narrow fin arête. A low crux around the 4th bolt and a high crux on the last 2 bolts. Harder if you stay left, easier if you embrace the exposure and hang over the arête.

2. _____
Pro:
An unfinished project. The right side and overhung aspect of the fin arête.

3. _____
Pro:
A deep crack corner on left face of the amphitheater.

4. _____
Pro:
A crack on the center face of the amphitheater.

5. _____   5.12- [?]
Pro:
An impressive extreme looking seam on face.

6. Mellow Drama 5.10c   ★
Gear to 2", route has 7 bolts
Start up an easy wide crack ramp to where the headwall steepens following discontinuous cracks and ledges. Follow the thin steep crack to the top, avoid the overhang on the top by going to the right through the narrow chimney to the rap anchors. A 60-meter rope will just barely get you back to the ground.

7. _____

✧ MT HOOD ROCK CLIMBS   393

ENOLA (THE SWINERY)

Primary beta by Jim Tripp, Tymun Abbott and associates

Enola (aka The Swine, aka The Swinery) is a well-established crag that holds a sizable selection of steep rock climbs on a bluff that faces directly west overlooking the tiny community of Rhododendron.

The bluff is composed of Tertiary pliocene andesite (Ta1) and is surprisingly steep in places. The rock climbing routes and quality vary from small finger edge face climbs to sloping pocketed sections interspersed with larger edges. A variety of climbing routes exist such as pure face routes while others are traditional crack climbs using natural/mixed pro. The climbing routes are typically 50' to 100' in length. The crag is well-suited for climbers who have solid 5.10 to 5.11 leading capabilities. The lesser traveled 5.9-and-under routes (and there are plenty) tend to be a bit mossy and dirty from lack of use. A few route names and ratings are not known at this time.

Seasonally the crag is generally limited to Oregon's reasonably good summer weather (May to late October) as it receives the brunt of most weather systems arriving from the west. Yet a mild breeze rolls up through the trees from the valley below the crag keeping the temperatures comfortable all season while generally keeping various pesky insects away.

Cliff Sections

This guide sub-divides the entire wall into recognizable sections for easy reference. The initial upper wall at the overlook is called Sunset Wall. The popular middle wall (with its stellar classics) is the Moonshine Wall (the alcove). A hidden Bench Area branches up left from the alcove on a steeply zigzagging trail. The North Point Wall is located about 400'

Dave leading *Burning Tree*, Enola Hill

394 CHAPTER 4 ✦ ORC

northward along a path from the second wall.

Directions
Drive east of Rhododendron 1¼ miles, then turn left onto road 27. Follow the paved portion east, then back up west on a very rough gravel road to the upper west most bend in the road at the 3000' elevation (total of 2⅓ miles from highway). Park on a small dead-end side spur road in a thick stand of fir trees.

From the forested parking area follow a level trail one minute west to a viewpoint overlooking the community of Rhododendron. Immediately below your feet is the Sunset Wall. Follow a narrow descending trail northward that zigzags down below the Sunset Wall.

SUNSET WALL (UPPER WALL)
The climbing routes are listed as if you are descending the trail. The first route described is the long arête climb on the left of the Sunset Wall.

1. **Pig's Knuckles 5.11d ★★**
   Length: 100', Pro: 8 QD's
   This is the bolted arête on left side of the wall. Great climb involving technical steep face climbing. Reachy mid section, and balancey on upper arête.

2. **Pigs Nipples 5.11a ★★**
   Length: 100', Pro to 2½" including cams & doubles
   This is a stellar crack that climbs a corner system to the immediate right of the arête. Route involves a tenuous layback through the middle crux section.

3. **Forbidden Zone 5.10a**
   Length: 90', Pro: nuts and cams to 2"
   This is the left direct crack leading up and right to merge with Tibbets.

4. **Tibbet's Crack 5.12a**
   Length: 90', Pro: nuts and cams to 2"
   A deceptively difficult crack system that starts under the left corner of a roof and powers up a tenuous thin crack. Merges with FZ.

   MOONSHINE WALL
   Continue to descend steeply down a narrow trail to the next wall. The first climb is next to a large maple tree. A short distance further lands at the main area. This wall offers a comprehensive selection of routes ranging from quality 5.9 routes, pumpy 5.10 routes, to stellar crimper 5.12 face routes. The alcove is the place where most first-time climbers come in order to experience the invigorating flavor of Enola.

5. **Calm Before The Storm 5.7**
   Length: 40' Pro: 4 QD's
   This is a nice climb on a fairly steep face that follows next to a minor crack on the upper part. Start behind a large maple tree.

6. **Granny's Got A Gun 5.12b**
   Length: 75' Pro: 8 QD's
   This climb is located to the immediate right of the toe of a minor sunny buttress that overlooks a boulder field. This climb zooms up positive holds to a 'knock-you-in-the-head' powerful crux move punching through the outer right edge of the overhang then merges into the classic Burning Tree route.

7. **Burning Zone 5.10c ★★★**
   Length: 75' Pro: 8 QD's
   This is considered to be one of the best routes at Enola. This stellar line gets plenty of sunshine in the afternoon hours. Climb starts at the toe of a minor buttress and ascends tricky face edges then angles up right above the lip of the large roof on good holds. Finish up a very steep rounded nose on interesting face holds.

8. **Samurai 5.10c ★★**
   Length: 75' Pro: 8 QD's
   This fine route branches up left from Burning Zone at the 3rd bolt, and continues directly straight up to its own belay. The crux is on BZ so this variant offers interesting face climbing that eases as you get near the belay station.

9. **Meatloaf 5.10c ★★**
   Length: 75' Pro: 8 QD's
   This high quality climb is completely independent to its anchor. Start just left of Burning Zone and climb up next to a bush, then gingerly surmount the wobbly block, and continue up sustained face climbing to a belay station.

10. **Hillbilly Hot Tub 5.12c ★**
    Length: 45' Pro: 4 QD's
    An extreme thin face climb immediately to the right of Scorpion.

Dave leading *Fifty-seven*

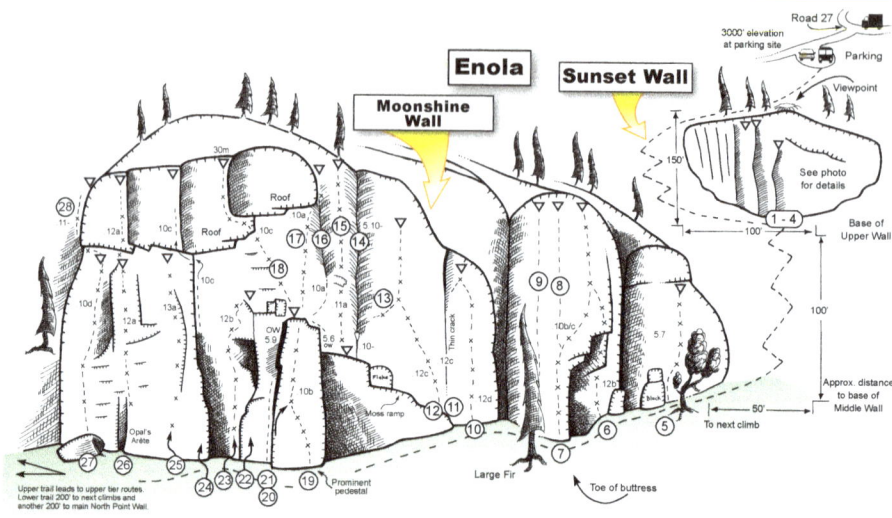

11. Scorpion BBQ 5.12c ★★★
Length: 45'
Pro: #3 TCU, #1 WC rock, #00 TCU (opt.), #5 nut, #0 TCU, 1½" Cam

A powerful thin seam lacking in real holds this quality climb is composed of painful side pulls, smears, crimps and long reaches. The climb eases at the bolt so don't peel off during the last few moves. Just use a biner on each pro piece.

12. Fifty-seven 5.12c ★★
Length: 70', Pro: 7 QD's

As in AGE fifty-seven not Heinz. A fierce edgy face climb that powers up left from the seam. Merges with the next route. Starts at the base of the grass ramp. The rating is based upon avoiding the thin vertical seam of Scorpion BBQ. This route merges into the upper portion of route #10.

Access the next three climbs on a long grass ramp ledge system by utilizing a belay anchor at a stance immediately above the large flake.

13. Serpentine Arête 5.10a
Length: 60', Pro to 2" then QD's

Scramble up the grass ramp past the large flake to a belay stance. Power up a vertical crack over the chock stone (crux) wedged in the crack, and then angle up RIGHT on the bolt line that ascends a vertical face. This route merges with the route Fifty-Seven.

14. The Easy Way 5.10a
Length: 60', Pro to 3" plus small cams & nuts

Walk up the ramp and hop up past the large flake to a belay stance at a single bolt.
Power past the initial chockstone (crux) wedged in the crack. Finish directly up the vertical minor

Brian is in for another Twenty Years 5.10b

crack corner system (5.9) on good edges and smears.

15. Calf's Gash 5.10c
Length: 60', Pro: QD's
From the same ramp belay stance power up past two bolts on a vertical flat face (crux), then power over a large block with a crack in it. Balance up a steep smooth face using delicate smears (bolts) to the belay anchor.

Access the next three climbs from the belay anchor on top of the prominent pedestal.

16. Mr. Hair of the Chode 5.10a PG
Length: 60', Pro to 2"
From the belay anchor at the top of the pedestal, step hard right and climb a poorly protected crack system with jug holds. The protection gets better the higher you climb. Exit past the right side of the roof to a belay anchor.

17. Jugalicious 5.10a ★★★
Length: 60', Pro: 5 QD's
One of the great quality routes at Enola totally worth doing. From the belay anchor at the top of the pedestal climb up RIGHT (bolts) using positive holds. Exit past the right side of the roof (crux) to a belay anchor.

18. SOTT P2 5.10c ★★★
Length: 60', Pro: 6 QD's & minor cams to 2"
This is P2 of Swine of the Times. From the belay anchor at the top of the pedestal climb up LEFT (bolts) on vertical terrain. Balance out left through the upper roof (some minor hollow rock) then continue climbing a vertical face (cam pro) to a belay anchor. A classic warm-up route when connected with the face climb on the outer side of the prominent pedestal.

The following two routes start at the base of the prominent pedestal at the 'Cove.

Tymun leading Grits & Gravy

19. Jethro 5.10b ★
Length: 50', Pro: 6 QD's
Face climb on the outer portion of the prominent pedestal. Climb direct from the ground on vertical face edges (bolts) all the way to the belay at the top of the pedestal. The first move can be protected with a small cam if needed.

20. Swine of the Times 5.10b ★
Length: 50', minor pro to 2" & QD's
This starts up Fat Crack, then steps right to send the last 3 bolts on the outside of the pedestal. Continue up to the ledge on a pedestal. SOTT pitch two launches off the top of the pedestal up left through a series of overhangs. Last moves need minor 2" pro.

21. Fat Crack 5.9
Length: 50', Pro: 2½"
Climb the obvious off-width on the left side of the pedestal. Usually top-roped. Another top-rope on a flat face just left of Fat Crack is called **Prohibition** 5.12c (TR).

22. Tipsy McStagger 5.11d
Length: 50', Pro: gear to 1", including small micro-cams
Climb the wide broken corner to a short left facing corner capped by a roof. Power over the lip and up a very thin crack (crux) till it eases onto a small ledge at a belay.

22b. Fortune Cookie 5.12b
Length: 50', Pro: 5 QD's
Climb a face just right of the previous route. Thin crux face sequence on upper ¼.

23. Grits & Gravy 5.12b
Length: 50', Pro: __ QD's
A wild face climb that balances up delicate face moves to a slight lip. The 'gravy' portion is below the small lip. The grits portion ensues at the lip where you must pull on small rounded edges and non-existent foot smears (crux).

This area is the very heart of the Alcove where most climbers congregate to plan for action.

24. Too Cool 5.10c ★★★
Length: 90', Pro: 3"
This is the stellar and obvious dihedral corner crack climb in the very center of this wall. The route powers directly up the crack on relatively holds, then launches into a small overhang. Move out and up left on precarious terrain to a tight stance, then out left again through the giant roof and then finish up a vertical corner groove to the anchor. Easy to get flamed out by the end of the climb at the top.

25. Psycho Billy Cadillac 5.13a ★★★
A powerful series of committing sequential moves utilizing the outer arête edge of a nearby dihedral. A strenuous series of crimps through the crux require excellent body core balance to connect the difficult string of moves.

26. Opal's Arête 5.12a ★★★
Length: 60' (P1), Pro: 7 QD's
Opal's Arête is considered to be one of the great classic routes at Enola. It is a tribute to the late Opal who owned what used to be called the "Food & General Store" in Rhododendron.

Ascend an initial short slot then launch up on a vertical smooth face using tiny edges and sharp knobby pockets. Use one of the methods listed below to power through the crux, then from a nice stance move either up right or up left for one move then clip into the belay anchor. Rappel.

Opal's Arête has several methods for ascent, so pick your style and go for it.

From the fifth bolt plant your right foot high onto a long narrow rail and using the right facing vertical rib pull up by rocking up onto your right foot.

Other option: From the fifth bolt plant an initial right foot on something, then reach out LEFT to the left arête. Slap up both blunt arêtes until you can stand on a narrow sloping right foot edge to clip the next bolt. Use the method that best suits your skill level, core body strengths and structure.

From the sixth bolt lean out left to use the left arête, or stay in close to the right rib.

Sea Hag Roof extension (5.12a) is the roof above Opal's Arête. Continue a few moves up from the belay anchor and climb out a large roof past 3 bolts.

27. Twenty Year Hangover 5.10d
★★★

Length: 60', Pro: 5 QD's

Twenty Year Hangover is certainly one of the more popular climbs at Enola. The route uses a minor crackless corner immediately left of Opal's Arête. The route has many unique face edges and pockets.

28. _____ 5.11a

Length: 25', Pro: 4 QD's

This route launches out up left from the belay anchor on 20YH around the left edge of the large upper roof to an upper anchor.

THE BENCH

This section can be accessed by a steep trail which starts next to Twenty Year Hangover. The trail zigzags uphill to a shaded steep wall

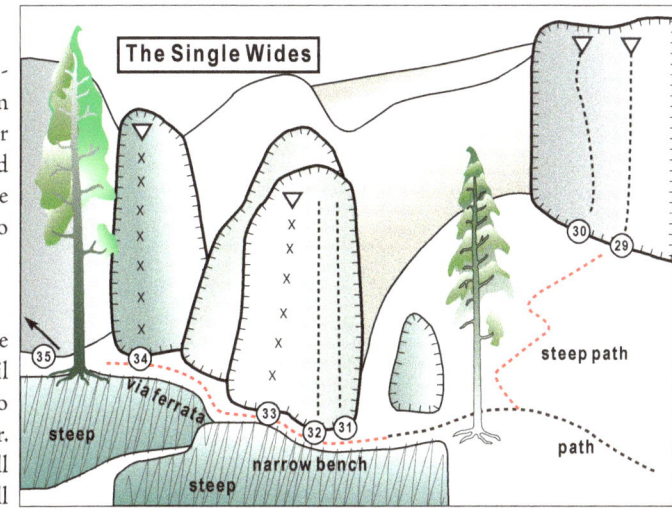

(80' tall) with the following two routes on it.

29. _____ 5.11 [?]
Length: 80', Pro to [?]
Climbs up steep face and crack corners, then powers through a bulge.

30. The Fang 5.10a
Length: 80', TR
Climbs up a steep face using minor seams, and then cruises up a crack on the left side of the overhang to the belay anchor.

The Single Wides Area

A string of routes along a narrow Via Ferrata ledge system are available by walking halfway up toward the Bench area and then stepping to the left. Each buttress along this ledge is tall like a bunch of single wide trailers stood up on end.

31. Shine 5.12d ★
Length 60', Pro: 5 QD's
A technical thin face climb on the right south facing aspect. The OW to its right has been TR'd and goes at 5.8.

32. White Lightning 5.11c ★★★
Length 60', Pro: 7 QD's
Climb past a prominent pocket up a rounded face through a techy thin crux at midheight. Thought to be one of the best routes here. FA: TA 2012.

33. Single Wide 5.12a ★★
Length 60', Pro: 6 QD's
A difficult face climb on the left side of the first tall buttress along a narrow ledge system.

34. Moonshiners Arête 5.13b/c
Length 60', Pro: 7 QD's
A face climb on the second pillar along this ledge. Start next to a large fir tree. Ascends a series of strenuous wave shaped features on the steep buttress. FA: TA 2012.

35. Tailgater 5.12a
Length 60', Pro: mixed QD's and gear to 2"
This is on the far left end of the Via Ferrata. Climb corner crack, step left to ramp, climb up ramp to upper left corner of ramp, then around a corner crux to nice crack on left headwall, then up crack to belay.

NORTH POINT WALL

Walk north from the middle wall for about 200' on a flat trail that follows the base of a mossy rock bluff. The trail ends at a steep rock scarp (see diagram). It has a small selection of climbing options that guide you up to several belay anchors on a higher ledge.

Reach the next three rock climbs via 5.4 easy steps to a belay anchor.

36. King of the Moes 5.9 ★★
Length: 120', Pro to 2½" including cams
Dash up the easy steps to the ledge anchor. Embark up left (bolts) then move up right under a large nose-shaped prow, and continue up a right facing thin crack system to the top. Rap from anchor.

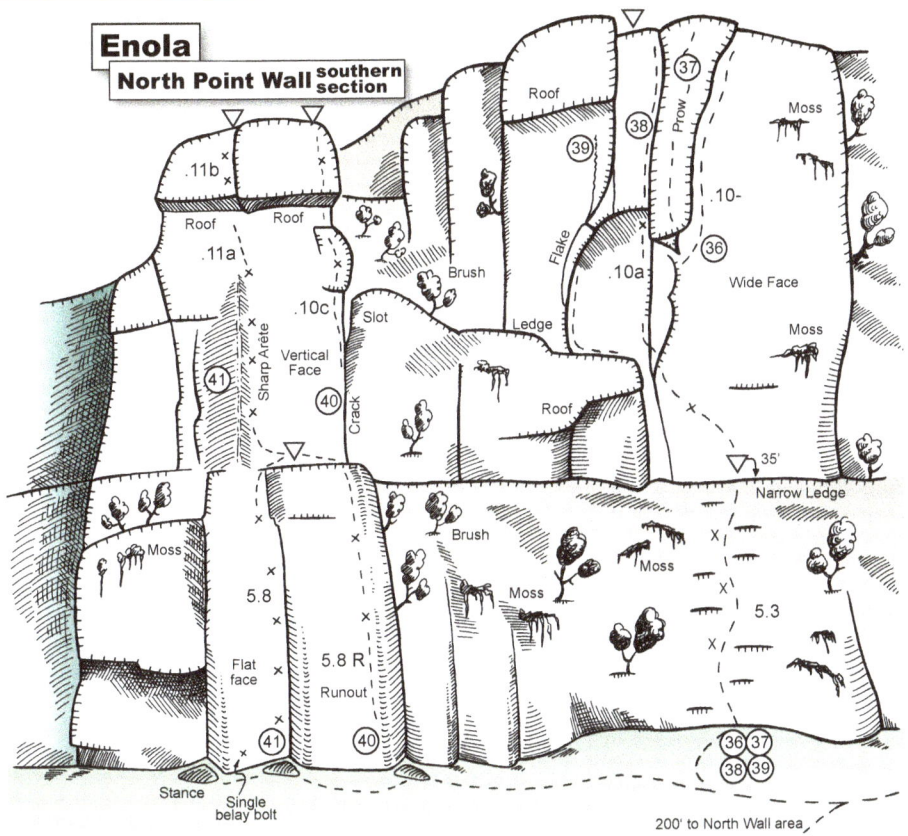

37. _____

Length: 60'

A potential route that can tackle the overhanging prow.

38. Dismantled Fears 5.10a ★★

Length: 60', Pro to 3"

From the ledge belay anchor launch up left on a face past 3 bolts to a crack, then climb up under a large roof (bolt). Power out the roof and up the double cracks above to an anchor.

39. _____

A potential thin seam starts up a right arching crack then punches up onto a steep blank face, but awaiting a potential buyer.

Access the next two climbs at the furthest point on this cul-de-sac trail.

40. Tres Hombres P1 5.8 R (avoid), P2 5.10+

Length: 40' 1st pitch (avoid), 50' 2nd pitch, Pro to 3" including cams

The first 40' is a mossy runout 5.8 R to the ledge with an anchor. Avoid this first pitch until someone safely fixes and cleans the climb better. Best to use the next 5.8 route to access a midpoint belay ledge (see topo). From the belay launch up right in a stiff 5.9 flared

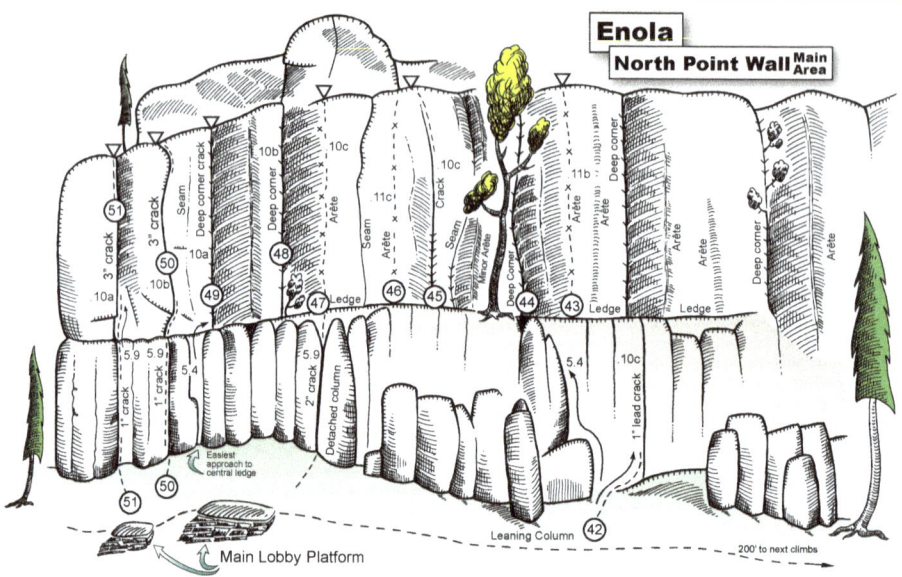

crack to a stance, then onto an odd arête (bolt) over a crux bulge (bolt) to the anchor.

Access the next climb from a single bolt belay stance on the ground at the very end of a narrow trail.

41. Welcome to the Swine P1 5.8, P2 5.11c ★★★
Length: P1 40', P2 50', Pro: P1 has 5 QD's, P2 has 8 QD's
A stellar arête climb considered to be one of the better routes at Enola. Walk out to the very end of the narrow trail to an exposed belay perch stance at a single bolt. The belayer should set up a belay here. Ascend up a delicate steep 5.8 face climb (bolts) to a large ledge with a belay anchor. Power up left onto the arête (5.11a) to a tiny no-hands rest stance under the roof. The crux roof is a height dependent (5.11c) inobvious riddle to solve. After you surmount the roof continue to an anchor at the top of the cliff.

The trail descends northward at an angle for about 100' then continues horizontally another 100' to a main amphitheater.

NORTH POINT WALL - MAIN AMPHITHEATER
The base of this wall has an open slightly contoured amphitheater with a string of twelve steep crack and face routes to select from (see topo). This section is broken by a midway horizontal ledge system which is very narrow on the left but is a wider ledge system for the routes on the upper right. The routes on the upper right tier can be accessed by several gear lead starts (see topo).

42. PB Direct 5.10c
Length: 40', Pro to 2"
Start up a 2" wide jam crack (5.10c) on the lower tier to a ledge & belay. Or squeeze up behind some blocks (5.4) just to the left of the thin crack.

43. Plum Butt 5.10d
Length: 40', QD's
From the midway ledge climb the quality bolted route on a double arête.

44. Thin & Lovely 5.10b
Length: 40', Pro to 1"
A thin seam crack corner system near a large maple tree.

45. This ain't yo momma's five-nine 5.9
Length: 40', Pro to 2½"
A vertical crack corner system.

46. The Plum Arête 5.10d
Length: 40', Pro: 5 QD's & gear
A bolted arête face climb with minor gear placements at the last move near a tree belay.

47. Plumberette 5.10+
Length: 40', QD's
A nice bolted climb on a minor rounded prow.

48. _____
Length: 60', Pro __
A steep crack corner system.

49. _____
Length: 60'
A deep corner crack system immediately above the initial rock step. Not developed.

50. EMF middle 5.9
Length: 60', Pro to 3"
This line ascends a thin 1" crack to a minor stance, and then launch into a slight bulge following a wide crack corner.

51. EMF left 5.9
Length: 60', Pro to 3"
A nice long wide jam crack on the left side of the main arena that ascends a thin 1" crack then powers into a wider crack on a vertical wall.

Tymun leading Psycho Billy Cadillac

KIWANIS CRAG

KC is truly a roadside crag with zero hiking distance. Composed of vertical Andesite the crag offers climbers a smattering of a dozen 40' tall top-ropes or lead climbs ranging in difficulty from 5.6 to 5.11+. The climbs are mostly crimpy face climbs or positive incut jug holds. Some routes take reasonable gear placements, while others are fully bolted routes or mixed bolt/gear leads. There are plenty of belay anchors, but for some routes you will need to sling a tree to belay.

The nature of the bluff is a short flat slice of well-worn smooth surfaced Andesite that is quite solid, but has a bit of moss on the infrequently traveled routes. Perhaps more climbers visiting KC will help to make this site more user friendly. The entire main wall tilts in-your-face about 2°, but each routes difficulty really depends on the size and quantity of holds. This particular grade of grainy surfaced Andesite is great for friction. Do not drop any gear (water bottles, belay device) because a roaring little stream (south fork Little Zigzag creek)is just beneath your feet a few steep yards away from the crag. Perhaps you know...what are the route

404   CHAPTER 4   ✧   ORC

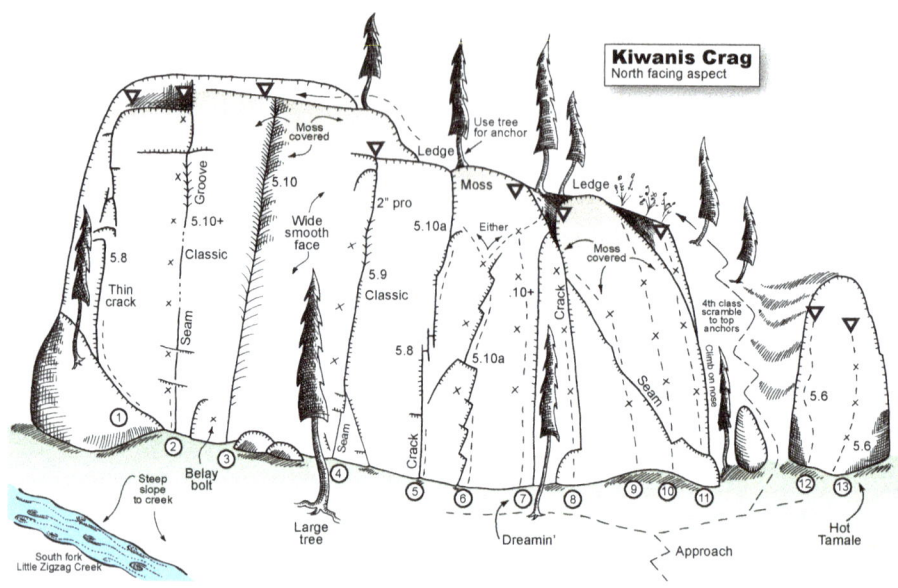

names and the other ratings?

Directions

Drive east of Rhododendron on US 26. Take #39 Road which travels east along the north side of Laurel Hill. Drive 1 mile along this road. Before you reach the Kiwanis Campground a small stream splits and runs under the road. The crag is located immediately south of the road next to the stream culvert. The site is ½ mile west of Kiwanis Campground, and ¼ mile east of the gravel road for Paradise Park Trailhead #778. Park alongside the road in a wide spot and have at it.

If you drove right past the little bluff on the way up #39 Road, don't be surprised. If you drive away even after locating the crag...again, don't be surprised. KC is not a destination crag, but the climbs will certainly keep you focused for a few hours.

The routes are described from left to right (see diagram).

1. **Newlywed 5.8 ★**
    The far left route smears up to a tiny tree, then dances up small edges (crux) to an anchor on a ledge. Using the tree reduces the rating to 5.8. It might be 5.9 without it. The crack is not easy to protect so leading it is not logical.
2. **Kiwanis Klassic 5.10c/d ★★★**
    Pro: 7 QD's and optional pro to ¾" (cams)
    The classic climb at KC and a must-do for everyone. Starts with balancy 5.9, then powers up a slightly hung face crux. As you near the upper pod slot do a crossover, then walk up into the pod. The final bulge is 5.9 and can be pinch smeared on the right to avoid the mantle onto the belay ledge.
3. **_____ 5.10- ★**
    Pro:
    A steep crack, but usually damp because of moss near the top (so clean it out). There is a single belay bolt at the start of this crack climb.

4. _____ 5.9 ★★★
   Pro to 2"
   Excellent lead route that starts with bolts and ends of natural gear. Powers up mostly positive jug holds and incuts on steep ground to a challenging ending.
5. **Sumthng Mssing 5.10c** ★★
   Pro to 1½" (cams are helpful)
   Starts as a great solid 5.8 then punches into a .10+ near the top. A bit mossy at the top.
6. **Kosmos 5.10b/c** ★★
   Pro: QD's (minor gear to 1½" if exiting left)
   A great starting climb with positive holds. At the third bolt you either break left (gear) or break right to #7 route to finish. Both exits are powerful and difficult.
7. **Dreamin' 5.10+**
   Pro: 4 QD's
   Although not a logical line, the difficulty focuses on a difficult series of balancy moves. Not easy to consistently stay with the line of bolts, but that's what makes it .10+. And the tree is very close!
8. _____ 5.9+
   Pro: 3 QD's and minor gear to 2"
   A prominent bolted closed up crack system that powers up good holds but ends in a widening slot with a bit of moss groveling to finish.
9. _____ 5.9 [?]
   A two bolt line that catches a seam mid-way up the face, then angles left to join route #8. Too much moss.
10. _____ 5.9 [?]
    A three bolt line that aims directly up through the dense moss madness.
11. _____ 5.7 [?]
    A three bolt line that aims directly up the nose at the far right edge of the cliff formation. Too much moss.

The last two climbs are on a small rounded knoll

12. _____ 5.6
    A project or perhaps it is already done?
13. **Hot Tamale 5.6** ★
    Pro: 3 QD's
    A surprisingly reasonable short route.

CASTLE CANYON

Castle Canyon trail #765 is a mere .9 mile gentle uphill hike (400' elevation gain) in a nice forested setting ending at a cluster of pinnacles composed of light colored volcanic breccia ash flow conglomerate. The rock is a sandy matrix with various sized rocks and boulders embedded with ledges covered in moss and grass. Potential hand holds simply come loose in your hand. The pinnacles are not your typical formations that one might desire to climb due to the detachable nature of the holds.

For those desperate few who relish the adventure here is some beta.

There are three primary pinnacles. There are narrow ridge features that provide tricky traversing along for views and some of these might offer further exploratory climbing. The First Lower Pinnacle is obvious as the trail weaves around its east flank and up to the saddle on the uphill side. The Second Pinnacle is just west of this first pinnacle, and is rather massive in size, standing nearly 150' on its longest side. The Third Pinnacle is a few steps up the trail and is quite apparent to the immediate east of the trail. It is like a cigar standing on end with a cannonhole next to it. Another minor point of rock exists on the far side of the third pinnacle. The trail ends on a narrow rib that overlooks the Second Pinnacle and offers great views of the valley.

Drive on U.S. 26 to Rhododendron, Oregon and then take a narrow paved road northwest of the community for ½ mile to the trailhead. A few yards up the trail you will enter the wilderness boundary. Since these rock pinnacles lack cracks (for gear) and has very, very old fixed gear, you might consider bringing an adequate selection of tools to get you up the pinnacles.

First Pinnacle 5.6 X
FA: Jim Nieland and Libby Kramm in 1969
Jaunt up the north rib past a bulge and cut up around left to top up.

Second Pinnacle 5.4 X
FA: Bill Cummins, Janet Marshall and Jim Nieland in 1968
Their original method of ascent was from the viewpoint but it is also feasible from as shown in the diagram to the saddle with the tree.

Third Pinnacle 5.4 X
FA: Jim Nieland and Libby Kramm in 1969
Start at the cannonhole and chimney up the space between the main wall and the cigar shaped pinnacle to a stance. Cut up around the east side to top up.

KINZEL TOWER

The Kinzel Tower is perched on the steep spruce covered slopes above the Still Creek drainage. Kinzel Tower area has been used lightly by climber's since the early 1950s. The second ascent of the cigar shaped Conkling's Pinnacle was in October 1951 by R. Conkling and Bud Frie.

To get there from Government Camp take the first road east of the State maintenance yard that leads down toward Trillium Lake. Take the surprisingly bumpy road F.S. #2613 southwest past Veda Lake trail, and on toward Kinzel Lake. The road is 10 long, slow miles, so expect 45-60 minutes driving

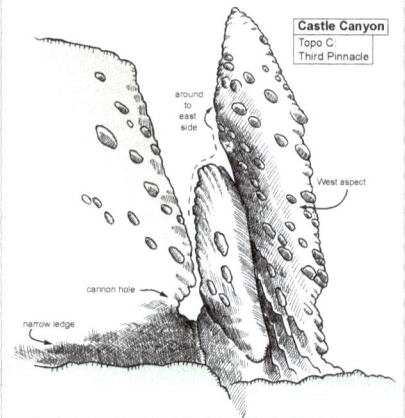

Libby Kramm on the Second Pinnacle (Castle Canyon)

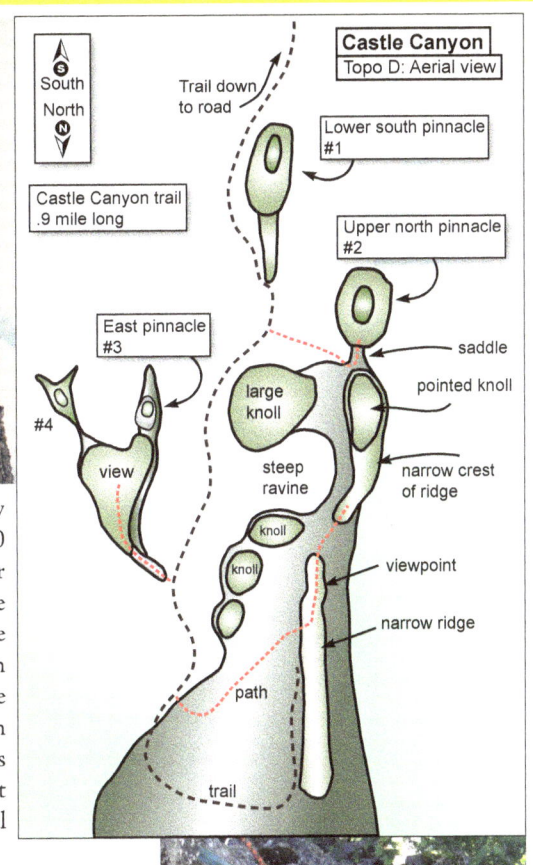

time from Government Camp. Follow the trail toward Devil's Peak about 10 minutes till you see the tower of your right. The main wall is on the east side including Conkling's Pinnacle. The tower is vertical on the east side, even radical in places. Most of the routes are ground-up affairs, and protection can be quite minimal at times so bring pins and bolts. The scramble to the summit from the south has a short 5.3 vertical section.

1. **Conkling's Pinnacle 5.8+**
   Length: 35' Pro: 4 QD's and minor gear to 1"
   A great, little thumb of rock with a few dicey moves near the top. A worthy ascent for everyone.

2. **Squeaky Alibi 5.8+**
   Length: 120', Bring hangers and pro to 3" including cams
   Ascends the right facing corner on the overhung NE face of the main tower, 50' from Conkling's Pinnacle. Excellent corner climbing that leads to a section of face climbing on delicate moves near the anchor.

Zac Reisner climbing on Conkling's Pinnacle

3. **Butterfly 5.9**
   Length: 120', Bring hangers and pro to 3½" including cams
   Nice route that starts same as SA, then angles up right to a belay on a ledge. Step up left, meander up technical ground then finish up 5.*easy* terrain near the anchor.

4. _____
   Unclimbed steep dihedral corner.

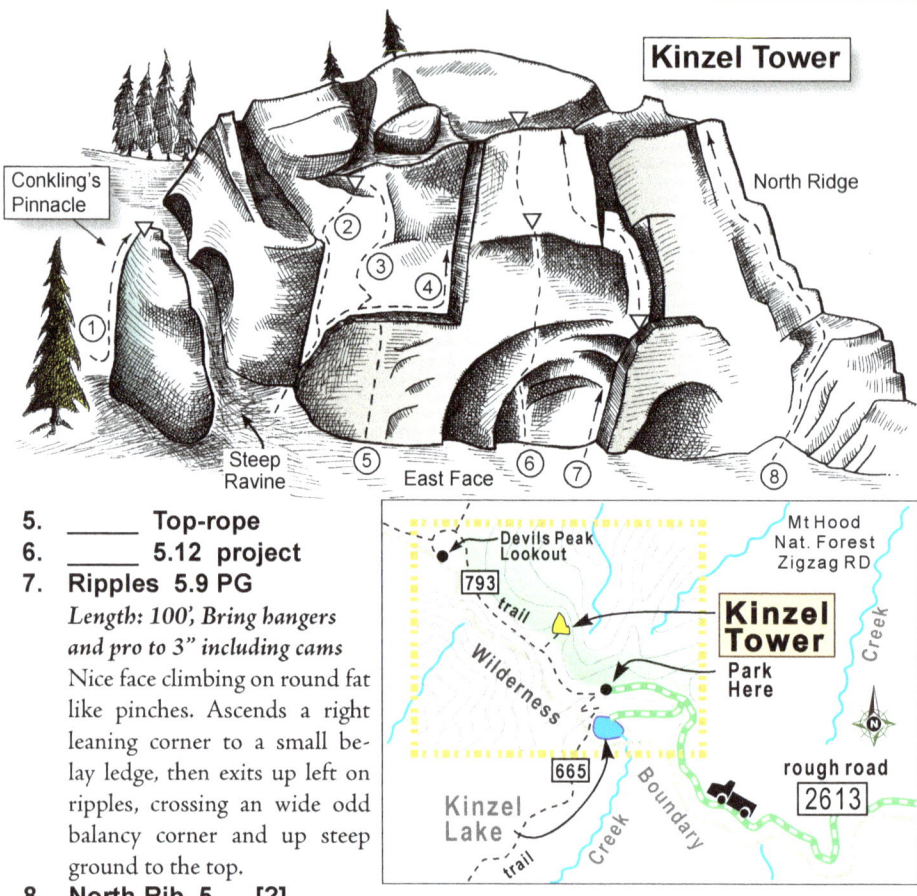

5. _____ **Top-rope**
6. _____ **5.12 project**
7. **Ripples 5.9 PG**
   Length: 100', Bring hangers and pro to 3" including cams
   Nice face climbing on round fat like pinches. Ascends a right leaning corner to a small belay ledge, then exits up left on ripples, crossing an wide odd balancy corner and up steep ground to the top.
8. **North Rib 5.__ [?]**
   An old anchor at top of rib indicates this may have been ascended.

MOSQUITO BUTTE

With a name like 'mosquito' it must be good. This site offers a very small but fine selection of climbing opportunities from 5.6 to 5.11, and fits a general theme suitable to most climbers: quick access, a nearby camping area, and a nice lake for swimming. An idyllic weekend retreat.

Mosquito Butte (aka Trillium) lightly forested rounded rock knoll is an eroded short steep little bluff composed of grainy textured Tertiary andesite (Ta1) from an old lava flow, eroded gradually to expose a steep little cliff. Route offer steep knobby holds or small edges for crimping.

This secluded west-facing bluff is situated in the high cascades in a quiet lightly forested slope, but is often sunny and climbable throughout the summer season from mid-May to October. The primary nuisance you can expect is the pesky mosquito during early summer. The bluff is about 40' tall but yields a cool selection of climbs from 5.6 to 5.11. Not all the climbs are described so you will find other fairly clean climbs in the area, because this small bluff has been utilized as a rock climbing site for well over 25 years. A short rock wall on the east side of this rounded butte also may yield 6-8 additional potential rock climbs, but has only been minimally used to date. Enjoy the scenic nature of this site; do not litter, and maintain the site for future generations. This site is best for small teams (1-4 persons), but is not viable for large groups.

Directions

Drive east from Government Camp on U.S. 26, and turn south on NF 2656. Park near the Trillium Lake Campground and walk to the north end, then follow a well-maintained round-the-lake trail. Near the northeast edge of the lake angle up toward a small bluff but angle around to its lower west side to access this small crag.

1. **Classic Arête   5.10c** ★★★

    A superb arête climb. Power start under an overhanging nose of rock. Reach around left then continue up using pockets and the arête. Ends on pumpy sloped holds near the top. Exit left along the rim to the anchor.

2. **Cool Crimps 5.10b/c**

    Quality face climb with a load of fun crimps.

3. **Pockets 5.8 ★★★**

    A great route with sloping pockets (crux) at the start on a steep face, then ends by using the left edge near top just before you reach the anchor.

3b. **Mosquito 5.5**

    On left flat face aspect is a minor bolt route.

4. **Easy Slab 5.3 TR**
5. **Fun Slab 5.7 ★★★**

    The standard popular route and a good introduction to the crag.

6. **Fun Run 5.7 ★★**

    A bit steeper for the first portion of the climb.

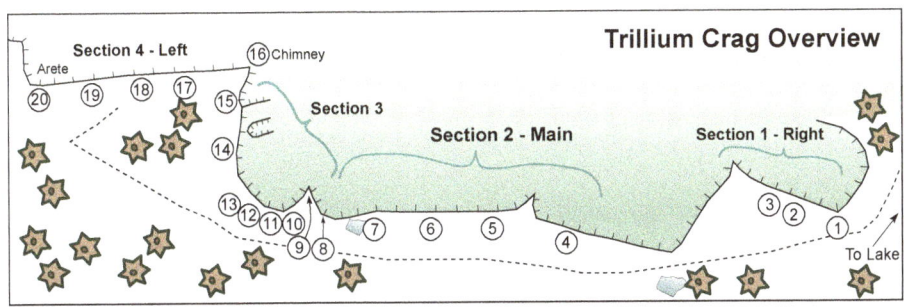

7. **Two Small Lips 5.7 ★★**
   Two variations on the lower part of this climb. Both are nearly identical in difficulty but most people enjoy the right variation. Fun climbing.
8. **Minor Prow 5.8**
   Located on the right face of a deep wide corner system. Starts up a steep slightly hung section but quickly eases.
9. **The Ravine 5.6**
   Pro to 3"
   Wide corner system (a bit mossy). Pro can be found on left side and in small cracks.
10. **Classic Tall Prow 5.8 ★★★**
    A roman nose rock feature that is an enjoyable surprisingly steep face climb.
11. **Nubbins 5.10b/c ★★★**
    Great climb that starts up a slight bulge then dances up plentiful small chickenhead nubbins on a very steep face to the anchor.
12. **Crimper 5.10d ★★★**
    Power up the initial jugs then crimp the remainder of the overhung moves in a timely fashion, then gingerly exit up right onto small knobs on the final slab.
13. **Steep Crack 5.11a ★**
    Balance up an odd steep crack in a slight overhang till it eases some.

Peter Neff at Trillium

◆ MT HOOD ROCK CLIMBS 411

14. Rock Horn 5.11a
   Route that ascends a face busting over a lip onto a steep prow on a tall rock horn.
15. Steep Face 5.11c/d
   A very steep face climb that ascends up the wall immediately right of a vertical off-width corner system.

16. Fat Corner 5.9
Pro to 4"
Obvious gutter ball mossy off-width corner system slightly hung near the top.

17. Right Crack 5.9
Pro to 3"
A overly mosssy thin crack next to the chimney corner system. The right most thin crack.

18. Center Crack 5.9 ★★★
Pro to 3"
This is the area classic and a must for every hunter who enjoys climbing a steep face using a variable sized thin crack on a flat face. The middle crack.

Hugh leading at *Trillium*

19. Left Crack 5.8 ★★
Pro to 2½"
Long left crack system that angles up to a belay near a large tree. Several bolts keep the last part of the climb reasonable.

20. Left Prow 5.8 PG ★★
Pro to 3" including cams (4" cam if you have it)
A great steep arête face climb on the far left side of this flat wall. Climb over two slight bulges to a stance. Wrap a very long sling around the large fir tree at this stance, otherwise it is a heady unprotected move to the belay anchor.

COETHEDRAL

Beta by Bill Coe

Unusual climbing on knobby rock welded in a black-gray igneous breccia matrix the Coethedral climbing site deep in the heart of the Clackamas River Recreation Area may be just the place for a wild climbing tour unlike the typical Oregon crag. Initially explored by Mr. Priestly he quickly teamed up with Mr. Coe and associates to establish a string of wild routes, some nearly 400' tall. If your rock climbing skills are not superb it is best to climb elsewhere. The site has comprehensive factors that require diligence for both leader and belayer.

How to get there

From the I-205 Clackamas exit drive east on Hwy 224 to Estacada. From the stop light in Estacada continue 21.8 miles along the Clackamas River on Hwy 224 till you are just past MP45. Where the road turns left onto a green bridge, you will go right up past the Indian Henry Campground on paved road FS4620 (Sandstone Rd.) for 10.2 miles total (five miles on gravel). At the five mile point the road becomes FS4622 and continues five miles on gravel as it winds uphill then northward. Park at a dirt berm and old gate with a closed sign affixed to it. Walk northeast along the old spur log road as it slowly descends around a minor butte to a slash pile at a viewpoint. You can see the Coethedral formation from here. Descend northerly along the forested ridge on a deer path to a saddle. Descend several switchbacks down the steep west side on the faint game trail to the base of the wall. Expect 15-20 minutes to walk to the site.

Requisite gear and site specifics

Wear a helmet, use thicker ropes such as a 10.5mm rope, QD's, and some gear. The rock is abrasive and can quickly abrade and ruin a climbing rope at this site.

Excessive hang dogging against the sandpaper like rock surface will affect the lifespan of your rope. Climb wisely as the site is an isolated area outside of cell phone range. Climb diligently because all the routes are serious, especially the easier routes even though they seem well bolted. When rappelling tie end knots for safety. Unless noted all routes are set so that a single 60m rope will get you down. Use longer slings where needed to reduce rope drag. Anticipate rock fall, particularly if you are at a hanging belay and your partner is climbing above you.

Coethedral is soft breccia matrix with larger stones of varying size (1"-5") welded into the gray groundmass. Lead bolts are typically ½" x 6½" stainless and provide the best long term usability margin. When adding another

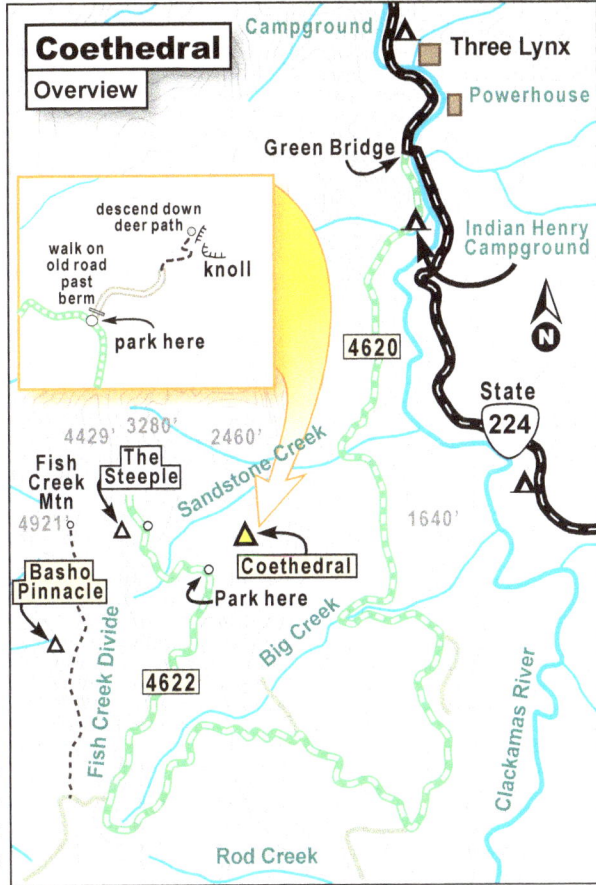

route or more bolts use similar type and standard. Consult local climbers who can assist you with recommendations for new additions, fixed gear spacing, or other hardware changes. The damp 3300' high altitude climate at Coethedral tends to aggravate lesser quality fixed hardware. If considering traveling here, the weather should be reasonably stable one day prior to your visit as the site is west facing and can stay quite damp, especially after a rain shower in the spring or fall season. The Coethedral climbing season is generally limited to the months from June-October. The grades are relative and can change due to key rock holds popping off. Climbing routes that are infrequently traveled tend to be more friable. Rock hand holds may be less stable after heavy rains because the porous breccia groundmass is weakened. Routes are listed from left to right.

1. **Coe-Priestly 5.10+** ★
   Length: 300+', Pro: 15+ Quickdraws, some minor gear, and slings
   Originally done as two pitches but is better when broken into three pitches. Expect loose rock in middle of P1 which mars this otherwise reasonable route. Start 40' uphill from the reading room cave at a single anchor bolt. Aim up slightly right for 26m to a belay. Needs more bolts on the first pitch. Pitch two is a short 5.9 lead on great rock. Pitch three is 100' long. Rap the route with a single 60m rope.

2. **Bewitched 5.9/5.10a PG13** ★★
Length: 300'+, Pro: 19 Quickdraws [for longest lead]
Pitch 1 is 100' (11 bolts) 5.9+
Pitch 2 160' (19 bolts) 5.10a [Bewitched Direct]

This route ends on top of the Old Witch Pinnacle. Pitch 1 100' (11 bolts) at 5.9+. Crux move getting off the ground and delicate steep knob climbing up to a roof, then step right at the roof into a wide chimney (bolts are near the outer edge) and stem up this deep corner till you exit left to an anchor. Pitch 2 (Bewitched Direct 160' 5.10a 19 bolts) punches directly over the intimidating overhanging roof. Climb directly up above the anchor on a very steep sustained prow. Pitch 3 75' (9 bolts) is 5.6 climbing up steep knobby terrain till it eases onto the spire. Tie off a knob with a sling for the last few moves. The bolt anchor is on the back side of the Old Witch. Rappel down to the notch 40' to the belay at the top of Excalibur, then rappel down into Trench Warfare for a total of four raps.

3. **Upskirt 5.9**
   Length: 170' (52-meters), Pro: 17 Quickdraws (or long slings), single 52-meter pitch
   Climb up the first short lead of Bewitched till it steps right under the roof into the chimney. Climb the chimney all the way up slinging knobs where possible. Exit through one of two holes on either side of a large unattached chockstone which used to be the belay stance for Trench Warfare. Belay at the Trench Warfare anchors..

4. **Excalibur 5.10a ★**
   Length: 174' (53-meters), Pro: 28 Quickdraws
   One of the better climbs at Coethedral with a prominent position on a steep knobby prow that offers sustained climbing with good rest points along the route. The first very long lead can be split by belaying at the Trench Warfare belay mid-route. The first full long lead ends on a rock point belay. Step over to a saddle, move up past the Trench Warfare second belay, and climb a 12 bolt knob face on the south side of the Old Witch to a small stance belay. Rappel down Trench Warfare in three rappels.

5. **Trench Warfare 5.10b R**
   Length: 166' (54-meters), Pro: 15 Quickdraws
   Climb the obvious deep rounded groove up vertical terrain past a bulge crux (optional belay point at 30m), and onward up an easier gully (sling knobs) till you land at a belay where Upskirt and Excalibur merge at a small ledge stance belay. The second pitch continues above the belay for 90' (12 bolts) to a small belay stance at the base of Salathe Highway. Rappel the route.

6. **Lava Flow 5.8 R ★**
   Length: multi-pitch, Pro: 24-26 Quickdraws
   Lava Flow is the easiest way to the top of the old Witch by combining the Gingerbread Shortcut to the Salathe Highway. Start slightly right of the arête and trend left to follow the gully straight up for 55m pitch (21 bolts). Tie knobs with slings to enhance margins. Pitch 2 (9 bolts) aims straight up to a rappel point at a large fir tree between the pinnacles. Rappel via Trench Warfare.

7. **Grey Ghost 5.7**
   Length: 50', Pro: 6 Quickdraws (more QD's for initial pitch from ground)
   Starts at top of second pitch of Lava Flow and steps right and up into a tough slot cleft (6 bolts) to the top of the Dragon's Spine Pinnacle. Sling some knobs.

8. **The Gingerbread Shortcut 5.7**
   Length: 50-60', Pro: 9 Quickdraws (more QD's for initial pitch from ground)
   From the P2 belay on Lava Flow aim left 10' to a large flake point, turn the corner and step into a gully, then race up the gully (9 bolts total) to a belay at the base of Old Witch.

9. **Salathe Highway 5.7 X ★★**
   Length: multi-pitch, Pro: nuts ¼" to 1", and cams to 2", but has no fixed bolts
   This is the original route to the top of the Old Witch with zero bolts.
   From the high point belay of Excalibur or Trench Warfare, this route squeezes up left through a gap between the two pinnacles, and then chimney up to the top where the lesser pinnacle ends (use slings on knobs). Step left then up around to the north side of the Old Witch following a minor break in the rock and onto the crest to a belay anchor at

the top. Rappel down to the notch belay, then rappel Trench Warfare.

10. Gothic Rocks 5.9
Length: multi-pitch, Pro: about 28-29 Quickdraws
Start on the ground between Lava Tube and Dragons Spine and follow the 28+ bolts a full pitch to the anchors. The mid-point rap anchors are visible 6' to the right of the route.

11. The Dragons Spine 5.8 ★★★
Length: multi-pitch, Pro: 24 Quickdraws
Some say 5.8; others say 5.10. **P1**: ascends an arête (24 bolts) straight up and near a spine, but wandering a bit (intermediate rap anchor on left at midway point) on knobs to a belay at 56m. **P2**: steps up right then up 15 bolts aiming slightly left to the top of Dragons Spine Pinnacle. Rappel either of three ways: this route, Grey Ghost from the top of the pinnacle off the north side, or aim down Gratitude in the gully behind the pinnacle.

12. Gratitude 5.8
Length: multi-pitch, Pro: 20 Quickdraws
The deep gully right of Dragons Spine route. Pitch 1 climbs a gully (15 bolts) 40m and steps right onto a small belay stance on a buttress. Pitch 2 aims up a gully tending up left (20 bolts) to a steeper headwall to a belay anchor. Descend from four single rope rappels down past Ujahns Delight.

13. Ujahns Delight 5.7 ★★
Length: 100', Pro: 15 Quickdraws (well protected)
Dance up the well bolted (15) face on numerous rock knobs on the right side of the buttress (right of Gratitude) to a belay.

14. Coecoenut Bridge 5.6 ★★
Length: 100', Pro: 11 Quickdraws
Bridge and stem (11 bolts) on lumpy coconuts in a deep 3' wide chimney to where you duck under a natural bridge 90' up in the buttress. Single rope rappel to ground.

15. Better than Sex 5.7
Length: 100', Pro: 15 Quickdraws (well protected)
Ascend plentiful rock knobs on well bolted (15 bolts) face up a nice low angle buttress where it merges with a knobalicious chimney up to the right. Single rope rappel.

16. Rad, Plaid and Glad 5.9 ★★
Length: 100', Pro: 14 Quickdraws
This is the 14-bolt radical buttress immediately to the right of Better than Sex. Is it better than sex. Single rope rappel to ground.

17. Runaway Weasel 5.8 ★★
Length: 100', Pro: 14 QD's
In the center of a buttress to the right of RP&G is this 14 bolt interesting route. Single rope rappel to ground.

THE STEEPLE
Length: multi-pitch, Pro: tie-off slings
Route was coined because of its similarity to other classic Beckey spire routes. From the parking site at the closed gate and berm you can visibly see several spire-like formations on the east slope of Fish Creek Mtn. The Steeple is the northern most formation (see map). To reach the Steeple continue driving on the gravel FS4622 road past the berm parking site till you are past a narrow spot that provides a view of Coethedral in the distance. Park at a minor spur, and scramble up brushy steep forested slopes to the upper side of the Steeple, staying left of a drainage till you encounter some small cliffs. Skirt the cliffs to the left till you reach the

northwest side of the Steeple. From the west side ascend 4th class 70m up a narrow gully to the notch and sling a big boulder and belay. The route aims straight up the big solid knobs (bring 20 slings) directly to the summit. Presently requires two ropes to rappel down west from the summit bolts, then rappel north from slings on a fir tree to ground. Alternate: rappel the "Brother Mike" route with one single rope.

A. Brother Mike 5.10- ★★★
Length: 400' (4 pitches long), 22 Quickdraws (some long ones are helpful), a single

60-meter rope
Located on the outer east facing aspect of The Steeple. The approach is the same as for regular route, but when you get near the cliff base traverse left to the east side aspect of this outcrop to reach the base of the route. A single 60-meter rope will suffice for both leading and rappelling. The climb is well bolted (1/2" x 5.5" stainless), not runout, and requires some minor natural protection for the first 60' (5.7) of the climb. The rock nuances are a characteristic mix between welded tuff and cobblestone (yet this particular outcrop is a slightly more solid form of breccia than the nearby Coethedral crag).

Basho Pinnacle

A minor 55' high summit on the southwest side of Fish Creek Mtn. that can be approached by the south side hiking trail and is visible about 300' below the trail in a forested ravine. The regular route (**Canine Conflict**) is about 5.7 and uses a minor choice of nuts and cams.

COLLAWASH CLIFF

The Clackamas River watershed region seems like one of the last places you would go to climb. But, even here along the Collawash River you can find challenging roadside "roadcut" climbs. There is not much there but if you happen to be in the area that day check it out.

When climbing at this crag wear a helmet and be wary of friable rock and tread carefully when using the steep, mossy slopes above the road. Just left of the main section of wall is a smooth near vertical 50' road cut which has one 5.10+ (TR), and two 5.11+ (TR). The favorite here is the **Johnson-Watt route** (5.9), which ascends 130' of rock on the main wall and is virtually all fixed with bolts. Bring some gear to 2" just in case.

Drive southeast of Estacada along the Clackamas River on Highway 224 to Ripplebrook, then south on FS46. Take the Collawash River road toward Bagby Hot Springs. Look for an extensive roadcut several miles up river. Near the upper left end of the roadcut you will find a few minor climbs. After the climb, and if the weather is hot you can step across the road to swim or fish.

5

EAST SIDE ROCK CLIMBS

Hood River Valley climbing crags and Cascade Mtns east slope crags

East side rock provides a formidable wealth of beta suitable to the needs of regionally based rock climbing enthusiasts. This information avenue to good east side rock climbing opportunities is a positive bridge that analyzes the sheer breadth, bulk and beauty of some of these favorite climbing crags situated in the rain shadow of the Cascade Mountain range east of Mt. Hood.

This open-air theater is an ideal forested climate that provides people with a significant opportunity to learn environmental awareness and good stewardship practices on valuable public lands. Through an ongoing level of commitment and cooperation, climbers who developed these climbing sites are interacting with Forest management agencies to ensure that long-term harmonized relationships are established to allow continuous recreational use at these rock climbing sites.

Thanks to this talented group of dedicated climbers, through their energy and momentum the fascinating climbing sites in this east side climbing chapter provide quality destination crags, each in their own reckoning.

Everyone who has visited the Hood River valley knows this region offers a plethora of extreme sport opportunities at your doorstep from windsurfing to skiing, from mountain biking to rock climbing; all in an area that boasts an ideal mix of sunshine and blue skies. This valley is your gateway to accessible climbing sites in the Cascade Mountain range east of Mt. Hood.

420 CHAPTER 5 ✧ **ORC**

GEOLOGY & BIODIVERSITY

Geology of east side rock scarp formations

The northern Cascade mountain geographic zone with its eastern sloping incline tends to experience a continuous cycle of seasonal hot and cold temperate fluctuations that strongly influence the process of mechanical and chemical weathering.

At Bulo Point in particular, chemically active water solutions tend to increase the process of granular decomposition of the superficial structures. Bulo Point fits the parameters of the typical northern state rock, igneous andesite, but with a visible dacitic-porphyrytic twist in a plagioclase matrix with phenocryst variances of light and dark-colored minerals. The formation is likely an extrusive lava flow or intrusive near-surface sill to be later exposed through erosional processes that removed the less resilient layers. A steady weathering process from water, heat and other factors gradually rounded the overall features of Bulo Point.

Bulo Point has a course-grained texture which, after weathering tends to make the overall bluff features well-rounded and the surface akin to a particularly rough grade of sandpaper. This does not necessarily make poor rock, but surprisingly increases edging friction ability so long as you are careful with how you jam your fingers or fists into rough-edged cracks.

Area 51 is composed of porphyritic andesite with large white crystals of plagioclase in a dense mesocratic matrix of light gray colored rock. It has weathered to a steep, slightly overhung bluff with angular layered strata rock cleavage.

Pete's Pile cliff formation is an andesitic formation with an abundance of large clear phenocrysts of plagioclase feldspar in a dense ground mass of medium-gray colored rock.

Seasonal Climatic Variances

The northwest U.S. has a temperate climate that receives an abundance of precipitation mainly because a warm subtropical air mass and a cold polar front jet stream air mass intermingle producing variant seasonal changes in the climate. This climatic diversity of marine and polar air, in conjunction with high mountain barriers provides prominent seasonal contrasts that make rock climbing on the east side of the mountains more attractive.

The western side of the Cascades tends to experience the greatest variance of rainfall. The Willamette Valley sees about 40 inches of rainfall yearly average, the northern Oregon Cascades 80 inches or more, while immediately east of the range in north central Oregon it decreases substantially to about 16+

Nicole leading the classic route *Jet Stream* **5.9**

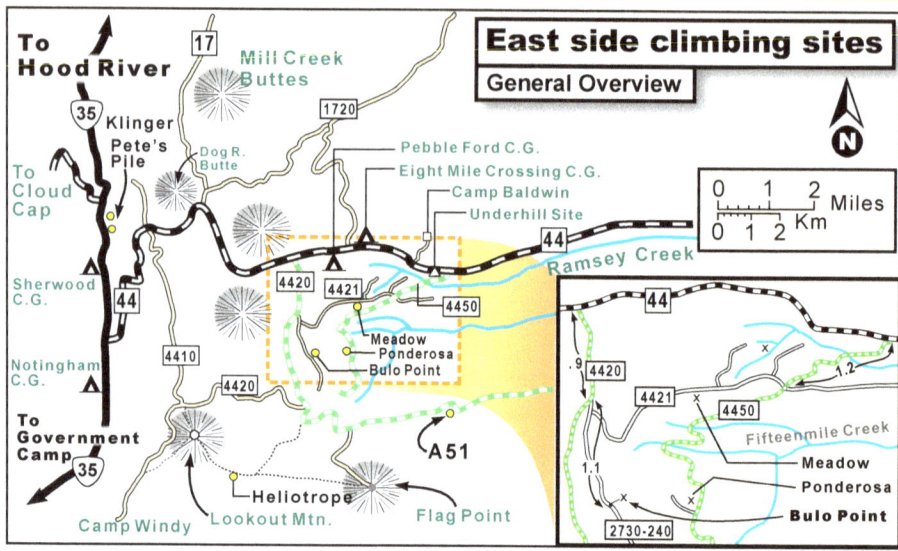

inches per year.

The effective rain shadow created by the Cascade mountain range allows east side climbing destinations to be your gateway to extended recreation opportunity.

Aside from the winter months when the cold jet stream funnels a steady series of winter snow and rain storms across the region you can find feasible rock climbing opportunity at some of the sites in this guide.

Bulo Point and Area 51 receive similar seasonal weather patterns and are usually inundated with deep winter snow from about November to mid-May, although it is possible to access A51 a bit earlier via county roads and NF2730 west from Friend, Oregon. Once the snow pack fully retreats sunny warm weather conditions usually prevail during much of the mid-May through October climbing season.

Bulo and A51 are ideally situated for rain shadow (in the shadow of Mt. Hood) climbing. Summer daytime temperatures peak in the 70°F - 90°F range. Night time summer temperatures can be cool (40°F +/-) and usually freezing (25°F - 35°F) in the Spring and Fall season because of clear skies and a relatively dry atmosphere typical of higher altitudes.

Since these climbing sites are situated close to the semi-arid Intermontane plateau of The Dalles-Madras-Bend region they tend to share similar daytime temperature characteristics, but are generally cooler than the usual boilerplate summer temperatures found further to the east of the range.

This region does enjoy a considerable amount of yearly sunshine and is highly favored by many rock climbers who enjoy venturing beyond the limiting confines of an urbanized rock climbing scene. Even with a tremendous number of sunny days it does occasionally rain even on the eastern sloping Cascade incline, partic-

Wayne on *Bag of Tricks*

ularly if a mid-summer thunderstorm develops.

So, if you live on the west side of the Cascades and the forecast calls for rain (you know the tune), consider driving east to the rain shadow of the Cascade Range to escape wet weather conditions. In essence, your visit to east side climbing destinations for great rock climbing opportunities is sure to be a success.

Biodiversity dynamics of east side flora communities

East side climbing sites offer climbers a quality climbing experience, and each visitor is encouraged to be an ecological partner. Responsible climbing on our part, in harmony with our natural surroundings, encourages good relations with the Forest managers. Become familiar with plant species at the local climbing sites you are visiting. Vibrant floral species provide beautiful blooms throughout the season, perfect for photographic opportunities.

Barney on lead at Bulo Point

This region holds a richness of flora diversity worthy of our commitment to study to understand the environs in which these plants thrive. By developing greater knowledge about indigenous plant species of the region in which we rock climb we gain a greater appreciation for environmental values at the rock climbing crags we treasure.

These east side climbing sites provide a life-cycle to all floras in a very short seasonal window of time before the snow returns. Plants bloom and propagate during these short warm months. As a visitor our duration is merely for a day or weekend, while the east side landscape is a year-round flora home.

The relatively dry rain-shadow climate of the eastern Cascade Range has a unique quantitative botanical diversity that helps to sustain this dynamic ecological landscape with a vibrant genetic population of species particularly suitable to this region. The fir-pine-oak woodland zone of the eastern Cascades sustains this network in a balanced structure for flora and fauna communities.

Land managers believe that a balance can be maintained between the regional ecological value and recreational integrity of these climbing sites. You are our partner in this endeavor and through your diligence we hope to promote a legacy of low impact activity vital to the long-term ecological sustenance of these sites.

Management plans are designed to promote a cohesive harmonic ecological balance in conjunction with rock climbing at these sites. Help be a part of the process to ensure a balanced coexistence between climber access and long-term habitat protection.

Environmental Considerations

The lightly forest covered riparian zone of this east sloping Cascade incline is extensively rugged and wilderness-like, except perhaps for the numerous roads that bisect the area. This entire regional resource is a popular destination for many visitors.

Low-growing vegetation and cliff dwelling plants are surprisingly fragile and visitors are encouraged to treat this vital region with care while climbing at these crags. There is much beauty to enjoy while walking in a forest of tall ponderosa pine. Mountain hemlock can be found at Bulo Point area, while gnarly Oregon White Oak or the bright leaves of the Douglas Maple can readily be seen at lower elevation climbing sites.

Many types of native micro-habitat flora inhabit this region, such as Balsamroot and purple Larkspur. The Microseris, Suksdorf's Desert Parsley, and certain Aster's compose just some of the species that make their niche in this ecological riparian zone between the semi-arid desert and high Cascade peaks.

Access and User Impact

Special efforts have been taken to provide a network of established user trails and base areas. Most foot trails are very well marked and have been creatively engineered with stone steps and stone belay platforms to minimize the erosional impact of visiting climbers in a dry, fragile environment. Please utilize the well-developed foot trails (no short-cutting) which provide convenient access to each climbing site and avoid unnecessary trampling of the local plant species. Concerned climbers have taken great strides to create trails designed to limit erosion problems.

Do not remove rare indigenous flora from the cliff, from the rock climb, or along the cliff base. Previous climbing route developers have occasionally left flora and moss in place on certain climbs because of the importance of the species. Certain sections of a bluff may be closed (such as at Pete's Pile) to protect and enhance the flora community. A low impact concept is encouraged for long-term viable use at these sites. Do your part to keep these sites a rare treasure for all climbers by packing out what you pack in.

Please seriously consider leaving your pets at home. A loose, rowdy dog is not everyone's best friend. It can cause more damage in five minutes than twenty climbers in a month, thus it is best to leave the pup at home.

Ethical Continuity

Pre-inspecting routes via rappel is normal business, so rappel bolting is the usual method (though not always) for route development at these crags. Removal of poor quality loose rock is a necessity for future climber safety. Refrain from chopping fixed gear, chiseling or altering holds, retro-bolting existing lines without permission, placing bolts next to quality gear placements, avoid developing 'R' or 'X' rated routes.

It is recommended to wear climbing helmets while leading or belaying. Some of the rock is less than stellar, even at Area 51. Use caution so as to keep your visit a safe journey free of an

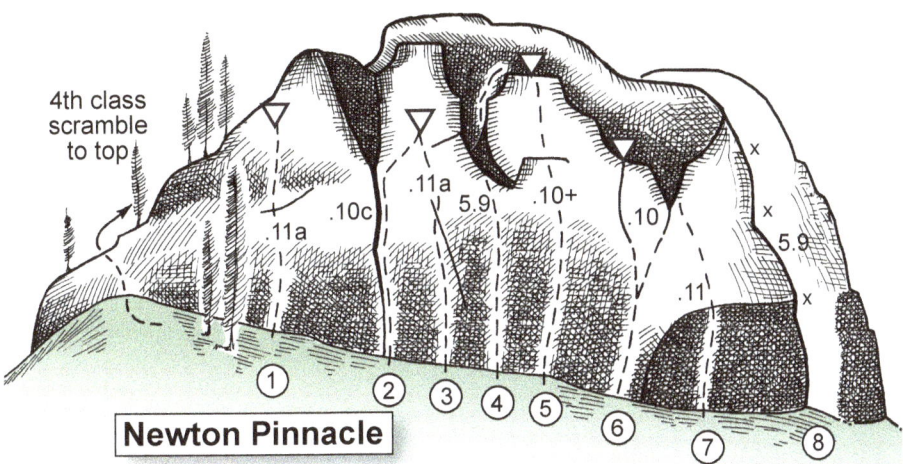

encounter with unidentified falling objects.

NEWTON PINNACLE

This secluded alpine rock pinnacle, is perched high along a forested ridge above the Hood River Meadows parking lot. From the community of Government Camp, drive 2 miles east on US Hwy 26, then at the three-way highway junction take state Hwy 35 toward Hood River. One mile east of Bennett Pass turn left onto the old Sahalie Falls road. Park near the entrance gate leading to the Hood River ski area. The small pinnacle is visible on the skyline northeast of the entrance gate. Hike northeast along an access road to trail #667 and follow this trail uphill to the ski run, then directly uphill through open forest to the pinnacle along the ridgecrest. A 30-minute approach hike. The northwest face is approximately 60' high, 150' wide and slightly overhung, but offers a liberal amount of hand holds. This site has been frequented for various climbing activity likely since the '50s-'60s based on several old hand-forged pitons found there.

1. **Wage Slave (aka Entropic Gravity) 5.11a** ★★
   A great short lead (just QD's) on a crimpy face.
2. **Poison Pill 5.10c**
   Clamber up past a big wedged block.
3. **Logisticon 5.11a** ★★★
   Follow the thin seam using tiny incuts. Great TR.
4. **Neophytes 5.9** ★★★
   Stellar climb that power straight up a vertical face to the large ravine.
5. _____ 5.10+ TR
6. _____ 5.10 TR
7. _____ 5.10+ TR
8. **Gravity Waves 5.9**
   On the far west end is this mixed gear-bolt route sending a face/crack corner past a hang. FA McGown and partner in early '90s.

LAMBERSON BUTTE

This extensive climbing area stands like a castle wall overlooking the majestic alpine slopes of the wooded Newton Creek drainage. Sheer rock cliffs, green forests of mountain hemlock, glacial moraines ablaze in red heather, and a view of the fearsome Black Spider combine to make Lamberson a remarkable destination for the veteran climber. The wall averages 150' to 200' high and is broken into several major sections offering rock climbing opportunities ranging from 5.8 to 5.12.

By far the most visible, and perhaps the most staggering is the **Great Pig Iron Dihedral** (5.12a, or 5.10 A2+). Like ocean waves this 160-foot undulating dihedral glimmers in the sunlight, even from afar. Another super classic is **Bag of Tricks** (5.10c), which ascends up ledges, thin corners, and face climbing next to a large slice of rock.

There are routes of every make and color: smooth-as-glass dihedrals, lightning bolt cracks, arête's, flake cracks and high-angle face routes.

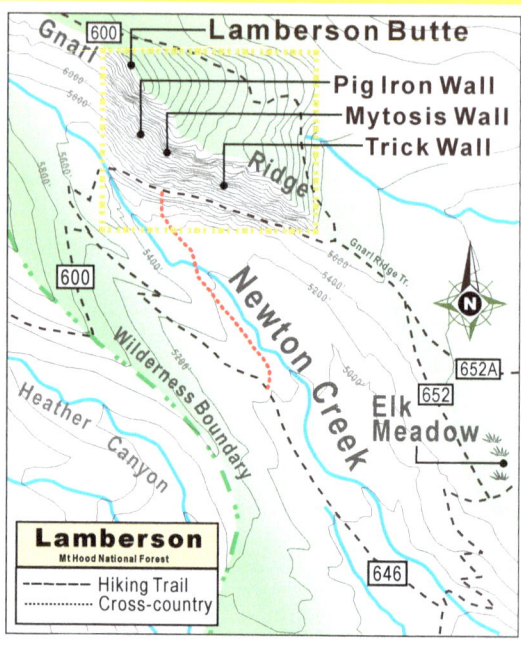

Several routes were accomplished by a ground-up means of ascent at Lamberson. Thin pitons, and bolts are usually necessary for success. Ground-up leading is bold, but also rewarding for those who like a fine mixture of free and nailing options. Beware of friable rock when you are exploratory climbing.

Directions

Park at the Hood River Meadows trailhead and hike toward Elk Meadows on trail #645. Take trail #646 following Newton Creek uphill to the Round-the-Mountain trail #600. A viable shortcut exists by hiking along the creek through light brush for the last ½ mile of the approach. Ford the stream and angle up toward one of the crags. The southwest-facing wall lies partway uphill overlooking the Newton Creek drainage. The hike is an easy 1½ hour 3-mile approach.

PIG IRON WALL

1. _____ 5.10+

A decent 150' top-rope climb if someone is into placing some fixed gear. Climb the main corner then launch out left into a long steep

EASTSIDE CASCADE MTNS

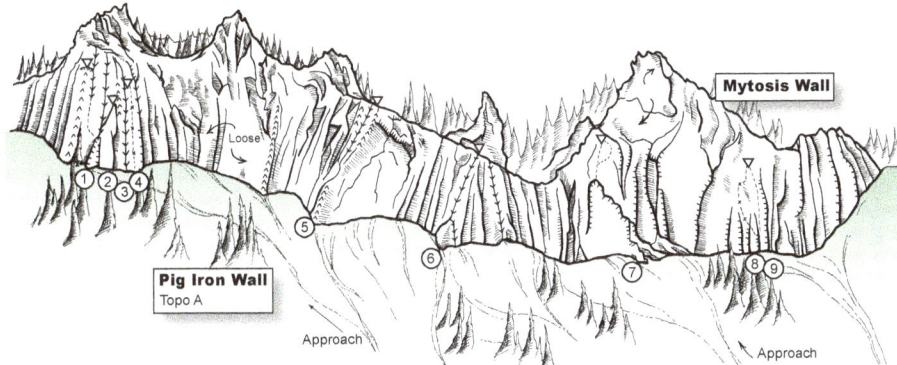

crack system.

2. **Pig Newton 5.10d**
   Length: 120', Pro to 2"
   A fine punchy line just left of Pig Iron. Wander up weird rock and corners, then out left (crux) and up right into the finishing crack to an anchor at a tiny perch.

3. **Great Pig Iron Dihedral 5.12a** ★★★
   Length: 150'
   Pro: KB, LA, TCU's and pro to 1"
   The Great Pig Iron is the most captivating corner climb at Lamberson. It radiates with a glimmer in the mid-day sunlight from afar. And it is certainly a must-do for any aid climber or free climber. The nailing line (5.10 A2) is a thin seam on the left face, but utilizes the lower and upper portion of the main corner. If you plan to free the dihedral (5.12a) just power your way directly up the corner past several bolts and gear placements to a belay anchor.

4. **Headhunters 5.11b PG** ★★★
   Length: 150'
   Pro to 1½" & TCU's, RP's
   Quite possibly the finest route at Lamberson. Climbs the very nose of the long buttress immediately right of Pig Iron. A stellar power packed line with many tenuous challenging sections and one very tricky crux move at about mid-height.

5. **Panorama 5.8**
   Length: 165', Pro to 3"
   Ascends a rock rib then follows a crack corner to the top of the bluff.

   MYTOSIS WALL

6. **Trafficosis 5.8**
   Length: 150', Pro to 2"

7. **Mytosis 5.10c**
   Multi-pitch, Pro to 2" Cams recommended
   Aim up left past a tree along a series of steps in a corner to an airy stance. Continue onto the flat

Wayne nailing *Pig Iron Dihedral*

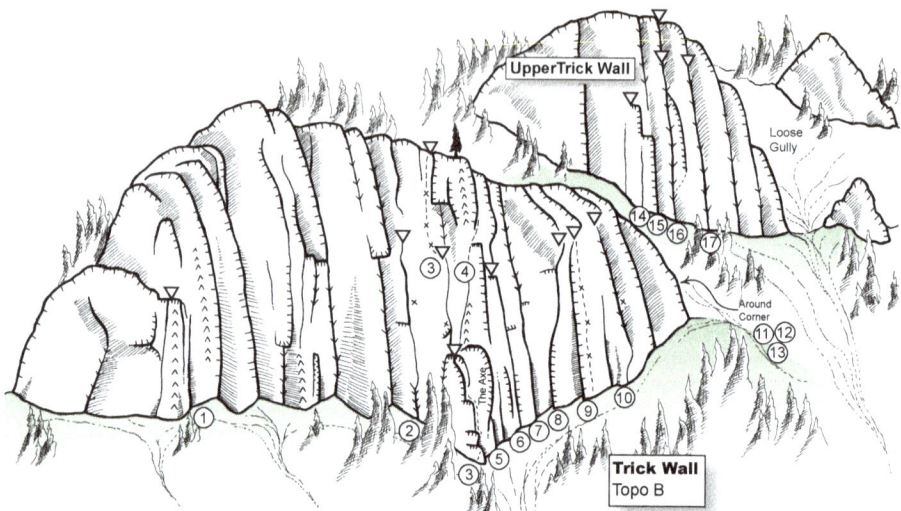

face above using thin cracks that angle up right. Power past a final small roof to a belay.

8. **Thirty-six Light Years 5.11b or 5.9 A2**
   Length: 155', Pro to 2" TCU's suggested
   A wild climb if you can locate it. Start just right of a broken corner system. Climb up to a long right facing thin corner crack till it ends. Power up right using face holds and thin seams on a wide flat face (bolts) till you reach easier terrain. Rappel.

9. **Catch Me If I Fall 5.11**
   Length: 165', Pro to 2½" & pitons

   TRICK WALL

1. **Poultry Picnic 5.9**
   Length: 60', Pro to 3"
   Way over on the left end of Trick Wall is a fine little climb on the right side of a steep minor nose. Aim for the notch to a tree belay on a ledge. Rappel.

2. **Crash of the Titans 5.10c ★★**
   Length: 100', Pro to 2½" & cams
   A stellar climb punching up a thin seam corner past a flake on a flat face. Rappel anchor.

3. **Bag of Tricks 5.10c ★★★**
   Multi-pitch, TCU's, RP's and pro to 3"
   This superb climb starts on the left side of the sharp blade-like rock feature at the base nose of a prominent buttress on the Trick Wall. **P1 60':** Begin up numerous steps and ledges to a ledge belay near the notch. **P2 50':** Power up left into a minor crack corner that runs up to a nice perch belay under a small roof at a small tree. **P3 50':** Smear up left (bolts) onto the blank face and continue (crux) up a thin crack to a left facing corner to exit onto the top of the

Wayne on *Momma Bo Jomma*

bluff at a large tree. Walk off.

4. **Upper Prow 5.10+**

   This is an interesting variation that ascends a thin crack up right from just above the first belay and above the 'axe' rock rib feature. Unconfirmed rating.

5. **Variation Start 5.10a**

   Length: 60', Pro to 1½" including pitons

   This starts on the south side of the blade-like rock feature by ascending a crack weakness to the notch. Merge with P2 Bag of Tricks and continue up.

6. _____ **5.11+ ?**

   Length: 80' TR

   Interspersed with a few ledges but has a long sustained smooth crux corner system.

7. _____

8. **Trafalgar 5.10c** ★

   Length: 80', TCU's, Friends to 3" required

9. **Arête 5.11b** ★★

   Length: 80', Pro: QD's

   A quality face climb that ascends a steep crimpy face on a minor rib.

10. **Test Tube 5.10a A0 R**

    Length: 80', Pro to 2" & pitons

    A long corner groove climb with some runout.

11. **Quantum Gravity 5.8** ★★

    Length: 60', Pro to 3"

    QG and the next two climbs are situated on the uphill southeast facing side of this wall. It faces toward the Upper Trick Wall.

    QG is a nice thin corner crack to a notch, where you face climb up another short distance to the bolt belay anchor shared by all three routes.

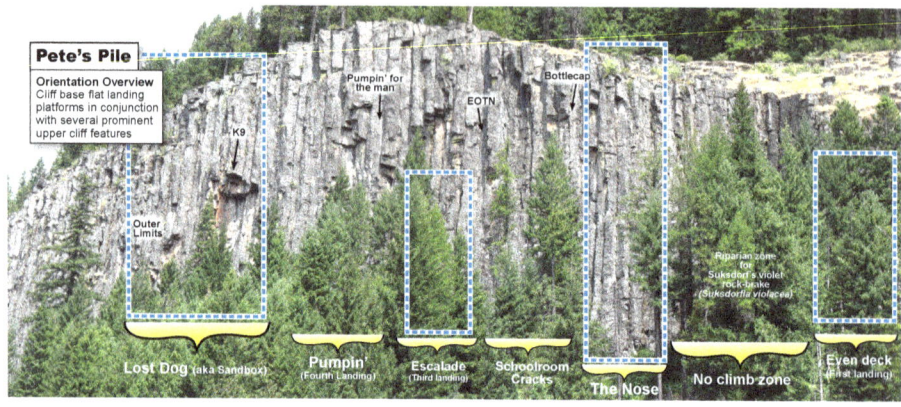

12. Pushover 5.10c ★★
Length: 60', Minor pro to 2"
Pushover is the center face climb immediately right of the crack corner.

13. Sunset Bowl 5.9
Length: 80', Pro to 3"
SB takes on the right side of this flat face mainly following the rib using some minor cracks along the way.

UPPER TRICK WALL
14. Lightning Bolt Crack 5.12 TR
15. Momma Bo Jomma 5.10c ★★
Length: 80', Pro to 3" & cams
A stellar climb. A deep dihedral corner system powers straight up with wide stems. As the crack widens place a piece high in the thin right crack, then launch out left into the offwidth moves and exit onto a stance where the Lightning Bolt Crack meets. Continue up a short chimney move to the bolt anchor and rappel.

16. World is Collapsing 5.10c ★
Length: 150', Pro to 3" & cams
Immediately right of Mamma.

17. Sanctum 5.10b ★★★
Length: 165', Pro to 3" & cams
Another stellar climb. A powerful steep corner stemming and face climbing extravaganza.

PETE'S PILE
Written by David Sword (Introduction and Beta)

History of the Area
It was the summer of 1984, and I was on the hunt for a job before ski season rolled around. I was sitting on the porch outside of the Mt. Hood Country Store when a baby blue '67 Nomad rolled up. A friendly faced Newfoundland stuck his head out the passenger window, and a stringy blonde haired man with Popeye sized forearms jumped out, fired me a quick handshake and said, "Pete's the name, and danger's my game." Two things I quickly learned about Pete Rue were that he was always game for climbing, and he was rarely seen without his dog, Andy.

Pete's early explorations took him all across the Hood River valley in search of climbing possibilities. One day he asked me along to explore a crag across from Pollalie creek. The rock here was messy and frightening. Broken, fractured, and unstable basalt was the norm, but plumb sections of pure joy offered a respite from the pain. Many near misses came during these initial outings, with both emotional and physical scars to prove it. During one first ascent, Pete lead through a tough vertical hand crack. "Watch the loose flake!", he yelled. Even twenty five years later I can see that flake buzzing past my head as my girlfriend climbed ahead of me. We finished the route at sunset and rappelled to the ground without headlamps. As with many of our early ascents, the route itself still stands, but the quick sketch topo made on the inside of a matchbook on the car ride home was lost long ago. Most of the early ascents were never recorded, and many of the original lines lay in repose, awaiting new motivations and adventurers to make their mark.

Later, we continued to the south and began to explore the vertical columns of what we now know as Pete's Pile. Any vision for an accessible climbing area came from Pete, and his obsessive bond with the Pile became almost legendary. Pete single-handedly put the crag on the map while most of us were driving to Smith Rocks or doing crack laps at Beacon Rock. Establishing a climbing area can be an arduous task. For some time Pete did much of the laborious work himself, including hauling in secretly quarried rock for the stairs. Eventually he found he could motivate locals by offering up lunch and beers in return for physical labor; and sometimes even a shot at a new FA. The name Pete's Pile became the local's reference for the outcrop, but other names, such as Pollalie Crags, Sunset Dihedrals, and East Fork Columns were discussed in the early development stages.

Surely ascended before the mid 1980's, climbers from the past left only tattered slings and a handful of fixed pitons; not exactly a clearly marked road map. There were rumors that some famous names had stopped by, and we wondered if perhaps Fred Beckey or Yvon Chounaird ever graced the crag. Most likely however, the fixed remnants were left by local pioneers who used the outcrop for aid climbing and rescue practice.

We taught ourselves how to aid climb and to rope solo from a well worn copy of Robbins' Advanced Rockcraft. Where the book fell short we would fumble around with the intricate details until it felt good. When a solid stance was reached, or when we ran out of rope or motivation to continue the grind, piton and stopper belay stations were built. As the sport climbing

David Sword leading at Pete's Pile

Pete's Pile
Route analysis for the upper cliff face

movement in America was still young and extremely controversial, most all the early ascents were accomplished from the ground up. The first permanent top anchors were placed at the top out of Pop Bottle (.10a), by Pete using a 22 ounce framing hammer and a handful of Rawl bolts poached from a construction job. Pounding anchor bolts into the hard Oregon Basalt led to severely blistered hands, but the man would not be swayed by such trivial set-backs. We taped over the wounds so Pete could top-rope the route later that same day.

As is common at climbing areas, there were controversies at the crag. When talks of further crag development evolved, area naturalists were worried about the effect it would have on a plant species known as Suksdorf Violet Rock-Brake (Suksdorfia violacea). At the time, the violet flowers were only found growing on a handful of northwest facing rock abutments. Active local climbers met face to face in an attempt to find common ground, and in conjunction with local USFS personnel, a climbers association was developed. One of the main tenants of the now defunct group, was to protect this rare flora. Even greater alarm developed when locals devised a powerful route cleaning technique for the dirt and moss choked dihedrals. By securing a fire hose to a seasonal drainage atop the crag, new routers could quickly pressure wash the rock, virtually eliminating the gargantuan efforts required previously. Clearer thinking, and more ecologically forward minds prevailed, and only a few routes sprouted from the Firehose era.

Climber's from the past and present who helped shape the crag include Pete Rue, Dr. Roger Stewart, JD Decker, Stewart Collins, Emily Kohner, Jim Thornton, Susan Nugent, Jim Opdyke, Deno Klein, David Sword, Reed Fee, Elmo Mecsko and the late Jeremy Flanigan. With the continued efforts of USFS personnel, and the continued adherence to local guidelines from the climbing community, the balance of recreation and preservation has been created and continues to move forward. As of today, the Suksdorf Violet Rock-Brake at Pete's Pile is growing stronger than ever, and has botanists reviewing its status as a sensitive species.

Dimensional Scope of the Crag

Pete's Pile is a hidden gem and one of only a handful of traditional climbing areas in the region. The crag is an excellent multi-season climbing area generally free of snow from April through October. Kept secret for a few decades, only recently has Pete's seen much traffic from outside the local community. Even today the crag remains a quite place to get your

EASTSIDE CASCADE MTNS 433

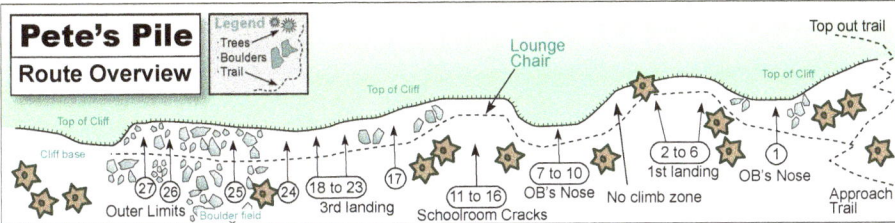

crack climbing skills up to par, and the scenic beauty is well worth the price of entry. Amazing views of the eastern and north slopes of Mt. Hood await you while climbing here. As the base of the crag sits a couple of hundred feet above the East Fork of the Hood River, once you climb to tree top level, the sense of exposure is spectacular. Most of the current routes are moderate (5.10 and under), and the potential exists for dozens of more climbs of various grades.

Guidelines for climbing here are straightforward and simple; 1) If you pack it in, you pack it out. This includes cigarette butts, food wrappers, TP, and tape; 2) Do not remove dirt or vegetation from cracks unless it is necessary to provide safe hand-holds, steps, or for placement of protection. The Suksdorf Rock-brake has continued to grow for years even in some of the established climbing areas because climbers have left the soils surrounding the plant intact. Suksdorfia violacea is found throughout the climbing area, and is most easily identifiable by it's puffy, round violet flowers that are reminiscent of something from the pages of Dr. Suess; 3) Stay on the established trail system to avoid soil erosion. This includes the access trail, the base area trail beneath the climbs, and the descent trail from the top of the cliff.

Geology Of Pete's

The exposed cliff line making up Pete's Pile is basalt made up from ancient flows originating from the Cloud Cap area of Mt. Hood. Geologist refer to the columnar formations as olivine-bearing basaltic andesite, which is common on the northern flanks of Oregon's largest volcano. Although vertically sliced, the broad band of basalt has many features conducive to climbing. The steep and sustained nature of the rock is softened slightly by incut edges, ledges and pockets, and the soaring cracks accept a multitude of traditional protection. Adding to the challenge are overhanging roof sections, which become more prominent as you move northward. Sections of loose rock exist and necessary precautions should be followed. A 60-meter rope is standard here, but 70m ropes are handy. A standard free climbing rack is sufficient for most climbs. Don't forget a nut tool for the gear gobbling cracks, and long runners or cordelette, which are useful for belays and top anchors.

Some routes can be approached from the top of the crag by setting up rappels and top ropes. The top of the crag is sloped and tiered, and anchors are neither marked, nor necessarily convenient for setting up top ropes. Extreme care should be taken for your own safety and for the safety of those below you! Route numbers begin at the right most portion of the crag (OB's Nose) where the approach trail first meets the rock, and proceed northward (left).

Directions

Drive south from Hood River on Hwy 35 for 23¼ miles toward Mt. Hood. Park at a dirt

pullout on east side of the highway (the pullout is ¾ mile south of the Cooper Spur Road and ¼ mile north of the East Fork Trail #650).

From Portland follow Hwy 26 to Government Camp. Take the Hwy 35 exit towards Mt. Hood Meadows ski area and Hood River. Park at a dirt pullout on east side of the highway

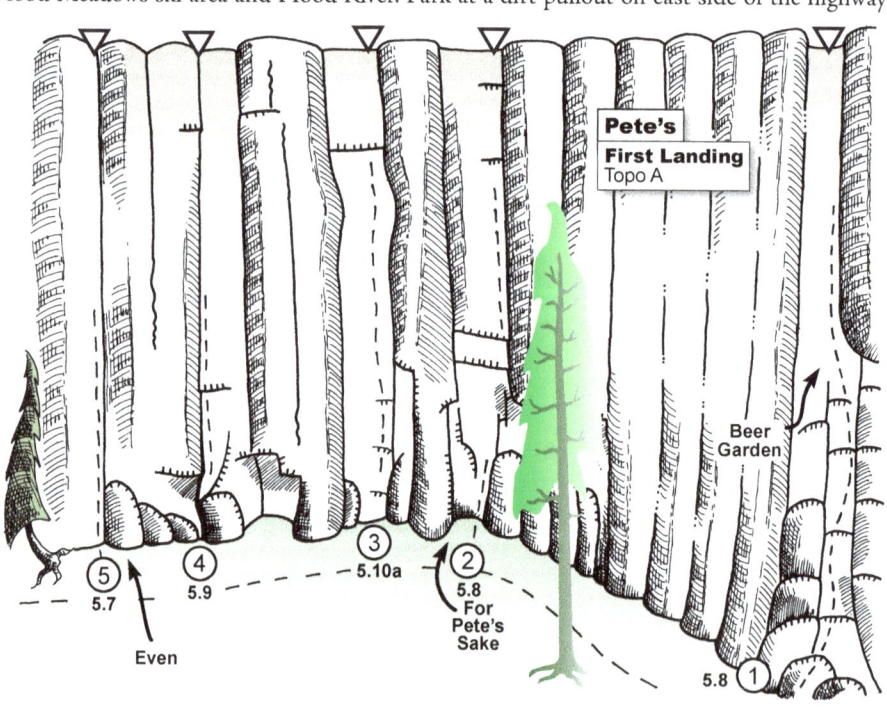

located 0.6 miles north of Sherwood campground.

Parking and Approach

At a small pullout on the east side of the highway access a parking area made from an old section of roadway. An unmarked trail ascends towards the crag. As you near the cliff, sign posts directs you to the left (base of the crag) or to the right (top access). Once at the base of the crag, the trail follows the cliff band, terminating at the northern end of the established climbing area (Sandbox). The climbing routes are listed from right to left as you first encounter the cliff.

SOUTH END

The first climb you encounter on the approach trail is the Beer Garden located on a minor nose of rock at the sound end of the main bluff.

1. **Beer Garden 5.8** ★★

    Length: 80' (30m), Pro to 2½"

    Beer Garden is a clean blocky route punctuated with plenty of steps and edges on the lower portion, and ending in a steep crack corner for the finale. It is a well traveled climb and rightly so because it protects reasonably well.

    Belay from the trail or 3rd class to a higher platform. Wander around on slabby moves until it gets steep, and then stick to the right side. Anchors at top sit back from the lip so bring cordellette for a TR or be mindful for rope cuts.

THE FIRST LANDING

As you ascend the trail northward you first encounter the cliff scarp at a large dusty landing spot at the base of a series of popular rock climbs.

2. **For Pete's Sake 5.8** ★★★

    Length: 92' (28m)
    Pro to 2½" including cams

    Another great moderate climb whose attention is well deserved. Although it starts up odd blocks

and steps it quickly fires into a superb steep corner crack that jams well and protects very well. This route is entertaining all the way to the very end with diverse moves on steep basalt with a crux section up high on the route.

3. **Guillotine 5.10a** ★★
   Length: 92' (28m), Pro to 2"
   A brilliant climb that tackles a steep dihedral and small roof resembling a guillotine. A great rest on the left welcomes you about 35' up the route, just before you pull over the roof and climb up the smooth surfaced crux section just above. A long section of sustained climbing with great jams takes you to the top of the bluff.

4. **Temptation 5.9** ★★
   Length: 92' (28m), Pro to 2½"
   With a crux close to the ground this steep 'niner is another gear gobbler worth its weight. The triangular roof visible from the ground is the crux. Diverse and challenging climbing all the way to the anchors.

5. Even 5.7 ★★★
Length: 92' (28m), Pro to 3"

A high quality moderate and certainly a must do route for every visitor. The route offers good protection with ample rest stances between the crux sections. Belay tree marks the beginning of the right facing book. Be mindful of some minor loose rock below and left of the belay bolt anchor.

NO CLIMB ZONE

Between the route called 'Even' and the route 'Mighty Mouse' but before you reach the Schoolroom Cracks, there is a protected riparian zone that is set aside for flora preservation purposes. The Suskdorf Violet Rock-Brake grows well in this dark water stained cliff scarp. Signage placed at both ends of this section reminds climbers that this is preserved as a 'no climb zone'.

Pete's Schoolroom Cracks
Map 8

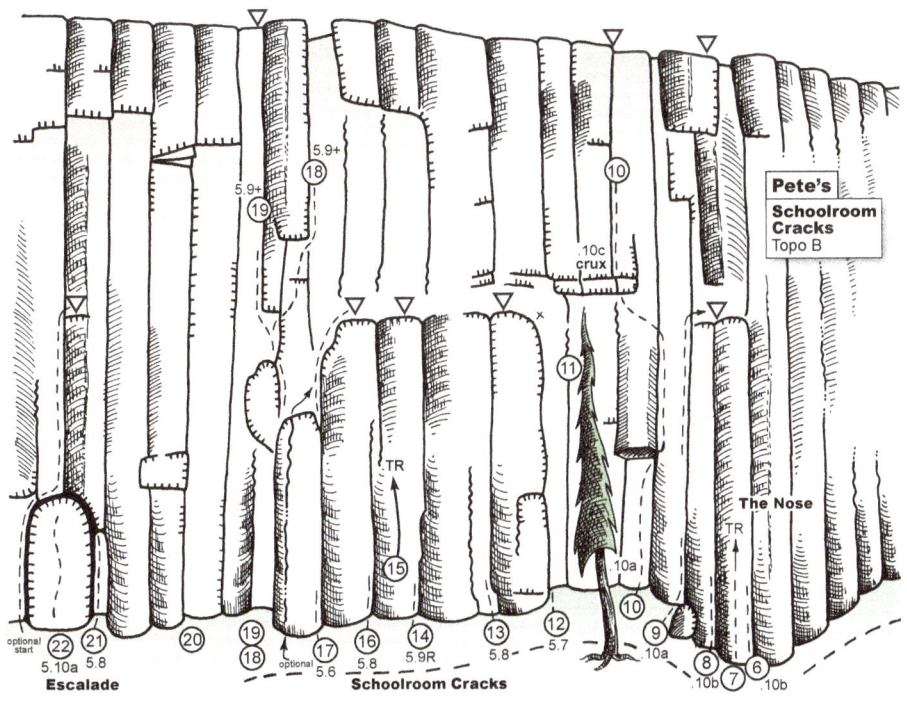

Pete's Schoolroom Cracks
Topo B

438 CHAPTER 5 ✧ ORC

NOSE OF MIGHTY MOUSE

A prominent feature at Pete's Pile is a buttress formation that dips low along the entire stretch of the trail just before you reach the Schoolroom Cracks area. This is the Nose of Mighty Mouse which provides a haven of classic lines that will surely challenge the crack climbing aficionado.

6. **Mighty Mouse 5.10b** ★★
   Length: 165' (50m), Pro to 2"
   This is a long steep sustained crack corner climb starting at the base of a sunny buttress of rock. Start up steps and launch into a long crack system to a bolt belay at mid-height. Continue up another crack system to the top of the cliff. Rappel from anchors. Originally given a sandbag rating of 5.9.

   Mighty Mouse Rappel
   The Mighty Mouse rappel is a single 60-meter rope rappel for descending down from the top of Pete's Pile. A cliff top anchor and a mid-point anchor offer a convenient means to rappel if you have only one rope and you have topped out on a nearby route.

7. **Stinger 5.10b**
   Length: 82' (25m) TR
   A wild top-rope problem on the nose of MM buttress. Start at absolute toe of the buttress and work thin moves up to the protruding arête. Climb the arête using smears and side pulls for 70'. Access to the black painted rappel anchors by climbing nearby routes or from lowering in from top of cliff.

8. **Tribes 5.10b**
   Length: 165' (50m), Pro to 2"
   Long steep sustained climb.

9. **S.T.A.R.D. (aka Pedestal) 5.10a**
   Length: 82' (25m), Pro to 2"
   STARD is an acronym for short, thin and hard. An apt description for this seldom traveled route. Begin up the shallow left facing dihedral with the pencil thin detached flake.

10. **Bottlecap   P1 5.10a, and P2 5.10c**
    ★★★
    Length: 165' (50m), Pro to 2½"
    You can recognize this route by the dark 'bottlecap' shaped overhanging roof 35' up the initial part of the climb.
    An old slider nut left during the FA remained fused under the crux roof for over a decade; a testament to both its difficulty and few ascents over the years. Bottlecap is the first 5.10 route established at the crag. This climb can be done in one long 165' lead to the summit anchors.
    Pitch 1 (82') 5.10a: Begin by climbing up

a steep crack till you are under the bottlecap shaped roof. Move right to surmount past this feature, and then continue another 20' to a stance. A belay anchor exists to the right on the next route if you choose to bail over that direction.

Pitch 2 (82') 5.10c: Continue up left to another smaller roof. Pull through this second roof and continue up very steep sustained crack with great finger and hand jams. If done in one long pitch it is a full 165' long. A great welcome-to-the-crag route with solid power packed punch to the entire climb.

11. Doctors Patient 5.10a
Length: 82' (25m), Pro to 2"

Start in mossy corner left of the Bottlecap roof. Ascend a mossy corner to the bottlecap roof, step left and climb a dirty crack to a cluster of broken roofs. Power through this roof and continue via jug holds and crack climbing to the belay anchors.

SCHOOLROOM CRACKS

The Schoolroom Cracks is the second large flat dirt landing area, and this section provides the most popular selection of climbs at Pete's Pile. A large wooden bench is available here to sit on while you are relaxing between climbs. The belay anchors (three total) for the next six climbs are located 70' up the cliff face. You can access all three belay anchors by leading up the route of your choice and traverse left or right to access the other anchors. By far the most ascended zone at the crag, many of these cracks were climbing in the 1980's, and have been named and renamed more than once.

12. Pop Quiz 5.7
Length: 70' (21m), Pro to 2½"

Though very dirty it is a seemingly viable method to the schoolroom cracks bolt belay anchors. Follow low angle crack up and left to anchors above Smokin'.

13. Smokin' 5.8 ★★★
Length: 70' (21m), Pro to 3"

A superb moderate climb that is totally worth leading. Though most first time climbers start with Dunce, Smokin' is an optimal warm-up climb with a plethora of edges, great jams and good protection placements. A second pitch ascends the slightly overhanging left facing dihedral to top of the cliff. It's rating is unknown, but is certainly a couple of grades harder.

14. Not For Teacher 5.9R ★★
Length: 70' (21m), Pro to 2"

Though less often led this shallow open book crack climb is great even as a top-rope. The

EASTSIDE CASCADE MTNS 441

route is unusually tricky with odd smears and small featured edge holds that keep climbers challenged all the way to the anchors.

15. Times Tardy 5.10a
Length: 70' (21m) TR

An eliminate top rope effort between Smokin' and Not For Teacher. Edge, smear, pinch and layback up the arête. Using crack on either side lowers the grade to 5.8

16. Schoolroom 5.8 ★
Length: 70' (21m), Pro to 2"

Schoolroom is no less challenging than its immediate neighbor to the right (Not for Teacher). A challenging shallow open book crack climb filled with jams, smears and tiny edge features. A route that will challenge your balance.

17. Dunce 5.6 ★ ★ ★
Length: 70' (21m), Pro to 3"

The most frequently climbed route at Pete's Pile since most visiting climbers head straight to the Schoolroom Cracks area first. Wander up a crack 15' and pull past the small roof, and then zen your way through a few tenuous moves to easier terrain and a wider crack. Large edges and steps make the last few moves a cruise to the bolt anchors. Climbers often traverse from this bolt anchor over to the next bolt anchors to set up a top-rope for all the Schoolroom Cracks routes, but if you do watch out for rope drag!

18. Dirt In Your Eye 5.9+
Length: 165' (50m), Pro to 4"
Though seldom ascended this is a unique climb with great history and character. The earliest route established to the top and Pete Rue's favorite. Begin by jamming up a crack corner to the left of Dunce targeting the obvious right facing chimney capped with a chockstone. Once you near the small roofs step over to the RIGHT side of the detached pillar and continue climbing a wide crack (beware the chockstone) on the right side of the long column to the top of the cliff. Fun and diverse movement.

19. Eye Of The Needle 5.9+
Length: 165' (50m), Pro to 3½"
EOTN takes the same start as Dirt in your Eye up to the roofs. From there it stays on the LEFT side of the detached rock pillar using hand jams and edges to ascend a wide crack dihedral system to the top of the cliff. Use a tree for a belay anchor.

THE SECOND LANDING

A few yards further along the trail past the Schoolroom Cracks is another large flat dirt landing area. A series of fine quality routes begin here including the classic and popular Escalade. After Ramble One the trail dips down a bit past another small cluster of routes before aiming north out onto an open boulder field slope below the Sandbox Area.

20. Unknown
Length: 70' (21m), Pro to 2"
Ascending a crack between Eye Of The Needle and Escalade, a 2 bolt anchor awaits those willing to roll the dice on this mysterious climbed route.

21. Escalade 5.8 ★★
Length: 70' (21m), Pro to 3"
A fun and challenging route also known as Abandonment Issues. Start on the right side of a large tall detached block. Stem up the corner, place wide pro to protect the slight bulge, and then slide out up left onto the top of the detached block to a nice stance. Continue to cruise up steep terrain with great pro and good edges to the bolt anchor. An alternative 5.6 start is on the LEFT side of the block which protects better and with smaller pro.

22. Reckless Abandon 5.10a
Length: 70' (21m) TR

This is the direct start to Escalade (outside face of large block). The bolts were removed by angry locals shortly after the first ascent. Climb a series of thin, bouldery moves past two bolts to the stance atop the large boulder, and then continue up the route Escalade.

23. Ramble On 5.7R
Length: 70' (21m), Pro to 1¾"

Another fun route that needs more traffic. A bit runout with some dirty sections, lead climbers should take caution. Begin up a short crack corner to a small overhanging roof, step left and continue to climb up the slabby column. Amble up left from the crack to reach the rappel anchors on a flat face.

THE THIRD LANDING

A few yards further north along the trail is a third flat landing platform. Pumpin' for the Man begins here.

24. Pumpin' For The Man 5.9 ★★★
Multi-pitch 195' (59m)
Pro to 2" on P1, to 3" for P2, and to 5" for P3

Pumpin' is a quality three pitch lead with energizing technical pitches from bottom to top.

Pitch 1 (60') 5.9: Begin out of the gate with a crux move off the deck by powering over the initial bulge to a stance under the larger roof. Carefully place some pro, then balance right and up into the long steep crack corner system. The first lead takes good small cams and nut protection. Power past a second small triangular roof, and then exit up left to a bolt belay anchor at a small perch.

Pitch 2 (50') 5.8: From the anchor continue up right in a crack past a small roof and 20'+ to a large ledge and belay at a bolt anchor. You are standing next to a long detached pillar.

Pitch 3 (90') 5.9: From the belay ascend a long sustained offwidth by climbing on the left side of the huge columnar pillar of rock. This lead is very wide and requires large width protection devices. Tremendously exposed! Belay anchor at summit.

Rappel route, walk off, or descend down the Might Mouse rappel.

25. Hamunaptra 5.9 A2
Multi-pitch 200' (60m), Pro to 3"

Originally climbed by aid and top roped, this multi pitch outing awaits insitu belays. Ascend left facing corner surmounting roof on the left side. Continue up ever-steepening crack to the cliff top.

26. Cryan's Shame 5.10b (2 pitches)
Multi-pitch 200' (60m), Pro to 2½"

Pitch 1 100' (30m): Start by climbing up on edges and thin finger jams below a broken series of small roofs. Surmount the small roof and climb up to a bolt anchor on a sloping ledge.

Pitch 2 100' (30m): Follow shallow open book to top of cliff. Use tree for anchors. A great route that could use some cleaning.

27. Acoustic Kitty 5.9 A3
Multi-pitch 200' (60m), Pro to 2½"

Another steep outing that awaits permanent belays and an all free ascent. Begin in crack

⬥ **EASTSIDE CASCADE MTNS   445**

system to the right of the large, red roof complex which houses K-9 Shanghai. Zig zag leftwards over a series of roofs with jams and footwork.

LOST DOG WALL (aka SANDBOX)

A large open boulder field is at the extreme north end of Pete's Pile. A vast sweep of vertical cliff scarp here provides some of the most challenging climbing at Pete's Pile, including the stellar K9 Shanghai route. Jeremy Flanigan nailed 5-6 unrecorded routes on the long crack systems, but little record remains of the original ascent.

28. K-9 Shanghai   P1 5.11a, P2 5.12a, P3 5.10a   ★★★
Multi-pitch 240' (73m)
Pro to 3½" including cams, doubles small & medium cams P1
FFA: Elmo Mecsko, Reed Fee 8-2008

K9 is one of the newer challenging climbs at Pete's Pile , putting into perspective the vertical possibilities for the ultra-initiated. The route is long, sustained and technical with demanding crux sections. The classic crux second pitch punches OUT and over a massive improbable looking yet surprisingly well featured overhanging double tiered roof.

Pitch 1 (100') 5.11a: The first lead is technically thin but fun with interestingly steep crack climbing that increases in difficulty the higher you climb. Climb past a small overhanging crux near the anchor.

Pitch 2 (60') 5.12a: From the belay ascend steep thin jams and smears, then launch out the double tiered overhanging roof using a variety of face holds and a finger-hand jam crack. Strength and pure thuggery will get you through the giant roof crux. Need a 3½" cam for crux (A2).

Pitch 3 80') 5.10a: From the belay anchor above the crux pitch, move right and climb the steep arête upwards with mixed gear. Finish through a small overhang moving up left to bolted anchors on a big ledge. An outstanding climb with unmatched position!
Rappel with two ropes only…or walk south and descend via another standard rappel.

29. Dunlap 5.9
Length: 80' (25m), Pro to 1½"

Follow the shallow face between 2 steeps cracks. Left crack accepts protection more readily. Sustained climbing eases as you near the anchors. Dunlap and its neighbor Outer Limits were developed by a gregarious and prolific local outdoorsman, the late Jeremy Flanigan…Good on ya' mate.

30. Outer Limits 5.10a
Length: 80' (24m), Pro to 1½"

The left most climb at Pete's Pile located at the northernmost end of the Sandbox area. Begin on the right side of a series of stacked blocks and ascend up easy terrain to a crack immediately above the blocks. Power up the short flat face via a nice jam crack and exit left to the belay bolt anchors. Rappel the route.

KLINGER SPRINGS

Klinger Springs is the next door kissing cousin to Pete's Pile, so if you like long columnar crack systems found at Pete's you are sure to like the nature of the routes here. The rock type is the same as Pete's, but the textural nuances are slightly different. There are a fair number of the quality climbs, both bolted and trad gear leads.

The site has held intrigue to local Hood River climbers for a long time (see Pete's Pile

intro), but recently Klinger has gained increased activity and popularity. The core route development enthusiasts are Elmo Mescko, Reed Fee, Rick Harrell and numerous others who have also found this place fascinating and enjoyable for climbing. The crag presently yields rock climbs ranging from 5.8 to 5.11 and there is certainly room for more. Seasonally the crag is great for rock climbing from May through October climbing under frequently sunny skies, but expect cold temperatures and snow in the winter months. As with many of the crags found of the east side of Mt Hood read the biodiversity section at the beginning of this chapter to familiarize yourself with the ecological nature of this region.

Review the local ethics concerning new anchor placements before starting a new project. Bring a trad gear rack if planning to climb here because about half of the routes are either trad gear leads or mixed gear/bolt leads.

Directions

Drive south of Hood River on highway 35 (about 20 minutes) till you pass NF3511 road that leads to Tilly Jane/Cooper Spur. Just as the highway crosses a small bridge, park at a small trailhead for Clinger Springs. Hike up this one minute, then take a faint path that continues upward steeply for about 15 minutes till you encounter the cliff. Most of the climbs are southward from the point where the trail meets the crag.

NORTH END
1. **Hanging Chad 5.7**
 Pro 6 QD's, Length 35'
 Bolted face climb (utilizing odd rock flakes). This route exists where the trail initially

meets the wall at the north end.

2. Hatchet Job 5.10-
6 QD's, length 45'

Just right of Hanging Chad on the same outcrop formation. Climb a series of underclings/sidepulls on flakes (first bolt is a tough clip to the far left). Continue via stem moves, then angle up left to a roof, then up a brief headwall, moving up right to meet the belay.

LAND OF SHADOWS

3. Hot Pockets 5.9
Pro 8 QD's, Length 50'

Easy climbing and shallow cracks. About 40' south of 'Hanging Chad' route.

4. Signs Preceding the End of the World 5.10
10 QD's, length 70'

Located at a cave-like section with numerous hanging blocky roofs. Begin below the blocks, power underclings/sidepulls past it till it eases to edge climbing for the remainder of route.

5. Cerberus 5.9
12 QD's, Length 80'

Long bolt face climb, but has optional trad start on left (5.9) and on the right (.10a).

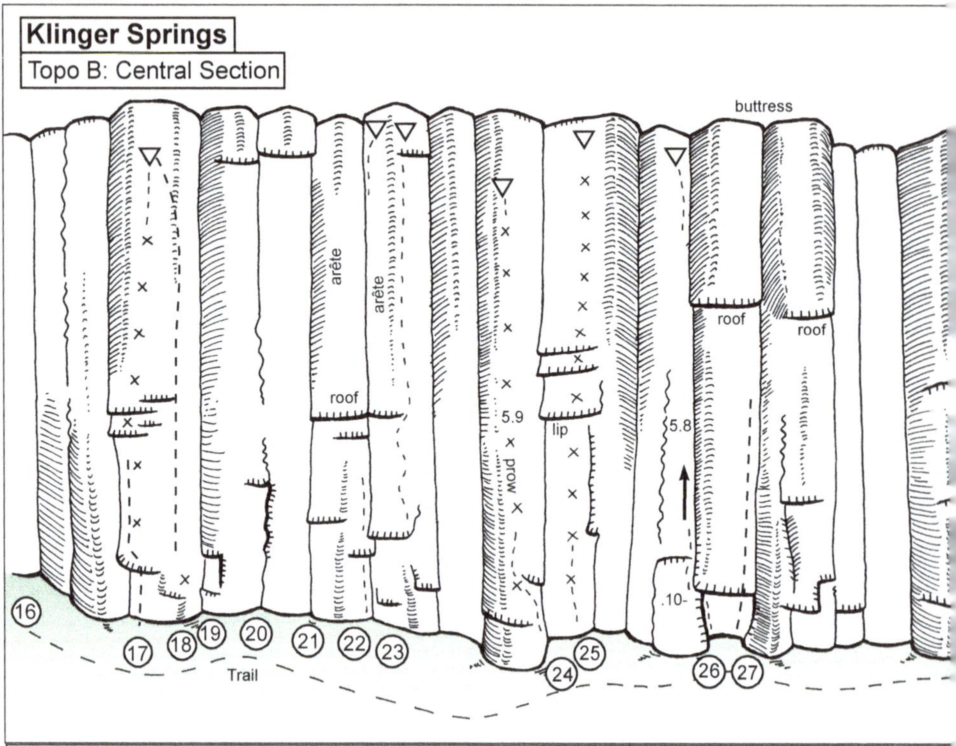
Klinger Springs
Topo B: Central Section
buttress
arête
arête
roof
5.9
prow
lip
5.8
roof
roof
.10-
16
17
18
19
20
21
22
23
24
25
26
27
Trail

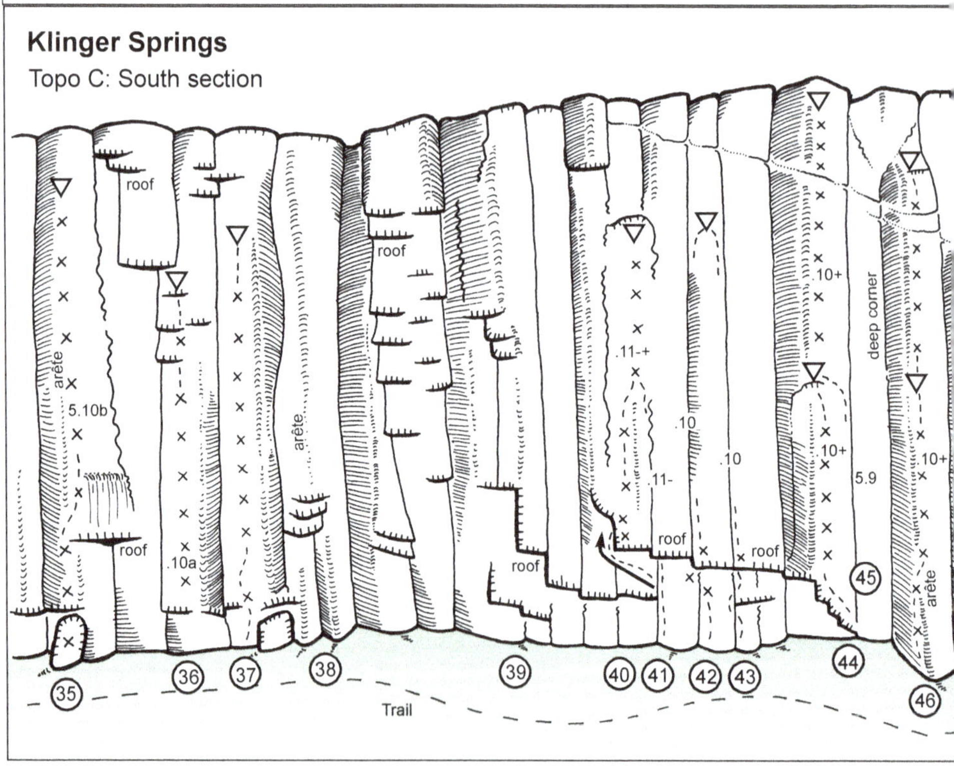
Klinger Springs
Topo C: South section
roof
roof
arête
5.10b
roof
.10a
arête
.11-+
.10
.11-
.10
roof
roof
roof
.10+
deep corner
.10+
5.9
.10+
arête
35
36
37
38
39
40
41
42
43
44
45
46
Trail

EASTSIDE CASCADE MTNS 449

6. **It's All Good 5.7 PG/R**
   Pro to 1½", Length 80'
   Climb 25' of Trad Dad route, step left (2 bolts), then climb a thin crack. Clip bolts for safety, or if not (gets R).
7. **Trad Dad 5.7**
   Pro to 3" (+ QD's), Length 80'
   Sustained 5.7 climbing for about 2/3 of route, then it eases. Located about 15' left of Bulge Boogy. Start in a low point in the trail.
8. **Bulge Boogie 5.10b**
   Pro: about ½" nuts and cams, 9 QD's, length 90'
   Start at a ground belay bolt. Climb fun moves through several crux bulges.

   ### AVIARY ZONE
9. **Eaglet 5.10**
   9 QD's, Length 70'
   Start near Kestrel, climb easy slab to small lip (above 4th bolt), then climb to belay underneath a giant roof. Rap.
10. **Golden Eagle 5.12c (the extension)**
    Pro 2 QD's, Length 16'
    From top belay of Eaglet, climb up over the giant horizontal roof. An extension.
11. **Kestrel 5.10c**
    9 QD's, Length 70'
    Climb up thru a crux balancy crimpy large plate of rock. The upper portion of route can be low-mid 10's depending on what part of the face you're climbing on.
12. **Osprey 5.10**
    13 QD's, Length 80'
    Start just to the right of large roof leaning out over the path. Has unique climbing style with crux puzzle.
13. **Felsschlüpfer (aka Rock Wren) 5.10d**
    10 QD's, Length 70'
    Techy climbing initially, thin crux at 4th bolt, and finish with face climbing to the belay.
14. **Blue Grouse 5.9**
    11 QD's, Length 70'
    Easy route involving a mix of underclings, laybacks and sidepulls. Located on same column as Rock Wren (to its right).
15. **You Me & Everyone We Know 5.10d**
    12 QD's, Length 85'
    Look for the first bolt pointing straight down under a low roof. Pull over the roof, and climb 45' of low-5.10's till you reach a stance below a slab. Climb the blank slab to a belay.

    ### WOLF POINT
16. **No Balls 5.10a**
    Pro a few cams 2-4", (8 QD's), Length 75'
    Move initially up left to the first bolt, climb up thru an easy roof, and continue up to a ledge, then (with pro) climb a wide crack to a belay.
17. **John Harlin II 5.11a**
    11 QD's, Length 90'
    Find a tall arête with 3 small lips on its right side. Climb the left side (bolts) of arete

(crux at midway), pumpy to end it to large ledge. From ledge continue up another 25' on a minor pinnacle to a belay. Shares belay with Ego Ex.

18. Ego Extension 5.10+
13 QD's, Length 90'
Climbs the right side of the same arête. Power thru the three small lips, continue up to a ledge, then up a final minor pinnacle formation to a shared belay (with previous route).

19. Bollocks 5.8
Pro to 5" (double rack), Length 90'
This is the crack next to Ego Ex. Reasonable climbing past several small lips. Shares belay with Ego Ex.

20. Good Sport Route (GSR) 5.7
16 QD's, Length 90'
Climb up to an arête (on its left side), continue up a face to a small lip, then move under the roof till you can pull over the lip using big sidepulls/jugs. Easiest route at KS.

21. Funkytown 5.9
Pro to 1", Length 70'
Stemming for the entire route. At top move left to attain GSR belay, then rap.

22. Shorty Got Wolf 5.9R
Pro to 4", Length 70'
Climb steep crack to a broken loose zone (sling a horn or runnout), continue with more steep variable sized crack climbing. Just left of Wolf Gang.

23. Wolf Gang 5.12
15 QD's, Length 80'
Initial odd opening sequential moves, then jugs run, and then power crimps to the belay. Located about 10' left of Wolf Point.

24. Wolf Point 5.9
9 QD's, Length 80'
Nice route on right side of arête. Climb face, then transition to the arête, and finish to a belay.

25. Bone-Eata' 5.10+
13 QD's, Length 90'
Power thru three roofs (in-a-row) using jugs. Located immediately right of Wolf Point.

26. Jugular Vein 5.10+
Pro to 4½" (+ cams), Length 90'
Initial crux moving under small roof-ish overhung section, then climb a steep corner, several minor bulges, to finish up a crack dihedral.

27. Bear Claw 5.10a PG
Pro to 5" (the wide stuff), Length 80'
Start same place as Jugular Vein. Initial opening roof crux section to start via edges and layback. The remainder of climb is a bit easier (wide pro is a +). Can avoid initial move by starting over on Jugular Vein route.

28. Lean On Me 5.10a
8 QD's, Length 75'
Start at the base of a leaning combination block tower. Climb the outside of the blocks, then continue up a brief bolted face above to reach a belay station.

29. **Point of Diminishing Returns 5.9**
   10 QD's, Length 90'
   Long sport route face (with a crux that can be negated by moving left around it).
30. **Solstice 5.10b**
   12 QD's, Length 90'
   Bouldery moves then jugs to a small rook, then move to the right side on a prow using crimps to finish on the prow.
31. **Dog Day Getaway 5.9**
   Pro to 3", Length 90'
   Quick start leads to a finger/hand jam crack. Move left at end to same belay as Solstice.
32. **Moss Covered Funk 5.10c/d**
   Pro to 3", Length 100'
   Pumpy crack climbing with stemming and finger jamming (a slight overhung section near top) and finish past a 'cap-stone' to a shared belay station (with Equinox).
33. **Equinox 5.10d**
   Pro 14 QD's, Length 90'
   Punch past an overhang to an arête, then up the arete on crimps till the holds fatten. A bit spacey near upper end.
34. **Delicate Sound of Falling 5.11a**
   Pro to 3" + QD's, Length 100'
   Crack punches past several small lips, then climbs up left under a large lip (bolts), then up left to an arte and face to reach the belay.

   ROOF UTOPIA ZONE
35. **RIP Kurt Albert 5.10b**
   13 QD's, Length 80'
   A thin, sustained balancy lead on a bolted arête left of Wet Spot.
36. **Wet Spot 5.10a**
   12 QD's, Length 80'
   A discolored wet spot area that is wet in late spring and early fall. Power face climbing with a finale crux roof to surmount.
37. **Campus Wolfgang Gullich 5.11-**
   12 QD's, Length 80'
   Climb the face (avoid crack & nearby arête) to get full deal. Begin on a shattered block about 10' up the cliff at an open book (left side of column). Belay shared with next route.
38. **Todd Skinner 5.10c/d**
   13 QD's, Length 80'
   Initial section of broken rock (15') then quality sustained face climbing all the way. Belay same as previous route. Aka the Right Arête.
39. **Twitch 5.11b**
   Pro to 3", Length 80'
   Begin climbing a crack, then switches to crimp edge face climbing for the upper part. Mixed bolt/gear lead.

The next three routes climb up, then out of the same broad big roof system.

40. Blockbuster 5.10a
___ QD's, Length 95'
Climb up to the big jutting roof, move left around the roof, and climb a long flat face.

41. Sequel 5.10b
Pro to ___" (+ ___ QD's), Length 95'
Climb up to and punch directly out the roof, then up a vertical face above.

42. Roofatopia Dope 5.10b
Pro to 3" (+ QD's), Length 90'
Climb through the initial hung roof (bolts) then up a long crack. Mixed bolt/gear lead.

43. _____
Pro to _"
Xxxx.

GODS AND MONSTERS ZONE

44. Taken 5.10c
Pro 20 QD's, Length 115'
A long arête with some tricky crimp climbing broken into to short leads (or 1 long lead).

45. Shaken 5.9
Pro to ___", Length 65'
Long finger crack climb landing at the P1 'Taken' belay station.

46. Power Child 5.10d
Pro 18 QD's, Length 115'
Long sustained powerful stellar bolted arête.

47. Oroboros 5.8
Pro to 4" (+ large cams), Length 60'
Climb a crack till it splits (and use either split), then continue up crack until you can peer right to find the belay station (also used by 'Dragon' route).

48. Morosoarus 5.10a
Pro to 3" + QD's, Length 60'
A second pitch of Oroboros. Ascend the 'Dragon' P2 to a trad gear spot, then move up left along a crack and face (left of the rock protrusion). Shares belay with next route.

49. Crouching Climber Ridden Dragon 5.11c
P1 = ___ QD's, Length 60'. P2 = Pro is small cams, Length 60'
A 2-pitch sport route that climbs a prow. P1 (5.12): start in BotB, then move left into a crux and climb powerful overhung moves to a belay. P2 (5.11c): Quick climbing gets you to a difficult rock protrusion, then finish across face to a belay.

50. Belly of the Beast 5.9
Pro to 3", Length 65'
Popular hand/fist crack to first roof, then left to a belay.

51. In Godzilla We Trust 5.10d
Pro to 3", Length 70'
Climb a crack up rightward through a difficult pumpy roof, then jams to finish to the belay.

52. Buddha Belly 5.10c
10 QD's, Length 65'
Second pitch option for previous route. Overhanging juggy sport route.

53. Getting It Up for the Crack of Dawn 5.10+
Pro to 3", Length 120' (total)
Just left of the tall rock pedestal is a long thin finger crack corner. P1 is 5.10c/d, and P2 is 5.10b/c.

54. Goddess of Virtue 5.11a
5 QD's, Length 40'
Short crimps face climb on the outside of the rock pedestal.

55. Monster Crack 5.9
Pro to 4" (5" is optional), Length 55'
Offwidth on the right side of the rock pedestal (with some tunneling for the last moves).

56. Medussa 5.9+
Pro to 2", Length 70'
Do a few moves of 'T.I.T.', then climb a small crack up left to shared belay.

57. Trapped in Time 5.9
Pro to 4", Length 70'
The second pitch of Monster Crack, offering a long crack with plenty of finger to hand jams.

58. Nosferatu 5.10-
Pro to 3" (optional to 4"), Length 110'
Long crack climb. Seam to start, then widens to fingers and hands, then widens to fist jams at a small roof (at 90'). The crack system widens to arm-bar status near the belay.

59. Sphinx 5.10c
Pro 17 QD's, Length 100'
Long steep sustained bolted arête with a small jug roof up high.

60. Red-headed Yeti 5.10+ PG/R
Pro to 2", Length 120' (total)
A multi-pitch lead. Long corner crack climb ending by climbing the big rock protrustion. Pitch 1 (5.8) and Pitch-2 (5.10c/d).

61. Yeti's Betty 5.7+
Pro to 3" (+ doubles), Length 110'
Long crack lead on a flat face.

62. Primal Institution 5.10b/c
12 QD's, Length 100'
Sustained face and arête climb.

SOUTH END OF CRAG

63. Crackalicious 5.9
Pro to 2" (small cams and nuts), Length 75'
Nice corner crack with finger to hand jams, and bulge finish near top.

64. Know What I Mean 5.8
Pro to 3" (small cams and nuts), Length 75'
A corner crack climb that shares same belay as previous route.

BULO POINT

The rocky crag of Bulo Point is a fascinating group of steep bluffs with quality rock climbing opportunities for leading and top-roping from mid-May to late October. Located roughly ten air miles east of Mt. Hood and a few miles south of FS44 this site offers enjoyable climbing from 5.6 to 5.11+. The site qualifies as one of the better backcountry climbing crags nestled in the ponderosa pine covered eastside crest of the Cascade mountains incline.

Nestled on the sunny eastern facing slopes overlooking the Fifteen Mile Creek watershed west of the small town of Dufur, Bulo Point offers visitors a quality selection of routes on surprisingly steep, 80' high rough-textured rock.

Although many of the rock climbs are sport routes, a fair selection of routes are traditional natural gear routes. Bring an adequate selection of cams and wires if you plan to lead any of the traditional climbs. Most of the climbing routes have fixed belay anchors which can be accessed from above for top-rope purposes.

Geological characteristics

The rock at Bulo is composed of heavily-weathered course-grained rock from old lava flows originating from the vicinity of Lookout Mountain. The outcrop is revealed later when the surrounding softer earthen layers are eroded away, leaving exposed bedrock that experiences chemical and mechanical decomposition from the principal reacting agents oxygen, water, and carbon dioxide.

The rough surface texture of the rock provides positive smearing friction opportunities along with numerous hand or finger edges. Moderate routes from 5.6 to 5.10 are plentiful, but the cracks tend to be shallow and flared, which can be challenging while placing protection on lead. The Point is a good place suitable for moderate to expert climbers.

These forested slopes provide recreational opportunities for hunters, hikers, mountain bikers, as well as rock climbers who find the Ponderosa pine covered Dufur watershed a delightful haven far from the madding crowd.

Many individuals were dynamically instrumental in developing this climbing site. Bulo Point has long been an established historical climbing site prior to the 1980s and a number of the routes were top-roped and some were lead climbs long before the era of fixed bolts. Do your part to keep this site a rare treasure for all climbers by packing out what you pack in.

Directions

To visit Bulo Point, drive south from Hood River, Oregon on Hwy 35. Drive east on FS44 for 8¼ miles and turn south (right) onto FS4420. Follow the paved road initially for ¾ mile. At the Dufur Watershed sign take a gravel road on the left onto FS 4421-240, which is a narrow dirt road. This road splits again within a few hundred feet. Take the right fork and drive for 1 mile to Bulo Point. Park at the roads end (being decommissioned beyond this point), and walk east down a footpath that leads out through the forest to the top of the crag. The crag is a one minute walk from your vehicle to the bluff top viewpoint.

The Viewpoint

The first string of routes begin at the Platform which is a common starting place where people arrive on their first visit to Bulo. Take the main trail out to the scenic viewpoint at the top of the bluff. Immediately downhill on your right side is an alcove platform with a short vertical east-facing wall. The routes at the Platform are listed from right to left. Only routes accessible from the Platform are listed here. **Jet Stream** and **Jet Wind** are listed in the Main Lower Lobby area.

To access the Platform routes scramble down exposed 4th class ramps to the alcove. Or

456 CHAPTER 5 ✧ ORC

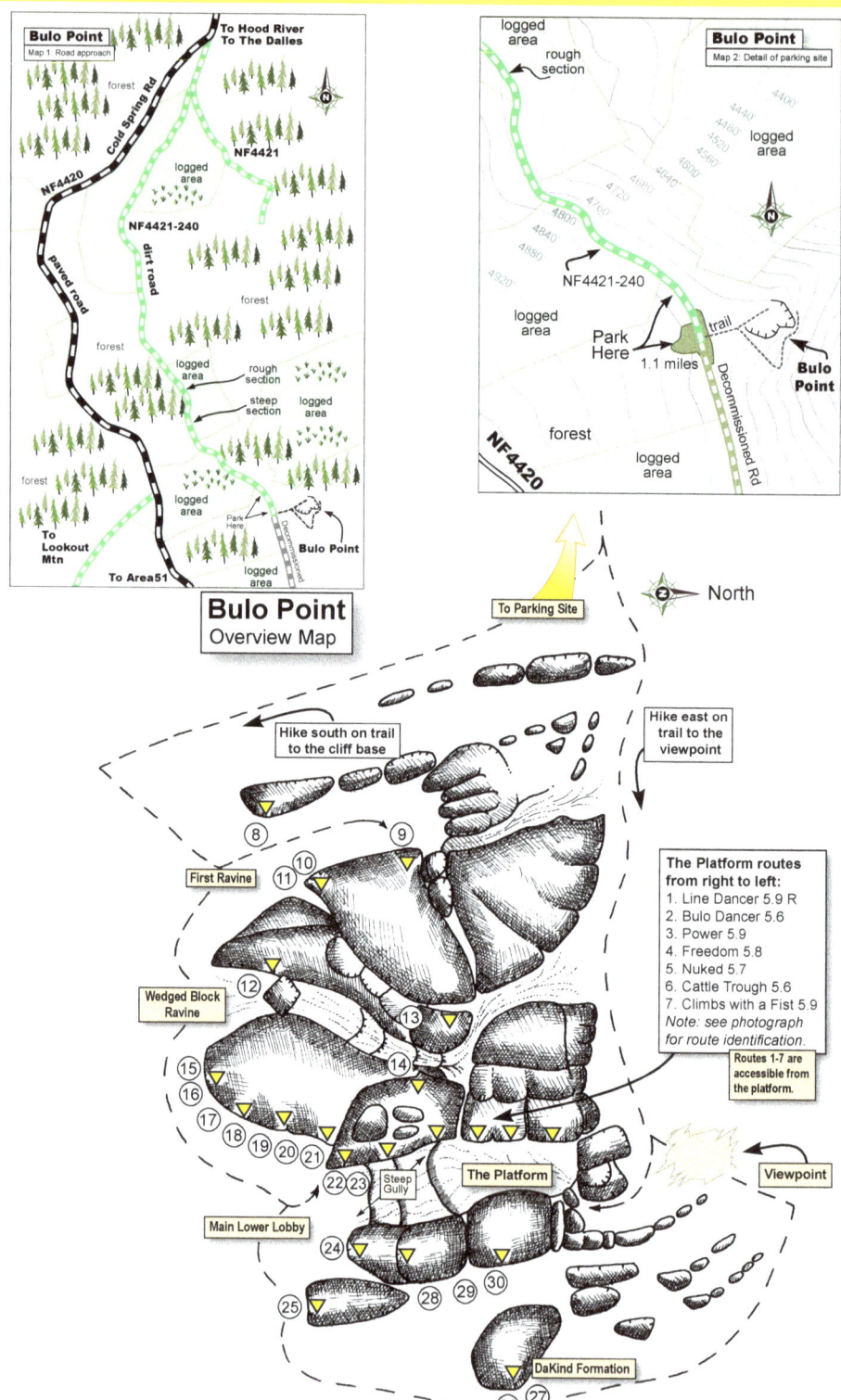

climb up onto the top of the higher bluff, set a top-rope and rappel down to the Platform. Be cautious if scrambling down to the alcove platform as it is surprisingly steep.

1. **Line Dancer 5.9 R** ★★
   Pro: Thin gear to 2"
   A sustained tricky thin crack on the upper right end of the Platform. This is the nearest route to the scenic viewpoint at the top of the bluff.

2. **Bulo Dancer 5.6**
   Pro: Behemoth gear to 5" or 6"
   This is the fat wide crack which is easier to just TR.

3. **Power & Politics 5.9** ★★★
   Pro: Gear to 2"
   Starts the same as Freedom, but launch up into the right thin finger crack. This line is a bit more difficult to lead. Does not need the additional bolts other than the first bolt to protect the initial starting move off the ground.

Nicolle leading at *Bulo*

4. **Cattle Guard. 5.8** ★★★
   Pro to 2"
   One of the best short face climbs at Bulo Point. Climb the steep edgy face past a bolt then up to the left jam crack. Only the first bolt is necessary. The remaining portion of the climb protects well using natural pro and does not need the other bolts.

5. **Nuked 5.7**
   Pro: QD's
   A minor face climb on the extreme left end and facing toward Cattle Trough.

6. **Cattle Trough 5.6**
   Pro: Behemoth gear
   A large chimney separating the outer buttress from the main flat faced wall.

7. **Climbs with a Fist 5.9** ★★
   Pro: QD's
   A face climb on the outer buttress immediately right of Jet Wind and facing Cattle Trough.

FIRST RAVINE

First Ravine offers four routes. You can access this ravine as you descend the hiking trail before you reach the Lower Lobby.

8. **Silence of the Cams 5.9** ★★
   Pro: QD's
   Located on the immediate left in the First Ravine as you descend the hiking trail. Climbs a short vertical face using small edges and finishing on jug holds.

9. **Inversion Excursion 5.10a** ★
   Pro: QD's
   Located at the upper end of the same ravine as Silence of the Cams. Begin up an initial

steep off-width crack, then step up right to finish up a low angle face to the belay anchor.

10. **Awesome Possum 5.11+/.12-**
Pro: QD's
An improbable face climb ascending the arête and ending at the same anchor as Separated at Birth. Located on the right side of the First Ravine. A powerful climb using small sloping holds on a substantial overhang. The upper bulge has another thin crux section on small edges just before you reach the anchor.

11. **Separated at Birth 5.10b R**
Pro: QD's
Located in the First Ravine on the right and utilizes the same anchor as Drawin' a Blank. This route stems up the large deep chimney using positive

face holds. Move up left on good face edges to a short hard steep face just before the belay anchor.

WEDGED BLOCK RAVINE

As you descend the hikers loop trail to the lower lobby you will see a narrow ravine with a massive wedged block in it. Atomic Dust Buster is next to the wedged block.

12. Atomic Dust Buster 5.10c
Pro: QD's
Starts on the left next to the huge wedged chockstone. Climb the short vertical face past a small lip to the anchor.

The next two climbs are visible uphill behind the giant wedged block. You can access both routes from several different places.

13. Barking Spider 5.8
Pro: QD's

14. Slice of Pie 5.9
Pro: Nuts to 2"
This is a crack climb located up left of Nook and Cranny on the upper west side of the buttress with a belay anchor at the top.

Main Lower Lobby is the primary destination for climbers because the popular Jet Stream is a must-lead route of stellar proportion.

15. Alice 5.9
Pro: Some gear and QD's
Located on the far left side of a lower lobby. Climb a flat face broken with cracks to a boorish one-move wonder over a bulge.

16. JRat Crack 5.8 ★
Pro: Wires and cams to 4"
The broad face is broken by a wide zigzagging flared crack. That's it.

17. Raiders of the Lost Rock 5.9 ★
Pro: Nuts to 2"
Immediately right of JRat is a low angle bolted face. Ascend easy steps to first bolt, then smear delicately up small sloping

edges till it eases.

LOWER LOBBY
18. Fat Rabbit 5.12b/c
Pro: 3 QD's
An very difficult route on a short vertical face.

19. Plumbers Crack 5.6 ★★★
Pro to 3"
An enjoyable deep corner crack system and a suitable lead for everyone.

20. Return of Yoda 5.10c ★★
A great balancy face climb with thin sloped edges that will keep you gripped. The final crux moves use some of the Nook & Cranny holds so in essence it is a bit squeezed at the end.

21. Nook and Cranny 5.8 ★★★
Pro to 2" including small cams
A popular crack climb immediately left of the long vertical arête. Rappel from belay anchor. Or if you are inclined step up around the corner to access an upper 5.8+ crack lead (Slice of Pie) that ends at the top of the bluff.

22. Jet Stream 5.9 ★★★
Pro: 10 QD's
Jet Stream is considered to be the best route at Bulo.

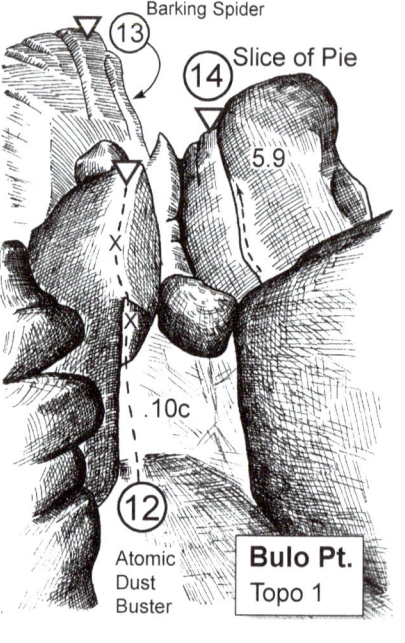

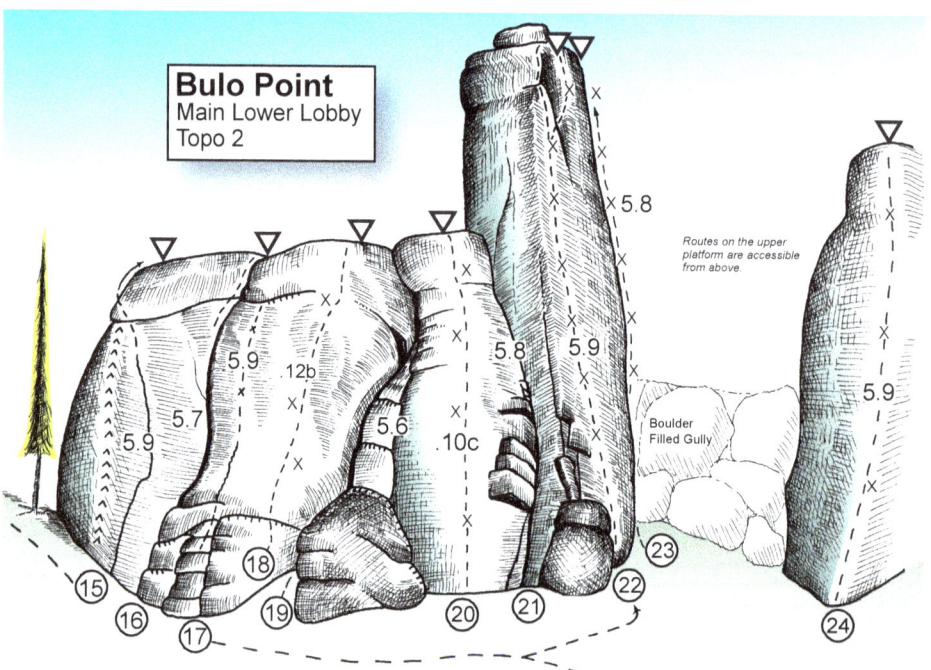

✧ EASTSIDE CASCADE MTNS   461

When standing at the main Lower Lobby you can easily spot Jet Stream because it is the long bolted arête route on the tallest buttress.

Ascend the prominent arête on small but positive face edges. Power through the first overhanging bulge crux section. Cruise up to the second overhanging crux section and aim right to get through this bulge (avoid the variation exit crack on the left). Finish on easier holds to the anchor at the top of the cliff.

Alternative route ending variation: If you plan to exit up *left* using the upper left exit crack variation it is called **Jet Stream Variation** (5.10a). Bring minor gear to 2" including cams. Climb Jet Stream, but at the second overhanging crux bulge jaunt up left in a minor crack to the top.

23. Streamlined (aka Jet Wind) 5.8 ★★★
Pro: 10 QD's (minor gear to 2")
A stellar long climb immediately right of Jet Stream on the same tall buttress formation. Start up a corner to a short crack (minor gear to 2") on a face, then continue to face climb up right (bolts) around a minor bulge on positive holds to the top of the cliff formation.

24. Black Market 5.10a
Pro: QD's
A insignificant climb on a minor arête on a minor bluff. The first several moves are awkward, but the rest of the climb is basic and in some ways a bit runout.

25. Don't Call Me Ishmael 5.11b ★★
Pro: QD's
At the far lower right end of the Lower Lobby is a wildly overhanging formation leaning out over the trail. This is Ishmael, a short but stiff seam/face climb that often gets free climbed, but also frequently gets 'dogged' by pumped climbers. Clipping the belay anchor is difficult.

DAKIND BUTTRESS

26. Scene of the Crime 5.10 C ★★★

Pro: QD's

Located on the left side of the DaKind Buttress formation, which is a large rock formation separated from the main bluff. Power up into a vertical short crack using face holds, then balance up right (crux) under an overhang. Attain better hand edges past the roof and cruise on up the belay anchor. Shares the same anchor with the DaKind route.

27. DaKind 5.9 ★★★

Pro: Minor gear to 3"

Located on the right side of the DaKind Buttress formation. Step up under an overhang using a crack, then lean out the slight bulge (pro) to grasp the edges above the overhang. Power past this initial overhang to better holds, and continue up slightly right on steep terrain with good holds to an anchor.

The last three routes are located uphill behind the DaKind Buttress formation. These routes are seldom climbed.

28. Who's the Choss? 5.9

Pro to 2"

This and the next two routes are located to the right and uphill on the east side of the same bluff of rock. Scramble up a steep dirt gully around DaKind to approach these routes.

29. Big Al 5.7 TR

A top-rope next to the previous route.

30. Rock Thugs 5.9

Pro to 3"

A crack climb tucked uphill and behind the DaKind rock outcrop formation.

THE MEADOW

The Meadow provides a nice selection of 'bumps' or minor rounded rock knobs and short bluffs composed of gritty sandpaper textured rock. The site has a minor string of bouldering opportunities and a few very short lead climbs. The knobs are scattered on a sunny Ponderosa forested slope, but is a reasonable place to escape the cloudy Spring weather of western Oregon. A little exploration and you will find other forested bouldering sites and minor rock bluffs.

To experience the flavor of this little area drive eleven miles east from Highway 35 on FS44, then take a sharp right turn (SW) onto FS4450. At 1¼ mile the Dufur City watershed sign will be visible at a 4-way intersection. Turn right on graveled road FS4421 and drive approximately 1 mile (elev. 3700').

HELIOTROPE

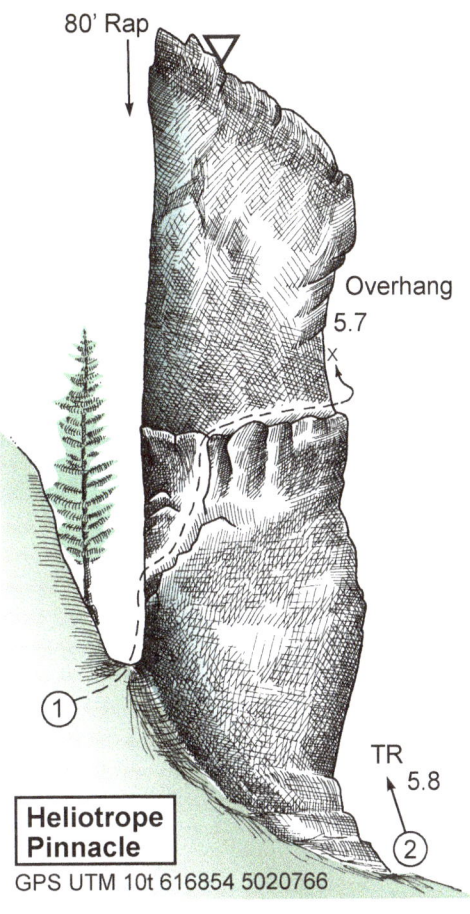

Heliotrope Pinnacle
GPS UTM 10t 616854 5020766

Another fascinating objective is this minor pinnacle located on a scenic hike east of Lookout Mountain on trail #458. About 1 mile east of the peak, and on the south-facing slope that drops into Badger Creek Wilderness is the **Heliotrope Pinnacle** (5.7) an 80' high pillar of rock that has a vertical aspect on all sides. The area is quite scenic and can be combined as a day hike in the area by starting at High Prairie, or at trail #456A, which starts at Fifteen Mile campground just south of Bulo Point. You can also hike the entire length of this trail starting from the east end near Flag Point. GPS: UTM 10t 616854 5020766.

AREA 51

Beta written by Kay Kucera and Paul Cousar

Area 51 is a great climbing crag that packs an energetic list of powerful rock climbs, all on a convenient south facing bluff. The site boasts unique advantages over other east side crags; it is great for early or late season climbing, and is conducive for rock climbers who are seeking a place to expand their skill level into the solid 5.11 range. The site tends to be dryer on overcast cold cloudy days when Bulo Point is too damp after a brief summer shower.

Area 51 is cast in a similar light as Bulo Point (proximity and seasonal temperatures) nestled in a forest of pine trees at the 4100' (1250m) elevation. Its southern exposure is advantageous in early Spring or late Fall. Area 51 is definitely a step beyond in terms of leading ability because the site has no easy routes under 5.9. Many of the climbs range in difficulty from 5.10c to 5.11+ and beyond, all on a very steep 80' high bluff. Many of the routes are mixed-sport routes in that you do need some specialized equipment (cams, nuts, etc.) to ascend the route without undue risk. The upper fixed belay anchors are not accessible from the top of the bluff so avoid trampling the fragile soils on the top of the bluff.

Area 51 was initially tapped as a climbing resource in the late '90s by several regional climbers. Others soon followed. Finding the site suitable for steep relentless climbing, they and friends quickly embarked onto creating a cliff where they could refine their climbing skills while enjoying the sport with friends. Paul Couser, Kay Kucera, and Jim Anglin were the primary route developers. They refined and enhanced the trail network, created stabilized platforms at the base of many routes, and placed an importance on climber awareness toward the ecological biodiversity of the Area 51 site.

Individuals who helped carry the dynamics of climbing into the 21st century were Dave Boltz, Jai Dev, Steve Mrazeck, Reed Fee, Matt Spohn, Adam McKinley, Kent Benesch, Elmo Mecsko, and other Portland area climbers.

Read the entire section on *Biodiversity Dynamics of East Side Flora Communities, Access and User Impact* and *Ethical Continuity* at the beginning of this chapter. With your dedication this partnership of low impact rock climbing activity continues to be an ecological legacy.

Several Area 51 reminder points from that article are:

1. Utilize the well-developed foot trails (no short-cutting). These user trails are well marked with stone steps and belay platforms to minimize the erosional impact.

2. The top anchors are not accessible from above so avoid walking on the fragile soils at the top of the bluff. Avoid unnecessary trampling of the local plant species. Do not remove indigenous flora from the cliff, from the rock climb, or along the cliff base.

3. Seriously consider

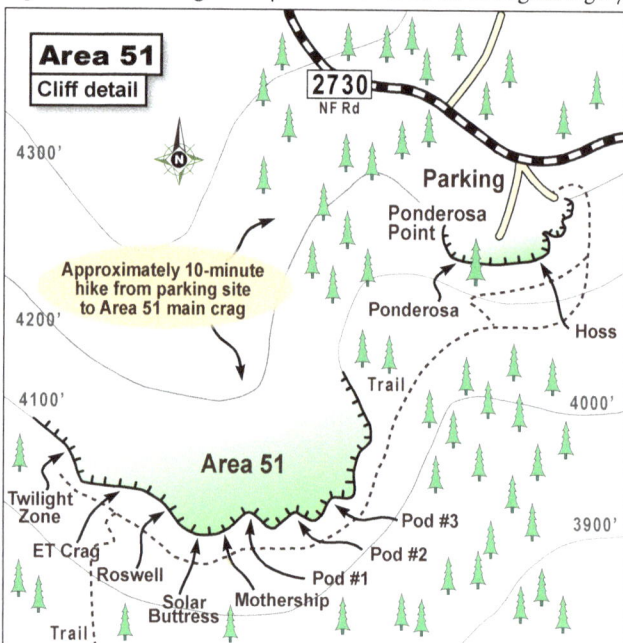

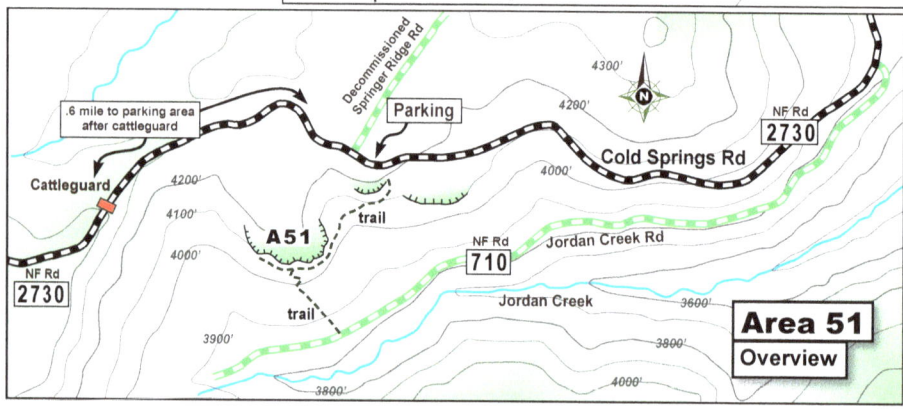

leaving your pets at home. A loose, rowdy dog is not everyone's best friend. It can cause more damage in five minutes than twenty climbers in a month, thus it is best to leave the pup at home.

4. Pre-inspecting routes via rappel is normal business, so rappel bolting is the usual method (though not always) for route development here. Refrain from chopping fixed gear, chiseling or altering holds, retro-bolting existing lines without permission, placing bolts next to quality gear placements, avoid developing 'R' or 'X' rated routes.

5. It is recommended to wear climbing helmets while leading or belaying.

Directions

Area 51 has good paved road access to the trail parking site. The site, though nestled in a pine forest at an elevation of 4,000' is often dry on cool rainy overcast days of Spring or late Fall.

Mackenzie Jones leading at A51

Directions from Hood River: Drive south from Hood River, Oregon on Hwy 35. Drive east on FS44 for 8¼ miles and turn south (right) onto FS 4420. Drive south on paved road FS 4420 past the Bulo Point turnoff. At a three-way junction drive south on FS 2730 past Fifteen-Mile Campground. The road descends eastward several miles and will cross a cattle guard. Continue for ½ mile and park in a large pullout on the south side of the road at Ponderosa Point. Take the descent trail as it drops downhill south below the parking site and aim west below Ponderosa Point. A ten minute walk will take you to the east end of the main A51 formation.

Directions from The Dalles: Area 51 can also be approached by driving south from The Dalles through Friend, Oregon and drive west on FS 2730 (see overview diagram).

Trail Approach: A fast ten-minute walk down below Ponderosa Point and along a path to the west will bring you to the east edge of the main A51 wall. An alternate but lesser used lower trail approach begins on FS 710 road and hikes uphill in 5-10 minutes to the base of the routes called Friend or Alien.

THE TWILIGHT ZONE

1. **Young Jedi 5.10a**
   Pro: 3 bolts and assorted gear
   Furthest west climb located 12' right of the "colonette cave". Start in crack left of Dreamland. Head right out crack through bolted bulge to common anchor.

2. **Dreamland 5.10b** ★
   Pro: 8 QD's
   Farthest left (west) bolted route on crag. Face climbing finishes out crack through bulge.

Gabriel leading *Wormhole*

3. **War of the Worlds 5.11a** ★
   Pro: 7 QD's
   WOTW is 15' right of Dreamland. Follows right side of slab to steeper overlaps up higher.

4. **Men in Black 5.10b**
   Pro: 6 QD's
   MIB is 25' right of Dreamland. Funky face climbing with a slab finish.

5. **Crash Landing 5.12c** ★
   Pro: 8 bolts, and gear to 1.5"
   CL is 15' right of MIB. Start left of wide crack. Increasingly difficult face climbing with overlaps that leads up to a 'crash landing' finish (.11d AO).

6. **Earth First 5.11a** ★
   Pro: 8 QD's
   Pocketed face right of crack. Begin in overhanging corner, and move right to face. Finish up steeper bulge.

7. **Shape Shifter 5.11a** ★
   Pro: 6 QD's
   Obvious right facing dihedral with steep start and involves technical stemming.

8. **Alien Lunacy 5.11b**
   Pro: 6 QD's
   Contrived variation of Luna. Stay left of bolts, and the crack is out of bounds. Crosses to right on upper face.

Jim Anglin leading at *Area 51*

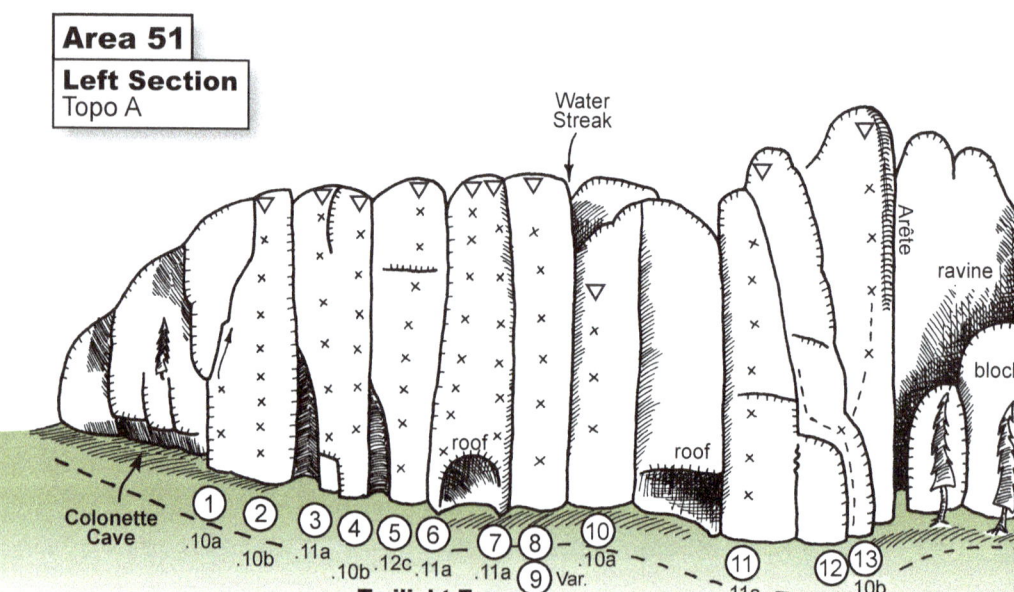

EASTSIDE CASCADE MTNS 467

9. **Luna 5.10c** ★★
   Pro: 6 QD's
   Face climb 10' right of Shapeshifter. Balancy crux at bolts #3-#4.

10. **Take Me To Your Leader 5.10a**
    Pro: 3 bolts, and gear to 2"
    Description: Broken arête and crack system right of wet streak. Mixed ice in winter.

11. **Cattle Mutilation 5.11a** ★★
    Pro: 7 QD's
    About 60' east of TMOYL. Crimp up sunny face with ledge midway.

12. **The Eagle Has Landed 5.10a**
    Pro to 3" [?]
    About 10' right of CM is a sharp edged left leaning crack. Ends at CM anchor.

13. **Erased Memory 5.10b**
    Pro: 5 bolts, and gear to 1.5"
    About 12' right of CM. Start on 'eagle' crack, move up and right to finish on a narrow pinnacle.

Tomma leading *Alien Observer*

ET CRAG
14. **ET (Extra Trad) 5.9**
    Pro to [?]
    Start from top of boulder 5' left of Phone Home. Follow the crack system.

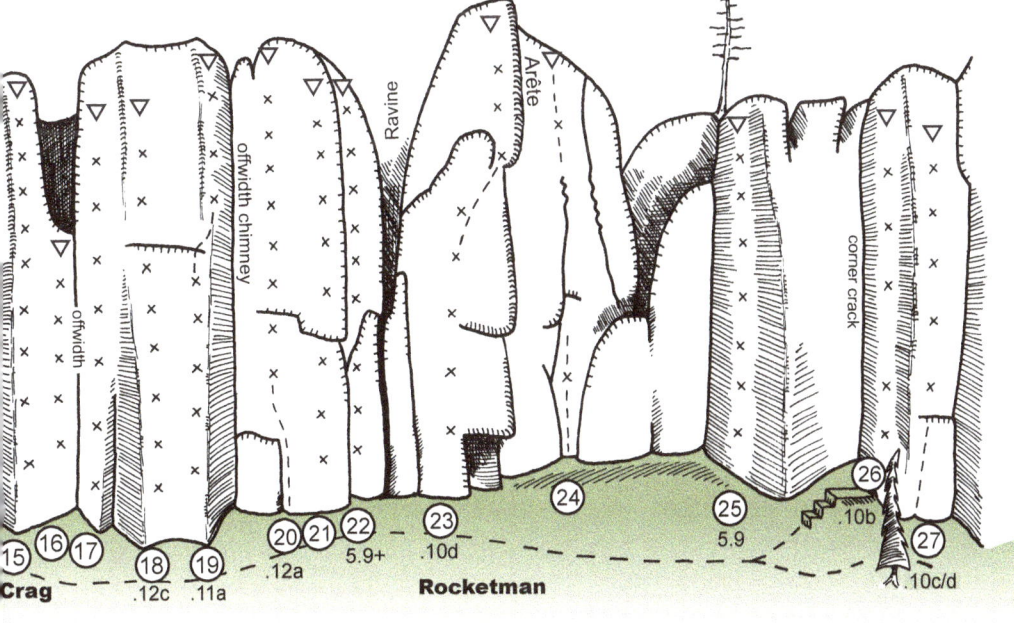

15. Phone Home 5.12b ★★
Pro: 9 QD's
Striking red arête. Steepening crimps to obscure finish.

16. Little Gray Men 5.11b ★
Pro: 5 QD's
Short face between Phone Home and Mars.

17. Mars 5.10d ★★★
Pro: 7 QD's
Beautiful red face on the right wall of open book that is broken by large horizontals. This route is west facing and involves 5.10d stemming, and offers a 5.11b direct finish.

18. Crop Circles 5.12c
Pro: 8 QD's
Located 6' right of Mars above lower approach trail. Start on left arête with smooth blank band. Stick clip past missing first bolt.

19. Friend or Alien 5.11a ★★
Pro: 8 bolts and gear to 2"
At the top of lower approach trail and 12' right of CC. Has some height dependent reachy moves.

20. Trouble With Tribbles 5.12a ★
Pro: 8 bolts and gear to 2"
Easy crack to bolted face with small overlaps.

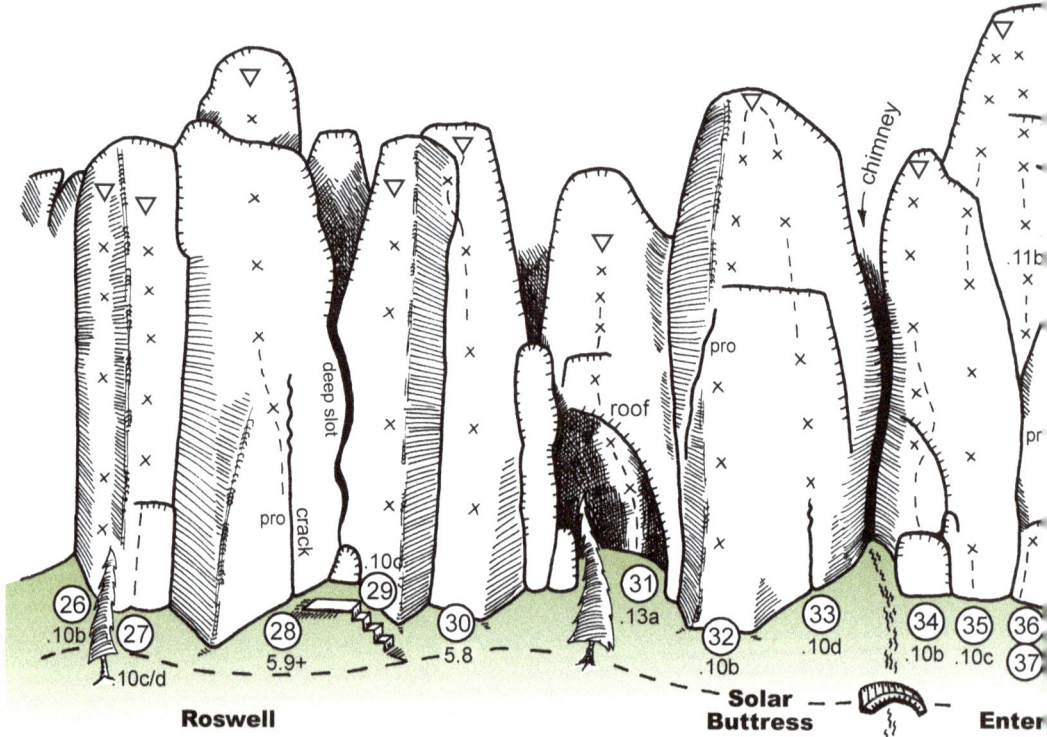

21. The Cover Up 5.12a/b
Pro: 8 QD's
Start up a slab 5' right of Tribbles. Move up right and work through bulge to featured face above.

22. Out Of This World 5.9+ ★★
Pro: 9 QD's
Located 7' right of 'Cover Up'. Climb 20' of wide fist crack to heavily featured slab above. Route is best accessed from off of the Rocketman platform.

ROCKETMAN FORMATION

23. Rocketman 5.10d
Pro: 8 QD's
Located 45' left of First Contact above and right of the 'Cover Up'. Climbs slabby face, then moves right to a wide crack up to a pedestal. Step right and finish on fun arête.

24. Major Tom 5._ [?]
Pro: [?] bolts [?]
Discontinuous cracks to the right of a steep arête to a thin face.

25. Cosmic Debris 5.9
Pro: 6 QD's
A minor face climb on the left side of a steep rounded rock slab.

26. First Contact 5.10b ★★★
Pro: 6 QD's
Short stairs just behind a huge stump takes you up to a platform at the base of this route.

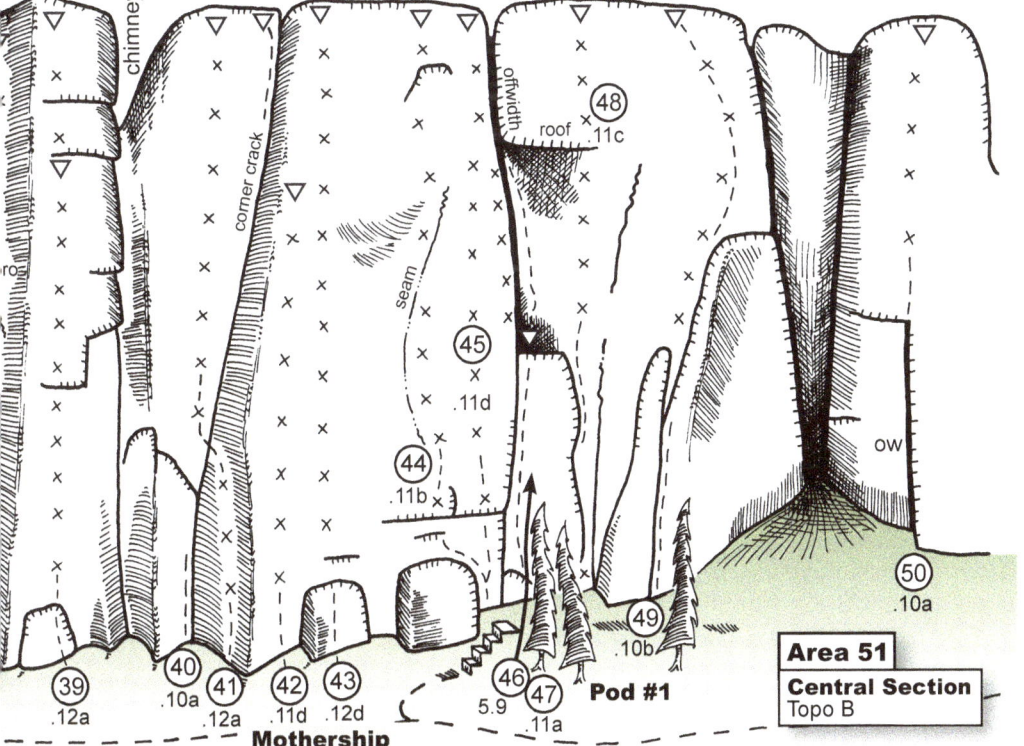

470 CHAPTER 5 ◆ ORC

27. UFO 5.10c/d ★
Pro: 5 QD's
Located 10′ right of First Contact. Climb up a hand crack left of some ledges and up to balancy moves on a bolted face above.

28. Roswell 5.9+ ★★
Pro: 5 bolts and gear to 2"
Located 20' right of UFO. Start up a 25' tall finger crack. Move left, and face climb to a bivy ledge, and then continue up the small pedestal to a chain anchor.

29. Uranus Has Rings 5.10c ★
Pro: 4 bolts and gear to 2"
Located 8' right of Roswell. Balancy moves down low on the lead, but casual climbing up top.

30. It Taint Human 5.8
Pro: 5 QD's
Located 8' right of UHR. Climb a slabby face on the right up to a dihedral using juggy crack holds. A bit dirty but will improve with use.

SOLAR BUTTRESS FORMATION

31. Journey To The Sun 5.13a
Pro: 6 QD's
Steep route in a short cave follows a bolt line to pull the lip and onward to a slabby face finish. There is an easier variation right of the bolt line.

32. Solar Flair 5.10b ★
Pro: 6 bolts and gear to 3"
Climb arête 15' right of JTTS. Finish on a steep face which quickly ends at the Sunspot belay anchor.

33. Sunspot 5.10d ★
Pro: 5 bolts and gear to 2"
Located on a sunny face 10' right of Solar Flair. Follow up some discontinuous cracks to cruxy face climbing above a ledge. The climb is a bit easier if you are tall.

THE ENTERPRISE

34. Vulcan Mind Meld 5.10b
Pro: 9 QD's
Located to the right of a drainage gully. Climb up large blocks to a roof. A vulcan mind meld might help with the perplexing moves above the roof. Finishes with adventurous climbing through questionable rock on blunt arête. Belayer should stay alert for flying objects.

35. To Boldly Bolt Where No Man Has Bolted Before 5.10c ★
Pro: 8 QD's
Located 5' right of VMM. Follow discontinuous cracks to finish on a blunt buttress. Route may be more difficult if you are short.

36. Live Long and Prosper 5.11b ★
Pro: 7 bolts and gear to 3"
Located uphill about 6' left of AA. Climb to the right of a vegetated crack up to another hand crack. At the 'Y' continue straight up on crimpy orange face holds to end at the belay anchor for TBBWNMHBB.

37. Captain Jim 5.10+
Pro to 3"
Start as for LLP but follow up a right trending crack to the anchors.

MOTHERSHIP

38. Alien Autopsy 5.10c ★★★
Pro: 7 bolts and gear to 2.5"
Located on an obvious west facing wall. Bolts and gear will protect a delicate series of face moves between discontinuous cracks.

39. Close Encounters 5.12a ★★★
Pro: 12 QD's
Located 10' right of AA. Multiple crux sections with varied climbing. It takes 10 clips to reach the first anchor, or continue past the first anchor by climbing through the roof past two more bolts to a short headwall to the upper anchor.

40. Black Ops 5.12a ★★★
Pro: 11 bolts and gear to 2"
Located 20' right of Close Encounters. Locate HAL which is the long right leaning crack corner. Black Ops start on a steep technical slab immediately right of HAL, and then cross over the crack onto the left where Black Ops powers up a vertical slightly hung bolted face with reachy, fun moves.

41. Open the Pod Bay Door HAL 5.10a ★★
Pro to 3"
This is the obvious long right leaning crack corner system starting next to the trail.

42. The Truth Is Out There 5.11d ★★
Pro: 7 QD's
Fun shallow dihedral that leads up to technical moves above a good rest.

43. Death Star 5.12d ★★
Pro: 11 QD's
Attacks multiple crux bulges on left side of a tall face with light colored rock.

44. Mothership 5.11b ★★★
Pro: 9 QD's
This is THE classic at A51. Located 18' right of HAL and to the left of Pod #1 at the base of the stairs. Clamber up onto the top of a large detached boulder. Step up to a bulge and power through an awkward crux mantle move. Delicate face climbing leads up left to a thin seam. Follow the vertical seam (crux) past a slight bulge to juggy holds. A few final face moves lands at an anchor.

45. Even Horizon 5.11d ★★★
Pro: 9 QD's
Start at the top of the stairs which leads to Pod #1. Climb far right side of light colored face just left of the blunt arête. Stay left at the 7th bolt for the full tick. Short aliens might not achieve liftoff.

POD #1

46. The Wormhole 5.9 ★
Pro to 3" (possible gear to 4" on upper part)
Climb a wide crack immediately right of EH to a large ledge called Denial Pedestal. Continue up the deep overhanging offwidth corner system up out left to an anchor at top of Stargate.

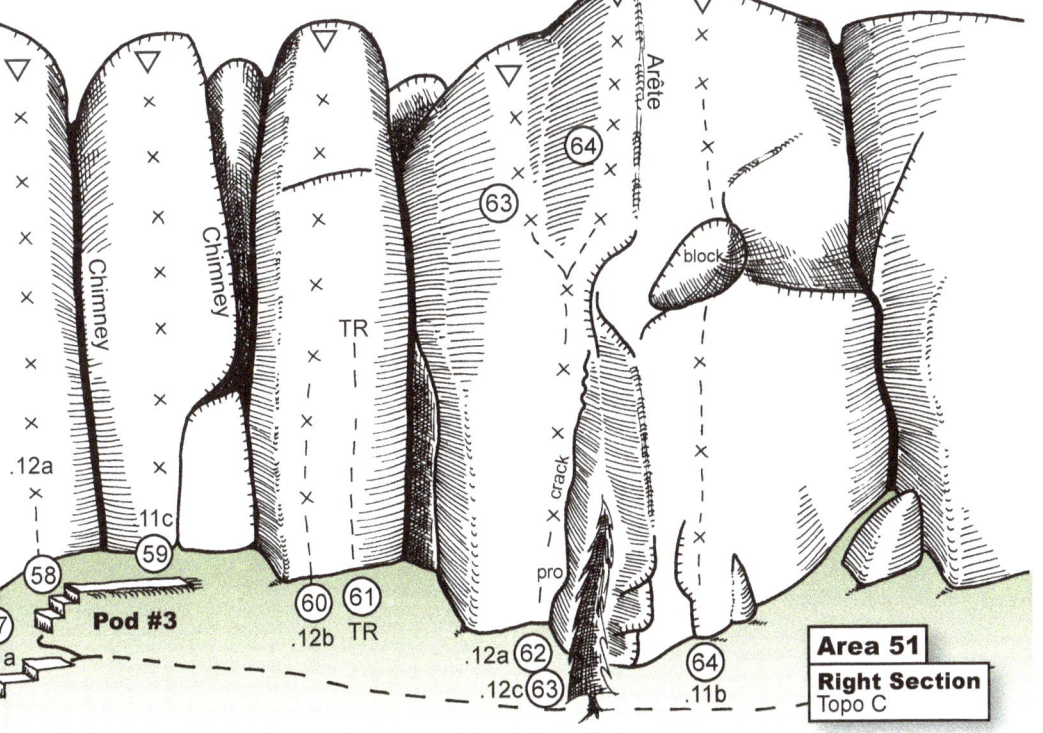

47. Stargate 5.11a ★
Pro: 7 bolts and gear to 2"
Walk up the stairs to Pod #1. Climb the first part of Wormhole to the large ledge. Stargate powers up a deceptively pumpy thin face off the ledge side of the ledge and merges in with the upper part of the wide Wormhole near the anchor.

48. Lies and Deception 5.11c ★★★
Pro: 7 bolts and gear to 3"
Walk up the stairs to Pod #1. A bolt protects the opening moves to an easy crack on the right side of Full Denial flake. Avoid Denial Pedestal, and climb a vertical reddish face to pass a roof on the right. Finish on technical crimps to an anchor.

49. Alien Observer 5.10b ★★★
Pro: 6 bolts and gear to 2"
Locate the Pod #1 area by walking up the stairs to the right to the landing. Start up a 30' hand jam crack that quickly widens as you near the flat top of a minor pedestal. Power off from the top of the pedestal up overhanging jug holds up right, and then up left to the anchor.

50. Probe 5.10a
Pro: 4 bolts and gear to 4"
Located on the right side of Pod #1 via the upper belay platform.

51. Dilithium Crystals 5.11b ★
Pro: 8 QD's
Crystal crimping up an obvious blunt face/arête. Start on main trail.

POD #2
52. Alien Invasion 5.10b/c
Pro: 5 bolts and gear to 2"
Located 9' right of DC in a right facing dihedral. Initial awkward moves lead to a finger crack passing a small roof on the left and ends on a fun slab above.

53. Abducted 5.10c ★
Pro: 6 bolts and gear to 1.5"
Begin on the highest platform between two wide cracks. Climb face and chimney (runout).

54. Taken 5.11d
Pro: 6 QD's
This is the direct no-stemming variation of Abducted. More difficult if you are short.

55. Glue Me Up Scotty 5.11b ★★
Pro: 8 bolts and gear to 2"
Located 30' right of AI. Usually starts from the low belay platform on the main trail. Climb a hand crack to the 'transporter' hold. Will Scotty beam you to the anchors? Stay tuned...

POD #3
56. We Are Not Alone 5.10d / .11a

★

Pro: 7 QD's
Located 5' right of 'Glue Me Up'. This route is the other side of the arête. Stay right of the bolts by using the pockets at start for the full value 5.11a stylin'.

57. The Borg 5.11a PG
Pro: 3 bolts and gear to 2"
Start on lower belay platform about 7' right of WENA. Belay on the trail. Starts in the crack/flake and ascends the bolted face above.

58. Lights Over Phoenix 5.12b ★
Pro: 7 QD's
Start on the upper belay platform 10' right of The Borg and left of the chimney. Technical climbing up a blunt arête.

59. Resistance Is Futile 5.11c ★★
Pro: 7 QD's
Located 8' right of LOP, but right of a mossy chimney on the upper platform. Mantle onto ledges leading up to a discontinuous crack system on a slightly overhanging face.

60. Covert Research 5.12b ★
Pro: 7 QD's
Located 14' left of Conspiracy Theory between two wide cracks. Surmount sloping ledge to a blank face above. Dude, if yo 6' or taller take off a letter grade!

61. Groom Lake (top-rope)
Pro: Top-rope
Located 5' right of Covert Research, and 5' left of Conspiracy. Power up a crack at the start which quickly leads to a hard boulder problem and micro flakes to an anchor.

62. Conspiracy Theory 5.12a ★★
Pro: 9 QD's
Begins on the far right wall in a steep, yellow dihedral. Climb up left past a small blocky roof to balancy moves on a blunt arête.

63. Conspiracy Lake 5.12c ★★
Pro: 7 QD's
Follows the initial part of Conspiracy Theory to the 5th bolt. Then it crimps out left and up a blank face past 3 more bolts to finish on the Groom Lake anchor.

OUTER LIMITS
Only one route, but with cleaning there could be more.

64. Dark Side of the Moon 5.11b
Pro: 6 QD's and pro
Furthest climb at the east end of the main crag.

PONDEROSA POINT
There are four known climbs here, but since the wall is 150' long it could certainly stand to see

Climbing at *The Meadow*

a few more.

65. Ponderosa 5.10b ★

Pro: 6 QD's

This is the right route on the buttress behind the BIG ponderosa pine. Climb up a shallow, featured dihedral and move up right around the flake.

66. Adam 5.10b

Pro: 6 QD's

Adam is the left climb on the right end of the formation. Shares the belay anchor with Hoss.

67. Hoss 5.10b ★

Pro: 6 QD's

The first climb encountered on Ponderosa Point approach trail.

This is the right-most of these two. Pull through a fun bulge at the start. Follow discontinuous cracks and finish with exciting moves on slightly overhanging face moves near the top.

THE LINK-UPS

Here are some wild link-ups to mix some flavor into your venue on your next visit to A51.

A. Men Are From Mars 5.11b ★

Pro: 7 QD's

Climb up 5 bolts on Little Gray Men, clip the anchor with a long QD, and then step right to finish on fun headwall of mars past 2 more bolts.

B. Alien Encounter 5.11b ★★

Pro: 8 bolts and gear to 2"

Climb to 5th bolt on the Autopsy, then traverse right to Close Encounters. Finish through the roof to the headwall clipping three more bolts.

C. Black Truth 5.11c ★

Start on Black Ops slab (.11c), and finish on 'The Truth' as belay anchors.

D. Starship 5.11b ★★★

Pro: 11 QD's

Climb past 4 bolts on Death Star, and then trend right onto Mothership. Long slings reduce rope drag. Clip 7 more bolts on your way to the anchor on Mothership.

E. Event Gate 5.11c ★★

Pro: 9 QD's

Start at the top of the stairs leading to Pod #1. Follow 'Event Horizons' route to the 7th bolt. Move right onto easier terrain to finish on Stargate. Short stature aliens may not achieve liftoff.

6

SANTIAM ROCK CLIMBS & SUMMITS

THERE ARE TWO GREAT RIVERS which gather the waters of the old Cascade range southeast of Salem — the North and South Santiam River. This region, known as the old or Western Cascades, are composed of older lava flows, tuffs and other intrusive rock formations. The hills surrounding these vast river drainages are characterized by steeply forested transition zones of vertical mountainous uplift. The crests of these rugged fog shrouded peaks, reach to an average height of 5,500', and hold many unusual gems of delightful beauty for avid adventurous climbers.

Stellar Sub-Alpine Climbing Options

People have for generations come to these forests to experience the natural scenic wonders that abound here. There are natural rock arches, large caves with splendid views, deep blue-green lakes for fishing, and even pinnacles for rock climbing. This section will focus on the pinnacle and rock climbing destinations of the North Santiam River. The North Santiam River region is located east of Salem along U.S. Hwy 22, while the South Santiam River climbing recreation area is southeast of Albany on U.S. Hwy 20.

NORTH SANTIAM REGION

Tumble Lake Area

This area has a variety of wild pinnacles perched high along the ridge overlooking Tumble Lake. Steep forested slopes embellished in deep green, rugged rocky spires that stand like lone sentinels, and majestic views of Mt. Jefferson create a perfect place for exploring, climbing and photography.

The common destination is Needle Rock. To get there drive east from Salem on U.S. Hwy 22 to a left turn onto NF2223 just prior to the town of Detroit, Oregon. Follow French Creek road NF2223 till it splits left onto spur road NF520 and continue to Sardine Pass. Trail #3380 begins at Sardine Pass and traverses southeast past Dome Rock en route to Needle Rock, then descends down to Detroit Lake.

NEEDLE ROCK

This spire is the premier classic of the entire Tumble Lake region. To approach this elusive pinnacle overlooking Tumble Lake, park at the Tumble Lake trailhead #3379, and walk over the initial brief hill, then hike southeast on trail #3380 for 1¼ miles east passing Dome Rock knoll. You will see Needle Rock below the trail on your right in the forest. When adjacent to the spire descend through open forest a short distance to the classic 160' spire. Needle Rock has seen just a mere handful of ascents since it was first ascended by Eugene Dod and Jim Nieland.

The Tumble Lake hills are accentuated with a unique forested structure composed mostly of Mountain Hemlock, Spruce, Douglas Fir and low growing Vine Maple. Clumps of stout Bear Grass are plentiful on all the slopes, while tiny Rock Ferns, alumroot, and colorful penstemon can be found on vertical cliff scarps.

1. **Nieland Route 5.8**
   Pro: Nuts and cams to 3"; single 60m rope

   The Dod-Neiland (North Prow) route of Needle Rock is a stellar climb. Commence by scrambling up the initial 5th class mossy section 40' up to a good stance at a single fir tree belay. Step past the tree and free climb up a vertical blocky face (4 bolts) for 30' over a slight bulge overhang (5.8 crux) to a belay anchor located right at the lip. Traverse right along a sloping ledge system (1 bolt) that faces to the west to the base of a prominent wide corner system (1 bolt). Climb the wide corner (5.8 crux) by initially stemming and jamming the overhung crack corner till it eases near the top. Expect some friable rock (helmets!) and surprisingly technical climbing. One 60-meter rope will suffice for the rappel.

2. **The Direct 5.10a R**
   Pro: Nuts and cams to 2½"

   This route starts by clipping the first bolt on the Dod-Nieland, then embarks up and left on vertical ground to attain the summit at the notch. Definitely runout with limited protection, and has seen only one on-sight ground-up ascent mainly because the route is inobvious and loose.

Hugh on Spire Rock SE Rib

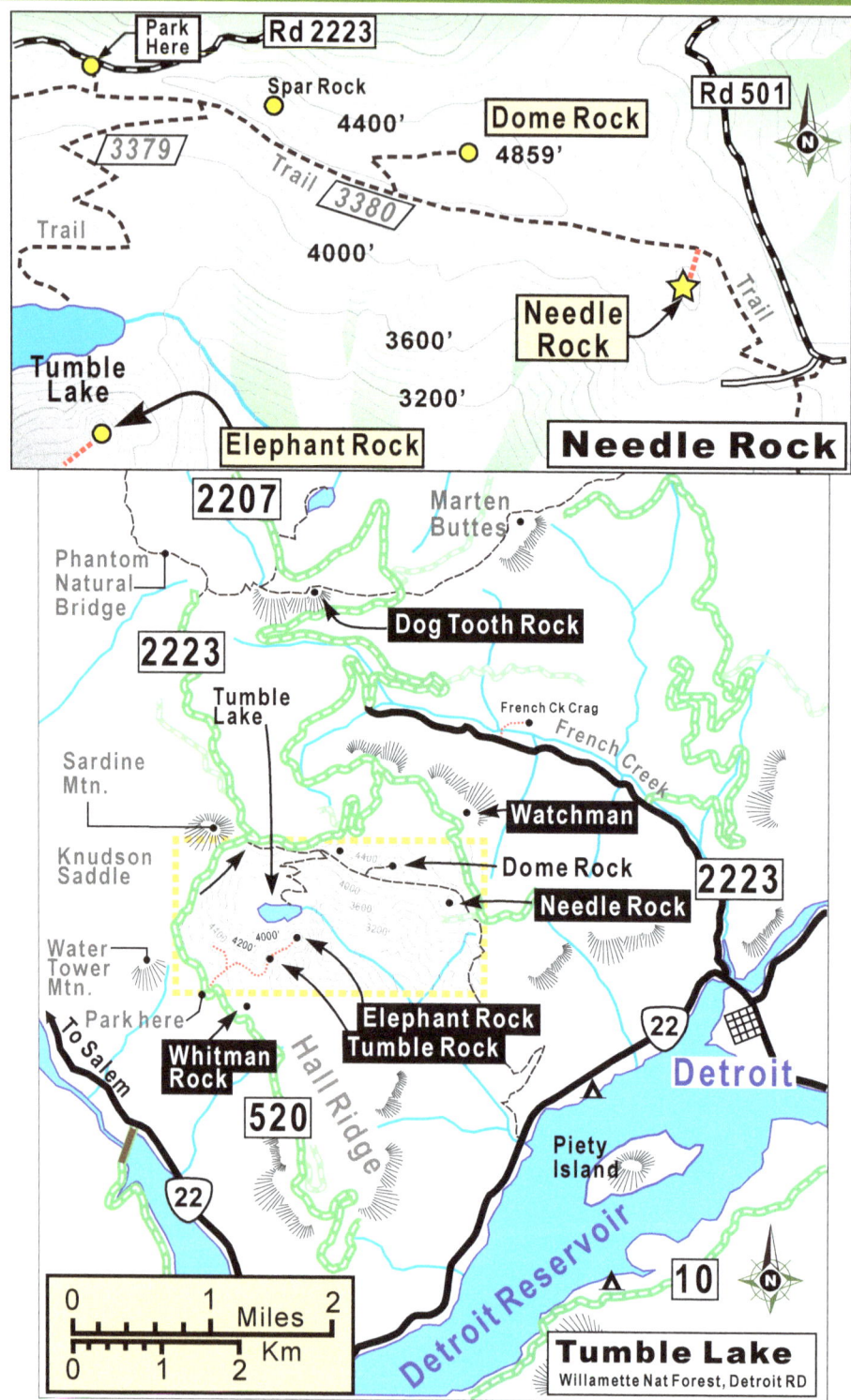

✧ SANTIAM SUMMITS   481

Needle Rock

Standard Route
5.8 Crux
Original Dod-Nieland

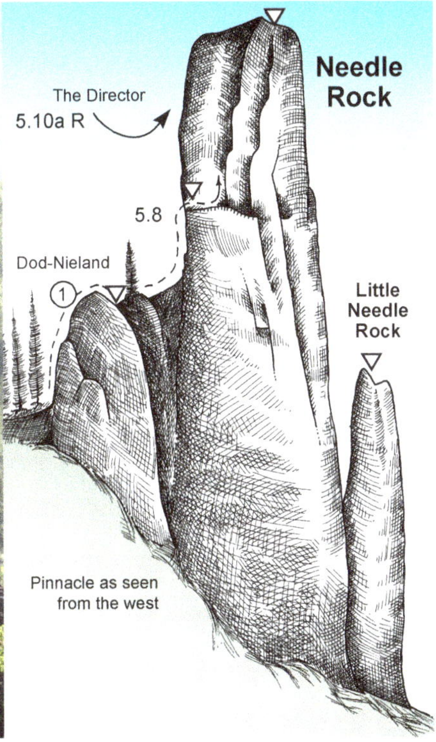

The Director 5.10a R
5.8
Dod-Nieland

Needle Rock

Little Needle Rock

Pinnacle as seen from the west

LITTLE NEEDLE ROCK

Yup, you gottr' right. There really is another pinnacle directly south of big Needle Rock. This little pinnacle is invisible till you take a tour down the slope on the east side of the main pinnacle. Then you realize there is actually something else here that is also a worthy objective.

Little Needle Rock is a 70' high crisp wafer thin spire that offers a well-protected (bolts) aid line from the saddle directly to the top. Though not free climbed at time of print it would likely go free at about 5.11-.

To aid the slightly overhung **Englund Direct** from the saddle follow the 5-bolt line (5.7 A0) using aiders, a few thin wires, cams, and perhaps a piton to gain access to the summit of this little forest gem. Here is the summit register up till June 2009: 1.) Brad solo 7-26-1997; 2.) Brad solo 8-1999; 3.) Brad solo 11-4-2002; 4.) Brad solo 7-19-2003; 5.) Brad solo 8-9-2003; 6.) Brad solo 7-30-2004. Yeowza! Way to go Brad. So...don't miss out on this De-

Needle Rock Topo B

5.8 crux
Dod-Nieland
5.8 crux

troit favorite with great views in the wild outback.

ELEPHANT ROCK

To explore the next area, continue driving on the gravel road southwest (approximately 1¼ miles from Sardine Saddle) along spur road #520 past Knudson Saddle and park at a pullout. From the parking site the summit of **Whitman Rock** is visible to the east above the road.

Hike uphill to the north on a minor ridge line through a thicket of rhododendron plants till you reach the main hill crest. From the open plateau knoll overlooking Tumble Lake walk east along the rounded ridge through a thick tangled forest southeastward till you are above a narrow ridge that descends down directly to the three summits.

The approximate distance from the vehicle to the spires is roughly ¾ mile. Descend the very steep ridge line directly down to **Tumble Rock**, **Split Spire** and **Elephant Rock**. The centerpiece of this high valley cirque is the deep and beautiful Tumble Lake.

Little Needle Rock

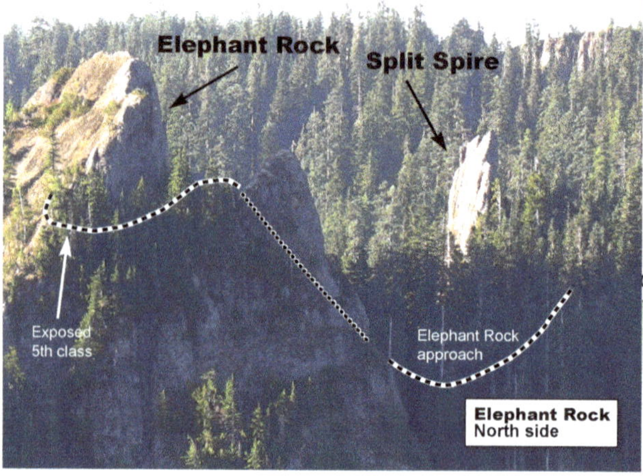

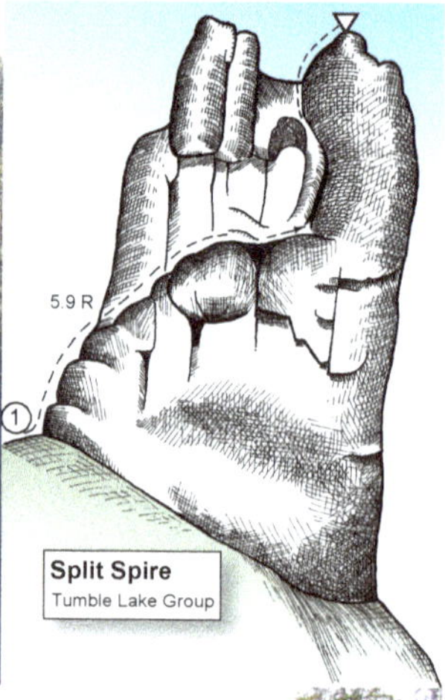

Needle Rock

Nieland's Needle (aka Needle Rock)
Summit register as recorded. There were likely 1-5 additional ascent parties from 1995 through 2008 who did not write in the summit register or were unaware of it. The summit register contents were water damaged beyond readability by 2008. As you can gather from the registry Needle Rock climbing conquistadors have been quite minimal.

Nieland's Needle 7-28-68 (Sunday)
Jim Nieland, Eugene Dod, Gerald Bjorman
Climbed 5th class up 1st pitch on west then on up right gully to top. It looks like someone else has been here.

10-22-80 (Wednesday)
Greg Ham, Teddy Lovett
Ketchikan, Alaska
Climbed 'Nieland's Route' using 4 pitons that were in place on 1st pitch. Clear, sunny weather, high 55° Low 29° Note: The price of this spiral notebook is about 49¢ in 1980!!

7-21-84 (Saturday)
Paul Harken - Lakeview, OR.
Brian Boswell - Victoria, BC
Sunny 7:50pm Peaceful
[On the] 2nd pitch took left (east) crack. Gerry & Terry here's your runner back (we found a tattered piece of webbing stuffed in the summit box).

1. **Tumble Rock 4th class**
   Pro: Rope, slings, and a few nuts
   Tumble Rock is a fun but exposed 4th class summit scramble. From the south saddle scramble up left on gravelly ledges passing a short step, and then up left amongst the trees on ledges to the top. The forested slope on the north side allows for an easier ascent.

2. **Split Spire   5.6 A1 or 5.10-**
   Pro: Versatile rack of nuts and cams to 4" plus pitons
   The infamous double summited Split Spire is rarely climbed. Start up from the west onto a gravelly ledge then angle to the right till you are under the notch between the two spires. On the right ascend a wide groove corner that angles up left to the notch. The toughest section is the free climbing moves from the shaky piton onto the notch. Step from the notch up onto the summit and belay. Expect some friable rock on this strangely classic summit. The technical part of the climb is less than 80' and you can rappel with one rope to the gravel ledge and rappel again from the bush to the ground.

3. **Elephant Rock 5.3 R**
   Pro to 2" and slings
   Elephant Rock is the lowest pinnacle of rock along this steeply descending ridge line. The climbing route is an exposed meandering line with considerable scrambling. Scramble up a 4th class section on the south side till you can follow a ledge around left to access the north side. Ascend the obvious easy 5.3R rib leading directly up to the top. This summit

is quite airy to attain yet yields exhilarating views once you are there.

DOG TOOTH ROCK

This minor wild jackal is a wild, friable adventurous endeavor on the French Creek Divide west of the pass just off FS2207 road. Take spur road FS2207 to the pass to access trail #3349. Hike west about ½ mile uphill to the eastern edge of the formation. Refer to the diagram and pick your weapon. This pinnacle actually has three minor knobs which can be gained by ascending a steep dirt and moss gully on the north side between two of the summits. GPS 44.78292° N / 122.22057° W Elev: 4490' / 1369m

1. **North Ravine 5.4 R**

   Pro: Minor nuts and cams to 1"

   Grovel up an exposed steep low 5th class dirty moss ramp (sling small cedars) 80' to access a notch separating the west horn from the middle knob. Drop down

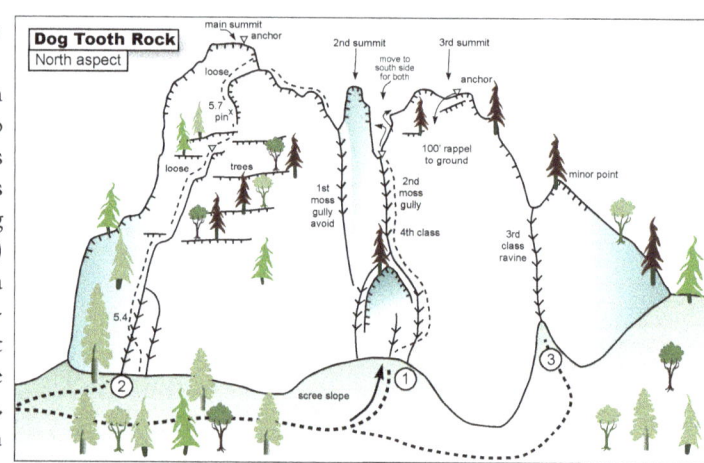

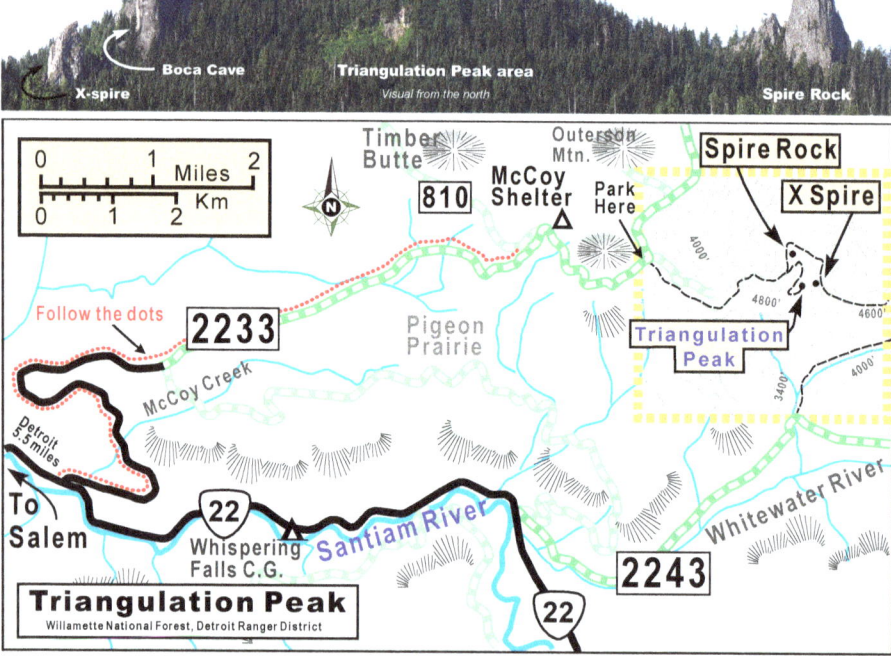

15' on the south side, traverse east along a ramp, then scramble up (180' lead) rocky steps to the east summit. Rappel back to the same notch belay, then lead up to the west knob on easy sloping ledges. Rappel anchor on west knob takes you back down the north side ravine to your original starting point.

2. **Nasal Mozz 5.7 R/X**
   Pro to 1" and pitons
   This east ridge route is a mossy ledge climb that starts at a series of minor corners and steps landing on a ledge (70') covered with small cedar trees. P2 (70') punches past a crux move then eases to loose mossy edges, so escape up right to the notch, then up the last step to the summit belay. Rap west to the notch belay, then rap from a small cedar tree down the North Ravine.

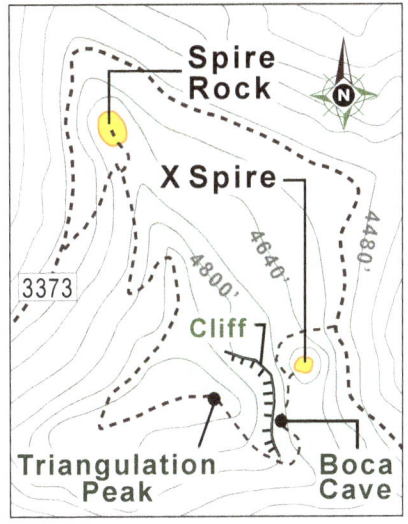

TRIANGULATION PEAK - BOCA CAVE

Two great pinnacles in the Detroit region majestically crown a lightly forested ridge crest alongside the Triangulation Peak Trail #3373, a scenic and popular 1½-mile hiking trail frequented by hikers en route to the famous Boca Cave. Perched on the crest of the ridge Spire Rock and X-Spire beckon the adventure climber. Great panoramic views of the Cascade Mountain range give the summits added value. Spire Rock fits the typical northern Oregon pinnacle geological composition of weather-worn grainy-textured andesite adequate for friction yet a little bit friable in plac-

Spire Rock

Spire Rock Map 1: South aspect

Directions

Drive east of Detroit on US Hwy 22 through Idahna and take road FS2233 left to the McCoy Creek shelter. Continue east from the shelter for another mile on gravel roads to the trailhead. Park and hike trail #3373 for 1½ miles east till it branches onto trail #3374. This trail zigzags uphill to Triangulation Peak.

SPIRE ROCK

1. SE Rib 5.4

Length: 160', Pro to 2½" and slings

The SE Rib of Spire Rock is the classic line on this pinnacle and the shortest climb. Spire Rock is the first pinnacle that the trail zigzags past on the way to the summit of Triangulation Peak. Hike initially up the first zigzag on trail #3374, and then scramble along a minor ridge*elette* to access the notch on the rib. Rope up at a tree prior to reaching the notch at the base of the cliff face. Traverse to the notch and around the large block. Climb up large steps and corners (fixed pitons) to a small ledge, angle up left to a slot, then aim up right for a belay anchor at the base of a dead tree. Scramble to the summit and belay at a bush. One single 60m rope will get you off the spire.

2. **South Face 5.4 R**
Length: 230', Pro to 3" including cams

Hugh on Spire Rock *SE Rib*

The south face is quite wide and offers a plethora of options for climbing on variable rock. Access is quick — just jump off the trail at the zigzag, rope up and start climbing. Pick a line that looks reasonably protectable. This is a fairly direct route to the summit although infrequently ascended and a bit friable in places.

3. **SW Buttress II 5.8 R**
Length: 500', Pro: Nuts and cams to 3" and several pitons

The **SW Buttress** holds the rare distinction for being the longest sub-alpine multi-pitch rock climbing route in the North Santiam Detroit region. Your first view of Spire Rock is the SW Buttress aspect. A serious climb involving difficult terrain navigation over friable rock and gravelly ledges suitable for the hard-core adventurer.

P1 120' 5.8R fixed gear: Start at the very toe of the buttress on the lower trail. Climb the initial steep slab, angle up right and surmount an odd vertical step (can be bypassed on right). Move up a groove and dance carefully up friable rock to a very steep vertical section of wall (crux). Balance up the crux section on small insecure sloping edges to easier terrain. Move up gravelly steps to a nice

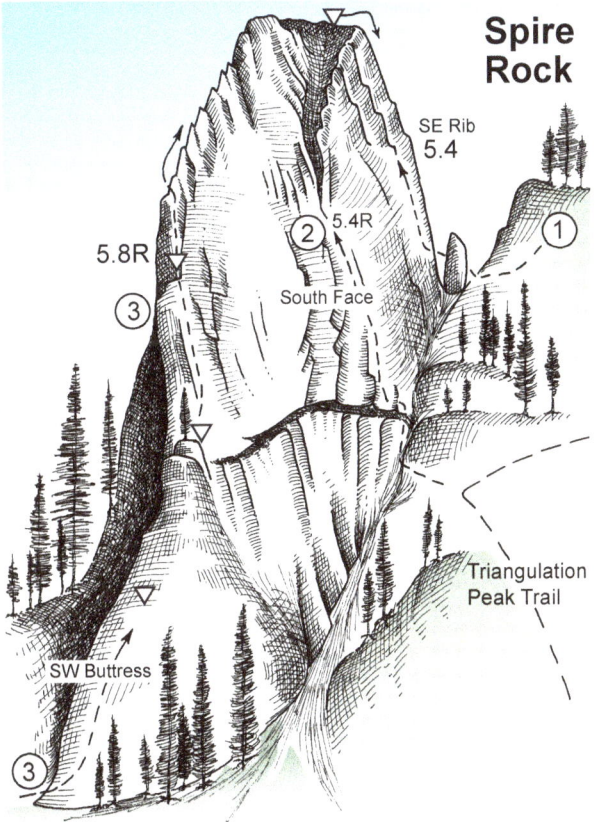

tree belay on a large ledge. Beware of friable rock.

P2 70' 5.4 pro to 3": Move up right on a sunny slope using steps and corners, move right under a large roof, then up a vertical corner to a tree belay on a ledge.

P3 100' 5.6 pro to 3": Start up an obvious crack using ample edges passing a small cedar tree. At a minor stance move up right into a crux offwidth slot crux. Place cams deep in the back and then surmount the slot carefully (best without a pack) and continue up to a belay anchor at a small stance.

P4 100' 5.4R pro to 2": From the belay ascend up right using a minor crack, then up steep steps (fixed pitons) and face moves onto the arête. Follow the arête (fixed pins) to a flat stance at a bolt where you can set a belay. Beware of friable rock.

P5 100' 5.4R pro to 2": Dance carefully along a tenuous narrow ridge crest then scramble along easy terrain to the summit. Expect 2 hours to ascend the entire buttress.

An alternative (Bypass Traverse 5.5PG) can be used to access the belay tree at the top of P2 and below the offwidth

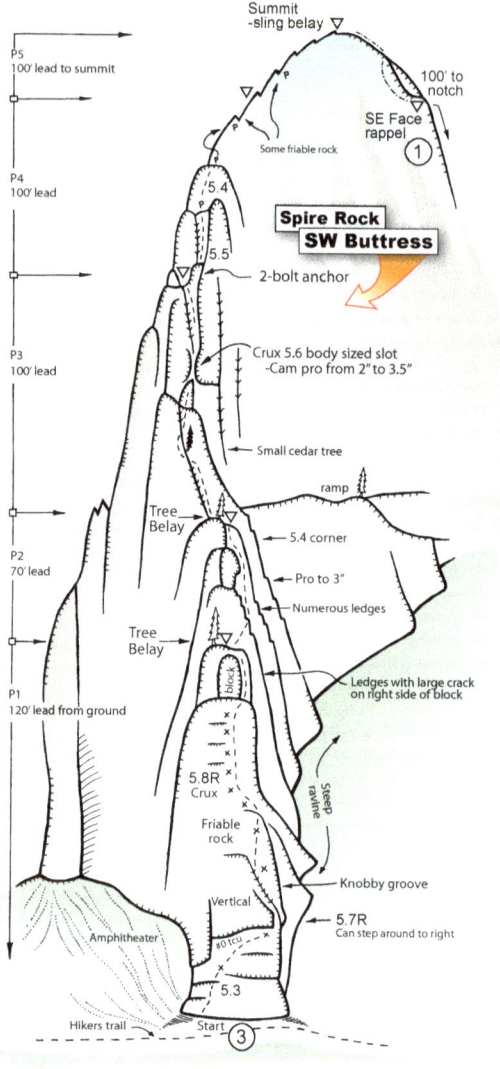

chimney on P3. It steps off the first switchback in the hikers trail and aims up along a rising traverse to a thin tree, then descends a bit to attain the belay tree at the top of P2.

Boca Cave

After climbing Spire Rock continue up trail #3374 to the top of Triangulation Peak, and then follow a rough descent trail eastward in a thick forest until the trail angles down steeply underneath a large vertical northeast facing rock promontory of Triangulation Peak. Tucked immediately under this promontory is the unique entrance to Boca Cave. Be sure to bring a camera so that you can take a picture of the rewarding view of Mt. Jefferson taken from inside the cave. For your next adventure look to the east, young man. On the far horizon you will see an elusive and barely visible pinnacle high up on the eastern slope of Olallie Butte.

X-SPIRE

1. **Regular Route 5.1**
Pro: Minor gear to 1"
A few hundred feet to the north of Boca Cave is X-Spire, an easy 5th class pinnacle. From the saddle step up onto a ledge and walk around to the right to the east side. Climb a crack-like weakness (the pro is sparse) on the east face that offers good steps and ledges. Belay near the summit at a rock horn and fixed piton anchor. The lower trail is immediately below this spire and can be attained by descending down the scree slopes immediately west of the pinnacle. Walk to the west past the base of Spire Rock to complete this adventurous loop hike.

BREITENBUSH EARS

While you are having lunch at the top of Triangulation Peak look to the northeast to see two tiny sharp profiled 'ears' on a long forested ridge connected to Devils Peak. Breitenbush Ears, though not a typical destination might just spark your musical bandwagon.

Logistics to get there are not quite so easy (trail #3345 is not maintained). Best to approach it utilizing road FS2231 (hot springs), then road FS870. Park at 4000' elevation about ¼ mile after the final road switchback and immediately below the saddle along the ridge crest north of the ears. Bushwack cross-country uphill through taller growth forest

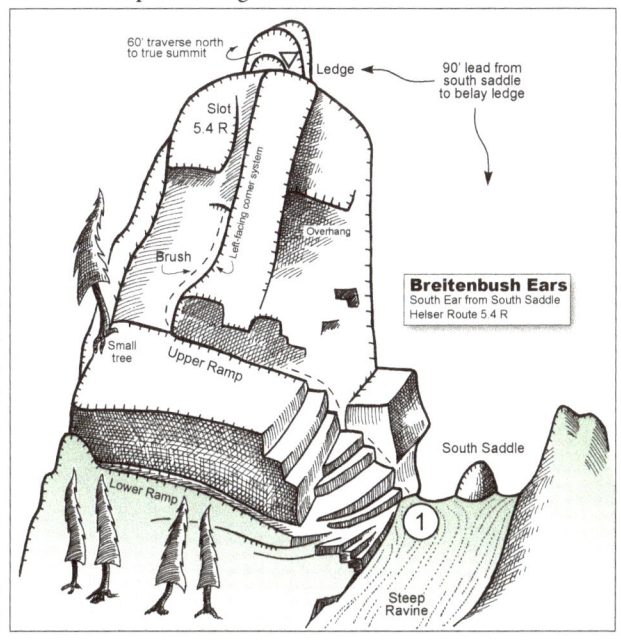

to the saddle, then aim south along the ridge. Cut east along the eastern base of the north ear and aim for a saddle next to the South Ridge of the South Ear and belay here.

The climb is definitely 5.4R and requires thin pitons or bolts to rappel off from the pinnacle. Use minimal gear from small cams to 3", a few pitons, and a few nuts to 1".

South Face Climb: Clamber up a few big steps, traverse left along a main ledge till near a large tree. Aim uphill to a left facing corner system on steep terrain with ample edges to a small stance. The crux 5.4R is a short vertical slot that can be body jammed and stemmed. Immediately beyond is a large wide sloping ledge (100' lead). Set a belay here using thin pitons.

From this belay move onto the SW side along a narrow ramp, surmount a 5.4 crux, then follow a poor rock ridge a total of 60' to the highest point. This lead is mostly a horizontal traverse with some minor gain. High point has no anchor or pro. From the belay at 100' rappel back down the ascent route to the saddle.

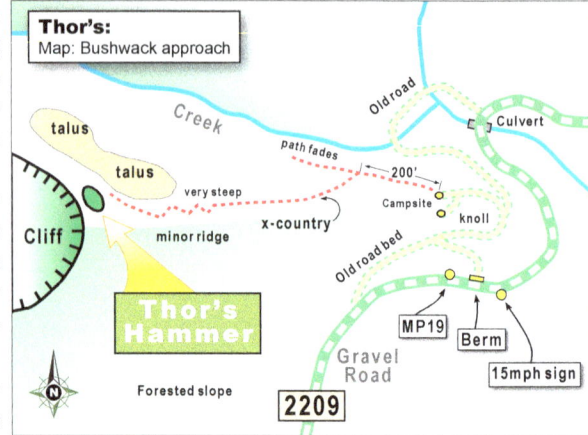

THOR'S HAMMER

Thor's is located on an east facing aspect of a large steep foreboding cliff formation on the lower east side of Henline Mtn. If you are an off-trail aficionado who relishes climbing rare summit objectives, then Thor's is worth a visit. Thor is the sky god in Viking lore, and Odin is the Viking war god. Thor's Hammer is one of the North Santiam's rare rock climbing gems. Boasting a forested thrash scramble approach this wild summit offers good views of the Little North Santiam River valley. The summit can be climbed by either the north ravine or the south ravine.

Directions

From Salem drive 25 miles east on Hwy 22 and turn left (north) onto the North Fork

Road SE which is one mile east of the small community of Mehama. Continue on FS2209. Park at MP 19 and step over the berm onto an old forest grade that meanders (see topo) up to a small knoll. Find an old miner's trace and follow this for about 200', then branch up onto a forested minor ridge crest heading due west following a game path. The uphill scramble gets steep as you draw nearer to the cliff base. **South Ravine:** bushwhack up left below the cliff to access the ravine. **North Ravine:** Angle rightward along the cliff base to a flat landing next to a mammoth fir tree.

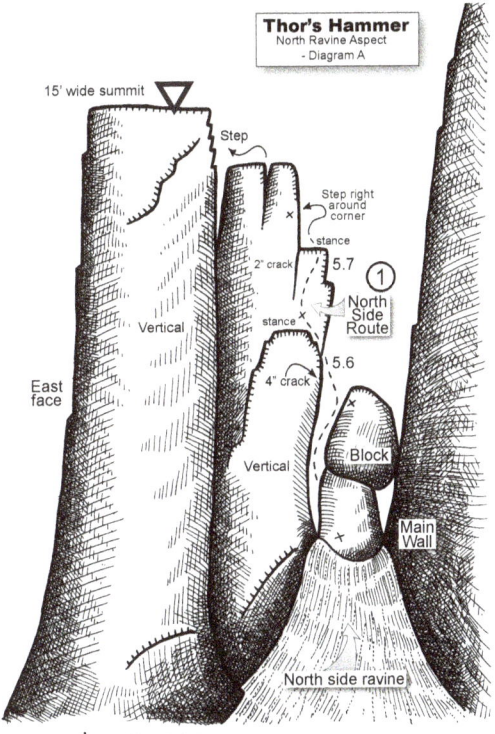

1. **North Ravine 5.7 R**

   P1: From the flat landing next to a large fir tree, rope up and lead up 5th class dirt and moss covered slopes 90' to a cluster of trees and set up a belay. This initial lead is not obvious so choose your path carefully as the terrain is very steep and trees to sling are limited.

   P2: Continue up 5th class terrain for 70' to another belay.

   P3: Angle left (south) up along a narrow 4th class dirt ramp for 70' to a third belay.

   P4: From here you can easily scramble up 3rd class terrain for another 60' to the notch between the main wall and Thor's Anvil. Expect some loose rock in the approach gully. Set up a belay at a fixed anchor at the notch next to a large chock stone. Both the North Ravine route and the South Ravine route meet here at the notch.

   P5 from the notch: Stem off the large chock stone and the pinnacle, placing pro in a very wide slot (4" to 5" pro) and make a diligent 5.6 move onto a small stance. Climb a steep crux section (2" crack) to another stance, then step right (south) around to the sunny side

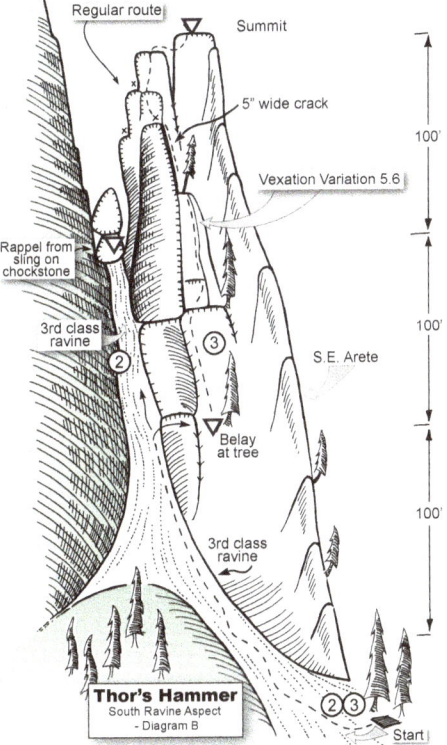

of the pinnacle. Ascend the steps and corners until you are on top of a separate pedestal.

Gingerly step across the void and balance carefully up some nice hand and foot edges onto the main summit massif. This summit is a gently sloping flat fifteen-foot wide ledge perfect for eating lunch and enjoying the scenic views of the region.

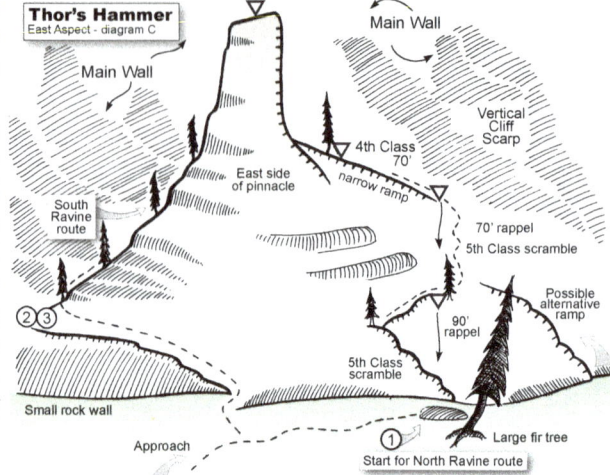

2. **South Ravine 5.7**
When the deer trace meets the base of the cliff and begins to angle right, break left and up along the rounded ridge crest until you reach the base of the sunny South Ravine.
Scramble 200' up the 3rd class south side ravine to the notch between the main wall and the spire. Continue leading 100' to the summit by referencing Route #1 (North Ravine route) from the notch belay at the large chock stone.

3. **Vexation Variation 5.6**
Ascends part of the south side ravine, but after the first 100' step right at a large tree and ascend a series of rock steps into a deep boxed corner system. At a small tree on a small ledge the V-shaped corner becomes vertical. Behind the tree on the left face is a short 5" wide off-width crack. Ascend this (5.6 crux) for 20' to a stance, clip a fixed piton, then balance up onto the next large ledge where this route merges with the Standard Route in the middle of pitch 5.

On the summit of Thor's

Thor's Anvil rappel challenges: The rappel back to the chock stone notch (100') is tricky and should be done with care so your rope does not get stuck in the process. The rappel involves descending over and around several edges and warrants careful rope management by a skilled leader. **Pro:** Minor gear to 2" and cams (4" if you have it). Take minimal gear; the technical lead portion on the pinnacle is only about 100' long. Bring long slings to reduce rope drag. One 60-meter rope is sufficient for climbing and rappelling back to the notch if just a party of two climbers.

STACK ROCK

The volcanic landscape of the Santiam valley yields a broad history of remnant volcanic flow activity composed of basalt, olivine andesite, basaltic or oligolclase andesite which form summit caps on certain higher elevation ridges from Martin Buttes to Mount Beachie west to the Henline Mountain ridge line and beyond. This volcanic cycle which ranges from about the middle to late Miocene epoch erupted mostly from a widespread series of dikes, plugs and related lava cones.

This cliff formation has infrequently seen a few ascents by hard-core climbers venturing here on the Little North Santiam River since the late 70s to experience big wall flavor. A friend mentioned the place to another friend who remarked, "Seen it, been there, done it!" Though seldom climbed the site provides sustained challenges for experienced climbers. Wear a helmet.

This wide valley region is filled with saturated colors of beautiful green, blue sky, and cold crystal clear streams rushing to the valley floor. The predominate tree canopy is composed of a dense growth of Douglas Fir, Western Hemlock, Western Red Cedar, and Vine Maple. The lower western region of valley has been logged and the forest you walk through to approach the wall is composed of second growth trees. Pacific Rhododendron dwells in the lightly shaded forest. Manzanita, Cascade Huckleberry, and Kinnikinnick thrive on certain slopes. A selection of vibrant floral colors dot the open slopes near the base of these crags. Indian Paintbrush and Mariposa Lily grow on open rocky slopes. The lightly wooded forest and steep rocky slopes provide a haven to saxifrage, alumroot, Mountain Parsley fern, Bear Grass, Salal, Twinflower, Sword Fern and Mahonia.

1. **Grand Alliance 5.9**
   Odd steps to a corner.

2. _____
3. _____
4. _____
5. **Steel and Stone (aka S&S) II 5.10b PG A2 (or 5.12+)**
   Length: 220', Pro to 3" including cams, and KB, LA
   S&S is a challenging route that ascends steep cracks, seams and face climbing till it powers through a large overhanging roof on the third pitch.
   P1 5.8 55': Start up a flaky minor corner to a ledge (piton). Climb up a steep broken 5.8 face (piton) past a small bush to a belay on a small ledge.
   P2 5.9 60': Climb directly up past the hueco into a crux corner pod, or step right to a left-facing corner and ascend it 20', then move back left.
   P3 5.10b A2 100': Crank up the thin seam 15', smear up the infamous smooth slab under the great roof. Aid directly out the 12' roof to surmount the roof lip, then continue up 25' past the last small bulge to a belay on a nice ledge.
   P4 5.7 20': Easier terrain quickly leads to the top.

6. **Monty Piton 5.10c R**

   Length: 220', Pro to 3" and cams

   P1: Start at a lone thin fir tree at the lower left edge of the prominent central buttress. Angle up left (fixed) on steep but reasonably easy 5.7 run out terrain to belay just below the right edge of the great

roof. **P2:** Step up and surmount the roof obstacle (5.10c R) and continue up (fixed) the obvious dark stained left-facing corner to the summit. The final exit moves near the end of the climb are highly exposed with considerable runout. Rappel the route.

7. **Eck-Rollings 5.8 A1**
Length: 220', Pro to 3½" including cams and pitons
Locate the main central headwall. To the immediate left is a crack corner system. The Eck-Rollings route is the next major corner system west of that. A lone fir tree stands at the base of the steep initial part of the first pitch. **P1 120':** Start at a belay stance and move left to a lone fir tree. Power directly up the crack system behind the fir tree, then move right and climb a wide (3-4") jam crack to a ledge. **P2 5.8 A1 140':** Aid up a slightly overhanging corner, step right and continue up low angle crack ramp system to the top of the wall.

8. **Adams Variant 5.8 A1**
Pro to 3½" including pitons
A direct variation joining onto Eck-Rollings route. **P1 5.8 A1 120'** to ledge where it merges with the above route.

9. **_____**
This is the first major corner system immediately left of the main central buttress.

10. **Dead Grouse 5.9 A1**
Length: 220', Pro: ?
This route is the huge deep chimney system on the immediate right side of the prominent central buttress. **P1:** Starts in a deep chimney and power up through an overhanging slot. Once above the crux this corner broadens onto a wide open face. **P2:** Face climb on the right of the crack on small edges in this large scooped out face.

11. **Stone Scared 5.10a**
Length: 250', Pro to 6"
To the right of the prominent central buttress is a smooth slab on the upper cliff. Stone Scared takes a crack system up to this smooth slab. **P1 90' 5.9:** Ascend the obvious crack below the slab then step right to a 2-bolt belay on the bottom of the slab. **P2 160' 5.10a:** Head up and right from the belay into the wide flare, make a tricky move pulling off of the slab (crux). Traverse left to the bushes, and pull over a small budge. Start in the right crack, then as it difficulty increases traverse back left on the slab to another crack leading to the summit and a tree belay after 30' of 4th class. Two double rope rappels to the ground.

SOUTH SANTIAM REGION

The old Cascades east of Sweet Home offer a particularly complex diversity of natural beauty. Hidden in these hills is a wealth of treasure for everyone to enjoy. The few active mines and numerous old mine shafts testify to a history of busy gold and silver exploration. These days the area is frequented by hikers delving in deep old growth forests, or searching for quartz crystals, or fishing, and rock climbing on unique andesitic and tuff formations.

THE MENAGERIE

A condensed guide to the Menegerie
From a manuscript by Jim Anglin

Several miles east of Sweet Home, Oregon, and near the community of Upper Soda is the unique Menagerie Wilderness Area, a small wilderness region that contains a wealth of tuffaceous rock spires, arches and cliffs of unusual shapes and sizes, even some monstrous spires in excess of 350' high. The majority of summits and cliffs tend to be concentrated in the Keith Creek drainage, but a healthy selection of additional spires do exist in the Trout Creek drainage to the west, and Soda and Bear Creek to the east.

The Menagerie Wilderness is not a crowded destination climbing site, partly due to its distance from a major metro area. Other factors that tend to limit climber interest is the variable quality of rock, which can range from excellent quality at the Rooster Rock group, to less than ideal on some of the upper wilderness spires. Some pitches can be of poor quality rock, but the remainder of the climb may be reasonable. Each section will detail some of the pros and cons on certain routes where quality is an issue.

This brief analysis on the Menagerie rock climbing opportunities fulfills the desire of Jim Anglin who thought it beneficial for regional rock climbers to have access to a condensed version of his original detailed thesis. He believed that through a condensed version climbers would be enabled to quickly access the more popular and favorite rock

climbing opportunities of the Menagerie Wilderness Area. This condensed version is dedicated to the memory of Mr. Anglin.

This brief study of the Menagerie is designed to provide route details for only the more commonly ascended rock routes. The focus of this section primarily points you toward spires and routes of greater value based on your likely time limitations, rock quality, technical difficulty and long-term user interest. Beware of dubious friable rock in the Menagerie, particularly the upper area. Numerous climbs, though not implied in the rating, are often R or X due to serious runout or lack of adequate pro options.

Directions

1.) From Sweet Home drive east on U.S. 20 for 22¼ miles and park near a state highway cinder yard. The 2.1 mile 2200' Rooster Rock Trail is an arduous hike from the parking lot on Highway 20, but if you can endure the steep approach hike the views from the top of the rock are beautiful.

2.) An alternative but longer 2½ mile trail starts at Trout Creek Campground and merges with the Rooster Rock Trail near the Rooster Rock pinnacle.

3.) To access the rock spires in the upper wilderness area, drive up FS2027, then park at the beginning of FS850 and walk along this overgrown road for ¾ mile (past a large landslide) to where the Rooster Rock Trail descends. The wilderness trail that descends from here to Rooster Rock is a bit faint in places, but is still reasonably easy to follow.

4) The common method to access the upper climbing sites is (see overview map) via FS2027 to FS850 which becomes FS857, then follow spur road FS856 to the landing, a nice overlook immediately above the wilderness. A short trail descends from the landing down to FS850 at the wilderness register sign.

At the registration sign your goal defines your direction: Go east along old FS850 to Turkey Monster, southeast to Rabbit Ears & Panorama Point, or south along the ridge crest trail to the Rooster Rock group. This upper approach to the Rooster Rock group is quite viable simply because the elevation and distance is considerably shorter than hiking 2200' from the highway in the valley.

Favorite climbs here are plentiful. The foremost is the Turkey Monster (III 5.6 A3 or 5.11a) is absolutely staggering, and has probably seen only a small handful of ascents since Eugene Dod, Dave Jensen and Bill Pratt completed it in 1966.

The most frequented pinnacles are Rooster Rock, Hen Rock, Rabbit Ears, Royal Arch, Turkey Monster and Panorama Point. A Peregrine Falcon seasonal closure is in effect for

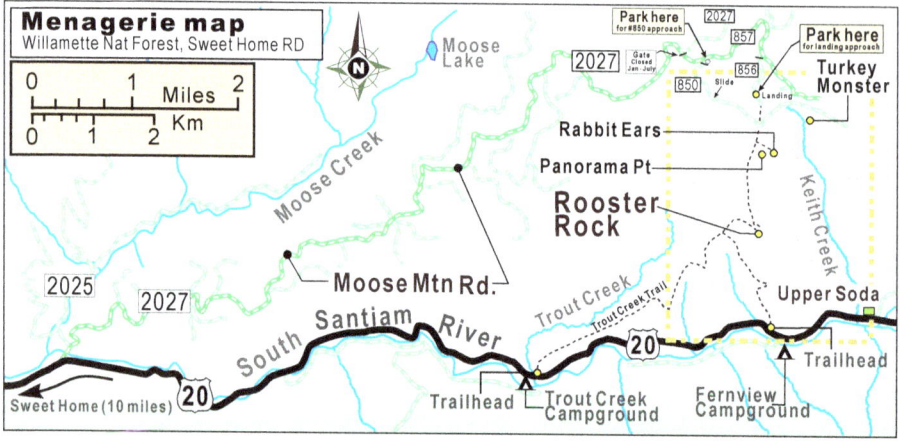

the upper portion of the wilderness which last until approximately August 1. Inquire at the Sweet Home Ranger Station about the status of the seasonal climbing closure concerning the upper wilderness access trails before driving to the Menagerie Wilderness.

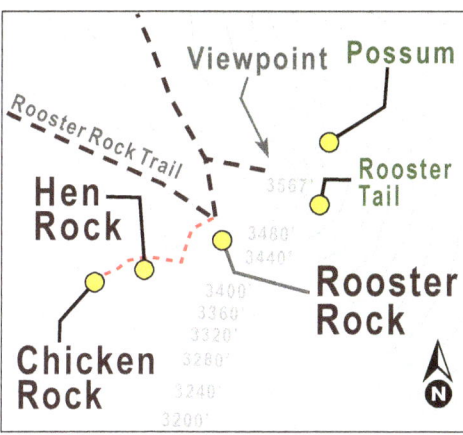

ROOSTER ROCK

The Rooster Rock group is the most likely destination for visitors and climbers who come to the region. The quality of the rock is good on all the spires in this group. The reasonable nature of the climbs provides climbers with a great venue of routes to choose from depending upon your skill level and time. Near the summit of Rooster Rock you will find a few remaining timbers and bits of rusted metal, which are the sole remnants of the small fire lookout that clung to the summit of Rooster Rock. There are a series of sturdy eye bolts still well-attached to the wall on the standard north side route which climbers usually clip into while climbing up this route to the summit. The first route on each pinnacle is the common line of ascent and descent unless other alternate descent options are noted. All the climbs generally require an assortment of gear to lead climb so bring a workable selection of wires and cams of various widths to suit your leading ability.

The Rooster Rock hikers trail encounters the north side of Rooster Rock at the 2200' level. This spire is the largest of a group of pinnacle in this area. From the trail step down right on a path for 30' and rope-up here for the regular North Face route.

1. **Standard North Face Route 5.4R**

    Minor pro to 3"

    The North Face route is the most frequently climbed route at the Menagerie and for good reason; conveniently reasonable climbing that quickly leads to a stellar summit view.

    Begin by stepping up past a mammoth eye-bolt to a short steep corner crack system. Use hand holds and friction smears on the right side of the crack until possible to move back left to the crack as you get near the notch. Clip another eye-bolt. Continue up easy large ledges past the old lookout timbers, and then angle right along the crest to the summit anchor. A single 60-meter rope will suffice for rappels off from Rooster Rock.

    The 5.6 variation is to simply use the corner crack directly for the entire way up to the notch. This is the better option provided you get good pro in the crack.

2. **North Face Jam Crack 5.8**

    Pro to 3"

    This climb starts a few feet to the right of the standard route, and begins upward from an obvious flake sticking out of the ground. Climb a crack corner to a rightward traverse and set a belay on the outer northwest point of the rock. Climb up right 30' on a moss covered ramp, and then up right to an obvious difficult overhanging jam crack. Carefully protect the upper section before committing to the moves.

3. **West Face Dihedral Direct 5.9+**

    Pro to 3"

    Considered to be the classic route at Rooster Rock this climb is a punchy hard route that in years past surprised the easier grade climbers because of its old underrated scale (5.8).

Descend west down slope (along the north side) to a notch between the northwest face and a large rock spur. Set a belay at the notch.

P1: Climb the west face via a steep crack which becomes an open chimney leading to a sloping ledge.

P2: Climb a flake to an overhanging crack, and then traverse left 15' to the crux. Surmount the overhanging crux section to a stance, and then lead up to a nice open book crack corner 30' to the summit.

Note: On pitch two, a direct start leading up to the overhanging crux can be attacked directly (5.10a/b) by placing pro up right before firing into the direct start.

4. **Frog Traverse 5.5**
   Pro to 2"
   About thirty-five feet up pitch one of West Face Dihedral Direct break up left using a traverse friction slab (5.5) which joins the ledge on the outer northwest point of the rock spire. From this belay follow route #2 upper portion (5.8).

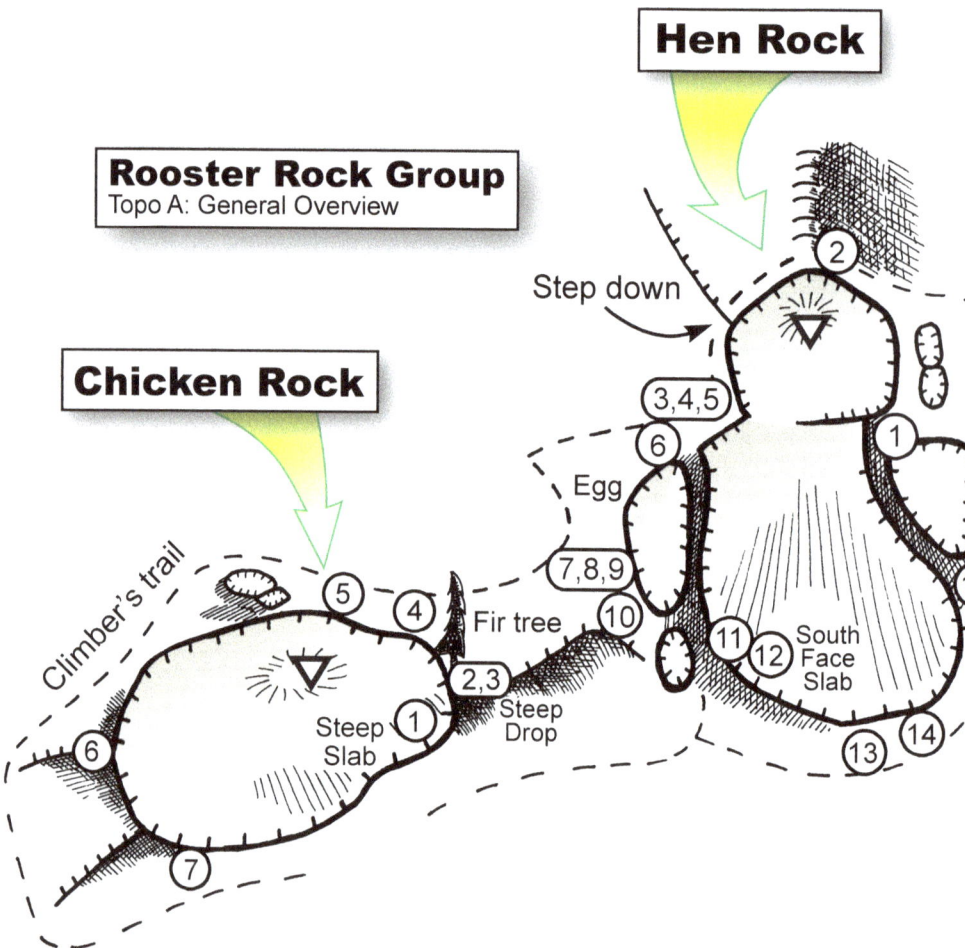

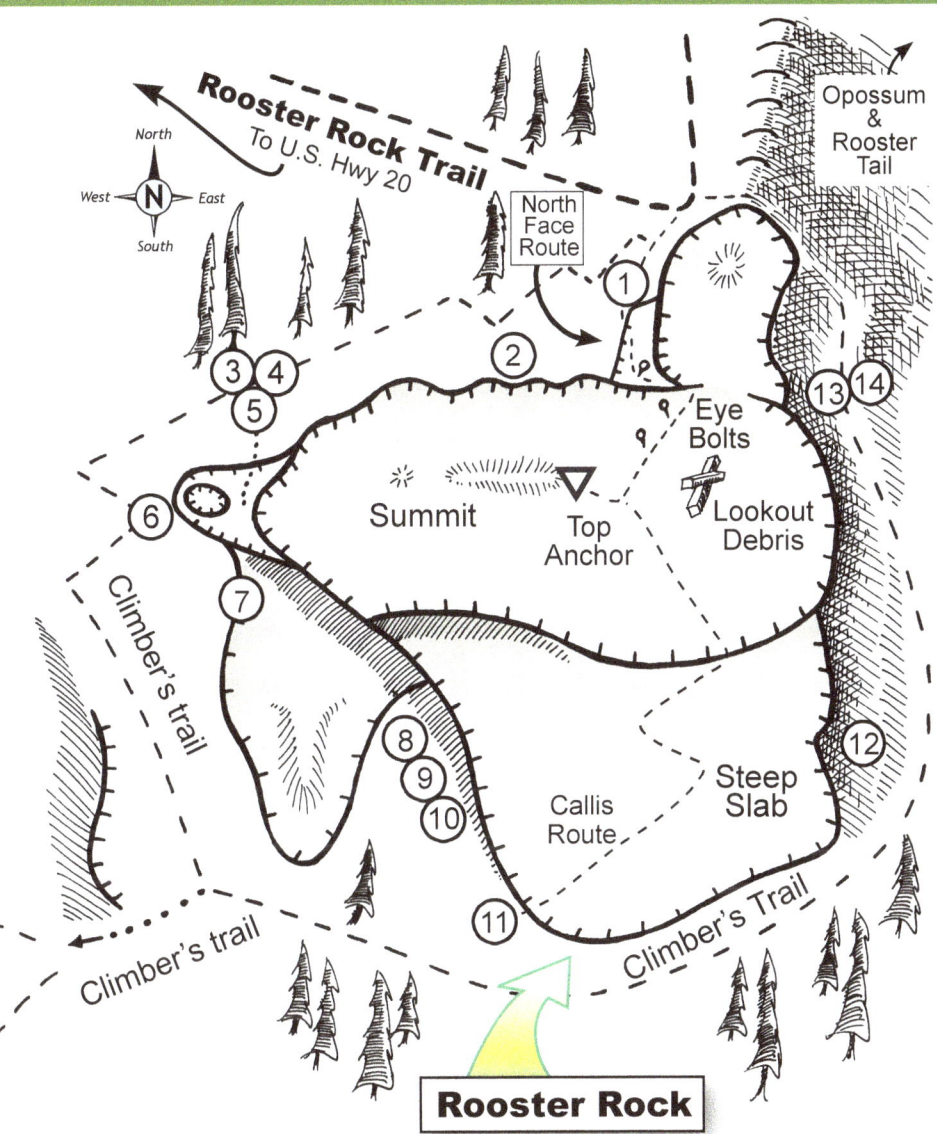

5. **NPG 5.11c**
   Pro to 2"
   P1: Climb approximately 30' of route #3 then aim up right onto a (bolted) hard steep face climb which leads to a crack and ends at a belay ledge.
   P2: Exit the right side of the ledge onto steep face climbing which leads to the summit.

6. **The Spur 5.11a**
   Pro to 1.5"
   A high quality route on the spur that forms the west end of Rooster Rock. Descend down to the west to a mossy ledge and a madrone tree. Climb a steep flake crack, clip a bolt and move left, then up (bolts) to a belay.

7. **South Face 5.9 A2**
   Pro to 1.5" including nailing gear
   Traverse above the large rock spur (mentioned in route #3) and angle around right onto the south face along a ledge above the large cave mentioned for the following routes. Belay.
   P1: Free and aid the crack above to a bolt ladder using more mixed climbing to a sloping belay ledge.
   P2: Move right around a corner onto a large south face sloping ledge (30') and then climb a rock step (5.5) continuing up a right diagonal crack 35' to another belay ledge.
   P3: Traverse right 25' and ascend a chimney to the site of the old lookout and finish to the summit.

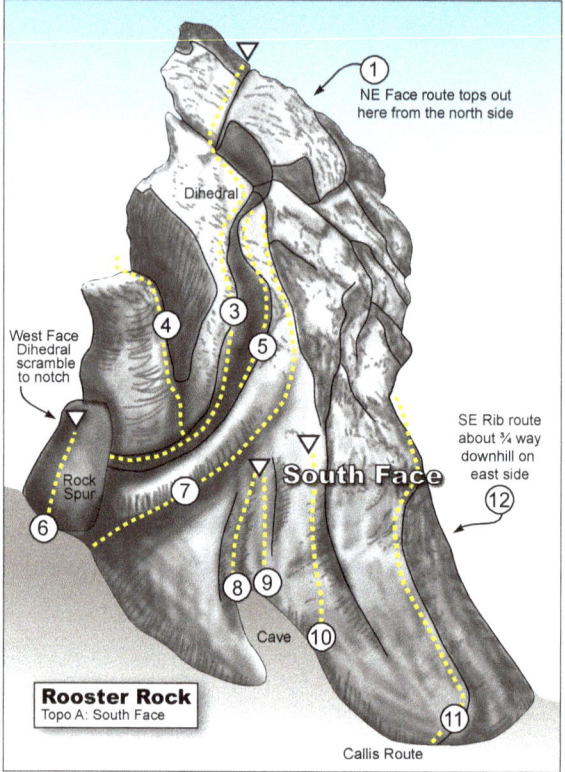

A Large Cave is located on the lower southwest side of the Rooster Rock formation. The next three climbs are located in or start on the right side of this large cave.

8. **Gizzard 5.10d**
   Pro to 2" and a cam to 4"
   In the deepest recesses of this prominent large cave is the Gizzard. Undercling out right (bolts) and up steep rock to a finger crack that becomes a chimney, and then escape by face climbing up left to the belay anchor.

9. **Old Flakes 5.10c**
   Pro to 1½"
   Power up the wall immediately right of the huge cave passing several bolts to a ramp. Rejoins the Gizzard route.

10. **Chicken Richard 5.11c/d**
    Pro: Mostly fixed but bring a few small nuts and cams
    A powerful line on a sweeping buttress of rock immediately right of the large cave. P1: Begin five feet right of the Old Flakes route. Climb a difficult and steep face to an easier slab which goes vertical to overhung at the crux. Rappel with 60m rope.

11. **Southeast Face (Callis Route) 5.7**
    Pro to 1" and minor gear to 3½" for the chimney
    A historic bench-mark route which established 5th class rock climbing at the Menagerie Wilderness and a good climbing route worth the adventure. If you have not done this yet, plan on it next time you are in the area.

Descend down around the west side of Rooster Rock to the south face. The first large cave is where you will find routes like the Gizzard. Walk to the right a bit along the south face and look high up on the cliff for another cave halfway up on the south face. The Callis Route starts at the ground below this other cave.

P1: Climb an initially mossy ramp up right passing several bolts. At the fourth bolt move left around a corner into a left facing dihedral and climb this crack (5.7) aiming toward the cave where you will find a bolt belay anchor just to the left. **P2:** Traverse rightward around a rock rib outcrop onto the southeast face (bolt), and ascend up a friction slab (bolts) to a wide chimney with several more bolts at its base. Ascend the chimney past a large fir tree and set up a belay.

P3: Continue stemming up the chimney crack and merge with the standard route on the ridge crest. Anticipate partner communication difficulties on the second pitch.

Options: An alternate variation exists starting at P2 by clipping the initial bolt to the right of the small cave, and then powers (5.9R) up and left to a small alcove, then to an exposed slab and upward to difficult face climbing to an undercling flake and jam crack leading to the summit.

12. Southeast Rib Direct 5.7
Pro to 3"

When descending about $^2/_3$ way down along the east side of Rooster Rock you will encounter an obvious 30' crack with an overhanging dihedral at its top.

P1: Climb 20' up the crack and exit left 15' (5.4) under the overhang and onto the main southeast face of Rooster Rock. Using smears friction climb up to the bolts at the base of the chimney on the Callis Route.

P2: Traverse left 15' onto a rock rib and climb the unprotected 5.7 rib for 40' which brings you to a jam crack (5.7) leading to the summit.

Note: You can skip the runout rock rib on pitch two by just climbing the upper Callis Route using the deep chimney.

13. Fred Hart Traverse 5.4
Pro to 1"

This is the other short viable alternate route on the north side of Rooster Rock that leads (nearly) directly to the summit. From the hikers trail step over onto the east side and follow a horizontal ledge system. When the ledge system ends, down climb a few feet and traverse left to a chimney. Climb the chimney 35' to the notch where it joins with the standard North Face Route #1 and continue another lead to the

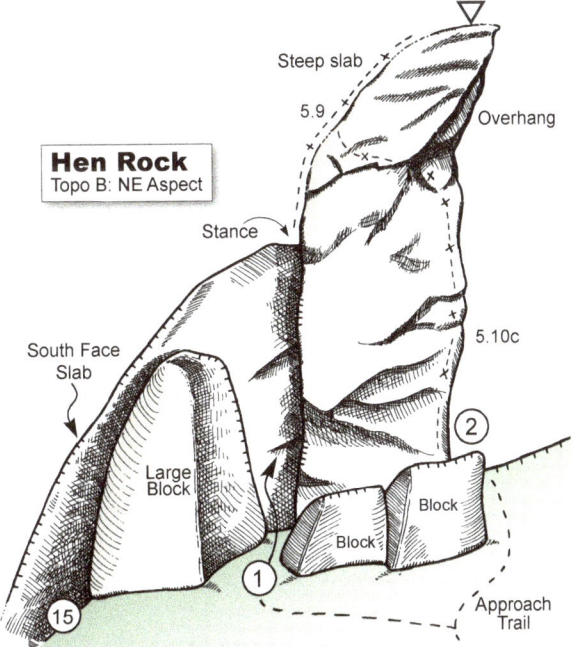

summit.

14. Fred Hart Lieback 5.9

Pro 1½"

This direct variation can be found by descending down the east side of Rooster Rock from the hikers trail 40' to a flake. Climb the steep flake (5.9) to where it meets with the Fred Hart Traverse ledge, and traverse left into a chimney and climb this for 35' to the notch, and continue another lead to the summit.

HEN ROCK

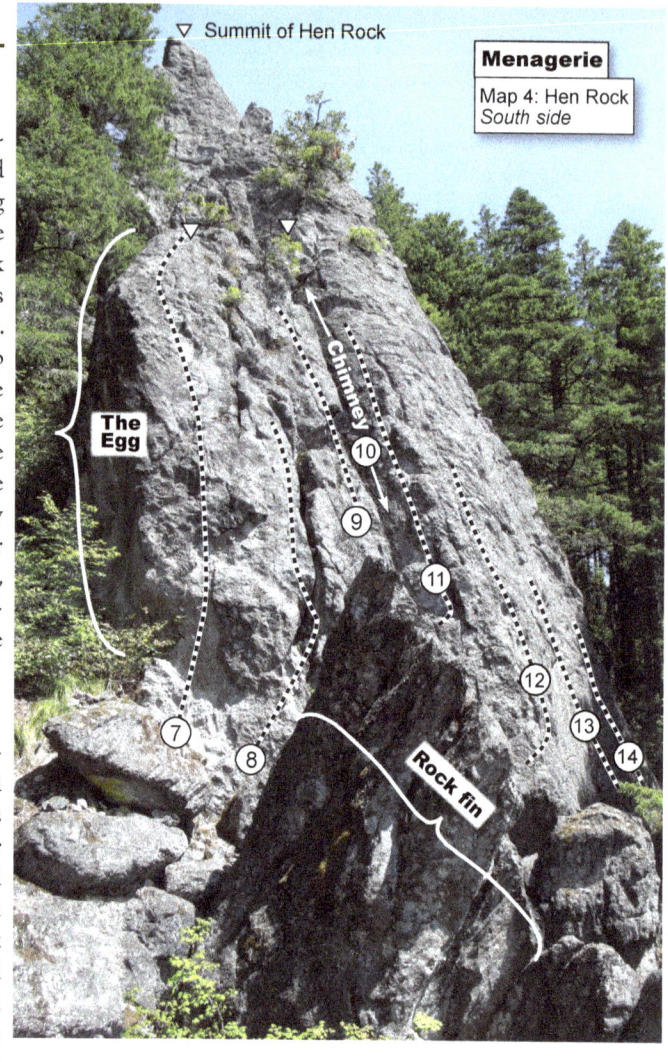

Hen Rock is a stellar rock formation and one of a cluster of spires forming the Rooster Rock group. It is located few hundred feet down west from Rooster Rock and can be approached by descending down a steep climber's path from the hikers trail next to Rooster Rock. Hen Rock has excellent rock and offers the highest concentration of sport routes in the Menagerie. If you plan to summit on Hen Rock rappel descend 75' down the vertical north side where route Eggs Overhard comes up.

1. Southeast Slab 5.9

Pro to 2"

A very popular and historic route way ahead of its time because it was first climbed in 1959.

Climb up a fun easy slab on the east side of Hen Rock left of a left facing corner that leads up to an airy stance. Smear up a deceptively hard and exposed steep slab (3 bolts) for 30' to the top. Rappel down the north side for all summit-bound routes on Hen Rock.

2. Eggs Overhard (North Face) 5.10c

Pro: QD's

This is the north face route on Hen Rock. Although the original ascent traversed up rightward to the first bolt it is best to just 'stick-clip' it first and boulder directly up the hard crux initial moves to the bolt. Power up hard, tricky face climbing, and then at the third bolt move up left until you are under the large roof. Traverse left again around the roof bulge until the angle eases and you can friction climb up a steep slab to the summit.

3. **Eggs Overeasy (Northwest Face) 5.8**
   Pro to 2"
   Begin about 15' right of the previous route starting on a mossy boulder in a corner. Climb up thin cracks and flakes (20') to a bolt, and then continue another 35' to an easy hand traverse leading right to a small ledge on the west face. Follow an overhanging rib (bolt) to the top. Route is seldom climbed.

4. **Wild West 5.10d**
   Pro to 1½"
   Great route on excellent quality rock. Scramble down onto the west side of Hen Rock to a large left facing crack corner with a bolt 20' up the route. Climb this past the bolt until you are above a chinquapin tree, and then traverse left onto the overhanging west face climbing up past bolts and a few cam placements en route to the top.

5. **Chinquapin Corner 5.9**
   Pro to 1½"
   Begin in the same large left facing crack corner as the previous route, but continue to climb straight up around a block until you can join Southeast Slab (route #1) at the airy stance. Finish up the steep bolted slab to the top.

The following five routes are located on a minor formation called the Egg

6. **Chimney 5.5**
   Pro to 1"
   On the lower west side of Hen Rock is a large block called the Egg. The chimney ascends between Hen Rock and this 'Egg' and then steps across the void onto Hen Rock to end at a tree belay. Rappel or continue up Hen Rock to merge with route #1.

7. **Sunnyside Up 5.11a**
   Pro to 1"
   This face route ascends the southern sunny outside of the Egg.
   P1: From the top of a pedestal slot a small nut, and then power up a series of bolt protected hard moves (crux). Place a cam and move left to a bolt, and then climb straight up to the top of the Egg. Step across the void onto the Hen and power up several hard moves to a large ledge.
   P2: Exit off the left side of the ledge but stay on the rib until you join route #1 en route to the top.

8. **South Crack 5.7**
   Pro to 4"
   This route also ascends the southern sunny outside of the Egg. Immediately right of route #7 (Sunnyside Up) is a crack leading to the top of the Egg. Climb this while gradually working leftward up the Egg.

9. **Poached 5.9**
   Pro: Mostly fixed with pins and bolts
   This is a route immediately left of the south side chimney of the Egg. Climbs a steep clean buttress to the top of the Egg and merge with the Sunnyside Up and continue to the top of Hen Rock.

10. South Chimney 5.7
Pro to 4"

This is the other side of the same chimney as (#6) the Chimney route.

The following routes are located on the south side of Hen Rock. The original wandering route that zigzagged up the wide sunny south face was called Winter Sunshine. Jim Anglin realized that the entire south face could yield a finer string on directisimo lines if they went straight up the wall instead. Therefore several seasonal sounding names were applied to a fine selection of three additional new routes for this stellar site.

11. Autumn Reigns 5.10b
Pro: 10 QD's if going to the top

This is the first of four routes on the clean south face of Hen Rock. Begin with a belay at the base of the South Chimney. Climb the right side of the chimney wall on the southwest side of Hen Rock. Steep powerful climbing (bolts) leads to a tree. Rappel or continue to the top of Hen.

12. Rites of Spring 5.10a
Pro: 10+ QD's and a medium sized cam

From the south chimney which separates the Egg from the Hen step out

right onto the top of a boulder. Step out from this boulder onto the south face of Hen, and climb upward (bolts) and aim up left. At the third bolt move right several feet, and then continue straight up passing two more bolts on the right of a small fir (place cam in horizontal crack). Continue upward past a large ledge which is on your left (bolt) to a lower angle slab, which you can move around using the left side of a block. Merge with route the Southeast Slab route #1 at the exposed airy stance and continue to the top.

13. Summer Rules 5.10c
Pro to 1" including QD's

This route begins immediately right of the lowest point of the sunny south face of the Hen Rock. Commence up left using a steep ramp (bolt). Climb straight up (bolt) and then past a difficult rightward move and over a small roof (cam placements). You will pass one of the old original ¼" bolts, but continue directly up the face to the next bolt and further up the face until you reach a crack. Pass a large loose looking block on the left and merge with route #1 at the airy stance and continue up the steep slab to the summit of Hen Rock.

14. Winter Sunshine 5.9
Pro to 1" and QD's

Winter Sunshine was the original zigzagging route on the south face of Hen Rock. It originally ascended crossing up left and back over to the right before joining into an upper route. Jim straightened the route to its present status as follows.

Begin 15' right of the very toe of the south face and climb past three bolts to a shallow trough (fixed pin) and climb past a loose block on its right where you will shortly merge with route #1 (Southeast Slab) at the airy stance.

15. Southeast Slab Direct 5.9
Pro to 1"

Uphill a bit on the southeast side of Hen Rock is a large moss covered boulder. Begin by climbing two parallel sided cracks for 20' and then over a large loose block (mentioned in route #14) to merge with route #1 (Southeast Slab) en route to the summit.

CHICKEN ROCK

Chicken Rock is located just a short spat downhill from Hen Rock. Though the standard 5.8 route is the easiest way to the top this pinnacle offers a selection of stout routes that will justifiably grab your attention. The rock spire is like a tall crooked finger with a broad flat south face. Several facets of the upper pinnacle tilt awkwardly to create difficult leading obstacles to pass over.

1. Southeast Face Slab 5.8
Pro to 2"

This is the original route and the easiest method to reach the summit of Chicken Rock. This route ascends this pinnacle in a clockwise fashion. Begin on the lower northeast side at a flat landing with an abrupt drop-off. Traverse out onto the exposed southeast face by diligently moving up leftward 40' to a large ledge on the south face. Move up 10' to a bolt, then a bit higher to a 2" jam crack and wander up right to a notch on the ridge crest. A final few moves of overhanging jugs on the ridge crest brings you quickly to the summit bolt anchors.

Line of Descent
The common descent from Chicken Rock is via a 75' rappel on the north side back down to the ground.

2. Sticky Fingers 5.10c
Pro: QD's

Two sport routes exist on the east face of Chicken. Sticky Fingers is the left route while Free Bird is the right route. Traverse a few steps up leftward onto the southeast face from the landing. Ascend directly up the southeast face on easy rock steps (bolts) to a ledge. Power up a very steep (bolts) face leftward to the top.

3. Free Bird 5.11a
Pro to 1" and QD's

Start on the east side of the pinnacle at the landing. Climb on the southeast rib on very thin face holds past three bolts on the lower section. A combination of pro and bolts leads up steep terrain to a final leftward leaning layback near the top.

Bob McGown on *Turkey Monster*

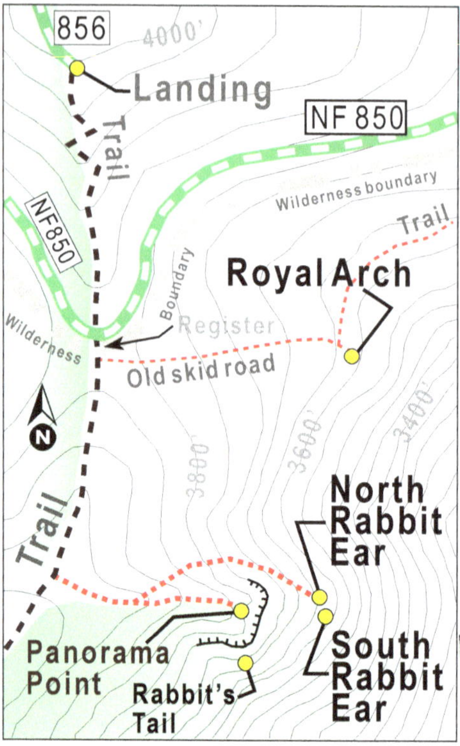

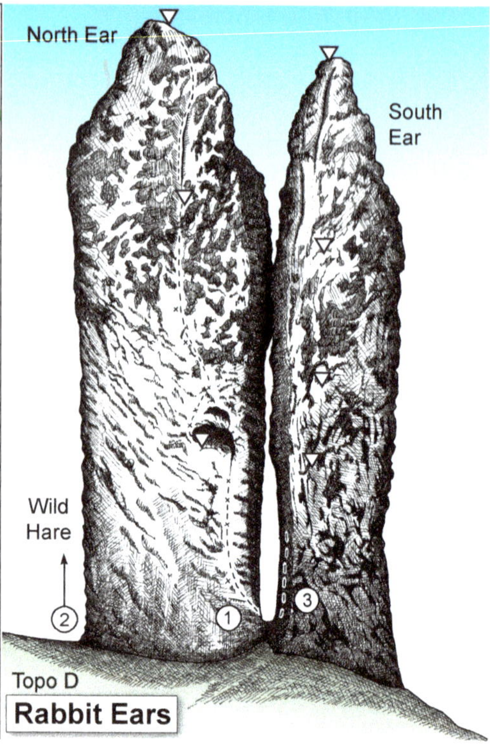

4. **Chicken Legs 5.11a**
   Pro: QD's
   A fine quality north side route on Chicken Rock that starts near a tall fir tree. The route is considered to be one of the best routes in the Rooster Rock group. Ascend a line of bolts directly up the shaded north side to a different set of bolt anchors on the summit. A 60m rope will suffice for rappel.

5. **West Chimney 5.6**
   Pro to 1½"
   This starts at the base of Chicken Legs, and traverses rightward on mossy ledge for about 30' to a shallow chimney.
   Ascend the chimney to the ledge on the crest where it merges with the standard route #1 Southeast Face Slab. Finish up a series of very steep holds on the crest that quickly leads to the

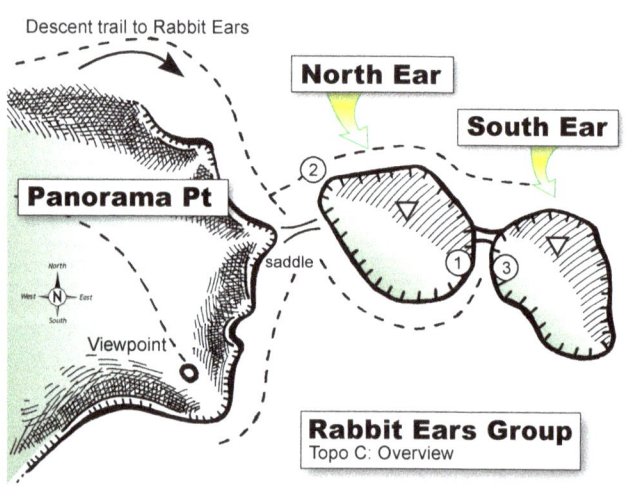

Rabbit Ears Group
Topo C: Overview

summit.

6. **Crystal Ball 5.11a**
   Pro: QD's
   Walk around to the west side of this pinnacle till you see a ramp. Climb the ramp to a bolt and then aim over a bulge onto the west face. Continue up left around several blocks (bolt) and aim up rightward to a ledge (bolt). Power up over a difficult mantle crux move and continue up steep rock (2 bolts) to the summit. The route has substantial runout. Note: A direct start variation exists from the first bolt by climbing directly up to the ledge below the crux.

7. **Southern Exposure 5.11c**
   Pro to 1½"
   Walk down around the west side of the spire to an obvious mossy rock rib that provides access to the south face. From the top of the rock rib climb up left following a steep left sloping ramp. At the end of the ramp ascend up to a large block and power around the left side of the block and traverse back right. A substantially overhung crux (3 bolts) leads to the large ledge of route #1. Finish up the crest on steep holds to the summit.

UPPER MENAGERIE WILDERNESS

The upper Menagerie Wilderness offers a wild selection of spires of astounding shapes and sizes. The quality of the rock varies considerably in the upper area and may be a factor that limits user interest to some of these sites. But in all there is a stellar small selection of spires totally worthy of your attention if you are well skilled for the adventure. The following list of spires is best when approached from the upper entrance at the "landing" at the end of FS856. From that access point you can easily descend the hiker's access trail down to the registration sign at the wilderness boundary. Again, beware of dubious friable rock in the upper Menagerie. Numerous climbs, though not implied in the rating, should be R or X due to serious runout

or lack of pro options.

The view from Panorama Point is absolutely stellar and provides an excellent visual bearing point for many of the spires in the upper Menagerie Wilderness. This panoramic viewpoint is such a superb site it is worth visiting even if you are out for a mere hiking trip.

To reach Panorama Point: From the registration sign hike the Rooster Rock trail uphill for ¼ mile till it levels off. Aim left (east) through open forest and out onto an open ridge crest (a bit hard to spot initially because of the forest) that offers a nice path leading to the rocky topped knoll of Panorama Point. From this rocky knoll you will be overlooking the two massive towers of the Rabbit Ears. Several other spires are easily visible from this location as well such as Turkey Monster and The Spire.

Wayne Wallace on P2 *Turkey Monster*

To reach the Rabbit Ears: From the registration sign hike the Rooster Rock trail uphill for ¼ mile till it levels off. A narrow path will descend eastward down an old clear-cut logging grade around the north side of Panorama Point. The path leads directly to the lower east side of Panorama Point where you will find the twin 300-foot Rabbit Ears towers. The first ear you encounter is the North Ear. To access the notch between the ears descend around the right side of the North Ear.

To reach Turkey Monster: Walk east along FS850 to the campsite. Continue a few hundred yards further along the old road, and then descend off trail directly down to the Turkey Monster. The off trail portion is tricky especially for first timers. A very steep bluff (Turkey Point) and a tangle of brush can cause some approach frustration if you are too far to the west.

NORTH RABBIT EAR
1. **The Cave Route 5.10a R/X**
   Pro to 2" and QD's

The Cave Route is usually the first climb of choice for climbers who are debating which route on the Ears to ascend. Beware, the 2nd pitch is serious R-rated, and the 3rd pitch is X-rated.

The first Ear you encounter on the descent hike is the North Ear. Descend down to the right around the North Ear to access the notch between both Ears. The Cave Route begins left of the notch.

P1 5.10a: Climb up a few feet, and then traverse left to a bolt. Climb directly up 80' (5.10a) to the cave belay.

P2 5.10a R: Exit out the left side of the cave (bolt) to a ramp and tread carefully up and rightward to a dihedral (loose rock). From a high bolt traverse up left out the overhang face (bolts) to a notch, and then directly up jugs to a nice belay ledge. Two 50m ropes will reach the ground from here.

P3 5.7X: Ascend a pro-less vertical groove system for a 90' past a bulge to an anchor, then cruise pro-less for 80' to the top of the Ear. Alternative: If you move left into route #2 you will find a tree ¾ way to the top.

Line of Descent:

A 90-foot rappel from the summit will bring you to the top of pitch 2. From there two 50-meter ropes will take you to the ground.

2. **Wild Hare 5.10b**

   Pro to 2" including one 4" cam, otherwise mostly fixed

   Wild Hare begins at the up-hill saddle on the spires west face.

   P1: Climb up and a bit left on steep face holds past six bolts to a short dihedral. Traverse left to the Piles belay ledge.

   P2: Follow a wide crack up and right until it ends. Continue over a bulge and then move right on a ledge to another crack and punch over another bulge. Belay on a sizable ledge above the previous bulge.

   P3: Easier terrain on good rock quickly leads up to the summit of the North Ear.

   SOUTH RABBIT EAR

   Sure enough, the South Ear is right next to the North Ear.

3. **West Face of South Ear 5.8 R**

   Pro to 4"

   Considered to be a near classic route, but is marred by some poor (crumbly) rock on the lower part and a healthy runout section starting the 3rd pitch. Although a great route, it is definitely NOT a simple climb for a casual 5.8 climber.

   P1: Begin at the notch between both Ears. Climb directly up for 25' on knobby rock to a ledge (bolt), and then traverse right 30'. Continue up 20' to a belay.

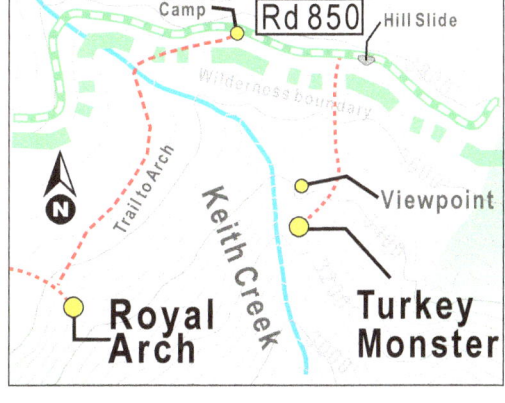

P2: Ascend the overhanging jam crack for 30' and belay at another small ledge.

P3: Traverse out right (5.7) for 30' and then straight up steep rock (5.8) to a chimney which leads up to a belay tree (bolts) at a ledge.

P4: Continue up this crack system 120' to the top of the Ear.

Line of Descent

Rappel with two 60-meter ropes from the summit down to the ledge with the tree. Rappel from the tree belay to the ground.

If you have only one single rope you will also need to rappel from the tree belay down to the small ledge belay at the top of pitch two. One more rappel will take you to the ground.

TURKEY MONSTER

Turkey Monster is certainly the most impressive tower in the Menagerie. An imposing sight standing nearly 400' tall on the downhill side it seems to defy the law of gravity with a summit larger than its base. First climbed in 1966 by Eugene Dod, Dave Jensen, and Bill Pratt this monster is definitely one of the more bold adventures to experience in the Menagerie.

Walk east from the campsite along the old FS850 road grade until you are directly above the monster. Descend brushy forested slopes slightly to the east of the tower.

1. **Dod Route (North Face) 5.11a (or 5.6 A3)**
   Pro to 3½"
   P1: From the uphill saddle (northeast side) move right a few feet, and then climb directly up (5.10a) for 80' to a belay at a small ledge in an alcove.

P2: Power up the large overhang (giant rotten bong crack) 5.10c. The rock starts out horrible but improves partway up the pitch. Follow a long crack (5.8) to a double flake belay at a tiny perch.

P3: Immediately above the anchor…muscle your way up and out the substantially overhung (5.11a and bolts) face surmounting this crux overhanging lip to another belay just beyond.

P4: Waltz up easy terrain the leads to the summit of the Turkey's head.

Line of Descent

Must have two 60m ropes. The common line of descent is via the Dod Route. Be certain to test-pull your ropes as there is good risk in getting the ropes jammed on pitch 2 or pitch 3. An alternate rappel is to descend the Wild Turkey route.

2. Southwest Face 5.10d A2

Pro to 3" including pitons

From the uphill saddle drop down a little to the west.

P1: Traverse out right past a bolt and around a corner 40' to a belay ledge.

P2: Very difficult climbing (5.10d) up a long 120' crack ends at a large roof. Turn this 5-foot overhanging roof on the left and belay on a small ledge (2 bolts).

P3: A 70' 5.8 crack leads to a belay on the left.

P4: Strenuous nailing leads up to 3 bolts and a runner on a flake leading over right.

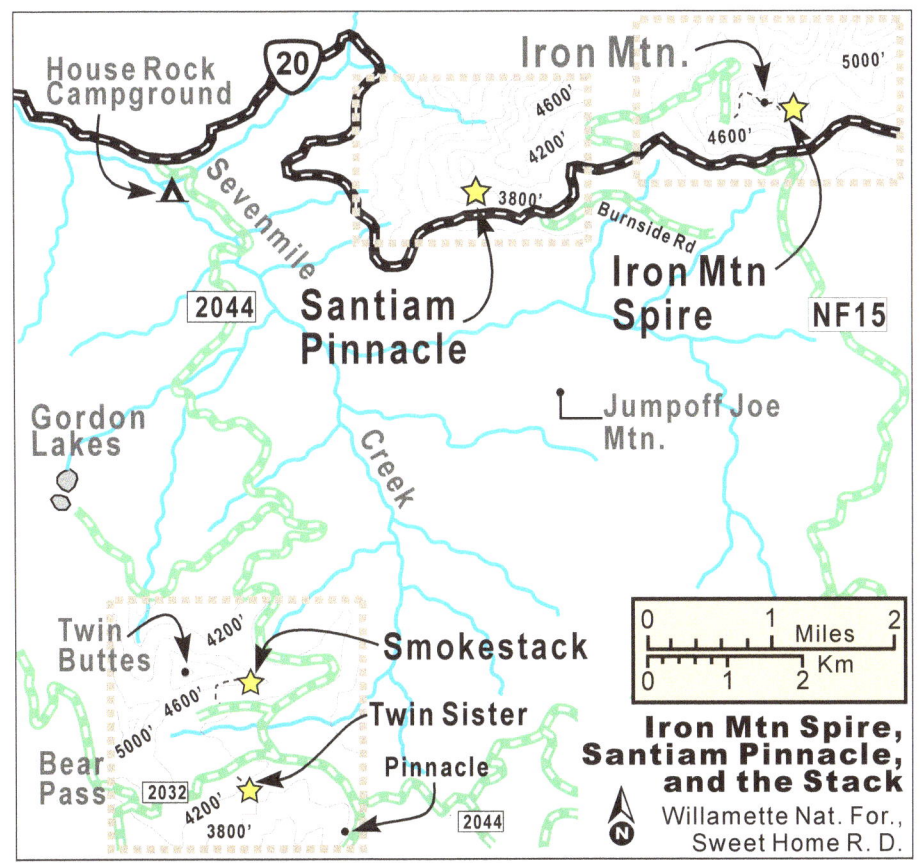

Iron Mtn Spire, Santiam Pinnacle, and the Stack
Willamette Nat. For., Sweet Home R. D.

Continue free climbing rightward around a corner then up left and then directly up to a belay ledge.

P5: A short easy pitch leads to the top.

3. Wild Turkey 5.8 A4
Pro to 4" including a selection of pitons, Rurps and KB's

Begin this route just to the east of the uphill saddle.

P1: Climb up a few feet to a bolt and traverse left (5.7) to a crack. A short section of aid (expanding A2) leads to free climbing (5.8) where the crack widens. Bolts lead left to a hanging belay left of an overhang.

P2: Move right into a crack above the overhang. Mixed (5.8 A3) climbing leads to a belay ledge.

P3: Difficult aid climbing (A4) leads rightward to a bolt. Climb up past more bolts and a runner to free climbing (5.8) that moves left and then up to a cave. Watch for rope drag.

P4: A short section of aid (A1) starts on the left and leads up to a chimney. Follow the chimney (5.6) to a large ledge just below the top.

P5: A final short easy pitch leads to the top.

SANTIAM PINNACLE

The Santiam Pinnacle (3500') is located east of Sweet Home, directly above U.S. Hwy 20 at Mile Post 60½, which is about 2½ miles west of Civil (Iron Mtn.) Road on the north side of the highway. Burnside road is ½ mile to the east of the pinnacle. GPS coordinates for the roadside pullout at the pinnacle are Lat/Lon 44.23322°N / -122.11784°W at the altitude 3416'/1041m.

The Santiam Pinnacle is easy to miss because it is slightly hidden amongst the trees. The south face route is by far the best climb here and is definitely worth visiting, especially when combined with other climbing adventures in the region.

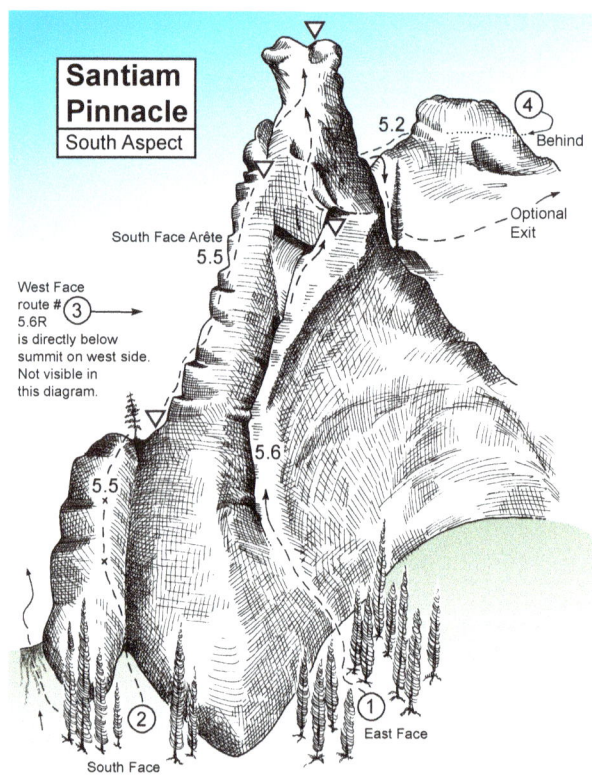

1. East Face 5.6
Pro: _ [?]

The East Face route ascends a friction slab, and then up a beautiful long crack to a belay nook. Exit left and up to summit.

2. South Face 5.6 ★★★
Multi-pitch, Pro to 2" and QD's

The stellar South Face route is a quality rock climb on a fabulous broad steep nose with airy section on excellent rock.

P1 80': Climb a chimney corner system on the lower west edge of the pinnacle. If the corner is too tough, step up left following the bolt line to a belay at the notch.

P2 60': Climb the wide arête past a steep section and belay at a stance in a corner on the upper west side.

P3 40': Continue up the outside face on knobs to the summit. Rappel from the summit toward the northeast to descend.

3. **West Face 5.6 R**

   Pro: Nuts and cams to 2"

   The West Face route ascends a crack to a delicate balance move right into a wide dihedral. Belay in the groove, then climb up left initially, to exit up right to a belay immediately below the summit. **Note:** There is a minor toprope route on the west face of Santiam Pinnacle. The **Water Buffalo** (5.11c) is to the right of the original West Face route on a vertical face below the summit.

4. **North Ridge 5.3**

   Pro: Minor gear to 1"

   From the upper saddle of the Santiam Pinnacle, traverse out onto the pinnacle using an exposed narrow ramp on the west side. Continue past the notch by walking along a ramp-slot on the west side just below the summit. Merge with the South Side route to top out.

   GONZO PINNACLE

   Gonzo Pinnacle is a very minor plug immediately west 100' of the upper edge

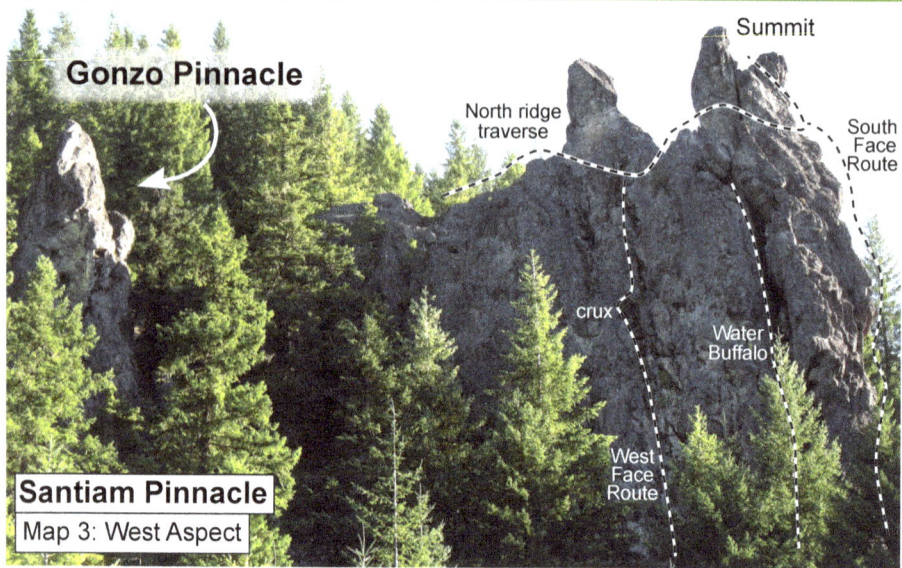

of Santiam Pinnacle. Virtually a boulder move from the upper side (5.4) you still might find this short (fixed) lead a worthy venture. A 4-bolt 5.7 sport route called **Archimedes** punches through an overhang on the east face of Gonzo Pinnacle.

IRON MOUNTAIN SPIRE

The Iron Mountain Spire is an exhilarating but rotten spire composed of welded tuff and crumbling basalt. The pinnacle is located several hundred feet south east from the top of Iron Mountain. The summit of this mountain has a lookout structure still in use by the Forest Service. Alpine forests, wildflowers, and superb scenic views of the Cascades create a beauty worth seeing from the top of Iron Mountain. The main south face was explored in 1971 by Joe Bierck, Paul Fry, and Dean Fry using a friable chimney system.

Directions

From Sweet Home drive 32 miles east on Highway 20 and turn left on Civil Road (FS035). Follow this gravel road for 2½ miles to the trailhead. Hike the 1½ mile trail to the summit of Iron Mountain and bushwack down the south east slope to the spire.

1. **Iron Mountain Spire 5.6 R/X**
   Pro: Nuts to 2" and pitons
   To ascend the spire requires a desperate instinct to survive and raw determination to summit on such a fine rotting massif. An 80' lead, then a 30' scramble to the top. The crux is a reddish bulge about ½ way up the lead. Gear placements are hard to find, and most hand holds are detachable. Belay at the shoulder, then work left on the scree covered ledge up to the top. Two rope rappel from the summit, or one rope rappel from the shoulder belay. Although

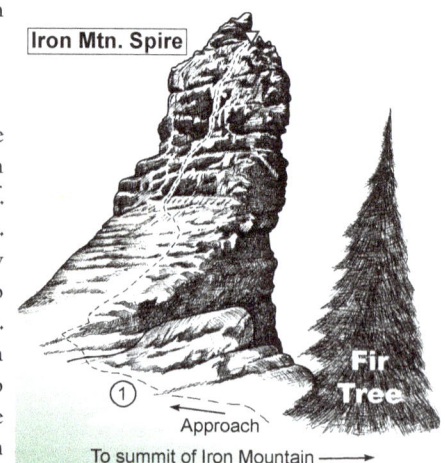

this is an easy rating for a climb, this is not a summit for a novice climber.

SMOKESTACK

What is it? A top hat...a smokestack? Few persons have climbed this ridge crest perched plug, but none-the-less it is a nice backcountry rock stack worthy of multiple routes. Though is has only one real climb, a mere 20 minute drive on gravel roads south of House Rock campground (east of Upper Soda) makes it a viable summit objective.

To access this smokestack like plug of rock drive south from House Rock Camp Ground on FS2044. It is located on the lower portion of a ridge line east of Twin Buttes. The smokestake plug and the Twin Sisters Pinnacle are short, enjoyable, and moderately easy rock climbs, and virtual neighbors to each other.

Park on a dead end side road south of the plug. The dense brushy thicket between the gravel road and the pinnacle is a bit too desperate to fight through. Instead, walk west 200' into a tall forest and hike cross-country up through the lightly wooded forest. When the slope steepens angle up right out of the forest onto the meadows. Walk along the sloping meadow east to the Smokestack.

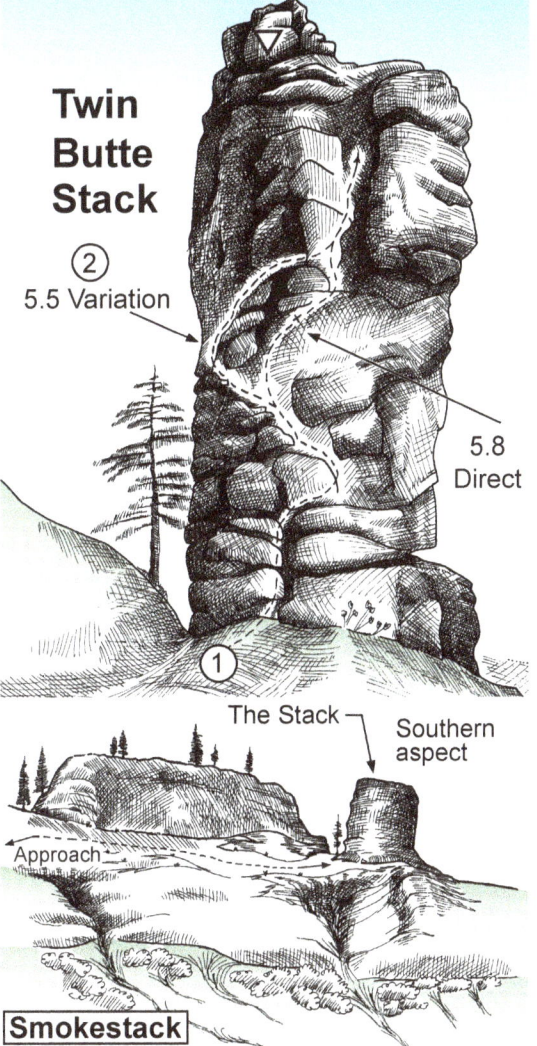

1. **West Face 5.8**
   Pro: Nuts and cams to 1½"
   This enticing and totally overhanging 80' plug of rock is perched directly upon a prominent ridge one mile east of Twin Buttes. Hike to the left in the deep forests, then up to the right on an open south-facing meadow to access the Stack. The west face nose route presently is the only way up at 5.8.
   A 5.5 R variation (#2) bypasses the crux on steep moss covered rock slope (cams to 3") by stepping left at the bolt crux move on the regular route. One 60m rope is sufficient to rappel.

TWIN SISTERS PINNACLE

Looking south from the summit of the Smokestack you will see the infamous Twin Sisters Pinnacle to the south ¾ mile in a clear-cut area along a ridge overlooking the Blue River basin. Though that pinnacle is not immediately visible from the place you park the vehicle along FS2032, a quick jaunt over a clear-cut slope leads to this spire.

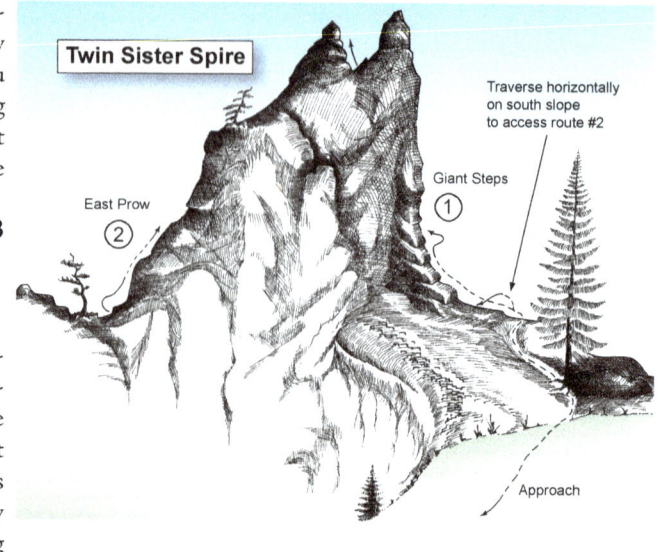

1. **Giant Steps** 5.3 R

   Pro: Minor gear to 3"

   This spire looks impressive as you approach it, but the standard southwest facing Giant Steps route is actually quite short. Finding good protection placements is a challenge.

   The **East Prow** is the only other known variation to the top. Scamper along sloping ledges around the southeast side till you can access the east ridge prow. Belay at a small tree then lead up friable unprotectable 4th class moves to the summit.

TWO GIRLS MTN

Rarely climbed raw adventure on double spires perched on a ridge crest overlooking the Two Girls creek valley on the upper eastern slope of Canyon Creek near Bear Pass. The pinnacles are composed of well-weathered crumbly Tertiary basalt with a variety of rock horns and rounded knobs (and occasional gear) for protection. The views from the top are great. There are two spires, the East Girl and the West Girl. The involved approach has a fair bit of cross country travel, some of it through rhododendron thickets, and very steep slopes. Expect loose rock (helmet country) and substantial runout sections on the 3rd and 4th class terrain.

Directions:

Drive east of Sweet Home on US 20 past Cascadia for a total of about 11 miles. Drive southeast of FS2022 along Canyon Creek 6 miles, then up FS2024 to access FS2024-250, and then FS2024-251 and travel up this as far as possible in a vehicle or

✦ SANTIAM SUMMITS 517

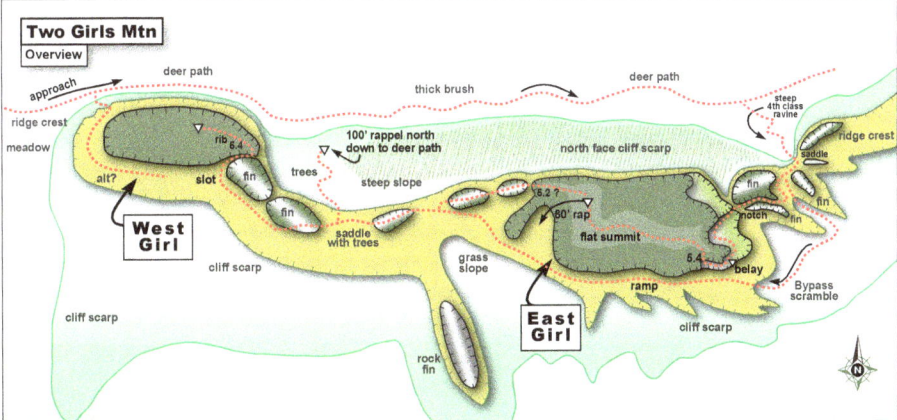

walk if the road is impassable. Where the NW ridge meets the road at 3700' cross-country up this forested ridge (800' approx.) to the main east-west ridge. Travel east to the Two Girls (¼ mile) to a meadow with a great view of the Two Girls. From here the adventure gets complex. Follow a deer trail that traverses left along the well-vegetated north slope of the spires next to the vertical rock face. Scramble up a 5th class ravine (ice axe and rope?) to land on the east flank (see diagram). You can either climb the East Buttress or use the bypass scramble on the south side for quicker access to the West Girl. There may be other ways to access these pinnacles so good luck. GPS N 44.326793 N / -122.297296 W Elev 4656' / 1419m

East Girl

East Buttress of East Girl 5.4 R
Mostly 3rd-4th class terrain with a short crux that takes good pro. Bring a few pitons.

West Rib of East Girl 5.1 [?] very short (50') and likely climbed. Easiest way to the top.

West Girl

East Arête of West Girl 5.5
This is the standard route. Takes the obvious corner up to a notch, then up a short rib to the top (pitons help).

Descent:
If you have climbed both summits it is easier to descend down near the east edge of the West Girl. Make a short rappel from one fir down closer to the final large fir trees. Two ropes easily reach to the base of the wall where the deer path traverse is located. By carefully selecting one of the lowest trees on the steep slope one single 60m rope (100' rap) will suffice in getting you down to the deer trail on the north slope. Round trip about 7 hours.

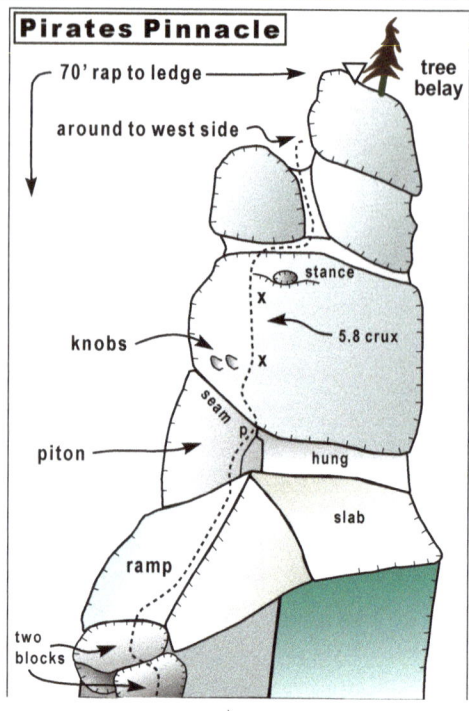

PIRATES PINNACLE

Pirates Pinnacle 5.8 PG
Pro: minimal nuts and cams to 3", a few thin pins, and some TCU's

A minor pinnacle on the east slope of Canyon Creek about 8 miles southeast from US Hwy 20 on NF 2022 road. This pinnacle is visible where the gravel road crosses the creek on a concrete bridge. Park just south of there and descend to the stream, cross it, then march up a long steep off trail

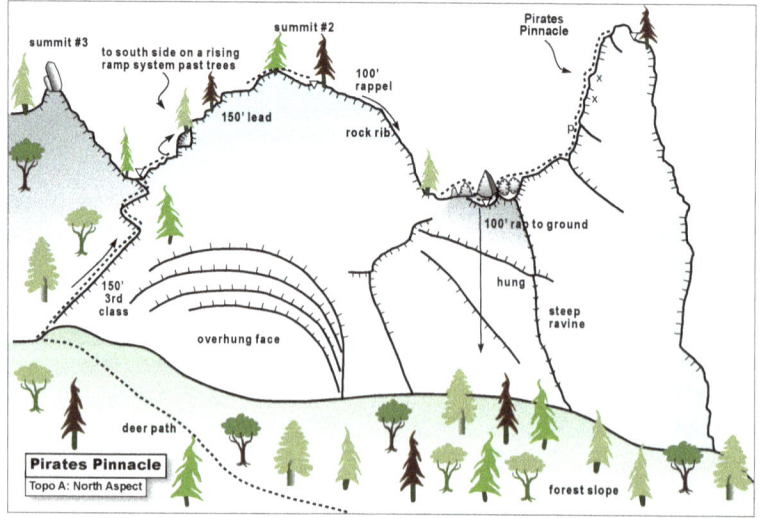

scramble 1050' uphill to get to base of pinnacle. It was odd to find no evidence of previous ascent for such as prominent minor pinnacle in this valley. Anticipate 1½ hours up hill, 2-4 hours to climb pinnacle, and 1 hour to descend back to car. See diagram for initial route beta, although alternative methods of ascent are feasible. Canyon Creek valley offers 2-3 more possible wild minor pinnacle climbs for the savvy adventurous climber.

HORSE ROCK PILLAR

Horse Rock Pillar (250' approx.) has a multi-pitch route on a wild looking gnarly spire similar in character to the infamous Turkey Monster. Rock composition is rhyolite similar to the spires in the upper Menagerie which should give you an advance clue of the rock type. Drive east of Sweet Home, Oregon for 11.7 miles, then southeast on Canyon Creek Road for 9.3 miles. The spire is visible on the road as you get near it but obscured by trees when directly below it. GPS 44°19'00" N, 122°20'15" W. See diagram/photo for visual.

Pro: Pitons, nuts and cams to 3", hangers, two 60m ropes; P1 5.8 80': a basic variable sized wide crack (partly fixed); P2 5.7R A2 130': mostly a fixed bolt ladder with a short spat of aid. Runout free climbing terrain near the top.

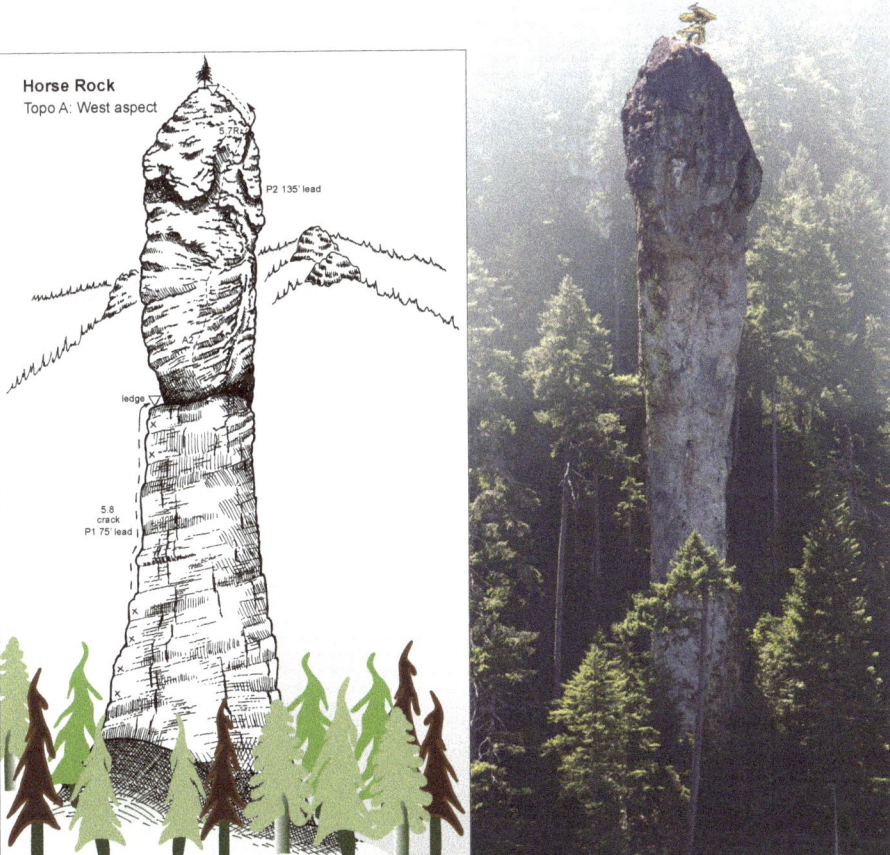

Horse Rock Pillar

7

SOUTHERN WILLAMETTE CRAGS

OREGON HAS MANY OTHER GREAT climbing destinations that involve a bit more driving time from Portland to visit but are well worth the venture when combined into an overnight climbing trip or a long fast day drive.

Make plans for an extended spring, summer or fall weekend journey around western Oregon state to experience some of these great climbing destinations. This chapter provides a selective analysis of rock climbing opportunities at several popular destination crags that continue to inspire and provide a great outdoor resource for everyone. Take the time and make the drive to the McKenzie region today. The following are a selection of climbing options near Eugene, Oregon.

SKINNER BUTTE COLUMNS

Written by Miles Noel

The Skinner Butte Columns are a group of relatively uniform high quality dark-colored columnar basalt which likely formed as a magma sill intrusion, then cooled to become gradually exposed through erosion, although a portion of the site was used for quarry material in the not-too-distant past. The bluff height is 45' tall and each column tends to lean leftward at a 70° degree angle. The cracks between the columns are excellent for various types of finger-to-hand-to-fist jams and present abundant opportunities to place rock gear protection while on lead.

The Columns at the butte have provided excellent training ground for rock climbers since the 1940s. Several near legendary climbers such as Wayne Arrington and Bob Ashworth used the site in the '70s, as well as other climbers like Gary Kirk, Ed Lovegren, Stu Rich and the Bauman brothers.

This climbing site is uniquely situated near the central core blocks of downtown Eugene, Oregon on the west slope of the Skinner Butte. With such convenient access this well-used crag offers climbers from beginner-to-expert good opportunity to refine their scope of rock climbing management technique. The University of Oregon Outdoor Program also instructs students here in the sport of rock climbing so expect the site to be busy on certain warm sunny weekdays and weekends, especially during the summer season.

The rock climb routes can be top-roped or lead on traditional gear. Many of the climbs are finger-size to hand crack-size and range in difficulty from 5.6 to 5.13a, while most are generally 5.8 to 5.10 in difficulty and include several face or arête climbs.

The Columns are available for year-round climbing and even though Oregon gets plenty of rain the small cliff does quickly dry because of the southwesterly orientation. Expect full sunlight on the rock face from about 10AM to sunset. You can usually climb 20-30 minutes past sunset with decent light. The site is not conducive to extensive bouldering but the ease of setting up tope-rope belays alleviates this.

Beta in Brief

Due to the close proximity of cracks and edges the rock climbs tend to be contrived to varying degrees, making each climb just a narrow stripe of vertical rock. The route and rating beta described herein assumes a crack climb keeps hands and feet in the crack, and a face climb adheres to the face of just one column.

Convenience and Accessibility

The site is within the boundary of the Eugene city park and features basic site improvements such as steel chairs, a sign board, and wood chip ground cover. Local climbers also provide some care for the site.

There are a series of easily accessible fixed chain belay anchors along the top of the wall so tope-rope climbing is a standard practice. Bring sufficient lengths of long sling as some of the belay anchors are set back from the upper edge of the bluff. Use the stair step trail on the left of the bluff to

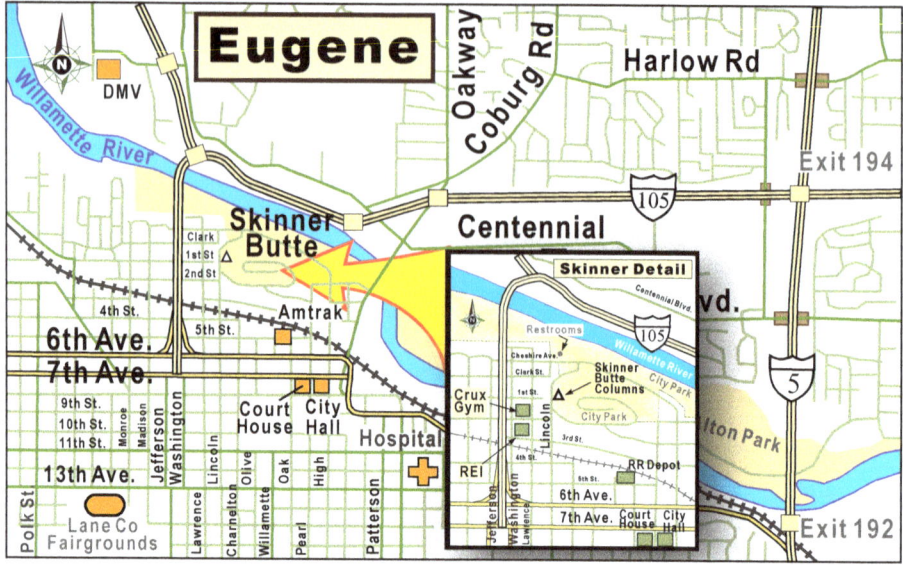

access the top-rope belay anchors.

Restroom facilities and water can be found at the nearby river front park to the north, on the west side of the playground. Just follow Lincoln Street north as is curves to junction with Cheshire Avenue. Turn left (west) and park in a parking area. The restroom facilities are next to the children's playground.

For sporting equipment needs or a rain-free indoor practice site the Crux Rock Gym is two blocks away while REI is three blocks away on 3rd and Washington. A city police precinct sub-station is located a block away which tends to deter transient activity, but you may encounter broken glass near the cliff on occasion.

Wildlife

Ladybugs and other insects nest in the rocks, but deep enough in that you don't need to watch out for them. All are harmless, but the ladybugs emerge by the millions and are attracted to the salty perspiration left from sweaty climbers' hands. Hummingbirds, bald eagles, peregrine falcons, red tailed hawks and starlings frequently ride the updrafts above the Columns. There is poison oak nearby in the brush and also near the 'closed' off limits area.

Directions

The columns are well-situated in the hub of downtown Eugene near the west slope of Skinner Butte on Lincoln Street where 1st street would be if it came through to abut up against the west slope of the butte.

From the I-5 freeway at exit #194 drive west on I-105 taking the city center exit till it merges onto 7th Street. Turn left onto 7th Street, drive east three blocks and then turn left onto Lincoln Street. Drive north (cross the railroad tracks) five blocks to the Columns.

The climbing routes are listed from right to left.

1. **LD 5.10b**
Use the crack and the column face to the left until left column ends, then finish as a face climb on the remaining column without using the top of the short column. This was a nice two star route until the top of the left column was removed in 2007. To top-rope this climb rappel down and over from chains above Hard Layback to the chains at the

SOUTH WILLAMETTE CLIMBS 525

top of LD.
2. **Satisfaction 5.11a/.12a**
   Jam up the crack for a fingertip cranking 5.12a, or add the face holds for a 5.11a. Mostly just finger jams, but with a couple hand jams at the top.
3. **Hard layback 5.9+/.10b**
   Jam up the crack for a really nice 5.10b, or climb it as a layback for a (strenuous) 5.9+.
4. **Fat Crack (Outer Column Jam) 5.8 / 5.9**
   This very uniform crack is perfect for learning to jam. Finger jams leading to hand jams. Hands and feet in the crack for a 5.9, or add the face holds for a 5.8.

5. **Arête Layback 5.12a**
   Strenuous and slippery, the name says it all.
6. **Left Crack 5.12+**
   Extremely thin fingertips crack immediately left of the prominent outer column.
7. **Grass Crack 5.10b**
   The start can be awkward and many people use a left foot smear, but try to stay true to the crack and stay off the face holds.
8. **Right Ski Track 5.10a**
   The crack forks, but stay to the single clear line through it for a nice 5.10a. Lots of protection opportunities.
9. **Left Ski Track 5.10b**
   This is a tricky bouldery route without many good jams, so using the occasional nub to the immediate left is fair game.
10. **Chimney Face 5.9**
    Face climb between Old Chimney and Left Ski-track until the holds peter out about 80% of the way up.
11. **Old Chimney (Main Chimney) 5.7**
    Climb the chimney using classic chimney technique or by stemming. Great beginner route.
12. **1st Column Face 5.10a / 5.11a**
    Climb the 1st column in the buttress without the crack for a slippery 5.11a, or with the crack for a 5.10a.
13. **2nd Column Right Jam 5.10a**
    Jam up the crack with hand and finger jams. This crack just gobbles up passive gear, offering bomber placement opportunities every few inches. Dyno past the thin, dirt-filled crack a third of the way up for style points.
14. **2nd Column Left Jam 5.9 / 5.10a**
    Jam up the crack with finger and hand jams. Keep hands and feet in the crack all the way up for a 5.10a, or let your left foot come out at the top for a 5.9.
15. **2nd Column Inclusive 5.7+**
    Climb using both cracks and the face holds on 2nd Column for a fun 5.7+. Great beginner route.
16. **3rd Column Face 5.8 / 5.10a**
    Face climb staying out of the cracks for a 5.8. The layback crux at the top can be height sensitive. Or climb it as a layback for the 5.10a barn-door layback variation.

Skinner Butte
Map B: Six Columns

SOUTH WILLAMETTE CLIMBS 527

Skinner Butte Map C

17. 4th Column Right Jam (Forthright) 5.10a
Jam up the crack keeping hands and feet in the crack for a nice 5.10a. Finger and hand jams, and lots of gear placement opportunities for small to medium passive gear.

18. 4th Column Left Jam (Sign Crack) 5.10a / 5.12a
Variant contrivances can be attained by climbing all the crack using all the holds or using focused emphatic limitations.

19. 4th Column Inclusive 5.7
Climb using both cracks and the face holds on 4th Column for a fun 5.7. Great beginner route.

20. 5th Column (Sign Face) 5.10a / 5.12a
Climb the face with both edges, staying out of the cracks, for a 5.10a, or climb the face only without either edge for a 5.12a.

21. 6th Column Jam (Bat Crack) 5.7+
Climb this wide irregular crack with hands in crack and feet on the face of 6th Column for a tricky 5.7+, or feet in the crack to

Ian Goss leading at *Wolf Rock*

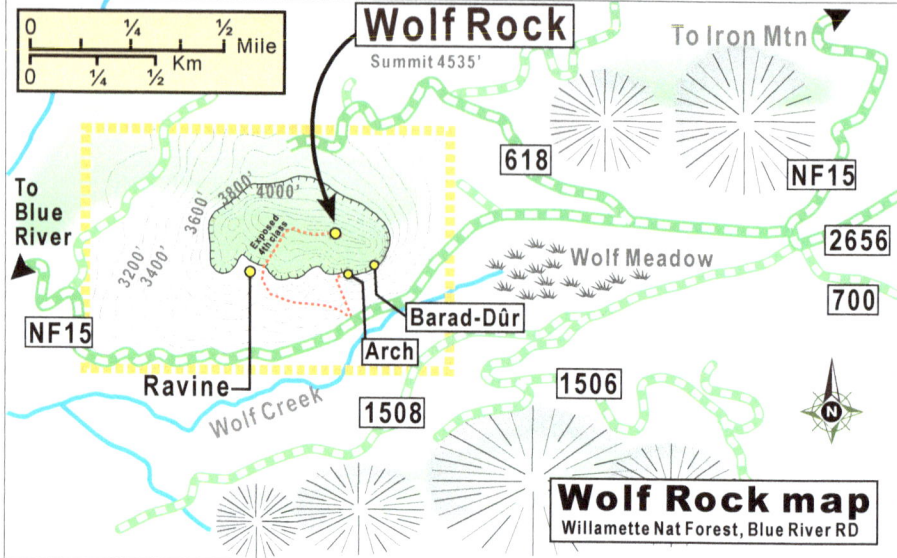

make it really awkward. This climb is sometimes wet or muddy deep in the crack, and frequently frustrates beginners.

22. **6th Column (Bat Face) 5.11a**
Face climb staying out of the crack for a 5.11a.

23. **New Chimney Jam 5.10a**
Jam up the crack in the right side of the chimney.

24. **New Chimney Column 5.9**
Face climb with edges up the column in the left side of the chimney.

25. **New Chimney Standard 5.8**
Climb the chimney using standard chimney techniques and face holds.

26. **One Note Samba 5.10a**
Face climb with right side crack. Mantle crux.

27. **Un-named 5.8**
Great face climb with a variety of holds. Immediately right of the bottomless column route.

28. **Bottomless Column 5.8**
Fun little roof problem, using column and edges. Don't worry about using the cracks. This is the detached bottomless column.

29. **Bugs! 5.7**
Climb this blocky 5.7 up past where the flying black bugs (flying ants maybe?) come out of the rocks. The bugs are totally harmless.

30. **Transportation Routes 5.6**
Blocky area that can get beginners moving, but not

Mackenzie on *The Arête*, Wolf Rock

great climbing.

WOLF ROCK

Wolf Rock is an impressive 900' volcanic andesite (Ta3) massif that ranks as the largest monolith in Oregon with a summit perched at an elevation of 4535'. This virtual mountain is an old volcanic remnant plug that was exposed after surrounding softer soils eroded away.

Wolf Rock is home to one of Oregon's outstanding classic rock climbing routes pioneered in the early '70s. Wayne Arrington and Mike Seely in a multi-day effort they established the 8-pitch grade IV 5.9 A2 (III 5.11a/b) route Barad-Dûr (Dark Tower) on the main 900' south face headwall. The route ascends very steep terrain up to the awe-inspiring dark roofs, breaking past the improbable roofs a few hundred feet below the main summit.

Many of the long established rock climbs at the Rock are traditional ground-up affairs with typically runout, down-sloping round-edged rock holds, and often marginal or limited protection placements. The established longer routes on the south face and north face offer similar obstacles and challenges.

The old north face climbs are seldom visited these days, but if you do decide to venture over there expect overgrown logging roads and very thick bushwhack thrashing just to get to the base of the wall. Expect difficulty finding the known routes and anticipate loose rock with moss covered down-sloping holds and limited protection options.

Today, most climbers suffice with faster rewards by aiming for the south side rock climbing opportunities. The standard scramble route to the summit (West Gully) is a great 1-2 hour uphill blast, but do expect several hundred feet of very exposed (3rd class) smooth rock slope terrain.

The Conspicuous Arch

For the sport minded climber a stellar selection of fixed bolt routes exists under the great Conspicuous Arch, a prominent feature on the sunny south side of Wolf Rock, just a mere 5-minute walk from your vehicle.

In all, Wolf Rock is a very fascinating place to visit whether just scrambling up the West Gully to the summit or climbing the classic Barad-Dûr. The Old Cascades are a delight to view and photograph from the top of this rock summit. The sheer bulk and magnitude of this rock, combined with lichen colored rock, dark-water stained ravines, vibrant green forest with vivid doses of yellow leafed Vine Maple provide a grand destination for everyone.

Wayne on Barad-Dûr, Wolf Rock

How To Get There

Directions from Eugene: Drive east 40 miles on Hwy 126 to the community of Blue River. Continue east another 2½ miles, then turn left on Blue River road (FS15). Follow this road up around the east side of Blue River Reservoir (paved along the reservoir) and past the Mona Campground. Turn right at the 'T' and follow this gravel road for a total of 12 miles to Wolf Rock. Park at a pullout below the Conspicuous Arch.

Trail Access

A very short 5-minute walk up a good trail leads

up from the gravel pullout to the sport routes under the Conspicuous Arch. If you are aiming for Barad-Dûr continue up eastward along the base of the cliff from the Conspicuous Arch till you are beneath the great dark roofs. This route can be difficult to locate for first time visitors. Wear a helmet on any multi-pitch route.

West Gully summit bound scramblers can start near the same trailhead and aim up west through the forest below the cliff. See route beta below for full specs. Wolf Rock is accessible for climbing about 5 months of the year, typically from mid-June through October, but if the weather is perfect you might find the site climbable a bit earlier or later than that.

Climbing Routes

The Wolf Rock routes of greatest interest to climber these days are Barad-Dûr and the single-pitch sport routes under/near

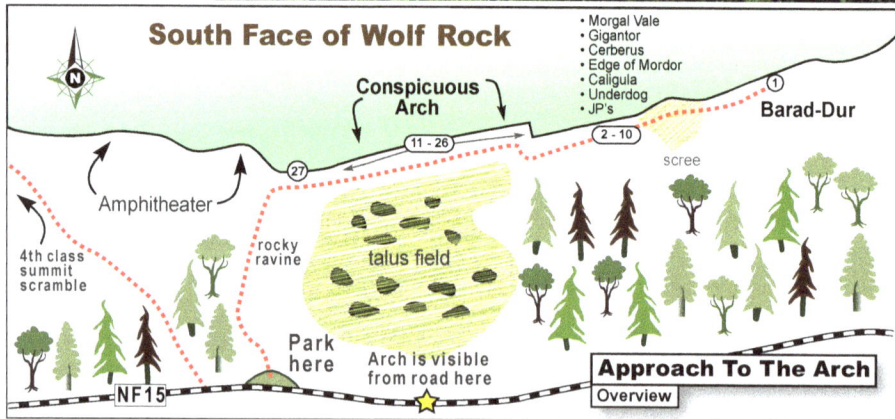

the great Conspicuous Arch.

Barad-Dûr is Oregon's great classic hardman route with long leads of moderate climbing up to the huge dark roofs which offer fierce exposure just to climb past. Hike a few hundred feet uphill east from the Conspicuous Arch to an open scree slope beneath a wide dark face. The routes Death March and Gigantor (upgraded bolt route) are located on this wide sweeping flat face starting from a large ledge just above the ground. Walk uphill east for another few hundred feet to find the start for Barad-Dûr. Look for a bolt about 5' above the ground. You should be standing directly beneath the great dark foreboding roofs high above.

1. **Barad-Dûr IV 5.9 A2 (III 5.11b)**
   Length: 1000', Pro: wires to 2", cams to 3", double cams at 1" and long slings. Aiders, and a few thin pitons if planning to nail the roof.
   P1 5.9+ 100': Climb directly up the face past five bolts using gear placements when you find it. Bolt belay anchor is at a little stance.
   P2 5.9 90': Aim up and to the right (bolts), and up to a left-facing dihedral corner system. Climb the corner system to a bolt belay anchor on a ledge.
   P3 5.8: Continue up and right (bolts) on lower angled slabs, and then up left (bolts) using gear when necessary (low 5th class) to a small belay nook on the far left.
   P4 5.9+: Climb up to the right on lower 5th class corner ramp, and then up left under a left-leaning overhang. Continue leftward till you can surmount (crux) the small overhang just before a bolt belay anchor on a tiny perch.
   Note: The fifth pitch involves launching into power climbing out a series of small bulge overhangs leading up to the final giant dark roof above.
   P5 5.10d 60' (or C1): Take a photo of your partner as he starts this lead! Traverse right from the belay on a sloped edge where the wall

leans out at you. Turn a blind corner and power your way straight up 50' to a hanging bolt belay anchor.

P6 5.11b 80' (or C2): Continue directly up an overhanging corner (bolts and KB) and power up over a small bulge crux. Begin a rightward traverse on a handrail under the final great roof. Turn the lip of the roof and waltz up to a bolt anchor belay on a large ledge.

Note: Pitch six overhangs nearly 15' from the belay. Be sure to place adequate protection for your partner to follow this safely.

Note: There is an A2-A3 variation which continues directly up the overhanging corner up leftward through the main roof from the pitch 6 belay anchor.

P7 5.4R: Climb up left (1 bolt) on steps with loose gravel making use of the natural features till you can reach a bolt belay anchor near the crest.

P8 Low 5th class: Continue up steps and corners along the ridge crest up west to the summit.

Line of Descent: Walk along the ridge crest for ¼ mile to descend the long smooth rock ravine called West Gully. Once at the treeline angle along the base

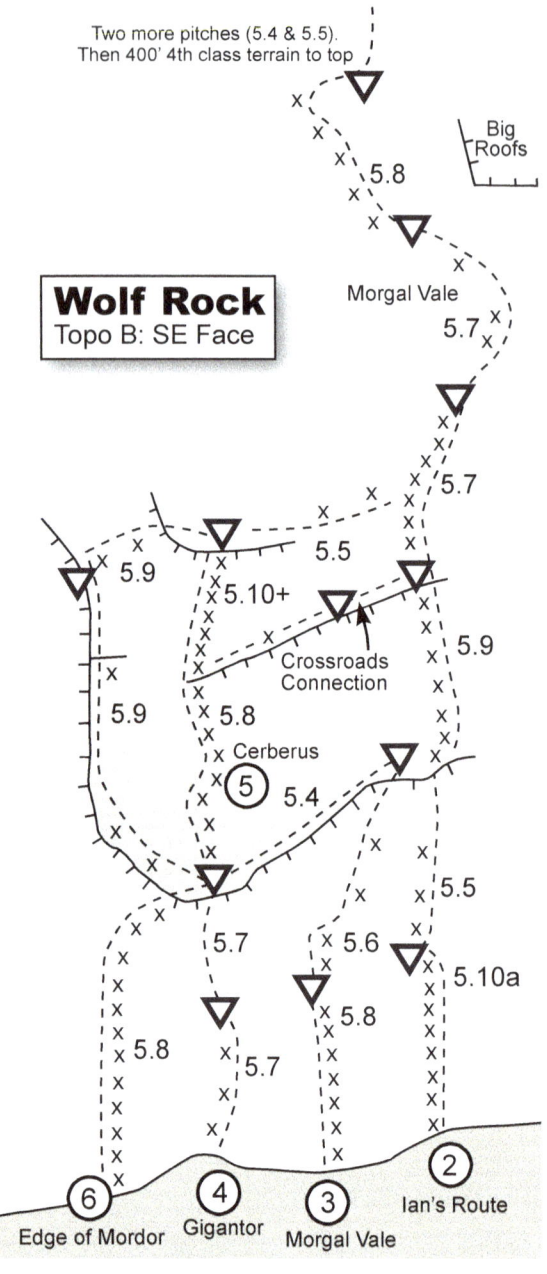

of the cliff but in the forest gradually descending downward to the FS15 and the parking site. Expect at least 45-minutes to descend.

2. **Ian's Route 5.10a**

   8-10 QD's, 2-pitch lead

   A quality addition to the long face climb routes in this zone. P1 is a 5.10a face climbing, and P2 is a 5.5 lead. It merges with Morgal Vale (bring more gear for this).

3. **Morgal Vale 5.9+**
Pro to 1½", about 10 QD's, Multi-pitch
A long multi-pitch lead that is becoming fairly common route to climb these days. P1 is 5.8, P2 is 5.6, P3 is 5.9, P4 is 5.7, P5 is 5.7, P6 is 5.8, P7 is 5.4, P8 is 4th class for 400' to top. See topo.

4. **Gigantor III 5.8 R**
Length: approx. 1000' Multi-pitch
Pro: __ QD's mostly, optional cams ½" to 1" and minor set of nuts.
Retro-bolted in 2010 so as to reduce the high risk runouts. The wide dark face has a series of steep sections broken with minor ramps and ledges. The base of this area (telltale lack of trees) is prone to volleys of loose rock so beware if climbing parties are above you. **P1:** an easy lead up rock steps to a ledge system. **P2:** where the face steepens, move right along easy ramp steps. **P3:** at a small light colored section of rock is a left-facing minor corner capped by a lip. Climb next to this directly up the face (crux). **P4:** is a short lead. **P5:** moves up left of the great roofs. Quality deteriorates; expect loose rock. **P6:** uses numerous ledges, traversing up left across loose terrain. **P7:** unprotected 4th-5th class slabs/ramp till the terrain eases to a scramble.

Wolf Rock detail
Map 2: Conspicuous Arch

534 CHAPTER 7 ✦ ORC

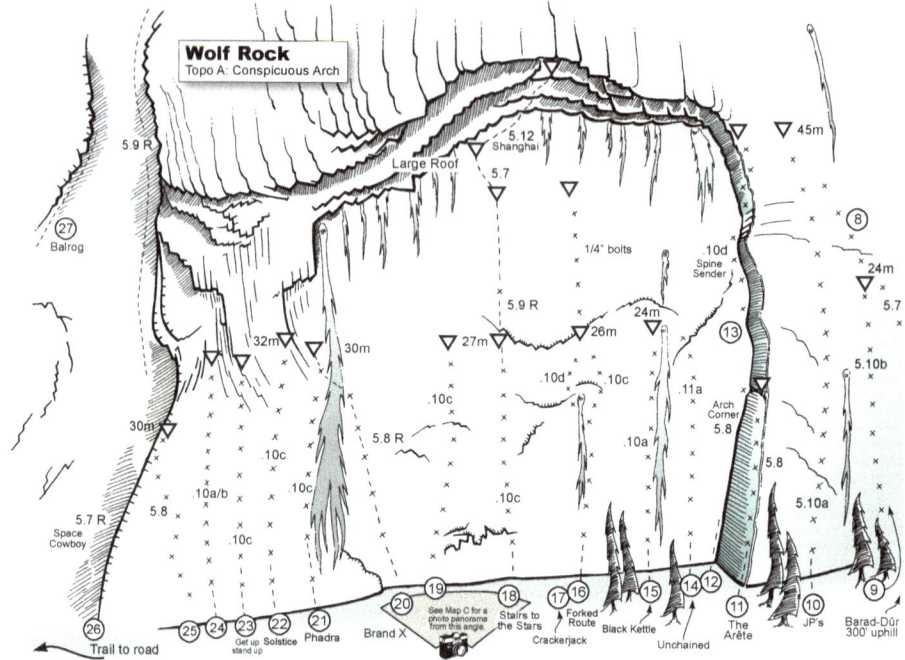

5. Cerberus 5.10+
16 QD's
A single pitch lead directly above the first pitch of Gigantor. Climb Gigantor to a ledge belay, then punch directly up this bolted face route.

6. Edge of Mordor 5.9
Pro __", and __ QD's, Multi-pitch,
This is a 3-pitch climb immediately left of Gigantor start. P1 is 5.8 face climb, P2 is 5.9 right facing corner. Belay, then do a short traverse moving rightward to another belay (used by Cerberus). Rappel. Or traverse further right to merge with Morgal Vale.
Note: Crossroads Connection is a minor traverse on a ledge system between routes.

7. Caligula III 5.7 R/X
Length: approx. 1000' Multi-pitch
To the right of the Conspicuous Arch is a low angled face and corner system leading to a prominent ramp system on top of the Arch. Climb down-sloping rounded edges to a chimney. Ascend the chimney to a dirt ramp and belay at an anchor. Follow this ramp system up left until reaching an obvious ramp traverse that continues up left. Exposed easy friction leads straight left to another major corner system where it merges with Space Cowboy. Climb up friable terrain to the top. **P1-P2** 5.7r/x, **P3-P4** 5.6/5.7r/x, **P5-P6** 5th class to 4th class.

Partial quote: *A Climbing Guide to Oregon, by Nick Dodge 1975*

CONSPICUOUS ARCH

The following are great quality face climbs located under the prominent south face arch. The climbs are listed from right to left (westward). All of the climbs are single pitch leads using a 60m rope. A 5.12 route powers into the roof and several lines on the far west end have difficult second pitch leads if you are so inclined to take them on.

8. _____ **5.7**
   Length: P1 70', Pro: 5 QD's for 1st pitch, 10 QD's for entire lead
   Walk 100' uphill east from the arête Spine Buster. This fine route angles up left on steep terrain with good holds till it merges at route #3 belay anchor. Continue up (5.7) a steep corner (5 bolts) till it merges with JP's Route and lands on a small stance at belay anchor. Rappel to previous anchor and then rap to ground.

9. **Underdog 5.10b/c**
   Length: 70', Pro: 9 QD's
   Just to the right of JP's Route is this quality steep face climb. Finesse up the initial moves, chill a second, then launch into the power moves at a slight bulge. Chill at the next tiny perch, then dance up small edges to the bolt belay anchor where it merges with route #2.

10. **JP's Route 5.10a**
    Length: 150', Pro: 15 QD's
    To the right around the corner (east) of the arch arête about 15' you will find a vertical bolted face climb. This route powers up a long steep face staying on the outside portion from the Arch. Rappel with two ropes or rappel to the midpoint belay on route #2.

11. **The Arête 5.8**
    Length: 60', Pro: QD's
    This is a classic arête climb that ascends the lower portion of the prow on great edges and quality rock. Good climb for everyone to lead.

12. **Arch Corner 5.8**
    Length: 60', Pro to 4"
    This is the inside crack corner of the lower right

Mackenzie leading *The Arête* 5.8

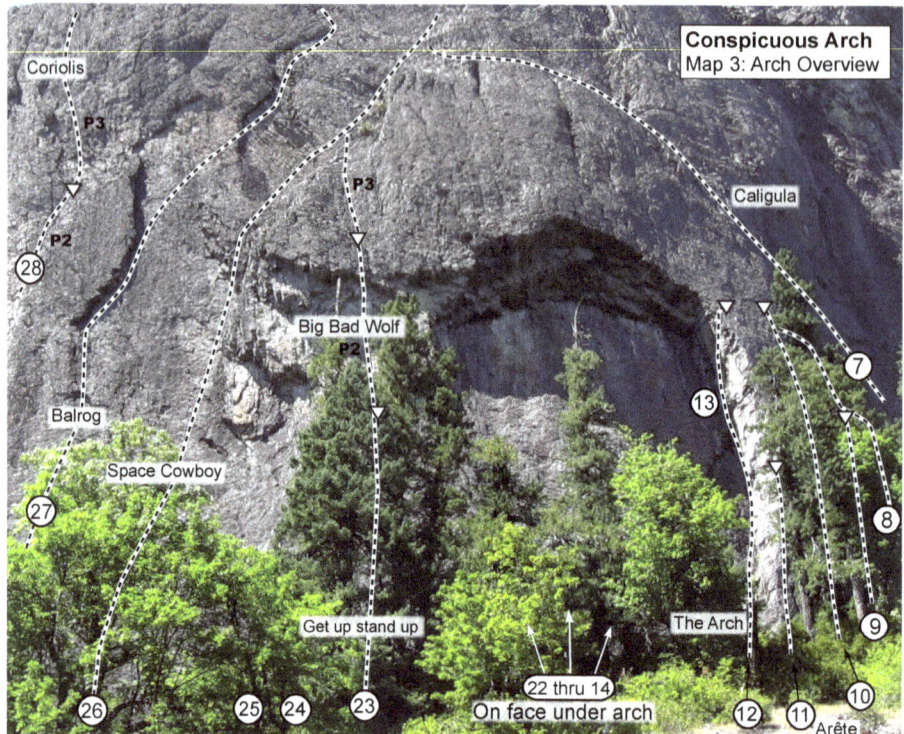

end of the Conspicuous Arch. Rappel from belay anchors on the The Arête.

13. Spine Sender 5.10d R

Length: 150' from ground including The Arête
Pro: QD's and small pro to 2"

This is the upper portion of the inside of the Arch or spine. From the belay anchor at the top of **The Arête** (5.8) climb up left close to the inside crack corner placing small pro for protection. At 25' clip the first bolt and climb a vertical face (bolts) up and rightward to exit to the outer edge of the prow to the bolt belay anchor.

14. Unchained 5.11a

Length: 80', Pro: 8 QD's

The first long face climb on the flat smooth face under the main arch and immediately right of the dark-colored water streak. There are three no-hands rests on this route. The crux is near the last bolt. Angle up left to the anchor on Cold Shut to belay.

15. Black Kettle 5.10a

Length: 80', Pro: 7 QD's

A classic route on steep rock, and has numerous positive holds once you are past the little roof. This route is easily recognizable by the obvious dark water streak. A shoulder jam at the little roof provides a no-hands stance.

16. Forked Route 5.10c

Length: 85', Pro: 8 QD's

A pumpy climb with two variations a mid-height passing a small lip and then merges at the bolt belay anchor. Forked Route takes the right line of bolts at the overhang.

17. Crackerjack 5.10d

Length: 85', Pro: 8 QD's

This is the harder left variation of the Forked Route involving a crux lip move and sustained climbing above the lip to the anchor.

18. Stairs To The Stars P1 5.10d, P2 5.9R, P3 5.7

Multi-pitch (P1 90'), Pro: 8 QD's 1st pitch

P1 5.10d 90': A nice first pitch with surprisingly demanding balancy start, and a crux at a small lip. Don't forget to use the no-hands rest at the crux lip.

P2 5.9R: An initial hard crux move, then clip the single bolt and dash up 5.5 terrain for 25' to the next anchor.

P3 5.7: Another short lead on large holds ending immediately under the giant roof.

P4 5.13a or C2 called **Shanghai**. A hardman route that pumps its way out the upside down giant roof of the Arch to an anchor. Use two ropes to rappel.

19. Captain Courageous 5.10c

Length: 95', Pro: 9 QD's

A reasonable route with some minor hollow hand holds just below the sloped ledge halfway up the route. Climb near a black water streak on the upper portion of the route to the bolt anchor.

20. Brand-X 5.8

Length: 100', Pro: 8 QD's

A stellar route and enjoyable to lead with a definite crux partway up. This route ascends the other dark colored water streak. Expect some hollow rock in places and well-spaced out bolts for the grade. Plenty of large steps and edge on the entire upper portion of the climb. This route was likely ascended using ground-up technique.

21. Phadra 5.10c/d

Length: 100', Pro: 8 QD's

A good climb with numerous small positive holds and a tight crux move on a short vertical section halfway up the wall. Shares same belay anchor as Brand-X.

22. Solstice Party 5.10c

Length: 105', Pro: 9 QD's

A steep power line ending at its own belay anchor slightly up left of the Brand-x anchor. Use two ropes to descend or jump over onto Brand-X to descend

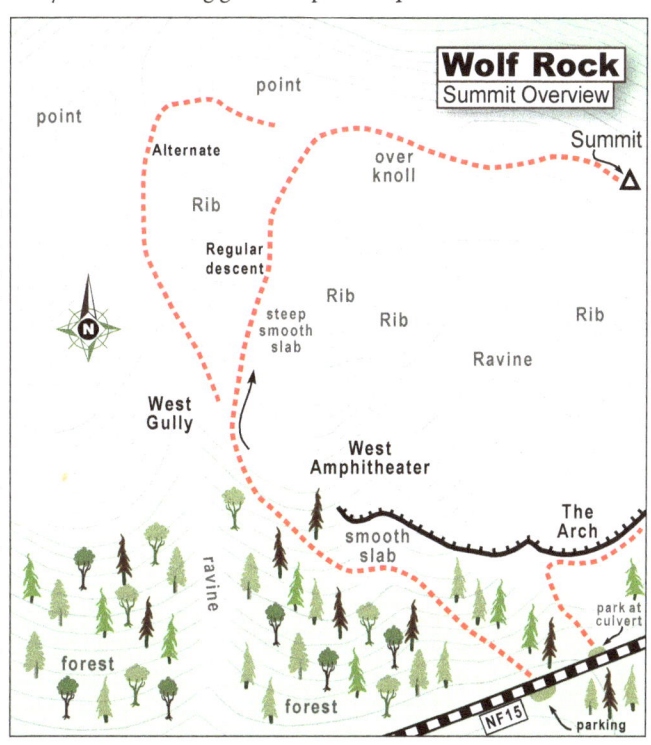

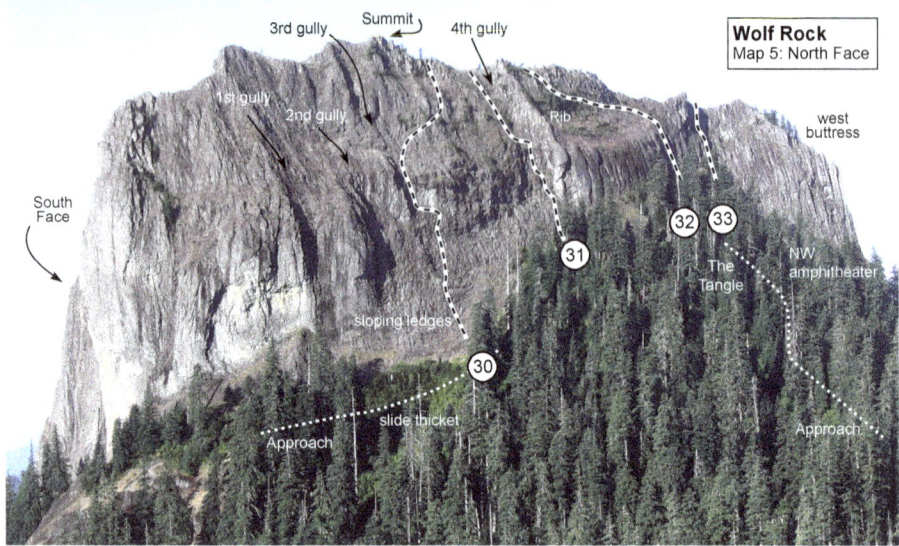

with one 60m rope.

23. Get Up and Stand Up 5.10c
Length: 100', Pro: 9 QD's

A cool sustained first pitch on numerous small edges. The **Big Bad Wolf** route continues from this belay anchor up through the roof above for an additional four pitches.

24. _____ 5.10a
Length: 100', Pro: 10-12 QD's

Another nice long face climb left of GUSU.

25. _____ 5.8+
Length: 100', Pro: 9 QD's

This route is lacking something, but at least it is easy-*ish*. Dance up mossy steps leftward, then up several steps rightward till the large edges end. Balance up left through a tricky section aiming to an easy right leaning ramp. Dash up the ramp to the belay anchor.

26. Space Cowboy 5.9 R/X
Multi-pitch

Bold climb for its time, with substantial runouts. P1 ascends a prominent left-facing stepped corner system. P2 continues up the left-facing corner. P3 powers past a steep section and dashes up a ramp. P4-P5 the angle eases but anticipate considerable runout terrain to the top.

27. Balrog 5.6 R/X
Multi-pitch

Located between Space Cowboy and Coriolis up high on the face is a right facing corner system. Balrog aims for this corner, then dances up right to another right-facing corner. Waltz along an exposed ramp up left to easier but loose terrain. Minimal pro options.

28. Coriolis Effect 5.9
Multi-pitch, Pro: 13 QD's & minor cams to 1½"

This is the first climb you encounter as you hike up the trail to the cliff scarp. Look for a right facing dirty corner at the ground with a bolt route 15' right of that. What the first pitch is lacking the second pitch makes up for it in stellar position and stellar quality. Rap with two ropes.

P1 5.8 120' 11 QD's: Climb a steep face with some hollow sections of rock till the terrain eases to large steps. Continue up another steep section to a belay anchor on a ledge.
P2 5.9 150' 13 QD's Cam/nuts to 1½": Move up right from anchor then dance up near vertical terrain on great hand edges and various small stances. A single hard move aims up to a crack then exits up right to a belay anchor. Pitch 3-5 has a few bolts, limited pro options, and is runout with friable rock. Best to rappel after the second pitch.

29. **West Gully (to summit) 3rd class**

    This is the scramble gully to the summit of Wolf Rock. From the parking site at a culvert follow a faint trail up left to a large stone cirque. Carefully prance across this wide smooth rock amphitheater and continue leftward up a narrow dirt path. The path ends next to a deep ravine gully system to your immediate west. Above is a broad slope initially of dirt and gravel slopes and a very long steep (3rd class) rock ravine aiming up and slightly right. There are several very steep sections on this long rock slope so be cautious going up and down (rope suggested). As the upper portion of the smooth rock ravine eases near the ridge crest begin to angle eastward near the crest aiming for Wolf Rock's highest point to the east. Time up will vary from 1-2 hours depending on your endurance. An alternative is to take the West Ridge that is between the West Gully and the Amphitheater. In either case, the ascent technicalities are about the same. Bring water and snacks and enjoy the view.

The following four climbs are located on the north face of Wolf Rock. The common method of approach is to hike along the base of the south face past Barad-Dur and curl up around to the north side. These routes are seldom climbed and should be considered of dubious quality with substantial runouts on mossy, down-sloping holds.

30. **North Face II 5.4 R**

    This route uses the second non-overhanging section east of the hogback and starts at the point where the vertical extent of the north face is greatest. Ascend for 100' and begin belaying. The first lead goes up and right for 130'. The next lead goes up for 20', then right for 130'. The next lead goes up for 20', then right to skirt an overhang, then up another 220' to a belay position on ledges below an overhang (pitons). The fourth lead is directly up a small, easy gully. From the top traverse right on ledges to heather and scramble to the summit. Anticipate about 4 hours for the ascent (Dodge, *A Climbing Guide to Oregon* (1975), pg 61-62).

31. **Barton's Gully II 5.5 R/X**

    Barton's Gully is the fourth gully on the north face when approached from the clearcut east of the rock. It is the most prominent of the four gullies. At a point east of the large overhanging bulge, climb sloping ledges and slabs to a belay point in a small Douglas fir 130' up in the gully. From here traverse left (east) 30', then climb straight up over mossy ledges to a poor piton belay 40'. Continue up 35' then traverse left 100' to a bush belay. From here continue straight up for 200' to the summit ridge. Anticipate about 6 hours (Dodge page 61-62).

32. **Hogback Chimney II 5.5 R**

    This route utilizes the deep chimney splitting the north face directly above the hogback. Ascend the chimney (30') and come out of a hole on the face of the cliff. Climb the face up and slightly left to a sloping belay ledge to the left of a small gully. From here diagonal up toward a low notch in the summit ridge (Dodge page 61-62).

33. **Hairy Tale II 5.7 R**
Traverse the base of the north face beyond the hogback past a dip in the base of the face to the top of the next rise. The climb begins above and left 40' of a small point separating rock terraces to the right and mossy slopes to the left in a left facing open book. Climb the book through a roof (5.6) and belay 10' above. Continue up to the second roof and climb 60' (5.4) to an awkward belay below a wall. Diagonal left, then right to a flared jam crack behind a flake. Proceed up this (5.7) crack. Gear to 3" including cams, and pitons. Anticipate about 6 hours to climb (Dodge page 61-62).

A Rock Climbing Guide To Moolack

Thad Arnold climbing *X Marks the Spot*
Photo archive: T. Arnold

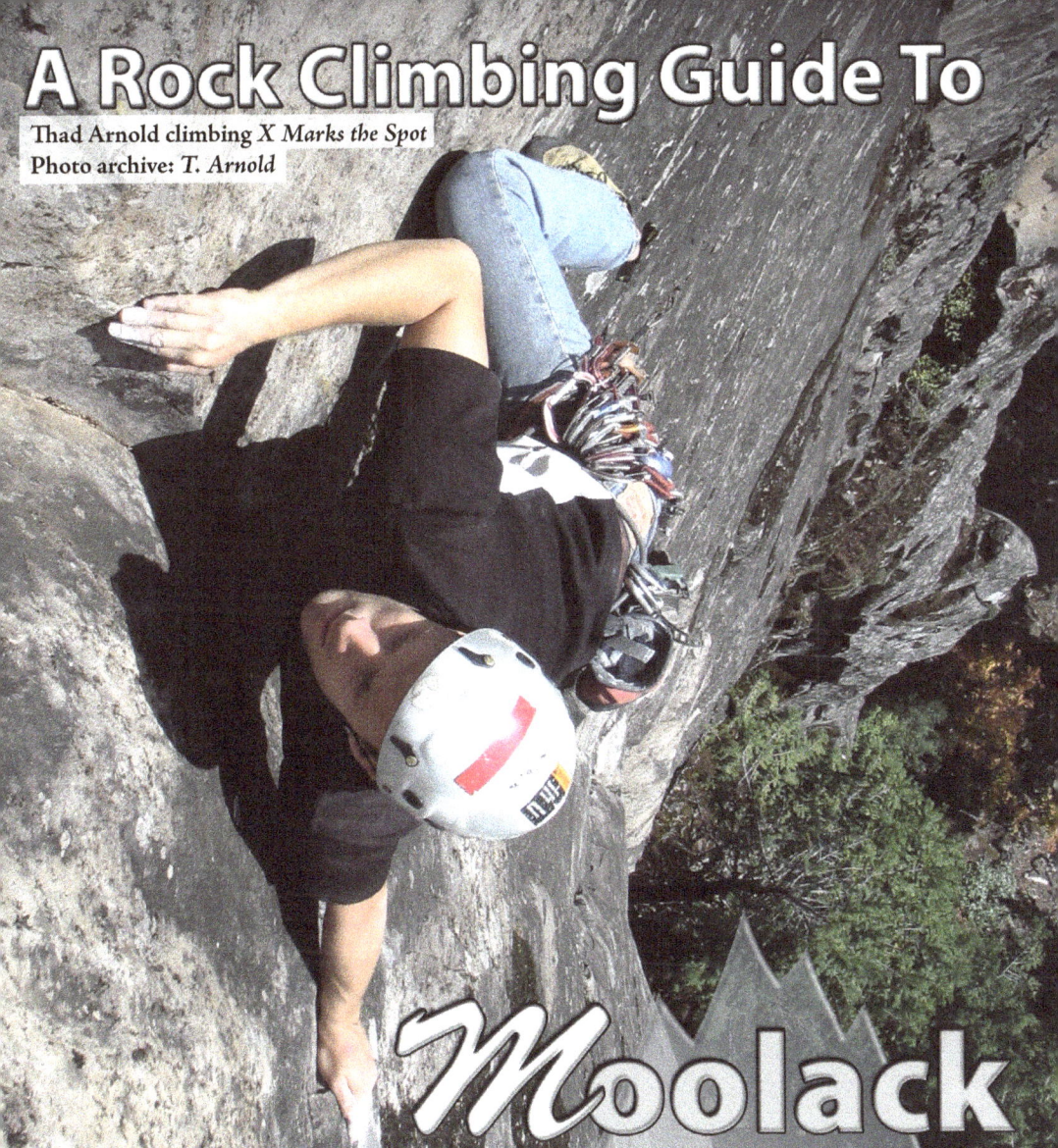

Original manuscript written by Paul Waters and Jennifer Mower (and dedicated to their daughter Eva)

Guidebooks have acted as the backbone to Oregon rock climbing for as long as the histories of ascents have been recorded. In 1968 Nick Dodge published *A Climbing Guide to Oregon* and since then a slew of guidebooks in Oregon have been printed ranging in quality. Great guidebooks have ascent information, discuss climbing history, and outline local practices (ethics, styles and tactics) of a particular crag in addition to providing readers with route descriptions. The traditional focus of the Moolack area creates a truly unique climbing experience, thus the traditional focus created a framework for this guide, from its first and second ascent information to its emphasis on a completely natural climbing experience. We aim to share the boltless standard and the uniqueness it has added to the experiences of those who have spent time at Moolack and those who will visit in the years to come. In summation, Moolack is an

* All Moolack photos courtesy of Paul Waters except where noted

Bill Soule leading *Gold 5.11b/c*
Photo credit: *Ari Denison*

inescapable and inherent part of the grand guidebook journey.

Moolack is for the moderate-to-experienced rock climber familiar with the concept of boltless climbing. Emphasis is placed on traditional on-sight, ground-up lead practices where feasible. Top-down new route development, including pre-practice to adequately prepare a route when needed (if the terrain has friable rock or has unknown difficulties or protection). Both methods are commonly practiced at Moolack. Even seasoned Moolack rock climbers still find it difficult to identify certain routes, so keep focused on the route you intend to climb and avoid uncleaned friable rock terrain. Moolack is a no-bolt crag, so categorizing established climbs and the individuals who developed a route necessitates information gathering usually in the form of a guide. Fixed gear implies provenance, so route development and first ascensionist establishment at a bolt-less climbing area would remain a mystery until written formulation is articulated.

For climbers less familiar with boltless climbing it is my hope to open your eyes to the thrill of traditional climbing in a pristine setting with zero visual interference from bolts. Finding crags with traits suitable for boltless climbing is rare, but rarer still if future generations of climbers have no awareness that zero-bolt standards do in fact exist. Sport and mixed-sport climbing that utilizes bolts as fixed gear is quite popular throughout Oregon, but Moolack's traditional style boltless climbing will continue to have appeal.

Bolts have historically been utilized at climbing areas of Oregon on land identified as protected wilderness areas, and in some cases appropriately so (e.g., Menagerie). At Moolack the boltless ethic exists primarily due to its geographic location in a "protected wilderness" region, making bolting here unlawful. But it is inappropriate to believe that making strides towards keeping Moolack boltless stops there. The Moolack climbing community has rallied around the boltless standard and it is not hard to see why. Moolack is completely conducive to non-bolted climbing because it has diverse cracks of all sizes with ample opportunity for ledges mid-climb for multi-pitch opportunities. Rarely has a hanging belay been implemented for even the longest of climbs. Finding unprotectable climbs is a greater task than finding readily protectable climbs. Those rare gems that haven't taken gear, are great top-rope problems. As for the cliff top, there are trees close enough to the cliff edge to provide quality top anchors, but far enough away to rarely encumber a lead climber when he tops out. Keeping Moolack boltless depends on stewardship abilities to express the Moolack standard, beyond merely localized community discussion.

Moolack is located in a quiet forested sanctuary. Climbing activity here is primarily due to its popularity and availability of route beta. In recent years evidence indicates that new climbers are being drawn to Moolack often with limited knowledge of the area. Not having a guide or a friend familiar with the area tends to limit the visiting climbers options resulting in crowding at the better known areas of the crag. A no-guidebook mentality to Moolack forces people to huddle around the same few rock climbs. I am promoting Moolack hoping that others are willing to be proactive in maintaining

Max Tepfer leading *Sideways*
Photo: *T. Arnold*

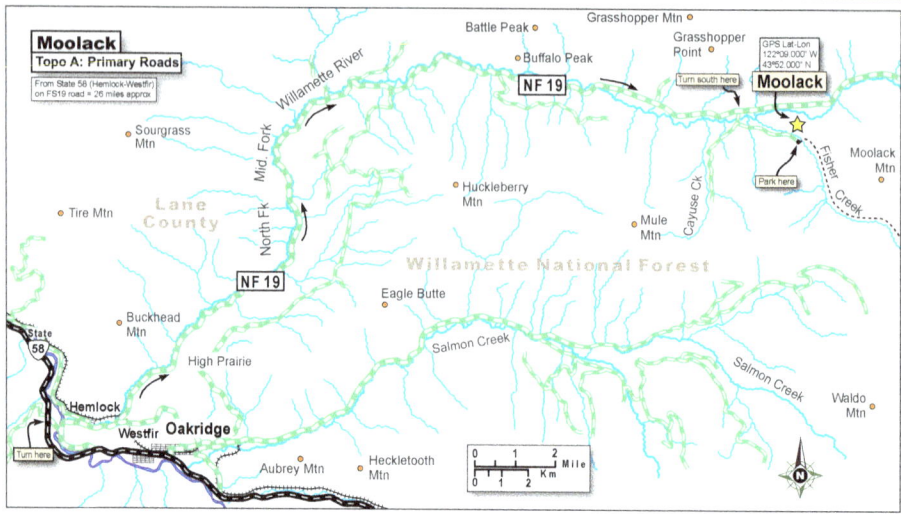

a user friendly environment on the climbing routes (moving some moss), and by being helpful to visiting climbers.

This book divides Moolack climbing into primary areas (e.g., Pedestal Area, Goldband Area) and within each area identifies routes in sequential order from right to left, east to west. Most climbs can be descended by rappelling or lowering from the top of the band, and some routes can be accessed by adjacent nearby routes. When topping out on a climb you can walk east along the rim top to descend via the cliffs termination on the east flank instead of rappelling.

This guide emphasizes the traditional practice of placing nuts, cams, tri-cams, hexes, sliding nuts, and sliding chocks (Big Bro) on lead, from the ground-up. Developing skills with a qualified and proficient friend or guide can lead to safe and well managed climbing at Moolack. Make sure you have plenty of long solid anchoring material (i.e. cord, webbing, static-rope) and avoid climbing over your traditional leading skill level unless you understand the risks. In the Southern Willamette Valley there are academic rock climbing classes, private lessons, and other areas used for practice of placing gear and building anchors with relatively easy access (e.g. Skinner Butte, Marys Peak). For top-down route access prior familiarity is beneficial in order to safely locate a specific climb.

Some route descriptions have abbreviated wording when discussing a nearby route, for example UOAP is Up on a Pedestal, EE is E.T.A. Eva, and OC is Orange Crush.

Moolack Mountain (5,490') a prominent rock hill northwest of Waldo Lake was formerly known as Elk Mountain because of the local abundance of that animal. It was renamed due to an abundance of Elk Mountains throughout the state. The Oakridge-Moolack region receives a substantial quantity of rainfall each year, which encourages profuse tree growth, lush dense brushy green foliage and thick brightly colored carpets of reddish-brown moss.

Moolack History

Bill Soule came to Moolack in the mid-to-late 1990s and started developing the approach trail and the areas earliest routes. Mike South, a Willamette Valley native also frequented the area. In these initial years Soule and South developed Lost Art, Up On A Pedestal, X-Marks the Spot, Perverts in Paradise and Geek on A Leash to name a few. Soule and South applied a

SOUTH WILLAMETTE CLIMBS

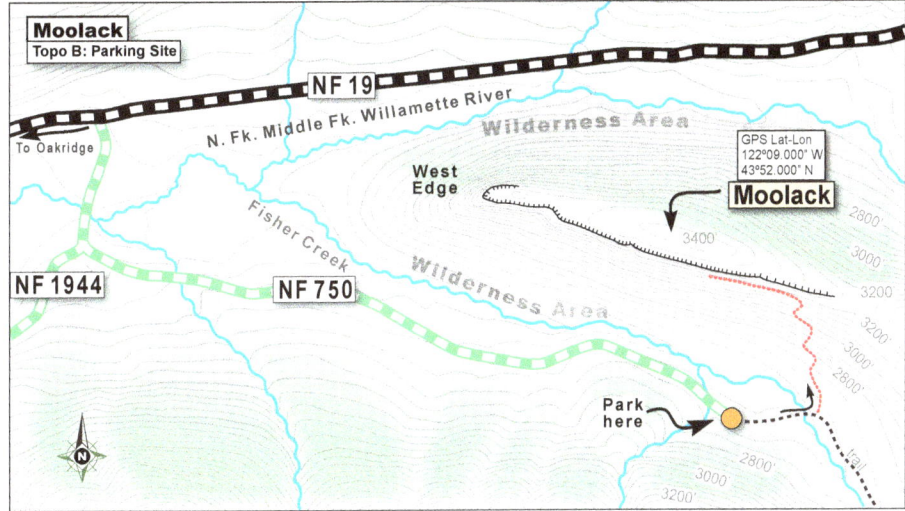

strict cleaning method that focused on retaining the natural wilderness aesthetic.

On-site, ground-up climbing was a primary focus for Soule-South from 1996 to 2000, but cleaning has always been a big part of safety. Around 2000 new parties made Moolack a regular climbing destination. Including Karsten Duncan, Jason Krueger, Paul Waters, John Brewer, Kimball Holloway, Dave Campbell, Cody Peterson and others began visiting Moolack. They replicated leads on established routes and began to clean and establish new routes. Other Willamette Valley climbers, many from the Eugene area began day-tripping the crag, but few climbers took to the gardening, the approach, the driving distance, and other unique aspects of Moolack. By 2003 there were over 14 known routes. During the winter 2005 season climbers/developers Lee Baker, Jeff Baldo, Criss Steiner and Brian Gilbert joined the process and by the end of spring 2006 known climbing routes from the eastern edge to beyond the Gold Band had increased to over 34. By the end of 2008 Moolack had attained 48 (30 single pitch and 18 multi-pitch climbs) developed routes, including an additional 12 incomplete project routes. By 2011 Moolack had 72 climbable routes; significant numbers considering the locale of wall.

The Climbers of Moolack

Bill Soule, considered to be the "Godfather" of Moolack, is an icon in the Oregon climbing community. Without Bill Soule there would be no Moolack. Beyond finding the area and committing tireless hours to its development, Bill had the foresight and experience to identify bolt-less climbing potential within Moolack. Bill Soule created a lasting legacy that endures with every climber that comes away from the area, with the understanding of the boundless opportunities within climbing and the satisfaction of climbing within a bolt-less climbing standard. In a time

Max Tepfer leading *Full Circle*
Photo: *Thad Arnold*

and place where Oregon rock-climbing was typified by bolting methods of various design on new routes, Moolack's progressive nature of not bolting at all broke the mold. The fortune of having all natural elements conducive to climbing top notch crack and face climbs, with a pure natural ethos, and zero application of bolts is rare. But to identify that these elements were in fact present at Moolack was truly visionary. Bill Soule's contributions to the climbing world are immeasurable; in the number of climbers he has inspired and the positive influence they in turn have on others.

To quote an article written by Dane Tornell in 'The Iceaxemen' (May 2009), a South Eugene High School climbing club, of which both Bill and Mike mentor, "Even if you are one of those that knows Bill or heard of him, you might not necessarily know the entire story. But, like Moolack with someone like Bill we'll never know all the secrets and mysteries."

Mike "Mr. Clean" South is a major steward to Moolack alongside Bill. Beyond setting the standard of relentless route-cleaning he has also set high route standards on everything from finger to fist climbs to wide body off-widths. Mike South gems can be found at any section of the Moolack band. Other heavy-weight players on the Moolack development scene are Karsten Duncan, Justin Kruger, Lee Baker, Max Tepfer, Thaddeus Arnold, Mark Koehler, Forest Weaver, Ball Oh, Kimball Holloway, Mike Holmes, Ryan Young, Evan Mikkelson, Matthew Jones, Dave Carr and others.

> "Although bolts are the lightning rods of ethical controversy, they are in fact only an emblem of the debate. Other problems, such as noise, litter, trail abuse, and graffiti, all threaten to creep into our climbing areas if we aren't vigilant."
> -- Don Mellor in Climbing in the Adirondacks, 1997

Thad Arnold leading Orange Crush Opposite page photo: T. Arnold

Moolack Ethics, Styles and Tactics

Moolack is a 'no-bolt' climbing area. Development practices at Moolack typically have two parts: (1) attempt the onsight after cleaning and (2) pass the route on to another in an effort to preserve a more pure onsight. If the route is not completed in its first attempt, most developers pursue subsequent top-down pre-practice of crux moves until a successful redpoint. Moolacks' route grades are subjective, but if you are familiar with the 'old-school 5.9' concept a competent leader can stay safe in this 5.9-5.10 level.

Soule and South epitomize a cleaning standard marked by leaving routes in a state that the random hiker wouldn't know we'd been there. In other words leaving the bottom 20' with moss relatively intact and the cracks relatively un-cleaned. This aims to preserve a natural aesthetic for non-climbers to the area. Cleaning should be done from the top-down as the majority of the danger lies at the loose top 20 meters of rock. Avoid cleaning sections that are of no route value to help maintain the natural aesthetics of the area. If unsure how much to clean on a lower section attempt it on top-rope. The climbing routes direction may be revised over time when better protection or a greater esthetic quality is found. The issue over cleaning and what is considered too much cleaning was discussed in 2001 by Soule and Jason Krueger. Karsten Duncan and Krueger cleaned and developed new routes at Moolack with a "to-the-base" cleaning concept. Other developers have adopted similar cleaning concepts while many still adhere to leaving routes mossy through their opening moves which are typically easy-to-moderate terrain.

Boltless climbing is not for everyone, and if we expect to maintain a no-bolt ethic at Moolack, the climbing community needs to acknowledge an alternative way to access routes. With a moderate-level of climbing knowledge, plenty of rock climbing can be done by top-rope on shorter sections of the cliff band. Sporty arêtes and blank faces provide amazing top-rope problems, with more to still be discovered.

Nailing at Moolack is uncommon and most developers tend to leave a route un-pinned to avoid degradation to the route or the rock. Aid climbing has been implemented for rainy months, and for would-be route cleaning on lead. Pins have been utilized during would-be free ascents turned aid for initial on-site leads, then followed up with later all free ascents. Sometimes the pin has stayed, sometimes it has been removed. Routes known to have utilized pins have been mentioned.

Moolack Geology

The Moolack cliff band is composed of Tertiary Basalt (Tb1) from the Pliocene Era (2-7 mil yrs) from an old volcanic vent source likely centered at a higher point about 1 mile southeast of the wall. Rock bluffs such as Moolack with a compositionally younger age structure tend to offer better quality climbing opportunities because weathering disintegration processes have had less impact on the feature, particularly if the cliff scarp has only recently sloughed into existence.

For climbers who know how to place protection and are familiar with a range of crack and face climbing techniques used at other columnar basalt or andesite crags, then you will be prepared for climbing the andesite here. Crack route systems at Moolack have an unrivaled number of protection opportunities that are unique for Oregon. Though Moolack is columnar it is a far cry from basaltic columns such as Skinner Butte or the Lower Gorge of Smith. Crack systems are non-uniform with rare reachable double-crack opportunities and minimal columnar structure, while the upper portion of the wall has horizontally layered fracturing. Each climb carries a style unto itself, like no other, again lending to the non-uniformity. Infrequent splitter cracks exist and do provide sustained finger to fist-size jam climbing. Most rock climbs blend a mixture of finger-to-hand-to-fist sized crack climbing with short sections of face climbing technique. Some visually prominent routes offer powerful wide cracks or burly off-widths certain to test your skill.

Oregon Rock Climbing in the 1990s

In the 1990s, during Moolack's earliest development, bolted routes outweighed traditional lines in Oregon. Smith Rock remained center-stage for not only Oregon, but nationally and internationally, as developers continued to push difficulty levels in sport climbing. Routes of all difficulty and ethos con-

Paul W. working a Moolack boulder

tinued to be added throughout Oregon with an emphasis on bolted lines. Oregon sport-climbing crags of the 1990s included but were not limited to The Callahans, Rattlesnake Crag, Hills Creek Spires, Area 51, Ozone, and coastal areas. Despite the popularity of sport climbing traditional routes emerged in the nineties and early 2000's. "New" high quality trad routes included but was not limited to Half Moon Crack, Crazy Crack, and Magic Blocks. A number of new trad-ish routes were developed at the Menagerie. Areas like Trout Creek, Beacon Rock, Cougar, Williamson River Cliffs and other rock formations of yesteryear saw continued climbing or in some cases routes were rediscovered. The climbing scene in Oregon was experiencing a trad climbing renaissance of sorts with new trad areas and new trad development in old areas every year. Time will tell how Moolack routes fare against other traditional areas in Oregon. Location, time commitment, gear requirements, and mossy routes may deter repetitive climbers. The nature of crack-climbing is apples and oranges when compared to places like Trout Creek.

Brian Gilbert on *Knife Fight*
Photo: Paul Waters

> "Without ethics there would be more cliffs like the Sport Park, in Boulder Canyon, with chiseled holds everywhere....every crack on the planet would be bolted. We need climbing ethics, as we all have such pig-headed opinions."
> -- Bobbi Bensman

Driving Directions

From I-5 at the south end of Eugene, Oregon take exit 188-A. Drive on US Hwy 58 for 34 miles (passing Lookout Reservoir) until you reach the Willamette Fork Ranger Station just west of the small town of Oakridge. At the Willamette Fork Ranger Station take a left onto the Aufderheide Memorial National Forest Service Road 19. In less than a mile you will cross a bridge and take a left turn. After the community of Westfir the road becomes windy but scenic. Turn right on Forest Service 1944. After crossing the bridge take an unmarked left turn onto graveled Forest Service road NFSR 750. The Moolack cliff band appears on your left high up on a hill. The road yields the best view of the cliff band. There is a single-car campground on the left side of the road with nearby river access. The road continues to a parking lot that also marks the beginning of the Fisher Creek Trail. The road ends just beyond the parking lot which accommodates about a half-dozen mid-size cars.

The NF19 corridor recreational drive is dedicated in memory of Bob Aufderheide, a past supervisor for the Willamette National Forest. Moolack Mountain (5490') is located in the Waldo Lake Wilderness. You can attain area maps, forest passes, and information at the Middle Fork Ranger Station on Highway 58 in Oakridge. The Fisher Creek Trail that takes you to Moolack also leads to the Waldo Lakes loop trail system.

Moolack distances from other points of interest:

Corvallis, OR	85 miles	Eugene, OR	44 miles
Portland, OR	150 miles	Seattle, WA	320 miles
Dunsmuir, CA	220 miles	Leavenworth, WA	430 miles
Almo, ID	620 miles	Squamish, BC	508 miles

Trail Approach

From the parking lot the Fischer Creek Trail immediately crosses a log bridge and drops into a campground. The Fischer Creek Trail heads away from the Moolack band just past this campground. A series of small paths connect camp sites to the left of the Fischer Creek Trail. These minor paths and downed logs intersect with an unmarked climber's trail that heads uphill past the Mane Boulder. This path skirts trees and brush and ascends up a steep scree field to a well-worn Z-path, then to a visible upper trail. The upper trail switch-backs up moderate terrain to a fork marked by a large flat rock. A right turn at the trail fork quickly leads up to the cliff band and ends at the cliff base trail under Lost Art. The left turn at the fork is an unfinished path that may eventually end at the cliffs mid-point. A secondary deer-path approach has been traveled from the Mane Boulder heading N-NW to the boulder field below the X-marks and Gold Bands.

This Guide To Moolack

With admirable commendability we recognize Alan Watts efforts to climbing 90% of the routes he describes in his Smith Rock guide. Other guidebooks with a "trad" focus like Red Rocks, the Adirondacks and the Squamish guide were written by authors who also climbed virtually all the routes in their books. However, I did not climb 90% of the routes in this guide. Route development and beta acquisition is a primary goal as well as enjoying rock climbing, though if time allows I may climb a greater number of routes at Moolack unfamiliar to me. This guide is a collaborative effort based upon the exploits and experiences of a group of climbers. This beta is based on first and second ascentist (and sometimes a third) knowledge, which may include anecdotes and physical characteristics associated with the route in question. Gear, though subjectively based on user preference is hopefully broad enough to meet your needs. With such details buried in the beta, some have expressed concern that I will take the "adventure aspect" out of Moolack. For the established routes no amount of beta can take away from the adventurous nature of Moolack's routes. If you want to know less, read less to attain your preferred spice level.

Max Tepfer leading *Sideways* Photo: T. Arnold

Cliff Top Access

Views from the top of the cliff make it one of the rare treats at Moolack, but accessing routes along the top of the cliff band can be challenging without prior understanding of start-to-end route configuration. Top-down route access methods usually require crag familiarity best learned with friends familiar with this crag. It is a poor place to learn anchor building, protection placement, or multi-pitch tactics.

Starting eastward along the base of the cliff from the end of the approach trail the initial opening rock climbs are Sophie and Gwenevere. Beyond, there is a 200'+ stretch of rock band that is shorter than the shortest route, yet too tall for safe bouldering. At the cliffs termination, there is a series of downed trees. Scramble up the slope, then walk westward along the cliff top till you see the madrone tree above Sophie and Gwenevere. This trail continues on to "The Hub", a popular tree anchor point usually slung with a bike tire tube or webbing wrapped 10.8 mm static rope with a simple chain rap ring. The Hub is the top anchor for Lost Art, Up on a Pedestal and other nearby routes. Tree anchors used for Zion Train and Sideways are visible from The Hub and are quite manageable with a 70-meter rope. Zion Train has a prominent outward leaning tree and obvious clean jug holds beyond the routes crux, visible from the top.

A large sun-baked column top after Pledge Crack marks the top of Fist-fighting Plumbers section, visible beyond a gap between the two columns. While Fist-Fight and Plumbers are easily defined and accessible, the top of Pledge crack is chocked with madrone trees. This section is usually climbed from the ground up due to difficult upper access points.

Looking past the very obvious Mushroom Band from the top of Fist-fighting Plumbers, the large black column split by Cleaned For Her Pleasure marks the end of the Fist-fighting Plumbers band. A small belay ledge tucked into a large tree marking the top of Fist Fight can be accessed past minor madrone trees, above the anchor tree via an easy but airy scramble down the columns top around negotiating the tree.

A large dead tree and nearby madrone's anchor mark the end of Where the Wild Things Are and Sasquatch (visible from Fist Fight top). A burnt-out old growth tree marks the top of One Flew Over the Cuckoo's Nest.

One very obvious single tree is the top anchor for all of the climbs for the Mushroom Band, but is down a slight slope below the cliff top trail. After Mushroom Band the trail continues extremely tight to the cliffs edge for a short distance. The locale for Mr. Clean and Pleasure Palace and nearby routes is difficult to gauge from above. There is a large dead old growth that marks the end of a 25 foot loose 5.3 section above the end of Mr. Clean. Leading Mr. Clean is a better way to familiarize access, rather than attempting to navigate it from above.

The cliff section beyond the Pleasure Palace slopes downward so the routes are best as lead climbs. They incorporate multi-pitch tactics, use mid-point belays which can be difficult to find other than bottom up, and many of the routes do not follow direct ground-to-top crack lines. The only other area that may be easily accessed top-down by first time visitor are routes on the Guillotine Band, because the tree anchor for Guillotine often has a webbing or cord wrapped in a tire tube at a clean ledge that looks out over the Guillotine double cracks and nearby tree also offers top belay stance for Pool Guy.

The anchor ledge for Dru's Cruise is visible from the trail. A dead tree marks the top of Age Before Beauty. This is a nice entry point to access some quality difficult routes. From Dru's Cruise to the Goldband it is best to lead the routes from ground up. Gold Gulley is just beyond Yay Climbing and before Sendero Sangre, and top-down access is feasible for routes like Sendero de Sangre and Slot Machine. Top-down access to Gold is possible, but not convenient. Most Goldband routes are best as ground up lead routes. Need more info...search Moolack Rock Climbing on the web.

> "It's crucially important that climbers don't hasten the inevitable by chiseling tomorrow's 5.15s down to 5/12c."
> -- Alan Watts

SOUTH WILLAMETTE CLIMBS 551

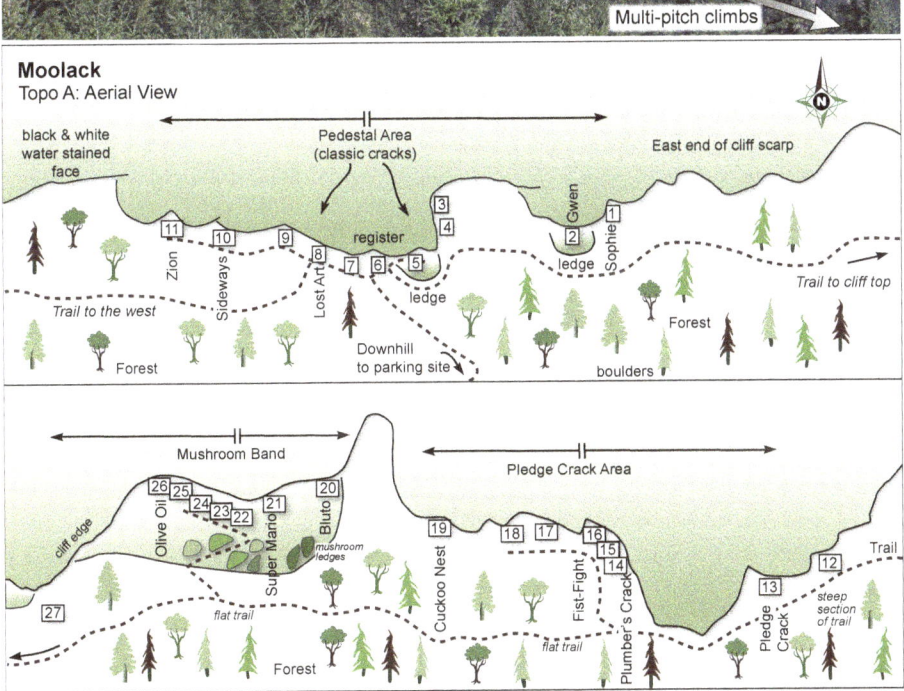

PEDESTAL AREA (CLASSIC CRACKS AREA)

The Approach Trail ends at the Pedestal Area (i.e. Classic Cracks). To the right are Scum Suckers, Bitch I Won, Gwenevere and Sophie. The routes are described right to left starting at Sophie. Continue on the trail past Sophie till the cliff band ends at a series of downed logs, then scramble uphill and back west along the top of the cliff to reach access points for various climbs. Lost Art is at the intersection of the Cliff Band Trail and the Approach Trail. Blood on the Cracks climbs the steep corner dihedral to the right of Lost Art. This area extends left

to the routes Sideways, Zion Train and right with Radical Sabbatical and Thaddalic.

1. **Sophie 5.7**

    Pro: Size 5"+ cams for opening moves, then minimal fist-to-finger cams and nuts
    A right-facing 90-degree open-book dihedral with a tree at its base. The crack starts wide, but utilizes a secondary thin crack to the right mid-climb for pro and jams. Two lie-back moves gain easy hand-jams and face holds. The last section of the climb has foot ledges and a twin crack. Belay at a low hanging madrone tree shared with Gwenevere.

2. **Gwenevere 5.7**

    Pro: ¾" to 5"+ large cams off the deck (#4-6 BD), TCU's and nuts for double crack
    Gwenevere is accessed via a short scramble using a tree left of Sophie. From below the ledge two awkward off-width moves utilize a wide crack. Access a small face

ledge with solid finger jams after initial moves, then easy hand-jams and foot ledges with good protection. The route ends on two ledges with a tree anchor hanging out over the second ledge, sharing the belay with Sophie. Can skip large pro if you're willing to stem across the initial belay ledge to the foot ledge and fist crack after the wide crack.

3. **Scum Suckers 5.10a** ★

   Pro: ½" to 5" cams, nuts, hexes and a Big Bro's for the top may ease top-out
   Start on a high saddle using a thin finger crack, foot-jams and ledge options on either side of a crack. It widens up higher from 3½" to 5"+, then after a gully finishes in a wide chimney. Beware of loose rock in the gully. The column separates from the cliff band when the crack ends; anchor to small trees at the top. *Originally called Hazeldell after the historic community now called Oakridge.*

4. **Bitch I Won 5.9** ★

   Pro: #00 to 5" cams, nuts, hexes and Big Bro for the top
   This route, parallel and immediately right of Scum Suckers, climbs a thin finger crack with delicate feet out on a face up to a dirty rock gully. Follow this to a dihedral with a small seam in back and a mini-roof at the top.

5. **Radical Sabbatical 5.10c** ★★★

   Pro: #00 to 4" cams, nuts, hexes, off-set TCU's
   This is a former 30' variation to Blood on the Cracks, but now with a new base direct. The new start is very steep off the ground with gear opportunities every foot or so, and horizontal jugs to grab the whole way. This 5.8 bottom section directly links into the steeper upper portion that makes for the 5.10c crux. The final layback is short, but stout, and pretty committing over the last 3" cam. This direct makes for a more quality first section than Blood on the Cracks.

6. **Thadallic 5.10+** ★★★

   Pro: #00 to 4" cams, nuts, hexes, off-set TCU's
   Thadallic formerly shared a start with Blood on the Cracks, but a direct start was added to offer 5.8+ to 5.9- climbing. From the base trail move up to a distinctive dihedral past a crux marked by a short, steep roof to the right of the dihedral. This upper dihedral is identified with flaring cracks and odd gear. It climbs like a gym route…may be height dependant, may be with an R rating, but offset cams really help. *When Baker was establishing this line his would-be belayer (Thad), overwhelmed by the areas potential missed*

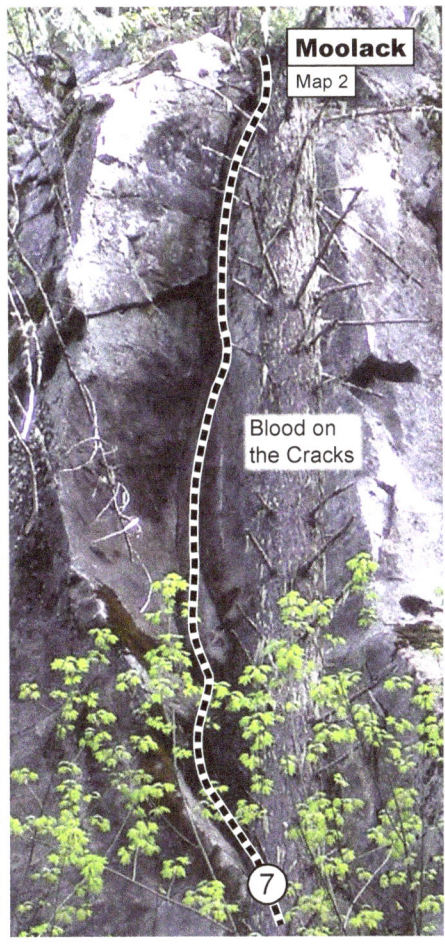

the routes inception when scouting further along the band. On a chance occurrence Bill Soule, always willing to lend a belay, was available to help with the FA.

7. **Blood on the Cracks 5.10c**
★ ★ ★

Pro: #00 to 4" cams, nuts, and hexes

Start up the first 3-meters of Lost Art, and move right to a ledge. Climb moderate 5.8 past three more ledges to a steep dihedral corner where the crack widens to fist-size jams. A second crack picks up mid route, which eases the level of difficulty. Stemming and solid fist jamming on steep terrain leads to a jug hand hold that ends the short 5.10c crux section on the last 5-meters of the climb. Multi-purpose top anchor serves 3 routes (LA, UOAP, and BOTC with extra tree runner).

8. **Lost Art 5.10c ★ ★ ★ ★**

Pro: #00 to 3½" cams, nuts; optional TCU at mid-climb directs rope out of crack

Start with stiff 5.8 thin finger jams and minor foot holds up a strenuous leftward arching crack with delicate feet (lower crux) to the routes mid-point roof and rest point. The upper crux section begins above the roof as the climb steepens using hand and finger jams. A fairly long, sustained crux section more so than UOAP. Multi-purpose top anchor serves 3 routes.

9. **Up on a Pedestal 5.10a ★ ★ ★ ★**

Pro: #00 to 4½" cams, nuts

The original line of UOAP shared the start with LA moving left to a dirty dihedral corner that leads to the 'Pedestal.' As the Pedestal Direct gained popularity in the mid-2000s the old start became overgrown and mossy. The direct starts up nice hand holds to a ledgy corner and up a wide 5.6 crack with hand and foot edges to a small stance below the Pedestal. From this small stance move up and connect to a short left arching splitter crack that ends on the Pedestal. From the Pedestal climb continuous crux 5.9 hand and finger jams till the route steepness eases, then finish on 5.6 pinches on a low angle slab to complete the route.

10. **Sideways 5.10a ★ ★ ★**

Pro: #00 to 4" cams; Pedestal Direct and Sideways

John on *Where the Wild Thing Are*

Direct use 4"+ gear

This line shares the first half of UOAP. A less traveled direct is feasible using fists to wide crack that links to the Sideways upper dihedral. Typically, you will start on UOAP route to the Pedestal ledge, and then make an easy 5.6 traverse leftward to the Sideways dihedral. Stem and jam up the dihedral past where the crack disappears for 10' on varied face climbing. The top is steep with semi-positive jams/stems. Slightly more technical but less pumpy than nearby climbs. The crux is a lie-back move and a reach/jam near the top ending with easy climbing off the ledge to multiple tree anchors.

11. Zion Train 5.9 ★ ★ ★
Pro: #00 to 4½" cams, nuts, hexes

The stance for Zion Train and Sideways Direct are 10-yds uphill from the base of The Pedestal. Easy 5.6 ledge climbing leads into a steep 5.9- corner that requires full stems with large face and foot holds through a chimney. Physical stemming, hand jamming, and face climbing opportunities lead up to a higher ledge beyond the chimney. From an upper ledge a crux 5.9 thin finger jam move links to the final 5.6 moves to a tree anchor. This last crux reach is considerably easier if you are tall.

PLEDGE CRACK AREA

The Pledge Crack will stand out even during the arduous approach hike. As you walk west away from the Pedestal Area the trail starts downhill. A large distinctive trailside tree stands just opposite of Pledge Crack before a rough section of trail. The wide Plumbers Crack to the west is the opposite end of Pledge Crack. To the climbers right of Compromising Positions is a wide black and white drainage wall.

12. Compromising Positions 5.10d ★★★
Pro: #00 to 2" cams, nuts and hexes
One hundred feet in length, this route contains a blend of chimney-moves, stemming, and difficult finger locking through steep terrain. The crux is marked by a short roof with finger locks. The roof was infested by hornets before cleaning. Baker explains it like this: Gain a stance via a few easy moves then pull over some vertical terrain and move up the groove toward the overhanging chimney. The crack eats up gear as you humbly wiggle up being forced into a rather exposed position. The 180° stemming move to gain the block is as good as it gets, then one more mantle, and up a layback flake to the final steep corner. Up and over gets you to the belay.

Brian Gilbert on *Eat Your Spinach*

13. Pledge Allegiance (aka Pledge Crack) 5.10d ★★★★
Pro: #00 to 4" cams, nuts, hexes, plus extra long slings for belay station
Climb 12' then move right through moderate (5.8/9) climbing up an often moist crack with odd flaring gear. Protect first portion before the traverse with long slings to avoid ropedrag beyond the tonsil later. After the start of the crux roof traverse, with low height jamming or lie-backing with an undercling technique moving up to a downward facing tonsil-like feature where the crack arcs to vertical. Transition out right onto the tonsil and up past it using small edges (mental/physical crux). Place adequate gear before and through this section to avoid a ground fall. Continue up to the left jamming, right facing corner crack, bear-hugging the tonsil, with small feet to the right until a small ledge marks the end of difficult climbing. Some fun 5.7 stemming with positive jams and holds is used to access a lower ledge. A small tree can be used on this ledge to avoid rope drag issues of belaying or top-roping from the cliffs top. An exposed 5.7 section links this lower ledge to an overgrown tree anchor at the cliff top.

FIST-FIGHTING PLUMBERS AREA
After Pledge Allegiance the trail wraps around a large column. The first visible large crack is Plumbers Crack, followed by Knife-Fight and Fist-Fight, Sasquatch, Where the Wild Things Are and lastly One Flew Over the Cuckoos Nest. The Mushroom Band is to the climbers left from here. From the cliff band trail a short uphill scramble lands at a series of belay stances for all Fist-fighting Plumbers Area routes.

14. Plumber's Crack 5.10+/.11- ★★★
Pro: ¾" to #6 cams (#4, #5 & #6 for the top) and Big Bro's (doubles recom.)
Early sections of moderate 5.8 fingers to fist crack climbing leads to a large off-width crack. Use your small gear for the lower part. The large off-width section runs for 60% of the route and requires intensive off-width technique including knee-bars, chicken wings, and other unique off-width techniques. Protection like Big-Bros and over-sized cams may hinder crucial jams that are otherwise more negotiable on TR.

15. Fist-Fight 5.9 ★★★
Pro: #00 to 4½" cams and nuts
An often uncleaned 5.6 low section gains a clean 5.8 crack that requires lie-backs, stems

Moolack Mushroom Band Map 6

and bomber finger-jams up a right facing dihedral corner. Move out onto a slab for a move, to a gain a great lie-back section leading to a rest point under a large roof. The climber is hidden from the belayer under this roof and through the crux. A bold exposed steep fist-sized crack traverse represents the routes crux. This crux can be jammed or lie-backed. The traverse ends on a small rest ledge before easily stemmed face holds and wide to the left, thin to the right crack climbing. The route ends with horizontal pro and tenuous stems to gain a small ledge with an encumbering large tree anchor.

16. Knife-Fight 5.10+ PG-13 ★★

Pro: #00 to 4½" cams and nuts, beaks, ball-nuts, and brass

An upper variation right of Fist-Fight. After the first lower crux of Fist-Fight (instead of following the crack left to the rest stance at the roof) move right to a short face slab leading to a thin ending crack. A hand-placed 'beak' protects a few sloping edges and tenuous balance moves. An essential finger slot represents the key hand match and protection through a set of bouldery moves to gain Fist-Fight's ledge above. 'Head-point' tactics, a TCU, and a hand-placed beak were adequate for FA.

17. Sasquatch 5.10+ ★★

Pro: #00 to 3" nuts and cams, sliding nuts and brass units for bottom, Big Bro's and 4", 4½" and 5" cams for upper pitch

From the stance, start a quick traverse on unscrubbed terrain to an obvious thin finger crack (sometimes moist). This initial crack marks the routes crux and a fall will land the leader back on the belay ledge. The second can bring up Big Bro's and big cams for the 2nd pitch wide crack. OW moves and edges outside of the crack make for a much more manageable wide crack climb than other test-pieces in the area. Requires multiple fist-sized pro to properly protect top, but some alternative ½" to 1" size pro in horizontal cracks is feasible.

18. Where the Wild Things Are 5.8 ★★★

Pro: #0 to 6" cams, Big Bro's size 4" and 6"

One of six climbs that start from a common base stance area. Easy climbing to access the inside of an arching, right-facing 5.7 finger jam corner. Before exiting the dihedral, physical chimney climbing with Big Bro's protect through the first crux. From incut jugs, mantle up to a rest ledge prior to the middle crux section. An arching finger crack (#0 or #1 TCU's) ends with a lie-back and a long reach to a jug crack, mantle and minor ledge stance. Lead past a less than protectable, airy second 5.9 crux, followed by a larger ledge by a wide, off-width crack with steep roof climbing offering alternating positive hand holds and body wedging rests outside of the crack at the last section. Non-cruxy ending. Use a curvy madrone tree for belay, prudently backed up to a larger tree 30' from the cliff's edge. *Formerly named 'Split Finger' after a split finger incident on the trail, postponing the free ascent a few weeks. The crux also has a short splitter crack.*

19. One Flew Over the Cuckoo's Nest 5.9 R ★ ★ ★
Pro: #00 to #6, and Big Bro's
Embark up a physical finger-to-fist flake crack to a large finger crack blocked by a small tree landing on a small slab. From the slab there is an 8" crack with fun 5.6 climbing and scary protection (Big Bro's), body jams and exposure. A large ledge at mid-climb is a poor location for a belay with big bros at your ankles and a crackless crux face section above. From the ledge a slab traverse using poor shallow thin gear protects exposed, risky moves to an exhilarating dead-point to an open finger jug (good pro) and a rest ledge. Bust through horizontal incut edges and multi-layered cracks up blocky steep roofy terrain for an amazing finish. Walk over to a large dead tree (directional), then over to the same madrone tree used for WTWTA. No redpoint to date because the crux section microplacements (and last available big-bro) involves a risky fall. *The infamous author Ken Kesey is intrinsically linked to the nearby city of Eugene, but beyond that his life was linked to Pleasant Hill, the last outpost for gas, food or coffee on the way to the Lack before Oakridge. The bus "Further" is still parked in the region and many in town acknowledge the man's huge influence there.*

MUSHROOM BAND AREA
The next seven climbs begin on the same stance ledge under a wide steep cliff face broken by a series of cracks, corners and face sections. Please use the winding, well trodden approach thru lower ledges and avoid cleaning alternate lines on lower scramble, for aesthetic preservation and ease.

20. Bluto 5.6
Pro: #0 to 3½" cams
From 8' below Super Mario's start veer hard right, ledge to ledge with easy protection through the path of least resistance. A short easy crack gives way to top. Less than stellar route. May be an optional get-to-the-top quick means for accessing other top-roping goals.

21. Super Mario 5.10- ★ ★
Pro: #00 - 2½", Multiple thin pro TCUs, nuts, brass nuts, and cams
A steep finger-to-fist sized crack climb on the right side of the band with gray and black rock. From the shared ledge stance, aim up and right on easy climbing that becomes steeper and the finger jams get thin. Shift to hidden hand holds in a crack that takes good

Chris Steiner leading *Mr. Clean*

SOUTH WILLAMETTE CLIMBS 559

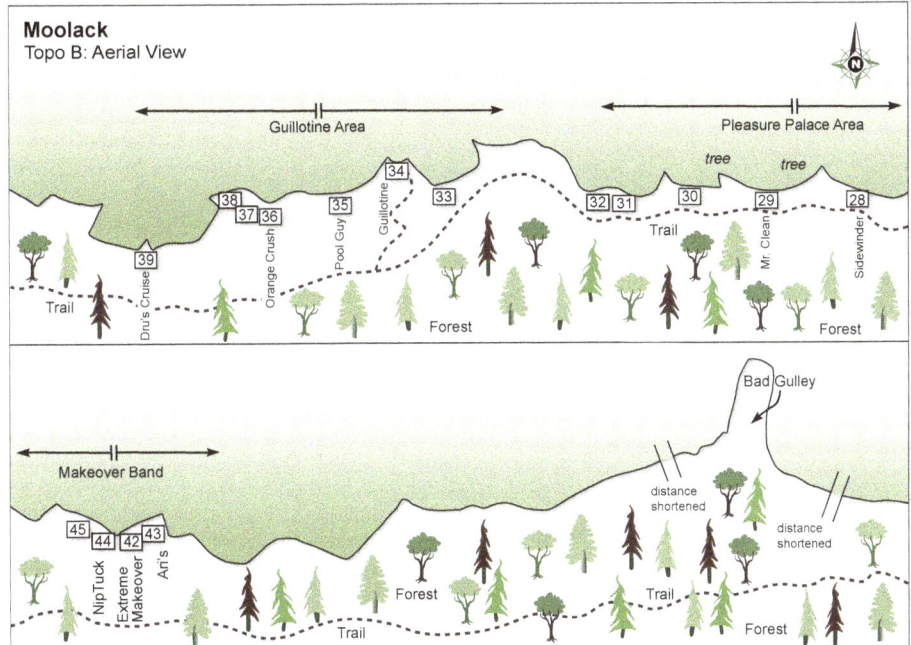

pro. After a short roof the upper section consists of stiff face climbing with thin pro (enduro crux). Holds are positive but well spread out with tricky to see, sometimes horizontal pro placements.

22. Eat Your Spinach 5.9 ★
Pro: #0 to 3" cams

A major crack splits the left middle section of the band marked by gray and white rock. Opens with jugs and ledges into fun finger jamming and great pro through the lower ledges. At the steeper first crux a series of thin jams offer either positive jams or positive protection (or place pro below your jams). Beyond moderate face climbing with occasional thin jam links to top section. The last bit of climbing is a shared roof finish with Stems and Caps.

23. Stems and Seeds 5.8 ★

Pro: #0 to 3½" cams, nuts, and brass nuts

Climb the lower easy portion of Eat Your Spinach, then before its crux you must move slightly left and climb an on-the-edge vertical minor seam with moderate movement on an incredible protectable face section immediately left of EYS. It merges with Stems and Caps at a small roof, then up right into EYS. Task intensive for the leader to protect yet remain on the vertical face and not move into the restful easier ramp nearby.

24. Stems and Caps 5.7 ★★

Pro: #00 to 4½" cams, nuts and micro nuts

A 40-meter climb on the left side of the Mushroom Band. From the shared base stance with Stems and Seeds and Super Mario veer hard left using large holds and ledges to a 4' by 4' ledge. Continue left a move or two utilizing a large 7" crack, then move out onto the face, with hand holds and foot smears through fracturing rock. Thin pro on easier terrain gains a low angle slab with hand jugs and a thin crack. Positive holds and foot edges gain easy stemming that gets harder through a steep roof to reach a ledge 5-meters from the top (at stance place horizontal micro-cam at hip level). Traverse right several moves on an exposed arête protected by this cam, then gain a large double crack that takes fingers to fist sized cams and nuts. A set of steep but easy roofs with jugs share an ending with EYS, S&S and Super Mario.

25. Sweet Pea 5.5

Pro: #00 to 3" nuts and cams

This line offers early easy holds and ledges with large protection followed by a single exposed move to face holds and a ramp with more pro opportunities. Only a utility route to gain top for other routes.

Thad Arnold leading *Orange Crush*
Photo: *T. Arnold*

26. Olive Oil 5.4
Pro: #0 to 2" cams
At extreme left side of the mushroom band is a large tree level with the base stance ledge of the Mushroom Band. This route of little resistance is an alternate means to reach the cliff top. Can be climbed in boots with backpack.

Pleasure Palace
Past the Mushroom Band the cliff height temporarily dips down, and then elevates again at a large black pillar indicating the top of the Pleasure Palace. The arching to horizontal hand crack of Sidewinder is unmistakable, and the top anchor tree of Hit and Run stands out at

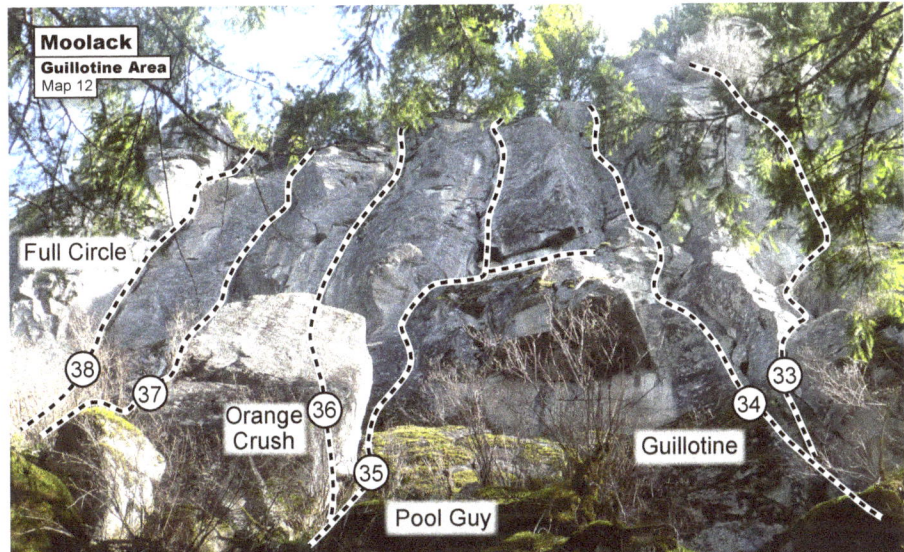

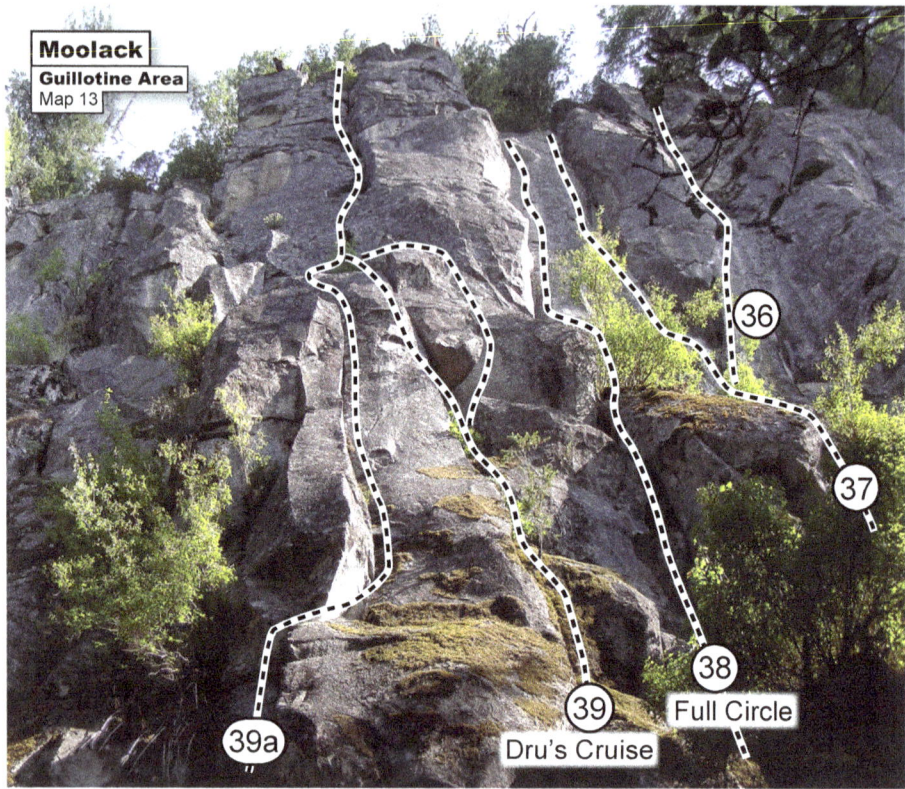

the cliffs edge.

27. Cleaned for Her Pleasure 5.10c ★★★
Pro: P1 ½" to 2½" cams & nuts; P2 is large fists to small OW gear and micro cams
The initial start of the climb is defined by a right-facing corner dihedral to the right of Sidewinder and includes jams of all sizes and a broad range of protection. From Olive Oil a ledge to ledge traverse right to left lands you on CFHP belay stance. This route and Sidewinder intersect ½ way under a large black and silver colored column at a ledge, followed by short moments of powerful climbing in the corner above.

28. Sidewinder 5.10c ★★★
Pro: #0 to 3" cams, nuts and hexes
A west facing and easily overlooked line, when focusing on a suffering trail. Sidewinder offers great short bouts of powerful climbing as it ascends a sideways arching, low angle crack wrapping around the large fractured column, left to right until the southeast flank is gained. Sidewinder is a half-pitch of great climbing before it traverses right under a large black and silver colored bulge of rock to intersect with CFHP at a rest ledge.

29. Mr. Clean 5.10c ★★★
Pro: #00 TCUs to 4" cams
Mr. Clean starts in an awkward finger jam corner. Climb to a C-shaped arch with a low crux move to access a small ledge. From this ledge unprotected 5.8 face climbing links to another group of ledges (pro) using a combination of arête moves and finger jamming. The ledges disappear as you enter the upper crux. A series of thin, awkward finger jams takes you to a thin ending flare crack. A hip-high foot crux move unlocks a difficult to

reach jam. Fun 5.8 climbing ends at large tree anchor.

30. Hit and Run 5.10a ★★★★
Pro: #00 to 3½" cams, nuts, brass nuts, and sliding nuts

A leaning column forms a small roof in the lower section. This route goes up the right side of this column. Easy to moderate climbing with frequent ledges, face holds, and a blend of off-width, stemming, chimney and crack climbing techniques access a ledge. From the midpoint unprotected but easy, fun lie-backing of a small free-standing fin accesses the upper portion of the crack system. The upper route, while having rest spots and positive jams, remains consistently difficult through the steep upper corner.

Variation on Hit and Run 5.10a ★★
Pro: #00 to 4½"

A linked roof variation through the middle crux of Hit and Run, avoiding M. South's original less than protected 5.8 fin slab that connects to the top 40-meter crack naturally. After the first crux, from a ledge veer slightly left to a steep chimney, climbing steep, juggy chockstones in larger protectable roofs.

Mike South leading *Extreme Makeover* Photo: M. South

31. Age Before Beauty 5.10b/c ★★★
Pro: #00 to 4½"

A left-facing book dihedral with an unknown first half that runs up a wide crack near the top. P1 offers 5.8 climbing that remains heavily vegetated. Beta intensive movement makes for difficulty at crux.

GUILLOTINE AREA

While UTBT, ABB and Two Beers and a Baby hide in tight forest cover, a large visibility window will expose Guillotine and its namesake flake. Once the Guillotine flake is found it is easy to locate the neighboring Pool Guy with its slasher finger crux. The upper right side portion of Guillotine's double crack has regrown moss. Guillotine Area, though tucked in a cluster of trees gets some sunshine and shade unlike the completely shaded Mosserati Corner or Pedestal Area.

32. Under the Big Top 5.10b/c ★★
Pro: #00 to 4½"

The crux is an overhanging lie-back off-width with some enduring run out. Tucked between ABB and TBAB, this line actually shares a finish with Two Beers and A Baby.

33. Two Beers and a Baby 5.10- ★★★
Pro: #00 to 4½"

This quality two-pitch climb shares the first 10' of Guillotine, and then moves right to a dihedral crack system. A 5.10- face move crux with funky pro is presented mid first pitch. Finishes in a corner dihedral immediately left of Under the Big Top. One of the better 5.10's here.

34. Guillotine 5.10a ★★★

Pro: Multiple #00 to 3½" cams, nuts, and hexes

A long well protected climb. From the base good holds lead up to a 5.9 stem and jam section linking a mantle move to access the mid-point ledge. Pool Guy is accessible from this ledge. Easy climbing leads to a distinctive undercling flake (the Guillotine) with finger-sized jams and jugs. Stem and utilize both left and right cracks of the Guillotine. After a section of lie-backs and jams the left crack offers 5.10a single crack line. Avoid the overgrown trees blocking the last 20-meters of the right crack. Continue up the left crack using large featured face holds and ledges with ample cracks for gear and occasional jams. At the end of the pitch there is a large tree anchor and belay chair. *Named after the undercling flake at half height. Warning: the flake may break loose; avoid using it after the crux by moving up to better edges by stemming.*

35. Pool Guy 5.11- ★★★★

Pro: #00 to 2½" cams and nuts

Pool Guy starts on the left side of Guillotine's mid-point ledge under a steep dihedral. Fun, moderate finger jams and toe edges offer classic climbing. As the bulge steepens foot holds disappear and the crack thins to just finger tips. A distinctive crux consists of a high reach fingertip jam off of thin toe jams, followed by more face hold options. Moderate climbing and protection to the tree anchor at the edge of the cliff band. A true classic for its relative grade. Hand size makes a definitive difference (small hands puts climb in .10+ range). *Possibly clean aided by Bobby Pool, a Eugene climber in early 2000s.*

36. Orange Crush 5.11
★★★★

Pro: #00 to 2½" cams and nuts

Stellar climb marked by a distinctive Z-shaped crack. This route shares its first 20' with Widespread Panic and has a large base stance. The shared start is a 5.9 flaring chimney. Where Orange Crush breaks right a 5.8 low angle crack leads to an overhung roof pod. A crucial rest is found before 25' of steep finger crack climbing (¾") ending at a large jug handhold. A 20' 5.9 finger crack in a ramp ends with a no hands rest. Move out left to 5.9 face climbing using widely spaced solid gear. The belay lies 30' beyond the cliff edge (static line suggested).

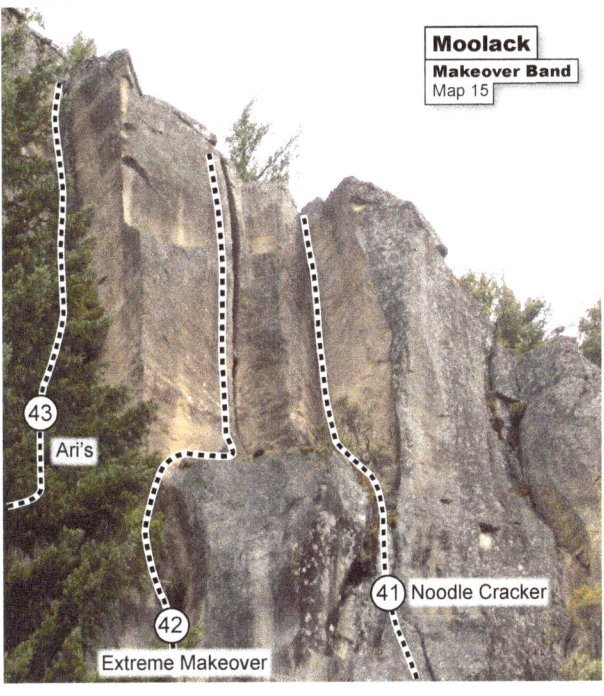

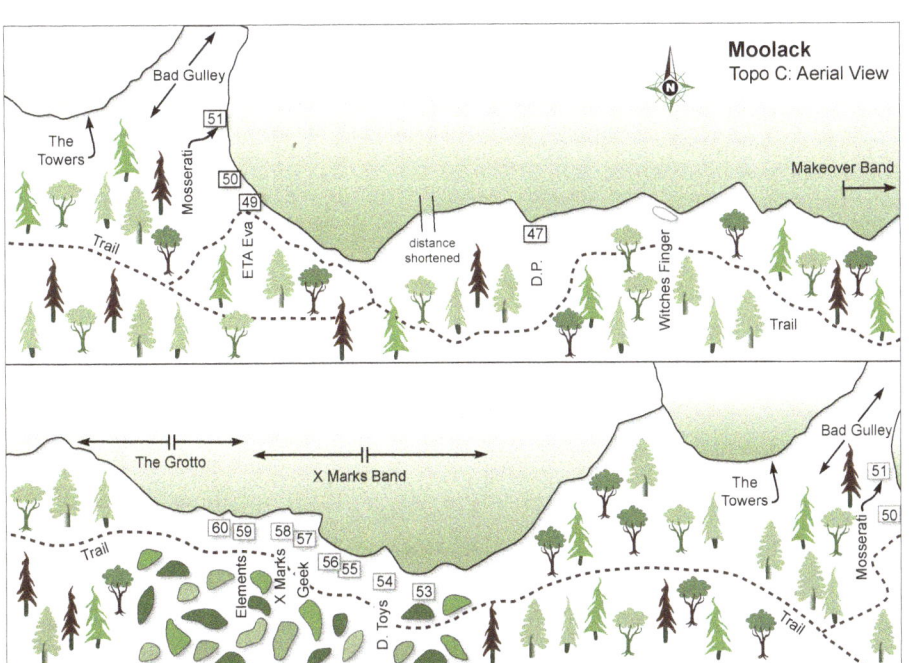

37. Widespread Panic (aka The Wave) 5.10c ★★★

Pro: #00 to 5" cams (1 small sliding nut, brass nuts, #5 RP at the crux)

Blends finger-to-fist size crack climbing with face climbing on minimal protection. From the base stance (also utilized for OC) the line starts with well spaced thin*ish* finger jams following the crack arching left. Some rest points with sustained climbing throughout. Pure face climbing technique is necessary as the crack becomes a seam (thin pro). When the crack widens the route steepens with awkward jams and stemming in a corner near the top. A tree belay marks the end of the line.

38. Full Circle 5.10b ★★★★

Pro: #00 to 3" cams, nuts, and hexes

Parallel and to the climber's right of Dru's Cruise, a large belay ledge 30-meters off the deck exposes a leaner left-facing dihedral above an exposed ledge. The slightly less than vertical  slab is tackled by well spaced finger jams in a crack heading left with small foot edges. These initial ledges are riddled with prickly Oregon Grape plants. The crack heads to a left facing dihedral with a steep overhead roof. One steep bulge leads to the next, all surmounted with bomber finger and fist jams. The middle crux section is awkward stemming and foot jams in a steep crack with some positive jams. The last 40' of the climb diverts right (primary crack), or can use a thinner left splitter crack (multitude of face holds). This ends on a small ledge, and a few scramble moves to the top of the cliff marked with a huge decaying tree that can be used as an anchor point. Use longer webbing for other nearby trees.

39. Dru's Cruise 5.10a ★★★★

Pro: #00 to 5" cams, nuts, and hexes

Pre-2009 this climb started by gaining a large ledge system utilizing dirty blocky climbing either right of the large roof visible from the base, or extremely left up an easy dirty 5.7. Bill Soule established the stunning 5.9 first pitch heading directly at Dru's distinctive off-the-belay-ledge crux visible from the base of the band. From the initial base stance after Bill's Dru's Direct 7-meters of fun, easy climbing to a large ledge with a yellow flake sets up the routes overall crux. A 5.10- crux move utilizes thin finger jams leaving this flake at its apex, onto a steep face with small*ish* feet. A reach and mantle move leads to another ledge. The upper 30-meters are exposed with a mix of 5.6 face and fist jams with available body jams. Once past a short bulge at the top the difficulty eases. Tree belay at the cliffs edge. *Name was coined after a student traveler cleaned the route in early 2000s, though he never attempted its lead.*

SOUTH WILLAMETTE CLIMBS 567

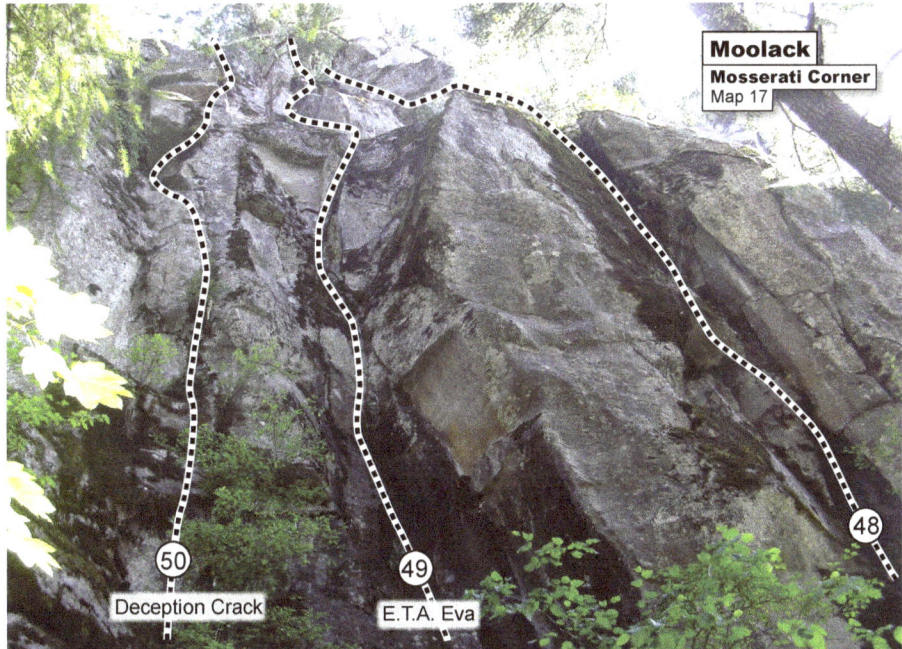

40. **Dru's Direct 5.9** ★★★
    Pro: ____
    The new direct leading up to the midway ledge. Protection consistent with Dru's but an extra couple TCU's may help for direct.

41. **Noodle Cracker 5.10a** ★★
    Pro: ____
    A 2-pitch climb near where the trail goes into a shady area and right up next to the rock.

BAD GULLEY

A trailside bright reddish-orange colored 40' pillar with a large trench below it (part of the trail) indicates end of Guillotine Area and its junction with Bad Gulley. The trail dips downhill into a shady brushy region beyond this pillar. Avoid using Bad Gulley (loose rock, dirt slopes). Subsequent Gulley's (e.g. Gold Gulley) have steep paths to the top of the cliff band. A second Gulley just after Mosserati is a bit more reasonable, but still a risky scramble with loose blocks, dirt and slippery leaves. The Gold Gulley is a feasible scramble with a minor trail that can be utilized to access the top. The east end walk-up is longer, but easiest and well traveled.

MAKEOVER BAND

There are routes (some not listed here) between Dru's Cruise and Extreme Makeover that are easy to miss because the trail runs flush to the cliff band

Mike South on *Perverts in Paradise*
Photo archive: *Mike South*

with minimal visibility. As the trail dips away from the cliff next, the highly visible wide cracks of Extreme Makeover, Dangerous Toys, and Nip Tuck/Tic Talk along with a large boulder field below, make Makeover Band a difficult to miss area. On a sunny day this area can be seen from road #750 campground.

42. Extreme Makeover 5.10+ ★★★★
Pro: ¼" to 6" cams, nuts, hexes, Big Bro's (70m rope needed)
A short uncleaned 5.6 section gains a small stance and the start of cleaned climbing. Easy finger jamming, alternating lie-back and stemming moves are used to access a ledge that breaks the continuous crack where the route splits in two directions. Continue left to access the ledge under a small tree (avoid going right into loose uncharted territory). Moderate climbing leads to a second ledge shared with a tree. This lower ledge sets up the 5.10- finger crux and mantle to a larger ledge. The upper pitch off-width should be set up with the belayer on this larger ledge. A chockstone breaks the off-width into two parts. The lower part of the crux is awkward and requires contorted leg jams. The mental crux involves nauseating exposure and awkward off-width movements in the upper pitch. Once the chockstone is gained the lead climber is prepared for the final crux off-width section. Anchoring at the top is best with big-bros or 4"+ cams or static line to bridge the distance from the tree to the edge of the band. *Before year 2000 this route was known as Dan's Chimney. Dan Crow, a Eugene guide had cleaned and TR'd the route.*

43. Ari's Dihedral 5.11 [?]
Gear: ¼" to 5" cams, nuts, hexes, and Big Bro's
Cleaned and likely TR'd in 2001 but never led. Access this upper thin finger crux from the same last ledge as Extreme Makeover's end crux. The upper pitch of Ari's is apparently more difficult, steeper than Extreme Makeover consisting of thin tips crack climbing. It is a micro thin crack in a 90° stem box. If people could get their fingers in it, it would have been lead by now. Tops out same as Extreme Makeover, with same anchoring considerations.

44. Nip Tuck / Tic Talk 5.10+, 5.11b/c ★★★
Pro: #00 to Size 6 cams, nuts, big bros
Mike South cleaned and climbed this route bottom to top in 2007. Karsten Duncan

had formerly cleaned and rappelled into and led large portions of the route in the early 2000's. This route is located in a dihedral near MWAD. It has two short crux sections. It has mostly thin pro. Karsten said this is the best and hardest line that he put up at Moolack, by first rap cleaning and removing a wedged keg-sized block before freeing the climb.

45. Morning Wood Afternoon Delight 5.10b/c ★★★

Pro: ½" to 3" cams, nuts, and hexes, multiples of ¾" sized gear

A multi-pitch climb (depends on rope length and rope drag) that shares a first pitch with Extreme Makeover. Led ground-up for the full length of the cliff band. When an obvious tree is encountered a 2" cam placement marks where the route deviates from Extreme Makeover. An OW chimney section in the upper portion is eased by a thin finger crack.

46. _____ (project lines)

While a multitude of potential route exist between Witches Finger and D.P., currently D.P. sits alone, amongst a series of uncleaned gem lines and the minimally cleaned Witches Finger. A distinctive column dubbed by Karsten when developing Mosserati a stone's throw away splits away from the band with a wide crack route up the fingers backside.

47. D.P. 5.10c ★★★

Pro: #00 to 6" cams, nuts, hexes, Big Bro's, doubles in larger size

This three pitch route is located just after the Witches Finger. The first pitch is a shallow dihedral at 5.8. The second pitch is a short 50' long 5.10b to a ledge, and the last pitch is an off-width/chimney for about 50'.

Beta in detail: P1 Climb a 5.8*ish* crack/corner system using the crack for hands and gear and the walls for feet/stemming (pro small/medium cams). The pitch ends at an obvious ledge/alcove where the crack widens and steepens quickly. The climbing is much cleaner from here onwards. P2 The crack starts overhanging and is a wide off-width most of the way. Lead out from the belay using medium cams (2", 3", 3½" etc.) with strenuous fist jamming (5.10b/c) and foot jamming, too. The crack straightens and gets

Mike Holmes leading *Bold Deli Flavor*
Photo: *Thad Arnold*

dead vertical using fist jams, hand jams, and a few edges. Traverse right from a crack a bit to a big ledge with a large flake (nuts and small cams for belay). P3 Traverse back across from the belay to the crack. Ascend an easier section of the crack (5.9*ish*) on good jams and holds to a bulging, overhanging chimney (5.10a) using feet on the right face. Place a #6 Camalot (or other big gear) and shuffle up till you clear the lip of the overhang and mantle up to finish the hard climbing. Belay from the trees and rap down. *D.P. stands for Dave Patterson who was involved with the development of the route, but not its FA. Thank you Julian Buck for the amazing route section by section breakdown.*

MOSSERATI CORNER

Mike South leading *Plumber's Crack*
Photo archive: *M. South*

Where the Makeover Band tapers down to long single pitch lines (before The Towers formation) small quality corner lines exist in a southwest facing orientation. Mosserati was the original line here and other lines added after 2006. This area offers many of the best parts of the Classic Cracks area: shade in the summer, and quality single pitch lines. The second tier of the Mosserati Corner does make it slightly taller, but little difficulty is encountered in the extra top section.

48. Project Helter Skelter 5.10b ★★
Pro: #00 to 4½" cams, hexes, and nuts

Top-roped during the final working of Eta Eva and Deception Crack, this Project missed out on its final send. Protectable and fun to climb. A bit easier than other lines in the

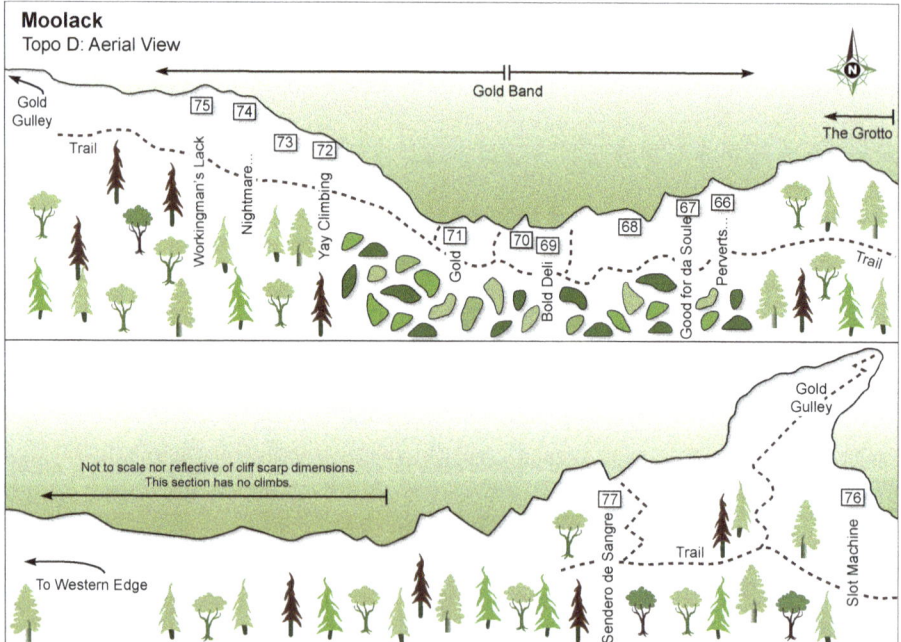

region.

49. Eta Eva 5.10b/c ★★
Pro: #00 to 4½" cams, hexes, and nuts

The crux of this route, like other nearby routes, comes in the first 30-meters. While seemingly steeper than the neighboring Deception Crack, this line provides secure crux jams with viable pro. Low angle terrain gives way to a series of ledges. Belay here if tackling the remaining 5.8 section as a second pitch. This ledge may be accessed via the first portion of DeCr. Rope drag is an issue in the upper reaches of this route if done in one pitch due to the low angled nature of the second half. A blank section of face up high between EE and DeCr may make viable 5.11 lead terrain (TR so far).

50. Deception Crack 5.10c/d ★★
Pro: #00 to 3½" cams, hexes, and nuts

Climb up edges and thin cracks to a ledge stance a few meters off the deck. A tricky 5.9 crux mantle gains this rest ledge (place #00's, brass units below it). A 1"-1½" finger sized crack offers pro and jams while stemming through a 5.10c/d crux. Move left of an overhead column bottom through a bulge past the second crux and up to easy terrain at midway ledges (EE joins here on ledges). Deception Crack avoids the TR boulder problem (mentioned in ETA Eva) by wrapping around left (ETA Eva wraps right) up easy jams to low angle easier terrain to the top. All routes in the Mosserati Corner are done in two pitches even with a 70-meter rope (lengthy stretch of rock from cliff top to tree anchors). *Named after Deception Creek in Westfir, and its manageable grade despite appearances.*

51. Mosserati 5.10a ★★
Pro: #00 to 4½" cams, hexes, and nuts

Mosserati climbs the relatively low angled fist-sized crack up to a horizontal break under a tree to the furthest left of the cliffband before a breach near The Towers. Move right into the corner that separates the pillar and main band. This route does not utilize the obvious tree as a mid-climb P1 belay point, but actually gains the second ledge staying left and avoiding the upper pitch of Deception Crack. P1 is a long first pitch and P2 is much shorter. This route offers high quality technique and movement. *Mike South mentioned that Slover had minimally cleaned and climbed this line. Originally minimally cleaned and climbed (unrecorded) by Shane "Parn" Slover. Duncan (inspired by this mossy line) re-cleaned and led the route. By 2008 the foliage and moss has returned. The start of Mosserati, though re-cleaned a third time in 2010 with the introduction of new lines in the area, retains a mossy start.*

THE TOWERS

52. _____ (project lines)

This amorphous lump of towers and wall offers climbing, but may offer top-roping challenges and more than normal fracturing than other walls. It is a short section of wall, offering a half dozen to dozen routes at most. Topping out, you may have to down-scramble back to sturdy ground for anchoring.

X-Marks Band

The X-Marks Band begins just after The Towers. The trail under it is visible from Mosserati Corner (The Towers is not very large). The X-Marks Band hosts a large sun-soaked open expanse of face and crack climbing with a sparsely wooded talus/scree field below it. Its possible to walk right past Dangerous Toys (faces southwest) due to foliage along the trail. Where the trail dips downhill and flattens, views behind you of the band reveal a large ledge 15' off the

572 CHAPTER 7 ✧ ORC

Map Photo #22 courtesy: Thad Arnold

deck that marks Dangerous Toys. Beyond both X-Marks The Spot and Elements of Style the trail reenters the woods limiting views of the Grotto. Routes at this part of the cliff band are very tall and can be difficult to distinguish one from another. An obvious 'X' is formed by two crack systems at a steep roof section acting as a guide to locate this and other routes in the area.

53. Project Happy Rapping 5.10+ ★★
Pro: #00 to 3" cams, nuts, and hexes (doubles in 1"+)
The face crack to the right of Dangerous Toys, and the common rappel for nearby routes. Happy Rapping has been TR'd, but not led free. A large ledge with a large tat wrapped

tree parallel to Dru's Cruises' midpoint crux transition is the end of HR's first pitch.

54. Dangerous Toys 5.10+ ★★★★
Pro: #00 to 3" cams, nuts, and hexes
From a large ledge roughly 15' off the trail finger jam and stem in a left-facing corner dihedral till you gain a mid-point ledge where the crack bends slightly left at a steep bulge. A large tree at this ledge (utilized as a rappel) is part of the PHR top-rope finger to fist jam line. The route splits at this ¾ mark; the right variation is Scared Alive, while Dangerous Toys traverses horizontally left via stems and face holds into the next dihedral (use care to avoid dislodging any "dangerous toys" loose rock). *Name coined from the loose rock avoided by the FAists by utilizing alternative crack and face holds.*

55. Scared Alive (variation) 5.4 C1
Climb P1 of Dangerous Toys taking a right variation at the ¾ point roof bulge, before DT's left deviation. A step-off ledge will avoid the loose roofs; walk out onto a thin ramp to a body jam OW (5.4) and continue to the top. *Name coined during a wet winter day solo clean-aid ascent. Loose rocks along the traverse fell and sliced the climber's rope at the ground anchor, momentarily stranded him on a ledge just short of the cliff top. An easy, but loose chimney gained the top resulting in the aided start with a free finish variant.*

56. Bag Full of Hammers 5.10+/ 5.11- ★★★
Pro: #00 to 4½" cams, nuts, and hexes
A start-less gem that can be linked into from Dangerous Toys' start. A P2 variant to Dangerous Toys. This line is further left than the normal Scared Alive and Happy Rapping.

57. Geek on a Leash 5.12a ★★★★
Pro: #00 to 4½" cams, nuts, and hexes
A three-pitch climb with a 5.12- crux (starts at a nice base belay stance). Climb to a small mid-point belay ledge. From the left side of a small ledge move and climb past a steep crux roof that has steep hand jams. The climb eases to 5.10a where the crack arcs and pinches down to finger jamming in another left facing

Moolack
Goldband
Map 21

Gold 71

dihedral. A four star classic at its grade.

58. X-Marks the Spot
5.11+/5.12- or 5.10 C2 ★ ★ ★ ★

Pro: #00 to 2" including a #1 BD C4, lots of RP's, Ballnuts, Brass (or aid gear C2)

P1 consists of thin finger-climbing. Crux section is visible in the black roof where the crack system forms a distinctive 'X'. P2 is steep 5.9 climbing, then a short bit of overhung aid (wet black streak), then more 5.10 climbing. P3 consists of steep crack climbing leading to an anchor 40' from the top. The route remained mixed free/aid till 2007/8, then true to good form Mike sent the route in free style, making quite a legendary story for Moolack. Can be done as a two pitch route (or one pitch using long runners). Less than suitable opportunities for belay before the routes ¾ mark. The crux consists of run-out difficulty past a #1 Ball-nut.

59. Elements of Style 5.11a ★ ★ ★ ★

Pro: #00 to 3" cams, hexes, nuts (Ball-nuts may help)

P1 has a low 5.11a crux in the first 30-meters. The line ends left of a log at the bands top edge between the two cracks. The route remains straight through P2 involving steep terrain with 5.10 crux followed by 5.9 jamming. Those who have climbed this route claim that, despite the appearance, the upper portion is manageable if you are capable of climbing the lower crux.

THE GROTTO

All views of The Grotto are obscured by tree cover along the trail. It is an area just short of the Goldband developed between 2008 and 2010.

60. Case of the Blues 5.11 ★ ★ ★ ★

Pro: #00 to 2", ball-nuts, RPs, doubles in thin pro (TCU's helpful)

Start to the left of Elements of Style and wrap into The Grotto, this route divides the two walls. While the top is often dirty, this route stands proudly with other classic lines of the region. One crux consists of 10 feet of thin hands.

61. Whiskey River 5.10+ / 5.11- ★ ★

Pro: ___

Located at the start of the Grotto where X-Marks Band ends, linking X-Marks to Goldband.

62. Jessie's Route, Wish That I Had 5.11+ ★★★★
Pro: #00 to 2" cams, nuts, RP's, brass nuts, and sliding nuts
An impressively proud two pitch line incorporating very thin pro on a thin crack line. The initial pitch is 5.11d and the top pitch is slightly easier at 5.11c. Located next to Whiskey River. From the bottom, this route is in between Case of the Blues and Perverts. Jessie's Route is two lines right of BKS.

63. Best Kept Secret 5.11a ★★
Pro: #00 to 5" nuts, cams, TCU's and Ballnuts
A new (2011) route with no beta other than its location and difficulty. A climber who's sent it rated it at ★★★ if it stays clean. Located two lines left of Jessie's Route.

64. Locked and Loaded 5. 11+/- ★★★
Pro: #00 to 3½" nuts, hexes, cams, RP's, and brass nuts
Lots of 5.10 climbing with an overhanging section of fingers, reminiscent to Pool Guy. Located 4 -5 cracks to the left of Jessie's Route.

65. False Alarmageddon 5.11b ★★★
Pro: #00 to 5" cams, nuts, hexes
Currently (as of 2012) the left most route in the Grotto. Belay from a small tree, or a small ledge 8' off the trail where medium cams suffice for an anchor. A bouldery start makes way to steep blocky moves that traverse right into a 5" crack. Jam and lie-back this crack to a minor stance with a roof over head. Exposed climbing out and around the roof leads to the next 20' of overhanging fingers. This finger crack ends with flaring hands when the steepness lets up. Another 20' beyond the cliffs edge finish the route at a tree anchor.

THE GOLDBAND
The most stunning swath of cliff band at Moolack, tall and loaded with plenty of stellar rock climbs. As unlikely as it may seem numerous untapped lines still exist here between completed routes and at the outer flanks of Goldband, before Perverts and after Gold. The upper cliff edge involves low angle technical (often unprotected) scrambling just to reach the forest above. Goldband has forged an energetic group of route developers into a commendable ground-up on-site movement involving risk, aid ascents, and free ascents, resulting in a historical legacy known far and wide, with plenty of room for more route lines. Average height of this section of wall is 240'.

66. Perverts in Paradise P1 5.10c, P2 5.10b ★★★★
Pro: ½" to 3" cams, nuts and hexes
Three pitches of flaring overhung crack climbing. A high quality climb. A friend proposed that it might be led as one single pitch, but this may require an 80-meter rope. Perverts In Paradise and Good For The Soule share the first 100' pitch with a slight leftward veer in a left-facing dihedral. The second pitch for both PIP and GFTS are within 10' of each other, GFTS on the left, PIP to the right, both finishing well right of the large obvious 2nd pitch pillar close to Southern Exposure. Perverts in Paradise is characterized as finger-to-hand-to-fist (mostly hands), while GFTS offers tight fingers.

67. Good for the Soule 5.10+ ★★★
Pro: ½" to 3" cams, nuts and hexes
This route shares the first pitch anchor with Perverts in Paradise. It has a low crux and a mid-route crux. The crux is "tight fingers and more of a fitness crux" than PIP.

68. Southern Exposure 5.11+/ 5.12- ★★★★

Pro: #00 to 3½" cams, brass nuts, sliding nuts helpful

This two pitch climb (235' high) sends one of the left-of-center lines on the Goldband. P1 is 5.11+, and P2 is 5.11 with three well protected cruxes. Expect some sections of 5.10 and a short section of 5.8 in the middle, and the last pitch is reminiscent to Orange Crush with a slasher finger crack. Originally done in two pitches, but with some rope drag. Breaking it into three leads presents crux/belay challenges. This route climbs the path of least resistance using variable options for gear, weaving in and out of the crack system.

69. Bold Deli Flavor P1 5.11-, P2 5.11 ★★★★

Pro: #00 to 3½" nuts, cams, and hexes, doubles in 2-3", triples ¾"-1½"cams. RP's and sliding nuts as well. (Full pro notes from FA'ist: RP's, blue, red and yellow Ballnuts, doubles from grey (#00) Metolius to yellow (#2), triples of orange (#3) Metolius, doubles above that to 2", one 3" and 3½" piece).

This route was initially climbed by Max as a 5.10 C1 with hangs on gear throughout the crux sections. Max returned and red-pointed the climb identifying the first pitch as 5.11- and the upper pitch as 5.11/5.10+. It breaks cleanly in half in two pitches at an obvious ledge beneath a left-facing dihedral. Use small gear on P1, and big gear for P2.

70. Baker's Dozen 5.12+/- ★★★

Pro:#00 to 2.5", many ball-nuts, RP's

To the climber's left of Bold Deli Flavor is this fine hardcore route that punches out of the biggest roofs at Moolack (at mid-route). Heady climbing up a clean white dihedral capped by a massive roof. This leads to mind-bending crux section up high. Merges with the upper right-facing corner of Bold Deli Flavor.

71. Gold 5.11 ★★★★★

Pro: #00 to 3½" cams, nuts and hexes (sliding nuts are helpful)

This route starts above an open area at the far left end of Goldband before the cliff band trail wraps around the Gold Pillar. The climb starts with easy moves and ample protection, but after 15' the route steepens using finger and hand jams splitting a face. Gear gets thin where a distinctive protected lower crux unlocks some easy climbing up to a ledge rest. Upper pitch is considered to be easier, but is steep and retains its 5.10+ difficulty. The route is longer than it appears from the base due to an extension from the top of the band to the tree anchor. After the business is over a 5.*easy* scramble runs for a long distance making it necessary to climb with a 70+ meter rope or splitting the route into pitches. *This 5-star classic readily compares to other Oregon climbs such as The Sickle and Hammer at Broughton Bluff, Delirium Tremens at Smith Rock, Dod's Jam and Blownout of Beacon Rock, J.R. Token of Trout Creek, Blackberry and Blueberry Jam of Rocky Butte and Crazy Crack at Medicine Rock, to name a few classics in Oregon. Even at Moolack, with*

Karsten leading *Sendero de Sangre*
Photo collection: *K. Duncan*

a plethora of high quality routes, Gold endures as "the" area classic.

72. Yay Climbing P1 5.8, P2 5.11 ★★★
Pro: #00 to 6" cams, nuts, hexes and Big Bro's
Nightmare on Madrone St. is to the left of this route. The distinguishing characteristic of this route is P2, which starts on a huge ledge, works an OW crack, powering through a crux using large fists to get over a bulge (20' above belay) into a tight squeeze chimney that gets wider all the way to the top. About ¾ up the corner the crack splits; one crack goes straight up the headwall (11a? with sporty moves and loose blocks). Climb out left further and up blocks in another crack to a gigantic ledge belay under a large overhang with a 4-6" crack in it (20' lead approx). Ideally (per FA-ists), a 5.11a P2 through the upper headwall will be the better finish for this gem. Leader took two 30'-40' whipper falls trying to lead the 5.11 headwall, ripping out a few wrist-sized trees during each fall.

73. Up an Alchemists' Sleeve 5.10+ ★★
Pro: #00 to 4" cams, nuts, hexes
Probably developed by Caleb at about the time that Workingman's Lack was completed. Another nearby route (Way of the Alchemist) also linked to the college student 'Caleb' indicate he set a few lines at Moolack. The route starts with 5.8- finger-sized crack climbing, bending to the right to access a large belay ledge marked by a gnarled tree. A consistent straight forward climb that ends at a brush choked pillar top (several yards from a tree anchor). *The Way of the Alchemist: Rumored ascent by Karsten Duncan, but FAist likely named the line after Karsten's influence. Karsten moved to Las Vegas and began developing all natural boltless lines and bolted routes in the Red Rocks Canyon and surrounding region.*

74. Nightmare on Madrone Street 5.10b ★★
Pro: ½" to 3½" cams, nuts, and hexes
Only P1 (80') has been established and was originally done ground up because the line looked inviting and naturally clean. P1 consists of fingers at the bottom, hand jams at the middle till the crack widens to wide hands at the top. Easy to identify with Workingman's Lack to the left of the dead tree, and NOMS to its right. Potential second pitch of overhanging OW.

75. Workingman's Lack 5.9 ★★
Pro: #1 TCU's to 3½" cams, nuts, hexes, sliding nuts (nice but not crucial)
Ground up first ascent that utilized the obvious dead tree at a mid-climb belay. From the base trail the route starts as a 5.8- finger-to-fist crack in a left leaning corner. The lower section ends on the ledge with the gnarled tree. Rather than heading right (NOMS) Workingman's Lack climbs behind the upper pillar, then aims slightly left in an arching crack with foot ledges and a large crack with flared sections. The top of the cliffband is choked with madrone and brush.

76. Slot Machine 5.10b ★★
Pro: #00 to 3½" cams, nuts and hexes
Slot Machine is the upper part of a single pitch wall with a convenient midway belay ledge. The route is located left of Gold on a short section of the cliff band. Begin up a 5.9 body slot chimney off the starting ledge to a two move mid-point crux (5.10b), then 5.9 jams to the end of the climb. A stellar line, but needs a base linkup as the climb has only been led via rappelling in from above. *Name coined after the 5.9 body-slot chimney off the starting ledge.*

SENDERO SECTION

After Gold routes on the Goldband are obscured by low foliage, however the Gold Gulley is easy to find as its the cliff bands next big break. The very obvious Sendero Tower is just beyond the Gold Gulley. Sendero De Sangre splits the center of the Sendero Tower. The non-existent trail wraps around Sendero Wall and heads slightly uphill. An unclimbed swath of route potential lay beyond. The Western Edge Turn-around and Shangri-La are all unclimbed "final" walls.

77. Sendero De Sangre 5.10d ★★★★
Pro: #00 to 3" cams, nuts, and hexes, doubles 1" to 1½"
The band height shortens but still has route potential clear to the Western Edge. To get to this route, scramble uphill from the non-trail to a small ledge at the base of this primary splitter crack (veers rightward). Thin finger/hand jamming with thin toe jams, but infrequent foot edges and smears. Viable pro opportunities in the horizontal features.

WESTERN EDGE TURN-AROUND / SHANGRI-LA
The remaining cliff formation over to the Western Edge Turn-around, while never developed, has garnished visual interest. Some obvious gems will eventually see development here.

78. On the Road to Shangri-La 5.10c/d (TR) ★★
The climb is located on the north flank of a large pillar near the cliffs western point. The route starts in a protectable crack from a short ledge leading up to positive holds on a steep face with sporadic odd minor cracks. A quality climb, minimally cleaned, but viable pro options feasible if cleaned further. TR only to date.

Index

Numeric

1st Column Face 526
1st Grade Problems 184
2nd Column Inclusive 526
2nd Column Left Jam 526
2nd Column Right Jam 526
2Trad4U 190
3rd Column Face 526
4th Column Inclusive 527
4th Column Left Jam 527
4th Column Right Jam 527
5th Column 527
6th Column 528
6th Column Jam 527
31 Feet of Pleasure 199
41 Feet of Pain 199

A

Abby Normal 386
Abducted 474
Abracadabra 375
Ace 88
Achilles 389
Acoustic Kitty 444
Adam 476
Adams Crack 189
Adams Variant 494
Aerial Display 136
Afternoon Delight 168
Age Before Beauty 563
Agent Orange 131
Aging Fags 222
Airtime 270
Alice 459
Alien Autopsy 472
Alien Encounter 476
Alien Invasion 474
Alien Lunacy 466
Alien Observer 474
Alma Mater 78
Alpenjaeger Route 258
Alpenjager 248, 249
Alpha 367
Alpine Route 239
Altered State 335
Amazon Man 75
Amazon Woman 75
American Eagle 331
American Girl 149
American Graffiti 39
Anastasia 51
Angle of the Dangle 184
Angular Motion 117
Ant Abuse 140
Apocalypse Needles 261
Apollo Column 261
April Insanity 374
Apron 276
Arch Corner 535
Archdeacon 387
Arch de Triumph 51
Archimedes 514
Arch Nemesis 97
Arcturas 51
Area 51 463
Arena of Terror 232
Ari's Dihedral 568
Arm Forces 141
Atomic Dust Buster 459
Autumn Gold 334
Autumn Joy 335
Autumn Reigns 504
Av's Route 221
Awesome Possum 458
Axe of Karma 232
Axe with a Passion 386

B

Back in 'Nam 129
Back in the Saddle 175
Bad Omen 62
Bag Ends 164
Bag Full of Hammers 574
Bag of Tricks 428

Baker's Dozen 577
Balloon Knot 369
Balrog 538
Banana Belt 146
Barad-Dûr 531
Barking Spider 459
Barramundi in a Billabong 336
Barton's Gully 539
Basho Pinnacle 418
Bat Crack 527
Bat Face 528
Bat Stupor 292
Battleship Arête 116
Bat Wall 59
Beacon Rock 201
BEACON ROCK 201
Beam Me Up Mr. Scott 136
Bear Claw 451
Bearded Lady 163
Bearhug 268
Bears in Heat 226
Be Bold or Not To Be 100
Beekeeper Magic 266
Before the Storm 165
Beginner's Luck 147
Beginner's Route 334
Bela Lugosi 60
Belly of the Beast 453
Berlin Wall 69
Best Kept Secret 576
Better than Sex 416
Bewitched 414
Beyond the Glory 167
BFD 46
Big Al 462
Big Dipper 180
Bikini 88
Bill's Buttress 89
Bill's Thrill 190
Birds of Paradise 106
Birds on a Shelf 285
Birthday Surprise 189
Bitches Brew 176
Bitch I Won 553
Bite the Bullet 83
Bitterroot 170
Blackberry Jam 106

Black Market 461
Black Ops 472
Black Prow 50
Black Raven 330
Black Ribbon 271
Black Truth 476
Bladerunner 214
Blarney Stone 358
Blind Ambition 290
Blind Deaf Old Goat 322
Bloodline 62
Blood on the Cracks 554
Bloodsucker 62
Blood Sweat and Smears 229
Blownout 224
Blownout Direct 222
Blueberry Jam 103
Bluebird 223
Bluebird Direct 221
Blue Grouse 450
Blue Highway 270
Blue Monday 122
Bluto 558
Boardwalk 205
Body Bionics 88
Body Language 87
Bold Deli Flavor 577
Bollocks 451
Bone-Eata' 451
Boo Coup 194
Bookmark 337
Borderline 224
Bottlecap 439
Bottle Rocket 268
Bottomless Column 528
Boulder Problem in the Sky 234
Boxcar 254
Boxtop 254
Boy Sage 97
Boys of Summer 233
Braille 276
Brand-X 537
Brandywine 164
Breakfast Cracks 105
Breitenbush Ears 489
Bride of Wyde 265
Bridge Cliff 55

Bridge of the Gods 224
Broken Arrow 220
Broken Hand 331
Broken Rock 68
Bronze Whale 330
Brother Mike 417
Broughton 33
Brown Rice 371
BSD 365
Bucket o' Ribs 283
Buckwheat 290
Buddha Belly 453
Buffalo Hunter 336
Bugs! 528
Bulge Boogie 450
Bullah Bullah 334
Bulo Dancer 457
Bulo Point 455
Bungee's Crack 271
Buried Treasure 281
Burning From the Inside 116
Burning Zone 395
Burrito 252
Burrito Killa 176
Bust A' Move 69
Butterfinger 269
Butterfly 407
Butt Shiner 291

C

Calf's Gash 397
Caligula 534
Callis Route 500
Call to Greatness 117
Calm Before The Storm 395
Camel Back 372
Campus Wolfgang Gullich 452
Cape Horn 262
Captain Courageous 537
Captain Jim 471
Captain She's Breaking Up 83
Carl's Route 291
Carrots For Everyone 172
Carver Bridge Cliff 109
Case of the Blues 575
Castle Canyon 405
Castle Crag's Direct 373

Cast of Characters 151
Catch Me If I Fall 428
Catharsis 136
Cathedral 390
Cattle Guard 457
Cattle Mutilation 467
Cattle Trough 457
Cave Man 372
Center Squeeze 194
Centurion 87
Cerberus 447, 534
Chain Mail 174
Challenger 123
Chaos 167
Chariots of Fire 122
Charlatan Salesman 357
Chemistry Slab 118
Cherry Cola 112
Chicken 148
Chicken Burrito 252
Chicken Legs 506
Chicken Richard 500
Chicken Rock 505
Child Abuse 198
Chimney 503
Chimney Face 526
Chimney Rocks 341
China Man 365
Chinese Finger Torture 94
Chinquapin Corner 503
Chockstone Chimney 40
Choix des Dames 356
Chopped Suey 174
Chop the Monkey 132
Chrome 155
Cinderella 38
Circus Act 46
Classic Crack 52
Claymation 100
Cleaned for Her Pleasure 562
Climbing Theme 371
Climbswell Butterflakes 242
Climbs with a Fist 457
Close Encounters 472
Closeout 196
Closet Nazi 69
Close to the Edge 104

Cloud Nine 219
Cloudwalker 144
Coecoenut Bridge 416
Coe-Priestly 413
Coethedral 412
Cold Hand of Technology 141
Collawash Cliff 418
Columbina 292
Comfortizer 131
Committed Convenience 270
Competitive Edge 104
Compromising Positions 556
Conga Line 266
Conga Variation 266
Conkling's Pinnacle 407
Conquistador 253
Conscious Haze 331
Conspicuous Arch 529, 534
Conspiracy Lake 475
Conspiracy Theory 475
Contrail Conspiracy 326
Coriolis Effect 538
Cornick's Corner 133
Corona Glass Houses 89
Cosmic Debris 469
Cosmic Dust 213
Cosmic Journey 329
Coucher du Soleil 355
Couch Master 213
Couchmaster Shuffle 266
Count of Monte Cristo 322
Covert Research 475
Crackalicious 454
Crackerjack 537
Crack in the Mirror 112
Crack of Dawn 233
Crack To Nowhere 226
Crack Warrior 97
Crankenstein 225, 366
Crash Landing 466
Crash of the Titans 428
Crazy Horse 218
Crime Wave 72
Crimson Tide 122
Critical Conundrum 384
Critical Mass 54
Crooked Finger 330
Crop Circles 468
Crouching Climber Ridden Dragon 453
Crowds of Solitude 338
Crown Point 247
Crows Feet 332
Cruise Master 213
Cruisin' 213
Cruisin' Direct Finish 213
Cryan's Shame 444
Crystal Ball 507
Crystal Hunters 150
Crystallin Slab 354
Cult of Personality 134
Cut and Dried 133

D

Dad's Nuts 182
DaKind 462
Dalle de Cristal 354
Damaged Circuit 88
Dancing in the Lion's Jaw 144
"D" and Rising 105
Dangerous Breed 156
Dangerous Toys 574
Danse Macabre 62
Dare 275
Dark Apron 276
Dark Arts 67
Dark Lord 183
Darkness Falls 67
Dark Shadows 68
Dark Side of the Moon 475
Dark Tower 38
Darr Route 258
Dastardly Crack 230
Day of Atonement 192
Dead Grouse 494
Dead Man's Curve 97
Death and Taxes 219
Death Star 473
Deception Crack 571
Deep State 172
Delicate Sound of Falling 452
Demian 49
Demon 64
Desdichado 217
Desert Dreaming 291

INDEX

Desert of Reason 382
Desperado 218
Devil's Backbone 230
Diagonal Desperation 219
Digital 117
Dihedral of Despair 148
Dilithium Crystals 474
Direct Start to Divine Wind 155
Direct Start to Flying Swallow 228
Direct Start to Tangerine Dream 131
Dirt In Your Eye 443
Dirty Dancing 142
Dirty Deeds 366
Dirty Double Overhang 226
Dirty Jugs 171
Dismantled Fears 401
Divine Wind 155
Djali 389
Doctors Patient 440
Dod Route 510
Dod's Deviation 230
Dod's Direct Finish 230
Dod's Jam 229
Dog Day Getaway 452
Dog Spine 276
Dog Tooth Rock 484
Do It Again 368
Domino Effect 142
Don't Call Me Ishmael 461
Don't Tread On Me 332
Dorian's Dilemma 240
Dorkboat 252
Double Dutch Left 137
Double Dutch Right 138
Double Eagle 356
Double Trouble 354
Doubting Thomas 233
D.P. 569
Dracula 60
Dreamcatcher 354
Dreamland 465
Dreamscape 122
Dream Weaver 89
Dr. Opus Goes Power Lunging 136
Dru's Cruise 566
Dru's Direct 567
Dry Bones 52

Dulcinea 189
Dunce 442
Dunlap 445
Dwarf Toss 198
Dynaflux 217
Dynamic Resistance 41
Dyno-mite 59

E

Eagle's Wing 56
Eaglet 450
Earth First 466
East Arête 257, 382
East Couloir 262
East Face 512
East Face Route 246
East Face South Tower 344
East Prow 516
East Ridge of South Chamber 375
East Route 250
East side Rock Climbs 419
East Wind 276
Eat Your Spinach 559
Eck-Rollings 494
Ecocide 77
Edge of Eternity 55
Edge of Might 88
Edge of Mordor 534
Edge of the Reef 123
Edges and Ledges 39
Eggs Overeasy 503
Eggs Overhard 502
Ego Extension 451
Eight is Enough 166
Electric Blue 269
Electric Everything 151
Elements of Style 575
Elephant Rock 482, 483
Elusive Element 219
Emerald City 367
EMF left 403
EMF middle 403
Emotional Rescue 97
Enchilada ala Carte 253
Endless Sleep 49
End of the Line 292
Englund Direct 481

Enigma 326
Enola 393
Enter the Void 75
Entrance Cracks 296
Entropic Gravity 425
Epitaph 64
E. Pluribus Pinhead 54
Equinox 452
Erased Memory 467
Escalade 443
Esmeralda 387
Espresso 106
ET 467
Eta Eva 571
Eternity 325
Even 437
Even Horizon 473
Event Gate 476
Eve of Destruction 88
Excalibur 225, 415
Exchange Student 196
Exodus 154
Extinction 144
Extreme Makeover 568
Eye in the Sky 92
Eye Of The Needle 443
Eye of the Tiger 154
Eyes of a Stranger 116
E-Z Corner 89

F

Face Not Friction 46
Fall From Grace 198
Fall Guy 222
False Alarmageddon 576
False Prophet 237
Fandango 86
Far East Wall 92
Far from the Edge 104
Far Side Crag 187
Fat Crack , 398
Father 69
Fat Rabbit 460
Fear of Flying 218
Feat of Clay 129
Felsschlüpfer 450
Fifty-seven 396

Fingers of a Fisherman 233
Fire and Ice 214
Fireballs 240
Fire Spire 261
Firestorm 77
Firing Line 142
First Amphitheater 298
First Contact 469
First Pinnacle 406
Fist-Fight 556
Fist-fighting Plumbers Area 556
Fisticuffs 154
Fits and Starts 147
Flakey Old Man 88
Flayel Bop 178
Flight of the Seventh Moon 94
Flight Time 228
Flying Circus 229
Flying Dutchman 226
Flying Swallow 227
Fool's Rush In 198
Forbidden Fruit 239
Forbidden Zone 395
Forest Circus Fiasco 292
Forest Fright 335
Forged In The Flames 77
For Heaven Sake 176
Forked Route 536
For Pete's Sake 435
Forthright 527
Fortune Cookie 398
Four Leaf Clover 358
Fourth Class Wall 133
Freak Freely 190
Freak Show 253
Fred Hart Lieback 502
Fred Hart Traverse 501
Free Bird 58, 505
Free For All 231
Free For Some 231
Free Ride 113
French Intern 196
French's Dome 361
Fresh Squeeze 231
Friction 55
Friend or Alien 468
Fright Night 61

Frodo's Journey 36
Frog Traverse 498
From Something to Nothing 46
Frozen Treats 214
Fruit Bat 57
Full Circle 566
Full Gold 67
Full Spank Mode 141
Fully Horizontal 254
Fun in the Mud 46
Funkytown 451

G

Gandalf's Grip 37
Ganesh 171
Garden Party 242
Gas Station Fashion 198
Geek on a Leash 574
Genesis 239
Genocide 70
Get It 291
Getting It Up for the Crack of Dawn 454
Getting Rich Watching Porn 254
Getting Your Kicks 182
Get Up and Stand Up 538
Ghost Rider 94
Giant's Direct 369
Giant's Staircase 39, 368
Giant Steps 516
Gigantor 533
Gillette Arête 380
Girl Crazy 154
Gitmo Love Machine 240
Gizzard 500
Glenn's Route 86
Global Warming 329
Glue Me Up Scotty 474
Go Back to the Gym 59
Goddess of Virtue 454
Gold 577
Gold Arch 67
Golden Eagle 450
Golden Shower 370
Golden Spike 261
Goldfingers 154
Gonzo Pinnacle 513
Good for the Soule 576

Good Sport Route 451
Good vibrations 194
Gophers Gone Wild 182
Gorilla Love Affair 73
Gothic Rocks 416
Grab 'n Go 165
Grace 183
Grace and Danger 41
Graduation 132
Grand Alliance 493
Granny's Got A Gun 395
Grass Crack 526
Grassy Ledges 217
Gratitude 416
Grave Digger 67
Gravity Waves 425
Great Barrier Reef 123
Great Pig Iron Dihedral 427
Great Wall of China 94
Great White Book 335
Green Scare 77
Grey Ghost 415
Griddle Cakes 328
Grits & Gravy 398
Groom Lake 475
Ground Effects 58
Ground Zero 227
Grub 92
Guillotine 436, 564
Guillotine Area 563
Gunsmoke 83
Gwenevere 552
Gym Droid 149
Gym Rats 147
Gypsy Dance 387

H

Habitual Ritual 53
Hairy Tale 540
Hammerhead Shark 330
Hammer, The 40
Hamunaptra 444
Hang 'Em High 48
Hanging Chad 446
Hanging Gardens Route 46
Hanging Gardens Wall 39
Hanging Judge 59

Hanging Tree 59
Hangin' with the Hunch' 388
Hangover 40
Hang up Your Hang Ups 176
Hanz Crack 285
Happy Crack 190
Happy Ending 198
Happy Trails 78
Hard Body 55
Hard Contact 88
Harder Than Life 106
Hardscrabble - South End 154
Hardscrabble Wall 148
Hard Times 234
Harlequin 83
Hatchet Job 447
Haunting, The 62
Hazy Daze 243
Head Case 239
Headhunters 71, 427
Heart of Darkness 74
Heatwave 276
Held Down 252
Heliotrope 463
Hell Boy 183
Helm's Deep 165
Hen Rock 502
Hidden Treasure 194
High and Mighty 219
High Plains Drifter 175
High Road to China 94
High Voltage 364
Highway Star 97
Hillbilly Hot Tub 395
Hinge of Fate 116
Hit and Run 563
Hit the Highway 53
Hogback Chimney 539
Hollow Victories 192
Ho' Lotta Shakin' 389
Holy Bubbles 99
Horizontal Delight 254
Horse Rock Pillar 519
Horsethief butte 295
Hoss 476
Hostile Old Hikers 290
Hot Donna 103

Hot Pockets 447
Hot Tang 106
House of Pain 165
Hugo 391
Hunchback Wall 383
Hunch sack 392
Hunger, The 68
Hung Jury 48
Hungry for Duress 136
Hyper Twist 97

I

Ian's Route 532
Iceberg in a Sauna 324
Icon 275
Icy Treats 214
Identity Crisis 128
Illumination Rock 373
Indian Summer 328
Indirect East Arête 382
In Godzilla We Trust 453
Inner Sanctum 268
Inner Vision 148
In The Black 129
Introductory Offer 188
Inukshuk 329
Inversion Excursion 457
Invisible Man 87
Iron Cross 234
Iron Maiden 227, 374
Iron Mountain Spire 514
Itchy & Scratchy 292
It's All Good 450
It Taint Human 471
It Takes a Thief 149
Ivans Arête 178

J

Jackie Chan 365
Jack of Hearts 86
Jackson's Daring Deeds 127
Jacob's Ladder 175
Jealous Rage 97
'Je' Mapel Jon Phillip 196
Jensen's Ridge 233
Jensen's Rimjob 234

Jessie's Route 576
Jethro 398
Jet Stream 460
Jet Stream Variation 461
Jet Wind 461
Jewel in the Crown 248
Jill's Thrill 217
Jimmy Cliff 264
Jimmy's Favorite 265
Jingus Jam 213
John Harlin 450
Johnson-Watt route 418
Joker, The 83
Journey To The East 230
Journey To The Sun 471
Joy Ride 103
JP's Route 535
JRat Crack 459
Jugalicious 397
Jugular Vein 451
Jumping Jack Thrash 58
Jungle Boogie 71
Jungle Cliff 71
Jungle Safari 113
Just a Freakin' Rock Climber 290

K

K-9 Shanghai 445
Kamikaze 172
Kashmir 54
Katanai Rock 259
Kestrel 450
Kiddy Litter 198
Kinetic Flow 197
King of the Moes 400
Kingpin 242
King Rat 122
Kings of Rat 254
Kinzel Tower 406
Kirkpatrick Route 258
Kiwanis Crag 403
Kleen Korner 92
Klinger Springs 445
Knife-Fight 557
Know What I Mean 454
Kung Fu 168
Kyles Big Adventure Gear 265

L

Labrador 89
Labyrinth 243
LaCamas Plug 349
Lamberson Butte 425
Last of the Mohicans 123
Last Tango 86
Latent Genes 285
Lathe of heaven 97
Lava Flow 415
Laverne 391
Lay Lady Lay 234
Leadhead 381
Leading Edge 103
Leaning Uncertainty 122
Lean On Me 451
Lean Years 40
Least Resistance 41
Left Cheek 190
Left Corner Wall 126
Left Gull 221
Left Ski Track 526
Leisure Time 164
Lemon Twist 106
Le' Premie're 355
Lethal Ejection 216
Lethal Ethics 98
Lever or Leaver 88
Levitation Blues 216
Lickity Split 69
Lies and Deception 474
Life As We Know It 149
Lightning Bolt Crack 430
Lights Over Phoenix 475
Line Dancer 457
Lion of Judah 192
Little Arete 98
Little Cougar Rock 255
Little Crow 332
Little Dipper 179
Little Gray Men 468
Little Needle Rock 481
Little Rauch That Could 175
Little St. Pete's 259
Little Wing 220
Live Free or Die 332
Live Long and Prosper 471

Live Wire 88
Livin' in Sin 69
Lizard Locks 188
Local Access Only 228
Locked and Loaded 576
Log Flume 284
Logisticon 425
Logjam 156
Lonely Climax 338
Long Wall 305
Loose Block Overhang 40
Lord Frollo 385
Lord of the Jungle 92
Lord of the Rings 143
Lost Art 554
Lost Boys 63
Lost & Found 65
Lost in the Delta Neighborhood 137
Lost Variation 219
Lost Wages 273
Lousy Putter 356
Love Supreme 176
Lower Sore Thumb 261
Low Voltage 369
Luck of the Draw 77
Luck of the Irish 358
Luna 467
Lunar Dreams 271
Lyle Tunnel Crag 294
Lyle West Crag 292

M

Machete 381
Madrone Wall 125
Magic 386
Magic Fingers 220
Magician 386
Main Vein 49
Major Tom 469
Makeover Band 567
Manic Madness 335
March Madness 375
Maria 228
Mark it Eight Dude 198
Marqueritaville 112
Mars 468
Masterpiece Theater 167

May Day 172
MC Direct 324
MD Route 174
Mean Street 97
Measure of Pleasure 282
Meat Grinder 175
Meatloaf 395
Medussa 454
Mellow Drama 392
Men Are From Mars 476
Men in Black 466
Mental Crisis 128
Metamorphosis 385
Meth Rage 182
MF Reunion 63
Middle Sore Thumb 261
Midget Madness 132
Midnight Warrior 86
Mighty Mite 270
Mighty Mouse 438
Milestone 40
Mind Games 92, 148
Minimancer 71
Mirage 385
Miss Adventure 149
Missing Children 64
Miss Kitty 83
Mists of Time 268
Mixing It Up 136
MJ08 188
Molly's Route 291
Momma Bo Jomma 430
Monkey Moves 188
Monster Crack 454
Monte Cristo Slab 311
Monty Piton 493
Moolack 541
Moonshiners Arête 400
More Balls Than Nuts 214
Morgal Vale 533
Morning Wood Afternoon Delight 569
Morosoarus 453
Mosquito Butte 408
Moss Covered Funk 452
Mosserati 571
Mosserati Corner 570
Mostly Air 234

INDEX

Mothership 473
Mothership Supercell 385
Motional Turmoil 269
Mountaineer's Route 150, 178
Mouse in a Microwave 285
Mowgli Direct 74
Mowgli's Revenge 74
Mr. Bentley 52
Mr. Clean 562
Mr. Denton on Doomsday 265
Mr Hair of the Chode 397
Mr. Noodle Arm (Goes Limp) 140
Mr. Potato 46
Mrs. Norris 183
MTV 88
Mujahadeen 77
Muriel's Memoir 218
Murky Water 388
Mushroom Band Area 558
My DNA 322
Mystic Pizza 64
Mystic Void 63
Mytosis 427
Mytosis Wall 427

N

Naked 269
Naked Savage 92
Nasal Mozz 485
Natural Mystic 64
Naughty and Nice 194
Necromancer 76
Needle Rock 479
Neophytes 425
Neptune 112
Never Mind 139
New Chimney Column 528
New Chimney Jam 528
New Chimney Standard 528
New Frontier Cliff 77
New Generation 113
Newton Pinnacle 425
New Wave 38
New Wealth 152
Niceline 270
Nieland Route 479
Nieland-Valenzuela route 351

Nightmare on Madrone Street 578
Night Music 275
Night Owl 164
Night Vision 113
Nip Tuck 568
No Balls 450
No Balls No Falls 214
No Leverage 100
No Nuts 182
Noodle Cracker 567
Nook and Cranny 460
Norseman, The 230
North Arete 257
North Couloir 259
Northeast Face 375
Northeast Ridge 375
Northern Lights 347
Northern Passage Lower 197
Northern Passage Upper 197
Northern Pearl 267
Northern Skylight 376
North Face 36, 246, 376, 502, 510, 539
North Face Direct 263
North Face Jam Crack 497
North Rabbit Ear 508
North Ravine 484, 491
North Rib 408
North Ridge 513
North Santiam Region 479
Northwest Face 503
Norwegian Queen 338
Nosferatu 63, 454
No Star Slab 271
Not For Teacher 440
Notorious 112
Notre Dame 389
Nouveau Riche 152
NPG 499
Nuggets 282
Nuked 457
Nuke-U-Later 227
Numb Nuts 182
NW Face (Nieland-Valenzuela) 351

O

Oasis 385
OCD 291

OH8 285
O.J. 131
Old Chimney 526
Old Flakes 500
Old Toby 163
Old Warriors Never Die 221
Olive Oil 561
One Flew Over the Cuckoo's Nest 558
One Half Shilling 358
One Note Samba 528
On the Loose 52
On the Move 234
On the Road to Shangri-La 579
Opal's Arête 398
Opdyke Crack 166
Open Space Plan 292
Open the Pod Bay Door HAL 472
Opus 55
Oracle 192, 76
Orange Crush 565
Orange Spice 106
Orange Wall 130
Orangotang 132
Orient Express 95
Orion 180
Orions Belt 347
Oroboros 453
Osprey 450
Outback BBQ 322
Outer Column Jam 525
Outer Limits 445, 475
Out Of This World 469
Out on a Limb 117
Outshined 178
Oz 367
Ozone Wall 159

P

Pacific Rim 205
Packin' Heat 99
Paleontologist 144
Panama Red 83
Pandora's Box 178
Panes of Reality 88
Panorama 427
Park Her Here 369
Party at the Moon Tower 166

Passing Lane 97
Passport to Insanity 116
Patrick's Dihedral 127
Paul's Route 291
PB Direct 402
PC 151
Peach Cling 38
Peach Cobbler 102
Pearl's Jam 267
Pearly Gates Route 258
Pedestal 439
Pedestal Area 551
Peer Pressure 49
Peloton 386
Penguins in Heat 123
Penstemon 291
Pernicious Picklefest 336
Persistence Is Futile 388
Persistence of Time 88
Perverts in Paradise 576
Pete's Pile 430
Phadra 537
Philanthropy 366
Phoebus 388
Phone Home 468
Phylynx 92
Physical Direct 53
Physical Graffiti 53
Pick Pocket 358
Piece of Cake 242
Pig Iron Wall 426
Pig Newton 427
Pig's Knuckles 394
Pigs Nipples 394
Pillars of Hercules 249
Pillow Talk 140
Pinhead 54
Pioneer Route 239
Pioneer Spirit 78
Pipe Dream 232
Pipeline 232
Pipeline Headwall 232
Pipen's Direct 37
Pirates 224
Pirates Pinnacle 518
Pissfire 252
Piton Variation 179

Plaid's Pantry 388
Plaidtastic 270
Plan B 68
Plastic Monkey 117
Playing Hooky 184
Playing with Fire 144
Play Palace 328
Pleasure Palace 561
Pledge Allegiance 556
Pledge Crack 556
Pledge Crack Area 555
Plumberette 403
Plumber's Crack 556
Plumbers Crack 460
Plum Butt 403
Pluto 99
Plywood Jungle 148
Poached 503
Point of Diminishing Returns 452
Poison Pill 425
Polar Vortex 55
Ponderosa 476
Pony Express 78
Poodle with a Mohawk 82
Pool Guy 564
Pop Quiz 440
Poultry Picnic 428
Power Child 453
Power & Politics 457
Power Surge 105
Predator 63
Pride and Joy 70
Primal Institution 454
Primary Gobbler 139
Primordial Soup 150
Probe 474
Progressive Climax 271
Prohibition 398
Promised Land 78
Psoriasis 369
Psychic Wound 225
Psycho Billy Cadillac 398
Ptero 285
Pumpin' For The Man 444
Pumporama 366
Punters in Paradise 150
Pushover 430

Q

Quantum Gravity 429
Quarry Cracker 97
Quasar 334
Quasimodo 387
Quesy 178

R

Rabbit Ears 263
Radical Sabbatical 553
Rad Plaid and Glad 416
Raging Sea 329
Rag Time 234
Raiders of the Lost Rock 459
Rainman 144
Ramble On 444
Ranger Danger 97
Rapunzel's Back in Rehab 352
Rasta Arete 178
Rats in the Jungle 117
Rattler 282
Rattlesnake 290
Rauch Factor 174
Raven's of Odin 332
Raven's Revolt 332
Razorblade Pinnacle 379
Reach for the Sky 103
Reasonable Richard 228
Reckless Abandon 444
Reckless Rookie 356
Red Dihedral 113
Red Fox 150
Red-headed Yeti 454
Redhorn Gate 165
Red Ice 233
Redneck Knuckle Draggers 334
Red Scare 141
Red Sun Rising 149
Red Wall 50
Red Zinger 106
Reed's Route 291
Regular Route 489
Reinhold's Dihedral 153
Repo Man 216
Resistance Is Futile 475
Resurrection 49

Retro Cognition 326
Return of Yoda 460
Return to the Sky 213
Revenant 67
Rhythm Method 205
Riders of the Purple Sage 123
Right Cheek 189
Right Gull 218
Right Roof Exit 344
Right Ski Track 526
Rime Dog 374
Rip City 234
Rip Grip 123
RIP Kurt Albert 452
Ripper 179
Ripples 408
Rise Up 231
Rising Desperation 136
Risky Sex 291
Rites of Passage 117
Rites of Spring 504
River Dance 358
Riverside 219
Road Face 364
Road Head 370
Road Kill 364
Road Rage 364
Robotics 88
Rob's Ravine 104
Rock Creek Crag 266
Rocketman 469
Rockgarden Wall 112
Rock Master 213
Rock Pirates 224
Rock Police 212
Rock Thugs 462
Rock Wren 450
Rocky Butte Quarry 79
Rolling Thunder 175
Ron Love Verly 290
Roofatopia Dope 453
Rookie Nookie 214
Rooster Rock 245, 497
Roswell 471
Route 66 182
Route Crafters 132
Recipe for Airtime 69

Reckless Driver 38
Red Eye 54
Remain in Light 64
Risky Business 38
Rubicon 123
Rude Boys 164
Runaway Weasel 417
RURP Traverse 248
Rusty Cage 178

S

Sacagawea's Route 291
Sacrifice 148
Sacrilege 219
Salathe Highway 415
Salmon 372
Salmon River Slab 371
Samurai 395
Sanctum 430
Sands of Time 269
Sandy's Direct 41
Sanity Assassin 113
santiam pinnacle 512
SANTIAM ROCK CLIMBS & SUM-
    MITS 477
Sasquatch 290, 557
Satisfaction 525
Save the Whales 136
Scared Alive 574
Scary As… 189
Scene of the Crime 462
Schmitz Route 261
Schoolroom 442
Scorpio 271
Scorpion BBQ 396
Scorpion Seams 49
Scotch and Soda 113
Scott Free 136
Scotty Hits the Warp Drive 138
Screaming For Change 167
Screensaver 151
Scum Suckers 553
Seagull 221
Sea Hag Roof 399
Seamingly Endless 98
Sea of Holes 113
SE Arête 341

Seasonal Anxiety 335
Second Pinnacle 406
Second Wind 224
Secret Maze 96
Sendero De Sangre 579
Sendero Section 578
Senior Moment 197
Separated at Birth 458
Separation Anxiety 242
September Morn 331
SE Rib 486
Serpentine Arête 396
Sesame Street 49
Seven Eleven 281
Seven Pearls 337
Seventh Sojourn 57
Severed Heads 133
Shadow Fox 116
Shady Personality 116
Shaken 453
Shandor 57
Shanghai 537
Shangri-La 579
Shape Shifter 466
Sharpen your Teeth 194
Shattered Dreams 148
Sheep Skinners Delight 189
Sheer Energy 55
Sheer Madness 97
Sheer Stress 52
Sheesh 127
Shine 400
Shining Star 48
Shining Wall 144
Shining Wall Section 141
Shire Wall 163
Shoot from the Hip 55
Shootin' 55
Short But Sweet 133
Short Circuit 58
Short Fuse 58
Short Straw 175
Shorty 291
Shorty Got Wolf 451
Shoulder Hop 196
Show Me The Money 48
Sickle, The 40

Siddartha 167
Sideways 554
Sidewinder 562
Siege Tactics 240
Sign Crack 527
Sign Face 527
Signs Preceding the End of the World 447
Silence of the Cams 457
Silence the Serenity 324
Silk Road 334
Silverback 77
Silver Bullet 86
Silver Bullet Wall 83
Silver Crow 232
Silverdyke 188
Silver Streak 366
Simple Twist 97
Single Wide 400
Sisters 155
Sisters of the Road 141
Skinner Butte Columns 523
Skookum Pinnacle 272
Skullduggery 38
Sky Fishermen 225
Sky Pilot 213
Sky's the Limit 328
Slanted and Enchanted 386
Slapfest 41
Slash and Burn 71
Slavemaker 92
Slice of Pie 459
Slim Pickins 337
Slippery Sage 134
Slot Machine 578
Slow Dance 267
Slow Train 243
Sluice Box 282
Small Nuts 182
Smears for Fears 96
Smerk 112
Smoke Signals 235
Smokestack 515
Smokin' 440
Smooth Dancer 226
Smooth Operator 122
Smooth Torquer 112
Snake 190

Snake Buttress 190
Snake Face 165
Snake Roof 166
Social Distancing 103
Solar Flair 471
Solid Gold 192
Solstice 452
Solstice Party 537
Sombrero 252
Something 46
Sophie 552
Sorcerer's Apprentice 221
SOS 172
South Chamber 375
South Chimney 504, 343
South Crack 503
Southeast Face 216, 500
Southeast Face Slab 505
Southeast Rib Direct 501
Southeast Slab 502
Southeast Slab Direct 505
Southern Cross 347
Southern Exposure 507, 577
Southern Skylight 378
South Face 245, 246, 487, 500, 512
South Face South Tower 344
South Rabbit Ear 509
South Ravine 492
South Ridge 257
South Santiam Region 495
Southwest Crack 345
Southwest Face 246, 511
South West Ridge 374
Space Cowboy 538
Spear Fishing in Bermuda 122
Spectrum 136
Speeding Down South 97
Sphinx 454
Spider Monkey 57
Spine Sender 536
Spiny Fish 239
Spire Rock 486
Spiritual Journey 98
Split Decision 78
Split Spire 483
Sport Court 116
Spring Breezes 292

Spring Fever 222
Spring Rock 57
Spring, The 58
Spud 40
Squall 357
Squatch's Travesty 336
Squeaky Alibi 407
Squeeze Box 231
Squeeze Box Direct 231
Squeeze Play 194
Squirrel's Stew 291
Stack Rock 492
Stained Glass 88
Stairs To The Stars 537
Stairway to Heaven 176
Stamina 153
Stampede 156
Standard North Face Route 497
Standard Route 259
Standing Ovation 181
S.T.A.R.D. 439
Stardust 213
Stargate 474
Star Gazer 179
Starship 476
Static Cling 68, 369
Steel and Stone 493
Stems and Caps 560
Stems and Seeds 560
Step and Fetch It 196
Stepchild 183
Steppenwolf 229
Stewart's Ladder 196
S#@t Fire 253
Sticky Fingers 505
Stiff Fingers 105
Stigmata 179
Stinger 438
Stone Rodeo 212
Stone Scared 494
Stone Soup 236
St. Peters Dome 257
Stranger Than Friction 88
Straw Man 366
Streamlined 461
Stump the Jock 99
Subway to Venus 138

Sufficiently Breathless 222
Sultans of Swing 137
Summer Daze 221
Summer Rules 504
Summit Scramble 341
Sundance Kid 83
Sunday's Best 325
Sunny Patina 301
Sunnyside Up 503
Sunset 355
Sunset Bluffs 353
Sunset Bowl 430
Sunset Strip 242
Sunspot 471
Super Burrito 253
Superchron 325
Superman 86
Super Mario 558
Supernatural 66
Superstition 63
Superstrings 137
Surfing with the Alien 133
Sutured by the Vampress 63
SW Buttress 487
Sweat and the Flies 116
Sweeping Beauty 171
Sweet _____ 196
Sweet Emotion 39
Sweet Pea 560
Sweet Surprise 189
Swine of the Times 398
Swiss Miss 108
Switchblade 214
Synapse 219
Synchronicity 234

T

Tailgater 400
Take Fist 227
Take Me To Your Leader 467
Taken 453, 474
Talent Show 122
Talk Talk Talk 129
Tangerine Dream 130
Tapestry 155
Tarzan 72, 89
Telegraph Road 97

Temporary Arete 87
Temptation 436
Ten-A-Cee Stemming 221
Tequila Sunrise 113
Termination 274
Test Tube 429
Thadallic 553
Thai Stick 52
That's the Way 55
The Arête 105, 188, 535
The Borg 475
The Bulge 178
The Bump 261
The Bypass 279
The Cave Route 508
The Chain Gang 291
The Conspiracy 54
The Cover Up 469
The Crumbling 183
The Darkhorse 194
The Dark Side 366
The Direct 479
The Dragons Spine 416
The Eagle Has Landed 467
The Easy Way 396
The Fang 400
The Far Side 198
The First 355
The Gap 292
The Gift of Time 144
The Gingerbread Shortcut 415
The Goldband 576
The Grotto 575
The Head Wall 196
The Humbling 183
The Lonesome Winner 190
The Long Alcove 303
The Martyr 196
The Maverick 254
The Menagerie 495
The Move 265
The Pin 188
The Plum 89
The Plum Arête 403
The Point 347
The Rat Cave 250
There and Back Again 172

There Yare 176
The Seige 366
The Short Bus 264
The Shuttler 292
The Spur 499
The Steeple 417
The Steppes 275
The Stiffler 253
The Swine 393
The Swinery 393
The Tallest Pygmy 385
The Trembling 188
The Truth Is Out There 472
The Tumbling 184
The Wanderer 94
The Warm Up 197
The Watchman 268
The Wave 566
The Wormhole 473
Thin Edge of Reality 285
Thin Line 194
Thin & Lovely 403
Third Pinnacle 406
Third Rail 228
Thirty-six Light Years 428
This ain't yo momma's five-nine 403
Thor's Hammer 490
Thoughts & Prayers 69
Three Martini Lunch 390
Thunder Road 98
Thunder Wall 357
Tibbet's Crack 395
Tic Talk 568
Tidewater 290
Tiger Pause 89
Tiger's Eye 96
Tilting at Windmills 385
Time Bandits 242
Time of Your Life 108
Times Tardy 442
Time To Kill 140
Tin Man 367
Tin Star 78
Tin Tangle 367
Tip City 40
Tipp Topp 176
Tipsy McStagger 398

To Boldly Bolt 471
Todd Skinner 452
Toe Cleavage 57
Tofutti Cutie 183
Tombraider 68
Tombstone Territory 223
Too Close for Comfort 221
Too Cool 398
Tooth Faerie 217
Toothpick 104
Toothpick Wall 102
Top O' the Bluff 358
Tornado 358
Tor the Hairy One 322
Total Depravity 77
Total Liberation 76
To the Edge and Beyond 218
Tottering Tower 261
Touch and Go 78
Tour de France 331
Tourist Attraction 243
Tourist Crack 243
Toveline's Travesty 338
Tower Rock 350
Toxic Waltz 89
Trad Dad 450
Trafalgar 429
Traffic Court 36
Trafficosis 427
Trailer Park Sunset 55
Transportation Routes 528
Trapped in Time 454
Trauma Center 138
Tree Frog 346
Trench Warfare 415
Tres Hombres 401
Tribal Therapy 198
Tribes 439
Trick Wall 428
Trinity Crack 172
Trinity Wall 69
Trivial Pursuit 83
Trix are for Kids 108
Trouble With Tribbles 468
True Grit 78
True Grunt 229
Tsunami 357

Tuffnerd 253
Tumble Lake Area 479
Tumble Rock 483
Tunnel Vision 194
Turkey Monster 510
Twenty Year Hangover 399
Twilight Zone 264
Twin Sisters Pinnacle 515
Twist and Crawl 70
Twister 357
Twitch 452
Two Beers and a Baby 563
Two Girls Mtn 516
Typhoon 357
Tyrolean Spire 263

U

UFO 470
Ujahns Delight 416
Uluru 324
Unchained 536
Uncle Rick 370
Uncola 112
Underdog 535
Under the Big Top 563
Under Your Belt 55
Un-named 528
Up an Alchemists' Sleeve 578
Updraft to Heaven 234
Up on a Pedestal 554
Upper Menagerie Wilderness 507
Upper Sore Thumb 261
Upper Trick Wall 430
Upskirt 415
Uranus Has Rings 471
Ur Baby's Daddy 190
Urban Cowboy 86
Utopia 273

V

Vampyr 64
Van Helsing 65
Variation 217, 223, 228, 235
Variation on Hit and Run 563
Variety 164
Vaudeville 102

Velcro Fly 58
Veranda 303
Verbal 129
Vertical Therapy 104
Vexation Variation 492
Vicious 166
Victor 390
Video Bluff 87
Vulcan Mind Meld 471
Vulcan's Variation 218

W

Wage Slave 425
Walk on the Wild Side 56, 325
Walk on Water 92
Wally Street 116
Wally Wedding 116
Wankers Columns 281
Warlock 77
Warmnerd 253
Warm Up 252
War of the Worlds 466
Warrior Wall 96
Water Buffalo 513
Waters Edge 243
We Are Not Alone 474
Wedged Block 342
Wedged Block Right Exit 342
Welcome to the Jungle 71
Welcome to the Swine 402
Well Hung 63, 197
Wendell's Big Mistake 282
West Arete 257, 346
West Arête 373
West Chimney 248, 506
West Face 513, 515
West Face Crack 273
West Face Dihedral Direct 497
West Face of South Ear 509
West Gully 539
West Wind 276
Wet and Dirty 199
Wet Spot 452
Whatever Blows Your Skirt Up 139
What's Your Motive? 156
Where the Wild Things Are 557
Where the Wild Things Roam 130

Whine and Cheese 170
Whiskey River 575
White Lightning 190, 400
White Rabbit 106
White Rabbit Buttress 106
Who's the Choss? 462
Why Must I Cry 164
Widespread Panic 566
Wild Blue Yonder 130
Wild Hare 509
Wild Turkey 512
Wild Turkeys 225
Wild West 503
Wild Wild West 78
Wind Dummy 291
Wind Mountain 273
Windows of Your Mind 150
Winds of War 150
Windsurfer 231
Windwalker 231
Windy Slab 275
Winema Pinnacles 255
Winter Delight 222
Winter Sunshine 505
Wisdom Tooth 108
Wishbone 230
Witch Hunt 66
Witching Hour 67
Wizard 92
Wizard Wall 92
Wobbegong 326
Wolf Gang 451
Wolf of the Steppes 134
Wolf Point 451
Wolf Rock 529
Workingman's Lack 578
Workman's Comp 274
World is Collapsing 430
Wounded Knee 189
Wretched of the Earth 74
Wrong Gull 220
Wushu Roof 192
Wyde Syde 269

X

X-Marks Band 571
X-Marks the Spot 575
X-Spire 489

Y

Yay Climbing 578
Yellow Brick Road 369
Yellow Wall 117
Yeoman's Work 147
Yeti's Betty 454
You'll Dance to Anything 97
You Me & Everyone We Know 450
Young Jedi 465
Young Warriors 205
Yum Yum 71
Zimbabwe 71

Z

Zabo's Delight 355
Zabo's Enchanteur 355
Zeeva 88
Zenith 103
Zeno's Paradox 388
Zimbabwe 71
Zion Train 555
Zucchini Route 247

International Rock Climbing Grades

The international rock climbing grading scale is a well established system. This chart provides climbers from other countries the opportunity to compare the standard YDS climbing grades with other common grading systems.
Local climbing crags grades may vary slightly in letter grade, yielding slightly 'soft' or 'hard' ratings, but as a whole the YDS grades used at each climbing site are generally comparable to the ratings shown on this chart.

YDS	British	French	Australian
5.3	VD 3b	2	11
5.4	HVD 3c	3	12
5.5	MS/S/HS4a,	4b	12/13
5.6	HS/S 4a	4c	15-17
5.7	HS/VS 4b	4c	15-17
5.8	VS 4c/5a	5a	18
5.9	HVS 5a/5b	5b	19
5.10a	E1 5a/5b	5c	20
5.10b	E1 5b/5c	6a	20
5.10c	E2 5b/5c	6a+	21
5.10d	E2/E3 5b/5c	6b	21
5.11a	E3 5c/6a	6b+	22
5.11b	E3/E4 5c/6a	6c	22
5.11c	E4 5c/6a	6c+	23
5.11d	E4 6a/6b	7a	24
5.12a	E5 6a/6b	7a+	25
5.12b	E5/E6 6a/6b	7b	26
5.12c	E6 6b/6c	7b+	27
5.12d	E6 6b/6c	7c	27
5.13a	E6/E7 6b/6c	7c+	28
5.13b	E7 6c/7a	8a	29
5.13c	E7 6c/7a	8a+	30
5.13d	E8 6c/7a	8b	31
5.14a	E8 6c/7a	8b+	32
5.14b	E9 6c/7a	8c	33
5.14c	E9 7b	8c+	34
5.14d	E10 7b	9a	35
5.15a	...	9a+	...
5.15b	...	...	...

ROCK CLIMBING

Notes

ROCK CLIMBING

Notes